Praise for *HP OpenView System Administration Handbook*

"I deliver training on all of the products covered in this book. I like to provide references for customers, and the more that people know about the products before arriving at my classes the better they are at the class. I will recommend this book to my students."

—Emil Velez,
Technical Consultant—Education, HP

"This is excellent! This definitely complements our courseware. We frequently have requests for reference material from customers attending courses. I think something like this has been the missing link for a very long time and I am anxiously awaiting the publication."

—Rose Lariviere,
HP Education Services

HP OpenView System Administration Handbook

Network Node Manager, Customer Views, Service Information Portal, HP OpenView Operations

Tammy Zitello

Deborah Williams

Paul Weber

Hewlett-Packard® Professional Books

HP-UX

Cooper/Moore	HP-UX 11i Internals
Fernandez	Configuring CDE
Madell	Disk and File Management Tasks on HP-UX
Olker	Optimizing NFS Performance
Poniatowski	HP-UX 11i Virtual Partitions
Poniatowski	HP-UX 11i System Administration Handbook and Toolkit, Second Edition
Poniatowski	The HP-UX 11.x System Administration Handbook and Toolkit
Poniatowski	HP-UX 11.x System Administration "How To" Book
Poniatowski	HP-UX 10.x System Administration "How To" Book
Poniatowski	HP-UX System Administration Handbook and Toolkit
Poniatowski	Learning the HP-UX Operating System
Rehman	HP-UX CSA: Official Study Guide and Desk Reference
Sauers/Ruemmler/Weygant	HP-UX 11i Tuning and Performance
Weygant	Clusters for High Availability, Second Edition
Wong	HP-UX 11i Security

UNIX, Linux

Mosberger/Eranian	IA-64 Linux Kernel
Poniatowski	Linux on HP Integrity Servers
Poniatowski	UNIX User's Handbook, Second Edition
Stone/Symons	UNIX Fault Management

Computer Architecture

Evans/Trimper	Itanium Architecture for Programmers
Kane	PA-RISC 2.0 Architecture
Markstein	IA-64 and Elementary Functions

Networking/Communications

Blommers	Architecting Enterprise Solutions with UNIX Networking
Blommers	OpenView Network Node Manager
Blommers	Practical Planning for Network Growth
Brans	Mobilize Your Enterprise
Cook	Building Enterprise Information Architecture
Lucke	Designing and Implementing Computer Workgroups
Lund	Integrating UNIX and PC Network Operating Systems

Security

Bruce	Security in Distributed Computing
Mao	Modern Cryptography: Theory and Practice
Pearson et al.	Trusted Computing Platforms
Pipkin	Halting the Hacker, Second Edition
Pipkin	Information Security

Web/Internet Concepts and Programming

Amor	E-business (R)evolution, Second Edition
Apte/Mehta	UDDI
Chatterjee/Webber	Developing Enterprise Web Services: An Architect's Guide
Kumar	J2EE Security for Servlets, EJBs, and Web Services
Little/Maron/Pavlik	Java Transaction Processing

Mowbrey/Werry	Online Communities
Tapadiya	.NET Programming

OTHER PROGRAMMING

Blinn	Portable Shell Programming
Caruso	Power Programming in HP OpenView
Chaudhri	Object Databases in Practice
Chew	The Java/C++ Cross Reference Handbook
Grady	Practical Software Metrics for Project Management and Process Improvement
Grady	Software Metrics
Grady	Successful Software Process Improvement
Lee/Schneider/Schell	Mobile Applications
Lewis	The Art and Science of Smalltalk
Lichtenbelt	Introduction to Volume Rendering
Mellquist	SNMP++
Mikkelsen	Practical Software Configuration Management
Norton	Thread Time
Tapadiya	COM+ Programming
Yuan	Windows 2000 GDI Programming

STORAGE

Thornburgh	Fibre Channel for Mass Storage
Thornburgh/Schoenborn	Storage Area Networks
Todman	Designing Data Warehouses

IT/IS

Anderson	mySAP Tool Bag for Performance Tuning and Stress Testing
Missbach/Hoffman	SAP Hardware Solutions

IMAGE PROCESSING

Crane	A Simplified Approach to Image Processing
Gann	Desktop Scanners

HP OpenView System Administration Handbook

Network Node Manager, Customer Views, Service Information Portal, HP OpenView Operations

Tammy Zitello
Deborah Williams
Paul Weber

www.hp.com/hpbooks

PEARSON EDUCATION
Prentice Hall Professional Technical Reference
Upper Saddle River, NJ 07458
www.PHPTR.com

Library of Congress Cataloging-in-Publication Data

A CIP catalog record of this book can be obtained from the Library of Congress

Publisher, HP Books: *William Carver*
Acquisitions editor: *Jill Harry*
Editorial assistant: *Brenda Mulligan*
Marketing manager: *Stephanie Nakib*
Marketing specialist: *Kathleen Addis*
Publicity: *Heather Fox*
Managing editor: *Gina Kanouse*
Production: *Specialized Composition, Inc.*
Cover design: *Sandra Schroeder*
Manufacturing buyer: *Dan Uhrig*

Published by Pearson Education
Publishing as Prentice Hall Professional Technical Reference
Upper Saddle River, New Jersey 07458

Prentice Hall PTR offers excellent discounts on this book when ordered in quantity for bulk purchases or special sales. For more information, please contact: U.S. Corporate and Government Sales, 1-800-382-3419, corpsales@pearsontechgroup.com. For sales outside of the U.S., please contact: International Sales, international@pearsoned.com.

Printed in the United States of America
Second Printing
ISBN **0130352098**

Pearson Education LTD.
Pearson Education Australia Pty, Limited
Pearson Education South Asia Pte. Ltd.
Pearson Education Asia Ltd.
Pearson Education Canada, Ltd.
Pearson Educación de Mexico, S.A. de C.V.
Pearson Education—Japan
Pearson Malaysia, S.D.N B.H.D.

How This Book Is Organized

Part I—Network Node Manager, Customer Views, and Service Information Portal

Chapter 1—Introduction to NNM, CV, and SIP

Provides an introduction to SNMP and the three products NNM, CV, and SIP.

Chapter 2—Why Network and Systems Management Systems Fail...

Chapter 3—Creating a Deployment Checklist

Chapter 4—Out-of-the-box Network Node Manager

Describes what NNM does without customization. Introduces the native GUI, the web interface, and Dynamic Views.

Chapter 5—Network Discovery

Describes how to seed network discovery, eliminate devices from discovery, and manual discovery. Reviews netmon and other NNM background processes.

Chapter 6—Customizing NNM from the GUI

Describes how to customize NNM submaps including background graphics, submap overlay, auto-layout, and symbol hiding. Also includes Internet submap partitioning, creating executable symbols, and creating MIB applications.

Chapter 7—Advanced Customization

Describes how to customize NNM with the registration files. This allows customization of the native GUI and the web launcher.

Chapter 8—Data Collection and Event Configuration

Describes how to collect SNMP data, store the data, and generate alerts based on user-defined thresholds.

Chapter 9—Scalability and Distribution

Describes several ways to allow NNM to scale to a large enterprise by the use of remote consoles, discovery filters, and collection stations.

Chapter 10—Customer Views

Describes the additional container views that are available with Customer Views. Provides examples of the ovcustomer utility.

Chapter 11—Service Information Portal

Describes the portal view of your enterprise available with SIP. SIP provides information such as Key Device Health, Router Health, and Server Health as configured with Customer Views.

Chapter 12—Introduction to OpenView Operation

Part II—OpenView Operations

Introduces the focal point of OVO, to monitor applications, resources, and services.

Discusses the three types of OVO users including administrators, operators, and template administrators.

Chapter 13—Out-of-the-Box with OpenView Operations

Describes what the typical system administrator needs to know to get up and running with OVO.

Chapter 14—Agent, Templates, and Distribution

Describes the internal components of OVO that are distributed to manage the enterprise.

Chapter 15—Smart Plug-Ins

Describes the essential instrumentation that will save time and resources in the implantation of OVO.

Chapter 16—Built-in Performance Tools

Describes the features that make it possible to monitor and report performance data from the managed resources and applications.

Chapter 17—Server Administration

Describes the critical success factors, tool and techniques for the typical OpenView administrator.

Chapter 18—Oracle for OpenView

Describes the engine that is the works behind the scene to store the configuration and run time data.

Chapter 19—Enterprise Management Flexibility with Multiple Servers

Describes the capabilities of the OpenView platform to span multiple management servers.

Part 3—Best Practices

Chapter 20—Security

Describes the user, system and network security standards that are supported by the OpenView platform.

Chapter 21—Plan, Document, Take Corrective Actions, Administer Changes

Chapter 22—Troubleshooting Tips and Techniques

Describes the various tools and techniques available to the OVO administrator to accomplish route tasks.

How This Book Is Organized

Part 4—OpenView Operations for Windows

Chapter 23—Introducing OVO for Windows

Describes the OVO management platform that runs on the Windows platform.

Chapter 24—OVO Windows and OVO UNIX Interoperability

Describes the capability of the two OVO management platforms to interoperate.

Chapter 25—OVOW Implementation Tasks

Describes some of the common tasks and tools available to understand where to begin with OVOW.

Appendix A—OpenView Commands Quick Reference Guide

Appendix B—Hostname Resolution

Appendix C—Resources

Dedications

This book is dedicated to my mother, Margena, and the memory of my father, Thomas B. Sealey, both of whom served in the U.S. Marine Corps during World War II.

—Tammy Zitello

This book is dedicated to my grandmother, Mary Jones, who inspired me with her wise words, "Nothing beats a failure but a try;" and my mom, Ms. S. E. Jones, who always said, "You can do anything if you just put your mind to it."

—Deborah Williams

This book is dedicated to my fellow men and women of the Armed Forces who are giving their lives in fighting the "Global War on Terrorism" so that Americans may continue to pursue "Life, liberty, and the pursuit of happiness."

—Paul Weber

Acknowledgements

Tammy Zitello—I would like to thank the students at Lockheed-Martin in Maine for inspiring me to write this book during my last teach of NNM. Thanks to my reviewers, including John Blommers, Karen Fritz, Emil Velez, Alan Greentree, Dev Norwood, and Bill Dooley. Thanks to my co-authors Deborah Williams and Paul Weber for driving this book to completion. Thanks to my editors Jill Harry and Elise Walter for making this book happen. A special thanks to my mentor, reviewer, and husband Stan (zman) for sharing his technical knowledge of NNM and helping develop the lab exercises.

Deborah Williams—I would like to thank the OVO students, who always asked good questions and were willing to push the limits of OVO during class. Thanks to the reviewers, some of whom are already mentioned (Emil and Bill), in addition Rose Lariviere, Kai-Uwe Jensen, Cherie Maurice and Thomas Gentsch. Special thanks to friends and family who remained patient and let me focus on this work. Thanks to Tammy and Paul, a great team to work with. Thanks to the editors Jill and Elise for many words of encouragement.

Paul Weber—I thank Ed Allen, Thomas Ross, and Daniel Uland for making me their protégé fifteen years ago as a "boot" UNIX system administrator. Steve Morga, who gave me my first Network and Systems Management white paper assignment that started my career in Network, Systems, and Service Management. These people, coupled with, above all things, "Talent on loan from God," have enabled me to be in the position to assist in writing this book. Special thanks goes to two wonderful ladies, Tammy Zitello and Deborah Williams, who have done the majority of the work and allowed me to interject my writing throughout the book. Thanks to all who have reviewed the book for accuracy, especially Kai-Uwe Jensen and Chris DeVita. Most importantly, my beautiful wife, Brenda, who has put up with her husband being away for both Hewlett-Packard and the United States Navy Reserve and then holed up in the basement till the wee hours of the morning.

Who This Book Is For

System and Network Administrators—*Network Node Manager* (NNM) provides a graphical representation of your network, device status, and SNMP trap alerting capabilities. NNM also collects and stores information retrieved from SNMP-based devices, including MAC address, equipment vendor, and model, that system and network administrators can use to troubleshoot the enterprise.

Network Design Architects—NNM can be used to collect statistical data for historical trending. Network architects can use this tool for capacity planning.

Application Administrators—OVO provides the capability for application monitoring. Smart Plug-Ins can be used to for monitoring specific applications such as databases.

Application Developers—OVO provides the capability to extend application monitoring by customizing templates. Application developers (or administrators familiar with the application log files and system resource requirements) can create templates to specifically monitor an application.

Database Administrators—OVO can be used to monitor many different databases such as Oracle®, MS SQL®, SAP R/3®, and DB2®. Database administrators may want to assist in configuring database templates so that they are alerted when database problems arise.

Information Technology Managers—While this book is primarily intended for technical implementation, management can use it to better understand what NNM, CV, SIP and OVO provide. References to additional OpenView products will be mentioned throughout the book.

Unix and Windows Administrators—NNM and OVO provide HP-UX®, Solaris®, Linux®, and Windows®-based solutions for monitoring your enterprise. Unix and Windows administrators can use OpenView tools for notification and troubleshooting in the enterprise.

Conventions Used in This Book

- **Boldface** is used for
  - Commands, pathnames, and filenames
  - IP addresses and URLs
- *Italic* is used for
  - New terms where they are defined
  - Emphasis on a term
- Brackets [ ] are used for
  - Buttons on dialog boxes, such as when the user clicks **[OK]**
- Arrows→are used for
  - Separation of menu items, such as the menu selection
  - **Edit→Find→Object By Attribute→isHTTPSupported**

Contents

Chapter 3
Create a Deployment Plan 23

Chapter 4
Out-of-the-box Network Node Manager 41

Chapter 7
Advanced Customization 111

Chapter 8
Data Collection and Event Configuration 147

Chapter 9
Scalability and Distribution 175

Chapter 10
Customer Views 219

PART I

Network Node Manager, Customer Views, and Service Information Portal

Part one addresses three OpenView products: *Network Node Manager* (NNM), *Customer Views* (CV), and *Services Information Portal* (SIP). NNM provides a highly customizable tool for the discovery, mapping, and SNMP management of network devices. Many OpenView products rely on NNM's underlying processes, including CV and SIP.

CV provides the ability to define which customers are affected by which resources, and is commonly used by Internet Service Providers, Managed Service Providers, and outsourcers to allow for customer-based management.

SIP is the glue that pulls many OpenView products together. It provides a uniform display method for OpenView products including NNM, OVO, OVIS, OVSN, OVPI, and OVSD. In addition to displaying your OpenView data, SIP also allows you to display content from your own applications. With SIP, you can create a segmented and custom look and feel to the portal views.

CHAPTER 1

Introduction to Network Node Manager, Customer Views, and Service Information Portal

OpenView *Network Node Manager* (NNM) is a *Simple Network Management Protocol* (SNMP)-based tool providing the capability to monitor networked devices and manage your enterprise. NNM provides discovery of IP devices, topological mapping of the devices, SNMP data collection, and the capability to receive and respond to SNMP traps. In addition to discovery, NNM can monitor some layer 2 devices while the Microsoft® Windows operating system implementation provides discovery and mapping of IPX devices.

OpenView is a framework providing the architecture for managing servers, workstations, databases, and networking devices. NNM is known as the "common services platform" because many OpenView products use the underlying processes and databases provided by NNM. More than 100 vendors have developed over 300 products that integrate into the OpenView framework.

This chapter covers background information on SNMP and introduces concepts of network management. The corporation presented in this chapter, Sealey Inc., is fictitious and is based on my experience as a system and network administrator. The theme will be carried throughout most of this book in an attempt to establish a real-world example of an NNM implementation.

1.1 AN SNMP COKE MACHINE

In theory, any device is SNMP manageable. Many networking devices have built-in SNMP modules, and most operating systems have SNMP agents available. Devices that do not have SNMP capability can use a proxy mechanism. Some years ago, a group of students at MIT® developed an SNMP interface to a Coke® machine. The purpose having of an SNMP-manageable Coke machine is that when the machine runs out of Coke, a notification can be sent. In this case, the notification mechanism is an SNMP trap sent to a network management station, such as NNM. The operator responsible for monitoring SNMP traps is notified that the machine is empty and refills the machine.

According to Rajeev Surati, MIT alumnus and a designer of the SNMP Coke machine, it contains a Motorola 6811 chip and is connected by a serial cable to an HP-UX box that acts as the SNMP proxy. A modified ftp server communicates between the Unix box and the Coke machine. You can query the status of drinks in the Coke machine at `http://www-swiss.ai.mit.edu/htbin/coke`.

In addition to problem detection, NNM can also be configured to resolve problems without human intervention. For instance, assume that the Coke machine is connected to a reserve storage bin of drinks. When NNM receives the trap indicating the machine is empty, NNM initiates an action directed to the proxy that triggers the bin to automatically release a lever that refills the machine. No human intervention is required to refill the machine. Ultimately, the Coke machine is never empty.

1.1.1 A Review of SNMP

SNMP provides the ability to query devices on your network. You can communicate with a device by retrieving information from the *Management Information Base* (MIB) on the device. The MIB is a hierarchical data structure containing information about the system, such as temperature, location, interface status, and interface queue utilization. The standard management MIB (MIB-II) is comprised of more than 300 variables.

The MIB tree defines the structure of the variables. Think of the MIB tree as a directory structure, as shown in Figure 1-1. The MIB-II subtree (.iso.org.dod.internet.mgmt.mib-II) defines the standard MIB variables as defined in RFC 1213. Vendors can extend the number of variables by defining vendor-specific MIB variables. Vendor-specific MIBs are defined under the private.enterprises subtree (.iso.org.dod.internet.private.enterprises). MIB variables have both a character and numeric representation.

Character representation	.iso.org.dod.internet.private.enterprises.hp
Numeric expression	.1.3.6.1.4.1.11

MIB variables define information such as the system description (sysDescr), interface traffic (ifInOctets, ifOutOctets), and the system object id (sysObjectID). The system object id, also referred to as the OID, uniquely identifies the equipment vendor and model of equipment. See Figure 1-1 for an example of the management branch of the MIB tree.

The SNMP agent uses community names (passwords) to restrict access to information provided by the MIB. To retrieve information from the MIB, you must know the community name of the device. Each SNMP device has a read community name and a write community name. The **snmpget** command allows you to query a MIB variable using the read community name. The **snmpset** command allows you to set a MIB variable using the write community name. Other SNMP commands include **snmpwalk**, **snmpbulk**, and **snmptrap**. **Snmpwalk** and **snmpbulk** both traverse the MIB tree, the latter reducing overhead by storing multiple responses in a single packet. The **snmptrap** command sends an SNMP trap, notification of a significant event, to an SNMP management station such as NNM.

Figure 1-1 This tree illustrates both the character and numeric representation of the management (mgmt) branch of the MIB tree. The management branch is the generic set of MIB variables as described in RFC 1213.

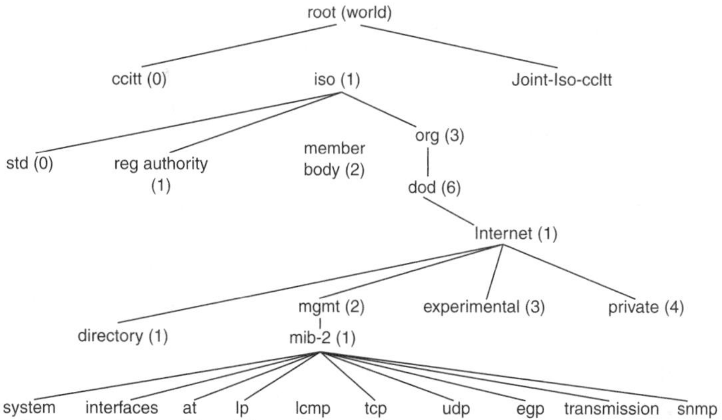

SNMP is a UDP[1] connectionless-based protocol. SNMP is not broadcast. NNM solicits SNMP information using the **snmpget** command. Devices respond directly to the NNM station using **snmpreply**. Unsolicited information is sent as a directed message (not a broadcast) to the NNM station to notify it that something important has occurred. This is known as an SNMP trap. SNMP traps may be directed to multiple SNMP management stations. The more SNMP traps a device provides the more information and automation NNM is able to provide.

For example, suppose you would like to page someone when a printer runs out of paper. The printer's vendor could help by providing a MIB variable to indicate the paper status. This could be as simple as setting a MIB variable to "1" when there is paper and "0" when there isn't. If this is all the vendor supplied, NNM would need to be configured to examine the variable at regular intervals and then send a message to the paging program when it detects a "0." However, if the vendor included an SNMP trap to indicate that the paper tray was empty, NNM does not need to poll the MIB, thus reducing the network bandwidth "footprint" of NNM. The device would send the SNMP trap to NNM with the relevant information from the MIB when the paper runs out. Thus, the more traps the vendor provides, the better you can manage the device.

1 User Datagram Protocol is a connectionless protocol that, like TCP, runs on top of IP networks. Unlike TCP/IP, UDP/IP provides very few error recovery services, instead offering a direct way to send and receive datagrams over an IP network.

1.2 WHAT NETWORK NODE MANAGER PROVIDES

Before getting into specifics, let's look at some concepts and terminology that will be used throughout this book. Then we will delve into the requirements of a corporation in search of a network management solution.

1.2.1 Continuous Status Monitoring of Managed Nodes

A managed node is a device that responds to ICMP echo requests (ping) and is actively being polled by NNM. This device may be discovered automatically by NNM or may be added manually. Optimally, the device is running an SNMP agent.

1.2.2 User and Administrator Interfaces

There are two types of NNM users: administrators and operators. An administrator manages the NNM installation and customization. An operator uses NNM to manage the network for the organization. An *administrator* accesses NNM from the native interface and requires full control of customization. An *operator* can access NNM using the native interface in read-only mode, which prevents permanent customization. The operator can also access NNM from the web-based Network Presenter, which provides limited functionality and read-only capabilities. Another web access method, Dynamic Views, allows full access, provided that it is executed from the NNM station that is running the NNM processes.

1.2.3 Integration with Trouble Ticketing Systems

Many corporations today have some means of tracking problems that occur within the IT infrastructure. This includes problems involving computer systems, environmental systems, network devices, and peripheral devices such as printers. These systems are commonly known as trouble ticketing systems because they use the paradigm of a ticket to track the problem from detection to correction. Depending on the size of the organization, these systems can become elaborate and include such capabilities as dispatching a person with equipment to effect a physical repair. NNM can tie into the trouble ticketing system. In this way, the system can be made aware of external detection and correction events.

1.2.4 Third-Party Applications

While NNM does not offer everything required for enterprise management, it is easily customizable and "open" to third-party applications. You can make customizations to NNM without modifying and compiling source code. NNM provides the ability to customize the *Graphical User Interface* (GUI) from within the GUI.

Many vendors develop product specific applications that integrate seamlessly into the OpenView framework. For example, CiscoWorks allows you to manage Cisco® networking devices and can be integrated into the NNM GUI. This application provides the ability to configure and manage Cisco devices from NNM.

The *HP OpenView Integrated Solutions Catalog*, available via `http://openview.hp.com/sso/isv/search`, provides a current listing of third-party software and device vendors that have integrated their products with HP OpenView solutions.

1.2.5 The Need for Network Management

Our rapidly growing business, Sealey Inc., provides managed services to its customers, including web hosting, systems monitoring, and notification. Although the company is based in Atlanta, there are co-locations across seven states. There are system administrators and router managers in each of the seven states who will need access to the data in their locations. The administrators typically use Windows systems and the router managers use a combination of HP-UX and Solaris systems, providing connections to their local network-monitoring software. The router folks expect to be able to use CiscoWorks 2000 to configure their routers and would like for the network management solution to integrate with these applications. The company also uses Service Desk as their trouble ticketing system and would like their network management application to automatically open a trouble ticket when certain events occur.

We need a network management solution that will allow Sealey Inc. to monitor customer networks proactively. For example, when a customer's Oracle database server becomes unavailable, the customer loses millions of dollars per hour. Most of the customer's servers are fully redundant with mirrored disk drives, dual power supplies, and contingency servers. However, the customers not only want the appropriate party to be notified when any components fail, they also want the ability to access this management information. The customers want to automatically page their engineers when necessary. Sealey Inc. needs a network management solution that will provide the following capabilities:

- Notification *before* a customer network device becomes overloaded
- Ability to monitor performance of database and application servers
- Capability for NNM operators to log on to the servers easily
- Access to network maps from Windows, Solaris, and HP-UX systems
- Access to network maps from a web browser
- HTML-based reports for the management staff
- Historical trending for network devices
- Ability to monitor up to 10,000 customer devices from a central location
- Ability to automatically open Service Desk incidents
- Integration with CiscoWorks
- Restricted customer access to network information
- Password-protected customer portal for remote access

The customers want their database and application servers to be monitored. Sealey Inc. will monitor the necessary MIB variables to keep track of memory and CPU utilization. Telamon® Telalert can be used to page the database administrators when problems are encountered on the servers. If network connectivity between application and database servers fails, a local network operator will need to be paged. Sealey Inc. can define thresholds for MIB variables and monitor these values in order to notify a network operator *before* the network becomes overly congested.

Sealey Inc. can give operators easy access to the database and application servers by creating buttons that will launch a telnet session to the server. NNM provides both a native (Motif) interface and a web-based interface. Anyone accessing NNM as an administrator can choose between the native ovw interface and the web-based Dynamic Views. The web-based version allows flexibility to run the application from any operating system in any location. Certain web-based tools provide read-only access and limited functionality, but can be used by operators to monitor the network. NNM also has the ability to generate and view web-based reports of devices and availability. See Figure 1-2 for the web-based General Inventory report available with NNM.

Figure 1-2 NNM provides web access to data such as General Inventory.

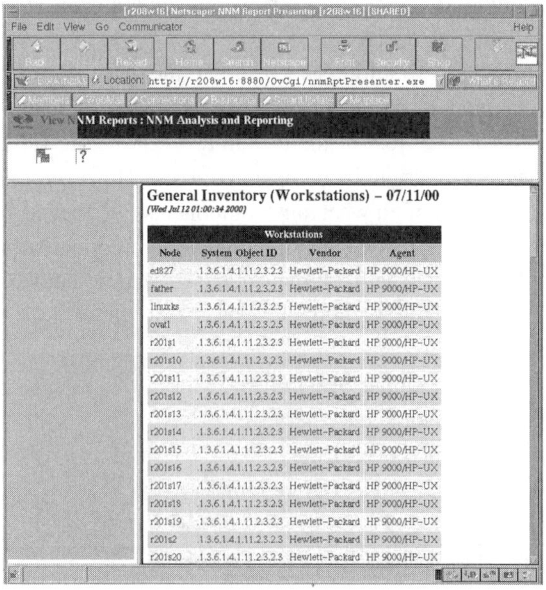

File Edit View Go Communicator Help

Location: http://r208w16:8880/OvCgi/nnmRptPresenter.exe

NNM Reports : NNM Analysis and Reporting

General Inventory (Workstations) – 07/11/00
(Wed Jul 12 01:00:34 2000)

Workstations			
Node	System Object ID	Vendor	Agent
ed827	.1.3.6.1.4.1.11.2.3.2.3	Hewlett-Packard	HP 9000/HP-UX
father	.1.3.6.1.4.1.11.2.3.2.3	Hewlett-Packard	HP 9000/HP-UX
linuxks	.1.3.6.1.4.1.11.2.3.2.5	Hewlett-Packard	HP 9000/HP-UX
ovat1	.1.3.6.1.4.1.11.2.3.2.5	Hewlett-Packard	HP 9000/HP-UX
r201s1	.1.3.6.1.4.1.11.2.3.2.3	Hewlett-Packard	HP 9000/HP-UX
r201s10	.1.3.6.1.4.1.11.2.3.2.3	Hewlett-Packard	HP 9000/HP-UX
r201s11	.1.3.6.1.4.1.11.2.3.2.3	Hewlett-Packard	HP 9000/HP-UX
r201s12	.1.3.6.1.4.1.11.2.3.2.3	Hewlett-Packard	HP 9000/HP-UX
r201s13	.1.3.6.1.4.1.11.2.3.2.3	Hewlett-Packard	HP 9000/HP-UX
r201s14	.1.3.6.1.4.1.11.2.3.2.3	Hewlett-Packard	HP 9000/HP-UX
r201s15	.1.3.6.1.4.1.11.2.3.2.3	Hewlett-Packard	HP 9000/HP-UX
r201s16	.1.3.6.1.4.1.11.2.3.2.3	Hewlett-Packard	HP 9000/HP-UX
r201s17	.1.3.6.1.4.1.11.2.3.2.3	Hewlett-Packard	HP 9000/HP-UX
r201s18	.1.3.6.1.4.1.11.2.3.2.3	Hewlett-Packard	HP 9000/HP-UX
r201s19	.1.3.6.1.4.1.11.2.3.2.3	Hewlett-Packard	HP 9000/HP-UX
r201s2	.1.3.6.1.4.1.11.2.3.2.3	Hewlett-Packard	HP 9000/HP-UX
r201s20	.1.3.6.1.4.1.11.2.3.2.3	Hewlett-Packard	HP 9000/HP-UX

By default, NNM does not collect MIB variable data. Data collection is easily configured and can be used for historical trending. Because Sealey Inc. manages customers that are growing rapidly, they need the network administrators to closely monitor the network activity to determine whether the networking devices are sufficient to handle the customers' growth. Data collection will need to be configured for select network devices. NNM can collect the data, graph the collected data, and configure thresholds to alarm on the data. Graphs can be used to spot trends in network activity and determine when network devices need to be upgraded. For example, the MIB variable ifInOctets measures activity coming *into* a network interface. You can collect, monitor thresholds, and graph MIB variables, such as ifInOctets, as shown Figure 1-3.

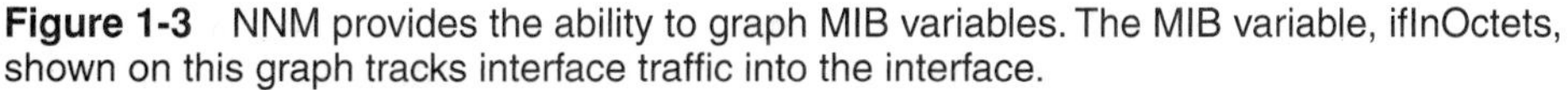

Figure 1-3 NNM provides the ability to graph MIB variables. The MIB variable, ifInOctets, shown on this graph tracks interface traffic into the interface.

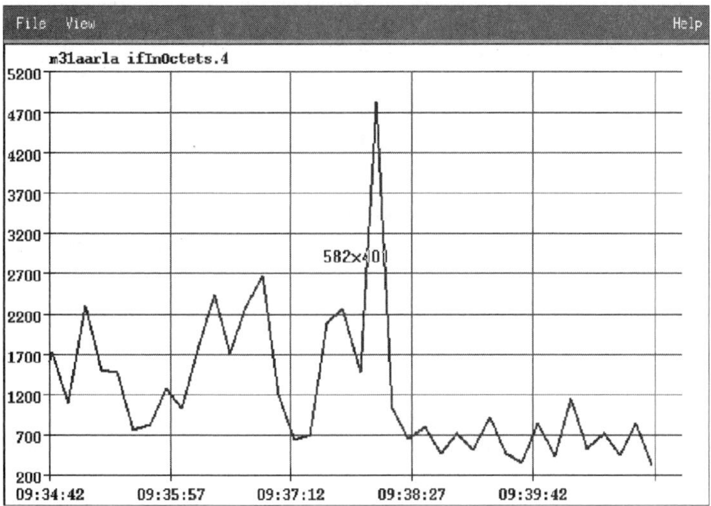

In addition to spotting trends, the staff can also configure thresholds for automatic notification. For example, thresholds can be configured for network interface traffic. When a threshold value is exceeded, someone on the network management staff can be paged. Telamon® Telalert can be integrated with NNM to provide automatic paging capability.

NNM can perform other automatic actions such as sending email. Sending an email can be a simple Unix script that passes the node name, the threshold value, and the sampled value. Another automatic action could be to open a Service Desk incident.

Because Node Manager has a practical limit of monitoring 2,000 nodes per NNM license, Sealey Inc. would need at least five NNM stations in order to manage up to 10,000 devices. This value is based on the typical polling interval used by NNM and depends on other factors such as network reliability and the amount of data being collected. The five NNM stations can be distributed throughout the network reporting to a central NNM station.

1.3 WHAT CUSTOMER VIEWS PROVIDES

NNM does an excellent job of displaying and monitoring the health of the network infrastructure. It provides a view of the physical network connectivity of an enterprise when you enable Extended Topology. What it does not do, however, is provide much of a customizable logical view. Though some customization exists within NNM, *Customer Views* (CV) extends the capabilities of NNM by allowing the administrator to define a logical hierarchy comprised of five additional views. Sealey Inc. will be able to grant restricted data access to each customer by grouping together each customer's devices in a separate hierarchy. CV provides the ability to define which customers are affected by which resources, and is commonly used by Internet Service Providers, Managed Service Providers, and outsourcers to allow for customer-based management. CV provides the five additional views from the top level of NNM, including:

1. **Key Resources**—Network devices that are deemed critical to the management of an organization.
2. **Customers**—A logical grouping of devices based on ownership of equipment.
3. **Devices**—Network devices that include routers, switches, and servers.
4. **Internet Links**—Devices that are provided to the customer by an external organization such as an Internet Service Provider.
5. **Sites**—A logical or geographical structure within an organization such as a city, building, or business structure (accounting, engineering, and so on).

CV must reside on the same system as NNM. The administrator plans the hierarchy, determines the customer and resource relationships, and identifies key resources. The CV command-line utility **ovcustomer** is used to define each of these components. This allows the administrator to define which systems belong to which organizations (Customers), where the systems are geographically located (Sites), and who the service providers are (Internet Links). Key Resources should be populated with the mission critical devices within an organization. Devices are automatically populated (based on SNMP responses) with network infrastructure devices such as network switches, routers, and hubs.

Sealey Inc. can configure CV to provide operators with a logical view of each customer network. This view will provide information regarding a customer by describing devices and key resources of a particular customer.

1.4 WHAT SERVICE INFORMATION PORTAL PROVIDES

Service Information Portal (SIP) enables service providers to give customers visibility into their environments by creating a "portal" view into each customer's services. The customer can access and customize their portal using a web browser that may be password protected.

SIP is configured using the **ovcustomer** utility (provided with CV) and the SIP administrator GUI. The SIP GUI enables the service provider to set up the information available for each customer in order to protect one customer's data from the other. The information provided in SIP may come from multiple sources from within NNM, including topology maps, events, performance summaries, network device health, and network performance graphs. In addition to NNM data, SIP provides data access to a variety of OpenView products including Operations (OVO), Service Desk (OVSD), and Performance (OVP) from a single tool.

Some of the features of SIP include

- Security by providing customer login
- Per-customer filtering of data
- XML template files for configuring customer portals
- An interactive interface for performing common tasks
- Tools for developing modules that present information other than NNM
- Presentation of NNM alarms, network device health and topology maps
- The display of NNM data collection graphs
- A message board to communicate information to the customer
- Online help for the administrator and separate help for the customer login

SIP provides customer access to a variety of data from a web page. SIP does not need to reside on the same system as NNM. The **ovcustomer** utility allows you to configure what to display on the portal. CV is not required to run SIP, but SIP integrates seamlessly into NNM with CV. For example, the device groupings configured in CV (Key Devices, Servers and Routers) are displayed as gauges on the portal. Portal configuration is done through an administrative web interface or by modifying *eXtensible Markup Language* (XML) files. After the configuration is complete for a customer, the administrator can disable modification of the interface by setting a flag in the XML file.

1.5 OBTAINING EVALUATION COPIES OF NNM, CV, AND SIP

Because this book is meant as a hands-on guide to these products, it is recommended that you obtain a copy of these products to enhance your understanding. Evaluation software is available from the web site `http://openview.hp.com`. Install documentation and product manuals can be also downloaded from the OpenView web site.

These can also be obtained from the web site `http://openview.hp.com` by selecting **Information library**, then **product manuals**. Select the product and platform **Network Node Manager for Unix** (or Windows) and select the **Quick Start Install Guide**. Repeat the process for Customer Views and Service Information Portal. After you've installed the product, the other manuals will be available online.

Note: This information was accurate at the time this book was written. However, the location and process of obtaining software is subject to change.

Check the Release Notes and Install Guides for current hardware and software requirements. Typically, you will achieve better performance by increasing the amount of physical memory on your management station. The number of nodes being monitored and the number of GUIs running on the management station will impact the performance.

At the time of this publication, the NNM management station is supported under HP-UX, Solaris, Windows 2000, and Windows XP.

1.6 ADDITIONAL OPENVIEW PRODUCTS

Hewlett-Packard offers a number of OpenView products. Listed here are a few HP OpenView products with a brief description of the products. While these products may be implemented independently, they can also be fully integrated into the OpenView framework.

The *HP OpenView Integrated Solutions Catalog* provides a current listing of third-party software and device vendors that have integrated their products with HP OpenView solutions.

1.6.1 HP OpenView Operations (OVO)

NNM monitors the network connectivity to your computer systems and network control devices. *OpenView Operations* (OVO), formerly ITO and VPO[2], monitors what is happening on your computer system by distributing an OVO agent directly to the computer system. While slightly more complex to implement than NNM, OVO offers the ultimate in flexibility of monitoring applications. OVO offers the capability of executing an automatic action when a significant event occurs. For example, the OVO agent can perform local actions as soon as it discovers that a process has died. You can define an automatic action to execute on the managed node that will do one or all of the following: restart the process, send a message to the operator, open a trouble ticket, and page someone. Similar to NNM, OVO has both a native GUI and a Java-based GUI.

1.6.2 HP OpenView Performance (OVP)

OpenView Performance (OVP), formerly PerfView/MeasureWare and Vantage Point Performance, is similar to Operations in that it relies on an agent installed on the computer systems to be monitored. While OVO is primarily used in monitoring the availability and problems (faults) occurring on these systems, OVP deals with the performance aspects of the system. The OVP agent collects approximately 300 metrics associated with the operating system on which it is running. The agent has the ability to extend these metrics to an application. For example, you might have a program collecting response times from a web server that you would like to view, notify, and summarize. This can be integrated into the data collected by the OVP agent.

The OVP management station is available on HP-UX, Solaris, and Windows 2000, while the Performance agent runs on HP-UX, Solaris, AIX, NT and several other operating systems. Refer to `http://openview.hp.com` for the latest releases of the Performance agent.

2 With every major release of OVO the product name has changed. The original name of OVO was *Operations Center* (OpC), The next release was named *Information Technology Operations* (ITO), and the next release was *Vantage Point Operations* (VPO).

1.7 SOME HELPFUL URLS

OpenView home page `http://openview.hp.com:80/`
OpenView Solutions Catalog `http://openview.hp.com/sso/isv/search`
OpenView Smart Plug-ins `http://www.openview.hp.com/downloads/downloads.html#spi`
OpenView Manuals `http://ovweb.external.hp.com:80/lpe/doc_serv`
OpenView Forum `http://ovforum.org`
MIT's SNMP Coke Machine `http://www.swiss.ai.mit.edu/htbin/coke`
CiscoWorks `http://www.cisco.com/univercd/cc/td/doc/product/rtrmgmt/cwparent/`
Telamon Telalert `http://www.telamon.com/products/telalert/index.php`
Unix Tools for Windows `http://www.cygwin.com/`
Google Search Engine `http://www.google.com`
Paint Shop Pro® bitmap editor for Windows `http://www.jasc.com`

CHAPTER 2

Why Network and Systems Management Systems Fail

Many factors can cause a network and systems management system to work differently from what you would expect. Maybe it is not being deployed as quickly as scheduled, deployment has halted, or it's not providing all the desired functionality required for a world-class management system. Some of the factors covered in this chapter might exist in your organization without causing problems; however, many readers will think, "That's happening to us!"

One reason for these scenarios is that network and systems management systems are not given the necessary attention by management to be world-class, fully functioning, fully staffed, totally automated systems. Network and systems management is often seen either as a "check box" that needs to be checked for the next promotion or as a minimal obligation. The "system" as a whole is not taken into account. Both management and the workgroup chosen by management to deploy network and systems management tools frequently have little knowledge of the complexity of their tasks. The workgroups managing networks and systems using products such as OpenView *Network Node Manager* (NNM) and *OpenView Operations* (OVO) generally include untrained or inexperienced personnel. The burden placed on them exceeds their abilities and they leave. They are replaced by more untrained personnel. It is like a revolving door.

Often, those given the responsibility to manage networks and systems aren't the same personnel who maintain the network. They may not even work for the same company, let alone even be in the same organization. Appropriate access to the systems for deployment of agents or even SNMP read access is hindered or forbidden by "the other" organization. This lack of cooperation between the groups slows deployment to a crawl.

The misconception exists that "anyone" can do the job. Sometimes the job is given to a person in the organization with the vision and the knowledge required to perform the tasks, but because of the complexity and time necessary to fulfill management's deadlines and requirements, the person suffers burn out and moves to another organization. The project then dies and the products are blamed for what is actually management's failure to provide adequate personnel, training and funding. Until network and systems managers and their personnel are given the same respect, attention, money, training, and certification as other professionals, network and systems management systems will continue to under-perform and be underutilized, keeping network managers and their teams in reactive mode.

2.1...TO WORK PROPERLY

Network and systems management systems most commonly fail to work properly due to a misunderstanding of how a product actually works and how it behaves when it interacts with parts of the operating system and other management systems within the management domain. The least understood part of the operating system also deserves the most attention and impairs the network and systems management systems from working correctly: the configuration of host name resolution in conjunction with an administrator's unique host-naming convention.

2.1.1 Incorrect Configuration of Hostname Resolution

Organizations can create some pretty unique host-naming schemes, and no matter what those "schemes" may be, they always seem to define one unique host name for every interface. There is nothing wrong with that host-naming scheme itself, it is the misconfiguration within each naming service that most frequently wreaks havoc on network and systems management systems and causes additional configuration problems elsewhere on each system. Appendix B, "Hostname Resolution," covers properly configuring hostname resolution to work with an administrator's unique hostnaming mechanism and prevent misconfiguration. Failure to correctly configure hostname resolution causes missed alarms or messages, event and message correlation, and synchronization.

Proper hostname configuration and resolution is documented in many places, including manual pages as well as other books on the configuration of NFS, NIS, and DNS and BIND. Yet it appears to be totally overlooked by system and network administrators. It is the first configuration item that is checked by any seasoned OpenView consultant before deployment of a network and systems management system. It is one of the first items checked during a call to the HP Response Center for an OVO agent communication problem. The proper configuration of hostname resolution is of the utmost importance for not only the network and systems management system, but for other system commands and processes such as the r-commands and NFS.

2.2...TO EFFECTIVELY MANAGE THE ENTERPRISE GROWTH

Effectively managing a growing enterprise requires forethought and planning the design of network and systems management systems. Improper planning of required resource requirements leads to an inability to manage networks and systems as quickly as management growth. How large the network is or how many nodes there are to "manage" is only part of the equation. "What" and "how much" is to be managed within the network and systems must also be entered into the equation. And "who" will implement and maintain it must be calculated as well. This means planning for resources that will enable the management system to go beyond managing the up or down status of individual systems as a whole and moving to managing individual processes and services. It means planning for system availability. These are all part of the requirements gathering process. Each must be an integral part of the deployment plan.

2.2.1 Lack of Hardware and Software Resources

There must be a plan for growth, high availability, speed, fault tolerance, and system upgrades. What is managed by the network and systems management system today will definitely not be what is managed next week, next month, or one or two years from now. More users, networks, nodes, applications, and services will be managed than originally planned. Not planning for growth can leave operators with sluggish consoles, cause *Network Management System* (NMS) polling to slow, or leave little storage for data collection. Overall, it reduces the ability of the system to immediately increase management upon demand.

When other organizations within the company learn that there is an organization effectively and proactively managing the network, they may to want to mimic it or piggyback onto that current system to save money. They might ask you to manage their systems. They will want to create a Service Level Agreement (SLA) with you and determine the resiliency of your system.What are your planned outages? What is the MTBF on your systems? What is the support contract on your systems—24×7? Are there fail-over systems in place? Are there enough resources to manage their systems as well? These factors must be an integral part of the plan.

Most organizations don't plan for future hardware and software upgrades and how the upgrades will affect customers. Purchasing systems that are easily upgradeable by processor or backplane swap will prevent rebuilding everything from scratch and restoring data. Upgrading hardware and software will be considered an outage; possibly several hours of outage. The ability to minimize an outage of the NMS should be in the overall design of the NMS system. Fail-over to another system in order to maintain the customer's SLA can necessitate the purchase of additional hardware and software in order to provide maximum uptime to the customers.

If possible, budget for development or "crash and burn" suites in order to test everything before placing it into production. Use the suites to test software upgrades, to fully test any procedure, and to avoid longer-than-planned outages, and even avoid having to back out of an upgrade. Implementing anything on production systems is precarious. One incorrect command can bring the testing of the recovery procedure to fruition.

2.2.2 Lack of Human Resources

Management products such as the OpenView suite of products don't behave as expected out-of-the-box. They are fully customizable. One can't simply install them, discover the network, deploy a few agents, magically generate a help desk ticket, page personnel fix the problem within the appropriate SLA, and automatically close the trouble ticket automatically when an alarm is cleared. It takes trained, knowledgeable personnel, and headcount to use and integrate these products.

Companies may have, at most, one to three people managing, developing, configuring, and deploying suites of OpenView products at multiple sites across the country. They perform all the design and implementation of each product. They are also responsible for being the system administrator (NT and UNIX), the database administrator (of many database flavors), troubleshooting, and backing up each system. Yet often, a year later, management asks why the entire enterprise is not being managed with all the "bells and whistles" they promised their customers. It's not the employees' fault; it's a lack of management expertise in the requirements to deploy, to deliver what was promised, and to know and hire the proper amount of people with the appropriate talents. It generally leads to a contract being made to a company that is experienced in OpenView product delivery.

The company forms a team with the appropriate skill sets to get the project on track and completed. It gathers the functional requirements and compiles a project plan and presents it to the customer. The project plan shows the steps and personnel required to complete the plan on time. The personnel most likely include a project manager, solutions architect, and a number of consultants knowledgeable in each product necessary to meet the functional requirements and for knowledge transfer to the customer to complete the project. A deployment team is also created to deploy the systems to multiple sites. Eventually, the project is completed and it is time for the knowledge transfer to those who will be managing the network and systems management system. How many people are provided who are properly trained in the products for which they will be administering? The answer to that question is usually "zero." The person or persons supplied may have had a class on one product, but have not been to a class for all the products. At this time, there isn't the breadth of knowledge about how each product works and integrates with another. It is nearly impossible communicate all the knowledge provided by skilled OpenView consultants and to a couple people before the project completion who can then train others on how the products and systems are configured and how they are integrated.

How many people should there be? That will depend on the number of different products, operating systems, databases, services, etc., at each site and on the terms of the SLAs. The term "products" should include the operating system, backup products, and so on. There is no magical number, formula, or algorithm for an exact number of people required. More often than not, there are too few people on the team with the appropriate skill levels to manage and deploy systems across large environments. Administrators of networks and systems that are going to be managed need to be involved in the various aspects of network and systems management. These aspects include what services need to be monitored, how they are monitored, when to alarm, when and who to page, and so forth. Get them involved.

2.2.3 Inadequate Training

Far too often, those who configure the products used within a particular network and systems management system are inadequately trained. They have some training on some products, but not enough to adequately deploy and maintain large environments. The more training that can be given to the personnel, the better it will be for them, the company, and the health and welfare of the NMS. Personnel who are given training classes will have a better understanding of each products capabilities and integration points. They will be able to architect and design a solution faster than they will from months of on-the-job-training. It boosts their morale and may make them less fearful to take on more responsibility as it pertains to the NMS systems and the systems they are managing.

While in class, they can network and discuss issues or possible solutions with the instructor and classmates who may have already resolved a similar problem. Many of these students have years more experience in network and systems management. Classroom training can prevent one from writing scripts for which commands already exist to provide the required functionality.

A common fear from management is that one will take the training and leave to find a better position for more money or responsibility at another company; thus, the lack of money most companies are willing to spend on training. It is generally junior personnel, who lack experience, who tend to jump ship after training and some months of experience. The technical interviewer at the company should detect a lack of experience, but the interviewer is not always technically sound. To avoid having employees leave the company after paying for training or certification, many companies have instituted policies that require a specific length of stay.

It is highly recommended that before attending an OVO UNIX training class that you first attend NNM training. OVO UNIX does not work without NNM! If any SNMP events (traps, alarms), especially Node Up, Node Down, Interface Up, Interface Down, etc., are to be seen in the OVO Message Browser, they will come through the NNM Event system. The NNM training class covers configuration of these events. Any installation of OVO UNIX requires a complete installation of NNM. NNM's processes run, discovery runs, traps are received, and some data collection occurs. Any solid OVO UNIX implementation requires a solid NNM implementation. In order to have a solid network and systems management system that encompasses both NNM and OVO UNIX, both classes should be taken.

If a company does not provide adequate training, find some practice time. Find a system, or systems, on which evaluation software can be installed and find out how it works there before implementing on production systems. The vast majority of all OpenView products come with an "instant on" license that is good for 60 days. Test all the theories and ideas before putting them into production. When not busy...practice! Learn all that can be learned about the products and how they function without worrying about breaking anything on a production system.

2.3...TO MANAGE EVERYTHING AT ONCE

A frequent mistake is configuring the network and systems management system to manage everything at once. Trying to integrate too many products at once and manage too many different services across the enterprise from the beginning, with lack of personnel, training, or hardware is destined for failure. It is too much, too fast, and it's done repeatedly at site after site. Network and systems management operators are then hammered with events and messages that cannot be managed at the rate they enter their browser. Tens of thousands of messages sit in the message browser and little is done about them. The operators no longer believe they are factual. Follow these steps to alleviate the problem:

1. Determine which systems, including network infrastructure, are going to be managed. Start with the NNM discovery process. Using discovery filters, the noDiscover files, or combination of both, configure NNM to discover only those systems.

2. For the discovered systems, ensure that hostname resolution is correct within the /etc/hosts file, NIS, and DNS. Correct means that the forward lookup of the short and fully qualified domain name returns every IP interface associated with that system and that the reverse address lookup of every IP address associated with that system returns the same fully qualified domain name. If this is not correct, then there is a 99.999 percent chance of something not working properly in the future. The following is a short list of things that can happen because of incorrect configuration of host name resolution services. The network and system management product does *not* cause these problems.
   - Messages not being seen in the OVO message browser
   - NNM events not acted upon
   - Multiple-node objects for the same node in NNM
   - Node names are different in each NMS product
   - Different node names in the Alarm Browser
3. If this is the first network and systems management project, start small. Add nodes to be managed by OVO agents to the OVO node bank. Turn off ALL events in NNM except Node Up, Node Down, Interface Up, and Interface Down. Set all the other events to "Log Only." Do the same for the OVO Trap template (after copying the default to a custom template). These four alarms are meaningful and are used by the majority of customers. Starting with only these four events prevents users from being inundated with a barrage of useless events coming from the network into the network and systems management system and having to delete them out of the NNM Alarm Browser. The operators will have confidence that the alarms received are meaningful. If they don't need to worry about a specific event, they don't need to see it as an alarm in the Alarm Browser!

After several weeks of running properly, peruse the log file for meaningful events and determine which events should be configured next. All the processes and procedures must be in place (such as a standard operating procedure, SOP for short) so that the operators will know what to do when the log file is received. If there is an automatic action that must be executed, it should be thoroughly tested. Operators will also need to know (through the instruction interface in OVO) what to do if the automatic action fails to correct the problem.

Determine the event requirements and integration points that will be provided by the additional products being added to the NMS. Add the products, one at a time, into the NMS. If adequate expertise exists, more can be done in parallel. Do not overwhelm the operators with useless events. The operator's browser should only contain useful and pertinent events (messages).

2.4...TO EVEN GET OFF THE GROUND

Managing networks and its systems is a great idea. Management likes the idea; corporate likes the idea; there can be return on investment and reduced cost of ownership, but who's going to fund it? What group is to be given responsibility for the project? More often than not, the organizational structure of a company is not conducive to allow a single group to design and deploy a network and systems management system for its enterprise. There are too many disparate groups who "do their own" networking and system administration who do not report to the group given the overall responsibility of network and systems management. The group needs to select and put into practice the right people, processes, and technology. Most of all, they have to have the authority to get the job done. The group selected may not be the best choice, it just happened to be the group who stated they would do it. The manager of the selected group also happened to have the appropriate high level degree such as a PhD… in orbital mechanics.

2.4.1 Layers 8 and 9 of the OSI Model

Just what are layers 8 and 9 of the *Open System Interconnection* (OSI) Model? Politics and money! Either one or the other or both will directly influence the whole NMS project (or any project for that matter). These layers decide who will do the project; when it will be completed; how much capital will be spent; and at times, even specify what products will be used. The combination of the former can get you a minimal system that barely meets the functionality requirements given for the project.

Even if a product doesn't meet the functional requirements, these layers can force its use within the NMS system and the outcome will be disappointing and only lead to building workarounds or not meeting schedule. The product doesn't meet expectations or specifications and is unusable. This can be caused by many factors, one being "Business Reciprocity," where someone within the management chain agrees to purchase the vendor's product in exchange for the vendor purchasing an equitable amount of services in return. The opposite can also occur when a vendor already has purchased a considerable amount of services and wants product in return. For the most part there is nothing wrong with this action; it's just good business. There are times when the exchange is not quite equitable and one party is left trying to fit a square peg into a round hole.

Egos can play a big part in preventing a project from getting started. Senior management in other departments may start jockeying for position in order to get a piece of the action after hearing that there is money to fund the project. Some even go as far as convincing management that their organization should have the project and "steal" the project, its funding, and the hard work from the first organization. Whether or not this is ethical is not the point. The point is *how* it was done. If it was done in order to gain notoriety within the company or to gain a promotion, it will only produce strife between the organizations within the company. Some might say, "That's just business." The following section is a direct result of the aforementioned situation.

2.4.2 Other Groups Won't Cooperate

As a direct result of politics and money, many companies end up with several NMS solutions, such as multiple help desks, all using different or possibly the same products as the other groups, none of which electronically interact with one another. This programming error generally occurs when there is an abundance of both layers within a company. The organizations involved do not report to the same top-level management, and each has its own budget, target customers, and management chain to appease. This wastes a lot of money on duplicate hardware, software, annual maintenance contracts, and consulting, thus increasing the total cost of ownership of the network and systems management system. Some companies have ended up with hundreds (yes, hundreds!) of little management stations running NNM with an enterprise license, none of which communicate with each other by any means.

How does this happen? There are many possibilities. One organization prefers one product because it has a specific functionality that is desired or because someone has been hired who already knows the product, making it easier and faster to implement. Perhaps a product does or doesn't run on a particular operating system on which they have an abundance of knowledge within their organization. But they have little knowledge on the product they have "evaluated" and wish to purchase. Most likely, they also have little money to spend on training; therefore, they have money allocated for capital expenditures and purchase what they believe is the right solution without regard for any synergy between organizations and products.

Business reciprocity is another possibility, which falls right in line with layer 8. Management agrees on an exchange of products for services and the entire company is forced to implement a product that in no way meets the criterion to fulfill their particular customer requirements. In order to meet customer demands and promised SLAs, additional products are purchased to provide the promised services. The original product then sits dormant on a shelf.

2.5 SUMMARY

One or a combination of all these problems could be the reasons a network and systems management project is failing in one or more areas; your organization may have yet another that hasn't been mentioned. The problems will not be fixed unless someone is ordered to do so by a high-level manager, or a new organization is formed to bring together all the organizations under a single manager who is responsible for network and systems management. At that point, the organizations all must work as a team, putting all misgivings aside and getting the job done. Select products based on today's and tomorrow's requirements. It could be the difference between promotion and demotion.

CHAPTER 3

Create a Deployment Plan

Before deploying *Network Node Manager* (NNM) and *OpenView Operations* (OVO), a deployment plan should be created to determine what and how the products will be configured. The plan includes what and how much of the network is to be monitored, collection station layout and management domains, manager of managers configuration, the products required to instrument the network for monitoring, and more. A good plan can be used to create other plans for system testing and acceptance of the final system and system hardware configuration, high availability, and so on. This chapter outlines questions that should be asked to successfully develop, deploy, and maintain OpenView NNM and Operations. It is not meant to be a complete list, but is generic enough to get started in tailoring one to your specific environment. Reviewing this list should stimulate more questions about the specific management domains that will be created.

This chapter emphasizes the importance of gathering all the necessary requirements for a network and systems management system, in order to design a system that meets or exceeds those requirements before purchasing anything. The requirements are gathered by those responsible for the systems being managed and those managing the management systems. Gathering all the requirements for the network and systems management system will place the project on the road to a successful deployment and implementation.

3.1 MANAGEMENT REQUIREMENTS

Gather the management requirements first. Ask the following types of questions; they should lead to many more questions: What will be managed? How it is to be managed? (Those two questions drive hardware and software requirements.) What problems are to be detected? How can the problems be detected? Can the problem be detected by an SNMP trap or by monitoring thresholds? Can the problem be detected by writing a shell script? When a problem is detected, what steps can be taken to automatically correct the detected problem? Can those steps be automated?

The term "managed" needs to be defined. What is managed on one node will be different than another. What is going to be managed? Will only network devices be managed or will servers and workstations be managed? How much is to be managed? Will only Up/Down status of systems and interfaces be managed? Will the status of processes need to be monitored on any given system? Will the resources of a system or resources a process is consuming need to be managed? These types of questions drive the size of the system and license requirements. And don't forget to gather the reporting requirements.

There will be a limiting factor on what will be managed. That factor is the budget. All the management requirements can be gathered and put in to a multi-year plan that takes into account the given budget.

3.1.1 Problem Detection

What problems require detection and thus an alert that the problem has been detected? Most likely, some event, catastrophic or otherwise, has occurred that led a company to determine that network and systems management needs to be deployed. Loss of revenue due to the unavailability of a network, system, or service is at the top of the list of reasons to deploy network and systems management product suites. But to what granularity of management does one need to have in order to be alerted of a particular problem? One can think of NNM as the manager of the "block diagram" of networks and systems. At a high level, NNM monitors the connectivity status of network interfaces of the network "block diagram" using ping and SNMP and problem detection becomes more granular from there.

OVO manages services and processes, and to some extent, Operating System and process resource utilization. The processes and resources are those that run on a "block" within the network block diagram. For more detailed process and resource utilization there is the coda subagent of the Operations Agent. And for even more detailed process and resource utilization, the *OpenView Performance Agent* (OVPA) can be purchased and configured. The OVPA will send "events" to NNM or OVO, using SNMP or Operations Center Messaging respectively. OVPA also collects and summarizes and maintains history of the resource data. How much detail is needed?

Specific service response time can be measured through *OpenView Internet Services* (OVIS). *OpenView Performance Insight* (OVPI) collects management data from NNM, OVIS, OVPA, and SNMP and contains threshold monitoring and forwards detected desecrations via SNMP.

The question again is, at what "point" must there be detection of the problem? Define the problem, and then determine the method of instrumentation to detect and report the problem to the management server. After the problem is detected and reported, decide what action must be taken, whether it is an automatic action taken by the product, or manual process by human intervention.

3.1.2 Software Requirements

Another reason for deploying management systems is to enable the company to become more proactive when it comes to managing networks and systems. Becoming proactive means the organization managing the networks and systems knows about the problem before the customer calls and notifies them of the problem. The ultimate goal is to know of the problem and fix the problem so the customer never knows there was a problem. This ultimate goal goes beyond the scope of this book because it entails the design of highly available networks, systems and services that are managed by the Network Management System. The goal of a network management team is to instrument the network in such a way that the problem is detected, alerted, and that any automatic or manual actions are taken to correct the problem. All these events are recorded within the NMS browser. What management software will help reach these goals? NNM and OVO problem detection and notification will be discussed here.

3.1.2.1 Network Node Manager

NNM's Alarm browser contains SNMP traps, or events. The way to get an alarm into NNM's Alarm browser is an SNMP trap. There are many ways that an SNMP trap can be generated. One is that a trap is generated from the SNMP agent on the managed node and sent to the trap destination. In this case, it is sent to NNM, but could easily be sent to a system that is designed for event correlation. SNMP traps are built-in to the SNMP agent from the vendor and are sent upon detection of an anomaly on the system. The associated traps are vendor, operating system, and product specific and are described in either the agent's documentation or the trap definition file. The traps are generally not configurable, though some agents allow for the customization of the data sent within the trap. HP OpenView's Extensible SNMP agent does allow for the creation of trap definitions.

HP's Extensible SNMP agent runs on HP-UX and Solaris and can be "enhanced" to provide additional data through customized *Object Identifiers* (OIDs) that operate through an **snmpget** or can perform system operations through an **snmpset**. The Extensible agent runs as a sub-agent to the HP's SNMP agent. The creation of customized OIDs and traps allow for detection of specific problems not available with the standard SNMP agent.

To use NNM to detect and notify that a specific problem has occurred on a node, check to see if there is a vendor-specific SNMP trap that will provide the problem detection. First, obtain the trap configuration file or documentation on the vendor's agent. The trap configuration file is an ASCII file and can be read with any editor. Using an editor makes it easier to search through the file for information rather than loading the trap definitions into the event database and looking down the event tree. Traps that meet the requirements can be loaded into the event database and configured through **xnmevents**. It is within **xnmevents** that actions can be configured when the trap is received.

A second way is to poll an SNMP agent for specific OIDs and create an internal trap within NNM based on a threshold. The OIDs can be found within a vendor's MIB definitions for the vendor's SNMP agent. These MIB definitions are text files and readable by an editor (brush up on reading ASN.1 syntax) and can be searched for a possible OID that can be retrieved to provide the needed information. The MIB definitions can also be loaded into NNM for reading in the MIB tree using NNM's MIB browser (xnmbrowser). They must be loaded in order to configure NNM data collection. When the MIB is loaded into NNM, configure NNM's Data Collection, Threshold, and Monitoring to retrieve SNMP data and internally create a threshold and rearm trap (event) based on checking the retrieved value against for the OID. When the threshold is broken, it sends an SNMP-specific trap. When the value for the OID returns to normal, the rearm trap (event) occurs. These traps will be viewed in the Alarm. If the information cannot be retrieved from the SNMP agent, another way will have to be devised, possibly through an OVO action, command, or monitor, or some other method or add-on product.

Tip: When using NNM Threshold and Monitoring, only numeric variables can be retrieved for status checking. Polling for changes in text cannot be done.

3.1.2.2 OpenView Operations

OVO is agent based, meaning that an agent is deployed to the node and alarms (messages) are sent to the OVO Management station based upon the templates assigned to the node. There are different types of templates that read log files, run monitor scripts, or intercept and format SNMP traps. Whatever the type of template, the template itself is used to retrieve the specific data and format a message based on a template string. The agents can only be deployed to specific operating systems and not to network devices such as routers, bridges, and switches. There are also *Smart Plug-ins* (SPIs) available, both free and at cost, that are designed to be deployed with the OVO UNIX agents to manage specific databases, operating systems, mail servers, and more. The templates and the actions, commands, and monitors they run are fully customizable. New templates, actions, commands, and monitor scripts can be created to do just about anything. If a script can be written to determine if there is a problem, it can be monitored through OVO. If a script can be written to properly correct a problem, it can be an automatic action. A trap template can be assigned to management server or collection station to send SNMP traps that are received by NNM's ovtrapd process to the OVO UNIX message browser via the OVO messaging system. The OVO message can be sent using the TCP protocol to ensure the message gets to the OVO management server.

Whether using NNM alone or in conjunction with OVO, it is recommended that Node Up, Node Down, Interface Up, and Interface Down events be enabled first, and everything else is turned off. If the OVO product is loaded and configured with the basic events and templates deployed, the system will be inundated with information about the monitored systems. Most of this information will be unwanted, unnecessary, and duplicated. Literally tens of thousands of events and messages can easily be generated on a daily basis if the default templates and traps are deployed out-of-the-box. It is virtually impossible to peruse through fifty thousand messages on a daily basis. The same concept applies to NNM. NNM will be flooded with traps from the nodes it discovers, especially if the discovered SNMP agent allows the management server to configure itself as a trap destination. Add alarms and traps as necessary within the product that is suited to detect, report, and act on the problem. If the operators monitoring the Alarm or Message browser are told to "ignore" what is presented in the browser, they will begin to lose faith in the system and its ability to provide alarms that are substantive.

3.1.2.3 Additional Management Products

Adding management products increases the complexity of the overall solution. Depending on the management requirements, there may be no way to avoid it. Don't add management capabilities if the other products are not working as expected. If the NNM alarm or OVO message browser contains unnecessary alarms, they need to be modified in order that the browser becomes state based. The more products that are added, the more memory, CPU, disk space, backup, and training requirements are needed. There will be more alarms coming if they aren't configured properly and implemented slowly. Keep in mind that some products have different methods of backing up the data, and some may not function in an MC/ServiceGuard or other High Availability configuration. Plus, not all the products can be managed remotely and require access to the system console for configuration. These items must be considered within the plan.

3.1.2.4 Functionality Overlap

There is the possibility of the overlap of functionality within each product. Determine which product has better functionality and use it. Both NNM and OVO have browsers that view alarms. NNM has the Alarm browser and OVO has the Message browser. When deleting alarms in the NNM browser, they are just that: Deleted! Acknowledging OVO messages in the active Message browser moves the message to the history table and remains there until downloaded. Until the message is downloaded from history table, it can be retrieved for viewing. Assigning the trap template to a NNM management console or collection station will forward the SNNP events into the OVO Message browser enabling the OVO Message browser to be primary viewer for alarms.

Note: By deploying an OVO Agent and trap template to a NNM management/collection station, SNMP traps can be sent from the NNM to the OVO via TCP, which guarantees delivery. After the trap has been converted to an OVO message, the message can be owned by an operator, escalated within OVO, text can be added for testing or instructions on what to do with the message when it is received, and so on.

3.2 DEFINE THE MANAGEMENT DOMAIN

There are many management "domains" when designing network and systems management systems. Each domain is uniquely defined, but they can also overlap each other. A domain can be defined by a geographical location, such as a building, city, state, country, or any combination of these. It can be administrative, such as who is responsible for maintaining the network and systems management system for a specific area. Networks, protocols, operating systems, or firewall boundaries can also define domains. These are also called demarcation points.

It's important to begin managing a small area, such as the local network, and expand the management domain slowly. Don't venture out into *Distributed Internet Discovery and Monitoring* (DIDM) out-of-the-box. Define exactly what is to be managed.

3.2.1 What Will Be Managed?

Nodes and Networks

Define which nodes are going to be managed with NNM and OVO. If the node will be managed with OVO, it must be managed by NNM in order to receive interface and node up/down traps through the trap template into the OVO message browser. Knowing the total number of nodes will determine the licensing requirements for NNM and OVO as well as other OpenView products.

Determine which nodes are most critical. Use this information to define the polling interval for the nodes.

Using the managed nodes IP addresses, the managed networks can now be determined. When NNM discovers an interface with an IP address, it has to create a segment and network object for that IP/netmask combination in which to reside. Are any networks more critical than another is? Use this information to modify the polling interval for those networks.

IPX Nodes

Will there be a need to manage Novell Networks using the IPX protocol? Discovering IPX protocol systems can only be done with NNM on Windows NT. These collected objects can be sent to NNM on UNIX running an enterprise license.

DHCP Hosts

How many network addresses are handled by DHCP, and will they need to be discovered and managed? NNM will discover employees' computers that are plugged into the network in the morning and obtain an IP address; that way, the employees can take the laptop home in the evening. When the employee shuts down the computer, NNM will show that system as down. If such addresses need to be managed they must be configured within NNM as DHCP addresses to be handled properly.

Level-2 Discovery

Is level-2 discovery a requirement for the network management system? Depending on your type of network, level-2 discovery will add hundreds if not thousands of objects into the NNM object database. NNM may show unused switch ports on some types of network switches in a down state, which will propagate that status upward through the submaps.

OVO Managed Nodes

How many nodes will be managed by OVO? The status of a system within the OVO Node Bank is based on the status of the messages for that system in the operator's active message browser.

In order to ensure that only meaningful alarms are displayed within an operator's active message browser, decide which two or three things (outside of Interface Up/Down and Node Up/Down) are "must-know" and must be managed through OVO's actions, commands, and monitors. Start by configuring a small set of alarms here, or else you'll be deluged with messages of unimportance that will begin to increase the size of the history messages table in the OVO database.

All acknowledged active messages are moved to the history messages table. The history messages table is the largest table within the OVO database. The number of received messages at the management server is based on the number of nodes managed and the number of templates that are distributed to those managed nodes. Messages from the nodes do not only notify of a problem, but also rectify it. They can also notify of normal behavior. The distributed templates have actions, commands, and monitors assigned that actually send the messages from the managed node to the management server based on what is checked by it. When, how often, and how many messages are sent from a node is entirely up to the person who configured the template.

How fast and large the history messages table is depends on the number of received and acknowledged messages and how often the history messages are downloaded out of the table. How often the history messages are downloaded is based on how long the information must be kept for examining messages over time, looking for troublesome nodes, or repeated events.

If the plan is to keep a lot of data for trending analysis, make sure the disk on which the database resides is fast and there is plenty of space.

3.2.2 Collection Station Requirements

Defining the number of required collection stations and management stations is based upon the overall design of the NMS itself. Does the design require overlapping management domains? The numbers of nodes within each domain, license requirements, slow network links, and so on are a factor in designing the system. Collection stations are used by NNM to remotely discover and monitor the network and report back node status and traps to an NNM management station.

3.2.2.1 Collection Domains

Use the defined management domains to determine the number of collection stations required to manage the enterprise. These management systems will be the "collection" domains for use with Distributed Internet Discovery and Monitoring. Any collection station is a management station. The difference between a management station and collection station is that an operator actively uses a management station NNM GUI to access NNM or integrated management products.

3.2.2.1.1 Will there be any Overlapping Domains?

Overlapping collection stations provide for monitoring redundancy, especially when the two collection stations use separate routes to the same destination. It also provides for continued monitoring in the event that one collection station requires maintenance or has experienced a failure. Don't confuse overlapping collection stations with automatic fail-over in a Manager of Managers situation. Overlapping collection domains for monitoring do not require an enterprise license. There are two management stations monitoring the same networks and/or nodes, but they do not replicate object data from one to another.

3.2.2.1.2 Will there be any Collection Station Fail-over?

Which collection stations need to fail-over for another? This scenario requires an enterprise license to operate. Here a management station "manages" another management station and uses it for a collection station. The acting collection station sends its object database through a topology filter (if defined) to the managing station. If there is no topology filter defined, it sends everything for which it is responsible for managing. The acting collection station does all status monitoring for those nodes. After it is replicated, only changes in topology or status are sent to the station(s) that managed it. If the collection station is no longer accessible by the management station, the management station can assume status polling of the collection station's nodes.

There are several traps that are pre-defined to be sent to the REMOTE_MANAGERS list. When a management station manages a collection station, its name is automatically placed in the REMOTE_MANAGERS list. Those traps are automatically forwarded to that list.

Knowing all the information documented thus far will assist with the purchase of the appropriate number and type of licenses and hardware requirements. Don't forget to account for future monitoring growth.

3.2.2.2 Distributed Internet Discovery and Monitoring (DIDM)

Distributed Internet Discovery and Monitoring means exactly that: The discovery and monitoring of the infrastructure is distributed across the enterprise. It is done by standing up separate collection stations to discover and monitor specific portions of the network by the defining discovery filters and noDiscover file entries. Whether or not DIDM is used, review the information in this chapter and decide how to handle map, discovery, topology filters, and noDiscover entries. Agree that only one filters file will be maintained and distributed to every management/collection station. Having one filters file makes the overall system more flexible and saves time in troubleshooting. If the systems are all HP-UX, think seriously about using Software Distributor for maintaining and distributing configuration files to all systems.

3.2.3 Distributed Consoles, Web Presenter, or the Java GUI?

NNM and OVO each provide a Motif Graphical User Interface for use by operators and administrators of the respective product. NNM can be configured to use distributed consoles and the web presenter to remotely distribute a display to present the network and node status, alarms, and reports. OVO has only a Java GUI for remotely distributing the display, and at this writing only the operator console is supported. The decision to use any or all of these requires *additional* system resources. Decide during the planning stages what is best method for distributing the presentation and removing the operator load on the management console, or plan to purchase enough hardware resources for all users to display Motif GUI from the management console to a local X server. No additional license is required to use any of these features.

3.2.3.1 Distributed Consoles

Configuring NNM to use distributed consoles allows the Motif GUI to be run from a console other than the management server. Third-party applications can be run from the client if the applications support a distributed console or are not dependent on access to NNM's database. To configure NNM to use distributed consoles, the management station must become an NFS server. In order for the NFS server to perform well, there are some kernel parameters that need to be adjusted, one of which is the amount of memory that is assigned to buffer cache. The default HP-UX setting for the maximum dynamic buffer cache (dbc_max_pct) is fifty percent. The maximum amount of buffer cache should not be more that 1GB on the NFS server and not more that 400MB on the NFS client. These are not minimum memory requirements; they are the maximum that should be used for maintaining NFS performance. Take this into account when calculating memory requirements. For more information on NFS tuning and performance see *Optimizing NFS Performance* by Dave Olker, published by Prentice Hall.

3.2.3.2 OpenView Web Interface

The OpenView Web Interface provides read-only access to maps and limited write access to events to multiple people simultaneously. Presented maps are updated dynamically. The OpenView Web interface requires an open **ovw** session on the management server for each map that will be displayed through the web interface. Logins to the interface are separate from those of a UNIX or NT login.

Only NNM information such as maps, reports, inventory, and alarms is available through this interface. No OVO information can be seen through this interface. Knowledge of web server configuration, authorization, authentication, access control, and performance tuning will be extremely helpful in its deployment.

3.2.3.3 Java GUI

The OVO Java GUI is installed and runs from an NT or UNIX client and provides an operator interface to the management server. Using the Java interface can offload memory requirements needed to run the same number of Motif GUIs back to an X server. The operator interface is fully functional for OVO. It can launch NNM applications from the management server and display them back to an X client. The administrator must still use the Motif interface for configuring the various OVO banks (node, application, and so on).

3.2.4 Data Warehouse and Data Collection

NNM provides everything necessary to export data collected within its various databases (topology database, event database, and SNMP trend data) to the data warehouse. The warehouse can be one of three databases: Oracle or NNM's internal database, or Microsoft SQL. These databases use *Open Database Connectivity* (ODBC), making it easier to create customized reports using spreadsheets or web pages. There are "canned" reports available through the Web Presenter and contributed spreadsheet reports. These are delivered with NNM.

For more information on the data warehouse, see the online manual *Reporting and Data Analysis with HP OpenView NNM*. It provides configuration and formulas to determine the approximate amount of disk space required.

3.2.4.1 Questions to Consider when Planning for the Data Warehouse

What types of reports are to be created?

What MIBs need to be collected to create the desired reports?

How much space is required based on the collected and exported trend data?

How long must the data be kept before archiving?

Is there a requirement to access archived data?

How many users will access the reports?

3.3 ARE THERE FIREWALLS WITHIN THE MANAGEMENT DOMAIN?

NNM, OVO, and the associated web server can be specifically configured to work through firewalls. Gather the firewall configuration requirements for all the products. Test procedures need to be created in order to ensure proper operation of each component that must traverse any firewall. A good test is to startup a secure shell daemon (or any daemon that logs connectivity to a log file) on the "other side" of the firewall on the specific port to be tested (sshd –p <#>). Telnet across the firewall from the management server to the node using telnet <host> <port #>. If a connection to the daemon is successful, then the connection will be logged in to the logfile (syslog). Whether or not full duplex connectivity was established, the important test is the directional connectivity and the establishment of the one-way connection. The same can be done in reverse (client to management server) using the appropriate port number with the daemon on the management server and telneting from the client.

As part of the configuration, those who managed the firewall will need to be contacted and given explicit instructions on how to configure the firewall for correct operation of the products. Be prepared to test and argue with them that the firewall is not configured correctly.

3.4 OUT-OF-BAND NETWORK MANAGEMENT

Is all system management traffic to be localized to a specific network? How can the management traffic be localized to a specific network? Here is where the *sortlist* of the /etc/resolv.conf file comes in handy (see Appendix B, "Hostname Resolution"). Configure the management station's /etc/resolv.conf file to include the sortlist feature and set the network to the out-of-band network:

```
domain hpc.hp.com
sortlist 192.168.2.0
nameserver 0.0.0.0
```

All multi-homed hosts will have the 192.168.2.0 network returned over any other IP on the system. In order for the client to talk to the server through the out-of-band network, each client will need an entry in its /etc/hosts file resolving the hostname of the management server to the IP address the management server's out-of-band interface.

If the resolver does not support the sortlist feature, the nameserver itself may support the feature. If the management server is a nameserver, add the sortlist to the named.conf file and test for proper resolution.

The last possible hope is creating one large /etc/hosts file on the management server. This entails configuring the /etc/hosts file with the IP address of each systems management atop any other IP address for that system.

3.5 BACKUP AND RECOVERY REQUIREMENTS

Define the method of backup and recovery for the network and systems management systems. These systems can be incorporated in the management domain or a single system can backup each if there is enough bandwidth and I/O throughput. Listed here are some of the questions that need to be asked about system backups. Backup and restoration have a direct effect on how much disk space to purchase and whether an additional backup product needs to be included in the NMS design. Bandwidth and throughput on systems and networks need to be taken into account. In order to do an online backup of the NNM and OVO Oracle databases, the database must be placed in archive mode. Configuring the database for archiving produces a large number of archive logs and the database server places them in the configured directory. These archive logs can take up a lot of disk space as the systems get busy. When using the ovbackup script supplied with the NNM and OVO, there needs to be enough temporary disk space available to copy the information for backup.

What organization is going to back up the systems and the data that is being collected?

Will a backup product need to be purchased or will standard back up products be used?

Will the organization backing up the systems want cost relief?

Is there anything peculiar in backing up certain products?

How much time will it take to back up the systems?

How often do the systems need to be backed up?

How is restoration tested?

Where will offsite backup tapes be held?

How fast can offsite backup tapes be retrieved?

Is it faster to design a recovery scenario through HP Ignite/UX or Sun JumpStart and then restore only data?

3.6 AUTHENTICATION, AUTHORIZATION, AND ACCESS CONTROL REQUIREMENTS

Is there a single sign-on requirement? Not all the products used to manage the network use the same authentication, authorization, and access control mechanisms. Authentication is the mechanism that is used to determine that a user is who he claims to be. Authorization comes after a person is authenticated and determines what access rights are permitted for the individual, which could be no access or full access. Access control controls the specific access to the resources.

Authentication is done in a variety of ways, but for network and systems management systems a login and password are the standard method. Many products can use the same authentication method, and most have individual authorization and access control mechanisms. NNM requires only the operating system login to run the **ovw** command. OVO requires the operating system login and a second login after the execution of the opc command. Authorization to execute NNM's ipmap can be given through the OVO application bank to unite the authentication methods of OVO and NNM. Using a product's web-based interface may provide the best ability to unite authentication, authorization, and access control.

3.7 EVENT CORRELATION REQUIREMENTS

With the advent of Message Correleation in OVO 7.x, message correlation is much simpler. Correlate messages within OVO whenever possible. Event correlation (NNM) using *Event Correlation Services* (ECS) is a whole project in and of itself and is not typically tackled during the first phase of an enterprise management project. Either way, when correlating events or messages, investigate the events and messages that have occurred over time within a specific network area and determine which of those could be correlated into a single event (message).

ECS does not prevent the events (traps to NNM) from coming to the network and systems management station, but takes the incoming events and, based on states or circuits, determines the possible problem and presents one event to an operator or none at all. At any point within a state or circuit an action could be taken to determine if there is still a problem, whether there was one in the first place, or take measures to retrieve more data or wait for more incoming traps before presenting anything to an operator. A myriad of possibilities exists for correlating events. Unless there is knowledgeable staff on hand to take on this task, event correlation with ECS should wait for a future project.

3.8 HIGH AVAILABILITY AND FAULT TOLERANCE REQUIREMENTS

Mirrored disks, fail-over sites, multi-computer fail-over, aggregated network links, active-standby systems and network links, routing protocols, alternate physical volume links, disk arrays, redundant power—these are just some of the possible requirements for high availability and fault tolerance. These requirements can be placed on the individual systems, multiple systems acting as one system, and systems acting in conjunction with one another in the overall design during an anomaly.

The amount of high availability and fault tolerance in the design is driven by the requirements, but what is actually implemented is driven by cost. The same can be said for the entire NMS plan. High availability and fault tolerance requirements will be driven by the necessity of continuity of operations. What is the importance of network and systems management to the organization during any type of outage to the NMS? How much high availability and/or fault tolerance can be purchased based on the capital spending allotted to the project?

Note: Always design a system that maintains data integrity over everything else, even over system performance. System performance should take precedence over ease of system administration.

If a disk array cannot be purchased due to budget constraints, at least purchase enough disks to mirror the data even if they are mirrored on the same bus. Replacing failed hardware components is much faster than having to rebuild the operating system or restoring data that is hours or even days old and being unable to manage the network during the process. There is also the fact that setting up software in a high availability/fault tolerance (HA/FT) environment works differently based on the product. Configuring the availability of SNMP traps sent to different NNM management stations is totally different than the configuring the availability of OVO messages sent from a managed node to different OVO management stations.

NNM can be configured in a Manager of Managers configuration to ensure continued status polling if there is an outage to a collection station. Any management station that has an enterprise license can be configured to manage and monitor another management/collection station and assume status polling for the systems for which the "managed" management/collection station is responsible. This configuration provides for the continued availability of status polling, but it is much different to provide for the continued availability of traps to a trap destination.

When a management station manages another management station to act as its collection station, it adds its name to the REMOTE_MANAGERS list on that collection station. Any trap received at the collection station that is configured to be forwarded to the REMOTE_MANAGERS list will be forwarded to each management station in the list without question. The collection station forwards only traps configured to be forwarded to either a REMOTE_MANAGERS list or to specific trap destinations. Otherwise, the traps "stop" at the collection station. Standard Operating Procedures has to be written in order to deal with this type of situation if there are operators manning each management station for incoming events.

But if an outage to a collection station occurs and a management station takes over the status polling for that collection station, it doesn't change the trap destination of all the SNMP agents within a collection stations management domain to send traps to the management station. The SNMP agents would have list the management station as a trap destination there will be no traps sent to the management station. Then all the SNMP traps are going to both the collection station and management station. If the collection station is used as a management station, such as there are operators managing and acting on the incoming events, and at the management station, there needs to be a defined Standard Operating Procedure as well. This limitation has nothing to do with OpenView NNM itself. It is the SNMP agent protocol that doesn't support the selection of trap destinations based on the availability or unavailability of the trap destination, or selection of a destination based on time of day and so on. Placing the collection station itself within a high availability solution allows for the NNM processes to be up on one of multiple systems within a cluster.

OVO can also be configured in a Manager of Managers configuration to ensure continued reception of messages from managed nodes. A managed node is given a responsible managers file (an actual file, but distributed with templates) that defines the OVO management consoles that are authorized to be a managed nodes' primary manager. The managed node will report to and take commands from only that primary OVO management station. A managed node will switch to being managed by another authorized management console when it receives the correct command from an authorized management console. The managed node sends its messages only to its current primary manager. It does not send it to all possible primary managers like the REMOTE_MANAGERS list or trap destination list configured in an SNMP agent. The appropriate number of managed node licenses is required at each OVO management console. This scenario allows for separate OVO management stations to be located in disparate geographical areas; each management station is able to assume the responsibility for the other for continuity of operations. Continuity of operations should also be part of the overall plan, but it is not discussed in this book.

An OVO managed node can also be configured, using a responsible manager's file, to send messages to different management stations at specific times of day. A managed node can also be configured to send messages of specific types to different management stations, send messages to assigned groups within the OVO console or combination of these. An OVO agent gives more flexibility than an SNMP agent does when it comes to the delivery of messages.

High availability support for a single instance of NNM or OVO is supported on HP-UX, Solaris, and Windows (OVOW) operating systems using the supported high availability product. This allows for NNM and OVO to run on a single system within the cluster and fail-over to another system within the cluster. The "fail-over" to an adoptive node can be done manually for maintenance on the primary node, or automatic due to hardware or network failure. Placing the products within a supported high availability product allows for continuous operation of the NMS.

3.9 CONFIGURATION AND CHANGE MANAGEMENT PROCESS REQUIREMENTS

Are configuration and change management procedures in place? Failure to have these in place and follow them could mean a disaster. Even for minor changes to the system. For example, if one maverick turns on level-2 discovery at a collection station that manages an entirely switched network infrastructure at a remote site, the upstream management servers' object database goes from maintaining 3000 objects to tens, if not hundreds, of thousands. It may seem like a "minor" change to one person but can mean downtime for many other operators because the upstream management station was not designed to handle the disk operations and the memory required to synchronize maps with that many objects. Stick to the developed C and CM processes to avoid unplanned downtime.

It is essential to test everything before deployment to production systems. If there is funding for test suites, purchase them. Use them to test deployment strategies, template distribution, alarm and automatic action testing, upgrades, patching and anything else that comes to mind. It will be well worth the money spent.

3.10 HARDWARE CONFIGURATION REQUIREMENTS

The functional requirements for the NMS drive both software selection and hardware selection. The software selection for the NMS has bearing on the hardware selection based on the operating systems on which it can run and the amount of memory required to run the applications. How much hardware to purchase is based on the overall design and how NMS is going to be instrumented for problem detection, high availability requirements, data collection, distributed consoles, and so on.

3.10.1 Memory Requirements

Gather all the information available about the running the server software, operating system, client software, databases, data collection, and so on, and calculate the memory requirements. Err on the high side. One can have all the virtual memory in the world configured on a system, but software cannot execute in virtual memory; it must be placed in *random access memory* (RAM) to run. It is better to have more random access memory than too little and have to swap out processes.

3.10.2 Disk Space and Disk I/O Requirements

Purchase fast disks, preferably arrays. Disk arrays allow for the creation of multiple LUNs. These physical volumes can usually be created smaller than the size of a physical disk within the array. How much space you need depends on many different variables. When using disks within a high availability solution, most likely all the products will be configured in an active/standby configuration. But will the products be configured on a single cluster node and when a fail-over is required they are shutdown on the first cluster node and started on another? Or will all the cluster nodes be used to run the associated products and any product can be run on any cluster node?

The latter will require more volume groups for configuration using a high availability product such as MC/ServiceGuard. Volume groups within MC/ServiceGuard are activated in "exclusive" mode and the logical volumes within that particular volume group can only be mounted on the system that has activated it "exclusively."

The chosen design may also require additional software licenses. For instance, a three-node cluster is created and a database server (using the same database product) is running on each system. Each database server is a serving a different database. Here, there needs to be three separate volume groups, and therefore three separate disks for the database data to be exclusive to its primary node. It also requires three database server licenses versus one system running a single database server that serves three databases. Check the license agreements.

From the standpoint of HP-UX, for every volume group, there must be at least one physical volume. Using *Just A Bunch of Disks* (JBOD) as storage can waste much-needed disk space and limits the flexibility of MC/ServiceGuard configurations. If 36GB drives are purchased in a JBOD configuration and minimum redundancy is required, two 36GB drives must be purchased in order to mirror the logical volumes to the second drive. These two disks are one volume group, and the volume group can only be activated exclusively on one cluster node. For the disk space to be used effectively, all products must be configured to run on the same cluster node to have access to the volume group. There is no way to configure JBOD into separate physical volumes that are smaller than the size of one physical disk.

An HP AutoRaid allows for the creation of only 8 LUNs (physical volumes) whereas an HP Virtual Array allows for the creation many more LUNs. The disk array is best suited for those who wish to have a multi-node cluster. Unlike JBOD, arrays allow for the creation of physical volumes smaller than the size of a single physical disk within the array. The ability to create more physical volumes within an array facilitates multi-node clustering; making it easier to distribute products over several systems that can provide fail over capabilities for one another.

How highly available must be my products (binaries) and data? This directly affects the purchase of the number of controllers in the system, the array or disk storage unit, the cache in the array, and so on.

The following are additional questions that will help plan for enough of the proper disk space and disk I/O:

Is the database in archive mode (Oracle)? (It should be for online backup.)

How large do the redo logs need to be?

How many users will be using the NMS system at one time?

Will they log into the NMS and display clients back to a workstation?

Will they use the Java GUI and Web Interface?

How many objects are in NNM's object database?

How many days of history must be kept in the OVO history table?

Where will the OVO history table be archived?

How much data will be accumulated with SNMP data collection?

Is there room for periodically defragmenting the OVO database?

Where will the SNMP data collection be archived?

Will NNM's data warehouse be used?

How much data will be online?

When using an HA product such as MC/ServiceGuard, how will the products be configured?

Will all the products be configured in single Active/Standby cluster configuration?

The high availability and fault tolerance requirements of products and systems and their inherent configurations will literally specify the amount of storage to purchase, its type, and required number of interface cards. The same can be stated for databases and product configuration. These too can force the amount and type of storage required. Various products can be configured on a single system to easily access and update its associated data on a single large spindle (disk). There may be no complaint from a user about data access or system performance. Multiple users, backup, and incoming events hitting a disk uses I/O. All these events occurring at one time will stack up the I/O queue of the disk. One network "hiccup" that prevents OVO messages from reaching the management server or causes additional messages to be generated from NNM traps can flood the OVO database with hundreds of thousands of messages. Correlating these messages for automatic acknowledgement or logging into OVO and bringing up the message browser takes, disk I/O, memory, and CPU. Incidents such as these are rare and one doesn't have to design the system around it, but it does prevent the use of the NMS until the database is purged of the messages.

3.10.3 One Database Vendor

This is not always possible, but a good goal to shoot for. Many companies want to utilize one database vendor, and rightly so. It reduces both purchase and support costs. HP OpenView standardizes on Oracle on UNIX and NT as well as Microsoft SQL on NT. It would be great if all the products used the same database vendor. Creating a single database server is a good idea, but if it is not configured for high availability and fault tolerance and there is a failure of some sort, then nothing within the NMS will be accessible. All productivity is halted.

3.10.4 Memory Amount and Kernel Parameter Requirements

To make things easier, obtain all the recommended memory, swap, and kernel parameter requirements from the installation instructions for each product and place them in a spreadsheet. Determine what each kernel parameter setting needs to be set to in order that the products will run properly at the same time on a system. This is especially true when clustering and systems are meant to fail over for one another. Not having the kernel parameters properly configured on each system can prevent processes from starting upon fail over. Be careful: Not all kernel parameters are "additive" and some only require the largest setting for all products. A product's documentation generally states the "minimum" required setting, and not all kernel parameters log to the syslog when the parameter has been expended. Certain kernel parameters will increase memory requirements, but that should be accounted for in the products stated memory requirements.

3.11 SUMMARY

There are several items that were not discussed in this chapter, such as the number of CPUs required in a given system or for a given product. Some processes will only use a single CPU and others will use multiple CPUs. Running multiple products that use only a single CPU could cause a CPU bottleneck. The ability to enhance disk I/O using JBOD, multiple channels and striping the logical volumes. Managing the management server itself, including the monitoring of its performance is important. These are just a few examples and there are more. Think of more, put them in the plan, and prioritize them. Prioritize all the required functionality and implement the functionality in stages. Don't manage everything at once. Unless there is experience, knowledge, and workforce to design and implement all the requirements, take it a step at a time. Try to design the system in order that minimal changes are required when moving from one stage to another. These include changes in design in hardware and software. It is not always possible to do so and downtime will be required. It will take product knowledge, experience, and trial-and-error to implement a world class network, systems, and service management system.

CHAPTER 4

Out-of-the-box Network Node Manager

Network Node Manager (NNM) is a *Simple Network Management Protocol* (SNMP)-based tool that provides discovery, mapping, and monitoring of all TCP/IP devices on your network. If a device responds to ping, NNM will display it. If it responds to SNMP queries, NNM is capable of displaying it more accurately. Information such as the vendor, model, the number of interfaces, etc. can be gathered through SNMP. This information is defined by the standard *Management Information Base* (MIB) variables as defined in RFC 1213.[1] Vendors can extend MIB variables by defining vendor/model specific MIB variables. For example, Hewlett-Packard provides MIB variables specific to HP network printers that determine when a printer is offline, out of paper, and when the paper tray is open. The more variables a vendor provides, the more effectively a device can be managed remotely.

Sealey Inc., our fictitious company, would like a network management application with the to ability discover and graphically display their customer networks. The application should be easy to navigate. It should allow the user to locate and query devices quickly from a GUI. Because many customer devices are SNMP manageable, the application needs to have the capability to accept and display SNMP traps. Sealey Inc. would also like to query SNMP MIB variables. Some of the operators will need read-only access to customer data. Many operators will access the network remotely and would like to have access via a thin client such as a web browser or a java interface.

This chapter describes out-of-the-box functionality provided by NNM that includes some basic functionality required by Sealey Inc. It provides details on accessing NNM data from the GUI and covers features that do not require customization, such as discovery and mapping of a network, reception of SNMP traps, and the different methods of accessing NNM including web access.

4.1 NNM DISCOVERY

Network discovery begins immediately after you install NNM. During discovery, NNM examines its own ARP (Address Resolution Protocol) cache and pings every device in it. The ARP cache is a list of the IP to MAC address translations of all devices a system has communicated with during the past 15 minutes. The ARP cache can be displayed as shown in Figure 4-1 by typing by typing the command **arp –a**.

1 RFC 1213 describes MIB variables that are not vendor specific. The RFC can be found in the $OV_DOCS directory. Refer to Chapter 5, “Network Discovery,” for a list of NNM environment variables.

Figure 4-1 The ARP cache includes the hostname, IP address and MAC address of systems that have communicated with this system in the past 15 minutes.

```
r207w100 (156.155.206.257) at 0:60:b0:b3:c6:37 ether
r206w18 (156.155.206.18) at 0:60:b0:e5:b2:12 ether
r208w15 (156.153.206.63) at 0:60:b0:a9:a9:13 ether
r203s16 (156.153.205.69) at 0:60:b0:22:c6:2c ether
r203w13 (156.155.205.17) at 0:60:b0:4e:c8:e1 ether
r203w12 (156.155.206.52) at 0:60:b0:98:28:35 ether
r203s14 (156.153.205.68) at 0:60:b0:d2:66:3b ether
r203w10 (156.155.205.150) at 0:60:b0:fe:c9:e9 ether
r205w15 (156.155.206.65) at 0:60:b0:c9:f8:3 ether
r206w100 (156.155.206.255) at 0:60:b0:c3:b6:3 ether
r206w10 (156.155.206.10) at 0:60:b0:e5:a2:16 ether
r208w15 (156.153.206.65) at 0:60:b0:a9:c9:13 ether
r202s16 (156.153.205.66) at 0:60:b0:22:36:3c ether
r205w13 (156.155.205.13) at 0:60:b0:3e:c8:e4 ether
r205w12 (156.155.206.62) at 0:60:b0:79:28:35 ether
$ █
```

After pinging a device, NNM sends a series of **snmpget**s to acquire more information about the discovered devices. One of the most important MIB variables that NNM retrieves is the system object id, also known as the OID. The OID uniquely identifies the vendor and model of the device. The OID is used by NNM as an index into a variety of its configuration files, one of which is **oid_to_type**. NNM sets the device type based on entries in the **oid_to_type** file. The **oid_to_type** file contains a list of well-known vendor devices. This list is a text file that ships with hundreds of predefined OIDs. HP OIDs are listed separately in the **HPoid2type** file. Both of these files indicate to NNM the device type that has been discovered.

If NNM determines that a device is a router, it examines the ARP cache of the router and pings every device in the router's ARP cache that is co-located with the NNM station. By default, NNM does not discover your network beyond the first router it encounters. Discovery beyond the first router requires either the use of a seed file, or manual discovery via the GUI or the **loadhosts** command. Network discovery is covered in Chapter 5, "Network Discovery."

Start the native NNM (ovw) interface and take a look at what it does out of the box. Start NNM by typing

Unix:

ovw&

Windows:

Start→Programs→HP OpenView→Network Node Manager

4.1.1 ovw: Maps and Submaps

The ovw interface uses the concept of a "map" to show you the network it has discovered. Because only the most trivial network could be represented on a one-page map, the ovw interface splits the map into multiple pages. The pages are known as submaps and have a simple hierarchical relationship. At the top of this hierarchy is the *root* submap, as shown in Figure 4-2a. There are only four other levels in this hierarchy. The submap levels include the root, Internet, network, segment, and node levels as shown in Figure 4-2a.

Figure 4-2a The root submap contains the Internet symbol. All submaps include a menu bar, title bar, display area and status line.

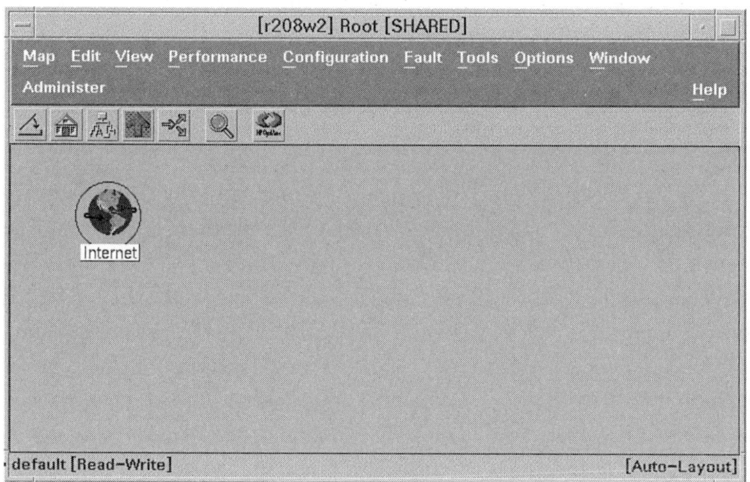

There are four additional levels in this hierarchy. The submap levels include the root, Internet, network, segment, and node levels as shown in Figure 4-2b.

Figure 4-2b The NNM submap levels are Root, Internet, Network, Segment and Node.

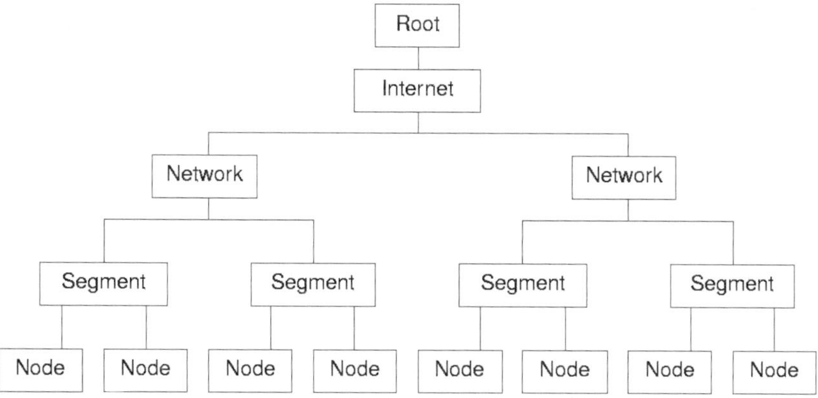

4.1.2 The Menu Bar

NNM has around 100 cascaded menu bar items, most of which will be covered in this book. Some of the most frequently used items can also be accessed through the toolbar. The menu bar can be customized by the use of *Application Registration Files* (ARFs), which are discussed in Chapter 7, "Advanced Customization."

4.1.3 The Toolbar Icons

The toolbar icons shown in Figure 4-3 can be used to navagate the submaps. The ***Close Submap*** icon closes the submap currently displayed, and if it's the only open submap, it will exit **ovw**. The ***Home Submap*** icon displays the submap defined as home, usually the one you visit most frequently and the one displayed on startup of ovw. Customization of the home submap is covered in Chapter 5. The ***Root Submap*** icon takes you to the root submap. The ***Parent Submap*** icon navigates up one level. Note that it is greyed out on the root submap because there are no more levels above root. The ***Quick Navigator*** icon displays a "standalone" (non-hierarchial) submap that can be customized for access to frequently accessed submaps. By default, the Quick Navigator is empty. Adding submaps and objects to the Quick Navigator is discussed in Chapter 5. The ***Pan and Zoom*** icon displays the panner/view port that allows you to zoom in on a submap. This is particularly helpful when you have a submap with many symbols. Finally, ***About OpenView*** provides version information on NNM.

Figure 4-3 The standard toolbar icons include Close Submap, Home Submap, Root Submap, Parent Submap, Quick Navigator, Pan and Zoom, and About OpenView.

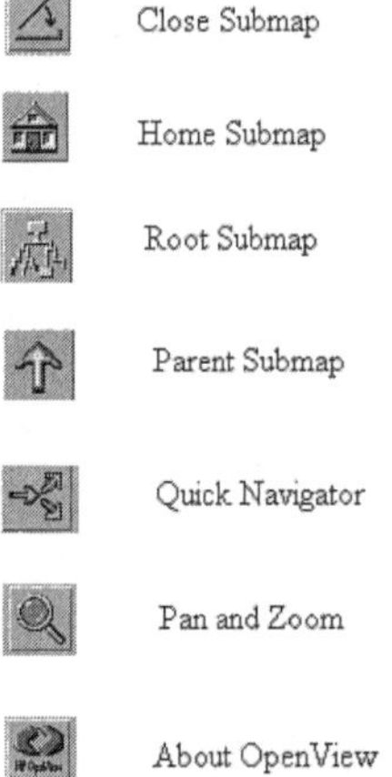

To display the version of NNM, click the About OpenView icon from the toolbar. This displays the "About HP OpenView" dialog box as shown in Figure 4-4.

Figure 4-4 The About OpenView toolbar icon provides the NNM version, the license document, and the NNM server name.

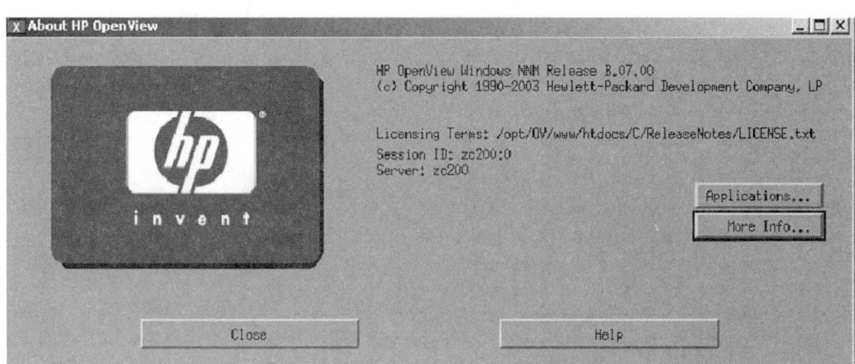

You can find integrated applications by clicking the **[Applications...]** button. License information may be obtained by clicking the **[More Info...]** button. See Figure 4-5 for the license type and node limit.

Figure 4-5 Click **[More Info...]** on the About OpenView window to display the license type and node limit. The license shown is an evaluation copy (InstantOn) of NNM with an unlimited number of managed nodes.

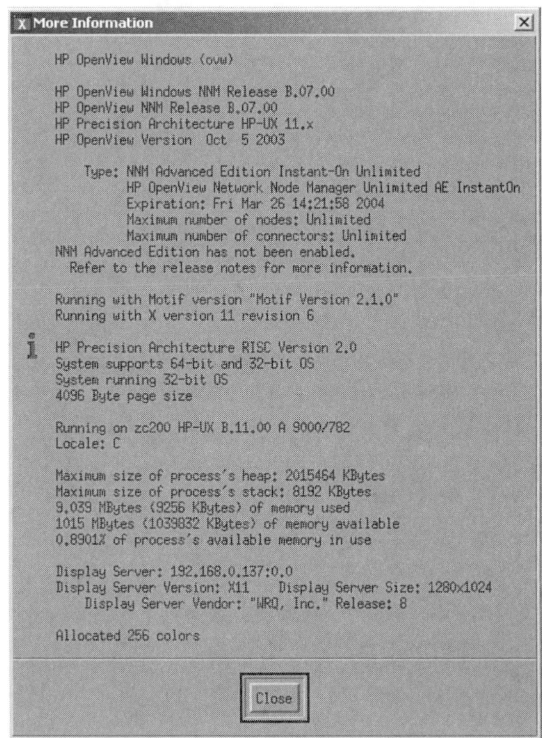

4.1.4 Pan and Zoom

Look at the network submap shown in Figure 4-6. Due to the number of symbols on a submap, sometimes you cannot see the internal symbol bitmaps and it may be difficult to read the symbol labels. By selecting the **Pan and Zoom** toolbar icon, you can get a close-up view of the submap.

Figure 4-6 Submaps may become cluttered when many devices are being managed.

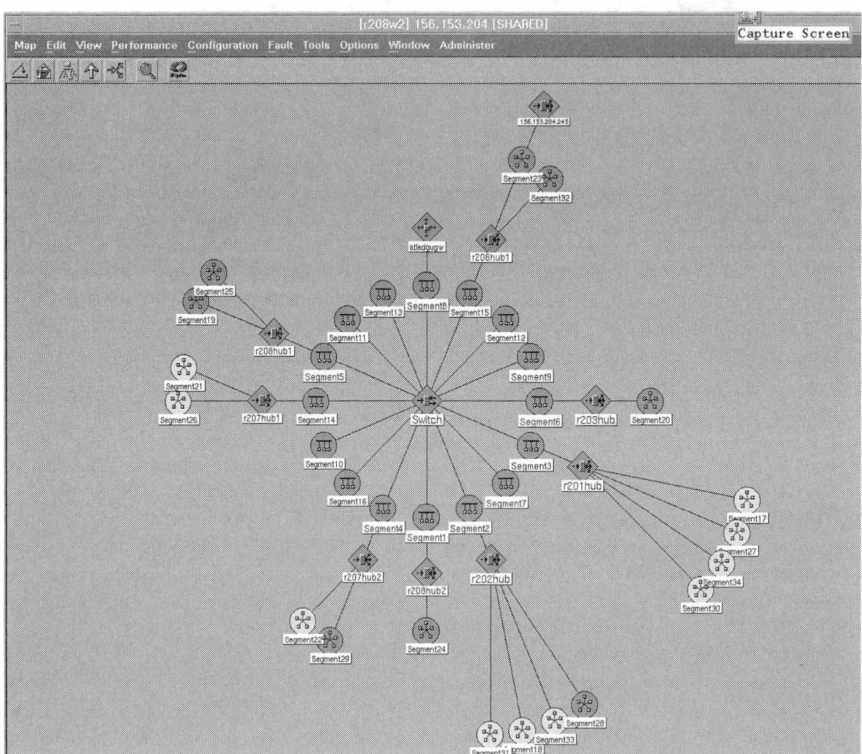

After clicking the icon, the panner/viewport is displayed on your screen as shown in Figure 4-7. To use this viewport, press and hold down the left mouse button, while dragging the mouse to draw a box in the panner/viewport around the symbols you want to zoom in on. Figure 4-8 shows the "zoomed in" effect of the panner/viewport. You can use the middle mouse button (both buttons together on a 2 button mouse) to drag the box, giving a panner effect to your submap view. If you keep the zoomed-in view, use the **[Close]** button on the panner/viewport. Click **[All]** to display the original view.

Figure 4-7 The panner/viewport can be used to zoom in on a submap. Zoom in on an area by drawing a box around an area of the submap with the left mouse button.

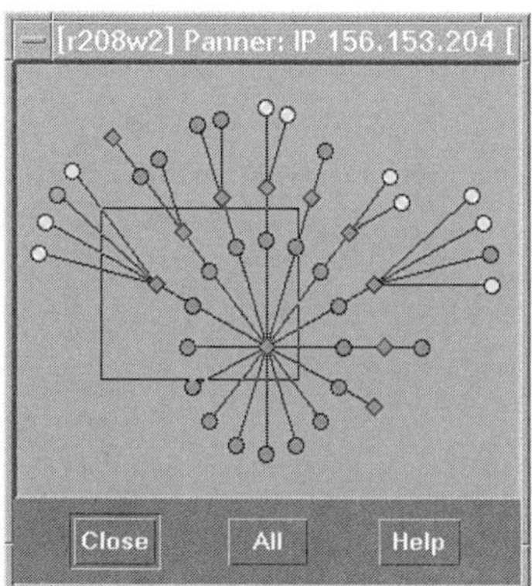

Figure 4-8 This submap displays the "zoomed-in" area as specified in the panner/viewport.

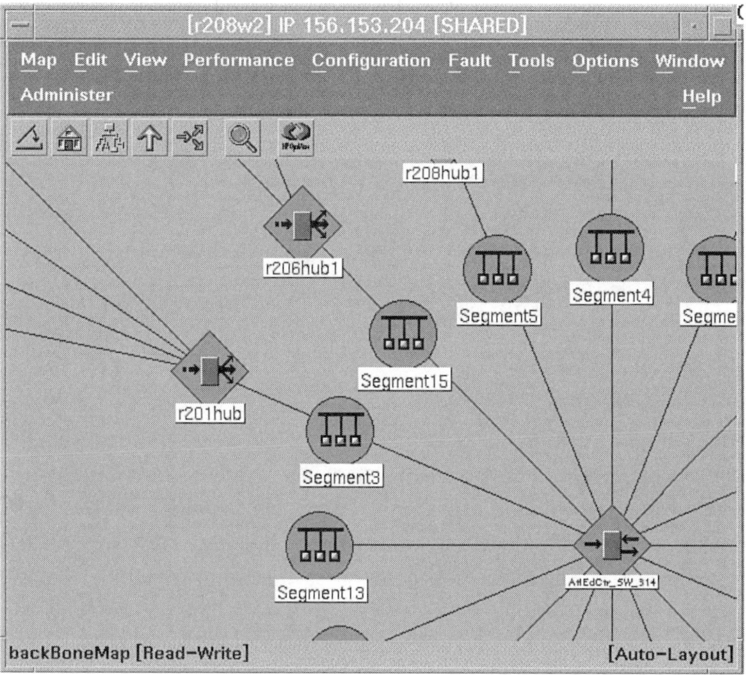

4.1.5 Map Navigation

To navigate through the GUI, double-click the symbols in the main viewing area to drill down to the next level in the map hierarchy and use the up arrow on the toolbar to access the parent submap. The symbols displayed with bitmaps are devices that have responded to SNMP, and NNM has successfully received configuration information about these devices. The symbols displayed without bitmaps have responded to ping but possibly not to SNMP, as shown in Figure 4-9.

4.1.5.1 Non-SNMP Devices

On occasion, you may encounter symbols with empty bitmaps such as the ones in Figure 4-9. This may occur for the following reasons:

1. The device is not running an SNMP agent. If the device is not running an SNMP agent, NNM has no way of retrieving the OID. Because it responded to ping, it is added to the object database, but because it did not respond to SNMP, it is assigned the default symbol type, a computer without a bitmap.
2. The agent has a community-name that is unknown to the management station. The community-name is used as a password and NNM must be configured so that it knows the community-names of all devices on your network. If the read community-name of a device is set to something other that "public" NNM must be configured with the device's community-names. If it's not configured, NNM will be unable to retrieve the OID.
3. NNM does not contain an entry for the device type in the **oid_to_sym** file. The **oid_to_sym** is a text file that maps the OID to a symbol type. An entry in the **oid_to_sym** file contains the OID, a symbol class, and a symbol subclass. The format of the **oid_to_sym** file is

   OID:Class:Subclass # Comment

   A sample entry in the **oid_to_sym** file is

   1.3.6.1.4.1.11.4.3.4.3:Computer:HP-UX # 800

The OID **1.3.6.1.4.1.11.4.3.4.3** is the numeric representation that uniquely identifies the device to NNM as a Hewlett-Packard series 800 computer system. The symbol class (**Computer**) defines the outside shape of the symbol. In this case, it is a square. The symbol sub-class (**HP-UX**) defines the bitmap for the symbol, in this case a monitor with the letters HPUX displayed and a keyboard, as shown in Figure 4-9. The colon (**:**) is a delimiter separating the OID, the class, and the sub-class. Anything following the pound sign (#) is a comment. The **oid_to_sym** file ships with hundreds of OID entries and can be extended by the administrator. Rather than modify the **oid_to_sym** file, the administrator should add OID to symbol mappings in a separate file. The file should be located in the **$OV_CONF/oid_to_sym_reg**[2] directory using the same format of the **oid_to_sym**. Errors in the **oid_to_sym** file or the **oid_to_sym_reg** directory will be ignored.

2 Refer to Chapter 5 for a description of environment variables available in NNM.

Figure 4-9 Symbols with empty bitmaps have not responded to SNMP, or NNM has no configuration information regarding the OID.

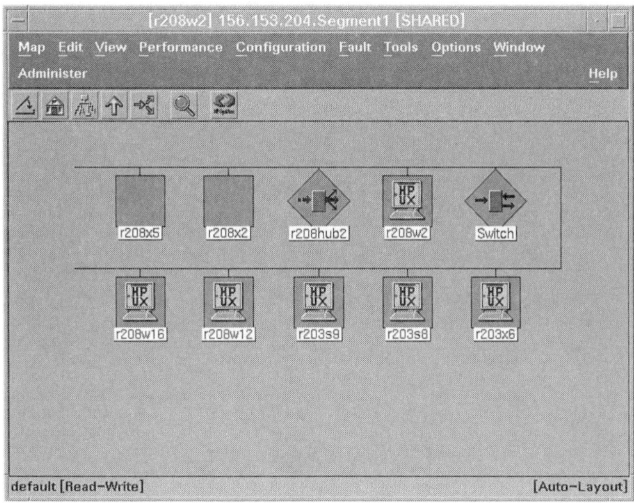

4.2 SYMBOLS AND OBJECTS

What lies below the graphical symbol displayed on a submap? When NNM discovers a device, an object is stored in the object database. An object can be a physical (a computer) or a logical entity (a segment). NNM uses a symbol as the graphical representation of that object. Each object in the database has attributes associated with it. We have already seen two *symbol attributes*, namely the outside shape (class) and the inside bitmap (sub-class). In order to see more detailed information, we will now look into the *object attribute.*

4.2.1 View and Locate Object Attributes

Look closer at the devices on the network. From the root submap, drill down to the Internet submap by double-clicking the Internet icon. Most networks contain at least one router or switch at this level. Assuming that your network contains a router (or a switch), place the cursor over the router symbol and click the right mouse button to display the symbol popup menu as shown in Figure 4-10. Select **Object Properties**.

The Object Properties dialog box contains five properties: 1) Capabilities, 2) General Attributes, 3) IP Map attributes, 4) Selection Name, and 5) Comments, as shown in Figure 4-11. The selection name is the unique identifier of the object of interest. If the object is a node and the hostname can be resolved, the selection name is set to the fully qualified hostname of the node. If the NNM management station cannot resolve the hostname, the selection name is set to the IP address of the node, as shown in Figure 4-11. The NNM administrator can add comments.

Figure 4-10 Object Properties are listed on the symbol popup menu. Hold the cursor over the symbol and click the right mouse button to access the symbol popup menu.

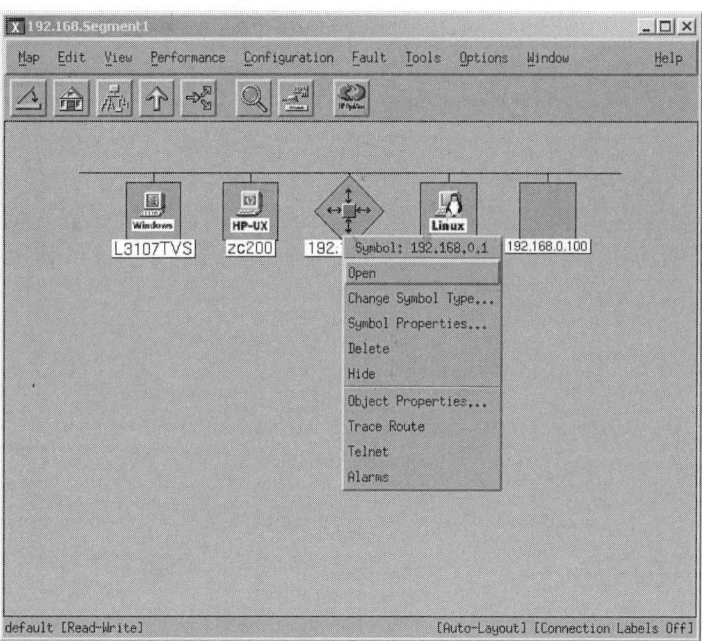

Next, double-click ***Capabilities,*** as shown in Figures 4-11 and 4-12. The Capabilities provide information regarding the device type stored in the NNM database. For example, the router shown has the attributes **isSNMPSupported**, **isIP**, and **isRouter** set to True. This indicates that the device is an IP router with an SNMP agent on it. Capabilities are set by NNM during discovery. They result from the SNMP request sent by the management station and response from the device. Notice that the Capabilities are "grayed out" indicating that they cannot be modified. They are set and controlled by NNM's controlling application, IP Map.

Return to the Object Properties dialog box and select **General Attributes**. General attributes are similar to capabilities, but apply to any object that might be discovered by NNM. See Figure 4-13 for the general attributes of the router. Note that the vendor of this router is Cisco Systems and the SNMP agent is also provided by Cisco. General attributes are also stored in the NNM database. Unlike the Capabilities, the general attributes may be modified. If you happen to have IP devices that do not respond to SNMP and you know the vendor information, you can manually make changes to the general attributes.

Figure 4-11 The Selection Name property is used to identify a device in the NNM database. If the NNM station can resolve the hostname, the selection name is set to the fully qualified hostname. If NNM cannot resolve the hostname, the selection name is set to the IP address as shown in this dialog box.

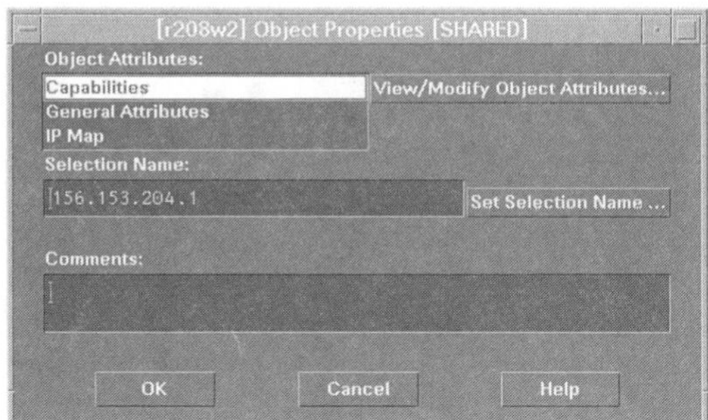

Figure 4-12 Object capabilites describe a device by defining attributes such as isSNMPSupported, isIP, isRouter. Object capabilities are set based on the SNMP response from a device and cannot be modified.

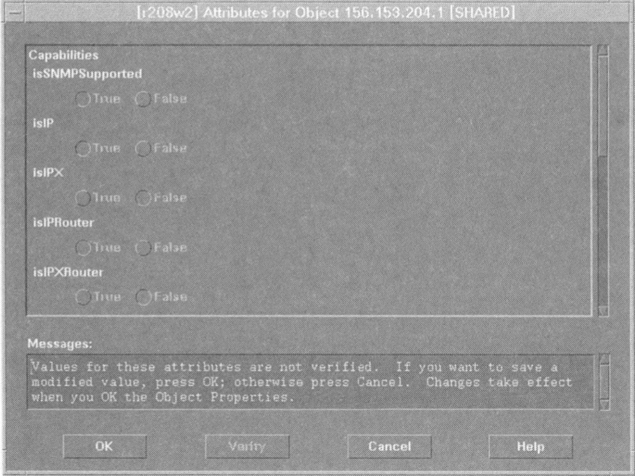

Figure 4-13 The General attributes also describe an object. General attributes may be manually modified. This is convenient when a device does not support SNMP or has a private SNMP community-name that has not been configured in NNM.

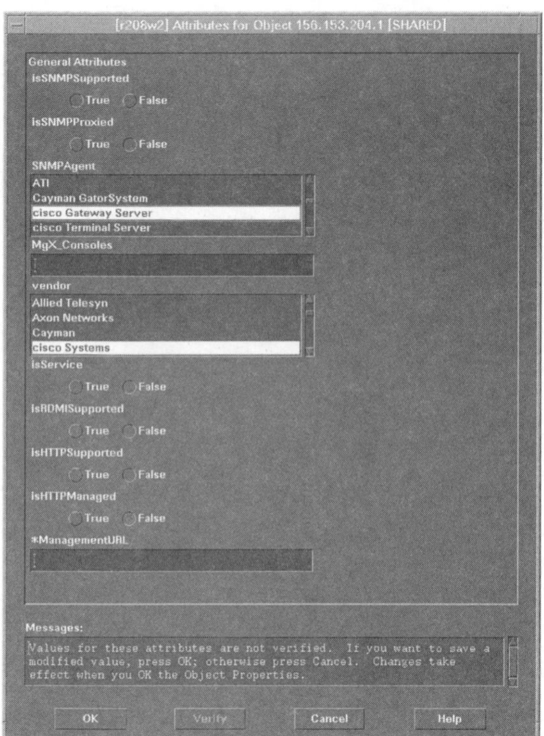

Return to the Object Properties dialog box and double-click **IP Map Attributes**. The information for a router includes the hostname, the device status, the interfaces (IP and MAC addresses), the system Description, and the System Object ID, as shown in Figure 4-14. This is the OID used by the **oid_to_sym** and **oid_to_type** files. You will also see the System Location and Contact for this device if they have been configured.

Navigate to the root submap and right-click the **Internet** icon. Select **Object Properties**, and double-click **IP Map**. This information will contain the number of ***IP networks, IP segments***, ***IP nodes***, ***IP interfaces*** and ***IP routers*** in your enterprise. With a couple of clicks you can find out how many IP nodes NNM is managing. Comparing these attributes to the IP Map attributes of a router, you can see that these attributes vary with the underlying object type.

Figure 4-14 IP Map attributes include the IP and MAC addresses of all device interfaces. The System Object ID, also known as the OID, is listed in the IP Map attributes. The OID for the device shown is .1.3.6.1.4.1.9.1.30, which identifies it as a Cisco device.

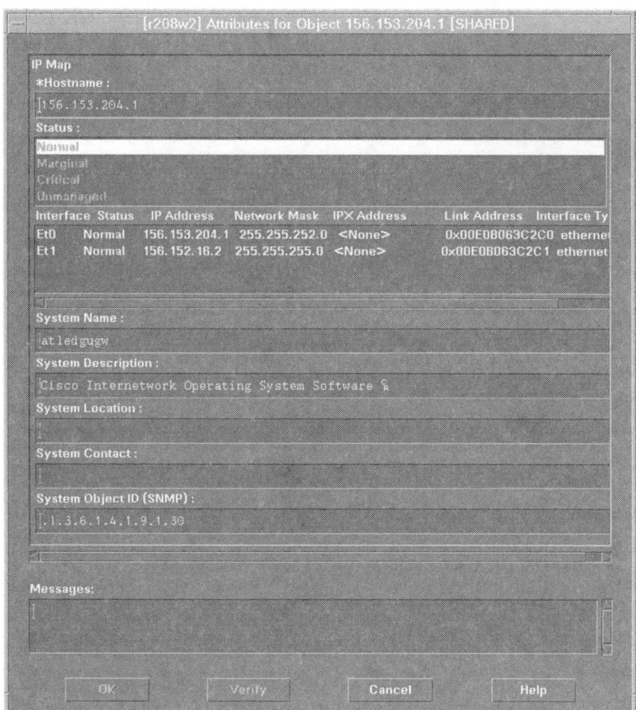

The attributes are set by NNM based on SNMP responses from the device. You can find the IP addresses of all interfaces of the router, the netmasks, the MAC addresses, the hostname, and the system OID. You can also find Boolean capabilities such as isRouter, isHub, isSNMPSupported, isHttpSupported, and vendor. You can search for objects based on the attributes in this list. For example, to list all systems running a web server in your enterprise, select the following from the menu bar:

Edit→Find→Object By Attribute→isHTTPSupported

This displays a list of all devices in your enterprise that have a home page running on Port 80. By double-clicking an item you can go directly to the submap on which the device resides. The labels of the located symbols will be highlighted (displayed in reverse video).

4.2.2 Symbol Status Colors

Symbol status colors can be displayed by selecting from the menu **Help→Display Legend →Operational Status Colors**. The color of a symbol represents one of the following levels of severity, as shown in Table 4-1.

Table 4-1 NNM uses the following status colors. The status color code indicates the severity of a symbol.

Status Color	Severity
Blue	Unknown (NNM did not discover this device and therefore is not managing it. When you manually add an object to a submap that does not respond to ping, the status color is blue.)
Green	Normal
Cyan (light blue)	Warning
Yellow	Minor
Orange	Major
Red	Critical
Off-white	Unmanaged (NNM is not actively polling this device for status. When you change the device status to unmanaged, NNM will no longer poll the device.)

4.2.3 Status Propagation Rules

Because submaps are part of a well-defined hierarchy, it makes sense that the aggregate status of a submap should somehow be reflected (propagated to) in its parent. NNM reflects this by applying color coding to symbols on a submap according to a set of propagation rules to the root, internet, network, segment, and node hierarchy. The propagation rules result in the assignment of colors to symbols in the main viewing area of the submaps. For the purpose of status propagation, a symbol on a submap that is not green or blue is considered of abnormal status. The default status propagation rules are described in Table 4-2.

Table 4-2 Status propagation rules determine the status color of symbols. The rules are defined on a per-map basis and may be modified. The default status rule determines the status color of the parent symbol.

Child Symbol Status	Parent Symbol Status Color
All normal	Green
1 abnormal, multiple normal	Cyan
Multiple abnormal, multiple normal	Yellow
Multiple abnormal, 1 normal	Orange
All abnormal	Red

If there is only one node on a submap and it is abnormal (red, orange, yellow, or cyan), the parent symbol will be red (all abnormal). If a node is *abnormal* and the interface connecting it to the segment is *down,* this will propagate as *multiple abnormal symbols*. The icon and connector symbols both contribute to the propagation rule. A yellow symbol indicates that the child submap contains *multiple abnormal* and *multiple normal* symbols. In order to determine where a problem resides, drill down into the network map by double-clicking abnormal symbols until you find the culprit.

A green segment symbol, of course, indicates that all child submaps have normal (green) symbols. This means that all underlying objects (for example, IP interfaces) are responding to NNMs polls. More simply put, they are all up! Taking this to its logical conclusion, our goal is to have the IP Internet symbol on the root submap always be green. Good luck!

4.3 ALARM CATEGORIES

In the upper right side of your screen you see the **Alarm Categories** as shown in Figure 4-15. This window consists of two distinct parts. On the right are the (user extensible) alarm categories and on the left are color-coded indicator buttons. The indicator color is based on the most severe event in that category received by NNM.

Figure 4-15 The alarm categories have color-coded indicator buttons that reflect the most severe event in each alarm category.

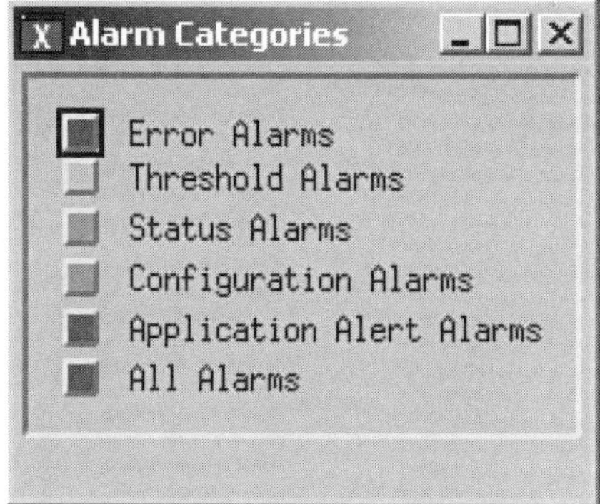

4.3.1 All Alarms Browser

You can display the message browser by clicking one of the buttons in the Alarm Categories. This shows an alarms browser that lists the most recent alarms from that category. The **All Alarms** category indicator button displays the **All Alarms Browser**, a list of all the alarms received by NNM, shown in Figure 4-16. These alarms are usually a result of SNMP traps that have been sent as directed messages from some device on your network to NNM. An operator can use alarms to determine problems that have arisen in your enterprise. Most of the events are color-coded indicating the severity of the event. By double-clicking an event, you unveil the submap of the device that sent the event. If the event message is longer than the browser, right click on the message and you will see the entire message without having to use the scroll bar at the bottom of the browser as shown in Figure 4-16.

Figure 4-16 The All Alarms Browser lists events received by NNM. Single-click an indicator button from the Alarm Categories to access this browser. Right-click a message to see the full text of an event.

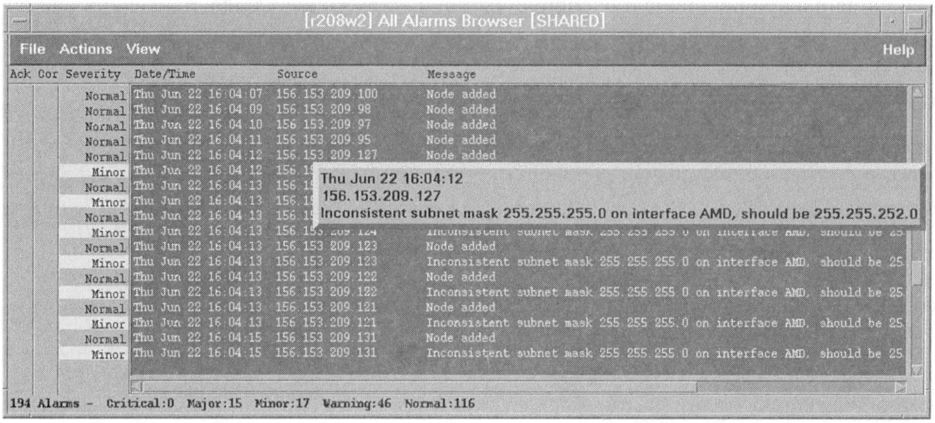

By default, NNM only color-codes events of the severity Minor, Major and Critical. Review some of the details of an event, as shown in Figure 4-16. The browser provides the severity, a timestamp, the hostname of the event, and the message. The browser is commonly used as a "to do list" for an operator. By left-clicking in the first column, you can acknowledge the event. If the event has an asterisk (*) in the **Cor** column, you can left-click the * to view correlated events. Another way to display correlated events is by selecting **Actions→Show Correlated Events**. NNM has a built-in event correlation engine to determine whether multiple events have the same root cause and automatically adds these as child events under the parent event.

Select Actions→Views to see a list of dynamic views related to solving the type of problem indicated in the alarm. Double-click the alarm to open the **ovw** submap showing the device involved.

4.4 QUERYING THE MIB

Why query the MIB? NNM stores just a few MIB variables in its database. Much more information is readily available from the SNMP agent on the managed node. For instance, to find out where the device is physically located and who is responsible for managing it, you can customize the MIB variables for **Location** and **Contact**. Commonly, the NNM administrator customizes these using NNM. This will be discussed in more detail in Chapter 9. Better yet, what if you want to look at interface traffic in real-time on a managed node? **ifInOctets** and **ifOutOctets** are MIB variables that keep track of traffic coming in and going out of each interface.

NNM provides a handy tool, the MIB browser, for browsing the set of variables on your network devices. To access the MIB browser, select from the menu bar **Tools→SNMP MIB Browser**

4.4.1 The MIB-II Subtree

First, let's take a look at the Management MIB subtree. The MIB-II subtree starts with the character representation

iso.org.dod.internet.mgmt.mib-II

You can also reference the MIB tree using the numeric representation

.1.3.6.1.4.1

Drill down to the MIB-II subtree and select "system" from the top portion of the MIB browser as shown in Figure 4-17. Type a valid hostname or IP address in the field labeled "Name or IP Address" and click **[Start Query]**. You should see the results of the query in the browser as shown in MIB Values section of the browser. If you get the error message "No response before timeout," it is likely due to one of the reasons discussed in Section 4.1.5.1, "Non-SNMP Devices."

Figure 4-17 The MIB browser allows you to drill down the MIB tree. The **[Start Query]** button sends an SNMP request to the specified host. This figure illustrates the system branch of the Management MIB tree.

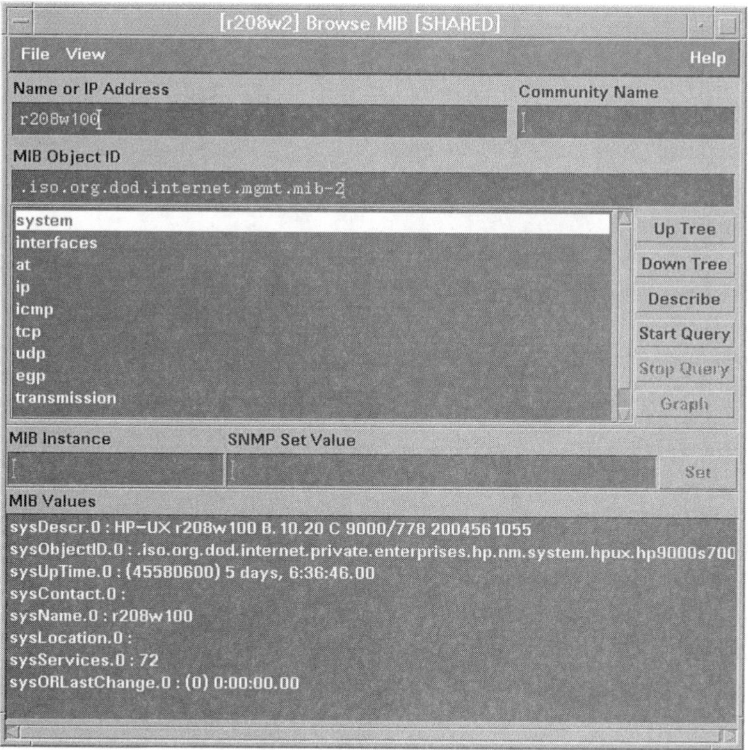

You can also query the MIB using the command-line utilities **snmpwalk**, **snmpbulk**, and **snmpget** that ship with NNM. Using these commands, you would specify the node and either the character or numeric representation of the MIB variable. I like the using the numeric representation because it frequently requires less typing. For example, to query the system subtree:

snmpwalk nodename .1.3.6.1.2.1.1

or **snmpwalk *nodename* system**

Now drill down to the **interfaces.ifTable.ifEntry** subtree. Select **ifInOctets** and click the **[Describe]** button displayed on the right side of the MIB browser. This displays the numeric representation as well as a description of the MIB variable you have selected. See Figure 4-18 for the description of the variable **ifInOctets**. This provides excellent online documentation.

Figure 4-18 The description of a MIB variable can be accessed from the MIB browser by selecting a variable and clicking the **[Describe]** button. Both the character and numeric representation of the MIB variable are displayed.

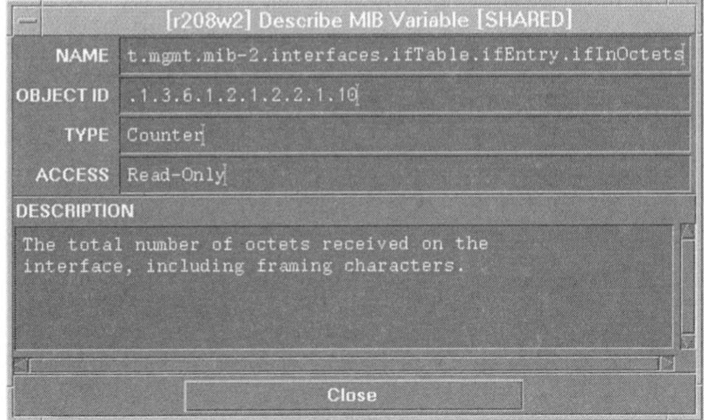

4.4.2 Graphing MIB Variables

You can use another powerful NNM feature to graph MIB variables. Select a MIB variable such as **ifInOctets** and click the **Graph** button. This displays a real-time graph of that variable. NNM is now sending an **snmpget** to the node you've selected and displaying the information on the graph. You can graph two or more variables at once by holding the control key and left-clicking the desired variables. Refer to the graph of **ifInOctets** and **ifOutOctets** shown in Figure 4-19.

For every IP network interface on the selected system (including the loopback interface) you will see a variable for **ifInOctets** and **ifOutOctets**. The .1, .2, .3 extensions each indicate a different interface.

Place the cursor over the graph and left-click it to customize it. You can zoom in, zoom out, page backward and forward. Further customization includes background color, time intervals, and polling frequency. When you right-click on the graph, you will see a timestamp line as shown in Figure 4-19. This can be used to align with interesting points (peaks and troughs) in network activity.

Figure 4-19 MIB variables can be graphed by selecting a variable and clicking the **[Graph]** button from the MIB browser. Multiple variables may be graphed by simultaneously pressing the control key and left-clicking to select the desired variables.

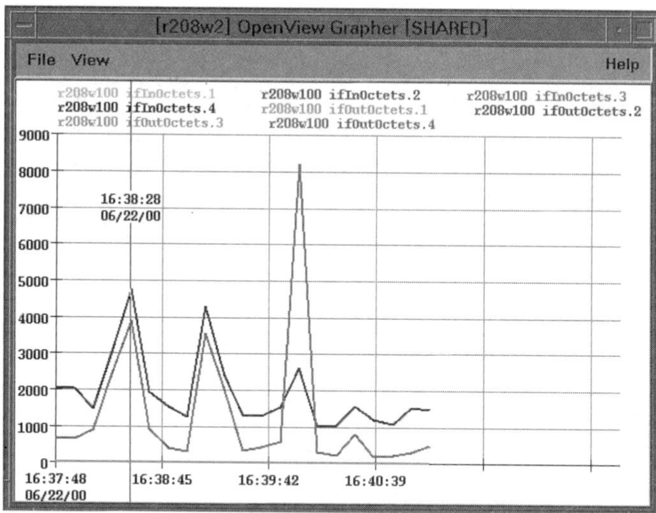

4.4.3 Loading Additional MIBs into NNM

NNM ships with a subset of vendors' MIBs. However, these MIBs are not necessarily up-to-date because vendors are always coming out with new hardware and new MIBs. You'll need to get the latest version of MIBs from the vendor, put them in the $OV_SNMP_MIBS/Vendor directory, and select **Options→Load/Unload** from the menu bar to load the MIBs into NNM. You will see the MIBS that are loaded in NNM as shown in Figure 4-20. To load additional MIBs, click the **[Load…]** button. Select **Vendor** and you will see a list the list from the $OV_SNMP_MIBS/Vendor directory as shown in Figure 4-21.

Note: Refer to the file ov.envvars.sh located in /opt/OV/bin for a listing of environment variables used by NNM. The $OV_SNMP_MIBS variable references the directory /var/opt/OV/share/snmp.

For NNM on Windows, the file is ov.envvars.bat.

For C shell users, the file is ov.envvars.csh.

The ov.envvars.sh can be configured in /etc/profile and ov.envvars.csh configured in /etc/csh.login to set the NNM environment variables for everyone, no matter what shell is preferred by a user.

Figure 4-20 Vendor-specific MIB variables extend the functionality of SNMP. They can be loaded into NNM by selecting **Options→Load/Unload** from the menu bar.

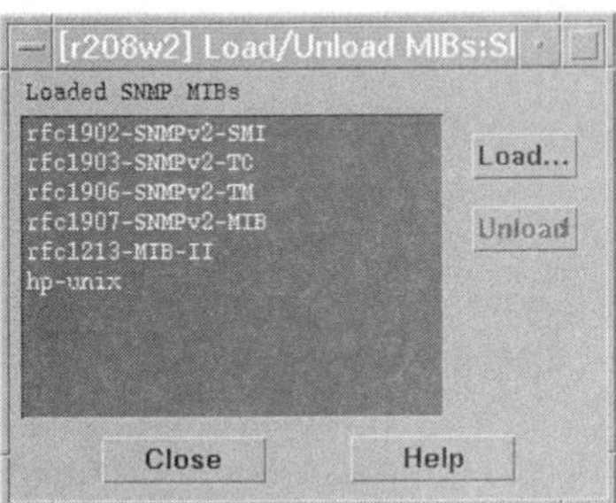

Figure 4-21 NNM provides a subset of vendor MIBs.

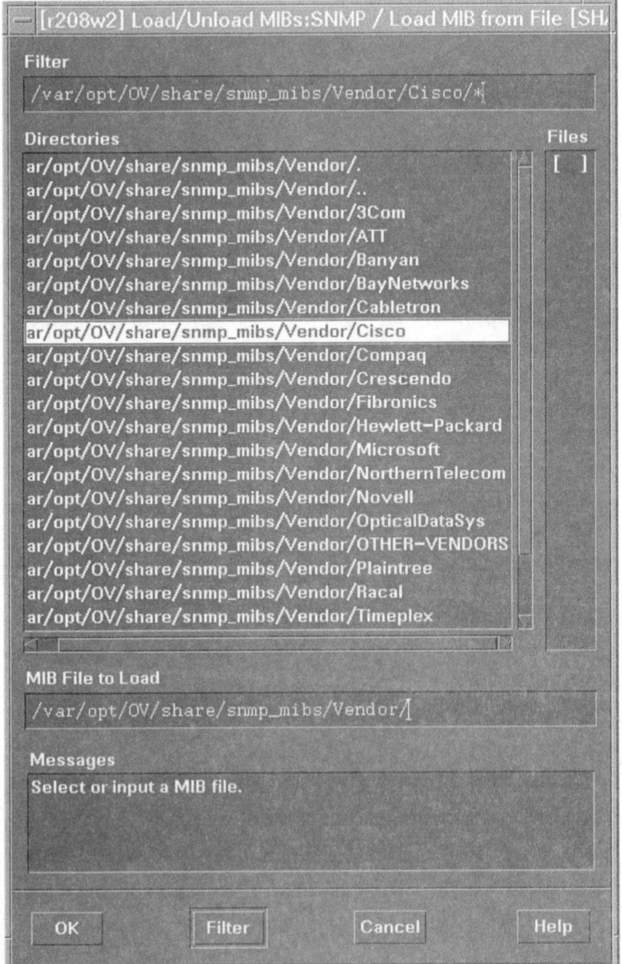

After you've loaded the MIBs into NNM, you can use the MIB browser to query and graph the vendor-specific MIB variables.

Some vendor software also includes trap definitions. If you are loading the MIB, most likely you will want to use the trap definitions that are assigned by the vendor. Otherwise, when the trap is sent it will be seen as "undefined" in the Alarm Browser. Follow the vendor-specific instructions to load vendor-specific traps.

4.4.3.1 The Need for Vendor-Specific MIBs

Because the standard MIB tree was written in a generic sense, it does not account for operating system-specific variables. Vendors can extend the functionality of SNMP by providing MIB variables specific to their equipment. Let's look at the Hewlett-Packard MIB variable computerSystemUsers. Use the MIB browser to navigate the private subtree to **iso.org.dod.internet.private.enterprise.hp.nnm.system.computerSystem.general**.

Assuming that you have an HP-UX system on your network, enter a valid HP-UX hostname, as shown in Figure 4-22.

Note: You can use the **Edit→Find** feature of NNM to locate a specific vendor's system. For example, to find an HP-UX device, select from the menu bar

Edit→Find→Object By Attribute→vendor→Hewlett-Packard

Figure 4-22 The HP-UX MIB variable **computerSystemUsers** defines the number of users logged onto a system. The numeric representation of this MIB variable is .1.3.6.1.4.1.11.2.3.1.1.2 and can be retrieved by clicking the **[Describe]** button.

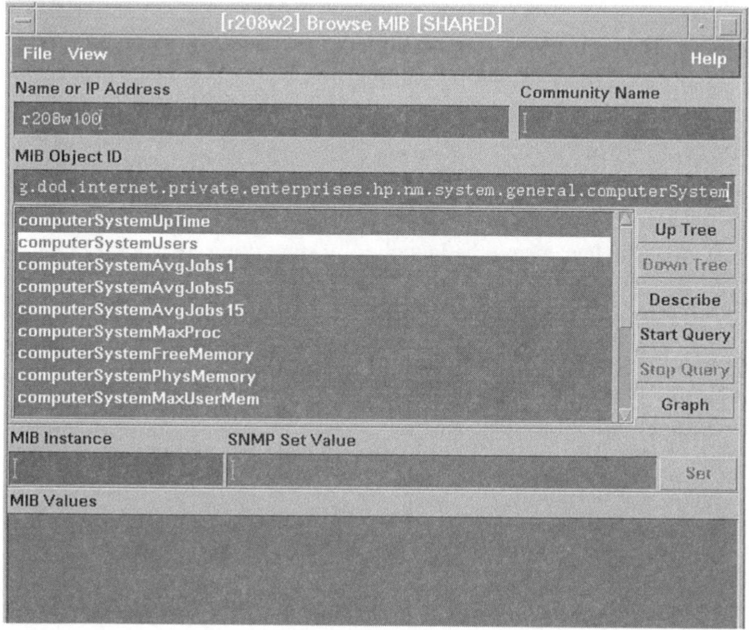

Select the variable **computerSystemUsers** and click **[Start Query]**. This will return the number of users logged on the system. While this MIB variable is specific to HP-UX, many vendors extend the functionality of SNMP by providing vendor-specific MIB variables.

When loading vendor MIBs, you may run into dependencies on other MIBs. You should follow the vendor instructions for loading these MIBs into NNM so they are loaded in the correct order.

4.4.3.2 Vendor-specific Trap Definitions

Vendors frequently provide trap definitions for their equipment as well. The trap definitions also provide NNM with the ability to better manage the vendors' devices. Recall the example discussed earlier in this chapter in Section 4.1, "NNM Discovery," of a printer sending an SNMP trap when it runs out of paper. By providing traps specific to their equipment, the vendors extend the functionality of SNMP. Thus, NNM is able to manage the device more effectively.

4.5 WEB ACCESS

With the advent of everything becoming web accessible, NNM ships with the Apache web and application servers in order to provide the ultimate in remote access. The web and application servers are both installed automatically when you install NNM. The web interface consists of three distinct components: the OpenView Launcher (Figure 4-23), the Network Presenter (Figure 4-24), and Dynamic Views (Figure 4-25). The OpenView Launcher and the Network Presenter provide read-only access to allow operators to remotely monitor the network via a web browser, while Dynamic Views provides flexible and full control of NNM.

4.5.1 The OpenView Launcher

Access to NNM via a web browser on Unix is slightly different than accessing NNM on Windows. You need to specify the port 8880 if NNM is running on a Unix system. To access the OpenView Launcher from a web browser, enter the following URL where *hostname* is the name of the management server running NNM:

For NNM running on a Unix system, enter `http://hostname:8880/OvCgi/ovlaunch.exe`. Access to the OpenView Launcher was changed in version NNM 6.3 (and later versions) to port 3443. For Unix systems, access the launcher by specifying the URL `http://hostname:3443/OvCgi/ovlaunch.exe`

For NNM running on a Windows system, enter the following URL *without* a port number: `http://hostname/OvCgi/ovlaunch.exe`

This displays the Welcome page and the Launcher window (Figure 4-23). The Launcher has five tabs located at the bottom third of the launcher.

Each Launcher tab provides Java-based access to NNM tools. The tabs provide the following functions from left to right:

- **Object Views**—Provides access to the SNMP MIB Browser and IP Network
- **Tasks**—Provides Event Correlation configuration and the ability to create, modify and schedule reports. Report templates include availability, exception, inventory, and performance
- **Information and reports list**—Provides the ability to list the reports generated from the Tasks tab
- **Tools list**—Provides access to the Network Presenter, Alarms Browser, Event Correlation Configuration, Report Presenter, Report Configuration, SNMP Data Presenter, SNMP MIB Browser, Unused IP addresses, and Home Base
- **Online help**—Provides online help for using all Java-based components of NNM. Online help can also be access by specifying the URL `http://hostname:3443/OvCgi/OvWeb-Help.exe` in your browser.

Figure 4-23 The web launcher provides limited access to data stored in the NNM database.

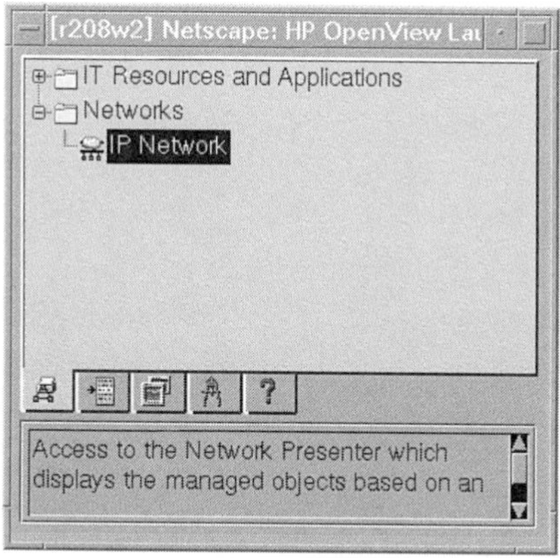

Some of the functions listed under the tabs include access to the submaps (the Network Presenter), access to the MIB browser, and access to the report generation and report display. The OpenView Launcher provides many of the commonly used tools that an operator may use in routine troubleshooting activities. For example, the tools tab gives you the ability to select a device and ping it. The Launcher can be customized using *Web Launcher Registration Files* (WLRF) to extend its functionality. WLRFs customization is discussed in Chapter 7, "Advanced Customization."

4.5.2 The Network Presenter

From the Launcher window, expand **IP Network** by clicking the "+" shown in the network launcher window. Double-click **IP Network** from the list and to launch the java applet Network Presenter. First you'll see the message that the applet is starting then you'll see the Network Presenter as shown in Figure 4-24.

Figure 4-24 The Network Presenter can be used for many tasks, including querying MIB variables, listing object properties, and testing network connectivity (ping, snmp, telnet).

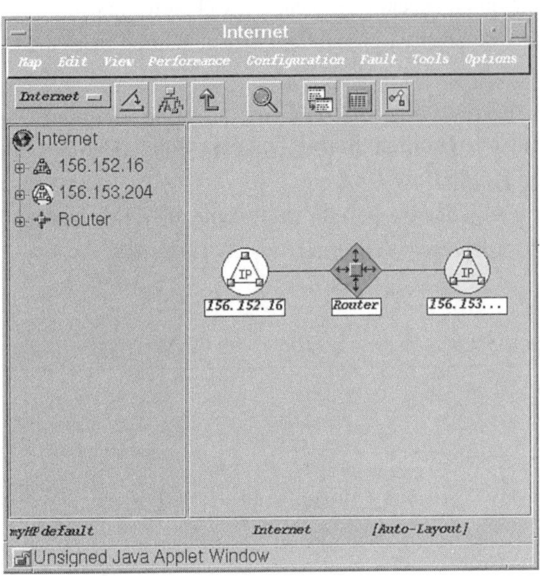

The Network Presenter is divided into two panes. Clicking the plus sign beside the network object expands the left pane. As you can see, the right pane of the network presenter looks similar to the ovw GUI. You can drill down into different submaps by double-clicking the symbols in the right pane. You can also use the toolbar icons in the same way as the native interface. Although some of the menu bar items are not present in the Network Presenter interface, this interface makes an excellent thin client. You are able to access NNM maps and troubleshoot networking problems with any supported web browser.

4.5.3 Dynamic Views

Dynamic Views provides the ability to present specific information based on user criteria from a Java-based web interface. It fully enables the network to be monitored remotely. Dynamic Views allow the network to be viewed from a single pane of glass as opposed to the hierarchical views provided by submaps. Dynamic Views provides flexibility to view the network based on what is interesting to the user.

Dynamic Views can be accessed from the ovw menu selection **Tools→Views**, from the Network Presenter selection **Tools→Views**, and from the NNM Launcher Tools tab. You can also access Home Base by typing the URL `http://hostname:7510` in your browser. When NNM is installed on your system, the Apache application server is started on TCP port 7510 in order to provide access to Dynamic Views.

Home Base, shown in Figure 4-25, is the launching point of Dynamic Views. Home Base lists the number of events of each severity (Critical, Major, Minor, etc.) contained in the Alarms Browser. It also shows the number of events and percentage of events in each severity. Home Base displays the node status summary of your network as a pie chart. As you place the cursor over a section of the chart, it displays the number of events of that severity.

Path View and Neighbor View are available from the drop-down list on Home Base. Click the **[Launch]** button to access a different view. By default, nothing exists in the dynamic views of the browsers. You customize them based on the criteria of interest.

Additional views that allow discovery of services, such as OSPF and VLANS, can be included added by installing and configuring the Extended Topology Discovery component of NNM. The Extended Topology discovery process is achieved by executing the PERL script **setupExtTopo.ovpl**, available on Windows systems in the directory %OV_BIN% and on Unix systems in the directory $OV_BIN.

Figure 4-25 Home Base is the launching point for Dynamic Views, providing a color-coded list of event severities, the actual number of events, and the percentage of events in each severity. It also contains a pie chart graphing the percentage of events in each severity. As you place the cursor over a section of the chart, it displays the number of events in that severity. This view of Home Base contains 34 events of Normal status.

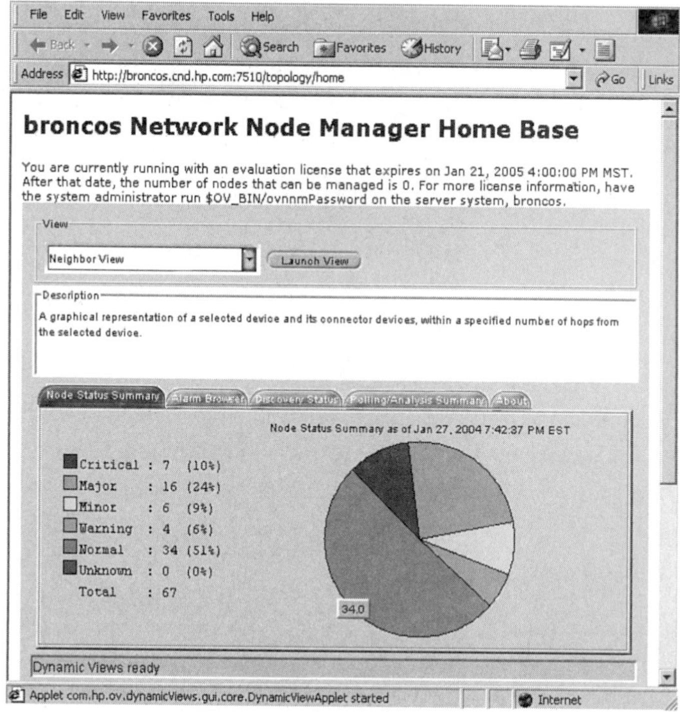

The default views available from Home Base include but are not limited to:[3]

- **Neighbor View**—Provides a graphical representation of the path between a specified device and its connector devices allowing a specified number of hops from the specified device (see Figure 4-26).
- **Node View**—Provides a graphical representation of a set of nodes as defined by the ovw filters file by selecting a minimum severity and IP address range (see Figure 4-27). Refer to Chapter 9, "Scalability and Distribution," for a list of pre-defined filters.
- **Station View**—Provides a graphical representation of the collection stations and management stations as discovered by NNM. This is applicable in an environment that uses more that one NNM station and is discussed in Chapter 9.
- **Internet View**—Provides a graphical representation of the networks in your IP Internet view. This allows you to view a high level of the overall status of your network.
- **Network View**—Provides a table presenting the segments in a specific network.
- **Path View**—Provides a graphical representation of the shortest path between two nodes.

Figure 4-26 The Neighbor View allows you to specify a device and all connector devices up to 9 hops from the device. It displays the connector devices up to the number of hops specified on a single pane of glass.

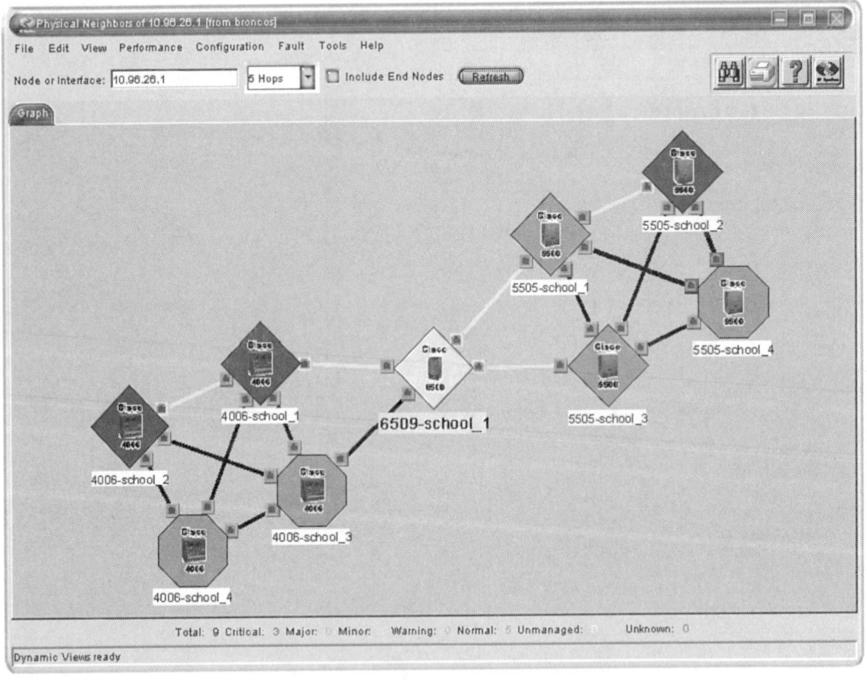

3 The Extended Topology component of NNM provides discovery and display of services such as OSPF and VLANS.

The Node View is another interesting view of your network. A number of filters can be selected from a drop-down list in order to narrow your display criteria. NNM filters are user-defined and are covered in Chapter 9. The Node View also allows you to specify and IP address range. The Node View shown in Figure 4-27 uses the filter NetInfrastructure with a minimum status of Warning in the IP address range of *.*.*.* (all devices).

The Network View provides a table presenting the segments in a specific network. This table lists the segment name, segment type, segment status, node name and node status, as shown in Figure 4-28. The Network View can assist in isolating network and system problems.

Figure 4-27 The Node View can be used to narrow the display criteria while allowing the user to view the network. The devices displayed in this Node View are defined by the NetInfrastructure filter and have a minimum severity of Warning.

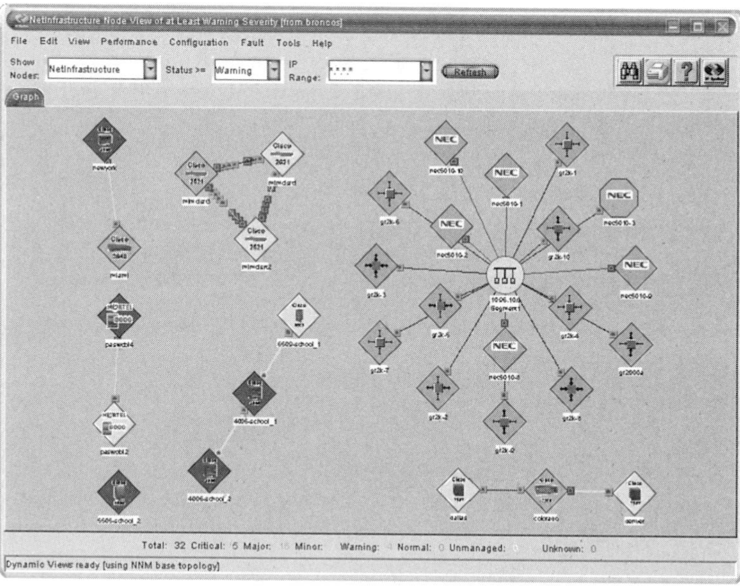

Figure 4-28 The Network View can be used to help isolate problems in particular segments. This view shows only one critical node in the segment.

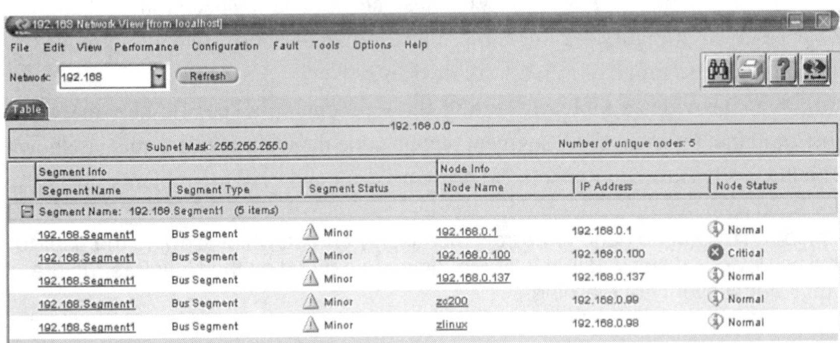

Detailed device information can be acquired by double-clicking a symbol in Dynamic Views. (Recall that double-clicking a symbol in the ovw GUI drills down into the next-level submap.) The most crucial information is provided when you place the cursor over a symbol, as shown in Figure 4-29.

Figure 4-29 The most crucial information of a device is displayed when you place the cursor over the symbol. The information of the device shown includes its IP address, hostname, hardware description, OS version, and a timestamp of the last status poll. Device detail can be obtained by double-clicking the symbol.

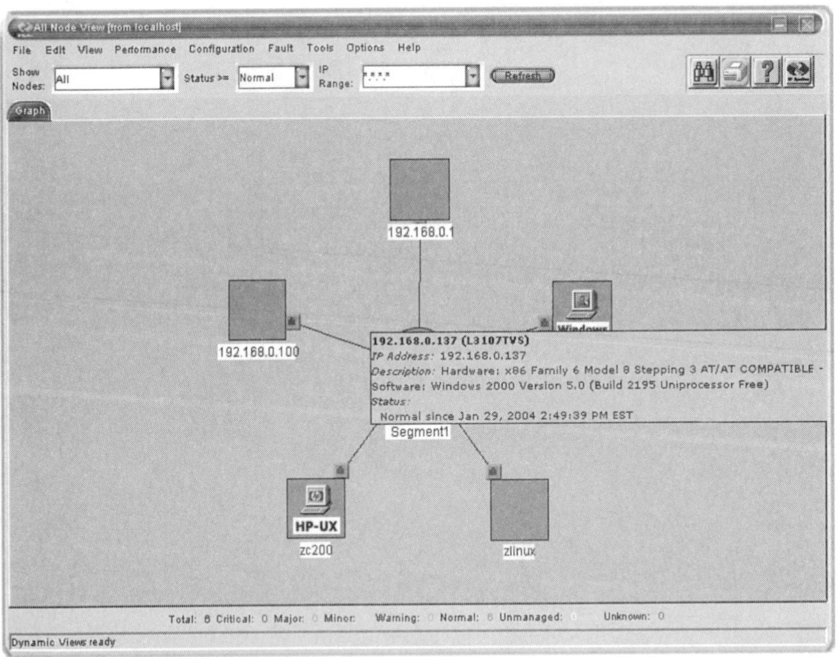

The symbol popup menu mentioned previously in this chapter is available by right-clicking a symbol in Dynamic Views. Note that the menu items available from Dynamic Views are slightly different than the menu items available from the ovw interface. The following menu options are available via the symbol popup menu in Dynamic Views:

- **Open**—Displays a tabular view of the symbol.
- **Details**—Displays detailed device information (hostname, IP address, hardware, etc.).
- **Poll Node**—Sends a configuration poll to the device.
- **Status Poll**—Sends a status poll (ping) to the device.
- **Test IP/TCP/SNMP**—Sends an IP, TCP, and SNMP request to test the device.
- **Trace Route**—Executes the traceroute command to the device to trace the path to the selected device.
- **Ping**—Send, five pings to the device.
- **Telnet**—Executes a telnet session to the device.
- **Expand Connecting Neighbor**—Expands only neighbors that are directly connected to the selected device.
- **Expand All Neighbors**—Expands neighbors.
- **Show Path to Additional Nodes**
- **Path View**—Provides a graphical representation of the shortest path between two nodes.
- **Neighbor View**—Allows you to specify a device and all connector devices up to 9 hops from the device
- **Launch View in New Window**—Displays all the above commands in a new window. By default, this is turned off so that a new window is NOT opened when executing the above options.
- **Manage**—Enables status polling to the device.
- **Unmanage**—Disables status polling to the device.

The Alarms Browser tab available from Home Base can be used to access the NNM Alarms, as shown in Figure 4-30. The Alarms Browser tab displays the alarm categories (Error, Status, Threshold, etc). To display alarms from any of the categories, click the category of interest. Select **[All Alarms]** to display all the alarms in the browser.

Figure 4-30 Select the Alarms Browser tab on Home Base to display the Dynamic Views version of the Alarms Browser. Click an Alarm Category to display the alarms. Messages can be sorted in this version of the browser by clicking the column label, such as Severity, Source, and Message.

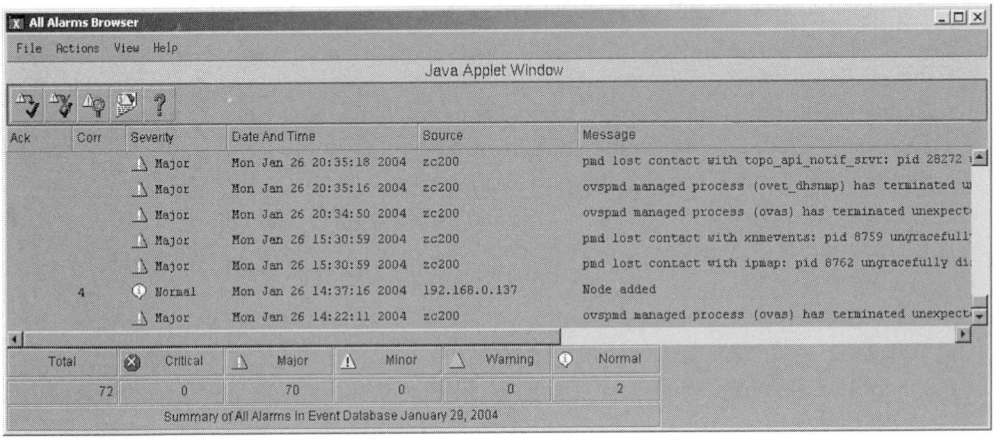

In order to allow better troubleshooting, you can display device detail from within the browser. Select **Actions→Views→Source Details** from the Alarms Browser menu bar to list device detail, as shown in Figures 4-31 and 4-32.

Information provided by Source Details includes the Hostname, the IP address, the hardware description, whether the device supports SNMP, the *System Object ID* (OID), and the type of network interfaces available on the device. The NNM Node ID used to internally identify the device is also displayed. Source Details for a device are shown in Figure 4-32.

Device Details is also available via the symbol pop-up menu by right-clicking a symbol and selecting Details. The same information can also be accessed by double-clicking the device from Dynamic Views.

Figure 4-31 Detailed device information can be displayed by selecting **Actions→Views→ Source Details** from the Dynamic Views version of the Alarms Browser.

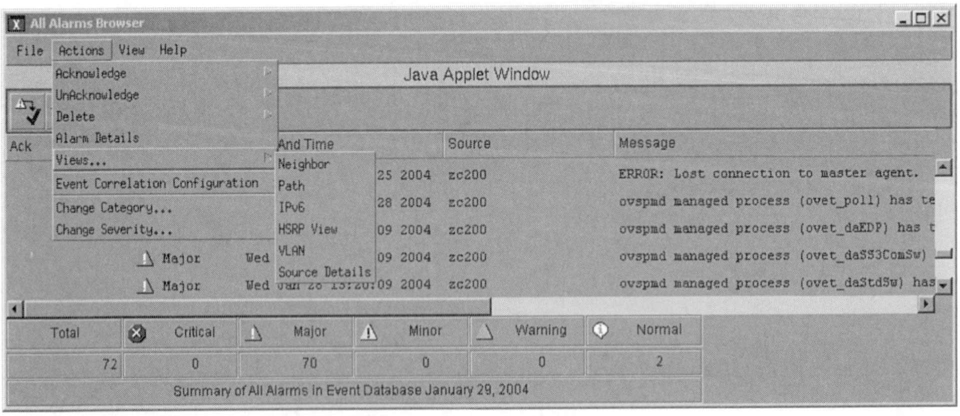

Figure 4-32 Information provided by Source Details includes the Hostname and/or IP address, the hardware description, whether the device supports SNMP, the OID, and the type of network interfaces available on the device. The system shown is an SNMP-supported Windows 2000 system with the OID of .1.3.6.1.4.1.311.1.1.3.1.1, a Microsoft MIB.

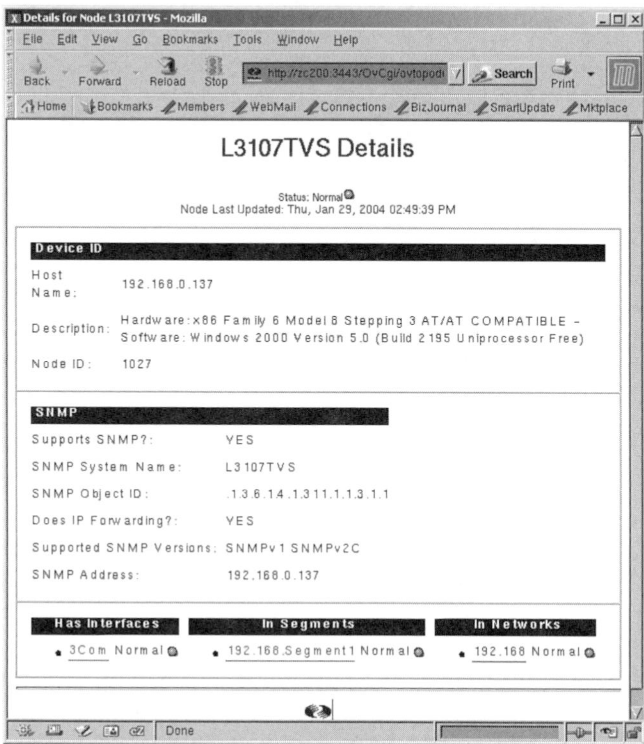

4.6 SUMMARY

NNM is an SNMP-based network management tool that provides discovery, mapping, and monitoring of your network. You can access NNM by several methods:

Unix ovw interface:

ovw&

Windows ovw interface:

Start→Programs→HP OpenView→Network Node Manager

UNIX Launcher:

`http://hostname:8880/OvCgi/ovlaunch.exe`(NNM 6.2 and before)

`http://hostname:3443/OvCgi/ovlaunch.exe` (NNM 6.3 and later)

Windows Launcher:

`http://hostname/OvCgi/ovlaunch.exe`

UNIX/Windows Dynamic Views:

`http://hostname:7510`

NNM collects inventory information via SNMP and allows the user to view the information from any location on the network. It provides the ability discover and graphically display your network. The NNM interfaces are easy to navigate. It allows the user to locate and query devices. NNM can accept and display SNMP traps to help determine glitches in the network. Operators can be limited to read-only access if necessary. Now, move on to Chapter 5.

CHAPTER 5

Network Discovery

The default behavior of NNM is to stop the discovery of the network at the first router relative to the discovery station (my IP address + my subnet mask). To prevent discovery of the entire Internet, NNM will not discover beyond the first router it encounters. Early implementations of network management tools had no limitations and would wreak havoc on the entire networked community. One important thing to remember when performing initial discovery is that it is extremely network-bandwidth intensive. Initial discovery is not something you should do during peak network traffic hours. The NNM station performs a ping of all the devices in the arp cache of the router followed by a series of snmpgets until all the devices listed in the router's arp cache are discovered. To list a device's arp cache you can execute the following snmpwalk command, providing the hostname or IP address of the device.

```
snmpwalk hostname at
```

This command traverses the **a**ddress **t**ranslation (**at**) branch of the Mib-II subtree, otherwise known as the arp cache. By using this command, you can get an idea of how much the discovery of this router will impact your network. Use **grep**[1] and **wc** to obtain the exact count of interfaces in the arp cache. The output of the following command will be a number indicating the number of entries in the arp cache of the specified hostname:

```
snmpwalk hostname at | grep atNetAddr | wc -l
```

One of the requirements for Sealey Inc. includes the capability of the network management application to discover remote networks. Local network monitoring is not required. Only customer networks need to be monitored. The application needs to automatically discover specified portions of the network. Because the customer networks are constantly changing, they also need the ability to manually add devices as necessary. On occasion, they might need to exclude devices from discovery to minimize the number of managed nodes discovered.

Many customers have private community names for security purposes. The application required by Sealey Inc. will need to provide access to SNMP devices configured with private community names. Another security issue is the use of firewalls. Sealey Inc. will need to determine how to handle access to customer devices through firewalls.

1 To perform these commands on a Windows system, you will need UNIX tools such as cygwin. Cygwin is a UNIX environment, developed by Red Hat for Windows.

Because network discovery and monitoring can be network bandwidth intensive, Sealey Inc. wants to be able to actively monitor the performance of its network monitoring solution. The company may need additional resources to handle all its customers.

5.1 SEEDING INITIAL DISCOVERY

Because the default behavior of NNM is to discover up to the first router, NNM provides a configurable way to specify a list of network devices that should be discovered. Because the local network may not be a very interesting (and possibly not a very useful) network, the discovery process can be augmented by the use of a seed file. The purpose of a seed file is to allow an administrator to define the portion of the network for NNM to discover and manage.

5.1.1 Setting NNM Environment Variables

When performing command-line tasks for NNM, it is advantageous to set the environment variables. For your convenience, NNM provides several environment variable files in the directory $OV_BIN on UNIX systems. A script exists for Bourne, POSIX, and Korn shell users (ov.envvars.sh), C shell users (ov.envvars.csh) and even one to be used from a Perl script (ov.envvars.pl). If you are using a Bourne, POSIX, or Korn shell you can source this file in your profile, /etc/profile, or from the command line by typing

/opt/OV/bin/ov.envvars.sh

making sure to put a space between the "." and the directory path/ filename. To verify that the variables are set, type

set | grep OV | more

Listed here is an abbreviated list of the variables available. Throughout this book variables such as $OV_CONF, $OV_LRF, and so on, will be referenced.

```
OV_BIN=/opt/OV/bin
OV_BITMAPS=/etc/opt/OV/share/bitmaps
OV_CONF=/etc/opt/OV/share/conf
OV_CONTRIB=/opt/OV/contrib
OV_DB=/var/opt/OV/share/databases
OV_DOC=/opt/OV/doc
OV_FIELDS=/etc/opt/OV/share/fields
OV_HEADER=/opt/OV/include
OV_HELP=/var/opt/OV/share/help
OV_LIB=/opt/OV/lib
OV_LOG=/var/opt/OV/share/log
OV_LRF=/etc/opt/OV/share/lrf
OV_MAIN_PATH=/opt/OV
OV_MAN=/opt/OV/man
```

For Windows systems, environment variables may be defined using the **ov.envvars.bat** file and referenced using %OV_CONF%, %OV_LRF%, and so on. The **ov.envvars.bat** file is located in the %OPENVIEW%\bin directory where %OPENVIEW% is the directory specified when installing NNM.

5.1.1 netmon: the Discovery Process

netmon is the background process responsible for discovering network devices.[2] The **netmon** configuration file, **netmon.lrf**, can be configured to reference a seed file. The seed file is a list of systems, typically routers that will direct **netmon** in the discovery of the network.

The seed file is an ASCII file containing a list of IP addresses and hostnames, one per line. The contents define the network management domain. Typically the devices listed in a seed file are routers, but they can be any devices containing an arp cache. NNM will discover and manage all interfaces for each entry listed in the seed file (barring a discovery filter or a **netmon.noDisover** file entry that excludes the specific interface).

The following is an example of a seed file:

```
128.1.1.1
128.12.2.1
128.15.5.1
128.22.4.1
mysys.hp.com
```

The entries in the seed file should include devices that have an arp cache and are SNMP manageable. For example, you could use a UNIX system running an SNMP agent as an entry in the seed file. If the community names of these devices are not public, NNM must be configured with the community names of the devices in the seed file. This will be covered in more detail later in this chapter.

When you use a seed file, **netmon** does not automatically discover its own node or network. This allows for third-party network monitoring. You are actually skipping over your network devices to the customer network. If you also want the management station and local network in your database, you need to include them in the seed file.

During the installation of NNM, you may be prompted as to whether or not you want to automatically discover the network depending on the installation method used to install NNM. The default answer is yes when using an NNM-specific CD-ROM and using the "install" command at the root of the CD-ROM. If you plan on seeding the initial discovery, make sure to specify NOT to automatically discover the network during NNM installation. If NNM has already discovered the network and you would like to redo the discovery using a seed file, refer to Section 5.1.4, "Re-discovering the Network."

2 NNM 7 has separate processes associated with extended topology discovery.

5.1.2 Excluding Devices from Discovery

If you have devices on your network that you do not want to discover, such as DHCP devices, you can set up a configuration file to exclude these IP addresses. DHCP devices are dynamically assigned, so the devices appear and disappear. DHCP addresses are dynamically assigned to devices. The addresses may migrate between nodes, confusing network management. To NNM this indicates that systems are down, when in reality someone has just gone home for the day. Also, the MAC and IP addresses of DHCP devices change frequently. Both addresses are associated with an object that is stored in the NNM database. When NNM determines an IP address and MAC address mismatch, it generates an internal event. If you're not responsible for managing DHCP devices, you can exclude them from discovery. If you do need to manage them for your service agreements, inform NNM of the DHCP address range using a DHCP filter. Filters are discussed in detail in Chapter 9, "Scalability and Distribution."

One way to exclude devices from discovery is to create the file **$OV_CONF/netmon.noDiscover**. Polling will not be performed on any device listed in this file. The **netmon.noDiscover** file uses the same format as the seed file. The file can include IP addresses and IP address ranges, with one entry per line. Hostnames are not allowed in the **netmon.noDiscover** file.

Another approach to handling DHCP devices is to implement a discovery filter. The use of a discovery filter allows you to limit the discovery of network devices. The configuration of discovery filters is discussed in Chapter 9.

5.1.3 Testing SNMP Connectivity

Before creating a seed file, it is a good idea to verify SNMP connectivity to all the devices you plan on using in the seed file. You can use the **snmpwalk** command to traverse the system subtree of the MIB. Execute the following command specifying the IP address of each entry to be used in the seed file:

```
snmpwalk <IP address> system
```

If you receive the error "No response before timeout," you must resolve the SNMP connectivity issue or NNM will not be able to retrieve the device's arp cache, the **ifTable**, or the **sysObjectID**. These are all important in the discovery and node identification process. One or more of the following reasons can cause this error:

1. The device is not accessible. Verify network connectivity by pinging the device.
2. The device is not running an SNMP agent. Contact the device's administrator.
3. The community name is unknown and must be configured in NNM (see Section 5.4, "Configuring SNMP Community Names"). Contact the device's administrator.
4. A firewall is blocking the SNMP port 161. Request that the firewall administrator open ports 161 (SNMP requests) and 162 (SNMP traps) between the management system and the managed nodes.

5.1.4 Re-discovering the Network

After NNM has discovered your network you may have a reason to re-discover the network using a seed file, **netmon.noDiscover** file, or discovery filter. Maybe you are interested in monitoring a third-party network only. You might want your management domain to include devices that are not directly attached to the network on which NNM station resides.

A seed file can also be used to prevent having to manually add devices via the GUI to your management domain. While you can manually add devices from the NNM GUI, it is much less labor-intensive to create a seed file and let NNM do the work. You can also use **loadhosts** if you don't want automatic discovery running at all.

If NNM has already discovered the network and you would like to completely undo what's been discovered, you can force re-discovery. This requires removing the NNM databases, configuring the **netmon.lrf** file, and restarting netmon. The following steps will allow you to rediscover the network:

Warning: The following steps will remove the all managed devices from the NNM database. Any map customizations you have made will be lost.

1. Create a file named **seed** in the directory **$OV_CONF**. This file can actually reside anywhere (and be called anything), but make sure to reference the exact location in the **$OV_LRF/netmon.lrf** file. Do NOT use environment variables in this file.
2. Modify **netmon.lrf** as shown here by adding the entry after the **–P** option. The following entry in **netmon.lrf** is on one line:
   OVs_YES_START:ovtopmd,pmd,ovwdb:-P ***–s***
   /var/opt/OV/conf/seed:OVs_WELL_BEHAVED:15:PAUSE::netmon.lrf
3. Execute the **ovstop** command to stop the background processes. (Refer to Section 5.1.4.1, "The Background Processes," for detail on this command.)
   ovstop –v
4. Remove the existing NNM database.
   UNIX:
   rm –rf $OV_DB/openview
   Windows:
   Select the **openview** directory from the %OV_DB% in Microsoft Explorer and click Delete. Then select **eventdb** from %OV_DB and click Delete.
5. Assuming that your environment variables are set, execute the command to update the configuration file **ovsuf**.
   ovaddobj $OV_LRF/netmon.lrf
6. Execute the command to start NNM background processes.
   ovstart -v
7. Execute the command to monitor background processes.
   ovstatus –c

8. Start NNM using the GUI or Dynamic Views and watch the discovery of your network using the seed file.
   ovw&
   OR
   `http://hostname:7510`

After you start the NNM GUI, drill down to a network submap and watch the network grow as it is being discovered. You may notice that all devices are initially put on segment1 until **netmon** receives enough information from SNMP to determine where to place them. **netmon** will parse the seed file, retrieve the arp cache of each device listed in the seed file, and start pinging the devices listed in arp cache followed by a series of snmpgets to the devices that responded to ping.

If you decide to implement a seed file after the discovery but want to preserve the devices that have already been discovered, you can skip only step 4, removing the databases. This will maintain existing devices and map customizations in the database and force the discovery of the devices in the seed file.

5.1.4.1 The Background Processes

After installing NNM, the discovery of the network begins. The background processes will automatically start, unless your installation method allows you to specify otherwise. The commands to check, start, and stop these processes are **ovstatus**, **ovstop**, and **ovstart** respectively. The "-c" command line switch for **ovstatus** lists an abbreviated version of the command output. The output of "**ovstatus –c**" will look something like this:

```
Name             PID      State        Last Message(s)
OVsPMD           18958    RUNNING      -
ovwdb            18992    RUNNING      Initialization
                                       complete.
ovuispmd         19285    RUNNING      Initialized. 0 ovw
                                       clients
                                       registered.
ovtrapd          19206    RUNNING      Initialization
                                       complete.
ovactiond        19207    RUNNING      Initialization
                                       complete.
ovsessionmgr     18994    RUNNING      Initialization
                                       complete.
ovalarmsrv       19208    RUNNING      Initialization
                                       complete.
ovdbcheck        18995    RUNNING      Connected to
                                       embedded
                                       database.
```

```
httpd           -       unknown     (Does not communi-
                                    cate with ovspmd.)
ovtopmd         19205   RUNNING     Connected to
                                    native database
                                    "openview."
netmon          19286   RUNNING     Initialization
                                    complete.
snmpCollect     19287   RUNNING     No values config-
                                    ured for collec-
                                    tion.
pmd             18993   RUNNING     Initialization
                                    complete.
```

This is a list of all the NNM background processes. What you see is the process name, the *process ID* (PID), the state of the processes, and the last message when the process was started. You want to make sure the process is in a running state. What would cause the process not to be in a running state? If you made an error in **netmon.lrf** for example, the netmon process may not start. If you make a simple syntax error in netmon.lrf, you can correct it and restart the individual process by typing **ovstart netmon**. If you've destroyed it beyond repair, you can find an original copy in **$OV_NEWCONFIG/OVNNM-RUN/lrf/netmon.lrf**.

Unix manpages are provided for both Unix and the Windows online help for each NNM process. The following paragraphs provide a brief description of each process. ovspmd is the process responsible for starting and monitoring all NNM processes. The configuration file for ovspmd is **$OV_CONF/ovsuf**. Never, under any circumstances, should you directly edit the **ovsuf** file. A corrupted ovsuf can render NNM unstartable. An entry is added to **ovsuf** when you execute **ovaddobj $OV_LRF/netmon.lrf**.

The database used by NNM has several distinct components, including what can be thought of as a separate object, topology, and map database. The object and topology databases are maintained by the **ovwdb** and **ovtopmd** processes respectively. Specific information from these three databases is proprietary and can accessed via the NNM GUI or the commands **ovobjprint**, **ovtopodump**, and **ovmapdump**. For example, when you display object properties you are viewing the information from the object database. When you view a submap you are viewing a graphical representation of the topology database.

The **netmon** process is responsible for new node discovery, configuration, and status polling of network devices. It uses the configuration file **netmon.lrf** to determine whether to use a seed file during discovery. **netmon** works as quickly as possible to discover each device on the network. **netmon** first sends a ping to each device in the arp cache. **netmon** issues a series of snmpgets to the devices. The **sysObjectID** is obtained via SNMP to determine the device type. **netmon** queries the ifTable and retrieves the interfaces, their types (Ethernet, ATM, FDDI, etc.) and their IP addresses. If the device has an arp cache, **netmon** repeats this process again to the devices in the arp cache.

The **ovuispmd** process keeps track of the number of ovw GUIs that are running. The **ovtrapd** and **pmd** process the SNMP traps. The **ovtrapd** process listens for traps, buffers them, and then passes them along to the postmaster daemon (**pmd**) for processing. This enables NNM to process around 2000 traps per second.

The process responsible for executing automatic actions associated with traps is **ovactiond**, which listens to **pmd** for events configured to execute automatic actions.

The **ovsessionmgr** process controls access to session information for web access. The **ovalarmsrv** is the process that serves all the alarm information. The **ovdbcheck** process controls access to the data warehouse, a relational database. From NNM, you can export information to the data warehouse from the topology, events, and trend data (data collected by snmpCollect). From the NNM GUI select **Tools→Data Warehouse** and one of the following: **Export Topology**, **Export Events**, or **Export Trend Data**.

The **httpd** process is the web server process. It keeps track of the users accessing NNM via the web. The snmpCollect process collects SNMP MIB data and can optionally compare the collected values to user-defined thresholds in order to generate events when the thresholds are exceeded. By default, NNM does not perform data collection; it must be configured to do so. The collected data is also referred to as trend data. This topic will be discussed in detail in Chapter 8, "Data Collection and Event Configuration."

5.1.5 The netmon.lrf File

The **netmon.lrf** file is the configuration file indicating the startup options for the netmon process. The lrf extension indicates that this file is a *Local Registration File* (LRF). LRF files are located in $OV_LRF. The first line of **netmon.lrf** describes the startup of the netmon processes. See the netmon (1m) manpage for startup options that can be included in the **netmon.lrf** file. If you plan to use a seed file, you must modify **netmon.lrf** and follow the steps previously discussed.

```
#
# @(#)netmon.lrf
# @(#)HP OpenView NNM Release B.06.10  Oct 27 1999
# @(#)Copyright  (c) 1990-1999 Hewlett-Packard Company
# $Revision: /main/PULSAR/PULSAR_REP/1 $  $Date: 1999/02/02
20:27 UTC $
#
# Local Registration File for Network Node Manager network moni-
tor daemon
#
# Arguments can be placed between the second and third colons
# of the second line.  See lrf(4) and netmon(1m)
#
# Run ovaddobj(1m), ovstop(1m) and ovstart(1m) after modifying
this file:
#   ovaddobj $OV_LRF/netmon.lrf
```

```
#   ovstop netmon

#   ovstart netmon
      #
          netmon:netmon:
OVs_YES_START:ovtopmd,pmd,ovwdb:-P -s
/var/opt/OV/conf/seed:OVs_WELL_BEHAVED:15:PAUSE::netmon.lrf
```

Note: The following should be on a single line. It is presented on multiple lines here due to the size constraints of this book.

```
OVs_YES_START:ovtopmd,pmd,ovwdb:-P -s
/var/opt/OV/conf/seed:OVs_WELL_BEHAVED:15:PAUSE::
```

Sample netmon.lrf and seed files are available for download from the server `http://www.phptr.com/title/0130352098` for both UNIX and Windows systems. Obtain the Readme file for this chapter for a description of the files available and install procedures.

5.2 ADDITIONAL DISCOVERY METHODS

You may be interested additional discovery techniques for a couple of reasons: Perhaps your network has limited SNMP devices, or maybe you missed a few devices in your seed file, or new devices have been added to the network that you would like to include in your management domain. Here are two additional ways to discover devices: you can use loadhosts, which is similar to using a seed file in that you must create an input file. You can also add devices via the NNM GUI, which can be labor-intensive if you plan to add more than a few devices. Neither of these two methods requires restarting background processes, which is required when using a seed file.

5.2.1 Discovery using loadhosts

After the network has been discovered, you can use the **loadhosts** command to add additional devices to the NNM database. Although the use of a seed file accomplishes the same end result, loadhosts is useful in the following situations:

- Only a few SNMP devices exist on your network (which means you are unable to retrieve the arp cache from these devices)
- You don't know the community names of the devices with arp caches
- You have a list of specific devices to manage in the file **/etc/hosts**
- You want to minimize discovery traffic
- You want to speed up the discovery of listed devices

If you have a list of devices with an arp cache and the SNMP community names are public (or you know the community names), either a seed file or **loadhosts** will work for you. If the devices don't have an arp cache or the community names are unknown, you will need to build a list of all devices (not just the ones that would be listed in the seed file) that you would like NNM to discover.

The input file for **loadhosts** is an ASCII file in the format of the /etc/hosts file. To use the **loadhosts** command, issue the following commands:

- **ovstop netmon**
- **loadhosts /etc/hosts**
- **ovstart netmon**

Each system in the file will be discovered by NNM and placed into NNM's databases and displayed on a submap and in Dynamic Views. NNM will perform the status and configuration queries on the device.

A sample loadhosts file is available for download from the server `http://www.phptr.com/title/0130352098`

for both UNIX and Windows systems. Obtain the Readme file this chapter for a description of the files available and install procedures.

5.2.2 Discovery via the NNM GUI

Manual discovery of network devices can be done from within the NNM GUI by adding devices to the appropriate submap. Why might you want to manually add a device instead of discovering it with a seed file or using **loadhosts**? You might be doing third-party monitoring and need to add a critical device that does not reside on any of the currently discovered networks and was not previously added in the seed file. The distinct advantage that the seed file provides is that you can put hundreds of entries in it and netmon will take care of the discovery of these devices. It may take hours to add hundreds of devices manually. The seed file requires stopping the background processes; manually adding devices does not. You probably wouldn't want to use the GUI to manually discover more than a couple of devices. Although, if you are adding a device such as a router, you may find that a great many more devices (located "behind" the router) are discovered. The seed file is also reproducible. If you ever need to delete the database, the seed file automates the discovery of specific nodes. If you've added nodes manually, you will either want to create a seed file or re-add them after network re-discovery.

To manually add a gateway or router, select from the Internet submap **Edit→Add Object** from the menubar. This displays a list of symbol classes and symbol subclasses, as shown in Figure 5-1. The symbol class denotes a symbol's outside shape (Application is oval, Computer is square, Connector is a diamond). The symbol subclass indicates the bitmap for the symbol (Gateway, Multi-port). Select the Connector symbol class and drag the subclass Gateway to the Internet submap and you will see the dialog box shown in Figure 5-2.

Figure 5-1 To add a router or gateway, select the Symbol Class Connector and drag the Symbol Subclass Gateway to the IP Internet submap.

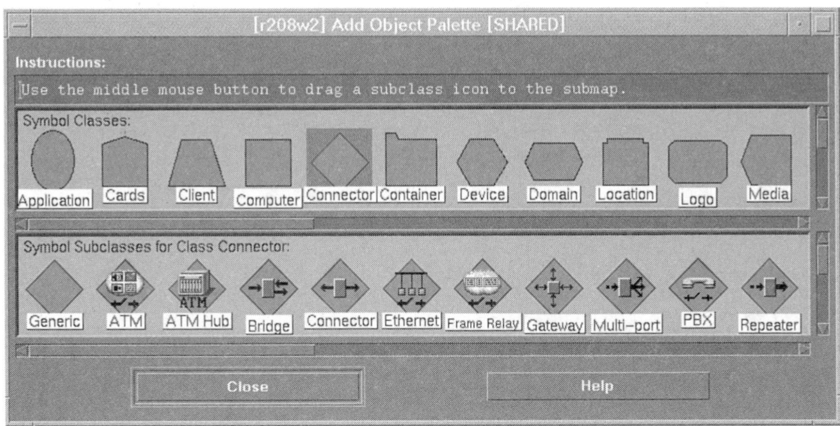

To add an object to be managed by NNM to the Internet submap, double-click "IP Map" from the Add Object dialog box shown in Figure 5-2. (You can also select "IP Map" and click **[Set Object Attributes]**.) You will see the set attribute dialog box shown in Figure 5-3. Fill in the device IP address and subnet mask and click the **[Verify]** button. After clicking **[OK]** in dialog box shown in Figure 5-3 and then in Figure 5-2, one of the following four things will occur on the Internet submap:

1. If the device responds to NNM's SNMP queries, all other fields in the dialog box will be populated, including the Selection Name and Label, and will be set to the hostname of the device.
2. If the device responds to ping but not to SNMP, the symbol will be set to the Computer Class and Generic Subclass.
3. If the device does not respond to ping or SNMP but is a valid device for the submap, the symbol will be added to the submap with a reflecting status of Unknown (Blue).
4. If the device is not valid for the submap, such as adding a Gateway to a node level submap, the symbol will display with shading around the lower and right edges. This is a visual indicator that the object resides in the user plane and is not being managed by the controlling application "IP Map."

Figure 5-2 To populate the router information, select the IP Map attribute and click the **[Set Object Attributes...]** button.

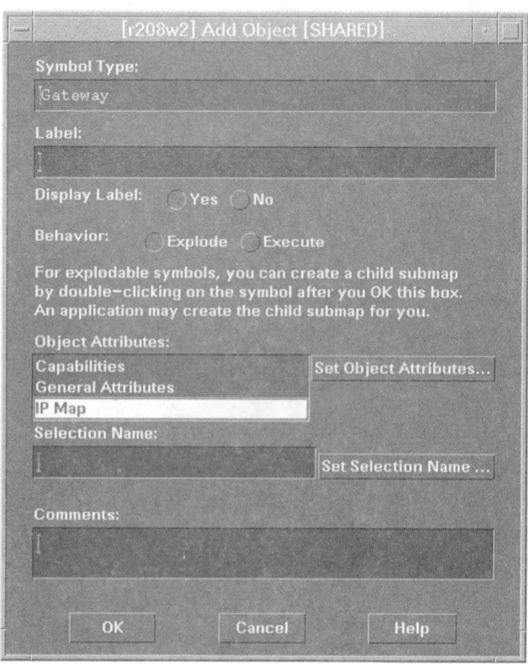

Figure 5-3 Set the IP address and Subnet Mask fields of the device and click **[Verfiy]**. At this point, NNM will send a series of SNMPGETs to the specified device. If the device responds, the remaining fields (Selection Name, Label, and Physical address) will be populated.

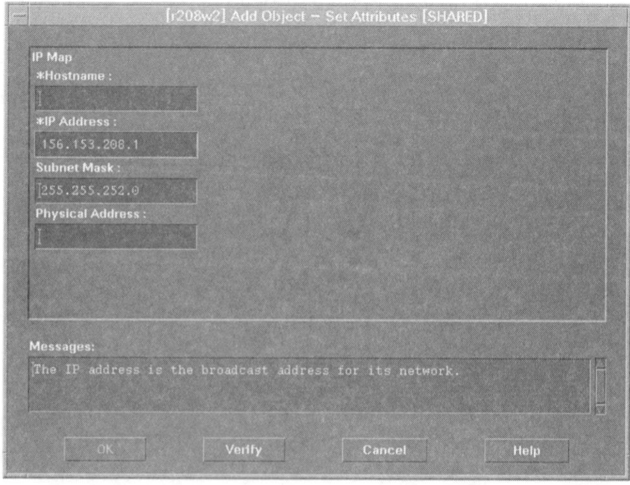

Note: Adding an Object to a Submap: When you add an object to a submap, NNM allows you to verify the validity of the object and will put it in the "IP Map" application plane if it is valid. Objects that are not recognized as valid will be put in the user plane, a visual indication that the object will not be managed by the ipmap process. Adding objects not managed by ipmap will be discussed in Chapter 6, "Customizing NNM from the GUI."

5.3 NETMON POLLING STATISTICS

Periodically you may want to check netmon's status. If you do this during network discovery you will find that netmon is very busy. You might also check when you suspect you have a network bottleneck or a network routing device is down. NNM provides a graphical representation of netmon's polling status, which can be accessed by selecting **Performance→Network Polling Statistics** from the menu bar. The Network Polling Statistics graph includes the following information:

- Seconds Until Next Status Poll
- Status Poll List Length
- Status Polls in Next Minute
- Seconds Until Next SNMP Poll
- SNMP Poll List Length
- SNMP Polls in Next Minute

The first variable, Seconds Until Next Status Poll, defines the number of seconds before NNM sends out an ICMP packet to determine the device status. By default, this type of poll is performed once every five minutes per device. This variable should always have a positive value. A negative value indicates that netmon is getting behind in its polling cycle. If a device does not respond to the status poll, netmon has a timeout (.8 by default, 800 milliseconds) and retry count (2 by default) that can cause the netmon polling cycle to get behind if a lot of devices are nonresponsive. This could happen for the following reasons:

1. A portion of the network is unreachable due to a routing device outage
2. Faulty network equipment causes heavy packet loss
3. Initial network discovery
4. Too many devices being managed by NNM[3]
5. A high incidence of node down/up events
6. Heavy network traffic

[3] Based on a five-minute polling interval, the practical limit of managed nodes per NNM station is 2000. However, you can increase the number of managed nodes by increasing the polling interval. For example, you can increase the polling interval for less critical devices to every 10 minutes instead of every 5 minutes.

The variable Seconds Until Next SNMP Poll may also be negative for any of the previously listed reasons. If either of these two values is consistently negative, take corrective action. Corrective actions may include managing fewer devices, increasing the status-polling interval for non-critical devices, or eliminating some devices using netmon.noDiscover. Implementation of multiple NNM stations may be necessary and is discussed in Chapter 7, "Advanced Customization."

The additional MIB variables displayed on the Network Polling Statistics graph include the number of devices in the list to be polled and the number of polls in the next minute. You will notice that these values increase during network discovery.

5.4 CONFIGURING SNMP COMMUNITY NAMES

Community names are passwords used by the SNMP agent to restrict access to information provided by the MIB. In order to retrieve information from the MIB, NNM needs to be configured with the community name of every device. The global default for community names in NNM is set to "public." This allows SNMP read access to devices that do not have a read community name configured.

5.4.1 SNMP Manager Configuration

You can configure community names in NNM by selecting Options→SNMP Configuration from the menu bar. In the center section of the dialog box displayed in Figure 5-4 you can see the entry for the global default for SNMP devices. Get Community is set to "public" and there is no Set Community name configured. The status polling timeout, retry, and Polling interval are also displayed. If you would like to modify the Global default, select the Global Default, update the values you would like to modify (Get Community, Set Community, and so on) and click the Replace button. To add a new entry, supply the Target (hostname or IP address), the Get Community, and the Set Community, and click the Add button. The example listed shows the hostname r208w100, the Get Community "mickey" and the Set Community "mouse." If you do not specify values for timeout, retry, and so on, the Global Default will be used.

Individual hostname targets will be listed in the top section of the dialog box, sub-titled **Specific Nodes**. You cannot use wildcards (*) when specifying hostnames. The next section of the dialog box, sub-titled **IP Address Wildcards**, permits IP addresses to be specified using wildcards (*) and also allows for the specification of IP address ranges. For example, if a certain type of network device in your enterprise ends with a 1 in the last octet and is configured with the same community name, you can specify the IP addresses using a wildcard:

```
156.155.*.1
```

Similarly, if you would like to specify a range of IP addresses with the same community name use the target

```
156.155.[201-210].1
```

You can also combine IP address wildcards and ranges:

```
156.[150-153].*.1
```

Figure 5-4 To configure the community name, provide the IP address or hostname as the Target, the get (read) community name, and the set (write) community name and click the **[Add]** button. If community names are not specified, the Global Default will be used. Wildcards and numeric ranges may be used only when specifying the device's IP address.

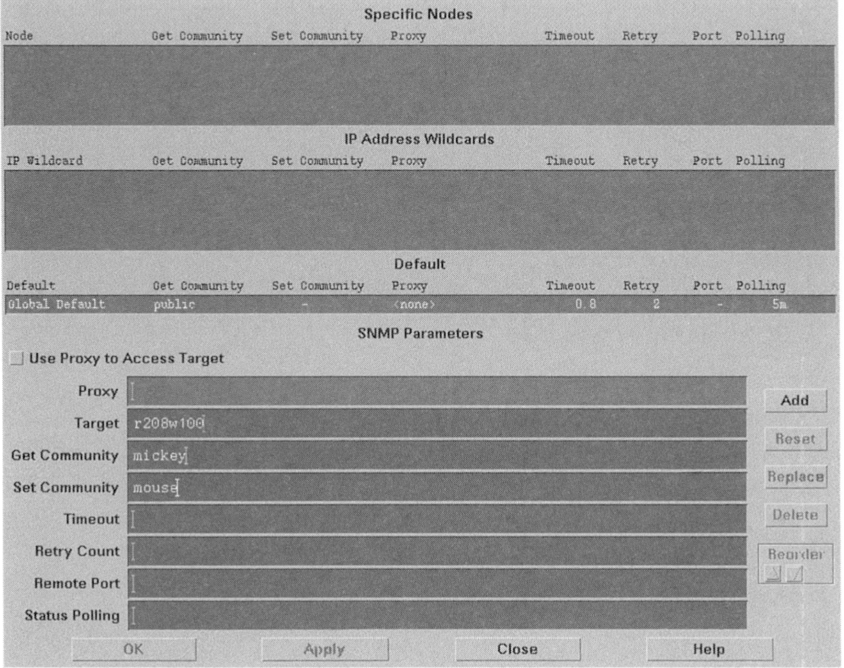

5.4.2 SNMP Agent Configuration

The agent configuration, not to be confused with the management station configuration, will vary based on the type of system. One area that may cause some confusion is the fact that the management station itself also must have an SNMP agent running on it. In this respect, it is just like any other managed node. Most Unix systems have a configuration file such as /etc/snmpd.conf. To configure the SNMP agent, modify the get-community-name and set-community-name entries. Sample entries in the snmpd.conf are shown. The trap-dest will usually be set to your NNM management station. This is the location to which to send agent initiated SNMP traps. Multiple trap destinations can be defined in this file in the case that more than one SNMP management station exists.

The SNMP agent configuration should include the following entries:

```
get-community-name: mickey
set-community-name: mouse
trap-dest: 156.155.204.8
```

After the changes have been made to the SNMP agent configuration, you will need to restart the SNMP agent. This process varies based on the agent you are running. NNM ships with the SNMP Research® EMANATE agent. This agent uses a master/sub-agent technology, which requires a restart of the SNMP master agent and the sub-agents. Use the following steps to add community names and restart the EMANATE agent:

UNIX:

1. Modify **/etc/snmpd.conf** with the get-community-name and the set-community-name.

   get-community-name: mickey

   set-community-name: mouse
2. Stop the master and sub-agents.

   /sbin/init.d/SnmpMaster stop
3. Start the master and sub-agents.

   /etc/snmpd
4. Verify SNMP communication to the hostname.

   snmpwalk <hostname> system

Windows:

1. Use the Notepad[4] editor to modify the file

   %OV_CONF%\ SNMPAgent\snmpd.conf

   with the get-community-name and the set-community-name as follows:

   get-community-name: mickey

   set-community-name: mouse
2. Restart the SNMP agent service. The **Services** are accessible from **Control Panel** for Windows NT and the **MCC** for Windows 2000. Scroll down the list until you reach the SNMP EMANATE Adapter for Windows and SNMP EMANATE Master Agent.
3. Select the **Windows Adapter** and **Stop** the process. You will be prompted for confirmation.
4. Select the **Master Agent** and **Start** the process.[5]
5. Verify SNMP communication to the hostname.

   snmpwalk <hostname> system

[4] Some editors cannot handle files with four character extensions.

[5] The Windows agent can also be stopped and started via the command line by typing **snmpdm stop** and **snmpdm start**.

If SNMP connectivity fails, refer to section 5.1.3 for troubleshooting. You can test the set-community-name through the NNM GUI by attempting to set a read-write MIB variable such as system contact. Follow these steps to test the set-community-name of a MIB variable:

1. From the NNM GUI, select a node that has a set-community-name configured and start the MIB Browser by selecting

   Tools→SNMP MIB Browser

2. Traverse the subtree:

   mgmt.mib-2.system

3. Select the variable **sysContact** and click **[Start Query]**.
4. Verify the MIB value. You should see the instance[6] **0** and no contact information unless the contact was previously set.
5. Set the **sysContact** by entering the MIB Instance 0, the set-community-name and click **[Set]**. The SNMP Set Value must match the set-community-name string you entered in the snmpd.conf (or the agent configuration) file.

5.5 FIREWALL CONSIDERATIONS IN NETWORK DISCOVERY

Many corporations implement network security to protect their resources. This may be achieved by using some type of firewall software such as Check Point FireWall-1. Most firewalls do not allow ICMP (ping) traffic to pass through, which means that by default, an NNM station cannot manage devices across a firewall. However, netmon can be configured to use snmp for network discovery (instead of ping) with the use of the configuration file netmon.snmpStatus. To configure SNMP discovery:

1. Create the configuration file in the following location:

   UNIX: $OV_CONF/netmon.snmpStatus

   Windows: %OV_CONF%\netmon.snmpStatus

2. Add a line to the netmon.snmpStatus file with the IP Address wildcards that you want to have SNMP status polled.
3. Restart netmon from the command line by typing the following:

   ovstop netmon

   ovstart netmon

Another solution to managing devices across a firewall is to implement a distributed model of NNM. This entails placing a Collection Station on one side of the firewall and a Management Station on the other side allowing management across the firewall. The communication between the NNM stations is SNMP. This topic will be discussed in detail in Chapter 9.

[6] The instance will always be 0 unless there are multiple instances for the variable. For example, if there are multiple file systems there will be a unique instance number for each file system and the instance will begin with 1.

5.6 SUMMARY

Network discovery can be customized in several ways. You can use a seed file to direct the discovery of your network. The seed file allows the administrator to define the portion of the network for NNM to discover and manage. You can also use the loadhosts command and the netmon.noDiscover file to limit the discovery of your network. Discovery can also be performed manually via the NNM GUI. Be aware that network discovery is bandwidth intensive and that it should only be performed at low network utilization times. Use netmon polling statistics to determine how well netmon is performing.

Because NNM relies heavily on SNMP access to managed devices, you should collect and configure the community names for devices you need to manage. In order to retrieve SNMP information, NNM needs to be configured with the community name of every device. If a device does not respond to SNMP, the device will be interpreted as a generic computer and the information collected for that device is limited to up/down status and its IP address.

Determine whether you need to manage across firewalls in your enterprise, and if so, what method you plan on implementing to manage across firewalls. Otherwise, NNM may discover a very simple and possibly not so useful network.

CHAPTER 6

Customizing NNM from the GUI

One compelling aspect of NNM is that the administrator can customize submaps from within the GUI. Some of the customizations include adding background graphics, saving window placement, hiding symbols, and creating MIB applications. While advanced customizations require file editing, NNM provides the flexibility to offer both simple and advanced customizations without source code modification and re-compilation. In fact, many modifications can be made on the fly without exiting the NNM GUI or restarting processes.

Sealey Inc. has a requirement to be able to make use of geographical bitmaps and customer floor plans. They would like to place certain devices in a specific region representing the physical locations of the devices. Certain devices are mission critical and they would like to configure the GUI with quick access to these devices. However, because each operator has different responsibilities, they consider different devices to be mission critical. Therefore, each operator may want a slightly different view of the network.

Sealey Inc. would also like to be able to graph SNMP MIB data real-time. Certain operators may frequently be required to access data from the same MIB variables. The network application should provide the ability to easily graph MIB data. This chapter details customizing NNM from the GUI.

6.1 CUSTOMIZING SUBMAPS

Submaps may be customized on a per-map basis to allow each NNM user to focus on specific needs. For example, a particular user might want to see the systems placed geographically on a submap according to the location in which the systems physically reside. A user might also want to create custom icons that will launch frequently used applications. The following sections include some of the commonly used map customizations.

6.1.1 Setting the Default Map and Home Submap

The *user default map* is the map that is open when a user starts the NNM GUI. If the specification of the default map is not modified, the map named "default" will be opened. The administrator can create as many maps as necessary, limited only by disk space.[1] Generally speaking, you

1 Maps are written to the directory $OV_DB/openview/mapdb. For UNIX systems, use du –k $OV_DB/openview/mapdb to view the sizes of the map databases in kilobytes. For information on the **du** command, refer to the UNIX man page on **du**. For Window systems, view the directory properties from Microsoft Explorer.

should never make customizations to the default map. A better practice would be to make a copy of the default map, saving it under a new name. Customizations should then be made to this new map. After making customizations to a map (such as background graphics, auto-layout, and so on), you may want to set this map as your user default map. The user can set his default map by performing the following:

1. Select from the menu bar **Map→Open…**
2. Select the map you would like as your default (see Figure 6-1).
3. Click the **[Set User Default]** button.

Figure 6-1 Select **Map→Open** from the menu bar to set the user default map. Select the map name and click the **[Set User Default]** button. The User Default Map shown here is the map named "default."

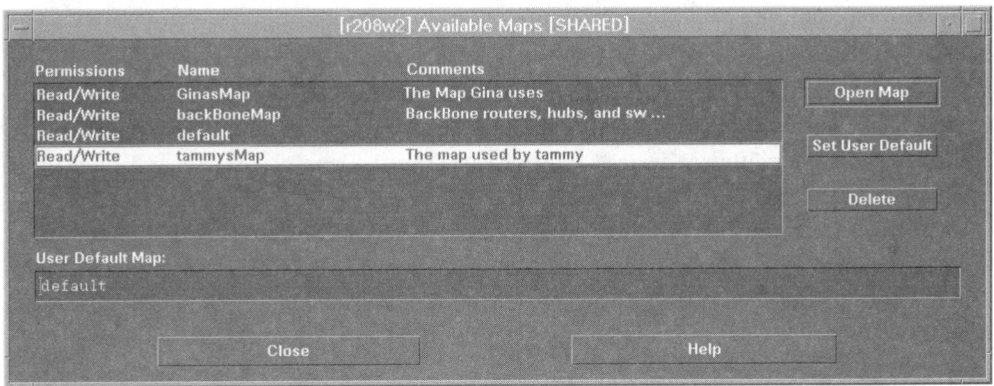

When a map is opened, the first submap to be displayed is the *home submap*. The home submap is also easily accessible by selecting the "house" icon on the toolbar. By default, the home submap is set to the root submap. The home submap should be set to the submap you access most frequently. Each map may have a different home submap. To set the home submap, navigate to your favorite submap and select from the menubar **Map→Submap→Set This Submap as Home**.

You can now use the toolbar icon to return to the home submap at any time. A user may have as many maps as desired and each map can have a different home submap.

Unused maps begin to contain stale topology data as the NNM topology database is updated over time. Even when **ovtopofix** and **ovw –mapcount** are run, you may encounter errors, such as "objects still in 4 maps." In order to correct this error, each map must be opened so that it synchronizes the current topology information into the map. Each map can either be opened individually or with a script run as root on the NNM server, depending on the number of maps you need to open to synchronize.

Don't open maps in NNM that are created by OVO! The following example "greps out" two default OVO maps:

```
export DISPLAY=displayhostname:0.0
for  map in 'ovwls -x | egrep -v "opcadm|opcop"  `
do
  ovw -map $map &
done
```

Check to ensure that every map was opened with read/write privileges. The map will not synchronize without being opened with read/write privileges. After the synchronization of the maps, run **ovw –mapcount**. This should run without errors.

6.1.2 Submap Overlay, Window Geometry, and Symbol Hiding

Many customizations may be made to a map, including the behavior of the submap overlay. By default, when you drill down through a map's hierarchy by double clicking, the child submap of the selected object replaces the current submap.[2] Likewise, when you click the up arrow icon from the toolbar, the parent submap of the current submap replaces the child. This prevents the user from having too many open submaps. If you prefer not to have this submap overlay feature turned on, you can modify this behavior on both a map and a submap basis by selecting from the menu bar

View→Submap Overlay→Off For This Submap

View→Submap Overlay→Off For All Submaps

Another user customization is the ability to save window size and placement. For instance, if you prefer the IP Internet submap on the left side of your monitor and a particular node-level submap on the right side, simply adjust the submap overlay to open multiple submaps, arrange the submap size and location to your liking, and save the window geometry by selecting **View→Window Geometry→Save For All Open Submaps**.

Further customizations can be made for personal preferences. Not all NNM users want to see the same view of the network. For example, a network manager may never want to see individual workstations or servers. By hiding symbols you can alleviate unwanted clutter from her view of the network. Hidden objects are still actively polled but their status will not be reflected on the maps in which they are hidden. If the network manager hides non-networking devices, she will not see when hidden devices are down by simply glancing at the appropriate submap. However, hiding a device does not prevent the **Node Down Event** from being sent to the Alarm Browser.

2 In earlier implementations of NNM, every time you double-clicked an object a new window opened. If you double-clicked twenty objects, you had twenty windows. This became a bit cumbersome to keep track of all the open windows. The submap overlay feature allows you to customize this per map and per submap.

To hide symbols, first select them[3] and then select from the menu bar **View→Hidden Objects→Hide Selected From This Submap**.

The status line at the bottom of each submap displays the number of hidden objects on the current submap, as shown in Figure 6-2. You may have a need to hide a particular type of object. For example, you may want to hide all Windows systems because they are all DHCP devices that appear to go down frequently. Follow these steps to hide all systems that have a common attribute such as the operating system:

1. Search for the object by the attribute.
   Edit→Find→Object By Symbol Type...
2. Select **Computer** class **Windows NT** subclass and click the **[Apply]** button.
3. Double-click one of the items listed under the "Located and Highlighted" section.
4. Select the items that were found.
   View→Highlights→Select Highlighted
5. Hide the objects that were selected.
   View→Hidden Objects→Hide Selected From This Submap
6. Hidden objects can be unhidden at any time by selecting
   View→Hidden Objects→Show Hidden On This Submap
7. Recall that the submap hierarchy is
   Root→Internet→Network→Segment→Node

Notice that the list includes the segment submap (objects) as well as node submaps. To more quickly and effectively hide the desired objects (in this case, windows NT nodes) we should concentrate on the segment submaps. When you double-click one of these, you are presented with the appropriate child submap which has all NT nodes "highlighted' (highlighted labels are displayed in reverse video).

While hiding objects is one way to deal with unwanted devices, filtering is a more elegant method of dealing with "undesirable" objects. A filter can be applied to on a per-map basis, which hides objects from the view while allowing them to exist in the object database and be actively polled. This type of filter is known as a *map filter*. While the result of applying a map filter is similar to hiding objects, the implementation is usually much faster and more effective. Other types of filters include *topology* and *discovery* filters, which are discussed in detail in Chapter 9, "Scalability and Distribution."

3 Use the control and left mouse button simultaneously to multi-select symbols. This also toggles the selection.

Figure 6-2 The status line displays the map name (default), the access mode (Read-Write), the number of hidden symbols (Hidden:8), and whether Auto-Layout is enabled.

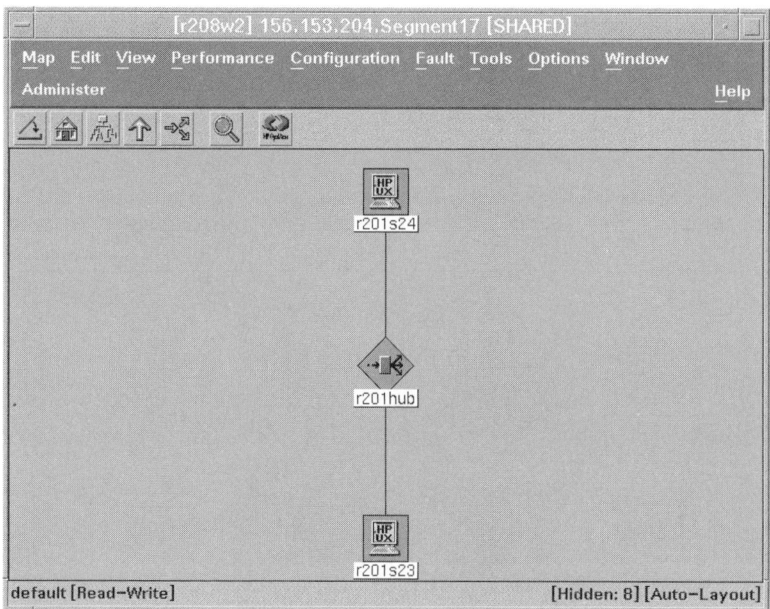

6.1.3 Setting Background Graphics and Automatic Layout

Background graphics can be used to enhance the appearance of a submap. They can be used to display geographic regions, floor plans, or organizational structures. A number of file formats are supported for submap background graphics. If you have a file that is not in the list, check the Release Notes for currently supported file formats. Supported file formats for background graphics are listed in Table 6-1.

Table 6-1 File types supported by NNM for submap background graphics.

GIF
TIFF
BMP
XBM
PCX
Image
Starbase
XPM
XWD
JPEG

Background graphics may be configured for a submap by following these steps:

1. Select **Map→Submap→Properties** from the menu bar.
2. Click the **[Browse...]** button listed by the Background Graphics section of the dialog box. This is located on the View tab for Windows.
3. Select a graphic as shown in the list of Figure 6-3.
4. Click **[OK]**.

Figure 6-3 The administrator can set a background graphic for each submap. Many of the provided graphics include geographic locations. The administrator can also import a custom graphic such as a floor plan.

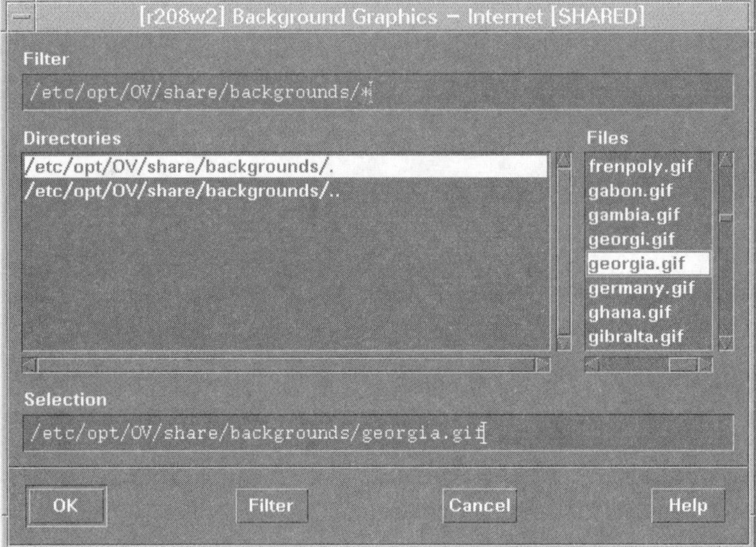

6.1.3.1 Memory Considerations when using Background Graphics

One thing to remember when setting background graphics is the amount of physical memory (RAM) you have on your NNM system. When you open a map, all objects, including background graphics, are loaded into memory[4]. The more objects in the database, the more memory required to load objects into memory. Similarly, the more complex the graphic, the more memory required. One way to tell if your system is memory-bound is if the synchronization process takes a long time (more than a few minutes) when you open a map. If synchronization is taking too long, try decreasing the number of objects being loaded into memory. One way to achieve this is by changing the persistence level of your map.

4 The default behavior of NNM on UNIX systems is to load all objects in to memory. The default behavior on Windows NT/2000 is to only load objects into memory on the IP Internet submap and higher.

6.1.3.2 Submap Persistence

The persistence level of a submap indicates the level at which objects are loaded into memory. If you select any choice other than **All Levels**, the objects appearing on submaps below that level are not loaded into memory until you open that specific submap. You can define the persistence level of a map by following these steps.

1. Select the map properties.
   Map→Properties
2. Select IP Map and click **[Configure For This Map…]**
3. Scroll down to the section that reads
   On-Demand: To what level should submaps be persistent.
4. Select one of the levels:
   All Levels
   Segment Level and Higher
   Network Level and Higher
   Internet Level
5. After selecting the persistence level, click **[Verify]** and **[OK]** in the IP Map configuration dialog box and **[OK]** in the Map Properties dialog box.

Tip: Any modifications you make to a submap will cause it to become a persistent submap, regardless of the persistence setting. For example, if you set your map persistence level to the **Segment Level and Higher**, only the root, Internet, and network level objects will be loaded into memory. However, if you make any of the following modifications to a segment or node level submap, you will cause that submap to become persistent:

- Submap Overlay
- Window Geometry
- Hidden Objects
- Background Graphics
- Auto-layout

Any objects contained in the submaps that have customizations such as these will be loaded into memory whenever the map is open. As another example, if you set your persistence level to **Internet Level** and set a background graphic on every submap, you defeat the purpose of setting the persistence level.

6.1.3.3 Automatic Layout

The purpose of automatic layout is to allow a device discovered by NNM to have its symbols placed on a submap without human intervention. When using background graphics, you may find that you would like to manually control the placement of symbols. When placing objects on a floor plan, for example, you can turn off auto layout and place the symbols where they physically reside. To turn off automatic layout for an individual submap, select **View→Automatic Layout→Off For This Submap** as shown in Figure 6-4.

Figure 6-4 This submap has been configured with Georgia as the background graphic. NNM ships with a GIF file for each US state and many countries. Turn off automatic layout to allow manual placement of symbols.

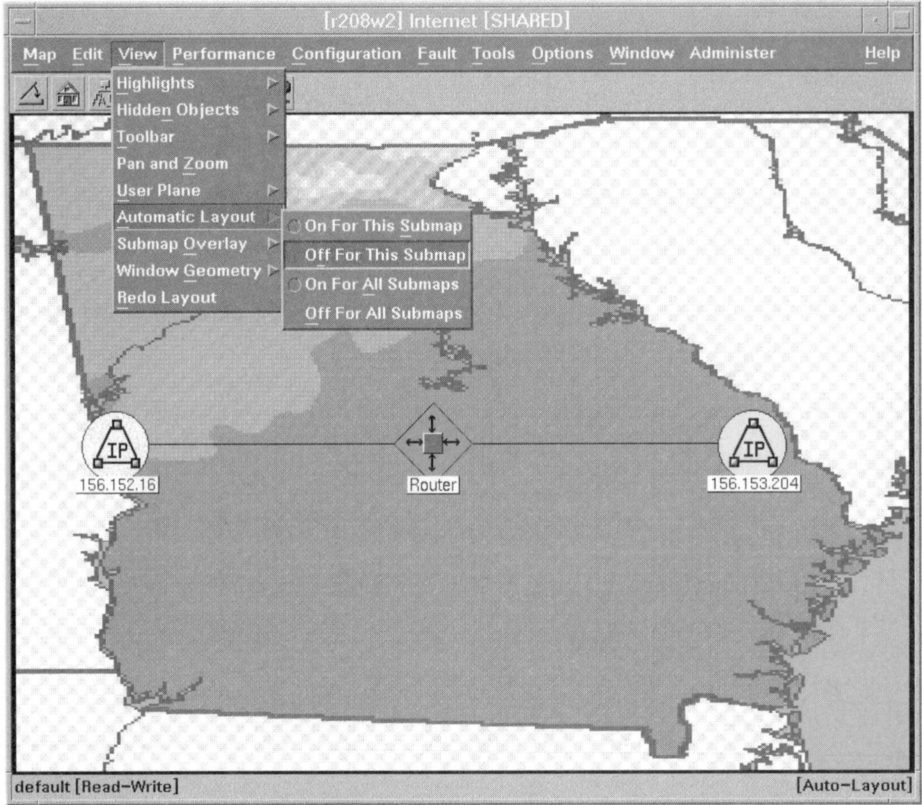

After you turn auto layout off, notice that **[Auto-Layout]** is removed from the status line and a "**New Object Holding Area**" appears at the bottom of the submap, as shown in Figure 6-5. When new devices are discovered that belong on a submap where auto layout is turned off, the newly discovered objects are placed in the New Object Holding Area. You must drag the new objects from the New Object Holding Area and drop them onto the desired location on the submap.

Figure 6-5 The **New Object Holding Area** is created when automatic layout is turned off. Newly discovered devices are placed in the New Object Holding Area. They can be manually placed on a submap by drag-and-drop.

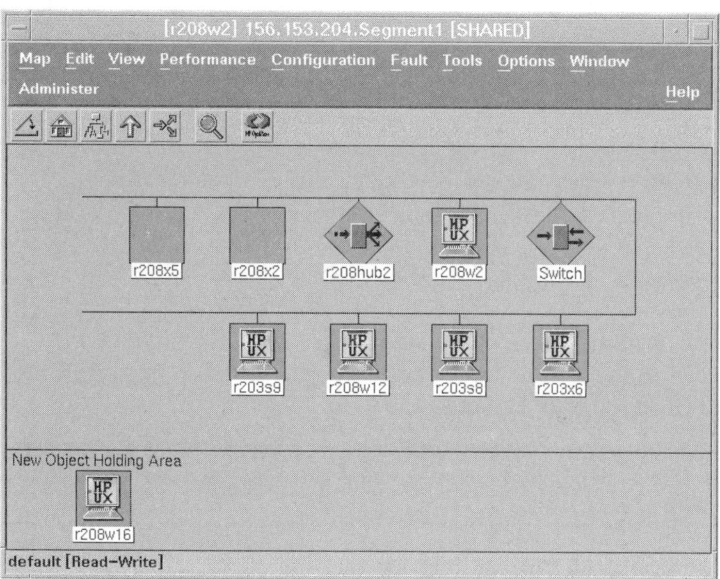

6.1.4 Partitioning the Internet Submap

NNM knows how to lay out devices based on the information provided by SNMP queries. The submap hierarchy from top to bottom is

Root
Internet
Network
Segment
Node

The layout of your network can be customized at the Internet level submap. The purpose is to allow partitioning of your network based on geographical or logical information. NNM does an excellent job of providing the physical connections of your network but makes no assumptions as to the organizational structure. This customization is known as partitioning the Internet submap.

Partitioning the Internet submap requires that you add a special type of symbol called a location symbol. The steps to partition the IP Internet submap are as follows:

1. From the Internet submap select
   Edit→Add Object
2. Select the Location symbol (Figure 6-6) and drag any of the subclass symbols to the submap.
3. Provide a Label and click **[OK].**
4. Repeat the creation of location icons until you have defined all necessary locations.
5. Drag each symbol and drop it in the desired location.[5] Connections will automatically be established between location symbols as shown in Figure 6-7.

Note: Location icons can be cascaded when partitioning the Internet submap. For example, you could add USA at the Internet level, add State under USA, and add City under State, and then add Building, Site, Room, and so on.

Figure 6-6 Location objects can be used to partition the IP Internet submap. Notice the location objects added to the submap shown (Japan and Australia) are in the application plane (no shading appears around the symbol).

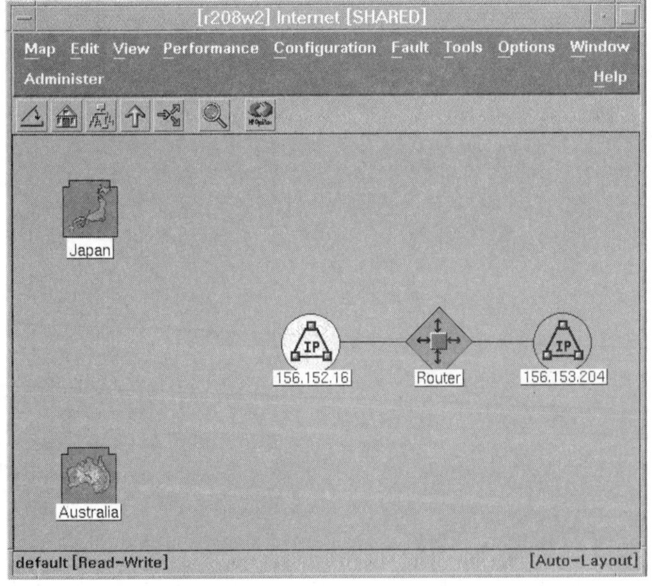

5 The Windows version of NNM requires using cut and paste instead of drag and drop.

Figure 6-7 When partitioning the Internet submap, connections between the locations are automatically established as symbols are moved into the location icons.

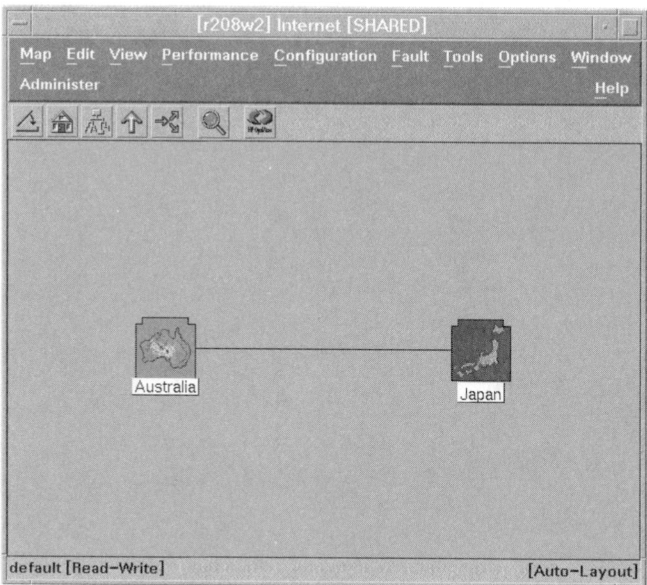

6.1.5 Creating Executable Symbols

By default, symbols on a submap spawn a child submap when double clicked. This behavior is referred to as "explodable." Symbol properties on a submap may be modified to launch an application when double-clicked rather than opening a child submap. This behavior is referred to as "executable." A number of pre-defined applications exist and are accessible in NNM. In fact, most applications available from the menu bar and the toolbar may be used in creating executable symbols. These applications are defined in NNM through *Application Registration Files* (ARFs). In addition to using the pre-defined applications, you can create your own applications by defining ARFs as discussed in Chapter 7, "Advanced Customization."

To make use of the executable symbol feature in NNM, follow the steps listed here. For this example, use a system that allows incoming telnet sessions.

1. Access the symbol properties by right-clicking and selecting **Symbol Properties** as shown in Figure 6-8.

Figure 6-8 The first step in making an icon executable is to place the cursor over the symbol, click the right mouse button, and select **Symbol Properties…** from the symbol popup menu.

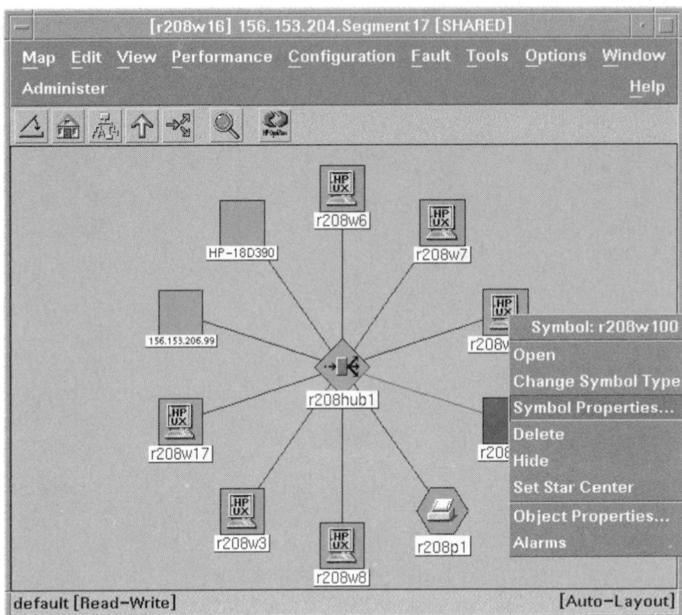

2. Modify the symbol behavior to **Execute**, as shown in Figure 6-9. Notice the list of Applications that appear under the section labeled "Application Action."
3. Scroll through the list and select the application **Terminal Connect: XTerm Telnet**
4. Click the **[Target Objects…]** button.
5. Click the **[Add]** button to include the hostname and click **[OK]** on the Target Objects dialog box as shown in Figure 6-10.
6. Click **[OK]** on the Symbol Properties dialog box and you will see the executable symbol as shown in Figure 6-11. When the symbol is double clicked it launches a telnet session to the system.

Figure 6-9 The second step in making an icon executable is to modify the behavior of the symbol to **Execute** and select to application to be launched.

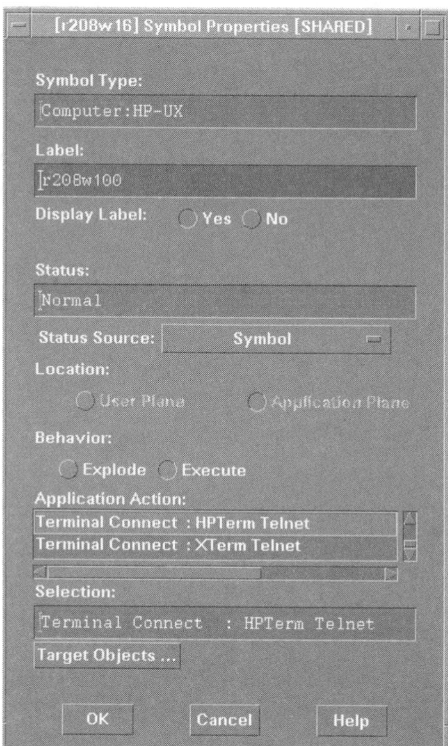

Figure 6-10 The third step in creating an executable icon is to click the **[Target Objects]** button, which displays the dialog box shown. Select the **[Add]** button to add the hostname as a target object.

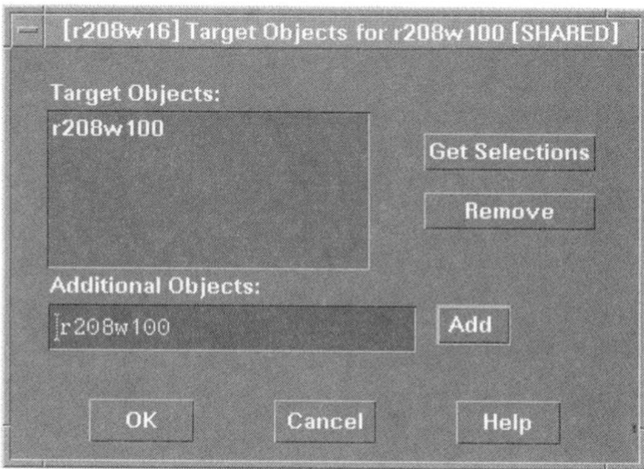

Figure 6-11 The executable icon (r208w100) shows up as a button. Double-click it to launch the application. You can also drag a symbol and drop it on the button to launch the application on another object.

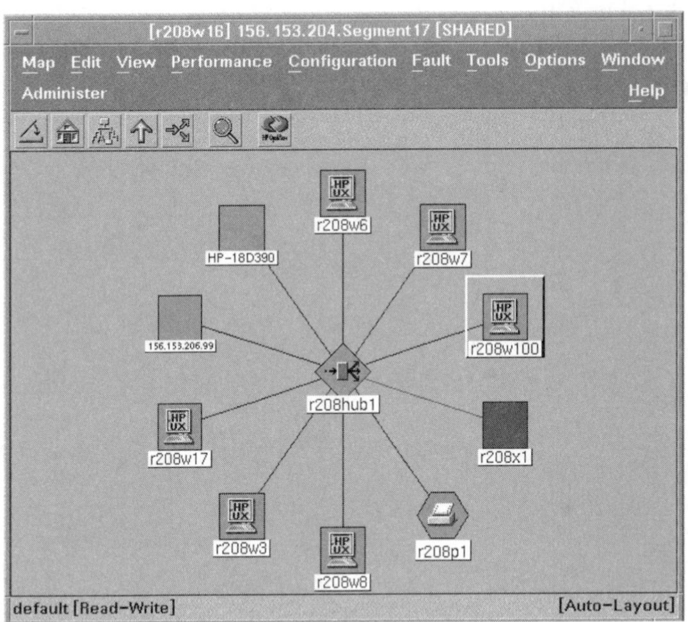

After you have created an executable symbol, you can drag other symbols and drop them onto the executable symbol. For example, if you want to launch telnet on a different system, simply drag the symbol and drop it onto the executable symbol. Making a symbol "executable" does not affect the symbol status set by ipmap. There is one caveat when changing an existing symbol's behavior to executable. After changing an existing symbol to executable, you will no longer be able to access the symbol's child submap by double clicking the symbol. Instead, the only way to access the child submap of the symbol is to use the submap open feature. You can do this by selecting **Map→Submap→Open...** You will need to drill down through the submap listings to find the modified symbol's submap. Select the modified symbol and click the **[Open Submaps]** button. For this reason, you can also create standalone symbols that launch applications. It is not necessary to modify the behavior of an existing symbol.

6.1.6 MIB Applications

Many of the options from the tool and menu bar access applications that communicate with the MIB. When launched, these applications send SNMP queries to the selected node to access certain MIB variables. Some applications create tables that contain the data and others generate real-time graphs. NNM provides many built-in MIB applications as well as the capability to create your own MIB applications via the GUI.

6.1.5.1 Built-in MIB Applications

Most MIB applications require you to select a node before launching. If nothing is selected, the menu items will be grayed out and unavailable. Let's look at some of the built-in MIB applications. Select a node and select from the menu bar **Performance→Network Activity→Interface Traffic: Packet Rate** as shown in Figure 6-12. This will display a real-time graph of the MIB variables for packet rate.

Figure 6-12 Interface Traffic is a built-in MIB application available from the menu bar. Select a node and select **Network Activity→Interface Traffic: Packet Rate** from the menu bar. This initiates snmpgets for specific MIB variables and displays them graphically.

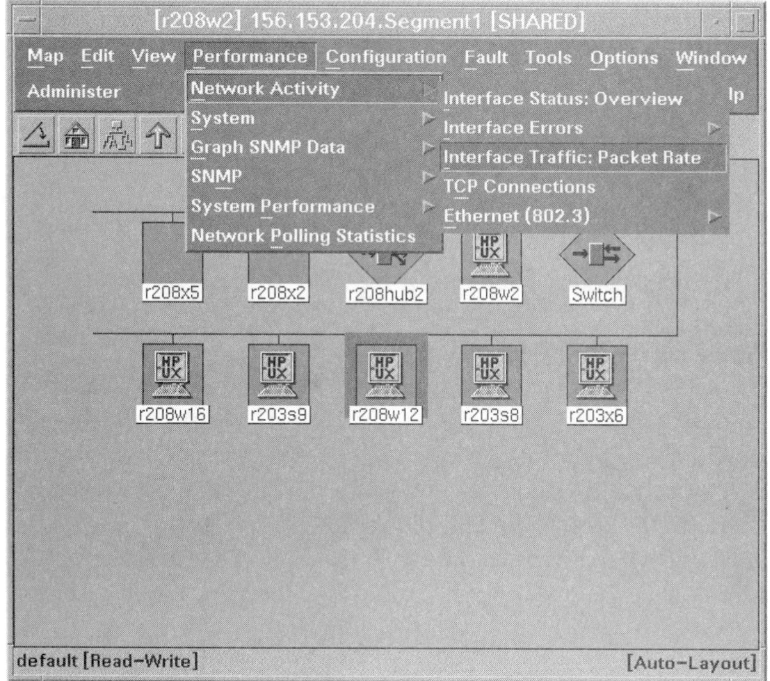

6.1.5.2 Creating MIB Applications

NNM provides the ability to create MIB applications that will be incorporated into the NNM menu bar. This can be achieved by using the MIB application builder.

The MIB application builder allows you to create custom graphs and tables by defining the MIB variables you want to be displayed.

Follow these steps to create your MIB graph:

1. Select **Options→MIB Application Builder: SNMP** from the menu bar. This displays an empty MIB application dialog box as shown in Figure 6-13.

Figure 6-13 To create a MIB application, select **Options→MIB Application Builder: SNMP** from the menu bar. The list will be empty by default. Select **Edit?Add MIB Application....**

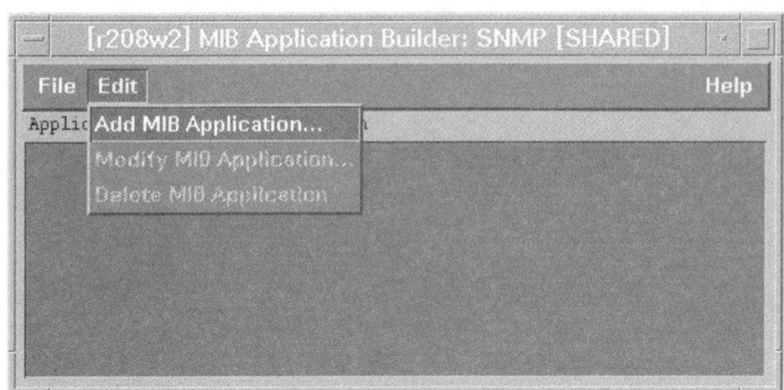

2. Select **Edit→Add MIB Application....** You will see the dialog box as shown in Figure 6-14.
3. Complete the following fields to define the MIB application:
   Application ID—This must be a unique ID not containing spaces or special characters. For this example, use **InVSOut**
   Application Type—Set this to table, form, or graph. For this example specify graph.
   Application Title—Name the application whatever you want. This can contain spaces and special characters. For this example, specify "In Packets VS Out Packets".
   Menu Path—This describes the cascaded menu bar for the application beginning with the top-level menu. This may also contain spaces. Use "->" to indicate cascading menus. For this example, specify *yourname* Custom Apps→In VS Out
   Selection Rule—The Selection Rule describes the node type for which this application will work. Until you are familiar with the filtering language described in Chapter 9, it is best to leave it set to the default. The default Selection Rule (**isSNMPSupported || isSNMPProxied**) will function on any device that supports SNMP or has an SNMP proxy.
4. Click the **[Add...]** button to define the MIB variables for the application.

Figure 6-14 Specify the Application ID, Application Type, Application Title, Menu Path and click the **[Add...]** button.

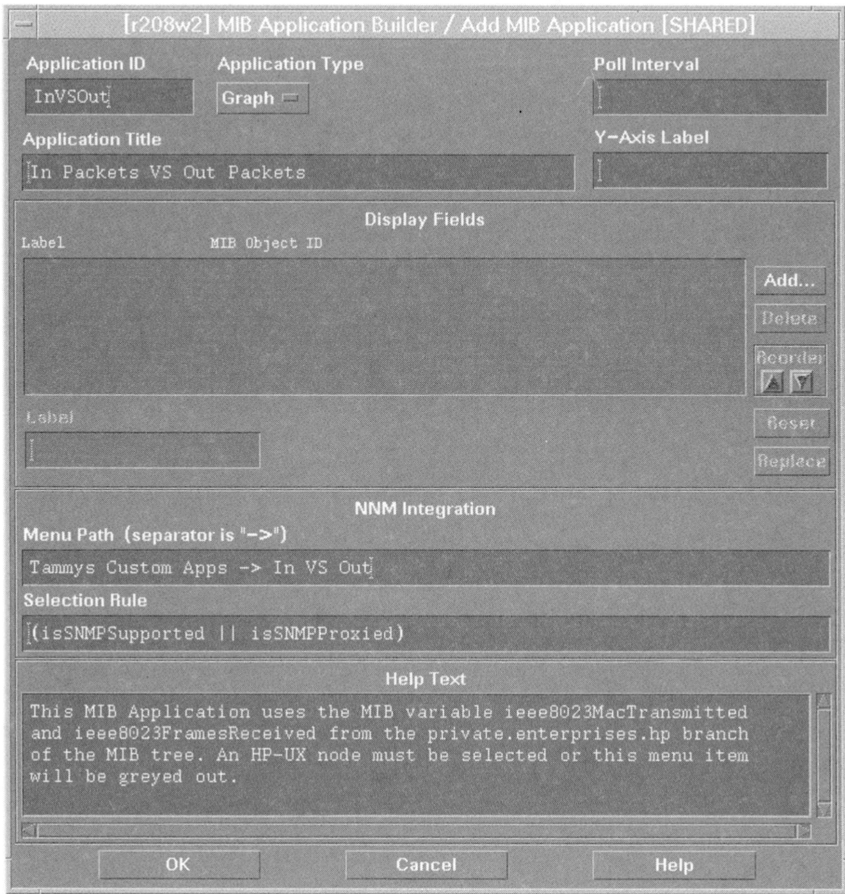

5. Traverse the MIB tree to include the MIB variables for the application. Use the control key and left mouse click simultaneously to select the desired variables. This example uses the MIB variables **ieeeMacTransmitted** and **ieeeMacFramesReceived** shown in Figure 6-15 under the MIB subtree private.enterprises.hp.nm.interface .ieee8023Mac.ieee8023MacTable.ieeeMacEntry
6. After selecting the desired variables, click **[OK]** from the Add MIB Objects dialog box.
7. Click **[OK]** from the Add MIB Application dialog box. You should see your custom menu as shown in Figure 6-16. You are now ready to execute your application.

Figure 6-15 You should be familiar with the MIB tree structure in order to create MIB applications. Press the control key and left click simultaneously to select multiple variables.

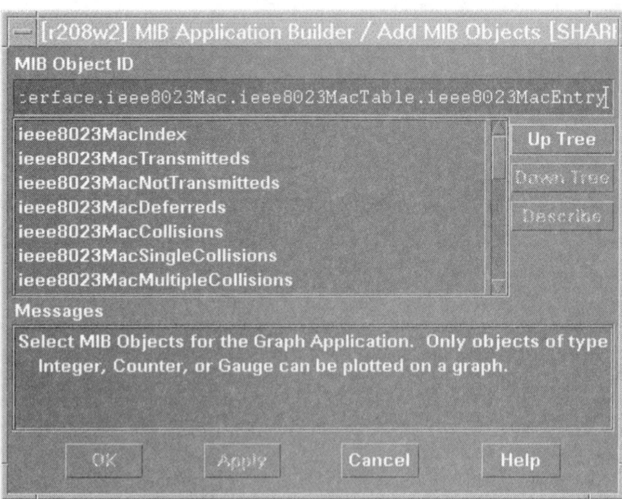

Figure 6-16 Select the node on which to execute the newly created MIB application. Select the application from the menu bar specified in the Menu Path of the MIB application builder.

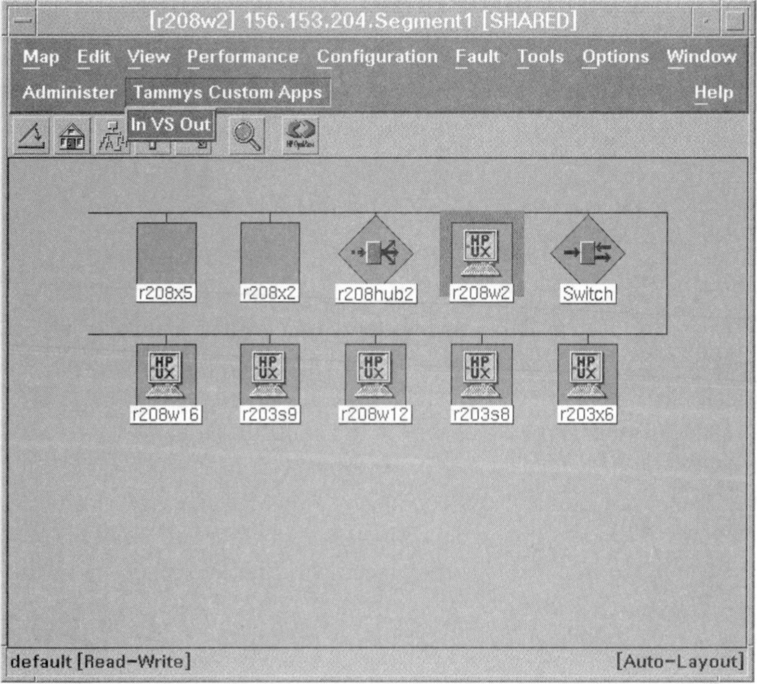

6.1.5.3 Use Your MIB Application as an Executable Symbol

After you've created an MIB application it becomes an NNM registered application. The MIB application can now be used when creating executable symbols. Add an object to a submap, change the behavior to executable, and check the list for your application. An *Application Registration File* (ARF) is created when you define an MIB application.

6.2 SUMMARY

Customizing the ovw GUI is both flexible and simple. Many customizations, such as adding submap backgrounds, automatic layout of symbols, symbol hiding, and creation of executable symbols, can be achieved from within the ovw GUI. These customizations allow each NNM user to tailor the environment based on job roles and responsibilities. Submaps are more easily managed, devices are more easily located, and frequently used applications can be easily executed with a double click (when executable symbols are defined). By allowing such customization, the NNM user can become more efficient at managing the network.

## CHAPTER 7

Advanced Customization

Advanced customization of NNM requires editing text files referred to as registration files. There are several types of registration files available for customization. This chapter covers the purpose of each type of registration file and provides examples of each. *Application Registration Files* (ARFs) allow the administrator to modify NNM's menu bar selections, the symbol popup menu, and the toolbar icons. *Web Launcher Registration Files* (WLRFs) allow the administrator to add menu items to the Web Launcher interface. *Network Presenter Registration Files* (NPRFs) allow the admin to customize the menu items on the Network Presenter. *Symbol Registration Files* (SRFs) allow the admin to create symbols with custom bitmaps. *Field Registration Files* (FRFs) allow the admin to add custom fields (isRouter, isHub, etc) to devices. Registration files are read dynamically (if placed in the proper directory) when a user starts an ovw session.

Sealey Inc. has developed several applications that they would like to integrate into the network management solution. These applications have been ported from HP-UX to Windows NT and Windows 2000. Many of the applications can be executed via a web browser. They would like the applications to be available from the web interface as well as the native interface.

Sealey Inc. manages a bagel company with SNMP-manageable toasters. They would like the ability to differentiate the SNMP toaster from other devices by using custom bitmaps. They would also like to quickly locate the toasters from the ovw GUI for troubleshooting purposes. The operators need to access online documentation, preferably via a web browser. This chapter includes details for advanced customization of NNM to satisfy the requirements of Sealey Inc. Examples described in this chapter are available for download from the server `http://www.phptr.com/title/0130352098`.

7.1 Application Integration using Application Registration Files (ARFs)

The purpose of an ARF is to incorporate applications into the native NNM GUI. Many OpenView products extend the functionality of NNM by supplying ARFs. An ARF may be used to incorporate an application onto the menu bar, the symbol popup menu, or the toolbar. In fact, you may have noticed that many of the available applications in NNM can be accessed from more than one location. For example, you can view an object's properties by selecting **[Object Properties]** from the symbol popup menu or by selecting the symbol and selecting **Edit→Object Properties...** from the menu bar. The ARF not only defines how the application is executed but also where in the menu structure the application appears.

7.1.1 Creating Your Own ARF

Whenever you add an ARF to NNM, it must be placed in the directory structure $OV_REGISTRATION/C. A better practice would be to create a separate subdirectory for new ARFs under the subdirectory $OV_REGISTRATION/C. When started, NNM parses all files and directories located under this directory tree. If any file in this structure contains syntax errors, NNM provides a detailed error message ignoring files containing syntax errors and continues to start.

Tip: Because NNM parses every file in this directory structure, you should never create a backup copy of an existing ARF in this directory. If duplicate definitions are detected, NNM displays errors but continues to execute. Backup copies of your ARFs should be created in a directory other than the $OV_REGISTRATION/C directory structure.

Refer to Section 7.1.2, "Zman's Sample ARF," for the description in the following list. The name of the application ("Database Information") indicates the beginning of the application definition in the ARF. Multiple applications may be contained in a single ARF. The ARF is broken down into the following blocks of code:

- **Version**—Describes the NNM version for which this application was written.
- **Description**—A brief description of the application.
- **Copyright**—Copyright information.
- **MenuBar**—If present, indicates the top-level menu for the application.
- **Menu**—If present, indicates submenus and references to action blocks.
- **Action**—Describes the device type, number of selected devices, and the command to execute the application.
- **PopupItem**—If present, indicates the item on the symbol popup menu.
- **ToolbarButton**—If present, indicates the toolbar icon for the application.

There are three basic functions that are used throughout the ARF:

f.separator—Indicates a menu item separator, which is a line between menu items.

f.action—Associates the call to the application or Action block.

f.menu—Indicates the name of the cascading menu.

In Figure 7-1, look at the area labeled 'MenuBar "Zman".' This defines the top-level menu bar from which the application is available. The name of the menu item is **"Database Information."** The **_D** defines the control key, in this case ctrl-D, that can be used to access the menu item instead of using the mouse. The Context describes the submap on which the application is available. "**AllContexts**" indicates that the application is available on all submaps. The **f.menu** is a keyword indicating a menu item named **"DB Info."** The menu structure defined by the **MenuBar** section is **Zman→Database Information→Object DB**, as shown in Figure 7-1. For details on submap context refer to the Section 7.1.4, "Limiting Menu Items by Setting the Submap Context."

Figure 7-1 The menu bar may be customized by using of ARFs. The Zman menu bar contains applications defined by the sample ARF listed in this chapter.

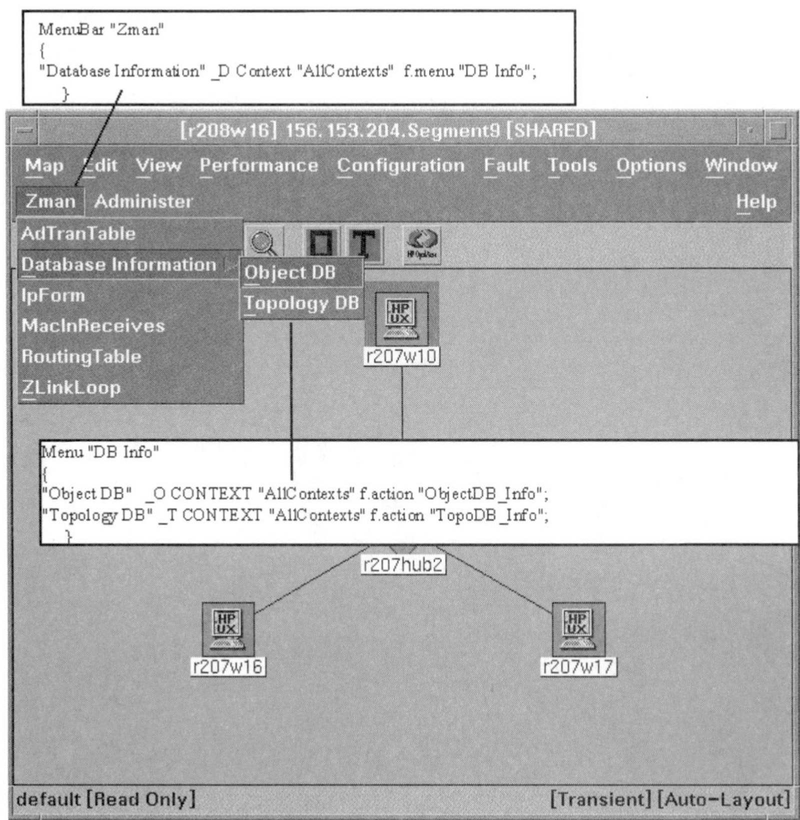

The next section, **Menu "DB Info,"** defines the actions that are executed when either of the two menu options (Object DB and Topology DB) is selected. The keyword **f.action** references the Action blocks **ObjectDb_Info** and **TopoDB_Info** that define the command to be executed.

The Action block **Action "ObjectDB_Info"** uses the selection rule to describe the type of devices on which this action can be executed. This action can be executed on a node that is SNMP supported, (isNode && isSNMPSupported). If the selected device does not meet the selection rule criteria, the menu item is not available. NNM uses menu graying to disable menu selections. For details on defining a selection rule, refer to Section 7.1.5, "Limiting Application Execution with the Selection Rule."

MinSelected and **MaxSelected** allow you to define the number of items selected by the user to be available for the application. This example requires the user to select only one symbol to enable access to this application. Use of **MinSelected** and **MaxSelected** also causes menu graying.

The **NameField** keyword indicates the object attribute that is passed to the command. In this case, the **IP hostname** or the **IP address** is passed through the variable $OVwSelections.

The **Command** is the actual call to the application to be executed by the ARF. NNM provides the utility **xnmappmon** to encapsulate the output of a text-based command into an X window, as shown in Figure 7-2. **xnmappmon** provides a scrollbar for the output and works nicely with tools that provide text-based output, such as **ovobjprint**. Execute **xnmappmon** from the command line by typing

```
xnmappmon -cmd ovobjprint selectionName
```

Figure 7-2 The xnmappmon utility wraps the output of a text-based utility, such as ovobjprint, in a scrollable X window.

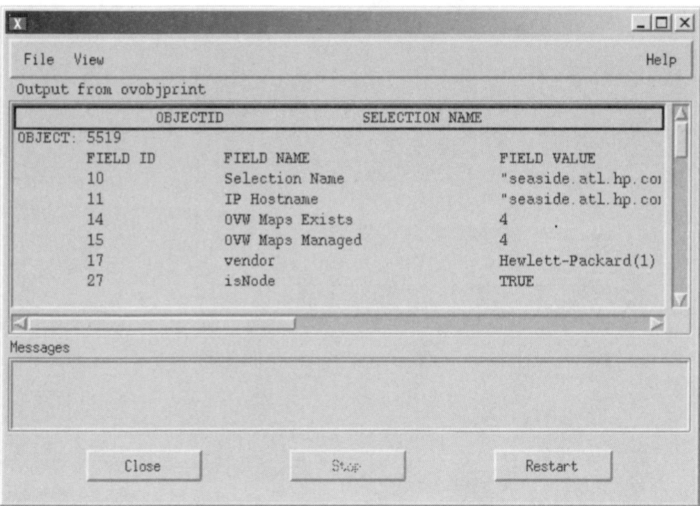

The **Command** in this example is a call to **xnmappmon,** which calls **ovobjprint** and passes the selected objects **$(OVwSelections)**. OVwSelections is a run-time environment variable that consists of a list of selected objects that have been selected from the NNM GUI. Refer to Table 7-1 for a description of environment variables available for use in ARFs.

Zman's Sample ARF uses two action blocks, one for the **ovobjprint** command and one for the **ovtopodump** command. The **ovobjprint** command displays information extracted from the object database. The **ovtopodump** displays information extracted from the topology database.

The PopupItem block indicates that the application is available on the symbol popup menu by right-clicking. **Zman's Sample ARF** adds two items to the popup menu: **Object DB Info** and **Topology DB Info**, as shown in Figure 7-3. The precedence value is optional and indicates where in the menu structure an item appears. The precedence value is a number ranging from 0 to 100. If no precedence is specified, the value is set to 50. If a menu bar item contains a precedence of 100, it appears as the left-most item on the menu bar. If two or more items have the same precedence, NNM orders the item alphabetically by the application name.

Table 7-1 OVw Run-time Environment Variables

OVw Environment Variable	Purpose
OVwSelections	A string containing the selection names of the objects in the selection list when the application is invoked. The names are separated by blank characters.
OVwNumSelections	The number of selection names in the selection list when the application is invoked.
OVwSelection*n* (*n*=1...10)	OVwSelection1 is set to the selection name of the first object in the selection list, OVwSelection2 is set to the second name, and so on. These strings are returned in the order in which their associated objects were selected. The selection list is limited to 10 elements.
OVwActionID	The name of the action by which the application is invoked. Actions are defined in the ARF and are described later.
OVwMenu Item	If the application is invoked via a menu item, this environment variable will contain the label of the menu item that caused the action. Menu items are described later.
OVwAppName	The name of the application that has started and is connecting to a GUI server.
OVServer	The name of the object database server host that stores the map database and runs the object database daemon.
OVwSessionID	The name of the GUI session identifier.

Context may be used to limit the submaps on which the item is available. You can specify the **TargetSymbolType** to limit the availability (menu graying) of the application. The **TargetSymbolType** may be specified as **ANY** or **SymbolClass:SymbolSubclass** in the ARF. For example, to limit an application to **HP-UX** systems you would specify **TargetSymbolType Computer:HP-UX**. View the symbol properties to find the class and subclass of an object. The keyword **f.action** references the Action block of the application to be executed. The keyword **f.separator** references a separator line that appears on the popup menu between the **Alarms** and **Object DB Info** items, as shown in Figure 7-3.

The **ToolBarButton** indicates that a toolbar icon is available to execute this application. The syntax of the **ToolBarButton** statement is similar to the **PopupItem**. If a precedence is specified, it indicates where the toolbar icon appears, 0 being the right-most and 100 being the left-most toolbar icon. The @"toolbar/objectinfo.24.pm" indicates the location of pixmap for the toolbar button relative to $OV_BITMAPS. The toolbar icon in this example is located in $OV_BITMAPS/toolbar/objectinfo.24.pm. The sample ARF adds two toolbar icons, the "**O**" for object information and the "**T**" for topology information, shown in Figure 7-4. **Context** is used to limit which submaps display the toolbar icon. The **f.action** keyword references the Action block for the application.

Figure 7-3 Items may be added to the symbol popup menu by defining the PopupItem block in the ARF.

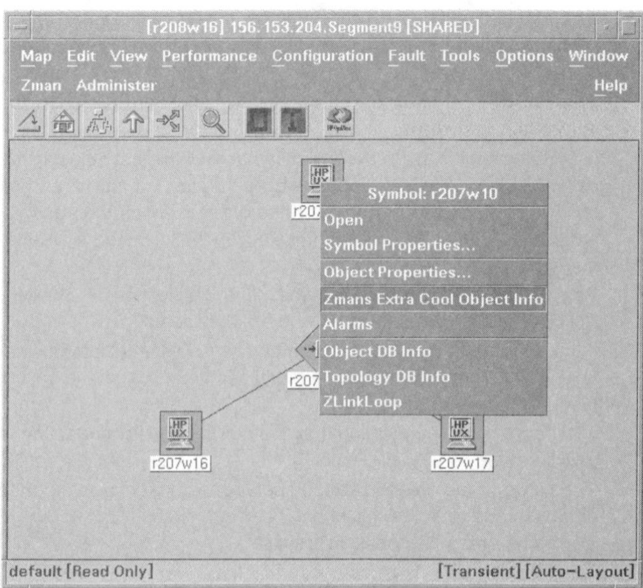

Figure 7-4 The toolbar blocks in the sample ARF create the "O" and the "T" toolbar items. The toolbar icons appear "grayed out" unless a symbol is selected (controlled by MinSelected keyword in the ARF).

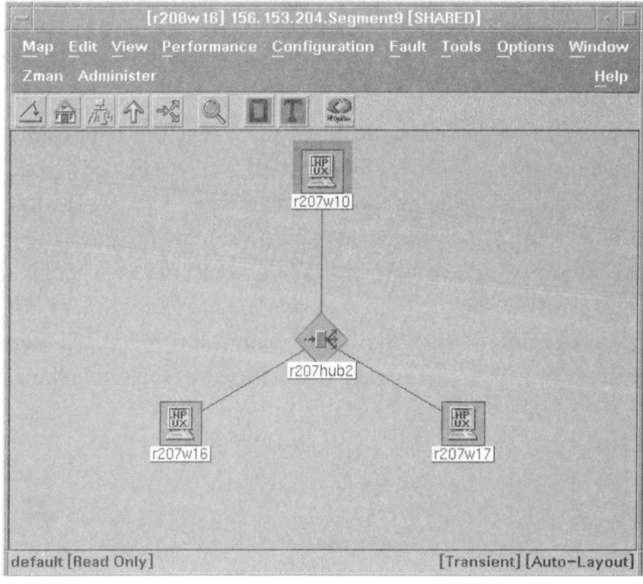

7.1.2 Zman's Sample ARF

The following ARFs are available for download from the server `http://www.phptr.com/title/0130352098` for both UNIX and Windows systems. Obtain the Readme file for Chapter 7 for a description of the files available and install procedures. You can parse a UNIX or Windows ARF to check for accurate syntax by executing the command **ovw –verify**.

```
Application "Database Information"
{
Version "OpenView NNM 6.01";
Description {
"ARF to print object.",
"Created by:",
"    Me",
}
Copyright {
"(c) Copyright 1997 Hewlett-Packard Co.",
"All rights reserved",
}

MenuBar "Zman"
{
"Database Information" _D Context "AllContexts"  f.menu "DB
Info";
}


Menu "DB Info"
{
"Object DB"   _O CONTEXT "AllContexts" f.action "ObjectDB_Info";
"Topology DB" _T CONTEXT "AllContexts" f.action "TopoDB_Info";
}

Action "ObjectDB_Info"
{
SelectionRule (isNode && isSNMPSupported);
MinSelected 1;
MaxSelected 1;
NameField "IP Hostname", "IP Address";
Command "xnmappmon -commandTitle \"Object Database Information\"
\
      -commandHeading \"Output from ovobjprint: \" \
      -cmd ovobjprint -s ${OVwSelections}";
}

Action "TopoDB_Info"
```

```
{
SelectionRule (isNode && isSNMPSupported);
MinSelected 1;
MaxSelected 1;
Command "xnmappmon -commandTitle \"Topology Database Informa-
tion\" \
      -commandHeading \"Output from ovtopodump: \" \
      -cmd ovtopodump -l ${OVwSelections}";
}

/*************************************************************
*************/
PopupItem <90> "PopupSeparator5" Context (AllContexts || Want-
PopupMenus) TargetSymbolType ANY f.separator;

PopupItem "Object DB Info" CONTEXT "AllContexts"
            TargetSymbolType ANY f.action "ObjectDB_Info";

PopupItem "Topology DB Info" CONTEXT "AllContexts"
            TargetSymbolType ANY f.action "TopoDB_Info";
/*************************************************************
*************/

ToolbarButton <80> "TBAR_SEP5"  Context "AllContexts" f.separa-
tor;

ToolbarButton <80> @"toolbar/objectinfo.24.pm"
           Context "AllContexts" f.action "ObjectDB_Info";

ToolbarButton <80> @"toolbar/topoinfo.24.pm"
           Context "AllContexts" f.action "TopoDB_Info";

/*************************************************************
*************/
}
```

7.1.3 Zman's Extra Cool Object Info ARF

The second ARF sample provides the popup menu item **Show Zmans Xtra Cool Object Info**, shown in Figure 7-3. This example consists of two files: an ARF and an executable script **showzmansxcoi** (**SHOW ZMANS EX**tra **C**ool **O**bject **I**nfo). The action block defined in the ARF calls the script **showzmansxcoi**. The script calls **xnmappmon** to encapsulate the output of **ovtopodump**, as shown in Figure 7-5.

Figure 7-5 The showzmansxcoi script calls xmnappmon with the **ovtopodump** command which passes the node selection from the ovw GUI.

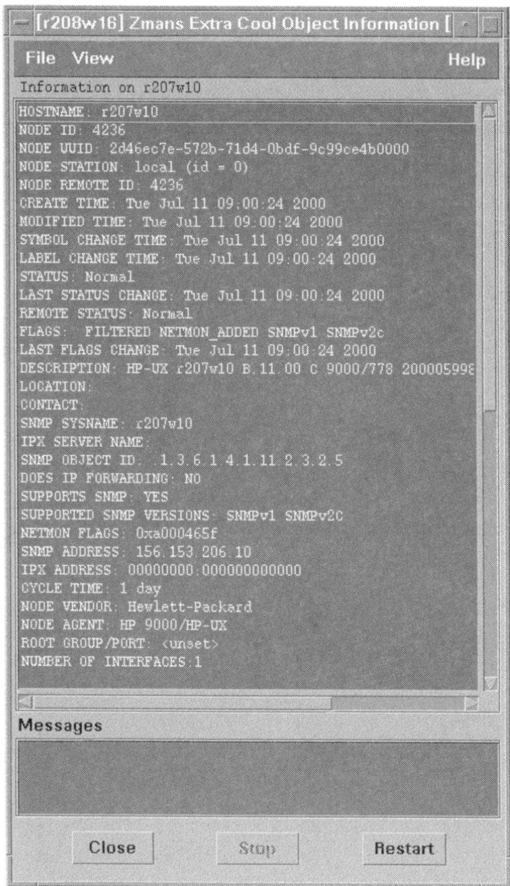

7.1.3.1 The Code For Zman's XCOI ARF

This ARF should be placed in a subdirectory under $OV_REGISTRATION/C. It will be parsed when you start ovw.

```
Application "Show Zmans Xtra Cool Object Info"
{

    Description {
      "HP OpenView Windows application"
    }

    Version "NNMGR 7.0";
```

```
    Copyright {
      "(c)Copyright 1992-1995 Hewlett-Packard Co."
    }


/*
      *  OVw Popup menu
      */

/*==============================================================*/
    PopupItem <100> "PopupSeparator2" Context (AllContexts ||
WantPopupMenus)
                     TargetSymbolType ANY f.separator;
    PopupItem <100> "Zmans Extra Cool Object Info" Context (All-
Contexts || WantPopupMenus)
                     TargetSymbolType ANY f.action
"Zmans_XCOI_4popup";
/*==============================================================*/

/*==============================================================*/
      Action "Zmans_XCOI_4popup"
      {
      Command "${showzmansxcoi:-/opt/OV/bin/showzmansxcoi} ";
      }
/*==============================================================*/

}
```

7.1.3.2 The showzmansxcoi Script

This script should be placed in the directory /opt/OV/bin or the directory referenced by the Command statement in the "Show Zmans Xtra Cool Object Info" ARF. The script needs to have executable permissions.

```
#!/usr/bin/sh
#
# Zmans show extra information for incorporation into
# the symbol popup
#
#
#
THECMD="ovtopodump -l $OVwSelection1"
THERESULT=`ovtopodump -l $OVwSelection1 2>&1`
THEERROR=`echo $THERESULT | cut -f1 -d" "`
if [ "$THEERROR" = "ERROR:" ]
      then
```

```
            THECMD="ovobjprint -s $OVwSelection1"
fi
xnmappmon -commandTitle "Zmans Extra Cool Object Information"\
        -commandHeading "Information on ${OVwSelection1}" -cmd
${THECMD}
exit 1
```

7.1.4 Limiting Menu Items by Setting the Submap Context

Submap contexts may be used to limit the occurrence of an application to a specific submap. When you specify a submap context other than AllContexts, the application is not available on submaps that do not meet the context criteria. You can define a custom submap context for an application by navigating to the submap you would like to customize and selecting **Map→ Submap→Properties** from the menu bar. Click the **[Submap Context...]** button and add a unique context such as **isMySubmap** to the context list. To use this submap context in an ARF, you would include **Context "isMySubmap"** in the ARF.

7.1.5 Limiting Application Execution with the Selection Rule

The selection rule can be used to limit devices on which an application may be executed. When specifying a selection rule, the menu item for the application is grayed out unless the selection rule criterion is met. For example, the selection rule **isNode && isSNMPSupported** indicates that the device must be an SNMP-supported node. A selected device must meet the criteria specified by the selection rule in order to execute the application. NNM plugin applications such as CiscoWorks® use elaborate selection rules so that menu items can only be executed on certain Cisco devices.

One way to obtain object attributes for the selection rule is to view the object properties of a device from the GUI. Right-click the device, select **Object Properties**, and view the **Capabilities** or **General Attributes**. Any attributes from either list may be used when defining the selection rule.

Object attributes may also be obtained with the command-line utility **ovobjprint**. The Selection Name of an object must be used with the ovobjprint command. The following example command lists the object attributes for the system r208w100:

```
ovobjprint -s r208w100
```

The output of **obobjprint** is similar to the output shown in Section 7.1.6.

7.1.6 Output of ovobjprint

```
OBJECT: 5519
FIELD ID FIELD  NAME                       FIELD VALUE
10              Selection Name             "r208w100"
11              IP Hostname                "r208w100"
14              OVW Maps Exists            4
15              OVW Maps Managed           4
17              vendor                     Hewlett-Packard(1)
```

```
27                isNode                   TRUE
29                isComputer               TRUE
30                isConnector              TRUE
31                isBridge                 FALSE
32                isRouter                 TRUE
33                isHub                    FALSE
37                isWorkstation            TRUE
52                isIP                     TRUE
53                isIPX                    FALSE
517               IP Status                Normal(2)
521               isIPRouter               TRUE
522               isIPXRouter              FALSE
523               isNetWareServer          FALSE
559               isSNMPSupported          TRUE
561               SNMP sysName             "r208w100"
562               SNMP sysDescr            "HP-UX r208w100 B.11.00
                                           U 9000/800 2007773835"
565               SNMP sysObjectID         ".1.3.6.1.4.1.11.
                                           2.3.2.3"
566               SNMPAgent                HP 9000/HP-UX(4)
578               TopM Interface Count     4

TopM Interface List
"lan0        Normal      156.32.122.21     257.257.248.0    <None>
0x001083F5D972  ethernetCsmacd       ""156.32.122.153 Normal
157.32.122.153   257.257.248.0   <None>  0x001083F5D993  ether-
net Csmacd       ""lan2        Normal      152.20.4.15
257.257.257.0   <None>        0x080009B8E98B  ethernetCsmacd
""lan1     Normal      <None>            <Unknown>        <None>
0x001083F5D928  ethernetCsmacd       "
586            isMcClusterMember           TRUE
587            isCollectionStationNode     FALSE
1514         isOPCmanaged                  TRUE
1515        OPC_ID                         "N:M315eb856-4910-71d4-
1c51-0f207a980000"
1533         isOPCnode                     TRUE
8053         isMCClusterObj                TRUE
8062         MCSGClusterID                 961088970
8063         MCSGClusterObj                Status  1
8067         isMCSGClusterNode             TRUE
8068         MCSGNodeID                    2
```

The operators in Table 7-2 may be used when defining a selection rule. Any of the object attributes listed by the **ovobjprint** command may be used when defining the selection rule. Most of the examples listed in Table 7-2 are self explanatory, with the exception of **"TopM Interface**

Count." "TopM Interface Count" indicates the number of interfaces listed in the topology database for the device. **"TopM Interface Count"** may be used to create an ARF that only executes on devices containing multiple interfaces by adding this statement to the ARF:

SelectionRule ("TopM Interface Count" > 1)

Table 7.2 Selection rule Operators

Operator	Description	Example
&&	Logical AND	isNode && isSNMPSupported
||	Logical OR	IsSNMPSupported || isSNMPProxied
==	Equality	vendor == "Hewlett-Packard"
!=	Inequality	vendor != "Sun"
>	Greater than	"TopM Interface Count" > 1
<	Less than	"TopM Interface Count" < 5
>=	Greater than or Equal to	"TopM Interface Count" >= 1
<=	Less than or Equal to	"TopM Interface Count" <= 5

7.1.7 Use Your ARF as an Executable Symbol

After you've created an ARF, the application defined by it becomes a registered application in NNM. The application can now be used when creating executable symbols. Add an object to a submap, change the behavior to executable, and check the list for your application. Refer to Chapter 4, "Out-of-the-box Network Node Manager," for details on creating executable symbols.

7.1.8 The ovw Application Registration File

The file **$OV_REGISTRATION/C/ovw** defines the entire menu structure, toolbar, and symbol popup items of the NNM GUI. You can limit user access to applications by modifying this file. As with any ARF, never make a backup of this file in the **$OV_REGRISTRATION/C** directory or it will cause duplicate error messages. In the event that you destroy the ovw file beyond repair, an original copy may be found in the **$OV_NEW_CONF/OVWIN/registration/C** directory.

7.1.9 Limiting Access to Applications using OVwRegDir

The **$OVwRegDir** environment variable can be set to define ARF directories for individual users. This is helpful when limiting access to applications. For example, a user might need access to applications that work only with networking devices. These applications might not need to be available to everyone. The ARFs can be located in any directory. For example, if custom ARFs are located in /etc/opt/OV/customRegDir on a Unix system, you would define the environment variable in a user's **.profile** as follows:

```
export OVwRegDir=/opt/OV/share/registration/C:/etc/opt/OV/
customRegDir
```

By defining this environment variable, you have limited the access to the ARFs located in /etc/opt/OV/customRegDir to users who export the **OVwRegDir** as specified. Registration directories are separated by a colon (:).

For Windows systems, you could add the custom ARF directory to the user's system variable list or modify and execute the **ov.envvars.bat** file.

7.2 Application Integration using Web Launcher Registration Files (WLRF) and Network Presenter Registration Files (NPRF)

WLRFs and NPRFs are similar to the ARF in that they allow custom applications to integrate with NNM. While ARFs are used to integrate the application into the native GUI, WLRFs are used to integrate an application into the web launcher, and NPRFs are used to integrate an application into the Network Presenter.

7.2.1 Creating Your Own WLRF

The purpose of the WLRF is to provide access to additional applications for users who use the web interface instead of the ovw GUI. You may develop your own WLRFs to customize the web launcher. The web launcher can be accessed by selecting **Tools→HP OpenView Launcher** from the menu bar. Figure 7-6 illustrates a customized version of the web launcher. The WLRF described in this section provides the customizations shown.

The syntax of the WLRF is similar to the ARF, and many of the blocks described in the ARF section (Description, Action) are also used in the WLRF. Two additional blocks are required in the WLRF: the *list block* which defines the list of items in the top portion of the launcher and the *tab block* which defines the tabs (or icons) in the lower section of the launcher. The lists in Figure 7-6 include "Configuration" and "Monitoring Tools." The tabs include the six tabs shown at the bottom of Figure 7-6. All WLRF files must reside in a subdirectory under $OV_WWW_REG/launcher/C. Similar to the ARF registration directory, this directory is dynamically parsed when the user starts NNM.

The Tab block corresponds to the MenuBar block in the in the ARF. The tab block in Zman's sample WLRF describes the custom toolbar icon and two folder items. Each item has an icon associated with it. The launcher icons are located in the directory $OV_WWW/htdocs/C/images/launcher. The three items contained in the tab block include

- **Management Tasks**—Toolbar icon (mgtarea.20.gif)
- **Monitoring Tools**—Folder icon (infofold.16.gif)
- **Configuration**—Folder icon (folder.16.gif)

The precedence of each menu item determines the occurrence of the item in the list. Since the precedence of **"Configuration"** is higher than that of **"Monitoring Tools,"** "Configuration" appears closer to the top of the list. The precedence value is 1 to 100, 100 being the top of the list.

The **ActiveHelp** keyword in the WLRF indicates the help message displayed in the status line as you pass the cursor over the item. Figure 7-6 displays the **Configuration tools** active help message for the **Configuration** tab item. The **f.list** keyword references the list block item.

Figure 7-6 The sample WLRF integrates the Event Correlation Configuration and the Full SNMP Data Access applications into the NNM web launcher.

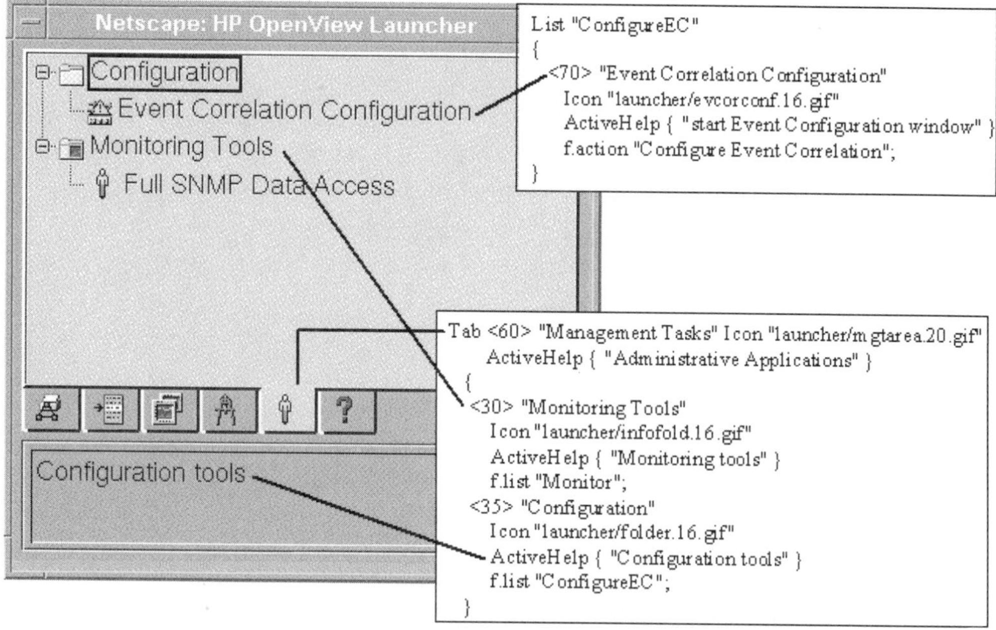

The list block describes the name of the item to be displayed, the icon, active help, and the action to be taken. The list block items correspond to items **Event Correlation Configuration** and **Full SNMP Data Access**, shown in Figure 7-6. The sample WLRF contains two list items:

- **Monitor**—Full SNMP Data Access
- **ConfigureEC**—Event Correlation Configuration

The **f.action** keyword in the list block references the action block that is executed when selected. Each of the two actions used in the sample WLRF call a URL provided by the implementation of NNM. No new applications have been developed for this example. The sample WLRF contains two action blocks:

- MySnmpPresenter
- Configure Event Correlation

The action for **MySnmpPresenter** provides full access to SNMP data. This functionality is similar to that of the SNMP MIB Browser in the native NNM GUI. See Figure 7-7 for the access to SNMP data provided by **MySnmpPresenter**. When a node name is given, **MySnmpPresenter** provides the ability to query any MIB variable for the given device.

Figure 7-7 The sample WLRF provides full SNMP data access via the web launcher.

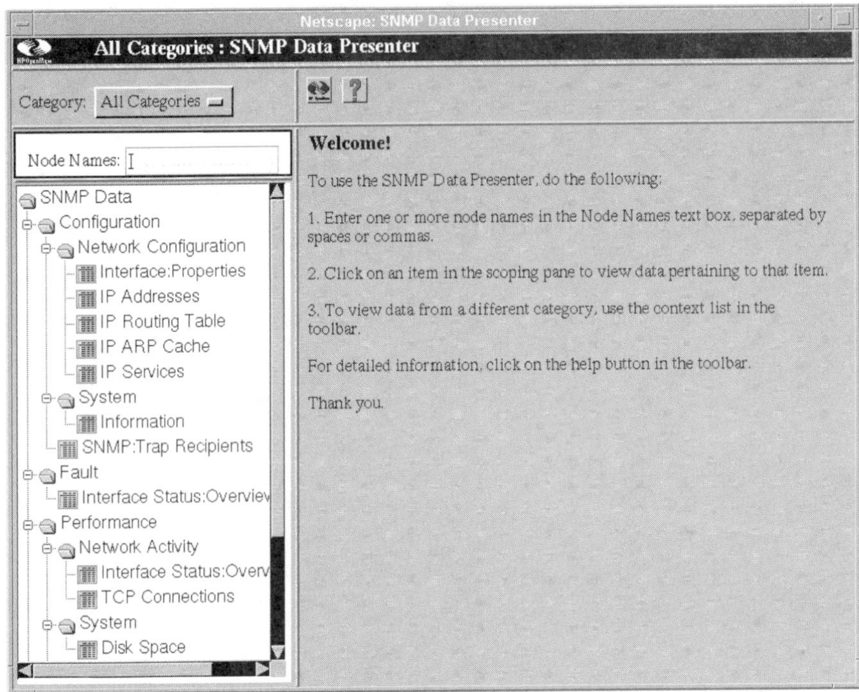

The second action provided by the sample WLRF, **Event Correlation Configuration**, is also a URL that exists in NNM. NNM provides five basic correlations to minimize the effects of event storms. Figure 7-8 displays the Event Correlation.

The WLRF provides access to the same URL provided by the native NNM GUI. Before discussing the WLRF access to the Event Correlation, a description of the pre-defined correlations follows. The Event Correlation may be accessed from the native GUI by following two steps:

1. Select **Options→Event Configuration** from the menu bar.
2. Select **Edit→Event Correlation** from the Event Configuration dialog box.

Figure 7-8 The sample WLRF provides access to Event Correlation Configuration via the web launcher. NNM provides five correlations that may be customized to reduce the number of events displayed in the alarms browser.

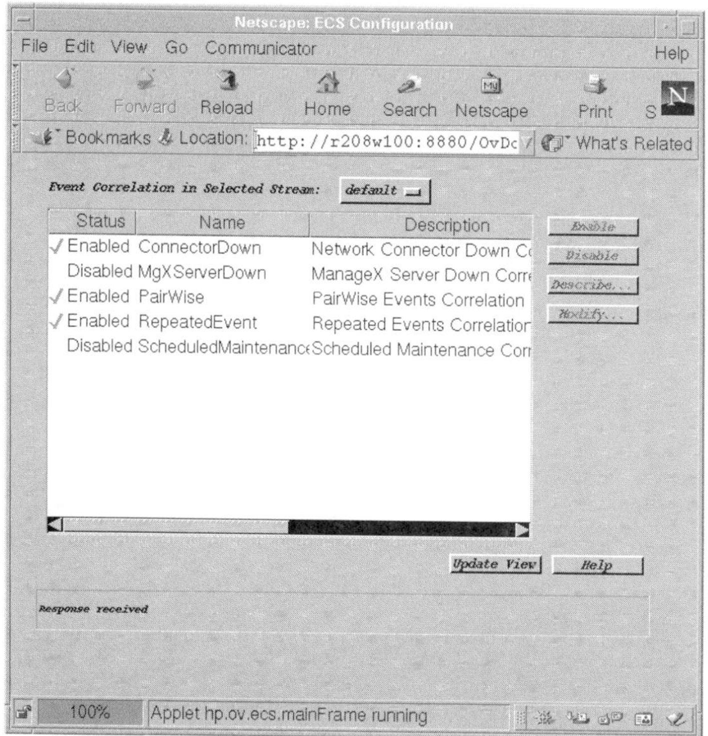

7.2.1.1 Configuring Event Correlation

The purpose of event correlation in NNM is to reduce the number of events received by NNM to a reasonable number of messages in the alarm browser. NNM includes the *Event Correlation Services*[1] (ECS) to help manage event storms and define relationships between different types of events. During an event storm, many events may be correlated into a single event. NNM provides five pre-defined correlations, three of which are enabled by default, as shown in Figure 7-8. The NNM administrator can customize the default correlations. The following paragraphs describe the default correlations.

1 The five correlations provided with NNM are ECS circuits that provide basic correlation functionality. Additional circuits may be built with the separately purchased ECS Designer product.

Network Connector Down

When a routing device's interface goes down, NNM automatically determines which device has malfunctioned and which devices are inaccessible due to the malfunction. The inaccessible devices are tagged as secondary devices. By default, NNM increases the polling frequency of secondary devices by a factor of two during an outage. If the global polling frequency is five minutes, the polling frequency for inaccessible (secondary) devices is set to ten minutes. The multiplier for secondary devices, as shown in Figure 7-9, can be configured by the following steps:

1. Select **Options→Network Polling Configuration: IP**.
2. Set the Configuration Area drop-down list to Secondary Failures.
3. Click the Secondary Failure Polling Options.
4. Modify the Status Polling Reduction Multiplier to the desired value. This value is multiplied by the global polling frequency to determine the polling frequency for secondary devices.
5. Click OK.

Figure 7-9 Secondary Failures include devices that become inaccessible due to a network outage. The Reduction Multiplier can be customized to reduce the polling frequency during a network outage.

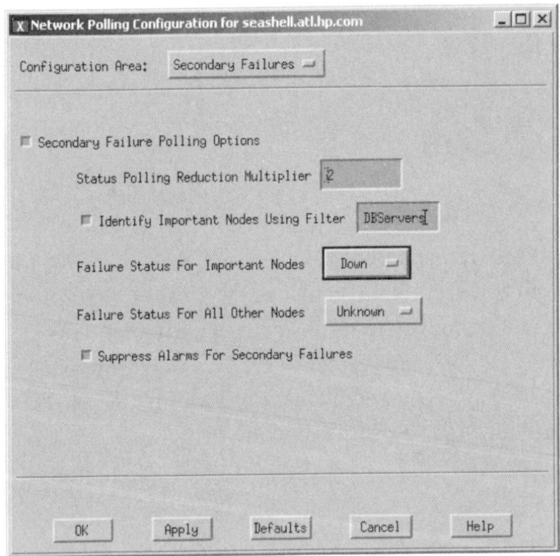

The administrator can also define a list of "important" nodes that should never be treated as secondary devices even though they are inaccessible due to an outage. For example, if you have a mission critical server such as a database server, you may want to treat it differently from other devices. If defined as an important node, it is always polled at the global frequency. A filter must be configured to define important nodes. Filter definitions are covered in Chapter 9, "Scalability and Distribution." After defining the filter, the filter name can be used in the Identify Important Nodes Using Filter field, shown in Figure 7-9.

The Secondary Failures dialog box can also be used to set the event status for important nodes to Down or Unknown. Failure for all other nodes (non–important) can be set to Down, Unknown, or Unchanged. Another option is to completely suppress events for secondary failures.

Correlation Composer

The correlation composer simplifies the process of modifying existing event correlations and allows you to define new ones.

Pair Wise

The Pair Wise correlation matches an event to one or more previous events. For example, if an interface were to go down and come up on a device within a reasonable amount of time, the two events would be correlated. The node up event causes a node down event to be removed from the alarms browser and correlated under the node up event. This correlation is enabled by default.

Repeated Events

The Repeated Event correlation identifies multiple events having the same root cause. When multiple identical events arrive from the same source, the repeated event correlation suppresses duplicates and displays them under the one alarm. You may include additional events that are correlated as repeated events, resulting in fewer (but more informative) alarms. This correlation is enabled by default.

Scheduled Maintenance

The Scheduled Maintenance correlation allows the administrator to configure planned network maintenance. Events generated by the specified devices during the scheduled maintenance period are excluded from the alarms browser. This correlation is disabled by default.

7.2.2 Zman's Sample WLRF

The following WLRF is available for download from the server `http://www.phptr.com/title/0130352098` for both Unix and Windows systems. Obtain the Readme file for Chapter 7 for a description of the files available and install procedures. You can parse the WLRF to check for accurate syntax by executing the command **regverify $OV_WWW_REG** on Unix and **regverify %OV_WWW_REG%** on Windows.

```
Application "Student Applications"
{

   DisplayString "Student Applications";
   Version "1";
   Copyright { "no copyright" };
   Description {
     "Module 3",
     "Stans fine application experiment"
   }

   Tab <60> "Management Tasks" Icon "launcher/mgtarea.20.gif"
          ActiveHelp { "Administrative Applications" }
      {
       <30> "Monitoring Tools"
           Icon "launcher/infofold.16.gif"
           ActiveHelp { "Monitoring tools" }
           f.list "Monitor";
       <35> "Configuration"
           Icon "launcher/folder.16.gif"
           ActiveHelp { "Configuration tools" }
           f.list "ConfigureEC";
      }

      List "Monitor"
      {
         <60> "Full SNMP Data Access"
            Icon "launcher/mgtarea.20.gif"
            ActiveHelp { "Access to the full SNMP data presen-
            ter." }
            f.action "MySnmpPresenter";
      }

      List "ConfigureEC"
      {
         <70> "Event Correlation Configuration"
            Icon "launcher/evcorconf.16.gif"
            ActiveHelp { "start Event Configuration window" }
            f.action "Configure Event Correlation";
      }

      Action "MySnmpPresenter" {
         URL "/OvCgi/snmpviewer.exe?Context=";
         WebWindow "My_SNMP_Data_Presenter" {
```

```
            Type limited;
            Width 800;
            Height 600;
        }
    }

    Action "Configure Event Correlation" {
        URL "/OvDocs/ecs/ecscmg.html";
        WebWindow "ECS_Event_Configuration" {
            Type full;
            Width 650;
            Height 500;
        }
    }
}
```

The WLRF listed previously could easily be modified to allow access to documentation to satisfy the Sealey Inc. requirement for online documentation.

7.2.3 Creating Your Own NPRF

The NPRF allows you to add custom applications to the Network Presenter. The sample NPRF provides access to the Object Database and Topology Database applications as defined previously by the ARF in this chapter. Applications implemented in the NPRF must be web-based (accessible via a URL) applications. This section provides the **Zman** menu bar shown in Figure 7-10. You can customize the menu bar, toolbar, and the symbol popup menu of the Network Presenter by defining a NPRF.

The sample NPRF calls the same utilities previously described in the sample ARF, including **xnmappmon**, **ovobjprint**, and **ovtopodump**. While the interface to the information is different, the resulting information provided by the application is exactly the same. The "**O**" and "**T**" toolbar buttons shown in Figure 7-11 are provided by the sample NPRF.

The two action blocks in the NPRF, **ObjectDB_Info** and **TopoDB_Info**, define the action to be executed when the associated items are selected. The output from the **TopoDB_Info** action is shown in Figure 7-12. The **TopoDB_Info** action is referenced from three locations:

The menu bar **Zman→OV Database Information→Topology DB**

The toolbar "T" button

The symbol popup item Topology DB Info

Both **TopoDB_Info** and **ObjectDB_Info** actions are available from all three locations.

Figure 7-10 The sample NPRF integrates the Zman menu bar providing access to the Object Database and Topology Database via the Network Presenter.

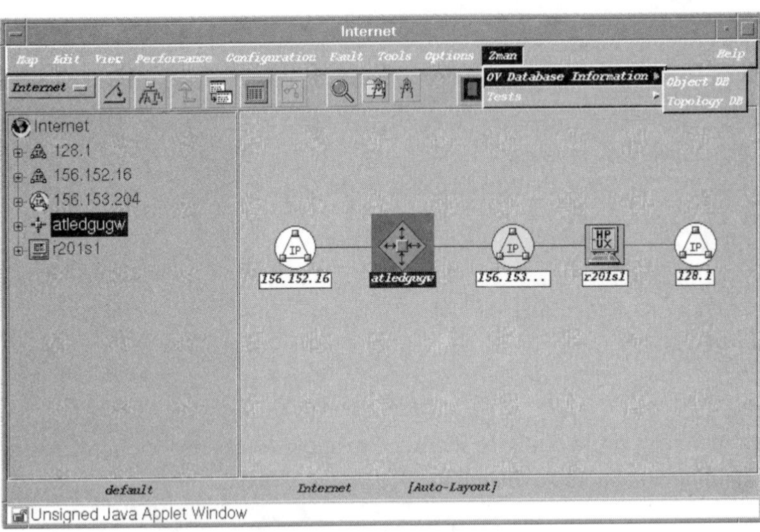

Figure 7-11 The sample NPRF integrates the "O" and "T" toolbar icons, providing access to the object and topology database information via the Network Presenter.

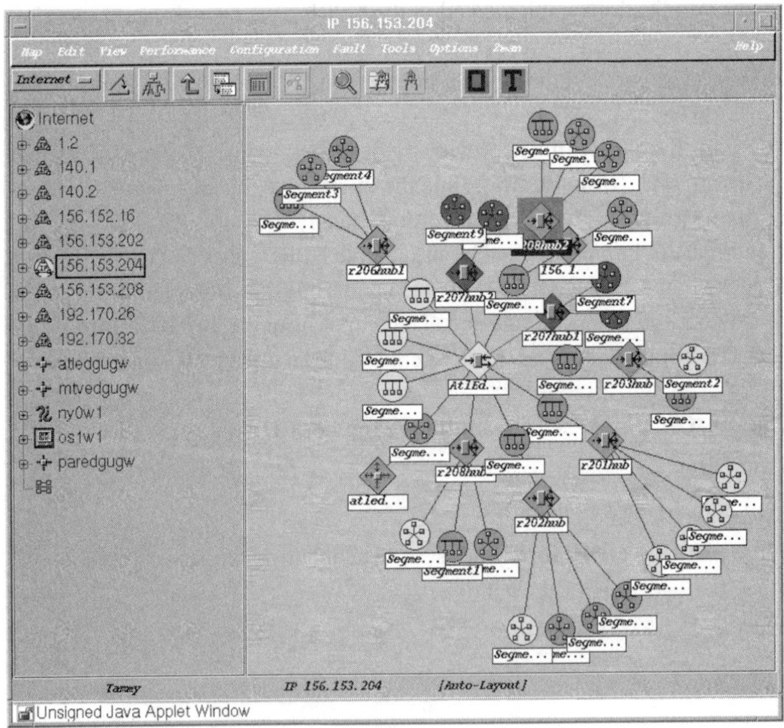

Figure 7-12 The output for ovobjprint from the NPRF (web launcher) displays the same information as the output using the ARF accessed from the native GUI.

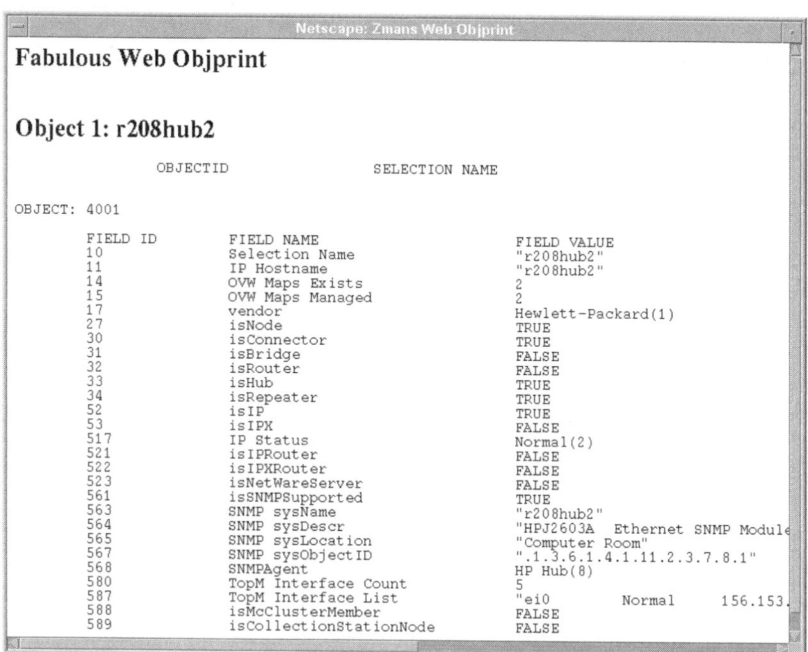

Netscape: Zmans Web Objprint

Fabulous Web Objprint

Object 1: r208hub2

OBJECTID SELECTION NAME

OBJECT: 4001

FIELD ID	FIELD NAME	FIELD VALUE
10	Selection Name	"r208hub2"
11	IP Hostname	"r208hub2"
14	OVW Maps Exists	2
15	OVW Maps Managed	2
17	vendor	Hewlett-Packard(1)
27	isNode	TRUE
30	isConnector	TRUE
31	isBridge	FALSE
32	isRouter	FALSE
33	isHub	TRUE
34	isRepeater	TRUE
52	isIP	TRUE
53	isIPX	FALSE
517	IP Status	Normal(2)
521	isIPRouter	FALSE
522	isIPXRouter	FALSE
523	isNetWareServer	FALSE
561	isSNMPSupported	TRUE
563	SNMP sysName	"r208hub2"
564	SNMP sysDescr	"HPJ2603A Ethernet SNMP Modul
565	SNMP sysLocation	"Computer Room"
567	SNMP sysObjectID	".1.3.6.1.4.1.11.2.3.7.8.1"
568	SNMPAgent	HP Hub(8)
580	TopM Interface Count	5
587	TopM Interface List	"ei0 Normal 156.153.
588	isMcClusterMember	FALSE
589	isCollectionStationNode	FALSE

The differences between the ARF and the NPRF are the use of bitmaps for the toolbar and the directories in which the files must reside. The Network Presenter requires XPM format for the toolbar icons. NPRF files must reside in the **$OV_WWW_REG/jovw/C** directory structure. Create a separate subdirectory for each application. If an NPRF application accesses a CGI file, the CGI must reside in **$OV_WWW/cgi-bin**.

7.2.4 Zman's Sample NPRF

The following NPRF is available for download from the server `http://www.phptr.com/title/0130352098` for both Unix and Windows systems. Obtain the Readme file for this chapter for a description of the files available and install procedures. You can parse the WLRF to check for accurate syntax by executing the command **regverify $OV_WWW_REG** on UNIX and **regverify %OV_WWW_REG%** on Windows.

```
/*
 * Danger, Wil Robinson!     This is a Zman Hack!
 *
*/
```

```
Application "Zmans cool cgi-boo apps "
{
   Description { "Zman", "Launch Zmans Cgi Applications" }

   Version "NNM Release B.06.00";

   Copyright {
        "Copyright (c) 1990-1999 Bogus Data, Inc",
        "Many reservations."
    }

   DisplayString "Zmans Launch Zmans Cool Cgi Apps thingy";

   MenuBar "Zman" _Z
   {
      "OV Database Information" CONTEXT "AllContexts" f.menu "DB
Info";
      "Tests" CONTEXT "AllContexts" f.menu "TestMenu";
   }

   Menu "DB Info"
   {
      "Object DB" CONTEXT "AllContexts" f.action
"ObjectDB_Info";
      "Topology DB" CONTEXT "AllContexts" f.action
"TopoDB_Info";
   }

   Menu "TestMenu"
   {
      "TestCgi" _C CONTEXT "AllContexts" f.action "TestCgi";
      "TestSettings" _S CONTEXT "AllContexts" f.action "TestSet-
tings";
      "TestObjprint" _O CONTEXT "AllContexts" f.action "TestOb-
jprint";
      "TestTopodump" _T CONTEXT "AllContexts" f.action "Test-
Topodump";
      "TestMapdump" _M CONTEXT "AllContexts" f.action "TestMap-
dump";
   }

   Action "ObjectDB_Info"
      {
      MinSelected 1;
```

```
      MaxSelected 10;
      URL "/OvCgi/zweb_objprint?$OVwNumSelections&$OVwSelec-
tions";
      WebWindow "zweb_objprint" {
         Type limited;
            Scrollbars on;
            Width 800;
            Height 600;
         }
      }

   Action "TopoDB_Info"
      {
      MinSelected 1;
        MaxSelected 10;
      URL "/OvCgi/zweb_topodump?$OVwNumSelections&$OVwSelec-
tions";
      WebWindow "zweb_topodump" {
         Type limited;
            Scrollbars on;
            Width 800;
            Height 600;
         }
      }

   Action "TestCgi"
      {
      URL "/OvCgi/test-cgi";
      WebWindow "TestCgi" {
         Type limited;
            Scrollbars on;
            Width 800;
            Height 440;
         }
      }

   Action "TestSettings"
      {
      URL "/OvCgi/test-settings?$OVwNumSelections&$OVwSelec-
tions";
      WebWindow "TestSettings" {
         Type limited;
            Scrollbars on;
            Width 900;
```

```
            Height 600;
         }
      }

   Action "TestObjprint"
      {
      URL "/OvCgi/test-ovobjprint";
      WebWindow "TestObjprint" {
         Type limited;
            Scrollbars on;
            Width 625;
            Height 250;
         }
      }

   Action "TestTopodump"
      {
      URL "/OvCgi/test-ovtopodump";
      WebWindow "TestTopodump" {
         Type limited;
            Scrollbars on;
            Width 620;
            Height 540;
         }
      }

   Action "TestMapdump"
      {
      URL "/OvCgi/test-ovmapdump";
      WebWindow "TestMapdump" {
         Type limited;
            Scrollbars on;
            Width 555;
            Height 555;
         }
      }

    PopupItem <0> "PopupSeparatorZ1" Context (AllContexts ||
WantPopupMenus)
      TargetSymbolType ANY f.separator;
```

```
    PopupItem <0> "ObjPrint" CONTEXT (AllContexts || WantPopup-
Menus)
      TargetSymbolType ANY f.action "ObjectDB_Info";

    PopupItem <0> "TopoDump" CONTEXT (AllContexts || WantPopup-
Menus)
      TargetSymbolType ANY f.action "TopoDB_Info";


    ToolbarButton <0> "TBAR_SEPZ1"  Context "AllContexts" f.sep-
arator;

    ToolbarButton <0> @"C/toolbar/objectinfo.24.gif"
      Context "AllContexts" f.action "ObjectDB_Info";

    ToolbarButton <0> @"C/toolbar/topoinfo.24.gif"
      Context "AllContexts" f.action "TopoDB_Info";
}
```

7.3 Defining Custom Symbols and Fields

Custom device symbols may be created and used in NNM submaps. The process requires creating the symbol using a bitmap editor, creating the class registration file (optional), and creating the subclass registration file. Both the class and subclass registration files are *Symbol Registration Files* (SRFs).

7.3.1 Description of the SRF

When creating custom symbols, you must decide whether or not to use an existing symbol class. To display existing symbol classes, select **Edit→Add Object** from the menu bar. The symbol classes are subdirectories located in **$OV_SYMBOLS/C**. SRFs must be located in this directory structure. Create a separate subdirectory for each symbol class. The symbol class and subclass files are located in the same directory.

The symbol class file defines the outside shape of the symbol. It also defines some basic attributes of the symbol such as the status source, **isComputer**, and **isNode**. The **Filebase** keyword references the basename of the bitmap to be used for the symbol. You only need to create a class file if you are not using an existing outside shape. Listed below is the **Computer** class file, which defines the outside shape of a square.

7.3.1.1 The Computer Symbol Class File

```
SymbolClass "Computer"
{
        Scale 7;
        Segment (-8, -8) to (8, -8) to (8, 8) to (-8, 8)
        DefaultStatusSource Compound;
        DefaultLayout RowColumn;
        Variety Icon;
      Filebase "computer";
        Capabilities {
                isComputer = 1;
                isNode = 1;
        }
}
```

The symbol subclass file resides in the same directory as the symbol class file. The **SymbolType** keyword defines the class and subclass of the symbol. While the name of the file is not used, the naming convention is *class_subclass*. For example, the **HP-UX** subclass filename is **Computer_hpux**. (The name of the class file is simply **Computer**.) The **Filebase** keyword references the basename of the bitmap to be used for the symbol. If a symbol subclass file exists, the **Filebase** listed in the subclass file overrides the **Filebase** listed in the class file. The subclass file can also set attributes such as **isWorkstation**.[2] Listed in the following section is the **HP-UX** subclass file.

7.3.1.2 The HP-UX Symbol Subclass File

```
SymbolType "Computer" : "HP-UX"
{
        Filebase "hpux";
        CursorSize 38;
        Capabilities {
                isWorkstation = 1;
        }
}
```

7.3.2 Creating Your Own SRF

SRFs require a symbol class file, a symbol subclass file, and bitmaps. If you plan on customizing bitmaps, obtain a decent bitmap editor. HP-UX ships with the **Icon Editor** application, which can be used to create and edit bitmaps. For Windows systems, obtain an evaluation copy of Paint Shop Pro® from `http://www.jasc.com`.[3]

2 Many object attributes are set by SNMP queries. Attributes may also be set in SRFs.

When creating custom bitmaps, it's easiest to copy an existing bitmap and customize it. The one used in this example is the **Mini computer** bitmap. The bitmaps for all computer subclasses are located in the directory **$OV_BITMAPS/C/computer**. The Unix implementation of NNM requires nine files for each symbol, two for masking and seven for submap resizing. You need to copy all nine files and modify only the *.pm files. The mini computer the files to that should be copied and modified are listed in Table 7-1.

Table 7-1 Bitmap Files for New Symbols

Existing file	New File
mini.16.pm	toaster.16.pm
mini.20.pm	toaster.20.pm
mini.26.pm	toaster.26.pm
mini.32.pm	toaster.32.pm
mini.38.pm	toaster.38.pm
mini.44.pm	toaster.44.pm
mini.50.pm	toaster.50.pm
mini.38.m	toaster.38.m*
mini.38.p	toaster.38.p*

* No modification required

Because this example uses an existing outside shape (Computer), there is no need to create a new symbol class file. The symbol class **Computer** is used. The basename of the bitmap described by the **Filebase** is **toaster**. The new object attribute **isToaster** is used to describe the new symbol. New attributes such as **isToaster** must also be defined in the Field Registration File described in the next section. Create a new subclass file named **Computer_toaster** in the directory **$OV_SYMBOLS/C/Computer** with the contents listed.

7.3.2.1 The Toaster Subclass File

```
SymbolType "Computer" : "Toaster"
{
        Filebase "toaster";
        CursorSize 38;
        Capabilities {
                isWorkstation = 1;
                  isToaster = 1;
        }
}
```

After creating the bitmap and defining the SRF, create or modify an existing entry in the **$OV_CONF/oid_to_sym** file. The OID used in this example is that of an HP-UX workstation. The **oid_to_sym** file entry for this example is:

```
1.3.6.1.4.1.11.2.3.2.5:Computer:Toaster   # The Toaster
```

After modifying the **oid_to_sym** file, exit the NNM GUI and update the database for all objects having the same OID by performing the following steps:

1. Stop netmon.
   ovstop –c netmon
2. Update the database entries.
   ovtopofix –a –o .1.3.6.1.4.1.11.2.3.2.5
3. Start netmon.
   ovstart netmon

The toaster symbol should be displayed as shown in Figure 7-13 for any object defined in the **oid_to_sym** file with the subclass **Toaster**.

Figure 7-13 The toaster is a custom symbol referenced in an SRF.

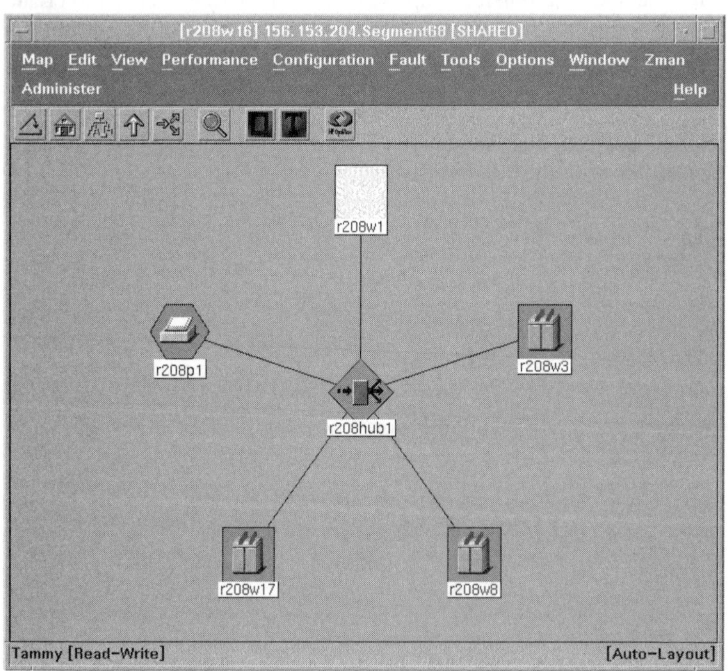

Verify that the newly added symbol is available from the symbol class in which it was defined. The **Toaster** symbol was defined in the **Computer** symbol class. Select **Edit?Add Object** from any submap. Then select the **Computer** class to display the subclass **Toaster**, as shown in Figure 7-14.

Figure 7-14 Custom symbols are available from the symbol class when you add an object. The Toaster is listed as a subclass of the Computer symbol class.

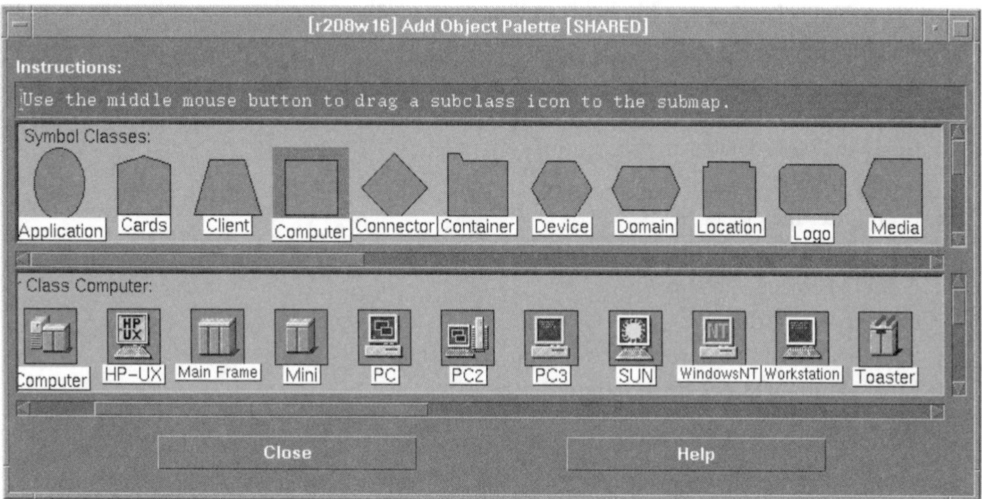

The toaster SRF file and bitmaps are available for download from the server `http://www.phptr.com/title/0130352098` for both Unix and Windows systems. Obtain the Readme file for this chapter for a description of the files available and install procedures. You can parse a Unix or Windows SRF to check for accurate syntax by executing the command **ovw –verify**.

While the toaster example might not be the most practical use of a custom symbol, defining symbols might actually be more useful. Tape libraries, disk arrays, and security devices frequently run SNMP agents. However, these devices are displayed with a generic computer when discovered by NNM because there is no custom symbol for the devices, unless the Vendor provides a plug-in application.

7.3.3 Description of the FRF

Field Registration Files (FRFs) can be used to define new attributes such as **isToaster**. Attributes are set in Symbol Registration Files as previously defined in the **Toaster** symbol registration file. Defining a field provides the ability to locate an object by the new attribute. The FRF listed in Section 7.3.3.1 assigns the Boolean attribute **isToaster**. The keyword **locate** in the FRF provides the ability to search on the field, as shown in Figure 7-15.

7.3.3.1 Creating Your Own Field Registration File

```
Field "isToaster" {
        Type    Boolean;
        Flags   capability, locate;
}
```

FRFs reside in the **$OV_FIELDS/C** directory. Whenever you modify existing FRFs or add new ones, you must re-register the fields in the object database. Perform the following steps to re-register the fields:

1. Exit the NNM GUI.
2. Stop the object database:
   ovstop ovwdb
3. Re-register the object fields:
   ovw –fields
4. Start the object database:
   ovstart –v ovwdb
5. Start NNM and search for the new field isToaster:
   Edit→Find→Object By Attribute
   IsToaster

Figure 7-15 Custom fields such as isToaster may be used as locatable attributes. To search by attribute, select Edit→Find→Object By Attribute from the menu bar.

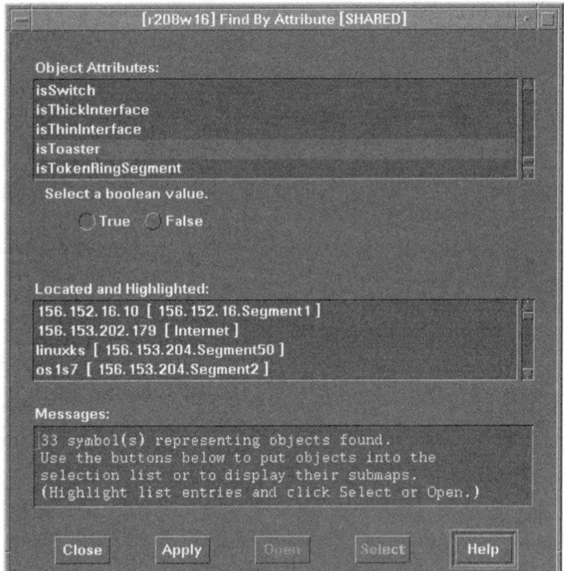

When the fields are re-registered, start up the NNM GUI and search for object with the newly defined attribute **isToaster**. If no devices are found, you may need to demand poll the device. Select the symbol and select **Fault→Network Connectivity→Poll Node**. Display the object attributes by right-clicking the symbol and selecting **[Object Properties]**, as shown in Figure 7-16. Double-click **[Capabilities]** to display the **isToaster** attribute, shown in Figure 7-17.

Figure 7-16 Check the Object Properties of the custom symbol to verify the value of a field.

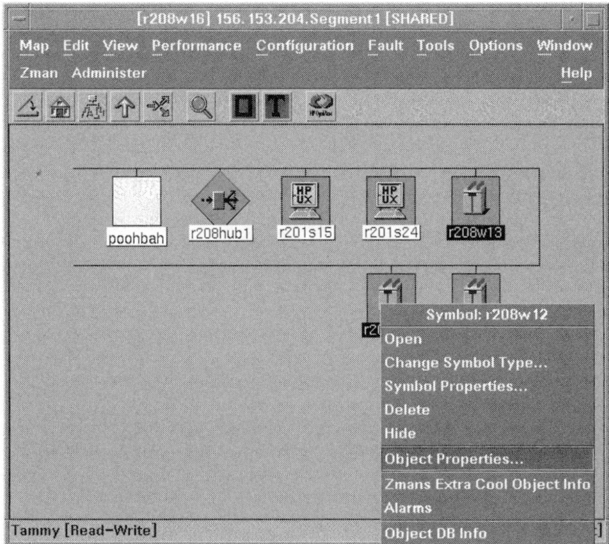

Figure 7-17 The isToaster attribute is set to TRUE for the toaster symbols. Fields are defined in the Field Registration Files and referenced in the Symbol Registration Files.

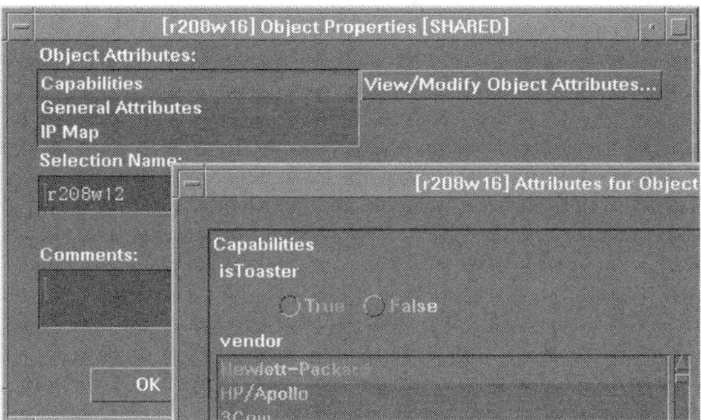

The toaster SRF, FRF, and bitmap files are available for download from the server `http://www.phptr.com/title/0130352098` for both Unix and Windows systems. Obtain the Readme file for Chapter 7 for a description of the files available and install procedures. You can parse a Unix or Windows FRF for accurate syntax by executing the command **ovw –fields**.

If NNM is used as your primary asset database, consider defining and populating fields such as Serial Number, Contract Number, or Product ID. The ability to track fields allows you to find the devices of interest more quickly, allowing better productivity.

7.3.4 Limiting Access to Custom Symbols and Fields

The **$OVwSymbolDir** and **$OvwFieldDir** environment variables may be set to define the symbol and field registration directories for individual users. This is helpful to limit access to symbols and fields. For example, a user might need access to applications that work only with networking devices. The symbols and fields for networking devices might not need to be available to everyone. The SRFs and FRFs can be located in any directory. For example, if custom SRFs are located in /etc/opt/OV/customSymbolDir and custom FRFs are located in /etc/opt/OV/customFieldDiron a Unix system, define the environment variable in a user's **.profile** as follows:

```
export OVwSymbolDir=/opt/OV/share/symbols/C:/etc/opt/OV/
customSymbolDir
export OVwFieldDir=/opt/OV/share/fields/C:/etc/opt/OV/
customFieldDir
```

By defining these environment variables, you have limited user access to the SRFs and FRFs. Symbol and field directories are separated by a colon (:).

For Windows systems, you could add the custom directories to the user's system variable list or modify and execute the **ov.envvars.bat** file.

7.4 Summary

Registration files integrate applications into the NNM user interface in order to tailor your environment to fit your needs. Applications can be made available to individual users as required by their job responsibilities. This type of customization allows network administrators be more productive. Creation of the following registration files allows for a highly customized NNM environment:

ARF	Modify the ovw menu bar, tool bar, and symbol popup menu
WLRF	Modify the Web Launcher tabs and menu
NPRF	Modify the Network Presenter menu
SRF	Include new submap symbols
FRF	Include new fields for searchable information

Many third-party products provide hooks into NNM with the use of registration files. While it is not required to develop your own registration files, NNM provides the ability to tailor your environment as necessary.

CHAPTER 8

Data Collection and Event Configuration

The purpose of collecting data is to provide an alarm on custom thresholds and to perform trend analysis. For example, interface traffic can be monitored for critical devices and configured to send a message to a paging system when a threshold value is exceeded. MIB variable data can be collected to determine a reasonable threshold value. Because NNM has no means of determining the critical devices, MIB variables, or threshold values within a given enterprise, NNM does not perform data collection until it has been configured. NNM provides the ability to

- Collect data without checking the threshold
- Collect data and generate an event when a custom threshold value has been exceeded
- Check the threshold value without storing the data

Collected data is stored in a proprietary database. NNM provides utilities to extract the data into ASCII format and store the data in the Data Warehouse, a relational database.

Sealey Inc. requires the ability to collect and graph SNMP MIB data in order to provide trend analysis for their customers. They also need the ability to specify custom thresholds for MIB variables that will generate events (SNMP traps) and interface with their paging software. Ideally, they wish to store the custom traps in a separate category from the SNMP traps shipped with NNM.

This chapter describes how to configure data collection from the NNM GUI, display and extract the collected data, and configure events based on custom thresholds. Events can be configured to interface with e-mail, audio alarms, paging systems, and trouble-ticketing systems.

8.1 CREATING A DATA COLLECTION

Before creating a data collection, decide which MIB variable best defines the information you are interested in collecting, whether to alarm on custom thresholds, and whether you want to store the data. Typically, you should store the data for analysis before defining custom thresholds. By storing the data over a period of time, you will have the ability to graph the data in order to collect statistics and spot trends. Graphing the data allows you to set more accurate threshold values.

The example described in this chapter collects on the Hewlett-Packard–specific MIB variable **ieee8023MacTransmitted**. Any MIB variable with a numeric value may be used when defining a data collection.

8.1.1 Defining and Displaying an MIB Collection

The first step in creating a collection is to define the MIB object (variable) for which you want to collect data. The following steps allow you to define a MIB object and collection for **ieee8023MacTransmitted** without checking a threshold:

1. Select from the menu bar **Options→Data Collection & Thresholds**, as shown in Figure 8-1.

Figure 8-1 Select **Options→Data Collections & Thresholds** from the menu bar to configure SNMP data collection.

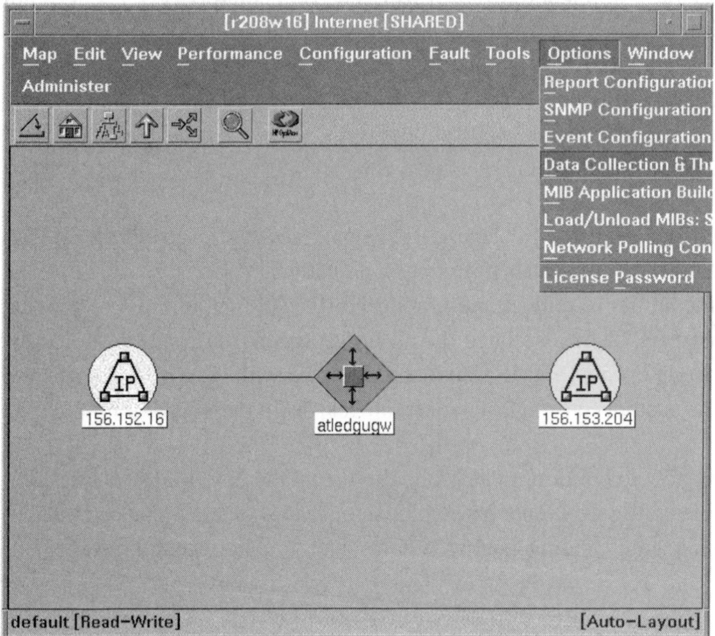

2. From the **Data Collection & Thresholds** menu bar, select **Edit→Add→MIB Objects...**, as shown in Figure 8-2.

Figure 8-2 Add a new data collection by selecting **Edit→Add→MIB Objects...** from the **Data Collection & Thresholds** dialog box.

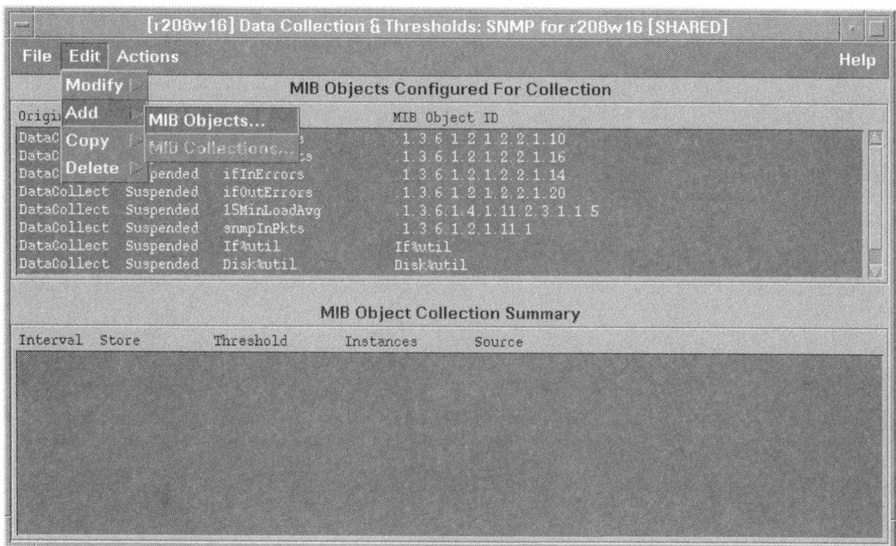

- While there are several pre-defined MIB objects, as shown in Figure 8-2, none of the collections for the objects are active. Notice that the second column in Figure 8-2 indicates "Suspended" for each of the defined collections. NNM cannot determine which devices are critical or which MIB variables are interesting in your enterprise. The implementation of NNM varies for each enterprise.

3. Traverse the MIB tree to the MIB object for collection. The Hewlett-Packard enterprise-specific MIB variable **ieee8023MacTransmitted** shown in Figure 8-3 can be found under the branch **.iso.org.dod.internet.private.enterprises.hp.nm.interface.ieee8023Mac.ieee8023MacTable**. Click **[OK]** from the **MIB Object Selection** dialog box.

Note: This example uses a MIB variable that has been pre-loaded in NNM. To use a custom MIB variable, acquire the vendor MIBs according to the vendor instructions.[1] The MIBs then must be loaded into NNM by selecting **Options→Load/unload MIBS: SNMP** from the menu bar. Click the **[Load...]** button, double-click **Vendor**, and select the desired MIB variable for data collection.

1 Vendor MIBs and traps may be available on a CD or downloaded via ftp or the web. Typically, the vendor supplies instructions on how to get the MIBs and SNMP traps loaded into NNM.

Figure 8-3 Traverse the MIB tree and select the MIB variable for the collection. The collection defined in this example is **ieee8023MacTransmitted**, which indicates the number of frames successfully transmitted.

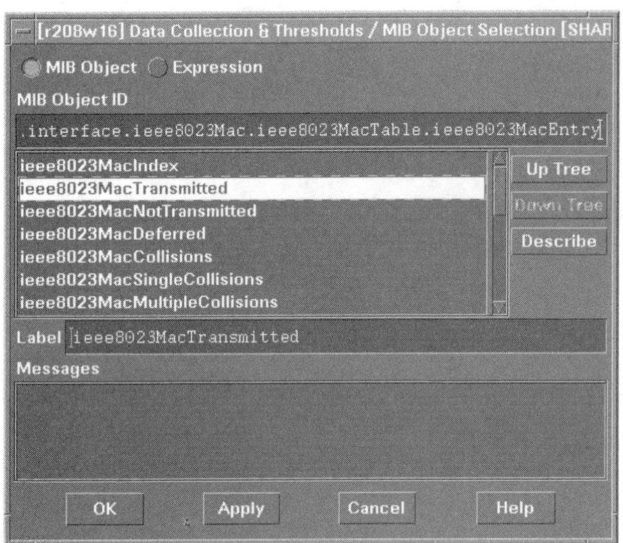

4. When you click the **[OK]** button (see Figure 8-3) from the **MIB Object Selection** dialog box, NNM displays the dialog box shown in Figure 8-4. Set the following fields in the **ieee8023MacTransmitted collection** dialog box:

Collection Mode	Store, No Thresholds
Source	The hostname for the system on which to collect
Polling Interval	5s

   Supply the hostname or IP address in the **Source** field and click **[Add]**. Click **[OK]**. Note that when the **Collection Mode** is set to **Store, No Thresholds**, the lower portion of the collection dialog box is grayed out.

Initially, you may want to test the collected data without defining thresholds. This allows you to analyze the data collected so you can set an accurate threshold value that generates events. You may also choose to use statistical thresholds and allow NNM to determine what is normal for each node and notify you if a data point is outside the range by some number of standard deviations. Statistical thresholds are useful for situations where you know that your load will increase over time due to growth.

Figure 8-4 When configuring a collection, define the **Collection Mode**, the **Source**, and the **Polling Interval** for the data collection. Type the hostname for the **Source** and click **[Add]**.

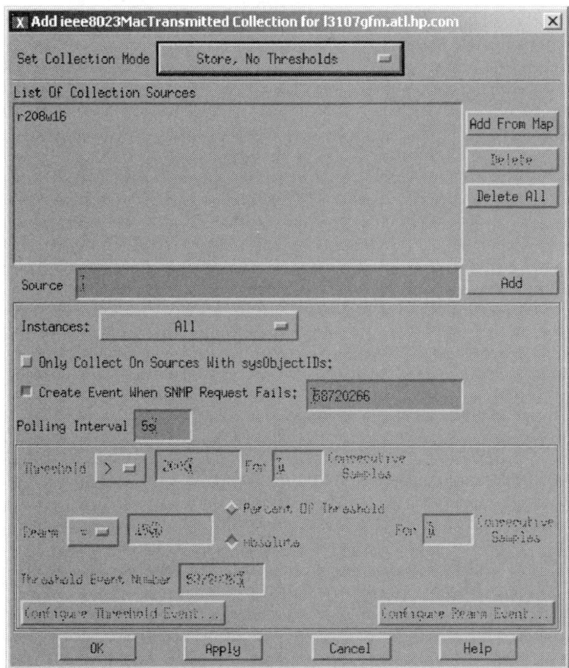

The source may be a hostname, an IP address, or a file containing a list of hostnames (one per line). Wild cards and ranges may be used with IP addresses. The following are acceptable IP address entries for the source:

..*.*	Collect on all possible addresses
15.6.212.*	Collect on all IP addresses on the subnet
15.6.212-220.*	Collect on all IP addresses on a range of subnets
15.6.212-220.177	Collect on the 177 machines on a range of subnets

You also may wildcard the source field, then constrain the nodes collected upon using a filter. Filters are available from the field **Collection Node Filter**. When you specify a filter, data is collected only from the nodes that meet the filter definition. For example, if you only want to collect data from your routers, select **[Routers]** from the drop-down list. Filter definitions are discussed in Chapter 9, "Scalability and Distribution."

Setting a polling interval of five seconds (5s) allows you to capture data quickly and verify that the collection is functioning properly. When the collection is functioning to your satisfaction, modify the polling interval to a more reasonable value, such as 30 minutes (30m) or 1 hour (1h). Polling too frequently takes additional bandwidth, CPU resources, and data storage space.

Additional fields available from the data collection dialog may be also customized. If a device contains multiple instances of an item such as file systems or network interfaces, **Instances** allows you to specify whether to collect on all or some of the instances. For example, if you have multiple network interfaces but only want to specify a collection for interface one and four, you would specify as the instance From List **1,4**.

You may want to limit a collection by nodes with a specific OID (for example, to limit to a specific vendor's equipment) by selecting the option. This works well when combined with specifying a group of IP addresses (158.153.*.1): **Only Collect On Sources With sysObjectIDs**.

By default, traps are not generated when the SNMP query fails. This may be enabled by selecting **Create Event When SNMP Request Fails**.

Field-specific help is available from this and many other dialog boxes. Selecting a field and pressing the F1 key accesses field-specific help. Detailed information may be obtained from any dialog box.

5. Select **File→Save** to save the collection. Select the newly defined collection and select the menu item **Actions→Resume Collection** and then **File→Save**.
6. Wait a minimum of two polling intervals (10 seconds, in this case) and select **Actions→Show Data** as shown in Figures 8-5 and 8-6.

Figure 8-5 To view the collected data, select the collection and select **Actions→Show Data...** from the **Data Collections & Thresholds** dialog box.

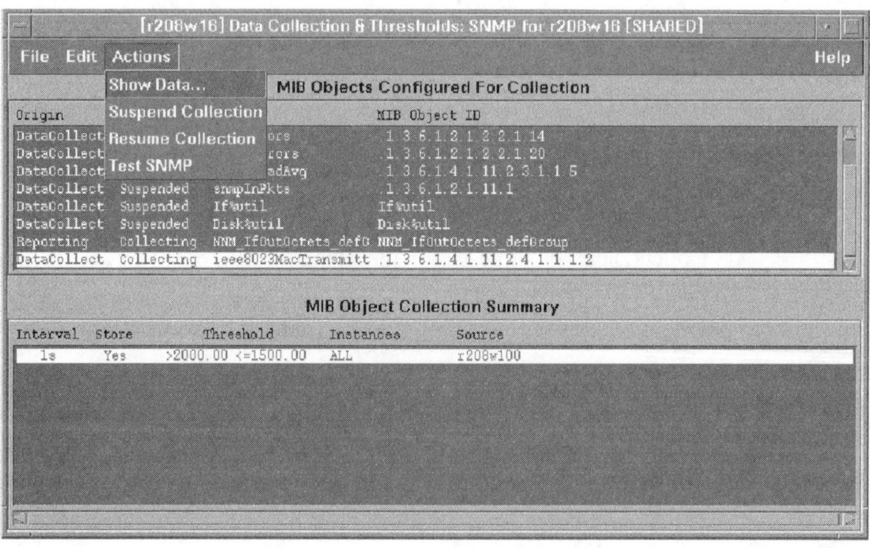

Figure 8-6 displays the data as it is being collected. Collected data is stored in the directory **$OV_DB/snmpCollect**. This directory should be monitored as the data collection files can grow without bound. You may want to set up a batch program to periodically archive and remove the data in this directory, or you can delete it as you export it to the Data Warehouse.

Figure 8-6 The data is displayed as it is collected. Note the five interfaces shown in the upper section of the dialog box. The data being displayed corresponds to the selected interface. Click the **[Graph]** button to graph the collected data.

[r208w16] Data Collection & Thresholds / Show Data [SHARED]

Type: COUNTER   Number Of Entries: 248

Instance	File
1	ifInOctets.1
2	ifInOctets.2
3	ifInOctets.3
4	ifInOctets.4
5	ifInOctets.5

Interval	Time	Source	Value
3s	Tue Jul 11 18:09:05	r208w15	0.00
3s	Tue Jul 11 18:09:08	r208w15	0.00
3s	Tue Jul 11 18:09:11	r208w15	0.00
3s	Tue Jul 11 18:09:14	r208w15	0.00
3s	Tue Jul 11 18:09:17	r208w15	0.00
3s	Tue Jul 11 18:09:20	r208w15	0.00
3s	Tue Jul 11 18:09:23	r208w15	0.00
3s	Tue Jul 11 18:09:26	r208w15	0.00
3s	Tue Jul 11 18:09:29	r208w15	0.00
3s	Tue Jul 11 18:09:32	r208w15	0.00
3s	Tue Jul 11 18:09:35	r208w15	0.00
3s	Tue Jul 11 18:09:38	r208w15	0.00
3s	Tue Jul 11 18:09:41	r208w15	0.00
3s	Tue Jul 11 18:09:44	r208w15	0.00
3s	Tue Jul 11 18:09:47	r208w15	0.00
3s	Tue Jul 11 18:09:50	r208w15	0.00
3s	Tue Jul 11 18:09:53	r208w15	0.00
3s	Tue Jul 11 18:09:56	r208w15	0.00
3s	Tue Jul 11 18:09:59	r208w15	0.00
3s	Tue Jul 11 18:10:02	r208w15	0.00
3s	Tue Jul 11 18:10:05	r208w15	0.00
3s	Tue Jul 11 18:10:08	r208w15	0.00
3s	Tue Jul 11 18:10:11	r208w15	0.00
2s	Tue Jul 11 18:10:13	r208w15	0.00
3s	Tue Jul 11 18:10:16	r208w15	0.00
3s	Tue Jul 11 18:10:19	r208w15	0.00
3s	Tue Jul 11 18:10:22	r208w15	0.00
3s	Tue Jul 11 18:10:25	r208w15	0.00
3s	Tue Jul 11 18:10:28	r208w15	0.00
3s	Tue Jul 11 18:10:31	r208w15	0.00

[Close] [Clear] [Stop Display] [Graph] [Help]

NNM provides a command-line utility **snmpColDump** to display the collected data in ASCII format. For each MIB variable instance collected, NNM creates two files: a binary file containing the data and an ID file containing information about the variable. The data file is named the *variable.instance* and the ID file is the same followed by an exclamation mark (!). To list the collected data for the fourth interface in ASCII format, type the following:

1. Set the current directory to the data collection directory.
   cd $OV_DB/snmpCollect
2. List the collected data for interface number 4 for the MIB variable ieee3023MacTransmitted.
   snmpColDump ieee8023MacTransmitted.4 | more

8.1.2 Defining an MIB Expression for Collection

A MIB expression may be used to define a collection. If no single MIB variable exists for the data you are interested in, you can define a formula using a combination of MIB variables. For example, if you are interested in the percent of available bandwidth utilized on an interface, this can be calculated using a combination of the variables received byte rate, transmitted byte rate, and interface link speed. The pre-defined MIB expression **If%util** defines the MIB expression for available bandwidth.

To display the MIB expression **If%util** and description, open the **Data Collection and Thresholds** dialog box. Select the **If%util** collection and select **Edit→Modify→MIB Objects** from the menu bar. Then click the **[Describe]** button. Expression calculations are in Reverse Polish Notation and can be a combination of variables and numbers. Figure 8-7 shows the calculation and description defined by the **If%util** MIB expression. You may select these expressions to add to the list available for configuring specific collections.

Now that you have collected data, you are ready to begin analyzing the information collected. During analysis, consider what values appear to be in a normal state verses an abnormal state. In doing this, you begin to define threshold and rearm values for your data.

Figure 8-7 The MIB expression **If%util** calculates the percent of available bandwidth.

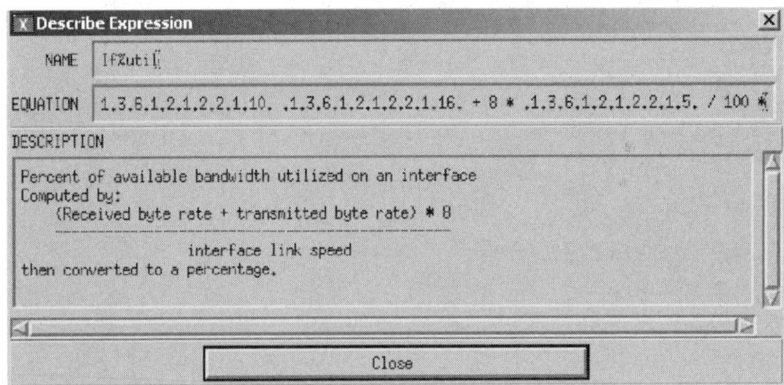

8.2 CREATING THRESHOLD AND REARM EVENTS

NNM provides default threshold and rearm events when custom thresholds are exceeded. The default events can be viewed in NNM's Alarm Browser or in the Exception Report but take no action by default. You can configure custom events to perform additional tasks such as sending a pop-up message to the management station or passing the information to an external application, such as a paging system. The purpose of a threshold event is to perform some action based on exceeding the custom threshold value. The rearm event allows you to configure another event based on the variable being monitored returning to normal.

Specific event numbers available to you are in the range of 1 to 10,000. Numbers outside this range have been reserved for vendor SNMP traps. Your organization should come up with a numbering convention for your enterprise. Threshold events should always be an odd number. The threshold event used in this example is 1001. The rearm event will always be an even number equal to one plus the threshold event number. 1002 will be the rearm event for the first example.

8.2.1 Defining a Threshold Event for Data Collection

When performing data collection, you should determine whether or not to alarm on custom thresholds for the data being monitored. You may wish to store the data for trend analysis and/or simply alarm based on exceeding a threshold without storing the data.

The following steps allow you to define custom threshold and rearm values for the previously defined data collection **ieee3023MacTransmitted**:

1. Select **Options→Data Collection & Thresholds** from the menu bar (see Figure 8-1).
2. Modify the collection **ieee3023MacTransmitted** by selecting it from the lower section of the **Data Collection & Thresholds** window. Then select **Edit→Modify→MIB Collection...** from the Data Collection & Thresholds menu bar.
3. Change the Collection Mode to **Store, Check Thresholds**. Notice that the bottom part of the dialog box is no longer grayed out. It activates when you check thresholds. It is only grayed out when the Collection mode is set to Store, No Thresholds. Fill in the following fields, as shown in Figure 8-8:

Collection Mode	Store, Check Thresholds
Threshold	> 2000
Rearm	< 1500
Threshold Event Number	1001

The values for threshold and rearm can be accurately determined by displaying the data described previously (**Actions→Show Data**). While viewing the data, use the **snmpwalk** command to generate interface traffic. The idea is to make sure you can exceed the threshold value to test the threshold and rearm values. To use the **snmpwalk** command, type **snmpwalk hostname**.

Figure 8-8 Set the **Collection Mode** to **Store, Check Thresholds** to generate events caused by exceeding a threshold value. Fill in the **Threshold** and **Rearm** fields. Change the **Threshold Event Number** to 1001.

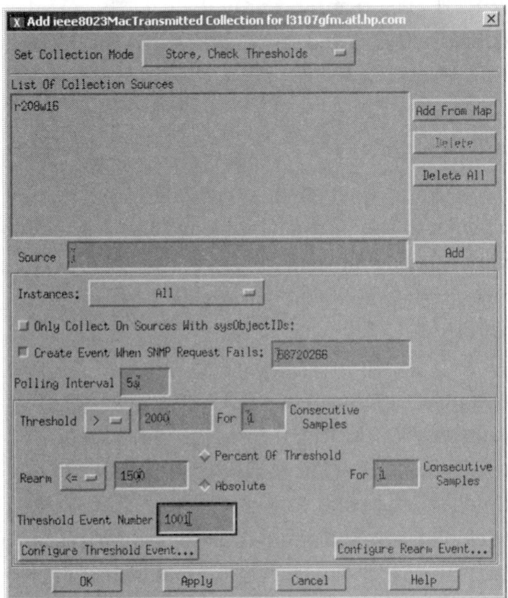

After populating the specified fields, click **[Configure Threshold Event…**. The dialog boxes shown in Figures 8-9 and 8-10 are displayed.

4. Acknowledge the dialog box **"No currently configured event for Event Identification "1.3.5.8.1.4.1.11.2.17.1.0.1001" sources: "hostname". Would you like to add this event configuration?"** shown in Figure 8-9 by clicking **[OK]**.
5. Acknowledge the dialog box **"Please add event configuration for Enterprise Identifier "OpenView". If you would like to have special event handling for sources "hostname," add them into the "Source" field of the "Add Event"** dialog shown in Figure 8-10 by clicking **[Close]**. The second dialog box indicates what to do if you would like to customize events on a per-node basis. In this example, we will not customize the event for a specific node.

Figure 8-9 When adding a custom event, you will be prompted to add a new event configuration for the Threshold event. Click **[OK]**.

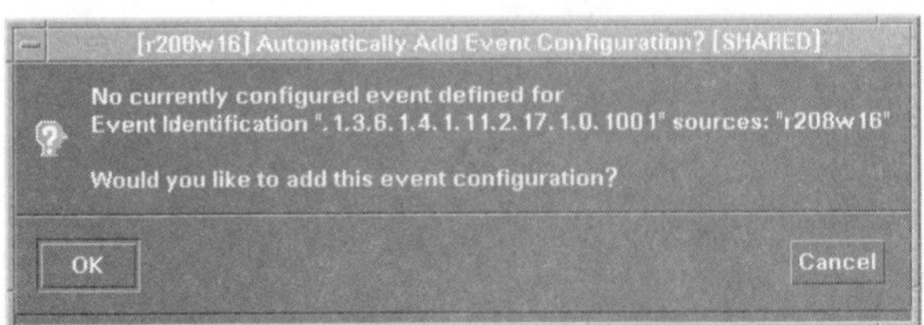

Figure 8-10 A second prompt is displayed with instructions on how to handle specific sources for the event configuration.

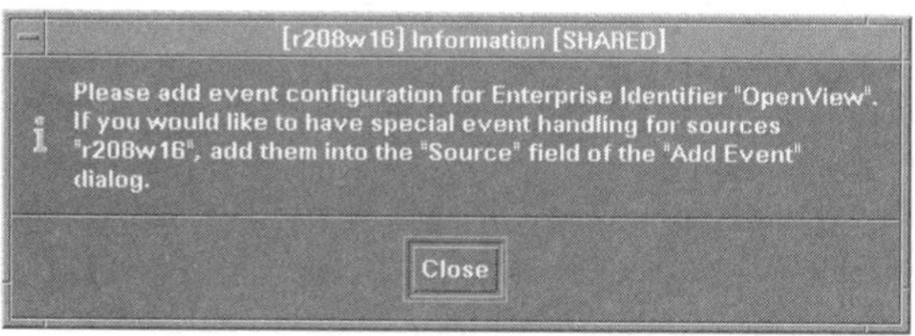

6. Upon acknowledgement of the two dialog boxes, two additional dialog boxes are displayed: the **Event Configuration** (Figure 8-11) and the **Event Configurator** (Figure 8-12). In order to propagate the Event number, select **View→Event Identifiers→ Display as SNMP Traps** from the Event Configuration menu bar, as shown in Figure 8-11. The Specific Trap number 1001 is displayed, as shown in Figure 8-12. Complete the following fields in the **Event Configuration** dialog box.

Event Name	TooManyPackets
Pop-up Notification	Too many packets $8 on $2

   If the event is displayed as an OID instead of a trap, you can change the events to be displayed as SNMP traps (described previously) or you must supply the event number in the format 0.event# (0.1001) in the OID field. This is due to the differences between SNMP version 2 and version 2C traps.[2]

   The **Event Description** shown in Figure 8-12 describes the variables available to be passed by the collection/configuration. These variables can be referenced in the **Event Log Message**, **Pop-up Notification**, and **Command for Automatic Action**. Use the dollar sign ($) in front of the number to reference the variable. For example, $2 references the hostname of the system on which the event happened.

   1. The ID of application sending the event.
   2. The name of the host that caused the threshold event.
   3. The HP OpenView object identifier, if available.
   4. The MIB variable in dotted numeric format.
   5. The name of the collection.
   6. The MIB instance.
   7. The threshold value.
   8. The sampled value.
   9. The highest sampled (peak) value.

2 The originally proposed SNMP version 3 was intended to provide encryption. Because the decision makers could not come to an agreement on which encryption method to implement in SNMP version 3, we now have version 2C with no encryption.

10. The time the highest value was sampled.
11. The lowest sampled (trough) value.
12. The time the lowest value was sampled.
13. The threshold operator.
14. The threshold count.

Additional variables are available for use in defining events. Select the Event Log Message field and press the **F1** key. Scroll down and select **[Variables]**. You will see the list of pre-defined variables available for use in the event configuration.

Figure 8-11 Select **View→Event Identifiers→Display as SNMP Traps** and the Event Number will be populated automatically for the Event Configuration.

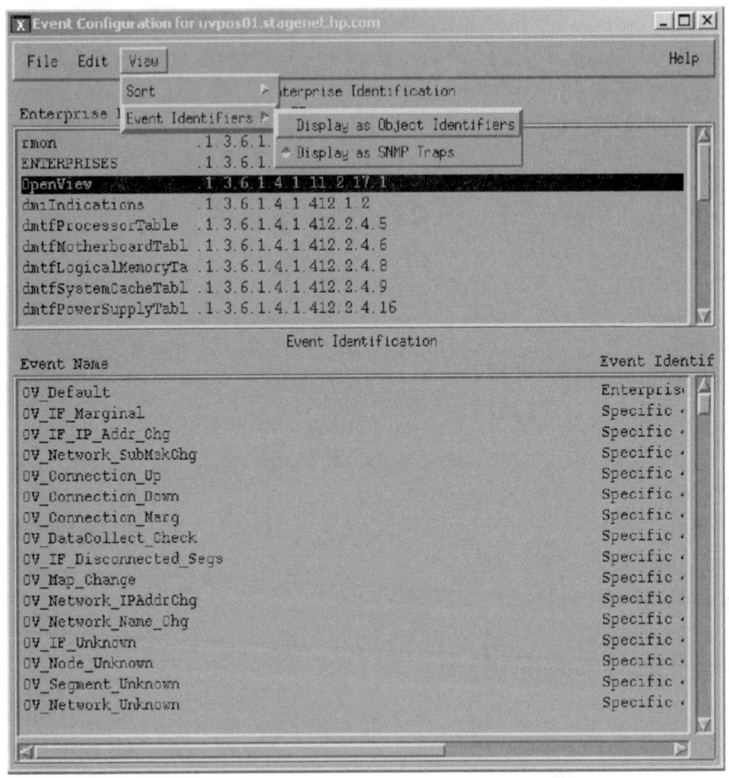

Figure 8-12 Provide the **Event Name** and an optional **Pop-up Notification** for the event. The variables listed in the **Event Description** can be referenced using $1, $2, $3, etc. $2 passes the hostname and $8 passes the sampled value to the pop-up notification.

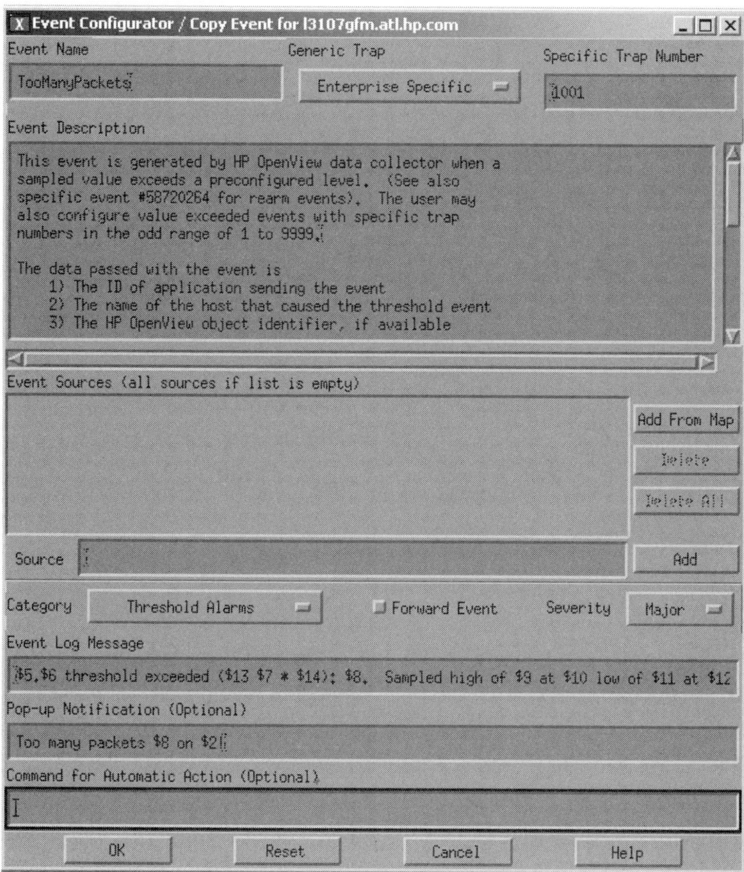

4. Save and close the Event Configuration dialog box by selecting **File→Save**, then **File→Close** from the Event Configuration dialog box, as shown in Figure 8-13. Only one Event Configuration dialog box can be opened at a time. After creating or modifying an event, always save and close the Event Configuration dialog box.

Figure 8-13 Select **File→Save** and **File→Close** from the Event Configuration dialog box after defining threshold and rearm events.

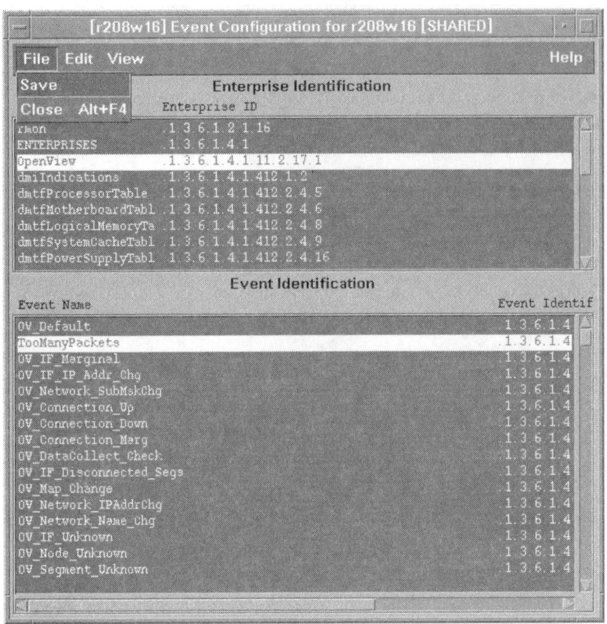

After creating a threshold event, you probably want to create a rearm event to indicate that things have returned to a normal state. The rearm event can be configured similarly to the threshold event to popup messages passing values to into the event message and the popup window.

8.2.2 Defining a Rearm Event for Data Collection

The steps required in configuring a rearm event for data collection are very similar to configuring to those of configuring a threshold event:

1. Select from the menu bar **Options→Data Collection & Thresholds** (see Figure 8-1).
2. Modify the collection **ieee3023MacTransmitted** by selecting it and select **Edit→ Modify→MIB Collection...** from the Data Collection menu bar (Figure 8-2).
3. Click the **[Configure Rearm Event...]** button (Figure 8-8).
4. Acknowledge the dialog box **"No currently configured event for Event Identification "1.3.5.8.1.4.1.11.2.17.1.0.1002" sources: "hostname". Would you like to add this event configuration?"** shown in Figure 8-14 by clicking **[OK]**.
5. Acknowledge the dialog box **"Please add event configuration for Enterprise Identifier "OpenView". If you would like to have special event handling for sources *"hostname"*, add them into the "Source" field of the "Add Event" dialog"** by clicking **[Close]** (Figure 8-10).

Figure 8-14 When adding a custom event, you are prompted to add a new event configuration. A second prompt is displayed with instructions on how to handle specific sources for the rearm event. The rearm event is always an even number: the threshold event number plus one.

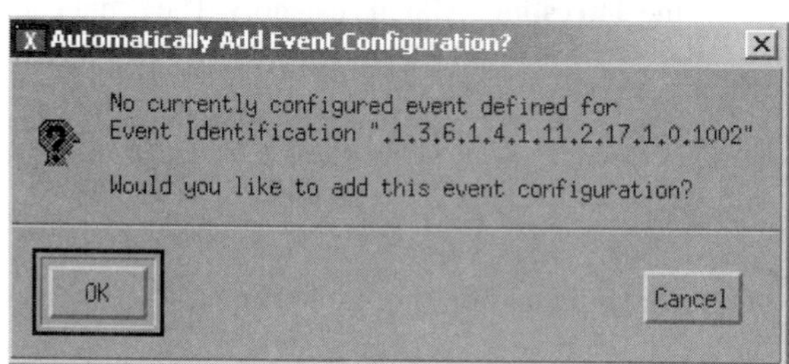

Note: The rearm event number will always be an even number equal to the threshold event number incremented by 1.

6. Provide the **Event Name** and a **Pop-up Notification** in the Event Configuration dialog box and click **[OK]**, as shown in Figure 8-15.

Event Name	TooManyPacketsRearm
Pop-up Notification	All is well on $2

Figure 8-15 Provide the **Event Name** and the **Pop-up Notification** in the Rearm dialog box.

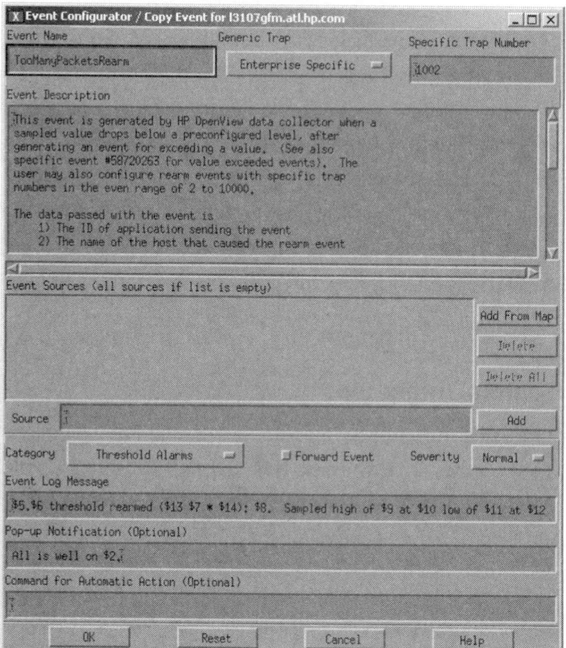

Because the threshold and rearm events are tied to data collection via the **[Configure Threshold/Rearm Event...]** buttons, predefined event messages already exist for both threshold and rearm events. The event message may be modified if you like, but it is not necessary. The default category for threshold and rearm events is the **Threshold Alarms** category. The event category may be modified by selecting from the drop-down list in the **Category,** shown in Figures 8-12 and 8-15.

After defining the rearm event, save it and perform the following steps in order to display the data collected:

7. Select **File→Save** from the Event Configuration dialog box (Figure 8-11).
8. Select **File→Close** from the Event Configuration dialog box (Figure 8-11).
9. Select **[OK]** from the Data Collection dialog box (Figure 8-8).
10. Select **File→Save** from the Data Collection & Thresholds dialog box (Figure 8-5).
11. The steps Select **Actions→Resume** Collection from the Data Collection & Thresholds dialog box (Figure 8-5).
12. Select **File→Save** from the Data Collection & Thresholds dialog box (Figure 8-5).
13. Select **Actions→Show Data** from the Data Collection & Thresholds dialog box (Figure 8-5).

This example triggers the popup notification "**Too many packets <sampled value> on <hostname>**" on the management station when the threshold value is exceeded. The sampled value is the value of the MIB variable **ieee3023MacTransmitted** for the hostname being monitored. The popup notification is generated every polling interval (5 seconds) until the value has crossed below the rearm value.

When the sampled value has dropped below the rearm value, the popup notification "**All is well on <hostname>**" is generated on the management server. If you want a threshold event to occur but do not want a rearm notification to occur, set the threshold and rearm values to the same number. After validating the data and the popup notification, remember to go back and change the polling interval to a more reasonable value (Figure 8-8). Depending on the number of collections defined and the severity of the collections, you may want to set the polling interval to 15 minutes, 30 minutes, or 1 hour. Always save the collection (**File→Save**) after making modifications.

For each threshold and rearm event configured and violated, an alarm occurs in the **Threshold Alarms** category.

8.2.3 Generating Actions Based on Custom Thresholds

When defining custom events, you can supply the command to be executed on the NNM system when threshold/rearm values are exceeded. Essentially, anything you type from the command line on the system may be used as an automatic action. This may be a script or a binary executable. Automatic actions are frequently used to send email, trigger audio alerts, alert paging devices, or pass information to a trouble ticketing system.

8.2.3.1 Automatic Actions for UNIX systems

Automatic actions are implemented in the **Commands for Automatic Action** field of the Threshold (Figure 8-12) and Rearm Event (Figure 8-15) configuration notification boxes. The command used in this field is executed on the management system. Any of the variables in the description field of the event may be passed in the automatic action. For example, the following action sends an email to root on a UNIX management station. The variable $2 is the nodename and $8 is the sampled value as described previously.

```
echo "$2 exceeded packet threshold: $8." | mailx -s "$2
Threshold Exceeded" root
```

The automatic action is executed on the management system unless you use a utility, such as **remsh**, to run the command on a remote UNIX system. [3]If the management server was configured to execute actions on the managed node with root access, you could issue the following as an automatic action. Assume that a process, such as **sendmail**, needed to be restarted after a particular threshold was exceeded. You could define an automatic action such as this to restart the **sendmail** daemon:

```
remsh remoteHost /sbin/init.d/sendmail start
```

Note: The OpenView Operations product actually is more capable of application monitoring than NNM. The point here is that NNM has the capability to execute automatic actions both locally and remotely if properly configured.

8.2.3.2 Automatic Actions for Windows Systems

Actions for Windows systems can also be defined in Data Collection and Threshold Events. For example, if you want to send a message to a remote windows system, include the following automatic action in the Threshold dialog box. The $2 variable translates to the hostname of the system on which the packet threshold has been exceeded. $8 is the sampled value.

```
"net send  " Node $2  " exceeded packet threshold:" $8 "."
```

Given a hostname of winxp256 and a packet threshold of 99999, the resulting command displays a popup message on the remote system similar to that shown in Figure 8-15a.

3 The remsh (REMote SHell) command requires a **.rhosts** file or **/etc/hosts.equiv** to be configured on a UNIX system. In many environments this is considered to be a security risk. For more details, refer to the UNIX man page on **remsh** for HP-UX and **rsh** for Solaris.

The capability to execute remote commands on Windows systems is available from the Windows Resource Kit command **rcmd**. The Remote Command Service (RCMD.EXE) provides a secure, robust way to remotely administer and run command-line programs. RCMD consists of client and server components. The client is a command-line program, RCMD.EXE. The server end, RCMDSVC.EXE, is installed and run as a service. Issued from the management server, the following example command starts the task scheduler service on the target system:

```
rcmd  \\hostname net start "task scheduler"
```

Figure 8-15a The **net send** command can be used to display a popup message on a Windows system.

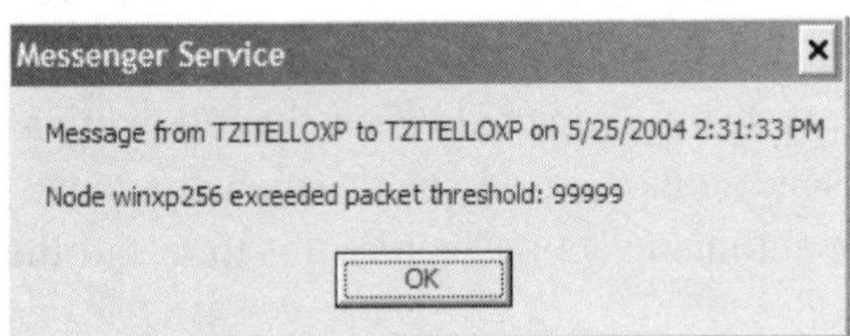

This command can be used in the automatic action field of threshold event configuration. NNM can automatically restart the task scheduler on the remote node without human intervention. Assuming that a MIB variable exists to indicate whether the task scheduler service is running, you could create a threshold event to monitor that MIB variable and configure an automatic action to restart the task scheduler service.

Note: By default, NNM only performs commands that are trusted commands. You must specify the command to be trusted in a file that resides in the trusted commands configuration directory:

UNIX: $OV_CONF/trustedCmds.conf

Windows: *install_dir*\conf\trustedCmds.conf

The format of this file is **Keyword=Absolute Path** and can include environment variables listed in the configuration file **ov.envvars.sh**. The following are sample entries for trusted commands file:

```
snmpnotify=$OV_BIN/snmpnotify
ovIfIndexRemap.ovpl=$OV_BIN/ovIfIndexRemap.ovpl
```

If the commands are not specified in the directory and are used in event configuration, NNM generates an error event and the action is not executed. You can override the trusted command feature by creating a file named ALLOW_ALL in the trusted commands configuration directory. After making modifications to the trusted commands directory, you must force the **ovactiond** process to re-read the configuration. This is accomplished by typing the following command:

```
xnmevents -events
```

8.2.4 Creating Custom Alarm Categories

As mentioned previously, the default alarm category for both threshold and rearm events is **Threshold Alarms**. When creating or modifying to an event, you can specify the category to which you would like it to be written. Custom alarm categories may be created for storing custom events. Follow these steps to create a custom category:

1. Open the Event Configuration dialog box by selecting **Options→Event Configuration**.
2. Select **Edit→Configure→Alarm Categories** from the Event Configuration dialog box, as shown in Figure 8-16.

Figure 8-16 To add a custom alarm category, select **Edit→Configure→Alarm Categories...** from the Event Configuration dialog box.

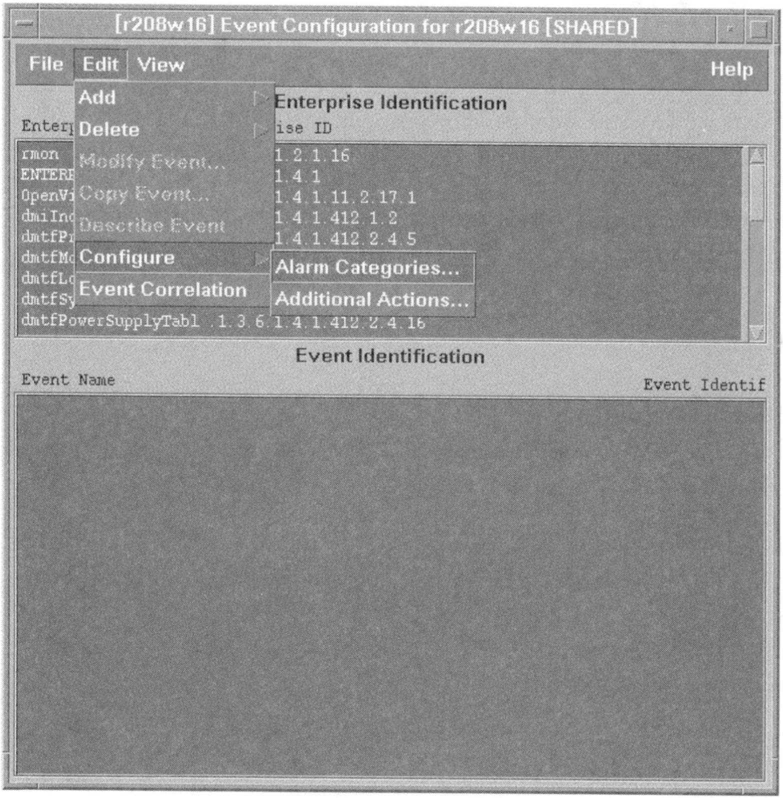

Type the name of the new alarm category and click **[Add]** and **[Close]**, as shown Figure 8-17.

Figure 8-17 Provide the category name (Tammys Alarms) and click the **[Add]** button. Then click the **[Close]** button.

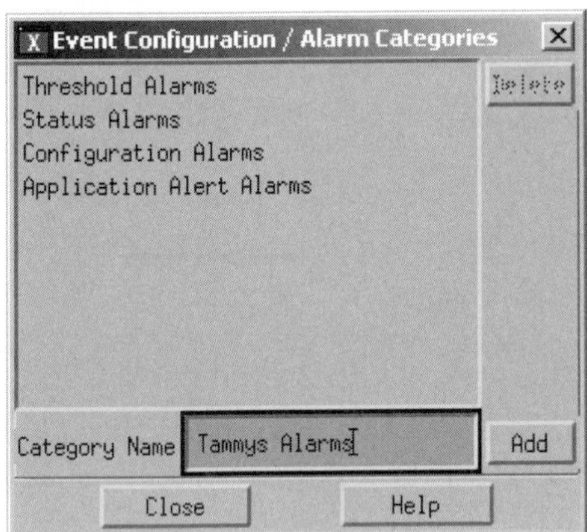

3. Select **File→Save** from the Event Configuration dialog box.
4. Verify that the new alarm category (Tammys Alarms) exists, as shown in Figure 8-18.

Figure 8-18 The new alarm category (Tammys Alarms) is displayed in the **Alarm Categories** window.

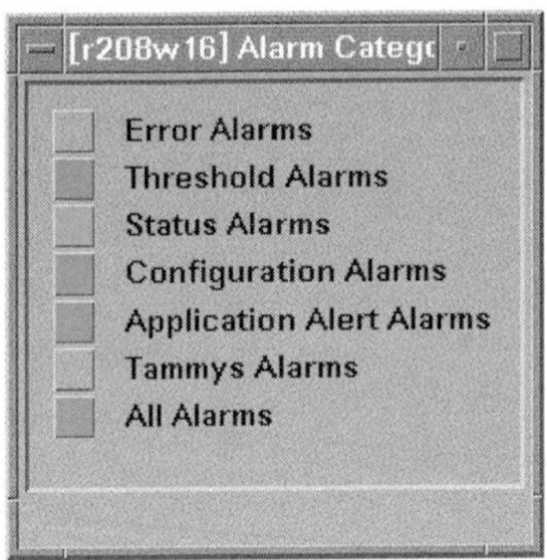

5. Modify the category for your custom threshold and rearm events by using the drop-down list in the **Category** field, as shown in Figure 8-19.

Figure 8-19 The **Category** of a custom **Threshold Event** may be modified to send Event Log Messages to a custom alarm category, such as Tammys Alarms.

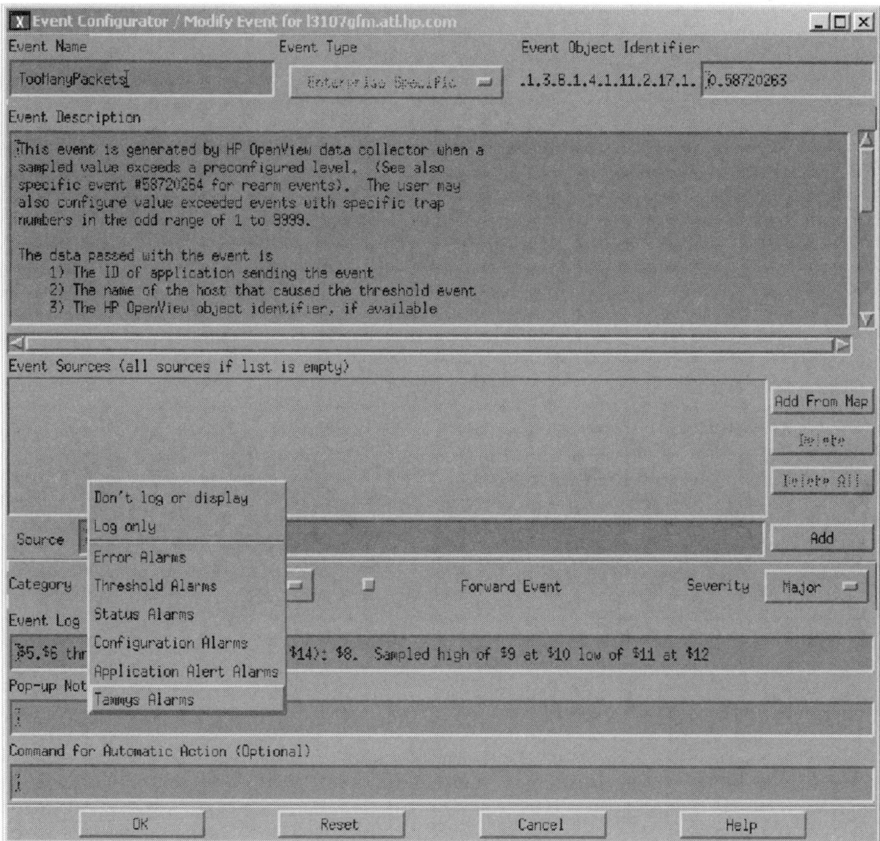

By default, events are sorted by Event Identifiers. Events may be sorted by name by selecting the Enterprise ID (**OpenView**) and selecting **View→Sort→Sort By Event Name**, as shown in Figure 8-20. Sorting by name makes it easier to locate an event by name.

Figure 8-20 By default, event configurations are sorted by the Event Identifier. Event configuration may be sorted by selecting **View→Sort→Sort by Event Name**.

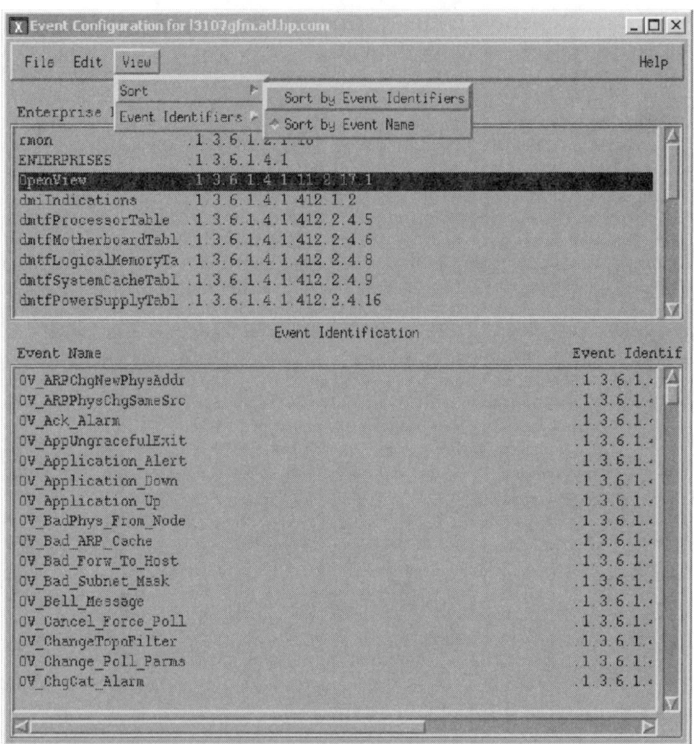

8.2.5 Accessing Events from the Alarm Browser

Another way to access an event is via the **Alarm Browser**. You can locate the event configuration that generated the message by selecting a message in the Alarm Browser and selecting **Actions→Configure Event...** as shown in Figure 8-21. You may then make modifications to the event, such as the **Category**.

Figure 8-21 Event Configuration may be accessed from the Alarm Browser by selecting a message and selecting **Actions→Configure Event....**

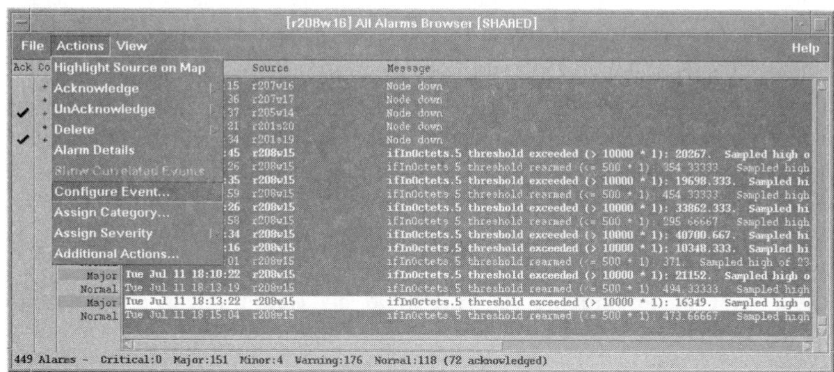

8.3 CUSTOMIZING EXISTING DATA COLLECTIONS

NNM provides many predefined collections that may be customized for your enterprise. By default, none of the collections are active. In order to activate them, copy and modify the collection. The example used in this section is the interface utilization collection, **If%util**. The **If%util** collection uses a MIB expression to calculate the available bandwidth of an interface, as described previously in this chapter.

The MIB collection can be customized by copying it. First, select the **If%util** MIB Object from the upper part of the **Data Collection & Thresholds** dialog box. Then, select the existing collection from the lower section of the Data Collection & Thresholds dialog box and select **Edit→Copy→MIB Collection**, as shown in Figure 8-22.

Figure 8-22 The **If%util** MIB Collection is copied by selecting **Edit→Copy→MIB Collections....**

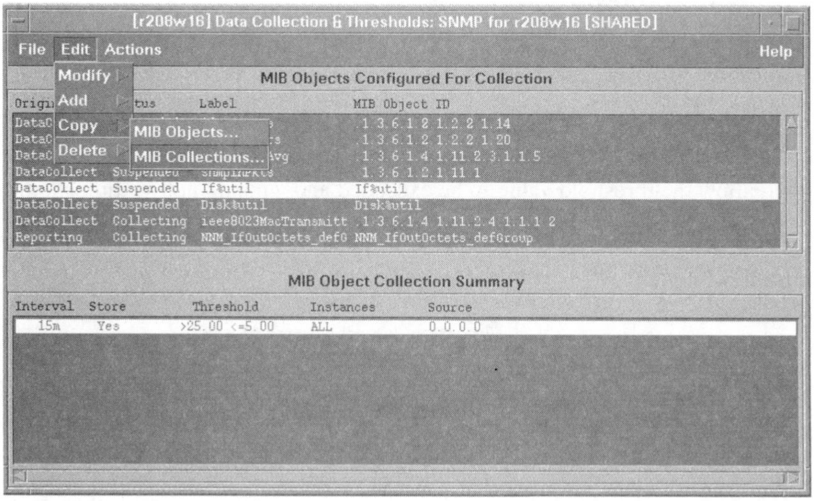

When you copy the collection, you see the data collection dialog box shown in Figure 8-23. Provide the **Source** (hostname or IP address) for the collection and click **[Add]**. Supply a **Polling Interval** of 3 seconds (3s). Specify the **Threshold** and **Rearm** values. If you wish to store and view the data in order to more accurately set these values, set the **Collection Mode** to **Store, No Thresholds**. Use the default **Threshold Event Number** (58720263). This event generates a message in the **Threshold Alarm** category. To customize an event for the threshold and rearm values, specify a unique event number and click **[Configure Threshold Event...]** and **[Configure Rearm Event...]**, as described previously. Then, click **[OK]** from the dialog box in Figure 8-23. Select **File→Save** from the Data Collection & Thresholds dialog box shown in Figure 8-24. Resume the collection (**Actions→Resume Collection**) and save it (**File→Save**).

Figure 8-23 Specify the **Source**, **Polling Interval**, **Threshold**, and **Rearm** values for the custom **If%util** collection.

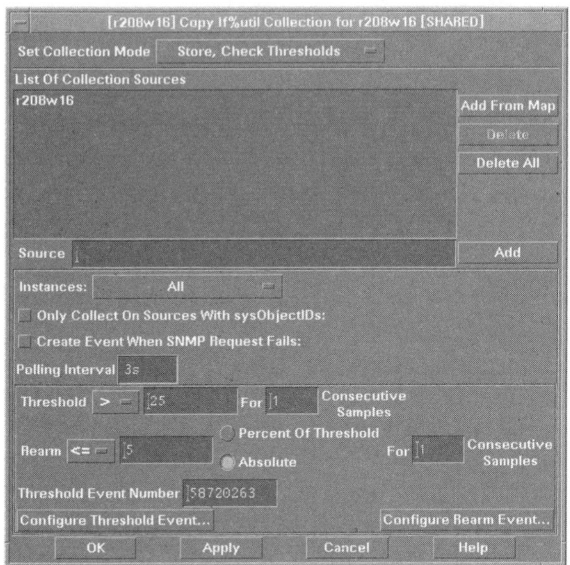

The **snmpwalk** command may be used to generate interface traffic when testing this data collection. This should allow the threshold value to be exceeded and a popup notification should be generated.

```
snmpwalk hostname
```

Figure 8-24 Start the new **If%util** collection by selecting **Actions→Resume Collection** and **File→Save** from the Data Collection & Thresholds menu bar.

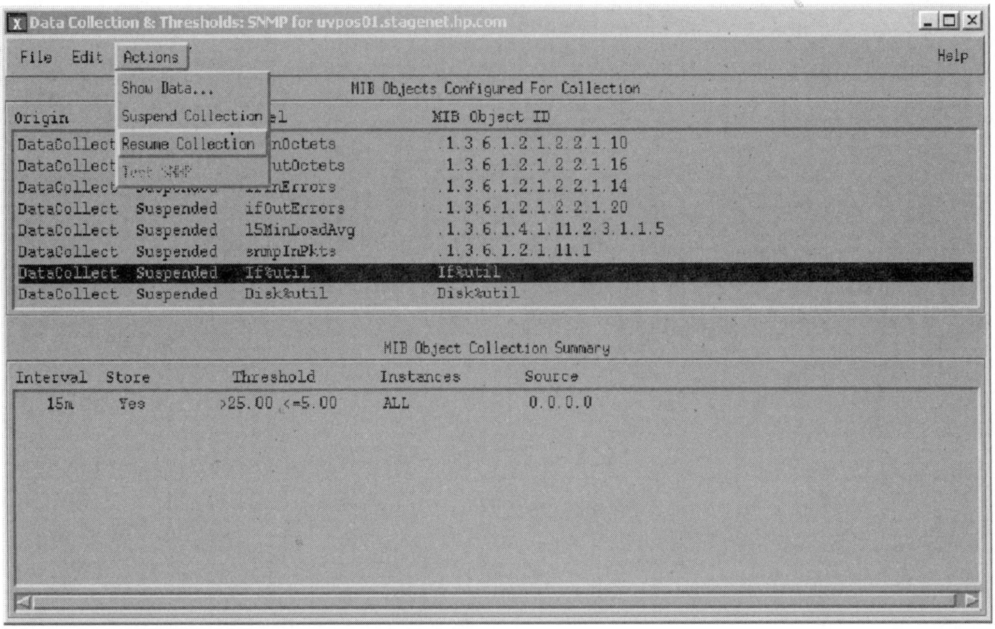

8.4 CUSTOMIZING EXISTING EVENTS

You can copy existing events and customize them for specific systems. For example, what if you would like to receive a pop up notification when certain devices are unavailable but only wish to receive a message in the Alarm Browser for all other devices? In order to do this, copy the **OV_Node_Down** event and modify it according to the following steps:

1. Open Event Configuration by selecting **Options→Event Configuration**.
2. Select the **OpenView Enterprise**.
3. Sort Events by name. Select **View→Sort→Sort Event by Name**.
4. Scroll down and select the event named **OV_Node_Down**.
5. Select **Edit→Copy Event...**.
6. Provide the event name **OV_Node_Down_Routers**, as shown in Figure 8-25.
7. Assuming that all routers contain a 1 in the last octet of the IP address, specify the source as **158.153.*.1** and click **[Add]**. This address must match your enterprise.
8. Add a pop-up notification, "The node $2 is down," and click **[OK]**.
9. Select **File→Save** from the Event Configuration dialog box.

This event triggers a popup notification on the management station for any IP address 158.153.*.1, and for all others the original **OV_Node_Down** event will be used.

Figure 8-25 Copy the **OV_Node_Down** event and modify it for specific nodes. Specify the source using an IP address wildcard, such as 158.153.*.1.

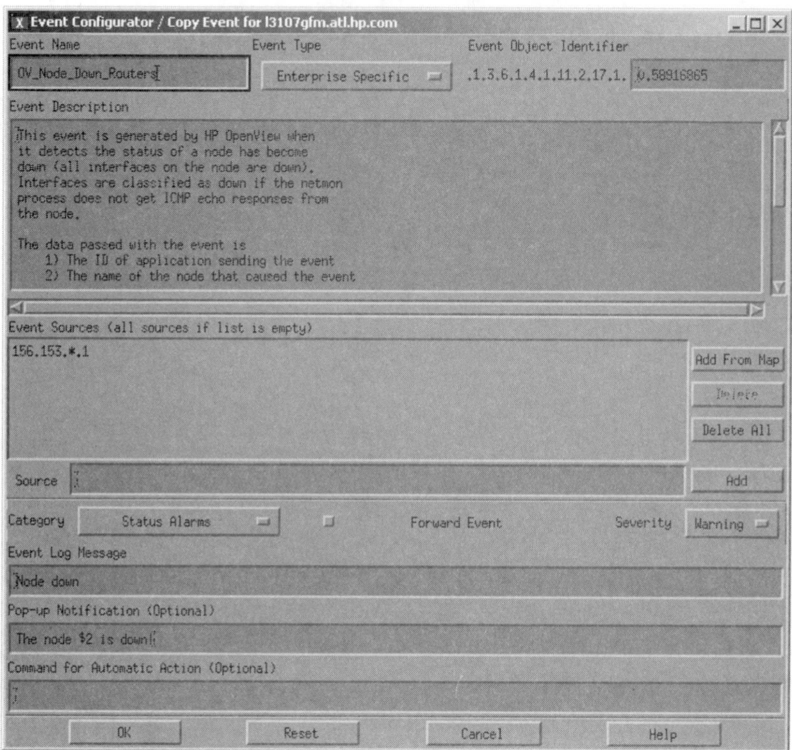

8.5 TEST YOUR KNOWLEDGE OF DATA COLLECTION AND EVENTS

This section is designed to help you understand the complete process of defining data collection and creating custom events. It reinforces the information provided in this and previous chapters.

Certain Hewlett-Packard printers contain SNMP variables to indicate when the printer runs out of paper. For this exercise you will need to

- Load the printer MIB
- Monitor the variable that identifies the paper is out
- Popup messages when the paper runs out and after the paper has been refilled

The basic steps are as follows:

1. Load the hp-np (HP Network Printer) MIB. This MIB ships with NNM.
2. Query the **private.enterprises.hp** MIB subtree to find an MIB variable that describes "Paper Out."

3. Locate an HP network printer to use for the data collection.
4. Define an event that will trigger a popup message when the paper is out. Hint: opening the paper tray on the printer gives the same result as "Paper Out".

If you are able to complete this exercise, you have a pretty good understanding of defining data collection and events. If you need assistance, refer to the next section of this chapter for a detailed solution to this exercise.

8.6 DETAILED SOLUTION TO NETWORK PRINTER EXERCISE

1. Select **Options→Load/unload MIBS: SNMP** from the menu bar.
2. Click the **[Load…]** button and double-click **Vendor** and **Hewlett-Packard**.
3. Select the **hp-np MIB**, then click **[OK]**.
4. Use the MIB browser to verify the value of the MIB variable changes when you open the paper tray. Select **Tools→SNMP Browser**. Traverse the MIB tree to
   private.enterprises.hp.nm.system.
   net-periperal.netprinter.generalDeviceStatus.gdStatusEntry.
   gdStatusPaperOut
5. Provide the hostname of the printer and click **[Query]** when the paper tray is closed. Open the paper tray and query the variable again. Verify that the value is 0 when the paper tray is closed and 1 when it is open.
6. Create a data collection by selecting **Options→Data Collection & Thresholds**.
7. Select **Edit→Add→MIB Objects…**.
8. Traverse the MIB tree to add the MIB object **private.enterprises.hp.nm.system.net-peripheral.netprinter.generalDeviceStatus.gdStatusEntry.gdStatusPaperOut**.
9. Complete the following fields in the Collection dialog box. Provide the hostname or IP address as the Source field.

   Source printername

   Collection Mode Store, Check Thresholds

   Threshold = 1

   Rearm = 0

   Event number 2001
10. Click the **[Configure Threshold Event…]** button.
11. Click **[OK]** and **[Close]** when prompted for new event creation.
12. Select **View→Event Identifiers→Display as SNMP Traps** from the Event Configuration dialog box.

13. Complete the following fields in the Event Configuration dialog box:
    Event Name: PaperOut

    Category: Tammys Alarms (or select your custom category)

    Popup Notification: $2 is out of paper.
14. Click **[OK]**, **File→Save**, and **File→Close** from Event Configuration.
15. Click the **[Configure Rearm Event…]** button in the Collection dialog box.
16. Complete the following fields in the Event Configuration dialog box:
    Event Name: PaperOutRearm

    Category: **Tammys** Alarms (or select your custom category)

    Popup Notification: The paper has been reloaded in $2.
17. Click **[OK]**, **File→Save**, and **File→Close** from Event Configuration.
18. Click **[OK]** in the Collection dialog box.
19. Select **File→Save** from Data Collection & Thresholds.
20. Select **Actions→Resume Collection**, **File→Save**, and **Actions→Show Data** from Data Collection & Thresholds.
21. Test the data collection and popup notifications by opening and closing the paper tray.

8.7 SUMMARY

Data collection allows you to focus on the aspects of your enterprise that are important to you. As the network administrator, you are able to collect data and configure threshold values to determine when a potential problem has occurred. When the threshold values are exceeded, NNM gives you the flexibility to configure automatic actions that may help resolve the problem that caused the threshold to be exceeded. Actions may be as simple as causing a popup message to display on a console window. The automatic action may link to a trouble ticketing system, send a message to a paging system, send an email message, or restart a process or service on a local or remote system.

Data collection also allows you to view information graphically and statistically in order to perform trend analysis and capacity planning. It helps determine the overall health and growth of your network.

Devise a plan for how your company can best use data collection. Determine which MIBs you need to monitor. Vendor-specific MIBs may allow you to better manage your network. Recall the SNMP Coke machine scenario from Chapter 1. If your company is in the business of refilling Coke machines, obviously you would like to have a method of being notified when the Coke machines need to be refilled. Implement the MIBs necessary to keep your business running smoothly.

CHAPTER 9

Scalability and Distribution

NNM provides a number of scalability features. This chapter discusses the features that allow the scalability and distribution of NNM. While scaling a product does not eliminate the necessity for hardware upgrades, it may reduce the amount of resources required for optimal performance. For example, if the synchronization of a map (loading objects into memory) takes a long time, this may indicate that the management station could use more memory. Before upgrading memory, try the options listed here that may reduce the amount of memory being consumed on the management station when maps are opened:

1. Configure remote consoles to distribute the display of maps. Maps that are opened from the remote console use the remote console memory to load the objects.
2. Modify the persistence level of the maps that are opened on the management station. This reduces the number of objects that are loaded into memory when a map is opened.
3. Implement a discovery filter to reduce the number of objects in the database. Because there are fewer objects in the database, the number of objects loaded into memory for polling and display is reduced.
4. Implement map filters to reduce the number of objects loaded into memory. The objects still reside in the database but are not displayed on maps containing filters. Assign different map filters to different maps.
5. Configure a collection station to discover a portion of the network. Maps displayed from a collection station only load objects that reside in the collection station's database.
6. Use the network presenter. Although this does not reduce memory on the management station because ovw must still be running, it does reduce the requirements on the display station.

Sealey Inc. needs a network monitoring solution that scales well. Because their customers do not currently have a monitoring solution, no one knows what the customer networks consist of (the number of nodes, routers, or the topology). Network operators have workstations (UNIX and Windows) that can be utilized to offload some of the resources from the management station.

Due to the network sizes and security issues, Sealey Inc. may be required to implement NNM stations on some of the customer networks. Many of the customers have firewalls between Sealey Inc. and their private networks. These firewalls do not allow ICMP and SNMP traps to pass through them.

Many of the operators have very specific skills that require them to monitor critical devices. They need custom maps that display only the critical devices. Custom maps allow the operator to monitor and troubleshoot the devices more efficiently.

If necessary, Sealey Inc. can ignore certain devices' types, such as DHCP devices. They would like to provide IP address ranges that will not be discovered or managed by their monitoring solution.

Many NNM features provide the capability to scale network management to the enterprise. This chapter provides technical details on the implementation of remote consoles, management and collection stations, and the different types of filters.

9.1 REMOTE CONSOLES

The purpose of configuring a remote console is to distribute the NNM ovw map display. Remote consoles communicate with the management station using either NFS or Windows operating systems file sharing. Whenever an NNM map is open on the remote console, all objects on persistent submaps are loaded into memory. The remote console utilizes its local resources (CPU and memory) when loading objects into memory. All databases remain on the NNM management station and all remote consoles access a consistent set of status and device information from these central databases. NNM supports up to twenty-five remote consoles from a single management server. Because NNM on UNIX uses NFS, the remote console must reside on the same LAN as the management station. While WAN links are supported for Windows file sharing, they are slow and should be avoided for NNM on Windows. See Table 9-1 for supportability of management server and remote console client.

Table 9-1 Supported Client/Server Configurations for Remote Consoles

Server	Client
UNIX Server	UNIX Client, Windows Client
Windows Server	Windows Client

9.1.1 Configuring Remote Consoles for UNIX

The following steps allow you to NFS export the required file systems from the NNM management station, provide client access to the file systems, NFS mount the file systems on the client, and run NNM.

Server Configuration

1. Export the NNM file systems **/var/opt/OV/share** and **/etc/opt/OV/share**.[1]
   Add the following entries to **/etc/exports** on the management server:

   ```
   /var/opt/OV/share -root=client
   /etc/opt/OV/share -root=client
   ```

2. Execute the command **exportfs -av**.
3. Add the hostname of the client to the **ovwdb.auth** and **ovw.auth** files to provide access to the database. Both files are located in the $OV_CONF directory. The "+" indicates any user can have access to the database.

   ```
   client +
   ```

Client Configuration

1. Install NNM on the client system, including all file sets.
2. Mount the server's exported file system.[2]
3. Add the following entries to the /etc/fstab file where server is the hostname of the management server:

   ```
   server:/var/opt/OV    /var/opt/OV
   server:/etc/opt/OV    /etc/opt/OV
   ```

4. Execute the command **mount -av**.
5. Run the **ovwsetupclient** script **ovwsetupclient** ***server***.
6. Start NNM on the client system and open a custom map that was created on the management server to verify access to the NNM database. Run **ovw -server** from the command line to display the hostname of the NNM database server.

1 NFS processes must be running on the UNIX client and server systems to configure a remote console. To check the processes, type ps –ef | grep nfsd. If the nfsd process is not running, enable nfs on HP-UX by modifying /etc/rc.config.d/nfsconf file with these entries:
NFS_CLIENT=1
NFS_SERVER = 1
NUM_NFSD = 32
NUM_NFSIOD = 16
Turn on NFS v3
After modifying nfsconf, execute the command /sbin/init.d/nfs.server start on the server and /sbin/init.d/nfs.client start on the client system. For more detailed information on NFS, refer to the UNIX man pages for nfs, nfsd, exportfs, and mount.

2 You can actually mount a file system on top of an existing file system and files will not be deleted or destroyed. However, if the server file systems become unmounted you will be using a local database. If you plan on using the remote console permanently you should remove the contents of /var/opt/OV, /etc/opt/OV, and /opt/OV on the client before mounting the server's file systems.

9.1.2 Configuring Remote Consoles for Windows NT/2000

Configuration for Windows to Windows is configured using the Windows file sharing software. The following steps document procedures for the server and client configuration for both Windows XP and Windows 2000 systems:

Server Configuration

1. Share the OpenView file system on the NNM management server. Typically, NNM resides in **\Program Files\HP OpenView** directory but it can be stored in a different location on your system. Make sure to share the directory in which NNM was installed. To share the directory, right-click the %install_dir% directory from the Windows Explorer. Select **Sharing...** and click the radio button **Share this folder** and click **[OK]**. Make sure the permissions are set to allow Full Control, Change, and Read access.
2. Add the client hostname followed by a plus sign to the **ovwdb.auth** file. The "+" grants access to any user on the client system.
   ```
   client +
   ```

Client Configuration

1. Verify that name resolution of the server is functioning on the client:
   ```
   nslookup hostname
   ```
2. Install NNM on the client using the Remote Console option. You will be prompted for the hostname of the server. NNM will establish connectivity to the server and provide access to the database.
3. Start NNM on the client and verify access by opening a custom submap that exists on the server.

9.1.3 Configuring Remote Consoles for UNIX/Windows

Remote consoles work in a combined UNIX/Windows environment only if the server is a UNIX system. This configuration requires installing NFS software on the Windows system. NFS software is available from the following vendors:

- Intergraph® DiskAccess
- WRQ® NFS
- Hummingbird® Maestro
- FTP® Software

Server Configuration

1. Export the NNM file systems /var/opt/OV/share and /etc/opt/OV/share.
   Add the following entries to /etc/exports on the management server:
   ```
   /var/opt/OV/share -root=client
   /etc/opt/OV/share -root=client
   ```
   Execute the command **exportfs –av**.

2. Add the hostname of the client to the **ovwdb.auth** and **ovw.auth** files to provide access to the database. Both files are located in the $OV_CONF directory. The "+" indicates any user can have access to the database.
```
client +
```

Client Configuration

1. On each system to be made an HP OpenView Remote Console (Windows), use your NFS software on the PC Remote Console to map the UNIX directories. Use Windows Explorer's "Map Network Drive" function. Be sure to consult your NFS software documentation about how to enable locking.
2. On each HP OpenView Remote Console system, insert the NNM installation CD, run setup.exe, and select "Remote Console Installation". Supply the two mapped drive letters configured in step 1.

9.2 CONFIGURING THE ON-DEMAND LEVEL FOR A MAP

The demand level of a map determines the level at which submaps will be persistent. All objects on a persistent submap are loaded into memory as long as the map remains open. A submap that is not persistent is transient. Objects on a transient submap are only loaded into memory when the transient submap is accessed. The demand level may be customized to affect the number of objects that are loaded into memory when a map is opened. When setting the demand level of a map, keep in mind that certain features of NNM, including third-party applications, may require an object to be persistent in order to function properly. For this reason, you may define a persistence filter to cause a submap containing any object that meets the filter criteria to be persistent. The persistence filter is applied in the same dialog box as defining the demand level, shown in Figure 9-1 (developing filters is covered in Section 9.4, "Defining Filters"). The following steps allow you to configure the demand level of a map:

1. Select **Map→Properties** from menu bar.
2. Select IP Map and click **[Configure For This Map...]**.
3. As shown in Figure 9-1, select one of the following levels beneath the section:
   - On-demand: To what level should submaps be persistent?
   - All Levels
   - Segment Level and Higher
   - Network Level and Higher
   - Internet Level
4. Click **[Verify]** and **[OK]**.

Figure 9-1 To modify the persistence level of a map, select **Map→Properties**, select **IP Map**, and click **[Configure For This Map...]**. Select the persistence level from the drop-down list as shown.

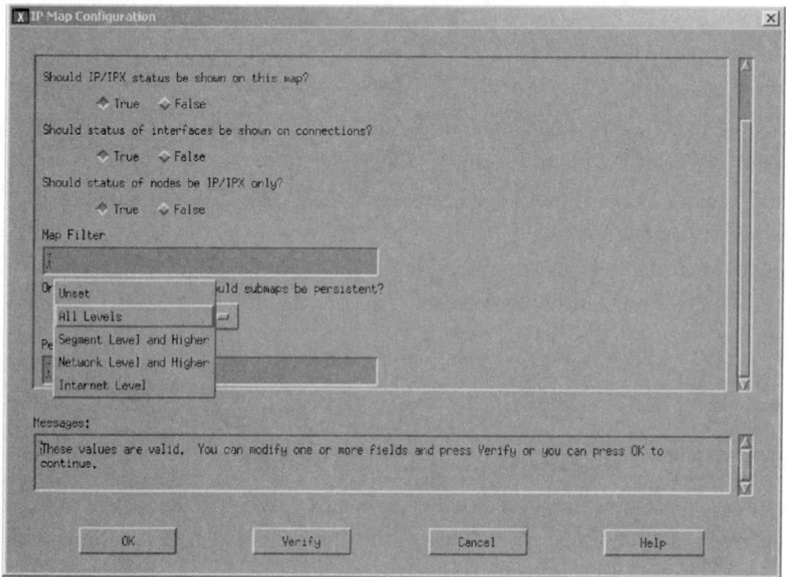

9.3 CONFIGURING THE POLLING FREQUENCY

The default status polling (ping) interval for all nodes is once every fifteen minutes.[3] As discussed in Chapter 5, "Network Discovery," the netmon polling statistics allow you to determine whether the management station is adequately able to poll the managed devices. Select from the menu bar **Performance→Network Polling Statistics**. If the MIB variable **Seconds Until Next Status Poll** consistently has a negative value, **netmon** is not adequately able to poll the managed devices. If your management station is unable to sufficiently poll all the devices at this frequency, you have several options:

Note: Earlier implementations of NNM define a five minute polling interval. Increasing the global polling interval to 15 minutes increases the number of devices a single NNM station can support because the station polls fewer devices per hour. However, a higher polling interval increases the time it takes to detect a node that has gone down. You may consider reducing the polling interval of mission critical devices. NNM 7 allows you to configure the polling intervals for classes of objects, such as routers or switches. Use the [Poll Objects...] button on the SNMP Configuration dialog box to configure class-based polling intervals.

3 Prior to version 7, NNM used a status polling interval of five minutes.

1. Increase the polling interval for non-critical devices.
2. Reduce the number of devices being polled by using discovery filters.
3. Configure a collection station to reduce the number of systems being polled by a single management station.

You can modify **netmon**'s polling frequency by selecting **Options→SNMP Configuration**, as shown in Figure 9-2. You can modify the polling frequency for all devices by selecting Global Default, or you can poll specific nodes less frequently. Hostnames and IP addresses may be used in the Target field. IP address wildcards and ranges may be used when specifying an IP address. Table 9-2 lists examples of specifying a Target.

Table 9-2 Hostnames, IP Addresses, IP Address Wildcards and Ranges

Hostname	**myhost.hp.com**
IP address	156.153.202.1
IP address wildcard	156.153.202.*
IP address range	156.153.[202-205].1

The other two suggested options, the use of discovery filters and collection stations, are discussed in Section 9.4.4, "Discovery Filters," and 9.5.1, "CS Configuration."

Figure 9-2 Configure the polling interval by selecting **Options→SNMP Configuration.** The polling interval for all devices is modified by selecting **Global Default**, changing the **Status Polling** field, and clicking the **[Replace]** button.

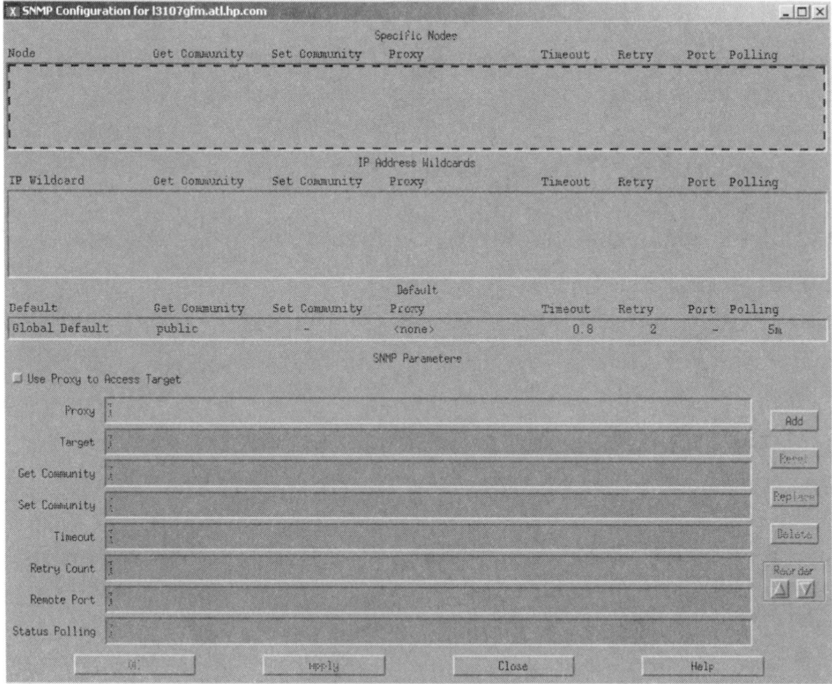

9.4 DEFINING FILTERS

Filters are designed to eliminate clutter on submaps and subsequently reduce the number of objects that are loaded into memory when a map is opened, sent from a collection station to a management station, or that are discovered by netmon. The type of filter (discovery, map, or topology) is determined based on how the filter is implemented. All filters are defined in the file **$OV_CONF/C/filters**. Filters are defined using the three building blocks: sets, filters, and filter expressions.

NNM provides a default filters file that can be used when defining filters. Refer to the sample filters file listed in Section 9.4.1, "The Default Filters File." The filters file must contain the following three elements in the following order:

Sets { }

Filters { }

FilterExpressions { }

To define a filter, determine a common attribute for the devices you are interested in capturing.[4] For example, a common attribute might be all the devices manufactured by a particular vendor. In some cases, you may not be able to capture all the devices with one filter definition. For example, what if you were interested in all devices by the same vendor or devices that include the network or segment attribute? You may also encounter a list of hostnames or IP addresses that have no common attribute. A set allows you to define lists of hostnames and IP address ranges. Listed are some examples used in the default filters file:

1. Devices made by Hewlett-Packard. These reside in the filters section of the filter file.

```
HPNodes "Hewlett-Packard nodes" { isNode && ( vendor ==
"Hewlett-Packard" )
```

2. Objects which represent either a network or a segment. These also reside in the filters section.

```
NetsNSegs "All networks & segments" { isNetwork || isSegment }
```

3. A list of hostnames. This resides in the sets section.

```
servers "Set of Servers" { "sv1", "sv2", "sv3" }
```

A filter must be defined to reference a set. This resides in the filters section.

```
ServersSet "Any designated Server node" { "IP Hostname" in
servers }
```

4. Object attributes may be listed typing ovobjprint -s selectionName from the command line. SelectionName is name of the object in the database. If necessary, use ovtopodump -L to list all objects in the topology database. Object attributes may also be obtained from the NNM GUI by right clicking the symbol, selecting Object Properties… and viewing the Capabilities, General Attributes, or IP Map attributes of the object.

4. Devices defined by at least one of the filters or sets above. These reside in the FilterExpressions section.

```
MyNet "HP nodes, nets, segs, or servers " { HPNodes || NetsNSegs
|| ServersSet }
```

Not all object attributes can be used in a filter or filter expression. NNM supports only a limited number of filterable attributes. Custom fields, described in Chapter 7, "Advanced Customization," cannot be included in defining filters. Filterable attributes are listed in Table 9-3.

Table 9-3 Filterable Attributes

isBridge	isConnector	isCollectionStationNode
isHub	isIP	isIPX
isNetWareServer	isIPXRouter	isIPRouter
isMcClusterMember	isNode	isRouter
isSNMPSupported	isRMON	isRMON2
isDS1	isDS3	isATM
isFrameRelay	isSONET	isCDP
vendor	IP Hostname	IP Status
Selection Name	NetWare Server Name	SNMPAgent
SNMP sysDescr	SNMP sysContact	SNMP sysLocation
SNMP sysObjectID	SNMP sysName	TopM Interface Count
isInterface	IPX Address	IP Subnet Mask
SNMP ifDescr	SNMP ifName	SNMP ifPhysAddr
SNMP ifType	TopM Network ID	TopM Node ID
TopM Segment ID	isbusSegment	isFDDIRingSegment
isSegment	isSerialSegment	isStarSegment
isTokenRingSegment	IP Segment Name	TopM Network ID
isNetwork	IP Network Name	IPX Network Hop Count
TopM Default Seg ID	TopM Segment Count	

9.4.1 The Default Filters File

```
//
// @(#)$OV_CONF/$LANG/filters
// @(#)HP OpenView NNM Release B.07.00  Oct 07 2003
// @(#)(c) Copyright 1990-2003 Hewlett-Packard Development
Company, LP
// $Revision: /main/NNMET/NC2.0/NCIII/2 $  $Date: 2003/05/15
20:58 UTC $
//
// This is the default filter file. These filters are
// examples which may be useful in your environment. Feel
// free to modify this file and/or add your own.
//
// You can check the syntax of this file after modifying it //
by running ovfiltercheck. See ovfiltercheck(1) for more //
details.
```

```
//
// You can check what nodes pass a filter using the ovfiltertest
command.
// For example, to see the nodes that don't support SNMP, run
// ovfiltertest -f NonSNMPNodes
// For more information, see ovfiltertest(1)
//
// You must stop and start openview processes after this file
has
// been modified (ovstop; ovstart), before changes will take
effect.
//
// See OVfilterIntro(5) for more information on this file.
//
// Sets are a simple way to list string values to test
// against in a filter. The "IN" operator tests a field value
// for membership in a set defined here.
//
// Sets {
//
// These are simple examples of sets.
// Sets are used to explicitly name a group of objects, such
// as a list of nodes to compare against. These set names are
// then used in Filters and FilterExpressions to test against
// an explicit list.
//
// servers "Set of Servers" { "sv1", "sv2", "sv3" }
// gateways "Backbone gateways " { "gw1", "gw2", "gw3" }
//
// Sets can include a filename that contains the entries.
// routers "Set of Routers" { /etc/opt/OV/share/conf/routers.set
}
//
// Filenames are useful for creating 'important nodes' filters,
which
// can easily group together your critical servers and network
// infrastructure. Comments are allowed in these 'set' files if
// the line begins with a '#'.
//
// On Windows, the 'set' file path must use forward slashes
rather
```

```
// than backslashes, and can include a drive specifier:
//  routers "Set of Routers"
//     { C:/Program Files/HP OpenView/NNM/conf/routers.txt }
//
// Important Node Sets
// ----------
//
// Explicit list of nodes (keep node list in this file)
// importantNodesHostnameList "Explicit Set of Important Nodes"
//          { "node1.myco.com", "node2.myco.com" }
//
// Windows format of a file in $OV_CONF:
//  importantNodesHostnameFile "Set of Important Nodes"
//          { C:/Program Files/HP OpenView/NNM/conf/important
            Nodes.txt }
//
// Unix format of a file in $OV_CONF:
//  importantNodesHostnameFile "Set of Important Nodes"
//          { /etc/opt/OV/share/conf/importantNodes.txt }
//
// For these Sets to be displayed in Node View, they must
// be incorporated into a "Filters" or "FilterExpressions"
definition.
// For example, see the "ImportantNodes" example below.
//
}
//
// Filters and FilterExpressions are used as Topology,
Discovery,
// Map or Persistence filters. Applications which use filters
// (like ipmap(1), ovtopmd(1m), ovtopodump(1), and
ovtopofix(1m))
// can take the name of a Filter or a FilterExpression.
//
Filters {
// The following filters are potentially useful as either
Discovery
// or Topology filters, or components for building Map filters.
//
// NOTES CONCERNING DISCOVERY FILTERS:
```

```
// Networks and Segments are not directly testing with Discovery
// filters (and so there is no need to include
// "isNetwork || isSegment" in these filters).
// However, it does not hurt to include networks or segments in
// a discovery filter, so long as you realize that they will not
// be acted on.
//
// Since nodes are only discovered in managed networks, the
network
// must already exist and be managed before the filtering test
// will be applied. New networks connected to discovered nodes
will
// be discovered unmanaged. For discovery filters,
// a node and all its interfaces can be thought of
// as a single object. If any interface or the node itself
passes the
// filter, the node and all of its interfaces will pass the
filter.
//
// ovtopofix -f follows the discovery filter semantics and only
// applies to locally monitored objects.  However, if a network
or
// segment is empty after the processing of the nodes with
the -f
// option, that segment or network will also be removed.
//
// ovtopodump(1) also follows the discovery filter semantic, and
// the filter only applies to nodes/interfaces.
//
// NOTES CONCERNING MAP AND TOPOLOGY FILTERS:
// For these filters, all objects are subject to filtering.
// One must specify the networks and segments to be passed.
// Furthermore, objects are displayed/included only if all their
// parent objects (submaps) pass the map/topology filter. For
example,
// if no networks would pass the filter ("isNetwork" is not
included),
// then all segments and non-gateways nodes would be filtered
out.
// Like Discovery filters, if any interface or
// node passes a Map filter, the node and all of its interfaces
```

```
// also pass the filter.
//
// See the FilterExpressions section for map and topology
// filter examples.
//
// Using Sets in Filters:
// An example of including a set, such as one that describes
// a file of important nodes would look like:
//
// ImportantNodes "Critical Servers and Infrastructure filelist"
//     { "IP Hostname" in importantNodesHostnameFile }
//
// where the set importantNodesHostnameFile was defined above
// in the Sets { ... } section.
//
Networks "Any network" { isNetwork }
Segments "Any segment" { isSegment }
Nodes "Any node" { isNode }
// The following filters are primarily for example purposes,
though
// they might be useful as discovery filters. They do not
generally
// make sense as map or topology filters because they do not
specify
// the inclusion of networks and segments. They also make sense as
// parts of a filter expression.
// Note: NNM considers any device that supports the Bridge MIB to
// be a bridge. This generally includes switches as well.
Routers "Any Router" { isRouter }
IPRouters "Any IP Router" { isIPRouter }
Bridges "Any bridge" { isBridge }
BridgesNSwitches "Any bridge or switch" { isBridge }
Hubs "Any multi-port repeater" { isHub }
SNMPNodes "Any node supporting SNMP" { isNode && isSNMPSupported
}
NonSNMPNodes "Any node NOT supporting SNMP"
                { isNode && !isSNMPSupported }
// The next filter is useful for defining map and topology
filters
// (see the FilterExpresssions section). It is not
// particularly useful as a discovery filter
```

```
// since all networks and segments automatically pass Discovery
// filters. Nor is it useful as a standalone
// map filter, since it doesn't pass any nodes.
        NetsNSegs "All networks & segments" { isNetwork ||
isSegment }
// This filter specifies that only objects that support IP
should
// be included. This filter should be used as a topology filter
on
// any collection station discovering non-IP information (Level
2
// or IPX only nodes or networks) that is forwarding to a
// NNM 4.X management station. This will not completely remove
// all non-IP information (e.g. IPX interfaces on a node that
also
// supports IP will come through), but will limit the impact on
the
// management station, and make migration to NNM 5.X easier.
IPOnlyObjects "Only objects that support IP"
      { isIP || isSegment }
// The following filters are examples that you can customize to
// match your environment.
// LocalLAN "Nodes with interfaces on the 15.2.112-119 subnet"
//    { "IP Address" ~ 15.2.112-119.* }
// NeighborLANs "Node with interfaces on the neighboring LANs on
site"
//    { "IP Address" ~ 192.1.2-10.* }
// HPNodes "Hewlett-Packard nodes"
//    { isNode && ( vendor == "Hewlett-Packard" ) }
// NonHPNodes "Non-HP nodes"
//    { isNode && ( vendor != "Hewlett-Packard" ) }
// These are example filters using the sets defined above.
// GatewaysSet "Any designated Gateway node"
//    { "IP Hostname" in gateways }
// ServersSet "Any designated Server node"
//    { "IP Hostname" in servers }
// The next filter is useful for defining map and topology
filters
// (see the FilterExpresssions section). It is not
// particularly useful as a discovery filter
// since all networks and segments automatically pass Discovery
// filters. Nor is it useful as a standalone
// map filter, since it doesn't pass any nodes.
//
```

```
// The network name below assumes an entry in /etc/networks.
// If no such entry exists, the actual network name will be
// something like “15.2.112”.
// MyNet “The network in which I’m interested”
// { isNetwork && “IP Network Name” == “yellow-lan” }
// This filter would be an example of a way to pass all objects
// contained in the subnet 15.2.112.0 with a subnet mask
// of 255.255.248.0 (so the subnet range is 15.2.112.0 to
// 15.2.119.255). Note that the inclusion of “isSegment” is
// not a concern, because all segments outside of this network
// would be filtered out because the networks containing them
// were filtered out. We must have some specification of
segments
// if we want the segment contents to be included.
// EngrLan “The 15.2.112 subnet used by engineering”
//     { (“IP Address” ~ 15.2.112-119.* ) || isSegment }
// This filter accomplishes the same thing, but is more
restrictive
// in the specification of segments to only include segments in
that
// engineering network. This assumes there is an entry in
/etc/networks
// such that the subnet gets the name “engr-LAN”, and hence the
segments
// in that network all have a name of form “engr-LAN.<something>”
// Generally, the above will accomplish what you want, but this
// may be necessary in some situations if you want specific
segments.
// In particular, it works well if you want to use this to
EXCLUDE
// the objects in this network. See the example in the Filter
// expressions below.
// EngrLan2 “The 15.2.112 subnet used by engineering”
//     { ( “IP Address” ~ 15.2.112-119.* ) ||
//       ( “IP Segment Name” ~ “engr-LAN.*” ) }
// The following are some sample DHCPFilters.
// They can be specified by using the Network Polling
Configuration
// dialog application, xnmpolling, on the Status Polling page.
// DHCPSubnet “Addresses in subnet 15.70.177 are DHCP allocated”
//     { “IP Address” ~ 15.70.177.* }
// DHCPNode  “A particular address is DHCP allocated”
//     { “IP Address” ~ 15.70.177.9 }
// DHCPRange “IP Addresses from 15.70.177.5 through
```

```
15.70.177.10"
//     { "IP Address" ~ 15.70.177.5-10 }
//
// Access to various nodes based on SNMP MIBs that have
// been discovered as supporting a particular MIB
//
CDPnodes "Nodes supporting Cisco Discovery Protocol" { isCDP }
ATMnodes "Nodes supporting ATM" {
    ( isATM ) ||
    ("SNMP ifType" == "ATM")  ||
    ("SNMP ifType" == "atmLogical") ||
    ("SNMP ifType" == "atmDxi") ||
    ("SNMP ifType" == "atmFuni") || ("SNMP ifType" == "atmIma")
}
DS1nodes "Nodes supporting DS1" {
    ( isDS1 ) ||
    ("SNMP ifType" == "T-1 Carrier (ds1)") }
    DS3nodes "Nodes supporting DS3" {
    ( isDS3 ) ||
    ("SNMP ifType" == "T-3 Carrier (ds3)") }
    SONETnodes "Nodes supporting SONET" {
    ( isSONET ) ||
    ("SNMP ifType" == "SONET") }
    FrameRelayNodes "Nodes supporting Frame-Relay" {
            ( isFrameRelay ) ||
        ("SNMP ifType" == "Frame Relay") ||
        ("SNMP ifType" == "Frame Relay Service") ||
        ("SNMP ifType" == "frameRelayInterconnect") }
    RMON1nodes "Nodes supporting RMON-1" { isRMON }
    RMON2nodes "Nodes supporting RMON-2" { isRMON2 }
// Short-hand for any RMON device
    RMONnodes "Nodes supporting RMON-1 or RMON-2" { isRMON ||
isRMON2 }

    MPLSnodes "Nodes supporting MPLS Protocol" { isMPLS }
    HSRPnodes "Nodes supporting HSRP Protocol" { isHSRP }
    IPV6nodes "Nodes supporting version 6 of the IP Protocol" {
isIPV6 }
    OSPFnodes "Nodes supporting OSPF Protocol" { isOSPF }
    BGP4nodes "Nodes supporting BGP4 Protocol" { isBGP4 }
    VRRPnodes "Nodes supporting VRRP Protocol" { isVRRP }
    STPnodes "Nodes supporting Spanning Tree Protocol" { isSTP }
```

```
    WirelessNodes "Nodes supporting Wireless Protocols" {
isWireless }
}

// FilterExpressions are simply combinations of filters defined
in the
// same filter file (above).  FilterExpressions make it simple
to
// combine filters without reproducing the expressions of each
// filter again
FilterExpressions {
// One can turn the filters defined above into viable map or
// topology filters by simply adding "|| NetsNSegs". (Doing so
// does not invalidate the filters as discovery
// filters. It just adds a superfluous test.)
    NetInfrastructure "Any network connecting device and what
they connect"
        { Routers || Bridges || Hubs || NetsNSegs }
    NetBackbone "Networks and gateways/routers"
        { Routers || Networks }
// The following combines the two set filters
// defined above into one FilterExpression.
// It works unmodified as a discovery filter.
// To work as a map filter, network and segment filtering
// must be added (see below).
// VitalNodes "All Gateways and Servers"
//    { GatewaysSet || ServersSet }
// One can turn the filters defined above into viable map or
// topology filters by simply adding "|| NetsNSegs". (Doing so
// does not invalidate the filters as discovery
// filters. It just adds a superfluous test.)
// VitalNodesMap "All nets & segs, but only gateway and server
nodes"
//     { GatewaysSet || ServersSet || NetsNSegs}
// LocalLANView "All nets & segs, but only local nodes"
//     { LocalLAN || NetsNSegs }
// Using the filters defined above that include only a specific
// network, we can also exclude the specific network like this
// Note the use of the more specific form to exclude only the
segments
// in the engineering lan. This could have been specified
directly
// as a negation in the filter part, but this form works well if
you
```

```
// have several networks to manipulate in this manner.
// EverythingButEngr "Everything but the engineering LAN"
//      { !EngrLan2 }
// Of course the above filter expressions, when used as
// map filters, pass all networks and segments. You
// may wish to see only a particular network. The following map
// filters accomplish this. Note that though segments
// and nodes from other networks will pass the filters, IP Map
// will ignore them because their parent networks will not pass.
// NOTE: These filters will not work as Discovery
// filters because all network and segments automatically pass
// Discovery and Topology filters.
// MyNetMap "Only the network of interest and all its con-
stituent parts"
//      { MyNet || Segments || Nodes}
// MyVitalNodesMap "Gateways, servers and segments in net of
interest"
//      { MyNet || Segments ||  GatewaysSet || ServersSet }
// This is a map persistence filter which ensures that
// all Ungermann-Bass are kept in memory and up to date.
// Note that this will also keep any containing submaps in mem-
ory.
// PersFilter "Objects to keep in map memory"
//      { HPNodes }
}
```

9.4.2 The Filters File Syntax

All filters must be defined in a file named *filters* and must reside in the $OV_CONF/C directory. This is the only filter definition file. The basic syntax of the filters file for each section is
`FilterName "Comment" { Filter }`

The FilterName is actually either a set name, filter name or filter expression name. It is the label used when applying the filter. In the previous example, HPNodes, NetsNSegs, and servers are all filter names. Comments can be used to describe the filter and are enclosed in double quotes (""). The filter is enclosed in curly brackets { } and can be any of the filterable attributes (listed in Table 9-3) combined by the operators listed in Table 9-4.

Table 9-4 Valid Operators for Writing Filters

Operator	Description
==	Equal to
!=	Not equal to
>	Greater than
>=	Greater than or equal to
<	Less than
<=	Less than or equal to
~	Like (used in pattern matching)
!~	Not like (also used in pattern matching)
IN	Is a member of the set

9.4.2.1 Attribute Value Assertions

The operators listed in Table 9-4 may be used in *Attribute Value Assertions* (AVA). An AVA is a statement used to describe a condition. An AVA statement evaluates to TRUE or FALSE and may use one of four types of operands:

Boolean	**isRouter**
Integer	**numInterfaces > 1**
String	**vendor == "Hewlett-Packard"**
Enumerated	**"IP Hostname" == "sv1"**

AVAs can be written in a number of ways. The following two examples evaluate the same way:

isRouter

isRouter == TRUE

These two examples also give the same result:

! isRouter

isRouter == FALSE

Wildcards and ranges may be used in defining conditions for IP addresses and SNMP OIDs. A wildcard may be specified using an asterisk (*) to capture all number. A range may be specified using a hyphen (-) to capture a portion of numbers. You can use wildcards and ranges independently or combined. When using wildcards and ranges, you must use the like (~) operator. Here are some examples:

"IP Address" ~ 192. 201. 10.*

"IP Address" ~ 192.201.1-10.1

"IP Address" ~ 192.201.1-10.*

"SNMP sysObjectID" ~ .1.3.6.1.4.1.11.*

"SNMP sysObjectID ~ .1.3.6.1.4.1.1-11.*

9.4.2.2 Testing Your Filter

NNM provides two command-line utilities to help you check and test filters. The first utility, **ovfiltercheck** allows you to check the syntax of the filters file. The **ovfiltercheck** command does not require any arguments. You simply type **ovfiltercheck** from the command line. If there are syntax errors in the filters file, the error and line number are written to standard out. If there are no syntax errors, **ovfiltercheck** lists all the sets, filters, and filter expressions by name. The output of the **ovfiltercheck** looks something like this:

```
Filter Table /etc/opt/OV/share/conf/C/filters
=============================================


Sets {
}


Filters {
  Bridges "Any bridge"  { (isBridge) }
  Hubs "Any multi-port repeater"  { (isHub) }
  IPOnlyObjects "Only objects that support IP"  { ((isIP) ||
(isSegment)) }
  IPRouters "Any IP Router"  { (isIPRouter) }
  NetsNSegs "All networks & segments"  { ((isNetwork) ||
(isSegment)) }
  Networks "Any network"  { (isNetwork) }
  Nodes "Any node"  { (isNode) }
  Routers "Any Router"  { (isRouter) }
  SNMPNode "Any node supporting SNMP"  { ((isNode) &&
(isSNMPSupported)) }
  Segments "Any segment"  { (isSegment) }
}


FilterExpressions {
  NetBackbone "Networks and gateways/routers"  { (Routers ||
Networks) }
  NetInfrastructure "Any network connecting device and what they
connect"  { (((
```

```
Routers || Bridges) || Hubs) || NetsNSegs) }

Defined Filter List
===================
Bridges
Hubs
IPOnlyObjects
IPRouters
NetBackbone
NetInfrastructure
NetsNSegs
Networks
Nodes
Routers
SNMPNode
Segments

Defined Set List
================
No sets defined
```

The second utility used in testing filters is **ovfiltertest**. This utility can be used to display the number of object passing the filter. For example, to test the number of objects passing the NetsNSegs filter type **ovfiltertest –f NetsNSegs** on the command line.

The output of the **ovfiltertest** command looks something like this:

```
Running filter NetsNSegs
PASSED: 15.32.120.Segment1
PASSED: 172.20.4.Segment1
PASSED: 172.20.4
PASSED: 15.32.120
Objects tested: 441, Objects passed: 4
```

Filter names (filters, sets, and filter expressions) are case sensitive. For example, if you had typed netsnsegs instead of NetsNSegs you would receive the message:

```
No such filter netsnsegs
No such filter
_______________

File: /etc/opt/OV/share/conf/C/filters
Error: "netsnsegs", filter not defined (-892)
_______________
```

Because NNM ships with a default filters file, both **ovfiltercheck** and **ovfiltertest** can be used without making any modifications to the file. You may try these utilities out before making any changes to the existing filters file. In the event that you destroy the filters file beyond repair and have made no backup, refer to the $OV_NEW_CONF/OVNNM-RUN/conf/C/filters for an original copy.

9.4.3 Map Filters

A map filter is one of the simplest filters to apply. The purpose of a map filter is to alter the view only. It does not remove anything from the database, only from the view of the map to which it is applied. A filter does not take effect until it is applied. Only one map filter may be applied to a map. Different maps can have different filters. Listed below are the steps to apply the filter named MyNet given the following filters file:

```
Sets {
servers "Set of Servers" { "sv1", "sv2", "sv3" }
}


Filters {
NetsNSegs "All networks & segments"  { ((isNetwork) || (isSeg-
ment))
HPNodes "Hewlett-Packard nodes" { isNode && ( vendor ==
"Hewlett-Packard" )
ServersSet "Any designated Server node" { "IP Hostname" in
servers }
}


FilterExpressions {
MyNet "HP nodes, nets, segs, or servers " { HPNodes || NetsNSegs
|| ServersSet }
}
```

1. Add the filter, set, and filter expressions to $OV_CONF/C/filters as necessary.
2. Test the filter expression using the ovfiltercheck and ovfiltertest utilities:
   ovfiltercheck
   ovfiltertest –f MyNet
3. When satisfied with the results, apply the filter expression **MyNet** as a map filter by selecting **Map→Properties** from the ovw GUI.
4. Select **IP Map** from Configurable Applications and click **[Configure For This Map…]**.
5. Using the filter name MyNet defined previously, type **MyNet** in the field labeled Map Filter. Refer to Figure 9-3 for the dialog box used when applying a map filter.
6. Click **[Verify]**.
7. Click **[OK]** in both dialog boxes.

Figure 9-3 To apply a map filter, select **Map→Properties**, select **IP Map** and click **[Configure For This Map…]**. Type the name of the map filter, **MyNet**, in the **Map Filter** field and click the **[Verify]** button and **[OK]** twice.

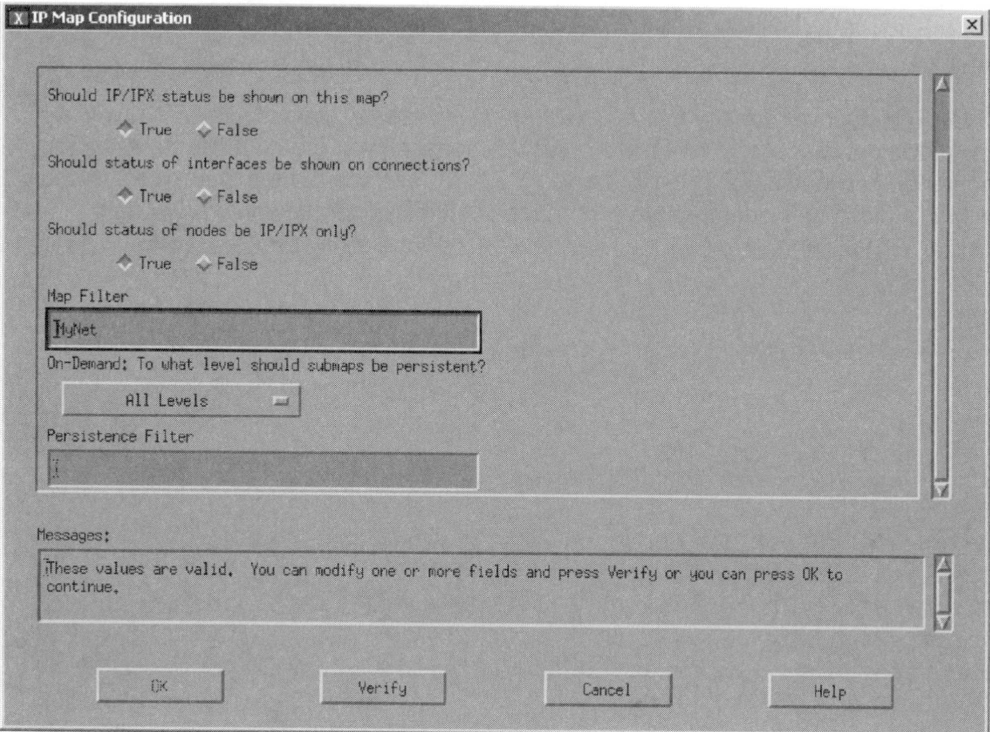

The resulting map displays the servers sv1, sv2, sv3, all network and segment devices, and all Hewlett-Packard devices.

Note: When writing a map filter, you must include network and segment devices as part of the filter expression. The default filters file includes the NetsNSegs that will include all network and segment devices. If you do not include network and segment devices, the map in which your filter is applied will be empty.

A map filter may be removed simply by deleting the filter name from the **Map Filter** field in the **IP Map Configuration** dialog box (Figure 9-3) and clicking **[OK]** twice. It is not required to remove the filter and filter expressions from the filters file in order to remove a filter.

9.4.4 Discovery Filters

A discovery filter actually affects which devices are added to the object database. Use a discovery filter to eliminate the discovery of specific devices. One example of a discovery filter would be if you were only interested in monitoring particular devices, such as network infrastructure devices and mission critical servers. Given the following filters file, here are the steps to apply a discovery filter:

Note: The discovery of any interface *automatically* creates its associated network segment and network object within the object database. If you create a filter to discover nodes on networks 15.2.112-199.* and 15.3.123.* and there are multi-homed nodes on either of those networks that have interfaces configured for networks *other than* 15.2.112-199.* and 15.3.123.*, all the networks will be discovered.

```
Sets {
servers "Set of Servers" { "sv1", "sv2", "sv3" }
}

Filters {
NetsNSegs "All networks & segments"  { ((isNetwork) ||
(isSegment)) }
HPNodes "Hewlett-Packard nodes" { isNode && ( vendor ==
"Hewlett-Packard" ) }
ServersSet "Any designated Server node" { "IP Hostname" in
servers }
ImportantNodes "Important systems" { "IP Address" ~
15.2.112-119.* }
}

FilterExpressions {
CriticalDevices "HP nodes, nets, segs, or servers " { HPNodes ||
NetsNSegs || ServersSet || ImportantNodes }
}
```

1. Add the filter, set, and filter expressions to $OV_CONF/C/filters as necessary.
2. Test the filter syntax using the **ovfiltercheck**.
3. Test the filter expression and check the results. Correct the filter syntax and retest if needed:
   ovfiltertest –f CriticalDevices
4. When satisfied with the results, apply the filter expression **CriticalDevices** as a discovery filter by selecting **Options→Network Polling Configuration:IP** from the NNM GUI, as shown in Figure 9-4.
5. In the General Configuration Area, toggle on the box labeled [**Use Discovery Filter**].
6. Enter your filter expression name, **CriticalDevices**.
7. Click [**OK**].
8. Stop the netmon process:
   ovstop netmon
9. Apply the filter to the existing database. This will remove devices in the database that do not pass the filter CriticalDevices:
   ovtopfix –f CriticalDevices
10. Start the netmon process:
    ovstart netmon

Figure 9-4 To apply a discovery filter, select **Options→Network Polling and Configuration: IP**. Toggle on the **Use Discovery Filter** found in the **General Configuration Area** and type the name of the discovery filter. Click **[OK]**.

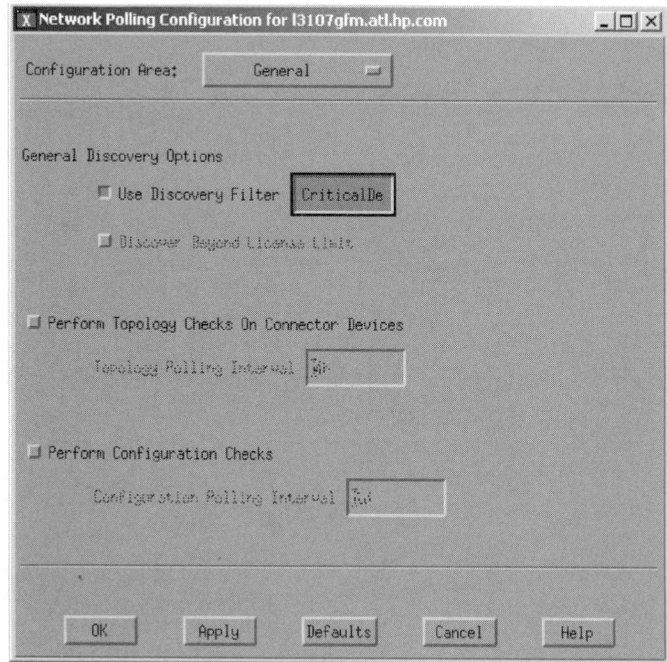

The resulting database will only include nodes defined by the **CriticalDevices** filter expression. This filter includes sv1, sv2, sv3, Hewlett-Packard devices, network objects, segment objects, and devices in the IP address range 15.2.112-119.*. The network and segment attributes are not required entries in the discovery filter, and it does not matter if they exist in your filter.

Because a discovery filter applies to the topology database as opposed to the map database, only one discovery filter may be defined per NNM system. It must include all the devices that any operator may want to see in any map. It may take several iterations to get the results you are looking for when writing a discovery filter.

A discovery filter can be removed by un-checking the **[Use Discovery Filter]** field in the **Network Polling Configuration: IP** dialog box and clicking **[OK]**.

9.4.5 Topology Filters

A topology filter resides on a *Collection Station* (CS) and determines which devices to pass to a *Management Station* (MS). In this way, you are able to limit the view of the CS from the MS by allowing only a subset of objects to be passed to the MS. The configuration of CS and MS will be discussed in more detail in Section 9.5, "Distributed Internet Monitoring." Using the following filters file, follow the subsequent steps to apply the **TopoFilter** filter.

```
Sets {
servers "Set of Servers" { "sv1", "sv2", "sv3" }
}

Filters {
NetsNSegs "All networks & segments"  { ((isNetwork) ||
(isSegment)) }
HPNodes "Hewlett-Packard nodes" { isNode && ( vendor ==
"Hewlett-Packard" ) }
ServersSet "Any designated Server node" { "IP Hostname" in
servers }
ImportantNodes "Important systems" { "IP Address" ~
15.2.112-119.* }
}

FilterExpressions {
CriticalDevices "HP nodes, nets, segs, or servers " { HPNodes ||
NetsNSegs || ServersSet || ImportantNodes }
TopoFilter "HP nodes, nets, segs, and important sys" { HPNodes
|| NetsNSegs || ImportantNodes }
}
```

1. Add the filter, set, and filter expressions to $OV_CONF/C/filters as necessary.
2. Test the filter expression using the **ovfiltercheck** and **ovfiltertest** utilities:
   ovfiltercheck
   ovfiltertest –f CriticalDevices
3. Verify the results of the topology filter with ovtopodump by specifying the hostname of your system and the topology filter name.
   ovtopodump –f TopoFilter
4. Add –f TopoFilter to the $OV_LRF/ovtopmd.lrf file.
   OVs_YES_START:pmd,ovwdb:-O –f TopoFilter:Ovs_WELL_BEHAVED:15:PAUSE
5. Execute the following commands to update ovsuf with the new topology filter.
   ovstop –v
   ovaddobj $OV_LRF/ovtopmd.lrf
   ovstart –v

A topology filter cannot be fully implemented until you have configured a separate NNM system as a management station. This will be covered in Section 9.5. Network and segment devices must be included in the definition of a topology filter. A simple way to test a topology filter on the CS is to apply it as a map filter. When satisfied with the results of the map, remove the map filter and apply it as a topology filter.

A topology filter may be deleted by removing the ***–f filtername*** from **ovtopmd.lrf** and executing **ovstop, ovaddobj**, and **ovstart** as described in step 5 of the previous list.

9.4.6 Persistence Filters

Persistence filters are used to include systems when the demand level is set to anything other than **All Levels**. Recall that the demand level determines which levels of the network hierarchy devices are to be loaded into memory for display in ovw. A persistence filter causes an object to be resident in memory when the map is opened. If an object passes the filter, the object and all devices contained in the submap on which the object resides become persistent. Listed in the following are the steps to apply a persistence filter.

```
Sets {
}

Filters {
HPNodes "Hewlett-Packard nodes" { isNode && ( vendor ==
"Hewlett-Packard" ) }
}

FilterExpressions {
}
```

1. Add the filter to $OV_CONF/C/filters file.
2. Test the filter expression using the **ovfiltercheck** and **ovfiltertest** utilities.
   ovfiltercheck
   ovfiltertest –f HPNodes
3. When satisfied with the results, apply the filter expression HPNodes as a persistence filter by selecting **Map→Properties** from the ovw GUI.
4. Select IP Map from Configurable Applications and click **[Configure For This Map…]**.
5. Using the filter name HPNodes defined above, type HPNodes in the field labeled Persistence Filter. Refer to Figure 9-5 for the dialog box used when applying a persistence filter.
6. Click **[Verify]**.
7. Click **[OK]** in both dialog boxes.

Figure 9-5 To apply a persistence filter, select **Map?Properties**, select **IP Map** from **Configurable Applications** and click **[Configure For This Map…]**. Type the persistence filter name in the Persistence Filter field.

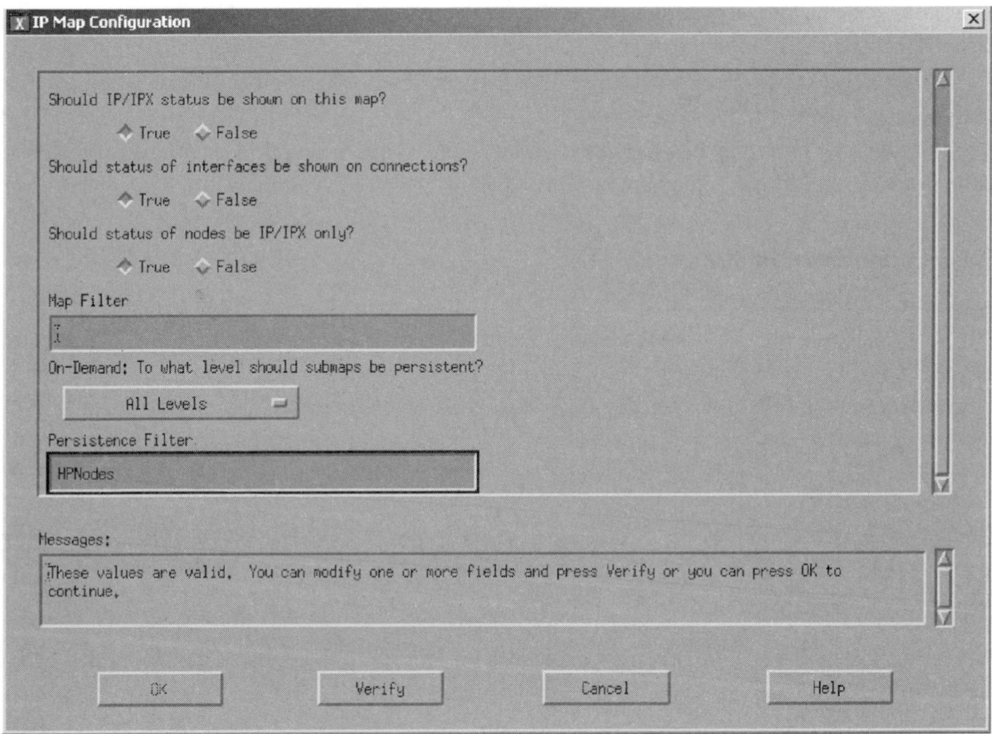

The resulting map contains all persistent submaps plus all submaps that contain Hewlett-Packard devices. Only one persistence filter may be applied to a map. Different persistence filters may be applied to different maps to allow a user to customize his or her map.

A persistence filter may be removed by deleting the filter name from the **IP Map Configuration** dialog box and clicking **[OK]** in the two required dialog boxes.

9.4.7 Important Nodes Filter

The purpose of an important node filter is to treat important secondary devices as primary devices during an outage. A secondary failure occurs when **netmon** cannot perform a status poll of a device because a connection device between NNM and the device has failed. For example, assume that you have a mission critical database server on a subnet other than the one on which NNM resides. If the connection device between NNM and the database server fails, the default behavior of NNM is to use the multiplier (2) to calculate the polling frequency for secondary devices. This means the database server and all other devices on that subnet would be polled every 30 minutes instead of every 15 minutes. Because the database server is mission critical, you may want to tag it as an important node.

An important node filter may be defined using the following steps:

```
Sets {
dbservers "Set of DB Servers" { "dbs1", "dbs2", "dbs3" }
}

Filters {
DBserversFilter "Database Servers" { "IP Hostname" in dbservers
}
}

FilterExpressions {
}
```

1. Add the filter, set, and filter expressions to **$OV_CONF/C/filters** as necessary.
2. Test the filter expression using the **ovfiltercheck** and **ovfiltertest** utilities.
   ovfiltercheck
   ovfiltertest –f DBserversFilter
3. When satisfied with the results, apply the filter expression DBserversFilter as an important nodes filter by selecting **Options→Network Polling Configuration:IP** from the NNM GUI, as shown in Figure 9-6.
4. Select **Secondary Failures** from the Configuration Area and toggle on the box labeled Secondary Failure Polling Options.
5. Toggle on the **Identify Important Nodes Using Filter** button and type the filter name **DbserversFilger** in the field.

6. Select the setting you would like for Failure Status of Important Nodes: Down or Unknown.
7. Click **[OK]**.

Figure 9-6 To apply an important nodes filter select **Options→Network Polling and Configuration: IP**. Select **Secondary Failures** from the Configuration Area. Toggle on the **Secondary Failure Polling Options** and the **Identify Important Nodes Using Filters** buttons and type the important nodes filter name in this field.

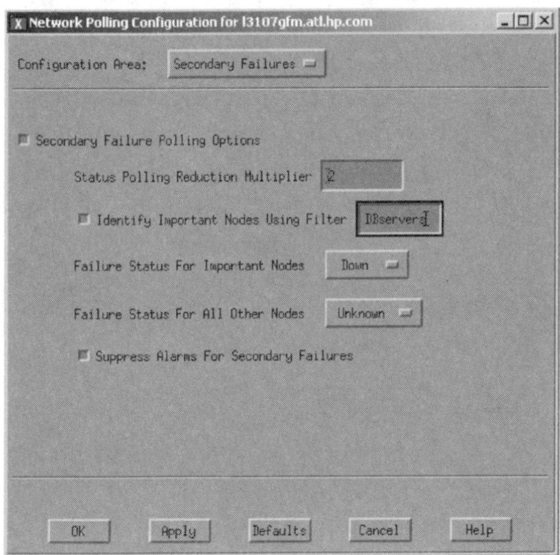

The resulting configuration polls the database servers dbs1, dbs2, and dbs3 with the same polling frequency as primary devices during a network outage. Only one important nodes filter may be applied per NNM station. More importantly, the alarms for the important nodes are displayed directly in the alarm browser, not correlated under the alarm for the primary failure. The important nodes filter may be removed by toggling off the **Important Nodes Using Filter** button.

9.4.8 DHCP Filters

Dynamic Host Configuration Protocol (DHCP) automatically assigns IP addresses and delivers TCP/IP configuration parameters such as the subnet mask and the default router. Typically, DHCP devices are mobile devices such as laptops. They might also be systems that are shutdown during nights and weekends. These devices appear in NNM as going down frequently, causing Critical alarms and "red" symbols. One way to handle DHCP devices is to use a discovery filter to completely eliminate them from the database. Another way is to treat them with a special set of rules by using a DHCP filter.

By default, NNM deletes a device from the database if it is down for one week, assuming that the device has been removed from the network. When defining DHCP devices, you may specify the window in which the devices may be deleted from the database. For example, if a DHCP device is down for 2 hours you may have it deleted from the database. The second "delete" field does not delete the record for the laptop from the database. It removes the IP address from the record so that the IP address can be assigned to some other record. When the IP address is removed from the record, the label reverts to the MAC address on the display. Listed here are the steps to apply a DHCP filter:

```
Filters {
DHCPnodes "DHCP nodes" { isNode && { "IP Address" ~ 15.2.112.* }
}
```

1. Add the filter listed previously to include the DHCP IP address range of your enterprise to $OV_CONF/C/filters file.
2. Test the filter expression using the **ovfiltercheck** and **ovfiltertest** utilities.
   ovfiltercheck
   ovfiltertest –f DHCPnodes
3. When satisfied with the results, apply the filter expression DHCPnodes as a DHCP filter by selecting **Options→Network Polling Configuration:IP** from the NNM GUI.
4. Select the **Status Polling Configuration Area**.
5. Toggle on the **DHCP Polling Options** button.
6. Toggle on the **Identify the DHCP IP Address Using Filter** field.
7. Type the filter name **DHCPnodes** in the field.
8. If you would like to modify the deletion window, modify the **field Delete Identified DHCP IP Addresses If Down For** field. The default is 8h (8 hours).
9. Click **[OK]**.

Figure 9-7 To apply a DHCP filter, select **Options→Network Polling Configuration:IP** from the NNM GUI. Select the **Status Polling** Configuration Area. Toggle on the **DHCP Polling Options** and **Identify DHCP IP Addresses Using Filter** buttons. Type the filter name in this field.

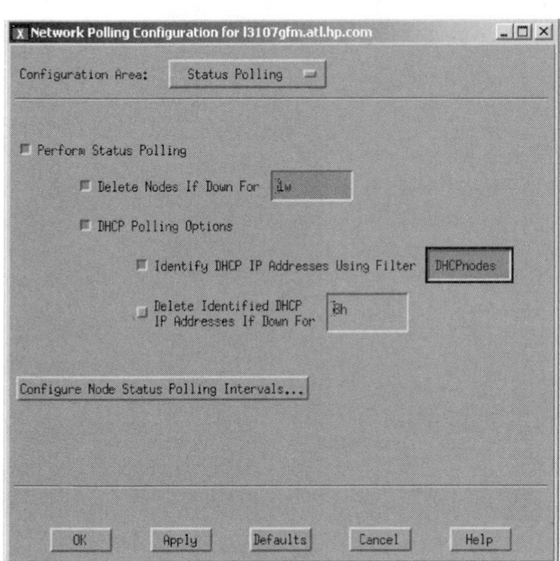

The resulting map will still have the nodes using DHCP displayed. If the IP address doesn't respond to status polling for 8 hours, the label reverts to the MAC address. Only one DHCP filter can be applied to per management station. To delete the DCCP filter, toggle off the **DHCP Polling Options** button.

9.4.9 Failover Filers

A failover filter allows an MS to pick up status polling responsibility for a CS that fails. The configuration for MS/CS is discussed in detail in Section 9.5. When defining a failover filter, you must first issue the command to enable failover. The **xnmtopoconf** command is issued on the MS, and *stationlist* is a list of CS(s) to be managed by the MS in the event of the CS failure.

xnmtopoconf –failover ***stationlist***

The failover filter must then be specified to include the objects to be polled by the MS. The failover filter is applied using the following steps:

```
Sets {
servers "Set of Servers" { "sv1", "sv2", "sv3" }
dbservers "Set of DB Servers" { "dbs1", "dbs2", "dbs3" }
}
```

```
Filters {
NetsNSegs "All networks & segments"  { ((isNetwork) ||
(isSegment)) }
HPNodes "Hewlett-Packard nodes" { isNode && ( vendor ==
"Hewlett-Packard" ) }
ServersSet "Any designated Server node" { "IP Hostname" in
servers }
ImportantNodes "Important systems" { "IP Address" ~
15.2.112-119.* }
DBservers "Database Servers" { "IP Hostname" in dbservers }
}


FilterExpressions {
FailoverFilter "HP nodes, nets, segs, and important sys" {
HPNodes || NetsNSegs || ImportantNodes || DBservers }
}
```

1. Add the sets, filters, and filter expressions to $OV_CONF/C/filters file.
2. Test the filter expression using the **ovfiltercheck** and **ovfiltertest** utilities.
   ovfiltercheck
   ovfiltertest –f FailoverFilter
3. When satisfied with the results, issue the following commands on the MS to enable failover and to specify the failover filter:
   xnmtopoconf –failover ***stationlist***
   xnmtopoconf –failoverFilter FailoverFilter ***stationlist***

   Failover can be disabled by issuing the following command:
   xnmtopoconf –nofailover
   You can remove the filter by typing
   xnmtopocof -FailoverFilter ""

A sample filters file is available for download from the server `ftp://ftp.prenhall.com` for both UNIX and Windows systems. Obtain the Readme file for this chapter for a description of the filters file provided at this site.

9.5 DISTRIBUTED INTERNET MONITORING (DIM)

NNM allows a single management station to manage tens of thousands of geographically dispersed nodes by implementing *Distributed Internet Monitoring* (DIM). DIM may be configured one of several ways. An implementation of DIM uses CS, MS, and MSs doubling as CSs to monitor specific portions of a network enterprise. These CSs are "managed" by one or more MSs. The topology and the status of each object are sent from the CS to the management station that "managed" each object. Any detected change in object status at the CS is sent to the MS, thus allowing a single MS to manage more nodes than if it were configured as a standalone system. The discovery and monitoring of the network are now distributed throughout the enterprise and may pass the information to one or more MS's acting central database location. SNMP traps can also be forwarded from the CS to the MS; some are automatically forwarded by virtue of the CS being managed by an MS. Multiple MSs can manage a single CS.

Note: At minimum, an Advanced Edition license is required for any system to be configured as an MS. A CS may use Starter Edition or Advanced Edition. An Enterprise license is required for a Management Station to configure and start the ovrepld process that allows the MS to "manage" a CS to replicate a CS topology.

The architecture of DIM may be configured hierarchically (shown in Figure 9-8) or peer-to-peer. In the hierarchical implementation, configuration data is passed from the CS to the MS. In the peer-to-peer implementation, both the MS and the CS exchange configuration data. Each station type (MS and CS) has a collection domain and nodes in which each is responsible for monitoring and collecting information. These domains may be completely independent or may overlap. This section describes DIM architectures, domain configuration, and the use of topology, discovery, and failover filters. The implementation and synchronization of MS/CS is also covered.

Figure 9-8 This diagram illustrates a hierarchical implementation of Distributed Internet Discovery and Monitoring (DIDM) using three CSs and an MS.

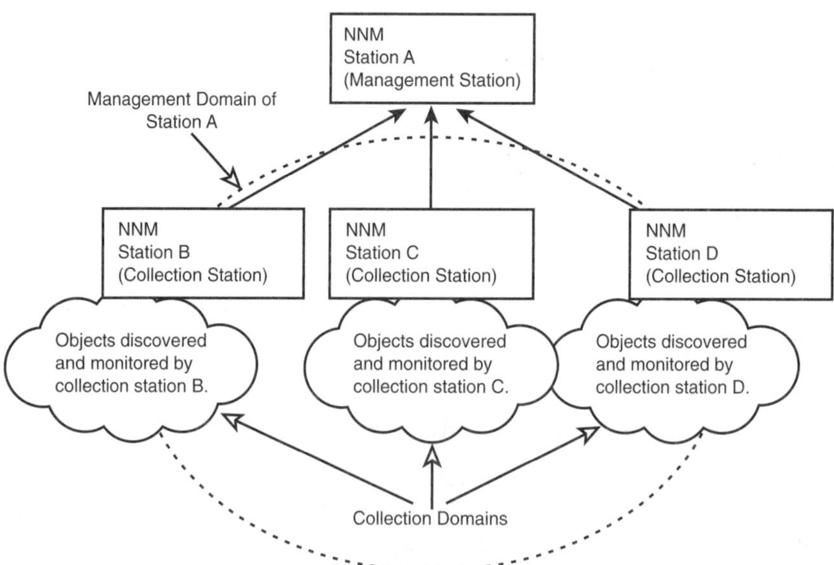

The role of a CS is to act as a collection point in the network management enterprise. A CS performs topology and status monitoring, threshold data collection, and event handling. CSs should be placed strategically in your enterprise to reduce polling traffic across expensive, slow, or congested links. A CS can also be used as a management console server.

The implementation of DIM partitions the discovery and status polling and dramatically reduces traffic on portions of the network. A fully deployed DIDM implementation should support up to 25,000 devices.[5]

Figure 9-9 Topology filters are applied on a CS to limit the objects that will be passed from the CS to the MS.

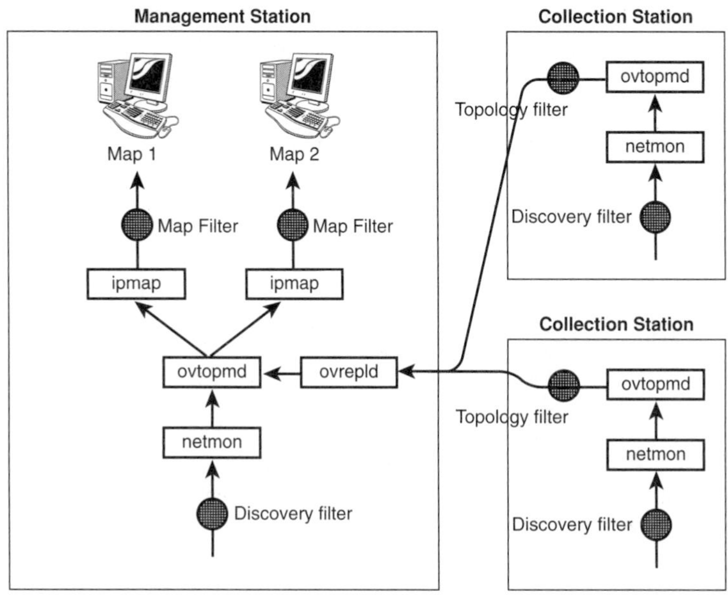

9.5.1 CS Configuration

The steps to configure a CS typically include the configuration of several types of filters. Listed here are the detailed steps in CS configuration:

1. Configure and apply a local discovery filter to define the collection domain. Make the required changes to the $OV_CONF/filters file. Be sure to test your filter for syntax errors and accuracy using **ovfiltercheck** and **ovtilertest**. Apply the previously defined filter expression **CriticalDevices** as a discovery filter by selecting **Options→Network**

5 The upper limit of managed devices depends heavily on the level of monitoring and data collection configured in an implementation. Hewlett-Packard derived this number for a CS containing 5,000 objects for a stand-alone CS with an object-to-node ratio of 2.4. This number varies for network maps containing a larger object-to-node ratio.

Polling Configuration:IP from the NNM GUI. In the **General** Configuration Area, toggle on the box labeled **[Use Discovery Filter]**. Click **[OK]**. Refer back to Section 9.4.4, "Discovery Filters," for details.

```
Sets {
servers "Set of Servers" { "sv1", "sv2", "sv3" }
}

Filters {
NetsNSegs "All networks & segments" { ((isNetwork) ||
(isSegment))
HPNodes "Hewlett-Packard nodes" { isNode && ( vendor ==
"Hewlett-Packard" )
ServersSet "Any designated Server node" { "IP Hostname" in
servers }
ImportantNodes "Important systems" { "IP Address" ~
15.2.112-119.* }
}

FilterExpressions {
CriticalDevices "HP nodes, nets, segs, or servers " { HPNodes ||
NetsNSegs || ServersSet || ImportantNodes }
}
```

2. Configure and apply a topology filter to determine which objects to be passed to the MS. Make the required additions to the filters file by including the TopoFilter definition below. Apply the filter by modifying the $OV_LRF/ovtopmd.lrf. Refer back to Section 9.4.5, "Topology Filters," for details.

```
FilterExpressions {
TopoFilter "HP nodes, nets, segs, and important sys" { HPNodes
|| NetsNSegs || ImportantNodes }
}
```

3. Configure the **snmpd.conf** for security. The MS needs access to both the get and set community names. Make the following modifications to the **/etc/snmpd.conf** file:

```
get-community-name: public
set-community-name: secret
```

Note: Configure the community names of the SNMP Agents on the MS and CS to different community names from the rest of the managed network.

4. Restart the SNMP agent by typing the two commands:

```
/sbin/init.d/SnmpMaster stop
/etc/snmpd
```

9.5.2 MS Configuration

Prior to configuring the MS, you need to obtain the hostname and get and set community names of the CS. The detailed steps for configuring, testing, and synchronizing with the CS follows:

1. In order to make the CS nodes more visible, turn off auto-layout on all submaps.
   UNIX:
   Select **View→Autolayout→Off** for all Submaps
   Windows:
   Select **Map→Properties**
   Select the **View** tab
   Un-check **Autolayout**
2. Configure SNMP to communicate with the CS.
   UNIX:
   Select Options→SNMP Configuration and specify the hostname of the CS as the target and the set-community name as defined on the CS in the **snmpd.conf** file.
   - Target: ***hostname***
   - Set **Community secret**
   - Click **Add**
   - Click **[OK]**

   Windows:
   - Select **Options→SNMP Configuration**
   - Select the Specific Nodes Tab
   - Click **Add**
   - Target ***hostname***
   - Set Community **secret**
   - Click **[OK]**
3. Test the communication to the CS with the **xnmtopoconf** command. Specify the hostname of the CS.
   xnmtopoconf –test *hostname*
   The output should look something like this:

```
Testing station cs1.hp.com.
                ICMP round trip time = 1 ms.
        Ping test to cs1 (192.50.100.20) succeeded.
                system.sysObjectID.0 :
.iso.org.dod.internet.private.enterprises
```

```
.hp.nm.system.hpux.hp9000s700
        Get sysObjectID test to cs1.hp.com succeeded
                Station description: HP OpenView NNM Release
B.06.10 for Unix Distributed Station
                Station filter:TopoFilter
                Station licensed node count: UNLIMITED
                Station managed node count: 50
                Station license expiration date: PERMANENT
        Get topology info test to cs1.hp.com succeeded
                Station is not currently configured to forward
events
        Set event forwarding test to cs1.hp.com succeeded
Test for station cs1.hp.com passed
```

4. Configure, test and apply a discovery filter to be used on the MS. Refer to the previous section on configuring discovery filters for details.
5. If the CS is not included in the MS's collection domain, add the CS to the MS domain using the **xnmptopoconf** command. Specify the hostname of the CS.
   xnmtopoconf –add –unmanage *hostname*
6. Start managing the CS and immediately join the synchronization process, specifying the hostname of the CS.
   xnptopoconf –manage *hostname*
   nmdemandpoll –s *hostname*
   You should notice the newly added devices from the CS in the new object holding area in ovw.
7. Display the topology of your system with the **ovtopodump** command.
   ovtopodump –RISC

9.5.3 Overlapping versus Non-Overlapping Domains

The simplest DIM configuration is to have completely separate collection domains. In this configuration, each device is monitored by a different NNM station. Each NNM station monitors a separate set of devices. Therefore, each database has a completely different set of data. However, it is not uncommon to have certain devices monitored by multiple collection stations. This configuration is known as overlapping collection domains.

When configuring collection stations, you may chose to have multiple stations poll the same devices. A redundant independent collection is a configuration in which two collection stations monitor all the same devices. This means independent discovery and management of the same network by two management stations. In this configuration, duplicate polling occurs on all devices.

Another DIM configuration is to have partially overlapping domains. For example, you might determine that certain important devices be polled by two separate collection stations. In this configuration, duplicate polling occurs only on the important devices that are managed by both collection stations.

Whenever overlapping occurs, an MS receives multiple versions of the same object from different CSs. The MS must choose one version as the primary. All other versions are treated as secondary versions. NNM uses the following nine rules, evaluated in order, to determine which version is the primary:

1. If only one station reports the object, it is the primary CS.
2. If an object is an interface (isInterface == TRUE), skip to rule 7.
3. If only one station reporting the object is managed and has noncritical status or has failed over, that station has primary ownership of the object.
4. If the administrator has expressed a preferred primary CS[6] (**xnmtopoconf – preferred CS object**) for the object, that station is the primary CS for the object.
5. If only one station reporting the object is managing the object, that station is the primary CS for the object.
6. If one station reports that the object is a gateway, that station is the primary CS for the object.
7. If the object is completely contained in another object, the CS for the container object is the primary CS for the object. For example, a non-gateway node should have the same primary CS as the network that contains it.
8. If one of only two stations reporting the object is non-local (not the MS itself), the non-local station is the primary CS for the object.
9. The first station to report the object is the primary CS for it.

You can determine whether objects are primary or secondary by displaying the topology database with the **ovtopodump –RISC** command. These options provide the following information:

R Print removed versions of objects. Removed objects will be tagged with an asterisk (*) before the object name (see the Table 9-5 for Special Output Character Tags).

I Print invisible versions of objects. Invisible objects will be tagged with an exclamation mark (!) before the object name (see the Special Output Character Tags in Table 9-5).

S Print secondary versions of objects. These objects will be tagged with an ampersand (&) before the object name (see Table 9-5, "Special Output Character Tags").

C Include the collection station for objects.

6 A preferred primary for an object may be configured by executing **xnmtopoconf – preferred** CS object on the MS.

NNM uses the special characters listed in Table 9-5 to identify objects that are non-local or do not appear in a submap. The output of **ovtopodump –RISC** will look something like the following:

```
OBJECT ID(S)    OBJECT                 STATUS     IP ADDRESS    STATION
1014    -                                         IP Internet   local
STATIONS:
1015    -       nnmcs1                 Normal         –         local
1038    -       dbserver               Unmanaged      –         local
NETWORKS:
1016            IP 15.50.168           Normal     15.50.168.0   local
SEGMENTS:
1019    -       15.50.168.Segment1 Normal            –          local
NODES:
1018            IP nnmcs1              Normal     15.20.19.1    local
1018/17         IP nnmcs1              Normal     15.20.19.1    local
1035            IP fs1                 Normal     15.20.10.2    local
```

Table 9-5 Special Output Character Tags

Character	Object Type	Description
&	Secondary object	An object whose primary manager is a remote CS.
*	Removed object	An object that has been removed from the database. For example, an object is removed when applying a discovery filter to an existing database that does not pass the object.
!	Invisible object	Invisible objects are objects that cannot be matched as primary/secondary with another object in overlapping domains. For example, when a network is monitored by multiple CSs the segments will not match up. Invisible objects will not show up on any submap.
@	Removed invisible object	Objects that have been removed and are invisible.

%	Secondary invisible object	An invisible object whose primary manager is a remote CS.
#	Removed secondary object	An object that has been removed from a remote station.
%	Removed secondary invisible object	A removed object whose primary manager is remote and does not match any object secondary object.

When you configure overlapping domains you must determine how to handle secondary objects. There are three choices in how to handle secondary:

1. **Allow Overlap**—Duplicate polling occurs
2. **Unmanage**—Duplicate polling does not occur, but the objects are stored in the database. This allows the station to quickly take over with a manual switchover if the primary station fails.
3. **Delete Secondary**—Eliminates duplicate polling and duplicate storage of objects in the database for non-connector devices. This does not delete network, segments, or routers that overlap. This is the default behavior with overlapping domains.

The **xnmtopoconf** command may be used to display and modify the overlap mode. To display the overlap mode, execute **xnmtopoconf –print**. The output will be something like this:

```
STATION     STATUS  INTERVAL  OVERLAP MODE     FAILOVER  FILTER
Local       Normal  5m        DeleteSecondary  off       <none>
nnmcs2      Normal  5m        AllowOverlap     off       <none>
```

The overlap mode may be modified by specifying one of three overlap modes with the **xnmtopoconf** command: **AllowOverlap**, **UnmanageSecondary**, **DeleteSecondary**. For example, to set the overlap mode to AllowOverlap, execute the following command on the management station:

```
xnmtopoconf -overlap AllowOverlap local
```

9.5.4 Troubleshooting DIM

Collection stations are identified by the object attribute **isCollectionStationNode**. When the remote station answers a MIB query for the NNM MIB, this MIB variable is retrieved. If a collection station is not in the collection domain of a management station, it is not displayed with **xnmtopoconf –print**. The collection station may be added. If you execute **xnmtopconf –add –unmanage** ***collectionStation***, the collection station is added to the topology database on the management station but is not managed (no topology is retrieved from it). If you execute **xnmtopconf –add** ***CollectionStation***, it starts the synchronization process between the management and collection station.

The SNMP set community name must be configured on the collection station. The set community name of the collection station must be configured in the NNM GUI on the management station. This can be verified by executing **xnmtopoconf –test *CollectionStation***. If this fails, you will not be able to synchronize with the collection station. This command performs four tests to the collection station including ping, two SNMP gets, and an SNMP set. Observe the output of the command closely to determine reason for failure. Refer back to Section 9.5.1, "Collection Station Configuration," and Section 9.5.2, "Management Station Configuration" for details on SNMP configuration.

Configuration of management and collection station overlap may take a couple of iterations before you get the expected result. You may reset collection station by issuing **xnmtopconf –reset *CollectionStation***. When you reset a collection station, the topology information is removed from the topology but the station itself is left in a managed state. To completely remove a collection station and its topology, execute **xnmtopoconf –delete *CollectionStation***.

When configuring automatic failover, the default interval is set to 5 minutes. When a status check of a collection station fails, the status is downgraded one level and an event is generated. After four status checks, or 20 minutes, the management station takes over status polling for the devices for which the collection station was the primary. During initial configuration you may want to set the interval to 5 seconds so you aren't required to wait 20 minutes during testing. You can modify the interval by executing **xnmtopoconf –interval 5s *CollectionStation***. Make sure to set it back to a reasonable interval when you've finished testing. The following intervals are accepted: seconds (s), minutes (m), hours (h), and days (d).

When troubleshooting the topology database, use **ovtopodump –RISC**. This lists removed, invisible, secondary, and collection station objects in the database. Another useful option is to execute **ovtopodump** using a filter name. You can determine which objects will pass a filter by executing **ovtopodump –f *FilterName***. Obtain a list of defined filters by executing ***ovfiltercheck.***

The **ovrepld** process must be running on the management station. It is not required to run on a collection station. To verify that **ovrepld** is running, execute **ovstatus –c** on the management station. You can also use **ovrepld** to log transferred topology information. All information can be logged to ovrepld.log by executing **ovrepld –p COWG**. This logs information for every device from the remote collection station. The specified options write the following information to ovrepld.log:

```
C - Collection station list
O - Report All Activity
W - Wait list: actions awaiting response
G - Global actions: ready queue
```

9.6 SUMMARY

NNM has the ability to function well in both large and small networks. Scalability features of NNM include configuring remote consoles to distribute the system load, defining several different types of filters to limit the device discovery, and configuring Distributed Internet Monitoring with multiple NNM stations. Individual users can reduce system impact by set the map persistence level or using the network presenter.

As your network grows, so must your network management solution. Depending on the growth rate of your enterprise, what works for you today may not be as ideal six months down the road. Networks evolve—so should your management solution.

CHAPTER 10

Customer Views

NNM does an excellent job of monitoring and displaying the health of the network enterprise. It provides a view of the physical network connectivity of an enterprise. However, it does not provide a logical view of the network because it has no way of determining the logical relationships that exist within a given enterprise. Although customization exists within NNM, *Customer Views* (CV) extends the capabilities of NNM by allowing the administrator to define a logical hierarchy comprised of five additional views. With CV, you can define which resources affect which customers. Internet Service Providers, Managed Service Providers, and outsourcers commonly use it for customer-based management. With the use of CV, a managed service provider is able to provide each customer with restricted access to their data by grouping together each customer's devices in a separate hierarchy. This chapter covers the concepts behind CV and describes the utilities used in configuring the environment.

10.1 THE FIVE ADDITIONAL VIEWS

CV allows service providers to group and access their network resource relationships by defining organizations. The organizations may be individuals, businesses, or any entity with network resource relationships to the service provider. CV provides two types of organizations, including

- **Customers**—Customers rely on the service provider for resource access.
- **Providers**—Providers supply access to resources.

When installed, CV adds five container symbols to NNM's root submap, as shown in Figure 10-1. These symbols provide the following five additional views:

1. **Key Resources**—Network devices that are deemed critical to the management of an organization.
2. **Customers**—A logical grouping of devices based on ownership of equipment.
3. **Devices**—Network devices that include routers, switches, and servers.
4. **Internet Links**—Devices that are provided to the customer by an external organization, such as an Internet Service Provider.
5. **Sites**—A logical or geographical structure within an organization such as a city, building, or business structure (accounting, engineering, and so on).

Figure 10-1 Customer Views adds five container symbols to the root submap, including Key Resources, Customers, Devices, Internet Links, and Sites. The Devices container is based on object attributes **isRouter** and **isConnector** and is automatically populated by CV. The additional containers must be configured with the **ovcustomer** utility.

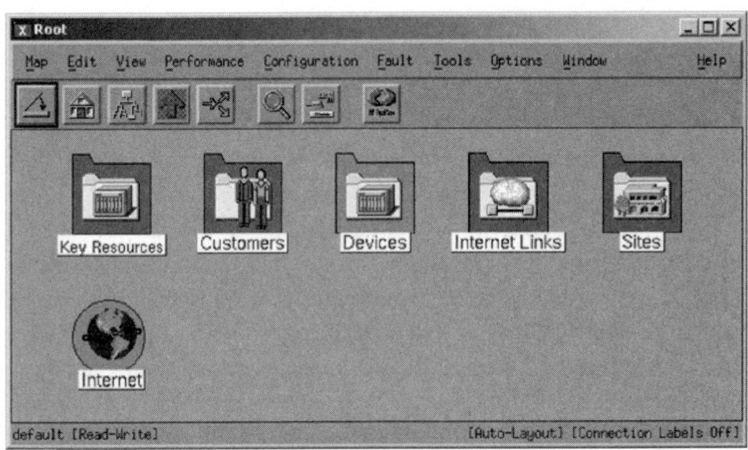

CV consists of two applications that are tightly integrated into NNM. The *Hierarchical Submap Builder* (HSB) application is managed by the **submBld** process. The HSB is responsible for the Sites, Internet Links, Customers, and Devices view. The *Key Resources* application is managed by the **keySys** process and is responsible for the Key Resources view. Because these processes integrate with NNM, CV must reside on the same system as NNM. These processes can be listed on a UNIX system by executing **ps –ef | more**. The processes are found in the task manager on Windows.

10.1.1 The Key Resources View

The purpose of defining key resources is to identify critical network devices. Key resources are identified by the object attribute **isKeyDevice**. This attribute is added to NNM by CV and appears under General Attributes, as shown in Figure 10-2. The attribute **isKeyDevice** may be modified via the NNM GUI. It may also be configured with the **ovcustomer** utility.

10.1.2 The Customers View

The purpose of defining customers is to allow logical, organizational groups of devices based on device ownership. NNM provides the physical layout of devices but has no way of determining which devices belong to an organization. With the **ovcustomer** utility, you can define customer organizations and associate devices that exist within the NNM database to an organization. The Customers view looks similar to that shown in Figure 10-3.

Figure 10-2 To modify the **isKeyDevice** object attribute, right-click the symbol representing the critical device, select **Object Properties...** and double-click **General Attributes**. Scroll down to the attribute **isKevDevice**. Select **True** and click **[OK]**.

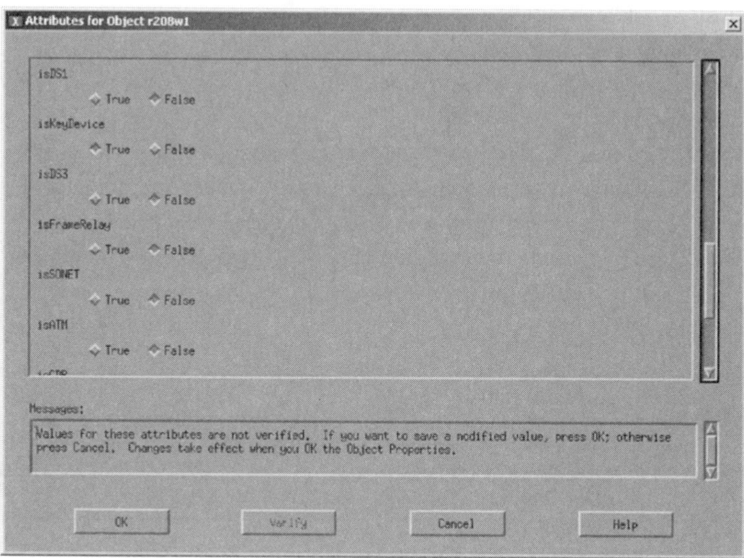

Figure 10-3 The ability to define customers allows logical organization of devices based on device ownership.

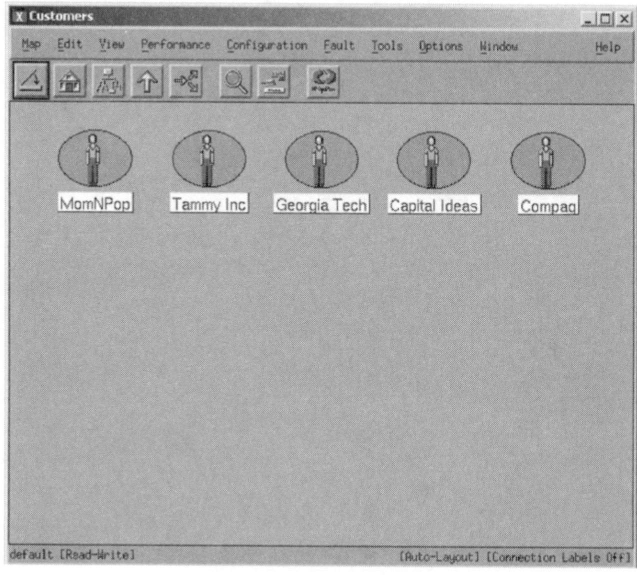

10.1.3 The Devices View

The Devices view provides three types of device groups, including

- **Routers**—Automatically populated by CV
- **Servers**—Must be defined with **ovcustomer**
- **Switches**—Automatically populated by CV

These three groups are shown in Figure 10-4. CV automatically builds the devices hierarchy when a map is created. This is the only CV hierarchy that is partially populated automatically. When devices are discovered by netmon, the device type is determined based on the object attributes listed in Table 10.1. The device type cannot be modified via the NNM GUI. The **ovcustomer** utility may be used to modify the device attributes.

Table 10.1 CV Device Types

Device Type	Attribute Value
Routers	isConnector == TRUE and isRotuer == TRUE
Servers	isServer == TRUE
Switches	isConnector == TRUE and isRouter == FALSE

Figure 10-4 The Devices view consists of the container objects **Routers**, **Servers**, and **Switches**. **Routers** and **Switches** are automatically populated based on the object attributes **isRouter** and **isConnector**. **Servers** must be defined with the **ovcustomer** utility.

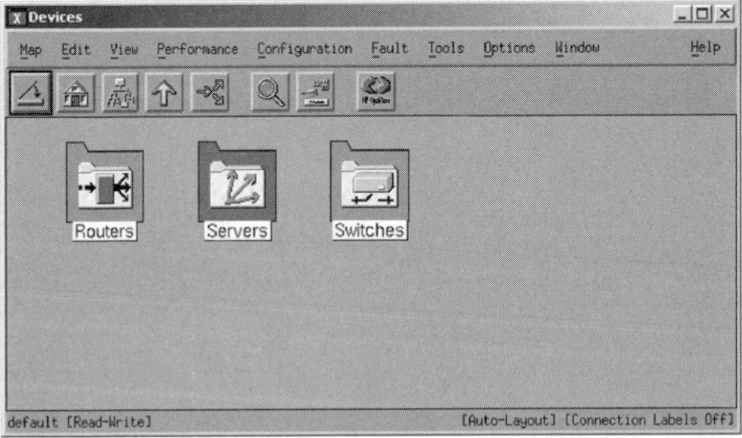

Because the object attributes **isRouter** and **isConnector** are set by NNM discovery, the Routers and Switches containers are automatically populated when CV is installed. However, CV adds an additional object attribute, **isServer**, to NNM. This attribute is used to identify servers that are considered critical to a customer's enterprise. The attribute **isServer** is added to the **Capabilities** section of the object attribute, as shown in Figure 10-5. The **isServer** attribute cannot be modified via the NNM GUI. In fact, the **isServer** field does not appear in the Capabilities or in the object database (**ovobjprint –s** ***selectionname***) until it is configured via the **ovcustomer** utility.

Figure 10-5 To view the **isServer** object attribute, right-click the symbol, select **Object Properties...** and double-click **Capabilities.** The **isServer** attribute cannot be modified via the NNM GUI.

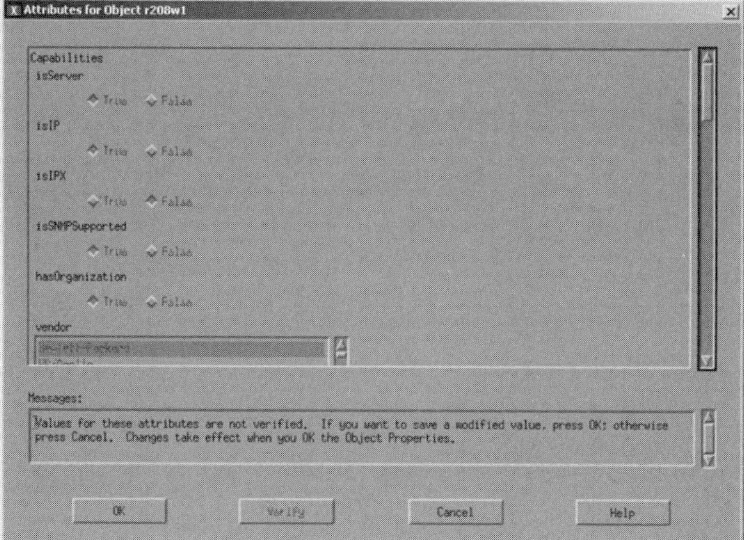

The Routers container consists of all devices having the object attributes **isRouter** and **isConnector** set to TRUE. The view looks similar to Figure 10-6. CV automatically populates the Routers container.

By default, nothing exists in the Servers container. This container is populated with devices having the attribute **isServer** set to TRUE. Because this attribute is added by the CV application, it must be configured. This attribute is configured with **ovcustomer**.

Figure 10-6 The **Routers** container is populated with devices having both **isRouterr** and **isConnector** attributes set to **TRUE**.

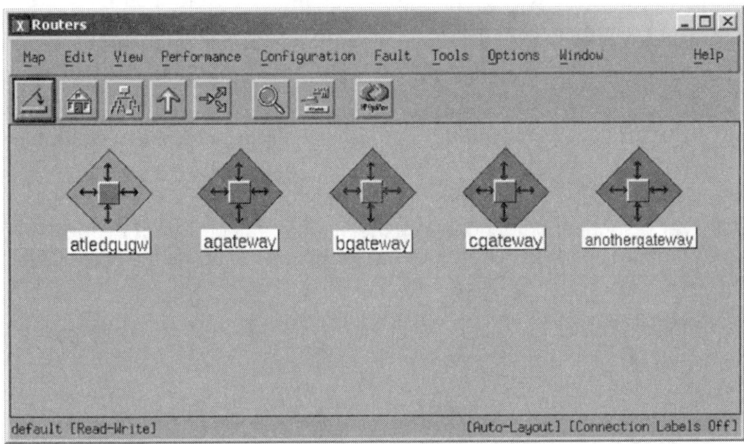

The Switches container consists of devices with object attributes **isConnector** set to TRUE and **isRouter** set to FALSE. It is automatically be populated by CV. The Switches submap looks similar to Figure 10-7.

Figure 10-7 The **Switches** container is populated with devices having **isRouter** set to **FALSE** and **isConnector** set to **TRUE**.

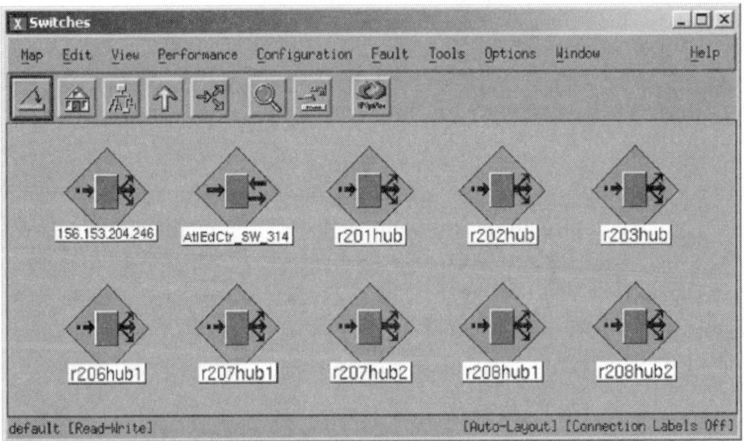

10.1.4 The Internet Links View

The purpose of defining Internet Links is to discern between customer and provider equipment. Two different types of organizations may be defined in CV: customers and providers. When a customer is defined with **ovcustomer**, the customer appears under the Customers container submap. When a provider is defined with **ovcustomer**, the provider appears under the Internet Links view. The Internet Links view is similar to the view shown in Figure 10-8.

Figure 10-8 A provider organization, such as an ISP, defined with **ovcustomer** appears in the Internet Links view.

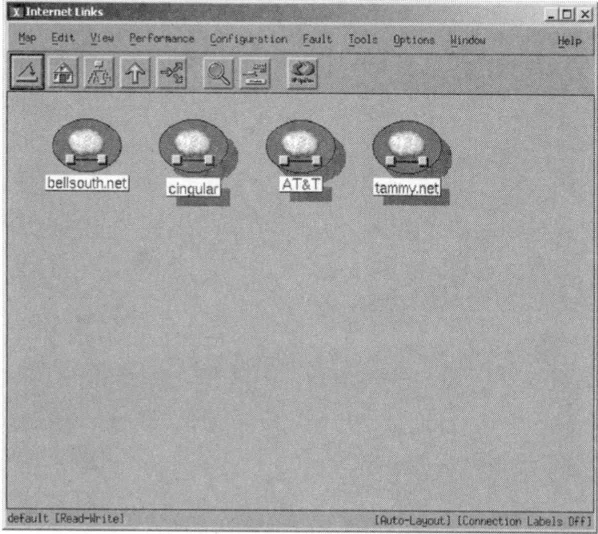

10.1.5 The Sites View

The Sites view shows the deployment of network devices in logical or geographical groups. Sites may be used to represent a building, a city, or a state, as shown in Figure 10-9. Location containers for the sites are created using the **ovcustomer** utility. Sites can consist of the following four location types:

- **Network Operations Center (NOC)**—A location for central resource management.
- **Point of Presence (POP)**—A location that extends the services area but it does not provide the services of an NOC.
- **Peering Point**—A location for sharing of service resources between service providers.
- **General**—A location, such as a city or state, that allows for customizing the Sites hierarchy.

Sites can be cascaded to represent a building within a city, and a city within a state. For example, Mass and Peabody are created as Sites. Peabody is associated with Mass such that Peabody appears in the Mass container, as shown in Figure 10-10.

Figure 10-9 Sites may be organized logically or geographically. Sites may represent a city, state, or building.

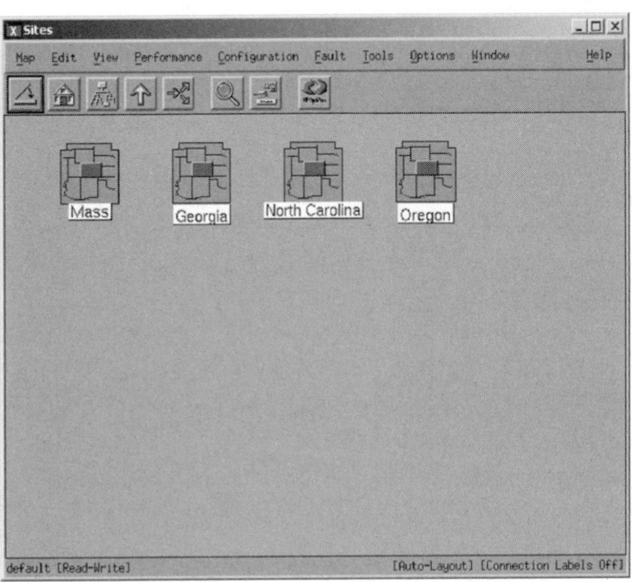

Figure 10-10 Sites can be cascaded to represent cities within a state. This submap reflects two cities within the Mass Site.

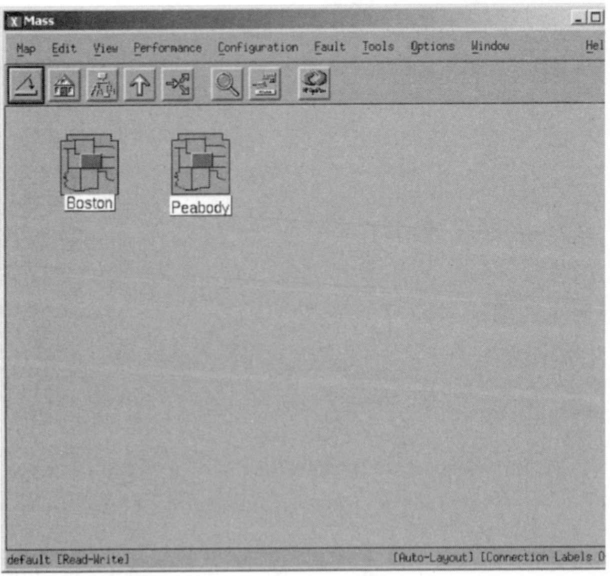

After the site hierarchy has been created, devices are associated with a site. Depending on the site type, the hierarchy looks similar to those shown in Figures 10-11 and 10-12. Peabody is a general site (Figure 10-11) and PeabodyNOC is a NOC site (Figure 10-12).

Figure 10-11 A site can be associated with other sites. In this example, Peabody is configured as a general site, PeabodyNOC is a NOC site, and PeabodyPOP is a POP site.

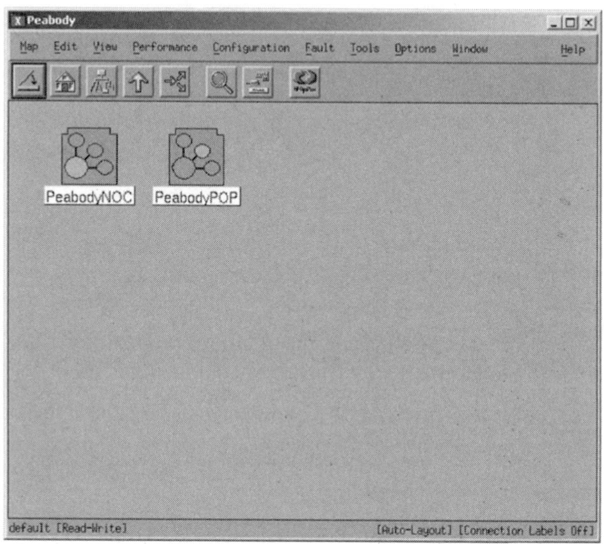

Figure 10-12 The PeabodyNOC site hierarchy includes the Customer Links, Devices, Internet Links, and LANs because the site type is NOC. NOC, POP, and Peering Point sites all have the same hierarchy.

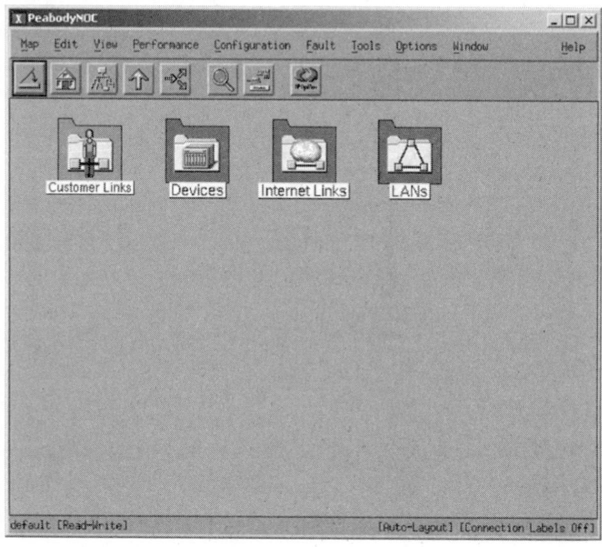

10.2 THE OVCUSTOMER UTILITY

CV is configured with the **ovcustomer** utility. Cut/paste and drag/drop functionality is not supported with CV. In fact, if you try to use the cut and paste or drag and drop functions, you may encounter undesired results. The **ovcustomer** utility must be used to define the hierarchy.

The utility is used in three ways: interactive command mode, not-interactively from the command line, or batch mode. The interactive method is helpful when you are first learning **ovcustomer**. The **ovcustomer** help menu list of supported commands and arguments that may be used with the utility. However, as you progress, you may want to create batch files to allow you to more quickly add customer configuration.

To obtain a list of commands available in **ovcustomer**, type **ovcustomer help**.

To obtain help on a specific command such as create_organization, use **ovcustomer help create_organization**.

10.2.1 Adding Customer Data

The following commands can be specified with the **ovcustomer** utility, both interactively and in a batch mode, to add customer data. To use **ovcustomer** interactively, simply type line **ovcustomer** at the command line.

The **create_organization** command requires a customer type and a customer name. Specify the type of organization (customer or provider), the customer name (use double quotes if the name contains a space), and an optional external key. The external key may be used to provide a keyed field. If a customer name already exists with a different external key, the external key is modified.

The **add_associations_to_org** command allows you to add the NNM selection name or IP addresses to the association. **add_associations_to_org** requires an organization name and selection name/IP address.

The **create_location** command allows you to define site types. The type must be one of the four: general, NOC, POP, or peering_point. The general may be used when defining a city, state, or building. NOC is used for a Network Operations Center, POP for a Point of Presence, and peering_point for shared equipment between service providers.

The **set_location** command is used to nest general locations and to add devices to locations. For example, **set_location Boston Mass** nests Boston inside the Mass container.

The **set_field** command allows you to set object attributes **isServer**, **isCPE**, and **isKeyDevice**. **set_field** requires the selection name, attribute, and value. For example, **set_field r208w100 isKeyDevice TRUE** sets the **isKeyDevice** field for the device r208w100 to true.

To use **ovcustomer** in batch mode, create a text file named custInfo.txt containing the commands listed in the next section and execute **ovcustomer** as shown. The actual name of the batch file can be whatever you choose. Use the following to execute **ovcustomer** using a file named **custInfo.txt**: **ovcustomer < custInfo.txt**.

The sample batch file, **custInfo.txt**, is listed in the next section. This batch file creates three organizations, adds some systems to the organizations, creates four types of locations, creates the location hierarchy, and configures the fields **isServer**, **isCPE**, and **isKeyDevice**. Make sure to include valid hostnames and IP addresses within your enterprise.

10.2.1.1 Sample Batch File custInfo.txt

Sample batch files for adding and removing customer data are available for download from the server `http://www.phptr.com/title/0130352098` for both UNIX and Windows systems. Obtain the Readme file for Chapter 10 for a description of the files available and install procedures.

```
create_organization customer MomNPop C-154
create_organization customer "Tammy Inc" Z-999
create_organization provider bellsouth.net
add_associations_to_org MomNPop r208w1
add_associations_to_org "Tammy Inc" r208w100
add_associations_to_org MomNPop 156.153.206.51
add_associations_to_org "Tammy Inc" 156.153.206.75
add_associations_to_org "Tammy Inc" 156.153.206.1
add_associations_to_org "Tammy Inc" 156.153.206.2
add_associations_to_org "Tammy Inc" 156.153.206.3
add_associations_to_org bellsouth.net 156.153.206.25
create_location general Mass
create_location general Boston
create_location general Peabody
create_location NOC PeabodyNOC
create_location POP PeabodyPOP
create_location peering_point BostonPPT
set_location Boston Mass
set_location Peabody Mass
set_location PeabodyNOC Peabody
set_location PeabodyPOP Peabody
set_location BostonPPT Boston
set_location r207w100 PeabodyNOC
set_location r208w100 PeabodyNOC
set_location r208w1 PeabodyPOP
set_location r207w1 PeabodyPOP
set_location r207w2 BostonPPT
set_location r207w3 BostonPPT
set_field r208w1 isServer TRUE
set_field r208w1 isCPE TRUE
set_field r208w100 isKeyDevice TRUE
```

10.2.2 Listing Customer Data

The following commands may be used to list CV information. These commands may be used interactively or in a batch file.

The **print _organization** command provides the organization type, organization name, and external key. If the organization name is provided, only objects within the specified organization are listed. If no organization is provided, all organizations are listed.

The **print_associated_organization** command also provides the organization type, organization name and external key. It requires the IP address or selection name of the associated organization.

The **print_associated_interface** command lists information about interfaces associated with objects. If an organization name is specified, interfaces associated with the specified organization are listed. If no organization name is specified, all interfaces associated with any organization are listed.

The **print_associated_node** command lists information about nodes associated with objects. If an organization name is specified, only list nodes associated with the specified organization are listed. If no organization name is specified, all nodes associated with any organization are listed.

10.2.3 Deleting Customer Data

The following batch file removes organizations, unsets and deletes locations, and resets fields that were set by the custInfo.txt file. It might be a good idea to create a corresponding batch file to similar to this when creating a batch file for creating the customer data. This allows you to quickly remove customer data in case you want to modify or remove customer data. Create a text file named **delCustInfo.txt** and execute the command **ovcustomer < delCustInfo.txt**

10.2.2.1 Sample Batch Fiel delCustInfo.txt

```
remove_associations_to_org MomNPop r208w1
remove_associations_to_org "Tammy Inc" r208w100
remove_associations_to_org MomNPop 156.153.206.51
remove_associations_to_org "Tammy Inc" 156.153.206.75
remove_associations_to_org "Tammy Inc" 156.153.206.1
remove_associations_to_org "Tammy Inc" 156.153.206.2
remove_associations_to_org "Tammy Inc" 156.153.206.3
remove_associations_to_org bellsouth.net 156.153.206.25
delete_organization MomNPop
delete_organization "Tammy Inc"
delete_organization bellsouth.net
unset_location Boston
unset_location Peabody
unset_location PeabodyNOC
unset_location PeabodyPOP
```

```
unset_location BostonPPT
unset_location r207w100
unset_location r208w100
unset_location r208w1
unset_location r207w1
unset_location r207w2
unset_location r207w3
delete_location Mass
delete_location Boston
delete_location Peabody
delete_location PeabodyNOC
delete_location PeabodyPOP
delete_location BostonPPT
unset_field r208w1 isServer
unset_field r208w1 isCPE
unset_field r208w100 isKeyDevice
```

10.2.4 Tips for ovcustomer

The **ovcustomer** utility accepts abbreviated commands based on the uniqueness of the command. For example, to obtain help on print commands, use the following commands:

List all print commands:	**ovcustomer help print**
List print_assocation commands:	**ovcustomer help print_a**
List print_location commands:	**ovcustomer help print_l**
List print_organization commands:	**ovcustomer help print_o**

The abbreviated commands may be used when creating, listing, and deleting information from CV.

For more information on **ovcustomer**, refer to the **ovcustomer** UNIX man page or the Window online help for **ovcustomer**.

10.3 CONFIGURING THE HIERARCHICAL SUBMAP BUILDER

The *Hierarchical Submap Builder* (HSB) is enabled on NNM maps by default. The HSB contains two configurations, only one of which may be modified after a map has been created. The two configurations include

- Should the hierarchical submap builder be enabled for this map?
- Should the hierarchical submap builder show ungrouped organizations?

The default value for both configurations is True. The first configuration, "Should the hierarchical submap builder be enabled for this map?" can only be set when a map is initially created. The second configuration, "Should the hierarchical submap builder show ungrouped organizations?" may be modified on a map that is opened in read/write mode. The following steps allow you to access and modify the HSB configuration:

1. Start NNM.
   ovw&
2. Select **Map→Properties**.
3. Select the application Hierarchical Submap Builder and click **[Configure For This Map…]**.
4. Select False to disable the ungrouped customer organizations. This enables organizations that have been grouped using the set_organization_group command in ovcustomer. This allows you to limit the customers displayed on a map if they have not been assigned to a group.
5. Click **[Verify]** and **[OK]** twice.
6. Assuming a customer named MomNPop and a group named small, assign the existing customer to a group:
   ovcustomer set_organization_group MomNPop small
7. Open the Customers submap from the NNM root submap. You should now see the group name "small" and no other customers. Open the "small" group to verify that MomNPop was added to the group.

10.4 SUMMARY

NNM provides a view of the physical network connectivity of an enterprise. CV provides a logical view of the network based on the logical relationships that you define within your enterprise. CV extends the capabilities of NNM by allowing the administrator to define a logical hierarchy comprised of five additional views. CV provides the ability to define which customers are affected by which resources, and is commonly used by ISPs, Managed Service Providers, and outsourcers to allow for customer-based management. With CV, managed service providers provide each customer with restricted access to their data by grouping together each customer's devices in a separate hierarchy.

## CHAPTER 11

Service Information Portal

Service Information Portal (SIP) can provide a wealth of information about your networking environment via a web browser. It can be customized to provide NNM topology submaps, SNMP data collection, and NNM alarms. SIP can also provide information such as Key Device Health, Router Health, and Server Health, as configured with *Customer Views* (CV). This chapter covers the demo portal provided with SIP, configuration of SIP users, and integration of NNM and CV. Although SIP provides integration of additional OpenView products, including *OpenView Operations* (OVO), *Internet Services* (OVIS), *Service Navigator* (OVSN), *OpenView Service Reporter* (OVSR), *OpenView Performance Insight* (OVPI), and *Service Desk* (OVSD), this chapter is limited to the integration of NNM and CV. For more information on the integration of OpenView products, refer to SIP documentation that can be found at `http://ovweb.external.hp.com:80/lpe/doc_serv/`.

IP is not required to reside on the same system as the applications that provide the portal data. In fact, you may consider separating the servers with the use of firewalls as depicted in Figure 11-1a. Given this scenario, a client accesses the data via a web browser located on the Extranet, an extension of the service provider's network. The SIP server resides on the DMZ, or demilitarized zone of the provider's network. The data servers, such as NNM and OVO, reside on the Intranet. Secure ports are opened between the Intranet, DMZ, and Extranet to allow necessary communication.

Figure 11-1a SIP is not required to reside on the same server as NNM or OVO. It can reside in a DMZ as shown.

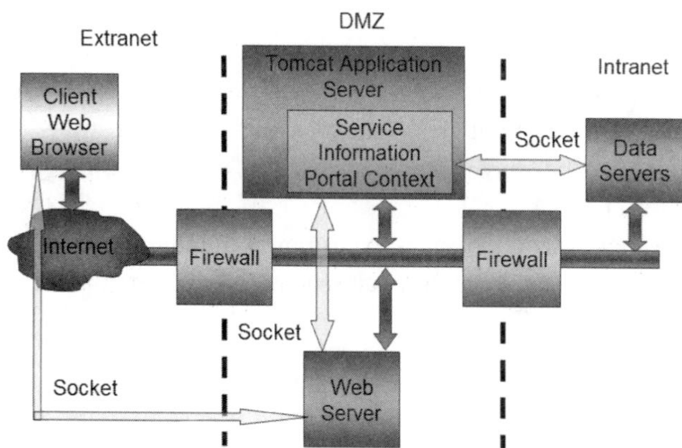

11.1 GENERIC NET DEMO

SIP is typically accessed via a traditional web browser. Limited information can be configured and viewed via wireless devices such as PDAs and WML-based cell phones. When you access SIP as a guest, you can see a demo version of SIP. The demo provides an excellent illustration of what SIP could look like after configuration. The data included with the Generic Net demo is fictitious and does not represent your network. The figures in this section illustrate the type of information that can be configured in your portal.

When you install SIP, the Apache web server is installed and configured to run on port 80. If you already have a web server running on port 80, it is necessary to change the port before SIP functions. Perform the following tasks to modify the port number:

1. Edit the file /opt/OV/SIP/apache/conf/httpd.conf.
2. Search for Port and change it from 80 to the desired port.
3. Save and exit the file.
4. Restart the web server as the user root:
   - HP-UX:
     ```
     /sbin/init.d/ovsip stop
     /sbin/init.d/ovsip start
     ```
   - Solaris:
     ```
     /etc/init.d/ovsip stop
     /etc/init.d/ovsip start
     ```

Note: The default port for secure communications (https) is 443.

To access the SIP demo, enter the following URL in a browser, supplying the hostname of the SIP server and the port defined previously: **`http://`*`hostname`*`:`*`port`*`/ovportal`**

At the SIP login page, provide the userid **guest** and click **[Login]**. The Generic Net demo portal shown Figure 11-1 should appear. The Network tab of the demo consists of the following five sections:

- **Network Device Health**[1]—This section provides gauges that indicate router health, server health, key device health, customer premises equipment, and interface health. The information is gathered from NNM and CV. Click any gauge to obtain a list of individual device information shown in Figure 11-2.
- **Message Board**—This provides a way to send messages to customers. It requires the administration function for the portal. The sipadmin user can send messages from the Message Board tab.

1 The NNM modules must be configured as described in Section 11.2, "Integrating SIP with NNM," for access to network device health, topology, and alarms.

- **Topology**—The topology gathered from NNM is displayed from the IP Internet submap of the default submap. The map must be open for the topology to be displayed. Drill-down capability is supported.
- **Bookmarks**—Bookmarks to other web links can be configured by the Bookmarks tab of the sipadmin portal login account.
- **Alarms**—The alarms module of NNM may be displayed on the portal.

Figure 11-1 The Network tab of the Generic Net demo displays fictitious data consisting of **Network Device Health**, **Message Board**, **Topology**, **Bookmarks**, and **Alarms**.

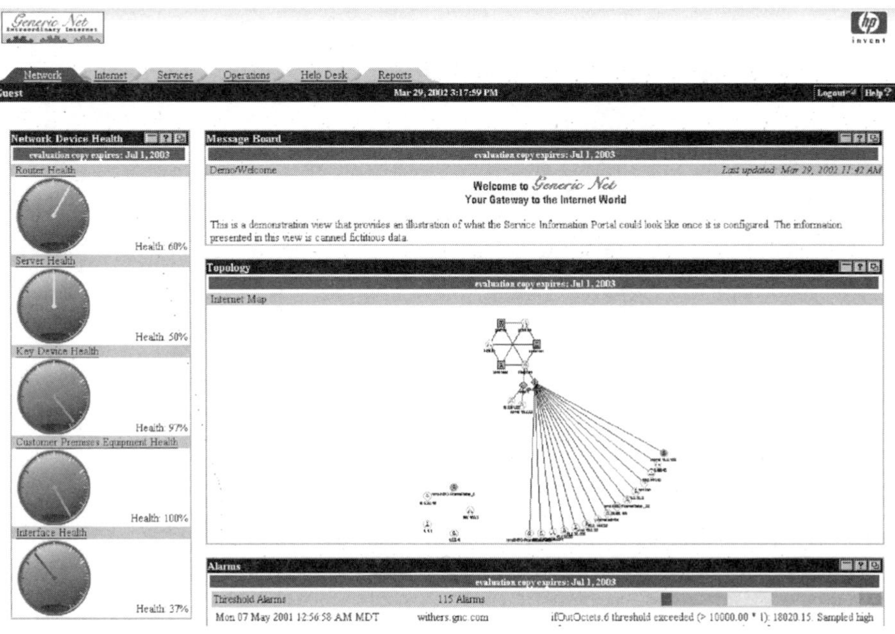

Figure 11-2 Click any device health gauge to display individual device information.

Generic Net
Extraordinary Internet

Network Device Health May 7, 2001 6:10:54 PM Home Help

Details

Router Health

Resource	Overall Health	Interface Health		CPU Utilization Health	
		Health	Raw Data	Health	Raw Data
fortuna.gnc.hp.com	0%	0%	0	Data unavailable	Data unavailable
withers.gnc.hp.com	100%	100%	100	Data unavailable	Data unavailable
warpspeed.gnc.hp.com	100%	100%	100	Data unavailable	Data unavailable
godfrey.gnc.hp.com	0%	0%	100	Data unavailable	Data unavailable
c4k1.gnc.hp.com	60%	60%	100	Data unavailable	Data unavailable
coal.gnc.hp.com	100%	100%	100	Data unavailable	Data unavailable

The NNM topology maps may be displayed in the portal, as shown in Figure 11-3. The map must be opened in the native NNM GUI to be accessed via SIP. Drill-down functionality is available by double-clicking a symbol.

Figure 11-3 SIP may be configured to display NNM Topology. The NNM topology module must be configured and the map must be open to access the topology.

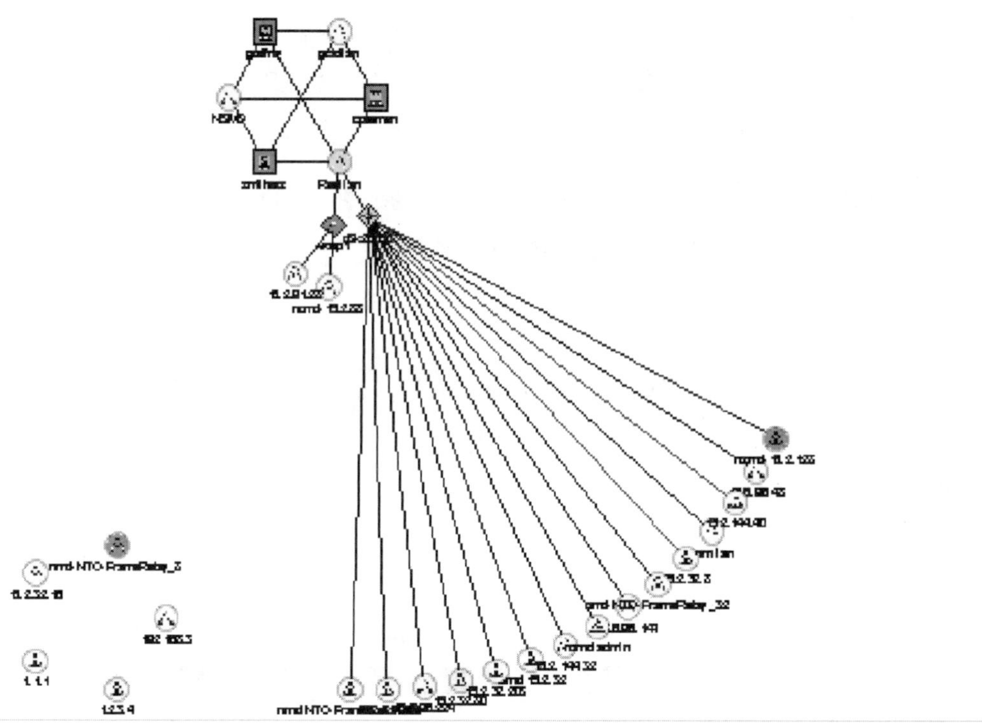

When configuring maps for different customers, you may want to use the filtering mechanism within NNM (as described in Chapter 9, "Scalability and Distribution") to create a separate map for each customer. A combination of map filters and CV configuration (covered in Chapter 10, "Customer Views") allows you to define exactly what a customer's map contains. After the map has been created, configure an SIP user to have access to the customized map. This prevents a customer from accessing the topology of another customer's network.

Network Health gauges may be displayed on the portal, as shown in Figure 11-4. The following fields defined from NNM and Customer Views can be displayed as gauges:

Figure 11-4 Network Device Health may be configured to include **Router Health**, **Server Health, Key Device Health**, **Customer Premises Equipment Health**, and **Interface Health**. These gauges can be displayed on a user's portal.

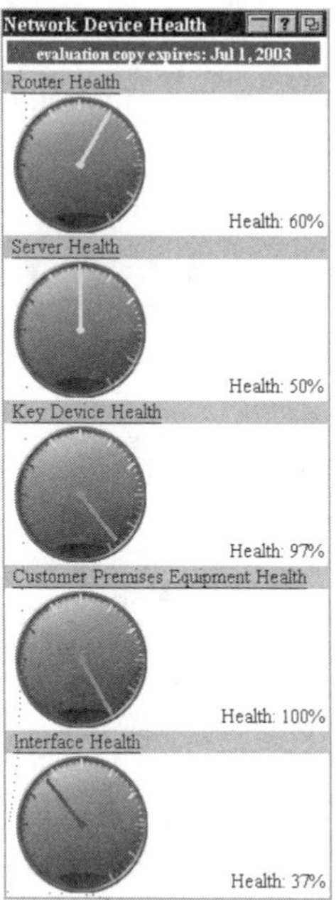

- **Router Health**—Devices with the attributes **isRouter** and **isConnector** set to TRUE. Determined by NNM upon discovery.
- **Server Health**—Devices with the attribute **isServer** set to TRUE. Defined by the ovcustomer utility.
- **Key Device Health**—Devices with the attribute **isKeyDevice** set to TRUE. Defined by the ovcustomer utility.
- **Customer Premises Equipment Health**—Devices with the attribute **isCPE** set to TRUE. Defined by the ovcustomer utility.
- **Interface Health**—Devices with the attribute **isInterface** set to TRUE. Determined by NNM upon discovery.

Detailed information for a device gauge may be obtained by clicking the gauge.

The alarms module of NNM may be displayed on the portal, as shown in Figure 11-5. This is essentially the NNM All Alarms browser, which includes SNMP traps and OpenView alarms generated by SNMP agents. You may want to limit the alarms customers have access to based on their systems. An easy way to do this is to configure an Alarm category for each customer within NNM (see Chapter 8, "Data Collection and Event Configuration"). Create an SIP user that has access only to a specific Alarm category. This not only hides alarms generated by other customer equipment, but also allows you to limit the alarms displayed to the customer. For example, a customer may not want to know when an interface goes down if it comes back within a short period of time. The configuration of the Alarm category is the key to what you wish the customer to see.

Figure 11-5 The Network tab may be configured to display Alarms received by NNM. The NNM alarms module must be configured to display alarms.

Alarms

evaluation copy expires: Jul 1, 2003

Threshold Alarms	115 Alarms	
Mon 07 May 2001 12:56:58 AM MDT	withers.gnc.com	ifOutOctets.6 threshold exceeded (> 10000.00 * 1): 18020.15. Sampled high of 18020.15 at Mon May 07 00:56:58.3 2001 low of 123.57 at Mon May 07 07:56:58.2 2001
Mon 07 May 2001 02:56:58 AM MDT	withers.gnc.com	ifOutOctets.6 threshold rearmed (<= 500.00 * 1): 158.12. Sampled high of 24188.41 at Mon May 07 01:56:58.4 2001 low of 158.12 at Mon May 07 02:56:58.3 2001
Mon 07 May 2001 10:21:44 PM MDT	sum01.gnc.com	If%util.15 threshold exceeded (> 25.00 * 1): 60.80. Sampled high of 60.80 at Mon May 07 22:21:44.4 2001 low of 0.30 at Mon May 07 21:36:44.4 2001
Configuration Alarms	**210 Alarms**	
Mon 7 May 2001 11:34:29 AM MST	HP-C97F	Node added
Mon 7 May 2001 07:14:55 AM MST	neto.gnc.com	Inconsistent subnet mask 255.255.255.0 on interface AMD, should be 255.255.248.0
Mon 7 May 2001 07:13:21 AM MST	gnc-gw1.gnc.com	test101.gnc.com reports a different physical address for gnc-gw1.cnd.com than reported by blueprobe1.gnc.com, changing from 0x00B096C2F0C to 0x00C00000C07A

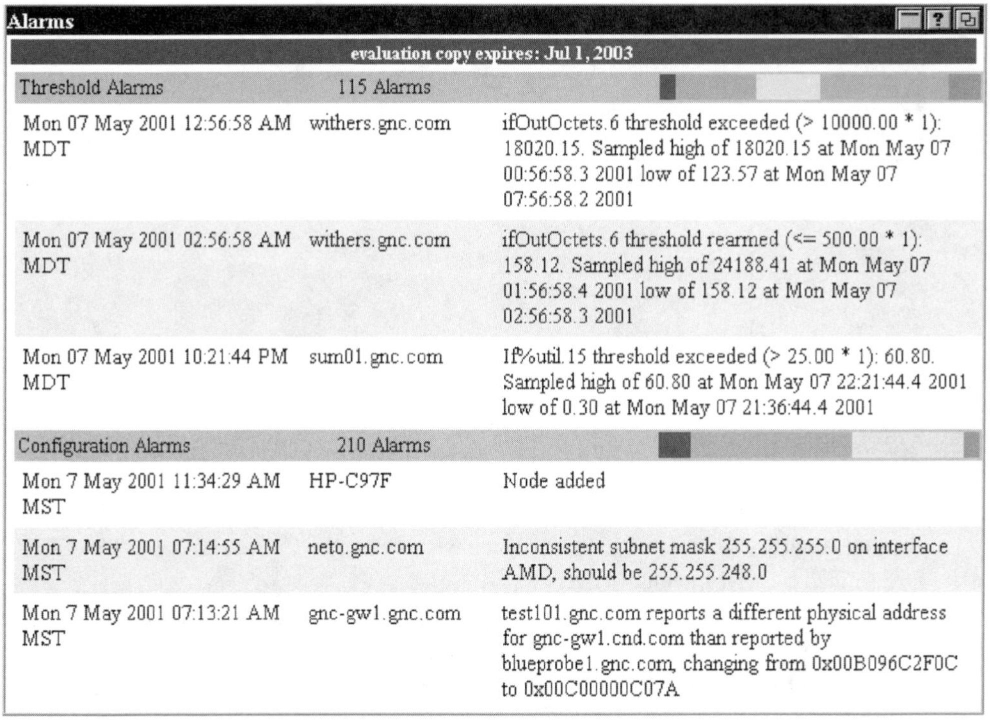

The Message Board shown in Figure 11-6 provides a way for an SIP administrator to communicate with users via the portal. Any user created with SIP administration capability can send messages to the board. The Message Board can be used to

- Create messages that include problem status information
- Change context of existing messages
- Delete messages from the board that should no longer be displayed

Bookmark links, also shown in Figure 11-6, can be used for quick access to documents and web pages. For example, you may want to provide access to OpenView documentation, software downloads, or internal web pages.

Figure 11-6 The Message Board and Bookmarks are displayed on a user's portal. The Message Board provides a mechanism for an SIP administrator to communicate status information to portal users. The Bookmarks provide hypertext links to commonly accesses sites.

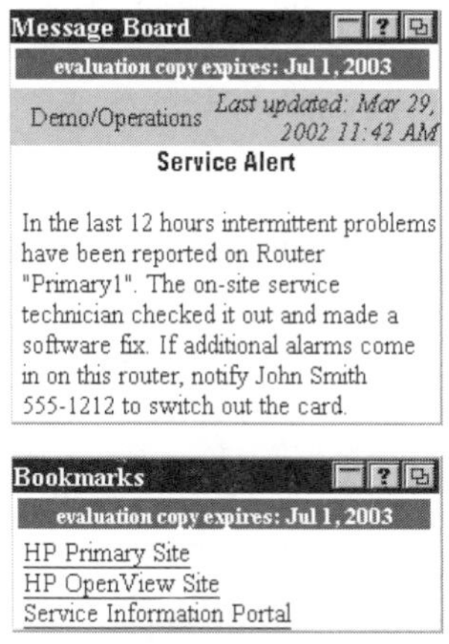

OpenView Internet Services (OVIS) allows you to monitor a customer's Intranet and network services. OVIS measures the availability, response time, set up time, and throughput of specific network activity. It can generate alarms and make them available to NNM. Information gathered by OVIS can be displayed on the portal, as shown in Figure 11-7. For more information on OVIS, refer to the Internet Services documentation available at `http://ovweb.external.hp.com:80/lpe/doc_serv`.

Figure 11-7 The Internet Tab of the demo is configured to display information regarding services such as **web page response time**, **availability**, and **SLO compliance** provided by OVIS.

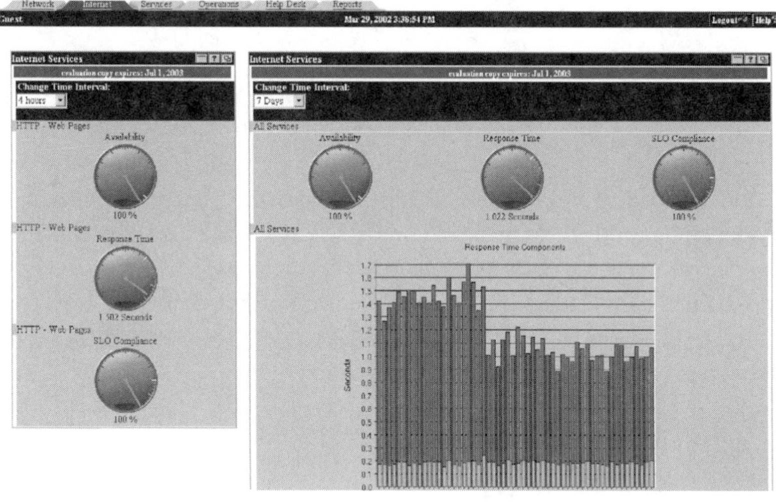

OpenView Service Navigator, an add-on component of OpenView Operations, allows you to configure services. A service is a group of processes or relationships between processes and systems. SIP can display Service Navigator-defined Service Cards, Service Graphs, Service Browser, and Service Health, as shown in Figure 11-8. For more information on Service Navigator, refer to the OpenView Operations section of the document server for the document **Service Navigator Concepts and Configuration Guide** available at `http://ovweb.external.hp.com:80/lpe/doc_serv`.

Figure 11-8 The Service tab of the demo is configured to display the **Service Browser**, **Service Graph**, **Service Cards**, and **Service Health** for services configured by OpenView Service Navigator.

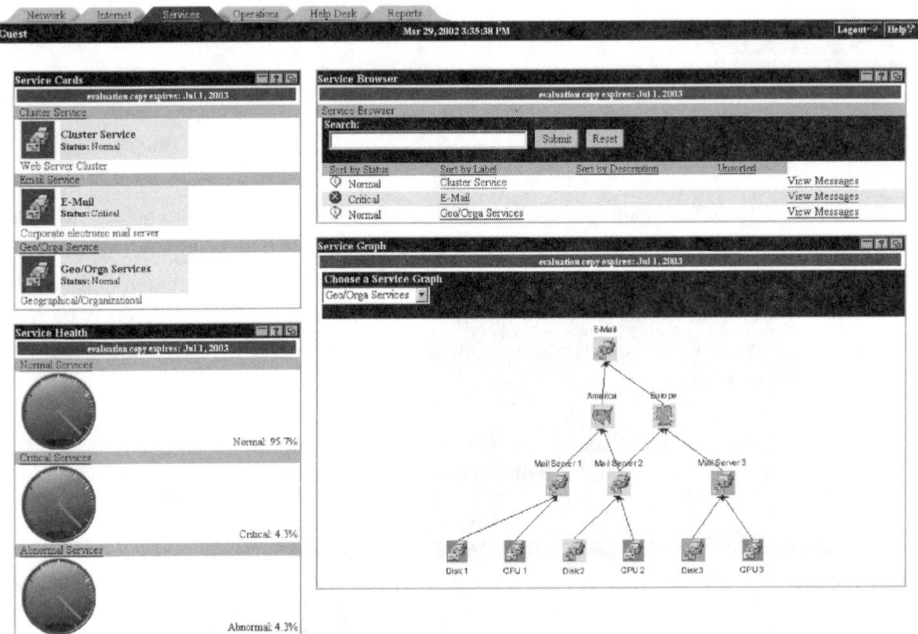

OpenView Operations (OVO) allows you to detect, solve, and prevent problems occurring in networks, systems, and applications. OVO agents are distributed to the managed systems. The OVO agents perform local monitoring of logfiles and processes. When the agent encounters a problem, it performs a local action and sends a message to the OVO manager. The message generated by the agent appears in the OVO message browser. The OVO messages may be integrated into SIP, as shown in Figure 11-9. For more information on OVO, refer to the document server `http://ovweb.external.hp.com:80/lpe/doc_serv`.

Figure 11-9 The Operations tab of the demo provides Messages generated by OVO.

Generic Net Extraordinary Internet

invent

Network Internet Services Operations Help Desk Reports

Guest Mar 29, 2002 1:14:46 PM Logout Help

OVO Messages

evaluation copy expires: Jul 1, 2003

All Message Groups	⊗	△	⚠	△	ⓘ	Total
Hardware	0	0	0	0	0	0
Network	0	0	0	0	0	0
HA	0	0	0	0	0	0
Job	0	0	0	0	1	1
OpC	141	0	0	1166	12	1319
Output	0	0	0	0	0	0
Performance	0	0	0	0	0	0
SNMP	0	0	0	0	0	0
Security	0	0	0	166	897	1063
OS	0	0	0	1186	0	1186
Database	0	0	0	0	0	0
NetWare	0	0	0	0	0	0
Misc	0	0	0	0	0	0

OVO Messages

evaluation copy expires: Jul 1, 2003

All Applications	⊗	△	⚠	△	ⓘ	Total
email_node1	1	0	0	0	0	1
Service Information Portal	0	0	0	0	712	712
Joe	1	0	0	3	1	5
syslogd	0	0	0	9	0	9
OpC	0	0	0	1172	0	1172
inetd	0	0	0	5	0	5
/usr/bin/su(1) Switch User	0	0	0	18	356	374
provport	0	0	0	0	3	3
email	8	0	3	4	1	16
/usr/bin/login(1) Login	0	0	0	148	541	689
SLB	0	1	1	0	1	3
Test	0	0	2	0	0	2
cl_lnode	1	0	0	0	0	1
HP IT/Operations	141	0	0	1166	12	1319

OpenView Service Desk (OVSD) provides an integrated set of support processes, including call management, incident management, and problem management. SIP can be configured to access OVSD data such as service calls, incidents, and so on, as shown in Figure 11-10. For more information on OVSD, refer to the document server `http://ovweb.external.hp.com:80/lpe/doc_serv`.

Figure 11-10 The Help Desk tab of the demo is configured to provide links to OVSD. SIP can provide access to **Service Calls**, **Incidents**, **Problems**, **Changes**, and **Work Orders**.

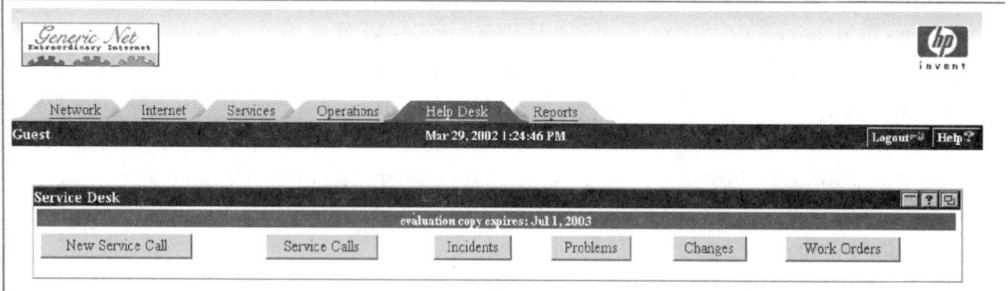

OpenView Service Reporter (OVSR) creates web-based reports from systems it discovers. A system running an OpenView Operations agent or an *OpenView Performance* (OVP) can be discovered by OVSR. It collects message and operator information from OVO. Reports for performance metrics such as CPU and memory utilization may be generated using OVSR. Reports can be displayed on the portal, as shown in Figure 11-11. For more information on OVSR, refer to the document server `http://ovweb.external.hp.com:80/lpe/doc_serv`.

Figure 11-11 The Reports tab of the demo is configured to provide performance data from OVR. Reporter provides data collected by OVO and OVP agents. This data includes performance metrics such as **CPU**, **memory**, and **disk utilization**.

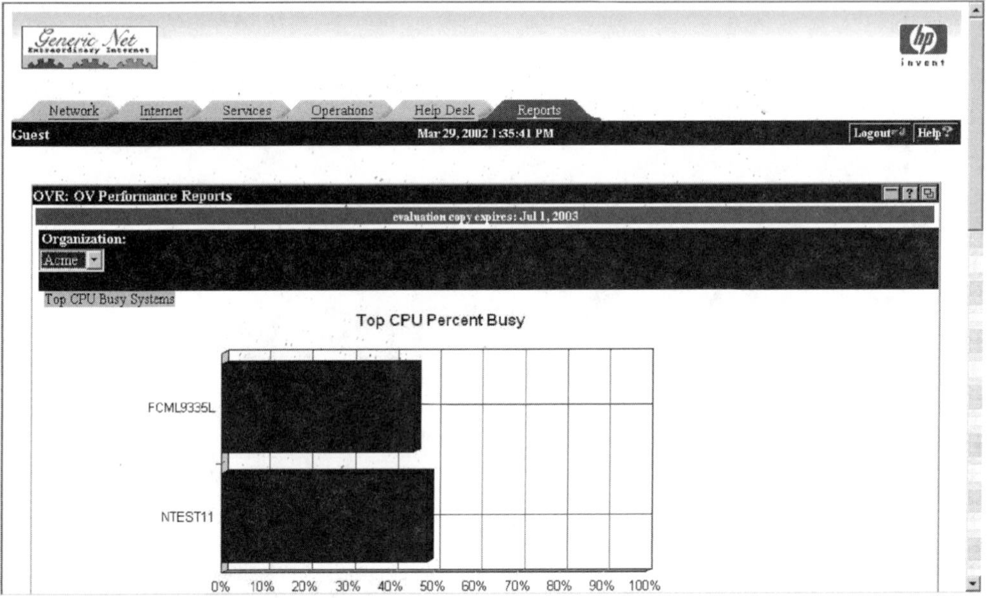

11.2 INTEGRATING SIP WITH NNM

SIP may be installed on the NNM management station or installed and configured on a separate server. It can be configured to communicate with one or many NNM stations. Three NNM modules may be configured in SIP, including

- **Alarms module**—Provides the alarm messages gathered from one or more alarm categories within NNM. You can filter the alarms so that only the alarms relevant to a particular user are displayed for an SIP portal view.
- **Network Device Health module**—Provides custom gauges that track the health of network devices so that your customers can monitor network performance at-a-glance. Predefined gauges such as router and server health are included. You can also write your own gauge definitions to monitor what is important.

- **Topology module**—Provides a collection of submaps from one or more NNM maps. Each map must be open on the management station before the associated submap can be accessed. Drill-down through the NNM submap hierarchy is available.

11.2.1 Configuring Users

Before using SIP with live data, you must first define SIP users and roles. Users and Roles are defined from the SIP Configuration Editor GUI shown in Figure 11-11. Roles are associated with users to differentiate what appears on a user's portal view. For example, you may have a technical user that is interested in always displaying the same data on the portal. You may have a number of NOC Operators that require the ability to customize their portal to view specific data. SIP supplies a technical user that cannot be customized from the portal and a NOC operator that allows the user to add modules from the portal. The SIP Configuration Editor is started by executing

UNIX: /opt/OV/SIP/bin/SIPConfig

Windows: Start→Programs: HP OpenView→Service Information Portal→Configuration Editor

All valid portal users must be associated with at least one role. A role defines what a user can see and do through the portal. If a user has been associated with multiple roles, he can switch between roles via a drop-down list on the portal.

SIP uses XML files to define users and roles. The configuration editor manipulates these files based on the information supplied in the GUI. Each user and each role consists of a separate set of XML files organized per user. Before defining a user, you should determine the responsibilities of the user. The basic roles of a user include

- A portal view—Determines what information the user sees. It is a configured set of modules the user has access to and how these modules appear on the tabs. It also includes portal attributes, such as name, in the button bar, refresh rate, default tab, and portal header and footers.
- An editing permissions level—Defines the interactive editing operations that a user can perform through the portal interface. There are three editing levels, including ReadOnly, UserPreferences, and ViewAdmin.
- A management data filter—Refers to information about resources such as services, nodes, interfaces, servers that you want to display through the portal. There are three options in filtering data: AllData, NoData, and a customized data filter (providing nodes, interfaces, and services).

Figure 11-12 Users and roles are defined in the **SIP Configuration Editor**.

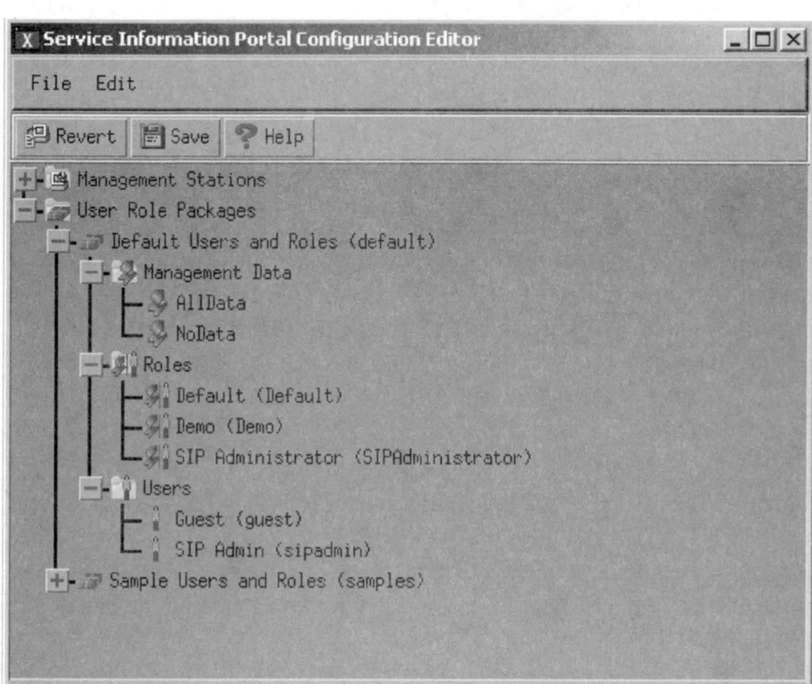

After determining the user roles, define a user. The following steps allow you to define a user with the existing role of a NOC Operator. The NOC Operator portal view contains a similar setup to the Generic Net view except that live data from your network is displayed. The NNM map must be open to access the Topology module.

1. Start the SIP Configuration Editor.
2. Right-click **Users** and select **New…**.
3. Provide the User Login Name **operator** and Display Name NOC **operator** on the **General** tab, as shown in Figure 11-13.
4. Select the **Roles** tab. Click the drop-down list for the **Initial Role:** and select **NOC Operator** as shown in Figure 11-14.
5. Click the **[Add]** button and select **NOC Operator** and **Technical** and click **[OK]** (see Figure 11-15).
6. Select **File→Save** from the main menu of the SIP Configuration Editor.
7. Open the default NNM map by executing **ovw&**
8. Login as the newly created user operator from the URL `http://hostname/ovportal`, specifying the SIP server hostname.

Figure 11-13 Use the **SIP Configuration Editor** to add users. Supply a **User Login Name** and a **Display Name** from the General tab.

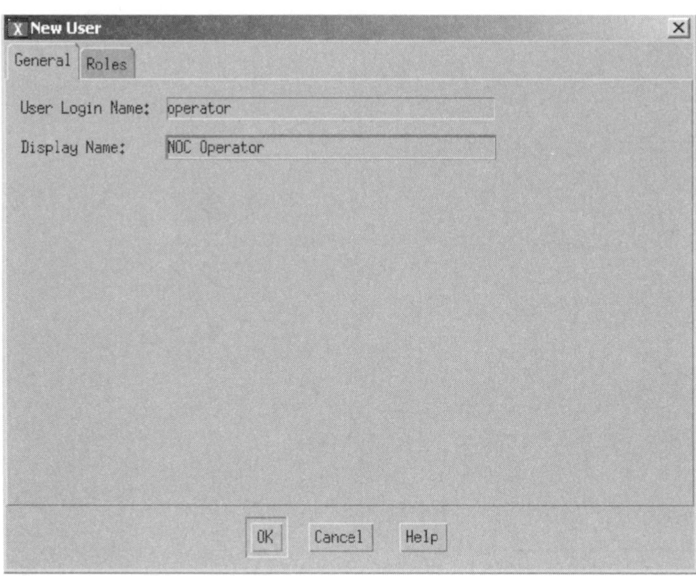

Figure 11-14 Select the Roles tab to define the **Initial Role** and **Other Roles** for a user. Select the Initial Role from the drop-down list as shown.

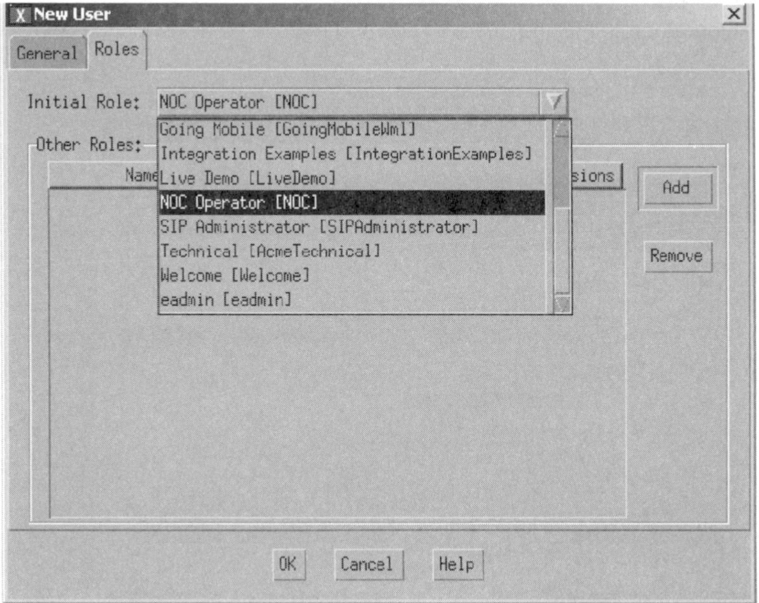

Figure 11-15 Select the **[Add]** button from the Roles tab to provide additional roles for the user. Select as many roles as required for the user.

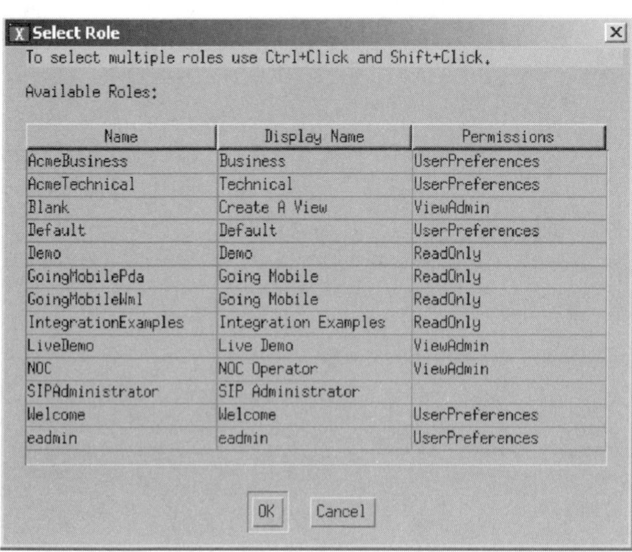

The NOC Operator role has the ability to add and remove modules as required for his job. Any user associated with the NOC Operator role has this capability. Figure 11-16 shows the drop down list of modules that may be added to the user's portal.

Figure 11-16 The NOC Operator role has the ability to add and remove modules to the portal view as shown above.

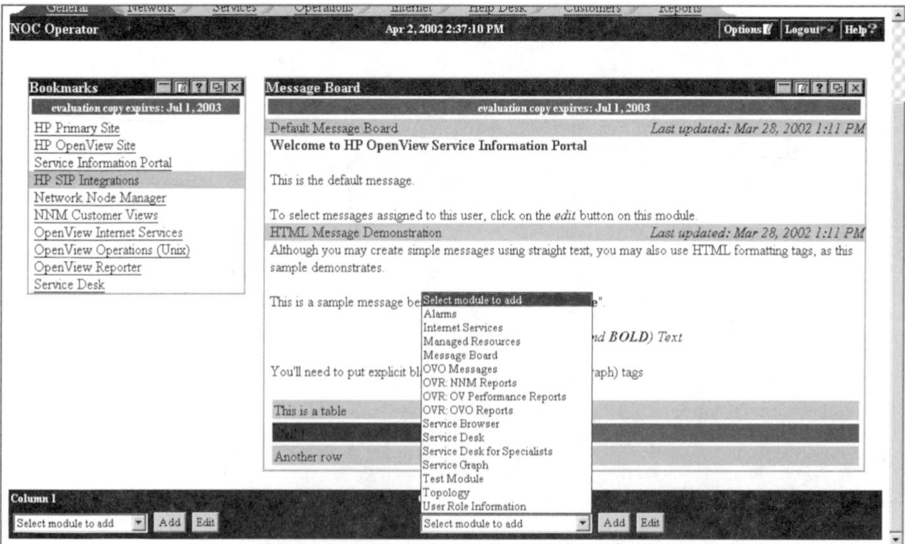

11.2.2 Configuring Roles

A role defines what the user sees in the portal view. Filters may be defined at the role level to hide data. This involves explicitly associating a filter definition with each role. The filter defines what data should be displayed when a user is acting in the given role. Three management data filters are available when defining roles:

1. **Show All Data**—Use this option if you do not want to segment data by customer organization.
2. **Show No Data**—Use this option if you do not want to display any real data through the portal, such as the Generic Net demo.
3. **Show Data for the Following Organizations**—Use this option if you want to configure a specific customer model that contains the organizations that you want to filter on.

Users and roles are configured in XML files. While these files may be manually edited, it is recommended that you use the SIP Configuration Editor to make changes. Certain advanced features are not available in the Configuration Editor and require the editing of the XML files. Roles can be modified using the following steps:

1. Start the SIP Configuration Editor.
2. Right click **Roles** and select **New...**.
3. Provide the **Role Name** and **Display Name** fields.
4. Select the Edit Permissions **ViewAdmin** as shown in Figure 11-17.

Figure 11-17 Supply the name of the XML file for the portal view relative to the views directory. Use the **[Browse]** button to search for the XML files. Sample XML files are provided in the **samples** directory.

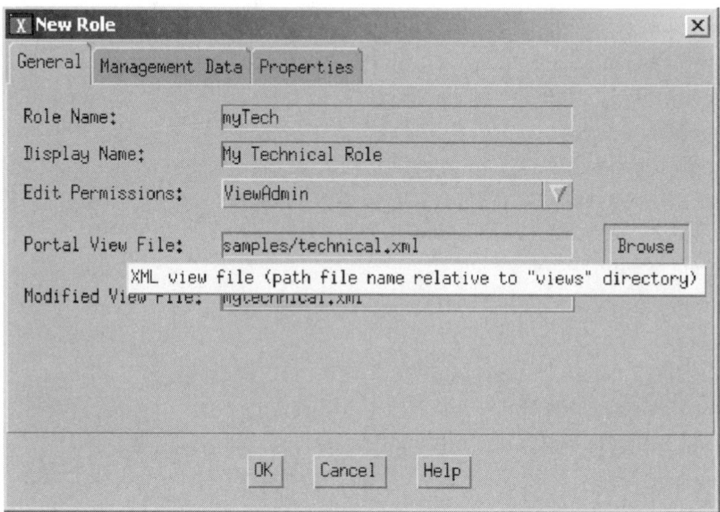

5. Click the **[Browse]** button and browse to the file samples/technical.xml.
6. Provide the Modified View File **myTech.xml**.
7. Select the **Data Management** tab shown in Figure 11-18.
8. Select **Use specific management data: AllData**.
9. Click **[OK]**.
10. Select **File→Save** from the main menu of the SIP Configuration Editor.

Figure 11-18 Select **Use specific management data** on the **Management Data** tab. Select **All Data** from the data drop-down list to give a user access to all customers.

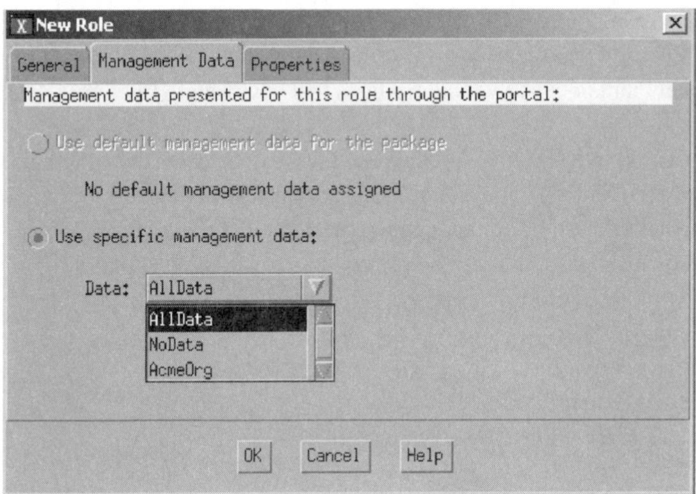

11.2.3 User Role Packages

In addition to providing the capability of defining users and roles, the SIP Configuration Editor may be used to group users and roles by organization. This type of grouping is called a user role package. Each user role package contains a set of users, roles, and management data. You can define all users and roles in a single package or partition them into multiple packages. For example, you may want to create a separate package for each customer. This package would contain the customer's role definitions, users, and management data. To create a package, follow these steps:

1. Start the SIP Configuration Editor.
2. Right-click **User Role Packages** and select **New…**
3. Provide the **Package Name:** Customer1
4. Provide the **Package Title:** Customer1
5. Select **Assign Default Management Data**.
6. Select **AllData** from the **Default Management Data** drop-down list.
7. Add Roles and Users to the newly created user role package, as previously defined.

11.2.4 Adding an NNM Station to SIP

Before accessing live data via your portal, you must establish connectivity between SIP and NNM. One or more NNM stations can be added to SIP. NNM does not need reside on the same system as NNM. NNM stations are configured with the SIP Configuration Editor.

1. Start the SIP Configuration Editor.
2. Right-click the **Management Stations** folder and select **[New…]**.
3. Provide the fully qualified hostname of the management station and click **[OK]**.
4. Select the **NNM** tab, as shown in Figure 11-19.
5. Select **NNM Is Installed On This System**.
6. Select the Version of NNM you are running.
7. Select the operating system (Windows or UNIX).
8. The port numbers do not need to be modified. They are populated when you save the configuration.
9. Select **Use As SNMP Data Source** to enable access to data for the Network Device Health Gauge module.
10. Select **Use As Alarms Data Source** to enable access to data for the Alarms module.
11. Select **Use As OVw Symbol Source** to enable access to symbol images for the Topology module and click **[OK]**.

Figure 11-19 To add an NNM server, start the SIP Configuration Editor, right-click **Management Server**, and click **New**. From the NNM tab, select **NNM Is Installed On This System** as shown.

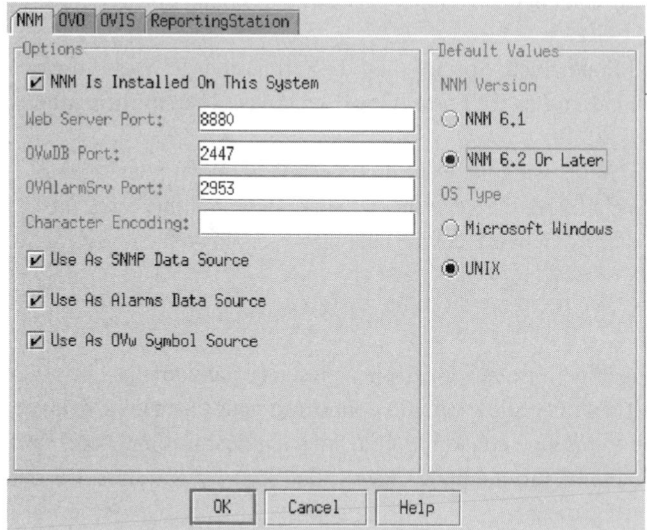

11.2.5 Integrating CV Organizations

The SIP program **getcvdata.exe** generates an XML file of the data from the CV database. Each XML file generated is an SIP customer model mapping conforming to the standard SimpleCustomerModel.dtd supplied with SIP. Configure CV as defined in Chapter 8 before this integration begins. The following steps allow integration of Customer Views defined data to be integrated into SIP:

1. Execute the command **getcvdata.exe**.
   UNIX: /opt/OV/www/cgi-bin/getcvdata.exe > /tmp/cvdata.xml
   Windows: \OpenView\www\cgi-bin\getcvdata.exe > c:\temp\cvdata.xml
2. Copy the **cvdata.xml** file to the organizations directory.
   UNIX:
   cp /tmp/cvdata.xml /opt/OV/SIP/conf/share/organizations
   Windows:
   copy \temp\cvdata.xml %SIP_HOME%\conf\share\organizations
3. Log into the portal as **sipadmin**.
4. Select the **Customer Model** tab and scroll down to **Customer Model Sources**.
5. Type **cvdata.xml** in the New customer Model Source URL field.
6. Click **[Add]** to integrate all customers from the **cvdata.xml** file.
7. Create a new package called BellSouth (assuming that you defined BellSouth as a customer in CV).
8. Add new management data specifying to **Show Data for the Following Organizations**. The drop-down list should now contain all customers previously defined in CV. Select bellsouth.net and click **[OK]** twice.
9. Create a new role named Bell South Tech. Specify the Edit Permissions as **ViewAdmin**. Browse to the **samples/technical.xml** as the Portal View File. Select **Use Specific management Data** and select **Bell South**.
10. Define a new user named BellSouth using the BellSouth Tech Role. When you login as the newly defined user, you see a filtered view of the network. Based on this filter, the view is limited to BellSouth alarms, network device health and topology.

11.3 SUMMARY

SIP can provide a uniform display method for many OpenView products, including NNM, OVO, OVIS, OVSN, OVPI, and OVSD. It not only allows you to connect to your OpenView management products, but also allows you to provide content to your own applications and data. With SIP, you can create a custom look and feel to the portal views. For security purposes, the displayed content can be segmented by customer.

CHAPTER 12

Introduction to OpenView Operations (OVO)

Many challenges lie ahead for communication service providers. While NNM addresses many of these challenges, it is difficult, if not impossible, for one product to satisfy all of them. Add-on products such as *Customer Views* (CV) and *Service Information Portal* (SIP) extend the functionality of NNM by allowing customization of the physical enterprise to reflect the logical enterprise. Service providers may require additional functionality to adequately manage extra resources, such as applications. In today's always-on infrastructure, there's a higher demand to keep all components of the enterprise up and running.

OpenView Operations (OVO) focuses on managing applications that run in the enterprise. OVO provides centrally configured intelligent agents that monitor specific applications. The OVO agent is supported on multiple platforms, including Windows and many versions of UNIX. This chapter introduces the three types of users, including the OVO Operator, Administrator, and the Template Administrator.

12.1 MONITORING THE ENTERPRISE WITH OVO

In the simplest form of monitoring devices, a management application can determine whether the device is up or down. NNM does an excellent job of discovering an enterprise and providing up/down status of the managed environment. In addition, NNM provides the ability to capture SNMP traps that are unsolicited messages indicating something on the device has a problem. Taken a step further, monitoring a system's running processes, services, or applications provides a more robust monitoring solution. OVO is designed to help administrators detect, solve, and prevent problems from occurring in the enterprise.

OVO runs in conjunction with the NNM processes in order to extend the management functionality to monitor processes, services, and applications. For example, some of the standard OVO offerings include monitoring **syslog** (UNIX), **rclog** (UNIX), and **iisadmin** service (Windows). The monitored environment can be configured to generate messages when certain errors appear in the **syslog** and **rclog** files. Messages can be generated when **iisadmin** service stops running.

The OVO agent has the ability to capture information from various message sources. These message sources are captured by one of the following interceptors: logfile encapsulator, SNMP trap interceptor, MPE Console, or OVO message interface,[1] as shown in Figure 12-1. The messages are assigned default attributes and presented in the OVO message browser. The message conditions are applied to the message to determine whether to suppress, prioritize, group, reformulate and correlate messages. The logfile encapsulator searches for specific patterns in a logfile. The trap interceptor captures SNMP traps that are sent to the management station and determines how to act on them. The MPE Console output can be monitored with OVO. The message interface is designed for template developers to customize templates that cannot be monitored with the previously mentioned methods.

Add-on components are also available to monitor specific applications and databases, such as Oracle®, Microsoft® Exchange Server, and PeopleSoft®. These add-on components are referred to as *Smart Plug-Ins* (SPIs). SPIs are very sophisticated and typically offer hundreds of monitoring options. SPIs frequently include commands and actions capable of restarting specific processes. SPIs also may incorporate application performance monitoring. For a list of available SPIs, refer to `http://ovweb.external.hp.com/lpe/doc_serv`.

Figure 12-1 OVO message sources are intercepted by logfile encapsulators, trap interceptors, MPE console, and the OVO message interface. The messages are assigned default attributes and presented in the OVO message browser.

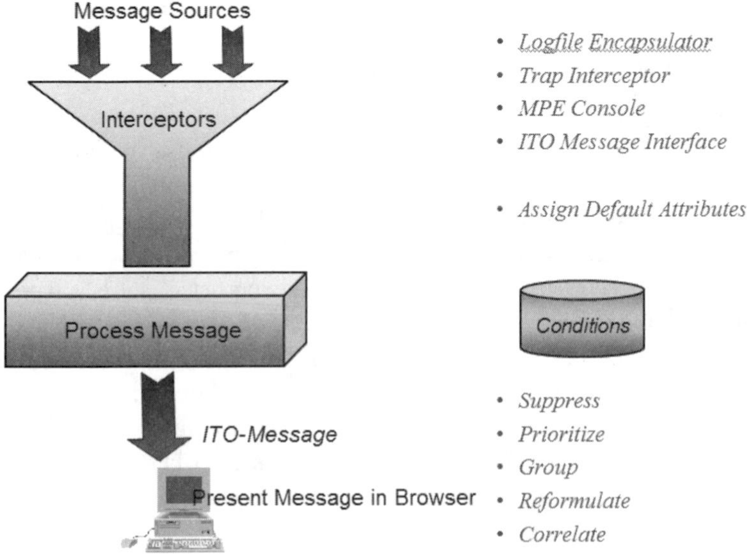

[1] The OVO message interface is the **opcmsg** command. This command may be used in a script or in a compiled program. **opcmsg** provide the ability for a template developer to adequately monitor an application.

12.1.1 OVO Terminology

OVO consists of a client/server solution that allows the configuration to be centrally managed and monitored. The monitoring process is distributed to the managed nodes. Problem resolution can also be distributed to the managed node by including automatic actions associated with the message source template that capture the problem. The messages or events appear in the message browser as shown in the diagram in Figure 12-2.

Figure 12-2 OVO consists of a client/server model that provides central configuration and distributed monitoring. Configuration is performed on the management server and the agents monitor the managed nodes.

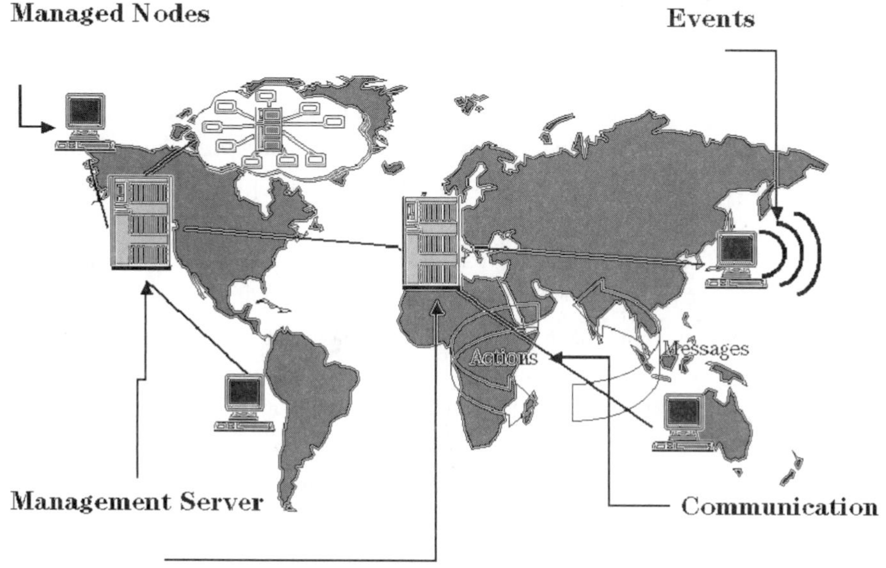

The following list describes OVO terminology that will be used throughout the remainder of this book:

Management Server—The OVO management server is the central location from which all configurations are performed. The management server consists of an Oracle database containing messages generated by the OVO agents.[2] Supported management servers include HP-UX and Solaris. Refer to the *Installation Guide for the Management Server* for a complete list of supported operating system versions for the management server and the agent available from `http://ovweb.external.hp.com/lpe/doc_serv`.

2 A management server running OVO also runs the underlying NNM processes. When OVO is installed, NNM is also installed. NNM performs the discovery of the nodes. OVO is responsible for monitoring applications running on the nodes.

Agent—OVO provides an intelligent agent that must be distributed to all nodes to be managed by OVO. The monitoring process occurs on the managed node. The agent is capable of performing local actions on the node. For example, you might want to monitor a process and restart the process if it stops running. The agent combined with the appropriate template provides this capability. Some of the currently supported OVO agent platforms include HP-UX, Solaris, Windows 2000, Windows XP, Linux, AIX, and Tru64.

Templates—A template defines the applications to be monitored by the OVO agent. Select templates are assigned and distributed to a managed node based on the applications to be monitored. OVO ships with default templates that provide monitoring for common operating system logfiles and processes. Templates can be developed by administrators to monitor most applications. SPIs extend the functionality of OVO by providing specific application and database templates for applications such as Oracle®, SAP®, and Microsoft Exchange Server®.

Message browser—The message browser is the focal point of OVO. Messages are events generated by an OVO agent indicating that something has happened on the managed node. Messages that appear in the browser are stored in an Oracle database on the management server.

Managed node—OVO managed nodes have an OVO agent installed. The agent monitors applications on the node based on the templates assigned to the node.

Events—An event is something that happens on a managed node. Events of interest might consist of a stopped process or service, an error message in a log file, or an application that is not functioning as it should. Events are detected by the OVO agent and templates assigned to the managed node.

Actions—The agent is capable of performing local actions on a managed node. For example, you may want to monitor a process and restart the process if it stops running. The agent combined with the appropriate template provides the ability to detect that the process has stopped running and automatically restart the process.

12.1.2 OVO, VPO, ITO, and OPC: They're All the Same

OVO was formerly named *Vantage Point Operations* (VPO). OVO was also formerly named *IT/Operations* (ITO) and *Operations Center* (OPC). The renaming of the product came about with major product releases. However, the original commands and processes have not changed since the original commands used for OPC. Much of the OVO product documentation still contains OPC, ITO and VPO references.

OVO is invoked by typing **opc** from the command line. The **opc** command does not require backgrounding (opc&). Backgrounding is handled by the command itself. When you start OVO, you should see the login window shown in Figure 12-3.

Figure 12-3 Start OVO by typing **opc** from the command line. The default operator login is **opc_op** and the password is **OpC_op**. Usernames and passwords are case sensitive.

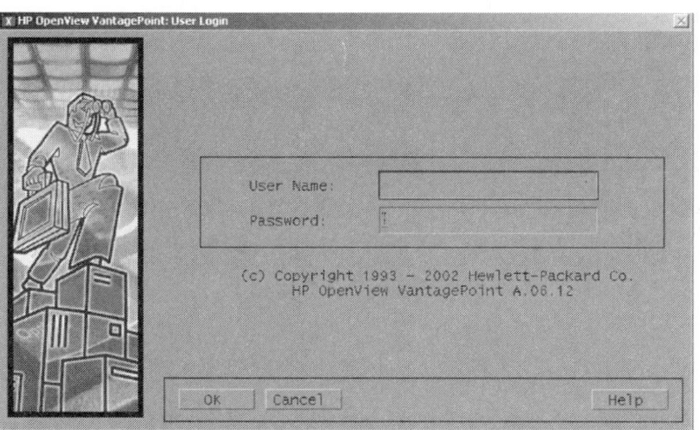

The default OVO logins include an operator (opc_op) and an administrator (opc_adm) user account. The default passwords are **OpC_op** for the **opc_op** account and **OpC_adm** for the **opc_adm**. The passwords are case sensitive. Note that these accounts are not affiliated with a Unix login. They are strictly used to login to the OVO application. The operator and administrator logins are described briefly in the following sections of this chapter.

12.2 THE OVO OPERATOR

The OVO operator is the user responsible for monitoring the environment. The message browser provides the operator with a view of messages and is the focal point of an operator account. The messages in the message browser indicate to the operator that an event has occurred. An event typically indicates that something in the managed enterprise has gone wrong.

The message browser contains ten columns, as shown in Figure 12-4. Each column provides indicators to the operator. At a glance, the operator can determine where the event originated, the severity of the event, and the type of event that occurred.

The operator login provides a toolset enabling the operator to perform a job. The job entails attempting to resolve problems listed by the events in the message browser. The operator login consists of five windows, described briefly in the following list:

- **Root**—The root window is a submap containing the hierarchy of all discovered devices in the enterprise.
- **Managed Nodes**—The Managed Nodes window contains the managed nodes assigned to the operator. An operator may be responsible for a subset of nodes in an enterprise. Operators are assigned nodes based on the monitored applications and the operator skill set.
- **Message Groups**—The Message Groups window consists of message groups assigned to the operator. Message groups contain events generated by OVO agents based on monitored attributes such as database, operating system type, or application name.

- **Application Desktop—**The Application Desktop contains applications and application groups assigned to the operator. Applications can be executed by the operator on a managed node without actually having to log into the system.
- **Message browser**—The message browser contains messages, message attributes, and status information sent by the managed nodes for which the operator is responsible.

OVO provides a Java-based GUI similar to that shown in Figure 12-5. The java client can be installed on Windows and Unix systems and configured to access the OVO server. The necessary components of OVO are available from the Java-based GUI for an operator to monitor messages and perform routine tasks.

Figure 12-4 The message browser is the focal point of OVO. The message browser contains events that indicate to the operator that something has happened. At a glance, an operator can determine the severity of the event, the event message, and node on which the event occurred.

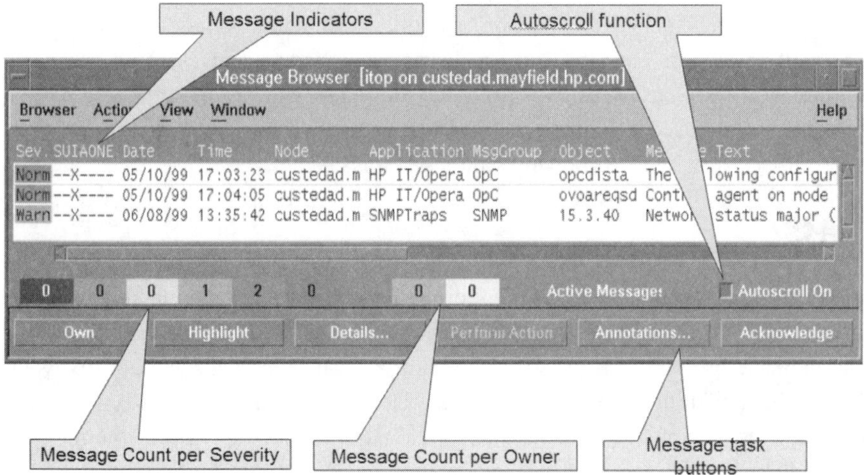

The operator has the ability to limit the messages in the view by setting the filter as shown in Figure 12-5. An additional feature available with the Java-based GUI is the ability to click on a column to sort messages. By default, messages are sorted according to the timestamp. If you were to click the **[Node]** button at the top of the Node column, the messages would be sorted alphabetically by node name.

Figure 12-5 The left pane of the Java-based GUI consists of an Explorer-like tree view of managed nodes, node groups, message groups, and applications. The right pane consists of the message browser.

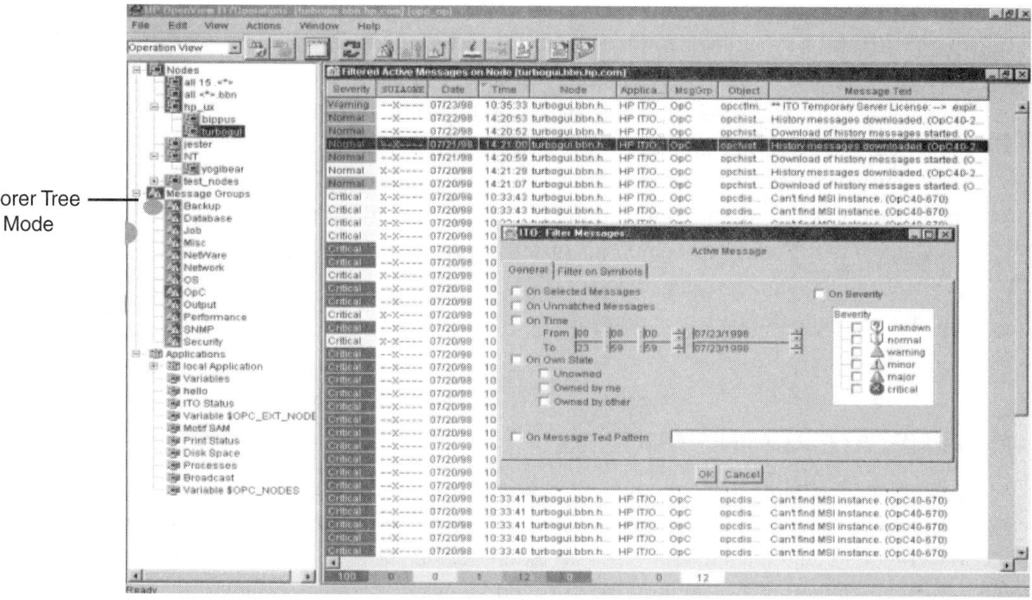

12.3 THE OVO ADMINISTRATOR

OVO makes no assumptions about a managed enterprise. Because of this, the OVO managed enterprise must be configured. The default administrator account is **opc_adm** and the password is **OpC_adm**. The administrator account provides the capability to configure the managed environment. The OVO administrator tasks of OVO include:

- **Adding managed nodes**—Devices connected to the network are discovered by underlying NNM processes (see Chapter 3, "Create a Deployment Plan"). However, devices are not automatically managed by OVO. The administrator must define the devices that to be monitored.
- **Creating node groups**—Node groups provide a logical means of managing systems. Nodes can be grouped based on attributes such as platform, application or customer. Node groups can be used to assign templates. Node groups are assigned to an operator based on the operator's skill set.
- **Creating message groups**—Message groups provide a logical means of grouping events that arrive in the message browser. Message groups are assigned to an operator.
- **Creating and customizing templates**—Templates are assigned and distributed to the managed node to determine what the OVO agent will monitor.

- **Creating template groups**—Template groups provide a logical means of organizing template. Template groups are assigned and distributed to the managed node to determine what the OVO agent will monitor.
- **Creating operators**—The default OVO operator account is **opc_op**. A typical environment will have a separate operator account for each OVO user.
- **Configuring operators**—The configuration of an operator includes defining managed nodes, applications, message groups. Each OVO operator may have a specific set of managed nodes and message group in which to monitor.
- **Distribution of agents and templates to managed nodes**—When the managed environment has been defined, the administrator must assign and distribute templates and the OVO agent to the managed node. This installs a process with a small footprint (less than 2% of the CPU) on the managed node. The agent process performs application monitoring and the templates define which applications to monitor.

12.4 TEMPLATE ADMINISTRATORS

OVO has one main administrator account, **opc_adm** that provides the ability to perform all necessary configuration. An OVO implementation may require additional users to assist with template development and customization. For example, specific applications require custom templates and may require a special set of skills and knowledge. Some examples of special skills include knowledge of applications and operating systems such as Oracle, Solaris, HP-UX, and SAP. Because these skill sets are diverse, many different administrators may be required to develop and maintain OVO templates for the corresponding applications.

The template administrator account provides the ability to create and maintain templates and template groups. The template administrator cannot assign or distribute templates. Templates contain parameters for monitoring including the name and location of a file to be monitored, a polling interval, and a set of conditions that capture or suppress messages. Templates also determine what to do with the message source after it has been intercepted. A template dictates whether to suppress, prioritize, group, reformulate and correlate messages.

Note: There is a command-line interface that allows you to maintain nodes, node groups, and template assignments. You must have root privileges to execute this command. For example, if you want to assign and distribute the existing template named OBAgent to the node ob001, execute the following two commands: opcnode -assign_templ templ_name="OBAgent" templ_type=EC_TEMPLATE node_name=ob001 net_type=NETWORK_IP opcragt -distrib -templates -force ob001

12.5 SUMMARY

OVO focuses on application monitoring. OVO provides centrally configured intelligent agents that monitor specific applications. OVO allows you to monitor processes, services, and applications by distributing agent to the managed nodes. The OVO agent runs on multiple platforms, including Windows and many versions of UNIX. OVO can be accessed from a Motif-based GUI and from a Java-based GUI.

OVO provides three different user types: an administrator to configure the environment, an operator to monitor the environment, and a template administrator to configure and develop the templates needed to monitor the applications. The focal point of the OVO operator is the message browser. A message in the browser indicates to the operator that something has gone wrong. It is the responsibility of the operator to attempt to resolve the problem and return the system or application back to a normal state. Good luck.

PART 2

OpenView Operations

In this section, we address the fundamental issues that face OpenView administrators. Many OpenView administrators have information technology and service management experience. Most of us can draw upon our skills in IT to help design and implement an OpenView solution to support the daily enterprise management tasks. So, whether you are new to IT or not, this section will help you with some of the fundamental concepts of enterprise service management and how they are implemented using the OpenView family of products.

The building blocks of the OpenView Enterprise Service Management solutions fit together like pieces of a puzzle. When all the essential pieces come together, you have a big picture that represents solutions for all aspects of enterprise and service management.

Inside the Network Services, solution is Network Node Manager. Systems and Services is where OpenView Operations is positioned. This book is written about these core products. Part 1 introduced Network Node Manager. Part 2 is dedicated to OpenView Operations. For Complete OpenView product descriptions, visit `http://www.openview.hp.com/solutions/index.asp`.

CHAPTER 13

Out-of-the-box with HP OpenView Operations

Installing an enterprise-wide system and services management solution begins with a plan. The plan will evolve as you refine the Service Level Agreements and objectives for the scope of work. After an analysis of the current business environment, you can gather the system and network management requirements and begin to work out the design and implementation details of the hardware and software. Whether you are working with a team or as a team of one, you should answer a few questions in the early phases of planning an OpenView implementation. Some of the questions are listed here for reference:

What services are provided by the business?

Who needs what type of systems and service availability information?

What are the security policies and concerns?

Is the current system management environment adequate?

Will the current system management environment map to OVO?

Is there a need to re-engineer the current environment (for example, moving off obsolete technology)?

Are there current system management tools that will readily integrate with the OpenView platform?

When your enterprise management plan calls for NNM and OpenView Operations (the focus of this book), it is important to collaborate with all the potential users, customers, managers, and other staff who will be impacted by this implementation. Root user access is required to install the agent software and components onto the managed nodes. In this chapter, we focus on some of the primary tasks of preparing the management server for the OVO domain. The topics covered include server installation, configuration, administrator and operator consoles and much more.

The OS platform of the OVO Management Server can either be Hewlett Packard (HP-UXHP-UX) or Sun (Solaris). Another management product is *OpenView Operations for Windows* (OVOW), a separate product for the Intel architecture. Here the Management Server runs on MS

Windows. Again, the managed nodes can be a heterogeneous mixture of various supported platforms.We cover more details about OVOW in Part 4 of this book, "OpenView Operations for Windows." After the management server hardware and software installation, you have only touched the tip of the iceberg for managing your enterprise with OpenView.

13.1 CONSIDER A SERVICE LEVEL IMPLEMENTATION

Businesses provide services to customers. The status of the service(s) is important at all levels of an organization. Service offerings might include email, web, or business-to-business. When a service is rendered unavailable, discovering the root cause and the impact to the business are critical steps in the service recovery process. Unplanned application, system, or device downtime may affect the business and the service delivery to the customer. With OpenView, it is possible to implement an enterprise management operations environment that will show you the status of the services that are supported by the back-end network, systems, and applications.

An overall view of the business from a service perspective enables faster resolution of any service impacting problems within the IT infrastructure. For example: You provide email services to customers (internal or external) using several mail servers that are located on different networks. The OV operator Java console can show you a graphical view of the email service. This view is possible as a result of the integration of OpenView Service Navigator at the management server. OV Service Navigator is a separate product but it is tightly integrated with OVO out-of-the-box and is available at no extra cost. The service configuration must be assigned to the operator before service views are visible within the operator's Java console. Figure 13-1 shows an example service view. The OpenView Navigator Concepts and Configuration Guide is available at the OpenView web site: `http://ovweb.external.hp.com/lpe/doc_serv/`.

Figure 13-1 Service graph.

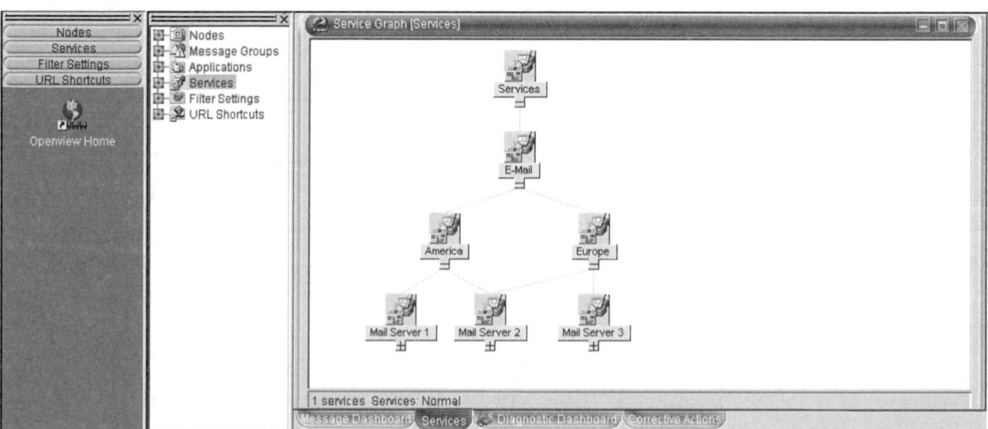

The OpenView product solutions guide available at: `http://openview.hp.com/solutions` is an excellent place to begin if you need to get a better perspective on how the OpenView solutions for Enterprise, Service Provider, and Adaptive Management ensure rapid deployment of the correct solution for your environment. Several of the solution categories are listed here for reference.

- **Enterprise Solutions**—IT service management, network services, service-driven operations management, windows management, web services and application management, and storage management.
- **Service Provider Solutions**—Wireless and mobile, fixed voice, broadband access and transmission, cable and multi-service operations, ISP and IP networks, network equipment provider, developers, service assurance, service delivery and fulfillment, service usage and billing.
- **Adaptive Management Solutions**—Analysis of the business and user demand for resources and uninterrupted, secure, dynamic allocation of resources.
- Other solutions are provided by HP Partner Products.

13.2 PRE- AND POST-SOFTWARE INSTALLATION SUMMARY

The OpenView products installed on the management server are delivered in CD sets. Oracle for OpenView is a separate CD set. The initial installation of the OpenView management platform includes the following software products:

- **OpenView Operations (OVO)**—Installed on a server hardware platform the OVO application provides central operations and problem management of multi-vendor distributed systems.
- **Service Navigator**—Add-on component of the OVO Java-based operator GUI. Service Navigator maps the incidents discovered by OVO to the monitored business or IT services. Provides views of the environment from the service perspective. Integrates with OVO out-of-the-box. (Requires a separate license.)
- **Smart Plug-Ins (SPIs)**—Pre-configured modules that provide out-of-the-box management of applications, components, services and daemons. The operating system SPI (OS-SPI) is included with the OVO software bundle. (Refer to Chapter 15, "Smart Plug-Ins," for more information about SPIs.)
- **Java Operator Console**—Integrates applications, tools, real time monitoring, service views, and much more into one secure operations console.
- **Remote Ovw Integration**—Starts OV applications and services (such as ipmap) on remote OV systems from the local client console.
- **Oracle for OpenView (OfO)**—Provides the data store for the run time OVO environment; after the database is installed, all record inserts, updates, and deletes should be done via the OpenView graphical interface, Application Program Interface(s), or using the OVO commands. (Separate CD set.)

- **Network Node Manager (NNM)**—Performs initial network discovery and monitors the network environment. NNM provides many tools for network management.

This section provides a high-level overview of the OpenView installation tasks. The list in Table 13-1 covers many of the tasks that you will perform during the OpenView implementation project. Depending on the scope of the implementation, you may choose to organize the tasks into one large or several small projects. Whatever you decide, it is important to document the plan and create operations procedures as part of the project deliverables.

13.2.1 Implementation Tasks

Table 13-1 includes implementation tasks you will perform through formal or informal planning. This list is just a start, and not all of the items will apply to every enterprise management scenario. The typical OpenView system implementation will include most but is not limited to only the items in the list. The important thing to remember is found in the form of the following quote: "Let us begin with the end in mind."—Stephen Covey

Table 13-1 OpenView Operations Implementation Checklist

Project Categories	Summary of Tasks
General	Project Plan.
	Budget for h/w and s/w purchases.
	Budget for h/w and s/w support.
	Budget for consulting.
	Read the OpenView Operations Installation Guide, Release Notes and Concepts Guide.
	Define the service management environment.
	Involvement and Information sharing with all affected parties.
	Training for system support staff.
	Training for operations staff.
	Review existing operations, security and support policies and procedures and how these will map with overall use of OpenView for systems and service management.
	Disaster Recovery Plan for OpenView.
Management Server Implementation Tasks.	Configure the hardware.
	Install the operating system (o/s).
	Install the o/s patches.
	Configure the o/s kernel for OVO.
	Configure the file systems for OVO.
	Create the OVO accounts.
	Install the Oracle database binaries.
	Install the Oracle database patches, if applicable.
	Install NNM and OVO.
	Install the NNM and OVO patches if necessary.
	Install the management server agent software and components.
	Install add-on OpenView products.

Project Categories	Summary of Tasks
	Backup the management server for disaster recovery.
	Obtain the permanent software licenses.
	Test the disaster recovery procedures.
Managed Nodes	Verify the managed node h/w and s/w requirements.
Implementation Tasks	Configure the nodes for the OV Installation.
	Verify the network communications between the node and management server.
	Verify name resolution consistency between the managed nodes and the server.
	Verify time synchronization within the network domain of the management server(s). Refer to the *Network Time Protocol* (NTP) documentation, `http://www.ntp.org`.
	Install agent software.
	Test the operation of the agents.
External Notification Services	Decide what external notification services (mail, paging or trouble ticketing) will integrate with the OpenView environment.
Service Policies and Components	Determine which services and applications will be included inside the OV operator environment.
	Install additional SPIs.
	Customize the service management components.
Messages and Events	Determine what events, errors and resource thresholds shall trigger messages, automatic or operator actions.
	Determine which events to correlate or message suppression.
	Define and organize the management environment (such as message groups, node groups, node hierarchies, application groups).
	Configure new and customize existing service policies and Instrumentation.
	Deploy the service policies and components.
	Deploy message-forwarding policies (if necessary).
Operator Environment	Determine which operators will have OpenView accounts.
	Define operator accounts.
	Define operator responsibilities; Includes node groups, message groups and applications.
	Test the operator accounts.
	Verify the operator responsibilities.
Security	Modify default account passwords.
	Implement user, application, data and network security policies.
Configuration Management	Configure periodic configuration download and data archiving.
and System Maintenance	Decide on an online or offline backup policy
	Implement and test the backup strategy.
	Optimize database operations.
	(See Appendix C for database-tuning resources.)
	Consider implementing OV configuration and change management policies and procedures.
Documentation	System Implementation Plan.

Table 13-1 OpenView Operations Implementation Checklist (Continued)

Project Categories	Summary of Tasks
	System configuration. System Operations Procedures. System Maintenance Procedures. System Upgrade Procedures. Backup and Restore Procedures. Disaster Recovery Plan. Determine if operations procedures and instructions will be implemented for each event or provided via an external application such as a web browser. Determine which additional reports are necessary, and whether they are produced via the built-in report system or If external reporting applications should be implemented (i.e. OV Reporter).

Note: This checklist assumes a standalone server configuration. Refer to specific OpenView High Availability Documentation for failover configurations.

13.2.2 Installation: Frequently Asked Questions

The following questions will help with some of the issues you may encounter during or soon after the installation is complete:

1. **Is it possible to change the initial database configuration parameters?** The initial database size is determined by the default configuration parameters for the tables and tablespaces, and is located in the file /etc/opt/OV/share/conf/ovdbconf which is called by the OVO configuration script /opt/OV/bin/OpC/install/ovoinstall. After installation, the database files can be recreated with different parameters with the command **opcdbreorg -consolidate**, and with new parameter values in the file **/etc/opt/OV/share/conf/OpC/mgmt_sv/oracle_sizing.cfg**. See the manual pages for complete syntax. Ensure that you have performed complete system and database backup prior to executing any commands that make structural changes to the database. Use the default configuration if your initial environment is small or medium with less than 500 nodes. Before taking any steps to tune the database for performance, it is a good idea to discuss the issues with a knowledgeable database expert or OpenView consultant.
2. **Should the database data and Index files be collocated on the same disk?** Tablespaces for data and indexes are generally located on different disks for performance improvements. Additional information and recommendations for OpenView Database Performance and best practices are discussed in Chapter 18, "Oracle for OpenView."
3. **Are there any documents that contain the database entity relationships and database schema?** The database schema and entity relationship documentation, Reporting and Database Schema, is available on the management server in the directory /opt/OV/www/htdocs/ito_doc/C/manuals. The manuals are also available online at `http://ovweb.external.hp.com/lpe/doc_serv/`. Although the schema is

published, it is not recommended or supported to modify the data without using either the provided utilities or APIs.

4. **What is the procedure to obtain the permanent software license or check an existing license?** The license is based on the IP address of the management server. There is a form available for getting a license in the directory /etc/opt/OV/share/conf/OVLicense/forms/opc. Also, the Installation Guide for the Management Server contains a licensing chapter. Obtain the license via the web at `http://www.webware.hp.com`. OVO will function using a built-in temporary license out-of-the box for 90 days. (If the server is configured in a cluster, use the IP address of the OVO package for the license.)
5. **How is the DISPLAY variable set for the Oracle and OVO Installations?** Users oracle and root set the DISPLAY variable prior to calling the Installation programs. If you are installing via an X-emulation program on a PC, remember to set the DISPLAY variable to the PC hostname or IP address. Example: **export DISPLAY=pcname:0.0**. If the display variable is not set correctly, the Oracle installer will produce an error message. Also, ensure that the X Display Manager will allow the GUI for Oracle to display on your terminal. Enable the X application permission to display with the command "**xhost +**". Refer to the man page for syntax details. Check the display setting with the command **/usr/bin/X11/xset -q**.
6. **What should you do if you have to re-start the Oracle Installer?** If there are any problems during the startup of the Oracle Installer program and you need to stop and re-start, you will need to do some cleanup first. Check for any programs started by the installer using the **ps** command. If necessary, shut down any of the Oracle Installer programs using the **kill** command. Remove the directories from /tmp created by the installer.

13.3 INSTALLING THE MANAGEMENT SERVER

The time it takes to install the OpenView software onto the management server will vary based upon your familiarity with the system hardware, network and operating system environments. Your experience with prior versions of the application will also prove beneficial with the installation of any new versions of the products. So, whether you are just starting or have the experience of prior installations, the first steps are listed here for reference:

- Develop a written plan.
- Share the plan with other peers, managers, customers.
- Review the impact of this installation into your test, development, or production environment.
- Prepare all the necessary resources.
- Re-read the installation procedures three times.

- Refer to the *OpenView Operations Installation Guide* for detailed instructions. The *OpenView Installation Guide for the Management Server* (HP-UXHP-UX or Solaris) is available at `http://ovweb.external.hp.com/lpe/doc_serv/`.
- Read the release notes.

HP-UX operating system examples are used throughout this part of the book. Any significant installation differences for the Solaris are indicated when appropriate.

13.3.1 Hardware and Software Prerequisites

The hardware and software prerequisite verification is the first step in the installation process. Taking the time to perform this important task ensures that your installation completes in a timely manner and without error. One method to verify the HP server configuration is with the command **/opt/ignite/bin/print_manifest**; this produces a report that includes information in the following categories:

- **System Information**—System type and build data
- **System Hardware**—System model, memory, processors, OS, LAN, SWID, and Language
- **Storage devices**—HW Path and Interface Name
- **I/O Interfaces**—Class, HW Path, Driver, and Description
- **Installed Software**—Product Name, Revision, and Description
- **Logical Volume Manager (LVM) File System Configuration**
- **JFS File System (JFS or VXFS) Configuration**
- **Disk layout**—LVM Disk, Device file, HW Address, size, and volume group
- **File System layout**—LVM device file, mount point, size, and file system type
- **Swap configuration**—Type, size, priority, and device/location
- **Kernel Configuration**—Drivers and Parameters
- **System Information**—Hostname, IP Address, Subnet mask, Gateway IP, and time zone

The **/opt/ignite/bin/print_manifest** command is only available if Ignite/UX client or server is installed. Installing OVO uses HP Distributor and runs a pre-installation check for kernel parameters, disk space, hostname, and so on during the installation. The output of the check can be read form the software distributor logfile.

Produce a similar report on a SUN Solaris server with the commands **prtconf** and **pkginfo**. Refer to the man pages for syntax details and optional command line parameters.

The specification and final configuration for the disk, memory, and swap resources depends on a number of factors, including:

1. How many user sessions will operate in parallel?
2. How many operators will use Motif GUIs?
3. How many operators will use Java GUIs?
4. How many active messages?
5. How many acknowledged messages?
6. How large is the IP network?

The disk, memory and swap minimum requirements are summarized in Table 13-2. The information in the table is based on approximately 500 nodes, 3,000 active messages, and 1,000 objects in the Service Navigator tree. The required parameters may vary with different OV software versions. The best practice is to review the most current installation guide.

Table 13-2 Disk, Memory and Swap Minimum Requirements

Binary and Data Files	Disk Space	Swap Space	RAM
Oracle Binaries	2400 MB	1024 MB	512MB
/opt/OV	700 MB*	512 MB	512 MB + 35 MB per OVO Motif
/etc/opt/OV	25 MB		GUI + 128MB per Java GUI
/var/opt/OV	135 MB		
OVO Data	800 MB		

* Although 700 MB is specified, it is recommended that you make available 1.5 GB.

Table13-3 is a listing of the recommended kernel parameters.

Table 13-3 Recommended Kernel Parameters for the Management Server

Kernel Parameter	Minimum Setting
Fs_async	= 0
Max_thread_proc	>= 1024
Maxdsiz	>= 0x40000000
Maxssiz	>= 0x4000000
Maxfiles	>= 256
Maxuprc	>= 256
Nfile	>= 5000
Mkthread	>= 6000
Nproc	>= 700
Semmni	>= 140
Semmns	>= 400
Shmmax	>= 0x80000000
Shmmni	>= 256

13.3.2 Prerequisite Patches

Verify that you have installed all prerequisite patches. The required patches are listed within the installation materials. Check or download OpenView patches from `http://support.openview.hp.com/patches/patch_index.jsp`. Vendor updates on the latest patches are available via email if you sign up for the email notification service.

13.3.3 Installing Oracle and OVO Software

The Oracle for OpenView software and the OVO software products are delivered on two different CD sets. Oracle must be installed prior to running the OVO install command, **ovoinstall**, which configures the database for use. The Oracle installation procedure is documented in the OVO Installation Guide. A standard version of Oracle is also compatible for use with OVO. After Oracle is installed, you can begin the OVO software installation. The script **ovoinstall** (new with OVO 8) will initialize a terminal window and begin the installation process with a series of prompts that allow the user to verify the prerequisite software patches, configuration parameters, and default settings, such as directory paths and environment variables. The installation default parameters are found in the file ovoinstall.defaults. An example of the file is listed here:

```
#cat ovoinstall.defaults
# This file is parsed by ovoinstall. Values may be changed in
this section
# Note: English text only.
BBCCLIENTS_PATH=/ovo_8/CD2/OV_DEPOT/HPOvOhttpsClients.depot
BBCCLIENT_PRODUCTS="OVO-CLT.OVO-UX11-CLT OVO-CLT.OVO-SOL-CLT
OVO-CLT.OVO-LIN-CLT OVO-CLT.OVO-DLIN-CLT"
RPCCLIENTS_PATH=/ovo_8/CD2/OV_DEPOT/HPOvOrpcClients.depot
RPCCLIENT_PRODUCTS="OVOPC-CLT.OVOPC-NT-CLT OVOPC-CLT.OVOPC-SOL-
CLT OVOPC-CLT.OVOPC-UX11-CLT"
CDROM_DEV=/dev/dsk/c0t0d0
CDROM_INSTALL=false
CDROM_MNT_PT=/SD_CDROM
DB_CHARACTER_SET=
DEFAULT_M10I_PATH=/ovo_8/CD1/OV_DEPOT/HPOvComponents.depot
DEFAULT_SERVER_PATH=/ovo_8/CD2/OV_DEPOT/HPOvOServer.depot
FORCED=false
LANGUAGE=C
M10I_PRODUCTS="HPOvLcore.HPOVXPL HPOvLcore.HPOVSECCO
HPOvLcore.HPOVBBC HPOvLcore.HPOVSECCC \
HPOvLcore.HPOVCTRL HPOvLcore.HPOVDEPL HPOvLcore.HPOVCONF HPOvL-
core.HPOVSECCC HPOvSext"
M10I_PRODUCTS_INSTFLAGS="-x enforce_dependencies=false -x autos-
elect_dependencies=false"
MINIMAL=false
```

```
ORACLE_HOME=/opt/oracle/product/9.2.0
ORACLE_DATA_DIR=/ora_db
PACKAGES_TO_ADD=
POLICY_DATA_TYPE=
REINSTALL=false
SERVER_PRODUCTS="OVOEnglish OVOSvcNavEng"
TAR_FILES=
this listing is truncated
HP-UXHP-UX
TAR_FILE_PATH=/ovo_8/CD2/OVOServer_patches

VERBOSE=true
TIMEOUT=5
INSTALL_DEVKIT=false

# NNM installation script options.
NNMINSTALL_SCRIPT_NAME=install
NNMDEPOT_PATH_CD1=/ovo_8/disk1
NNMDEPOT_PATH_CD2=/ovo_8/disk2

NNM_DISC_NETWORK=n
NNM_SHOW_UI=n
NNM_SNMPCOMMUNITY=s
NNM_BROWSER_PATH=s
NNM_VIEW_RELEASE_NOTES=n
NNM_INST_JAPANESE=n

# Values below here will not be read by ovoinstall when running
in silent mode
ORACLE_PW_OPC_OP=opc_op
ORACLE_PW_OPC_REPORT=opc_report
ORACLE_PW_SYSTEM=manager
ORACLE_USR_DBA=oracle
ORACLE_AUTODBSTART=y
ORACLE_SID=openview
ORACLE_USE_CURR_DB=y
ORACLE_NET=ov_net
ORACLE_BASE=/opt/oracle
ORACLE_DB_REINIT=y
ORACLE_IDX_DIR=/ora_db
#
```

The **ovoinstall** installation program writes progress messages into the log file /var/opt/OV/log/OpC/mgmt_sv/install.log. The software installation process uses the **swinstall** command, and you can monitor progress in the log file swagent.log with the command **tail –f /var/adm/sw/swagent.log**.

13.4 AGENT SOFTWARE INSTALLATION

The first-time agent installation is onto the management server. This enables the server to become the first managed node. If requested by the user, during OVO server installation process, the default agents and components are assigned and distributed to the management server automatically. Subsequent distributions can be performed from the OVO administrator console or the command line (refer to the man page for the command **opcragt**). After the initial server components are distributed, messages from the server begin to appear in the message browser. Refer to Chapter 14 for more information about agents and components.

13.5 OPENVIEW STATUS CHECKS

The processes that run on the management server and managed nodes indicate the health of the OpenView environment. If you experience any problems with the standard operation of the OpenView product, check to ensure that all the necessary processes are running. Below are three examples of checking the status of the OpenView processes. Refer to Chapter 18, "Oracle for OpenView," and Chapter 22, "Troubleshooting Tips and Techniques," for information about commands to check the Oracle and Operating System processes. Descriptions of the OVO processes appear later in this chapter.

13.5.1 Check the OpenView Services (NNM)

The OV service processes must be running in order for the OpenView server to function properly. Refer to Chapter 4, "Out-of-the-box Network Node Manager," for more information about the NNM processes. Check the status of the NNM processes with the command **/opt/OV/bin/ovstatus –c**.

```
Name                 PID   State           Last Message(s)
 OVsPMD              1422   RUNNING          -
 ovsessionmgr        1424   RUNNING         Initialization complete.
 ovwdb               1425   RUNNING         Initialization complete.
 ovuispmd            1484   RUNNING         Successful restart. 0 ovw
clients registered.
 ovtrapd             1455   RUNNING         Initialization complete.
 ovactiond           1456   RUNNING         Initialization complete.
```

```
 syslogTrap            -   NOT_RUNNING       -
 ovalarmsrv         1457   RUNNING        Initialization complete.
 pmd                1427   RUNNING        Initialization complete.
 genannosrvr        1458   RUNNING           -
 httpd                 -   unknown        (Does not communicate with
ovspmd.)
 ovtopmd            1453   RUNNING        Connected to native data-
base "openview".
 netmon             1485   RUNNING        Initialization complete.
 snmpCollect        1486   RUNNING        Initialization complete.
 ovas               1492   RUNNING        Initialization complete.
 ovrequestd         1430   RUNNING        Initialization complete.
 ovdbcheck          1459   RUNNING        Connected to embedded data-
base.
 ovctrl                -   unknown        (Does not communicate with
ovspmd.)
 ovoacomm           1490   RUNNING        Open Agent Service Server
Initialization Complete. For details about Open Agent Service
use 'opcsv'.
 opc                1772   RUNNING        OVO Server Initialization
Complete.
For details about OVO Manager Processes use 'opcsv'.
#
```

The processes are initialized during system startup or manually controlled with the commands **ovstart** and **ovstop**. Refer to Chapter 4 for the NNM process descriptions. The **ovstop** command will stop NNM and all OVO server processes. This will not stop the agent processes running on the server. When the server processes are down no user logins are allowed, and agent processes will buffer messages until the server processes are restarted.

13.5.2 Check the OVO Server

The operation of the management server depends upon the functions provided by the operating system, Oracle, NNM, and OVO. Descriptions of the OVO processes are provided later in this chapter. Check the status of the OVO server processes with the command **/opt/OV/bin/OpC/opcsv**.

```
# opcsv
OVO Management Server status:
Control Manager      opcctlm     (4807) is running
Action Manager       opcactm     (4814) is running
```

```
Message Manager       opcmsgm      (4815) is running
TT & Notify Mgr       opcttnsm     (4816) is running
Forward Manager       opcforwm     (4817) is running
Service Engine        opcsvcm      (4822) is running
Cert. Srv Adapter     opccsad      (4820) is running
BBC config adapter    opcbbcdist   (4821) is running
Display Manager       opcdispm     (4818) is running
Distrib. Manager      opcdistm     (4819) is running

Open Agent Management status:
Request Sender        ovoareqsdr   (4801) is running
Request Handler       ovoareqhdlr  (4804) is running
Message Receiver (BBC) opcmsgrb    (4805) is running
Message Receiver      opcmsgrd     (4806) is running

Ctrl-Core and Server Extensions status:
Control Daemon                ovcd       (4314) is running
BBC Communications Broker     ovbbccb    (1467) is running
Config and Deploy             ovconfd    (4315) is running
OV Certificate Server         ovcs       (4802) is running
#
```

Server processes that do no appear in the output of the **opcsv -status** command include the following processes that run to support the user sessions and DCE-RPC data transfers:

- **opcuiwww**—Java UI Manager (one instance per for each connected Java GUI)
- **opcuiadm**—Administrator UI
- **opcuiop**—Operator UI (one instance for each operator session using the MOTIF GUI)
- **opcuiopadm**—Administrator's Operator UI
- **ovw**—OV platform GUI session (one for each MOTIF GUI - admin+oper)
- **opccmm**—Subprocess of Message Receiver for bulk transfers (only if needed temporarily)
- **opctss**—TCP Socket Server

13.5.3 Check the Agents

There are two commands available to check the agent status: **/opt/OV/bin/OpC/opcragt** and **/opt/OV/bin/OpC/ovc**. Both commands report the status of the primary agents responsible for intercepting events, collecting performance data, filtering and forwarding messages. The following example lists the output from the **opcagt** command:

Execute the command: **/opt/OV/bin/OpC/opcagt**

```
opcmsga   OVO Message Agent          AGENT,EA(5129)   Running
opcacta   OVO Action Agent           AGENT,EA(5130)   Running
opcmsgi   OVO Message Interceptor    AGENT,EA(5131)   Running
opcle     OVO Logfile Encapsulator   AGENT,EA(5133)   Running
opcmona   OVO Monitor Agent          AGENT,EA(5135)   Running
opctrapi  OVO SNMP Trap Interceptor AGENT,EA(5137)   Running
opceca    OVO Event Correlation      AGENT,EA         Stopped
opcecaas  ECS Annotate Server        AGENT,EA         Stopped
coda      HP OpenView Performance Core      (3657)   Running
#
```

The command **ovc** (-start, -stop, -kill) also controls the agent processes from the command line. Refer to the man pages for **ovc** complete syntax. The command **/opt/OV/bin/OpC/opcagt** is now a wrapper for **ovc**. The output from the **ovc** command for HTTPS-based agents is listed here.

```
# ovc
ovcd    Control Daemon                            CORE (4314)   Running
ovbbccb HP OpenView BBC Communications Broker CORE (1467)  Running
ovconfd HP OpenView Config and Deploy      CORE (4315)   Running
ovcs    HP OpenView Certificate Server SERVER            Aborted
opcmsga OVO Message Agent                 AGENT,EA (4321)   Running
opcacta OVO Action Agent                  AGENT,EA (4322)   Running
opcmsgi OVO Message Interceptor           AGENT,EA (4323)   Running
opcle       OVO Logfile Encapsulator    AGENT,EA (4325)   Running
opcmona     OVO Monitor Agent           AGENT,EA (4327)   Running
opctrapi    OVO SNMP Trap Interceptor AGENT,EA (4329)   Running
opceca      OVO Event Correlation       AGENT,EA          Stopped
opcecaas    ECS Annotate Server         AGENT,EA          Stopped
coda        HP OpenView Performance   Core  4331)         Running
```

The output shows the processes that are responsible for overall control **ovcd**, HTTPS communications **ovbbccb**, distribution and configuration changes **ovconfd**, and security authentication **ovcs**. The **ovc** and **opcagt** commands work locally, **opcragt** executes on the management server (both for DCE and HTTPS agents). The **ovc** command exists only on HTTPS nodes.

13.6 OVO AUTOMATIC STARTUP AT BOOT TIME

You should become familiar with the automatic startup and shutdown process for the management server and the managed nodes. During server startup, it is necessary for several services, such as the Internet services or DNS, to start prior to the OpenView processes. If for some reason the prerequisite services are not enabled, you will experience problems with OVO. Information about the specific startup and shutdown files for Oracle, NNM, and OVO is provided here for reference. In general, the order of startup for the OpenView platform is operating system communication programs, Oracle database, NNM services, OVO server, and OVO agent.

- **/sbin/init.d/ov500**—This script controls the startup of the OpenView server processes, including OpenView NNM and OpenView Operations. OVO processes start after NNM because the file opc.lrf is registered with the NNM ovsuf startup environment. Refer to the NNM documentation for details about the registration files. You can also check that the opc program was initialized with the command **ovstatus –c**. During startup the script is called with the following option: /sbin/init.d/ov500 start. This causes the operating system startup program (called rc) to check the file /etc/rc.config.d/ov500 for the variable OV500=1. If the variable is set to the number one, the rc program will initialize the OpenView environment. If the variable is set to zero, OpenView will not start. The paths may be different on other platforms (such as /etc instead of /sbin on Solaris).
- **/sbin/init.d/OVCtrl**—This script controls the startup of the OpenView agent processes.
- **/sbin/init.d/ovoracle**—This script controls the startup of the Oracle processes. The rc program is responsible for checking for the startup variable OVORACLE=1 and OVORALISTENER=1 in the configuration file /etc/rc.config.d/ovoracle.

Refer to the operating system documentation for HP-UXHP-UX or Solaris for details on startup and shutdown procedures.

13.7 THE ADMINISTRATOR CONSOLE

Initiate a new OVO session with the command **opc** and use the administrators' login account and password (i.e. opc_adm, OpC_adm). It is recommended to change the default password for the administrator and the default user accounts after the server is installed. During the first administrator or operator login, the password change is enforced. When you initially log into the management server you see two windows, Root and Node Bank. Figure 13-2 is an example of the administrator login session.

Figure 13-2 OVO administrator login session.

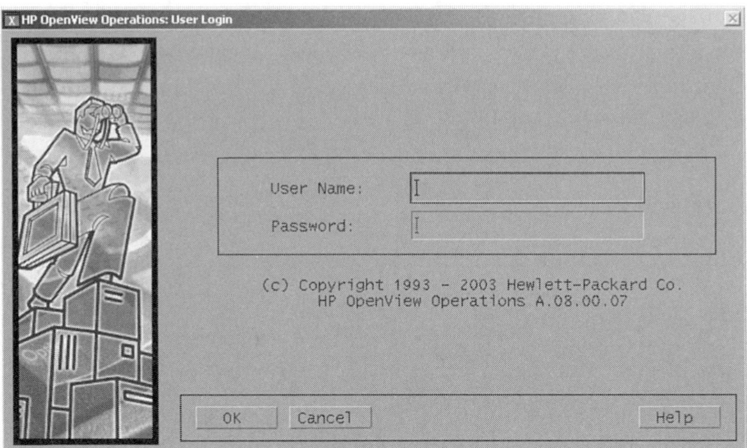

13.8 WINDOWS AND MENUS

After the administrator logs into the OVO console, two windows appear by default after login authorization. However, there are many other windows available for the administrator to control and configure the OVO environment. Select the menu item "Actions" or "Window" to access the full set of administrator windows from the Node Bank. It is important to get to know all of the administrators' configuration windows. The windows are also referred to as Banks. The description and examples of using the configuration windows are covered in more detail in Sections 13.9 through 13.15 of this chapter.

The administrators' primary windows include Root, Node Bank, Node Group Bank, Message Group Bank, User Bank, Profile Bank, Node Hierarchy Bank, Message Source Templates, and Message Browser. Each window contains default icons, or you can add an icon to represent a part of the configured components for your environment. When you select an item from the menu, a pull-down menu opens. The pull-down menu contains other actions or configurable components.

Select or highlight an icon with the left mouse button and click once. You will know the icon is selected if a shadow box appears around the symbol. While the symbol is highlighted, activate a pop-up menu and hold down the right-mouse button. The pop-up menu lists items that can be executed against only the highlighted symbol and the object it represents.

Select multiple nodes, hold down the control key, and select multiple icons with the left mouse button. Another method to select multiple nodes is to create a square window around the nodes. Hold down the left mouse button in the upper left corner of the window you want to make around the nodes. Drag the mouse to the right and down, and you will see a box surround the nodes. When the box includes the nodes you want to select release the left mouse button. The nodes that were inside the selection box are highlighted. This is a fast method to select many nodes for tasks that require drag and drop. Figure 13-3 and 13-4 are examples of the Root Banks

Figure 13-3 The Root Bank contains the symbols and icons that represent all of the configuration components.

Figure 13-4 The node for the management server is in the Node Bank by default after OVO software installation.

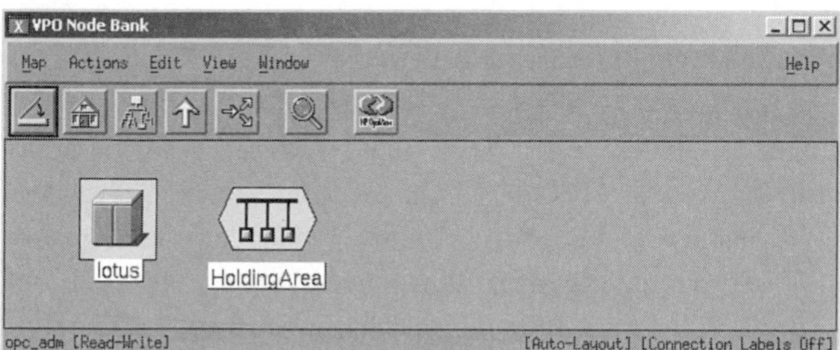

Node icons in the Banks and Groups represent managed nodes in the OVO domain. The Actions and Window pull-down menus at the top of the Node Bank lead to the configurable components or the Message Browser. The messages from the managed nodes will appear in the Message Browser window. Figure 13-5 is a view of the primary message browser window. The messages in the browser are identified with attributes that are listed at the top of the browser window (for example, Severity, Duplicate Count, Flags SUIAONE, Date, Time, Node Name, Application, Message Group, Object, and Message Text). The messages remain in the browser until they are manually acknowledged or automatically acknowledged using message correlation.

Figure 13-5 The Message Browser contains the list of messages from the managed nodes and the management server.

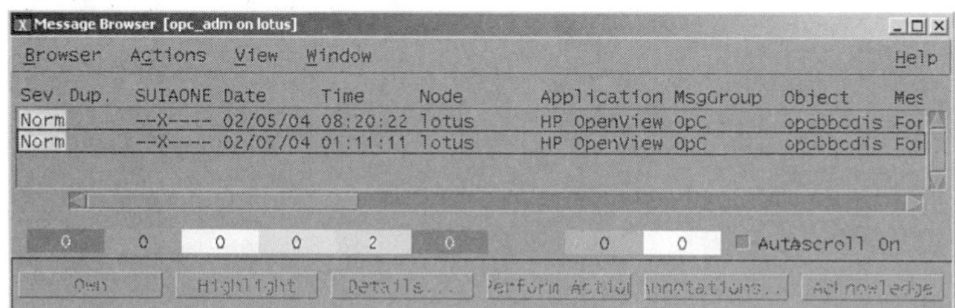

Table 13-4 lists the configuration components available from the Actions and Window pull-down menus. These menus are repeated on each of the administrators' windows (except the root window). This has the advantage of providing quick access to configuration components. These menu items are used often to add, change and remove configuration components. In the case of the Action menu item, it is context-specific depending upon the current active window.

Table 13-4 Actions and Window Menu Items

Actions Menu Items	Window Menu Items
Node	Root
Set Defaults	Home
Add	Parent
Add for External Events	Quick Navigator
Add Node Layout Group	Node Bank
OVO Certificate Requests	Node Hierarchy Bank
	Node Group Bank
	Message Group Bank
Agents	
Assign Templates	Application Bank
Install/Update SW & Config	User Bank
Deinstall	User Profile Bank
	Message Source Template
Subagents	Message Browser
Install/Update	
Deinstall	
Server	
Start Services	
Stop Services	
Assign Templates	
Install/Update Server Templates	
Regrouping	
Configure	

Table 13-4 Actions and Window Menu Items (Continued)

Actions Menu Items	Window Menu Items
Download Configuration	
Highlight	
Utilities	
Reports	
Database Maintenance	
Notification Service	
Trouble Ticket	
Instruction Interface	
Inform Operators	
Send Message to Operators	
Change Passwords	
Message Browser	
Start/Reload	
Stop	

13.9 NODES, NODE GROUPS, NODE LAYOUT GROUPS, NODE HIERARCHIES

Looking at an OpenView domain is overwhelming at first glance if there are many nodes shown as individual icons inside the Node Bank. There are many components within the Administrator's GUI that help you organize the look and feel of the OVO console. You can organize the nodes by using the built-in tools, such as node groups, node hierarchies, and node layout groups. The next sections explore some ideas on how to organize the nodes within the administrator and operator consoles.

13.9.1 Nodes

Deciding which nodes to manage is one of the OpenView administrators' primary tasks. Different types of nodes managed by OVO are brought into the configuration, including

- **Controlled**—Agent installed and allows remote logins, actions and monitoring.
- **Monitored**—Agent installed but does not allow remote logins or remote actions.
- **Message allowed**—No agent, node sends SNMP traps (for example, router or printer).
- **Disabled**—Node is not monitored for status, sends no messages.
- **External nodes**—Only send events via SNMP that will be processed and transformed into OVO messages. These are referred to as nodes for external events inside the GUI.

After you determine which nodes and or node type to manage, add the node to the Node Bank. Unlike NNM, OVO does not manage any node automatically. You must add the desired node to the Node Bank first. Adding a node can be done by either using the menu in the OVO Node Bank, or even more convenient, by drag/dropping from the NNM ipmap.

If the node is fully managed, a Node Configuration window appears and waits for you to verify the default settings or make changes. After you click OK, the information about the node is stored in the database. The node is not yet installed with the agent software; you will perform this task after the node configuration is complete. (Refer to Chapter 14 for agent installation techniques.) If the node is only sending events to OVO in the GUI, use the Add Node for External Events window. Although the GUI method is described here, there are commands to accomplish the same tasks. The Add Node configuration window is shown in Figure 13-5a for reference.

Figure 13-5a Add Node configuration window contains the fields used to describe information about the managed node.

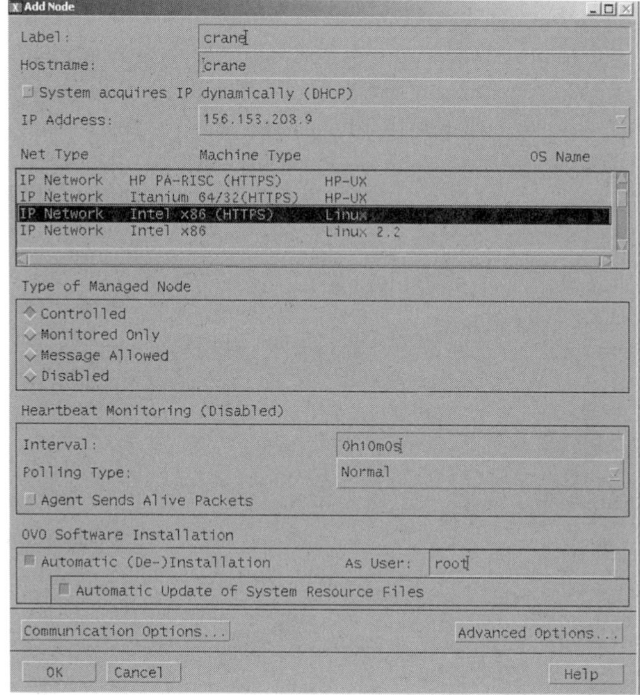

There are several methods to add nodes to the Node Bank. (Refer to *the OVO Administrator's Reference, Volume I* for more detailed information.) Examples of the process to add nodes to the Node Bank are shown here for reference. Each example assumes that a selection is made from the menu.

Example 1: **Actions→Node→Add**

This method is ideal for installing one node at a time. You need to provide the hostname of the node you want to add. OVO then attempts to determine additional attributes (IP address, system type, and so on) by querying the node's SNMP agent. If an SNMP agent is not running on the managed node, you will need to set the machine type manually in the configuration window.

Example 2: **Edit→Copy**

Locate the node in the root map, by selecting **Edit→Find→Object by Selection Name** (or some other attribute; see the list in the Selection Window). Once you have identified the node, select the node, and from the menu select Edit. In the OVO Node Bank, select the menu item **Edit→Copy**. The new node appears in the Node Bank. A drag/drop from the ipmap would also work to add the node to the Node Bank.

Example 3: Open the Node Group Bank, double-click with the left-mouse button on a node group icon, and then select from the menu, **Actions→Node→Add**

Add a new node to the node group and it will automatically appear in the Node Bank (Holding Area). Here you could also use the Menu option **Edit→Copy, Edit→Paste**. Node Groups are covered in more detail in Section 13.9.2.

Example 4: **Actions→Node→Add for External Events**

Use this method for managing devices that typically do not have the OVO agent installed but are capable of sending their events to a node that does have an OVO agent (a proxy node) or directly to the server. When the event arrives on the managed node, it is transformed into an OVO massage and sent to the server. A use case is to manage SNMP devices like routers, bridges, network printers this way. The external events icon changes status as the messages from the external nodes are processed on the server. When the window "Add Node for External Events" opens, provide a label name for the icon in the GUI. The dialog box for external events is shown in Figure 13-6.

Figure 13-6 Add Node for External Events dialog box.

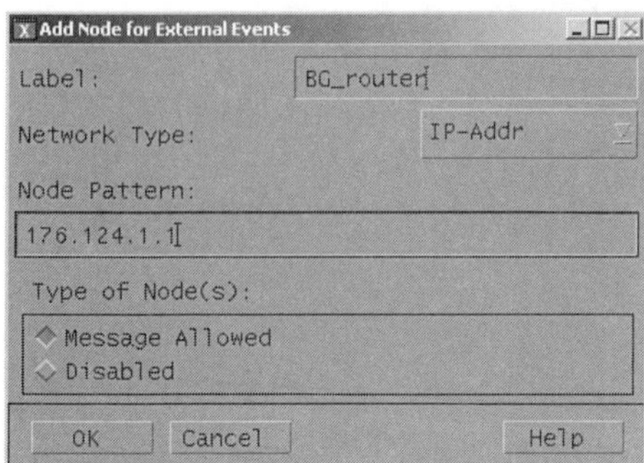

Select the Network Type, IP-Addr, IP-Name, or Others. This determines what type of entry you will use in the Node Pattern field. For example, if you use IP addresses in the Node Pattern Field, select IP-Addr. Provide a Node Pattern, which is actually a node name pattern (such as *.hp.com). The Node Pattern field can contain wild cards for the IP address range if there are many nodes on one a network that will send events to the server (i.e. 192.14.*.*). Other options for the address range can include and exclude specific IP numbers (i.e. 192.14.123. <5 –le [<#>] –lt 72>. Finally, select the Type of Node, Message Allowed (in order to enable the events from the external node(s) to appear in the browser). The external node icon is located in the node bank with the other node types as shown in Figure 13-7. Configure the external device to send SNMP events to the OVO server.

Figure 13-7 Nodes for external events in the Node Bank.

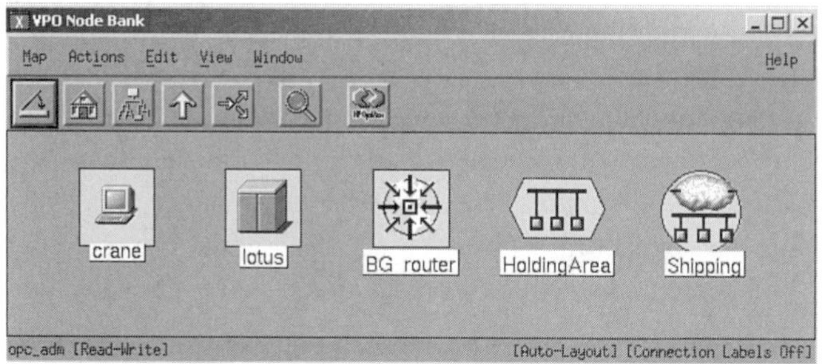

Example 5: Upload the node configuration from the command line. (Refer to Chapter 17, "Server Administration," for details on this method)

Example 6: Command line method, see the man page for **opcnode**.

13.9.2 Node Groups

All the nodes you plan to manage with OVO must appear in at least one Node Group. This is important because the Node Groups (shown in Figure 13-8) are assigned as part administrators' responsibilities and part operators' responsibilities. For example, if you add a node to the node group and the node group is assigned to the administrator or operator, they will begin to see messages from the new node after the next login session. Simplified administration is another advantage of organizing the nodes into a Node Group. For example, you may have a Win2K server (node) running IIS and an Oracle database. This node might appear as a member of multiple Node Groups (such as W2k, Oracle or Database). Also, assignment of Template Groups to node groups as the domain grows helps simplify distribution and configuration changes. Select **Window→Node Group Bank→Add**.

Figure 13-8 Node Group Bank.

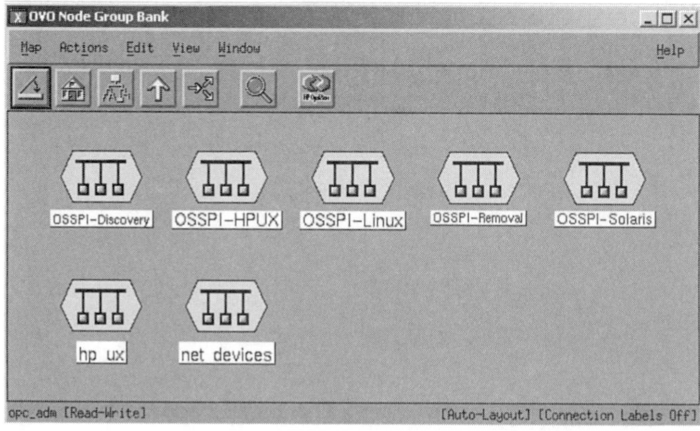

13.9.3 Node Layout Groups

Use this concept to pre-arrange the nodes within a window hierarchy for your operators. By default, OVO presents all managed nodes in a single, "flat" window (Managed Nodes Window) in the Operator GUIs. When there are so many icons in a window, it is difficult to distinguish which node manages what environment. For example, in the node bank, you might have several hundred nodes in the domain and the icons appear very small. Creating Node Layout Groups lets you create a hierarchy of windows where, for example, you organize your managed nodes by location or geography, by the role these systems fulfill, or by other custom criteria. You could use the features of the window to pan and zoom or create a quick navigator window, but you could also organize the nodes inside the current window.

Create a Node Layout Group from a window that contains individual node icons or other Node Layout Groups. From the menu, select **Actions→Node→Add Node Layout Group**. Add the name, label and description in the dialog box (Figure 13-9). The icon for the Node Layout Group is now in the window. In this example, we use the Node Bank window.

Figure 13-9 Node Layout Group dialog box.

Create a Node Layout Group for each physical location, department, or type of application (see Figure 13-10). Drag and drop the nodes onto the Layout Group Icon. This allows you to see only the Layout Group icons in the window when you login and open the Node Bank. Drill down into a Layout Group and double-click the left mouse button. Node Layout Groups may contain other Layout Groups.

Figure 13-10 Node Bank Layout Group.

13.9.4 Node Hierarchies

A node hierarchy is used to configure what organized view in the Motif GUI the operators see when they open the Node Bank. To customize a node hierarchy, use the Node Hierarchy Bank. For example, if the nodes are located in different regions, states, or departments, you can build a node hierarchy to represent the logical organization of the nodes for the operator's console.

For example, from the Node Bank, select **Window→Node Hierarchy Bank**. Within the Node Hierarchy Bank, select **Actions→Node Hierarchy→Add**. After you enter the name, label, and description, the new symbol for this Hierarchy appears in the Hierarchy Bank (see Figure 13-11).

Figure 13-11 Add Node Hierarchy dialog box.

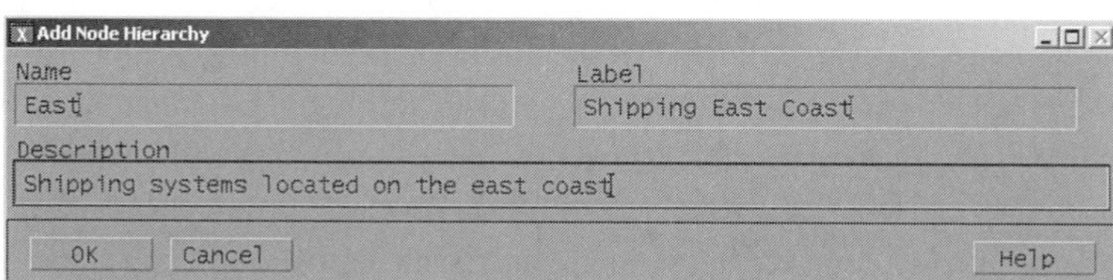

Double-click on the new symbol to view a Holding Area Symbol. All the nodes are available for use within the Node Hierarchy. A Node Hierarchy is assigned to the operator and provides an organized view of the operators managed node responsibilities, for example, Shipping East Coast (see Figure 13-12). A procedure to assign the Node Hierarchy to an Operator is outlined here.

Figure 13-12 Node Hierarchy Bank.

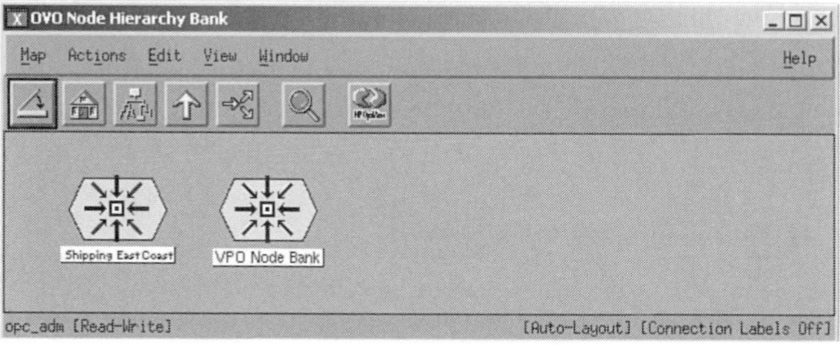

1. Highlight the Node Hierarchy icon.
2. Open the User Bank.
3. Select the operator account to modify.

4. Select the **Node Hierarchy** button in the Operator Configuration window. (You cannot type in the Node Hierarchy Dialog Box.) Select the **Get Map Selection** button; this transfers the name of the highlighted Node Hierarchy into the Operators Configuration the next time the Operator logs into the OVO via a Motif GUI. The node bank will be organized into the Layout Groups you defined in the Node Hierarchy. The operator is assigned only one Node Hierarchy at a time.

A Node Hierarchy defines "how" a user will see their assigned nodes. The assigned Node Groups in the user's responsibility matrix define "which" nodes the user sees.

13.10 MESSAGE GROUPS

Message groups are an important part of the configuration. An OVO message contains all of the important attributes that help determine who will need to see this event in their message browser. One of the attributes is the message group. For example, a message might contain the message group attribute called Database. The message group attribute of an OVO message will be defined by the OVO administrator as part of the agent's template configuration. See Chapter 14 for more information about templates. If an operator's configuration includes the message group Database, the message will appear in the operator's message browser. All messages must be organized into logical categories called message groups. The default message groups are Backup, Certificate, Database, HA, Hardware, Job, Misc., Netware, Network, OpC, OS, Output, Performance, Security, SSP, and SNMP.

The message group "Misc" plays a special role by catching all undefined messages. If an arriving OVO message contains a message group attribute which is not part of the Message Group Bank, it will be assigned to all OVO users who have the message group "Misc" assigned. However, the original message group value (as part of the OVO message) will be displayed in the message browser.

An example of how to create a new message group is shown here for reference. Select from the menu **Actions→Message Group→Add**. Enter the name, label, and description for the message group (see Figure 13-13). Click **OK**. The icon for the new message group appears in the window (see Figure 13-14).

Figure 13-13 New message group added to Message Group Bank.

Figure 13-14 Message Group Bank.

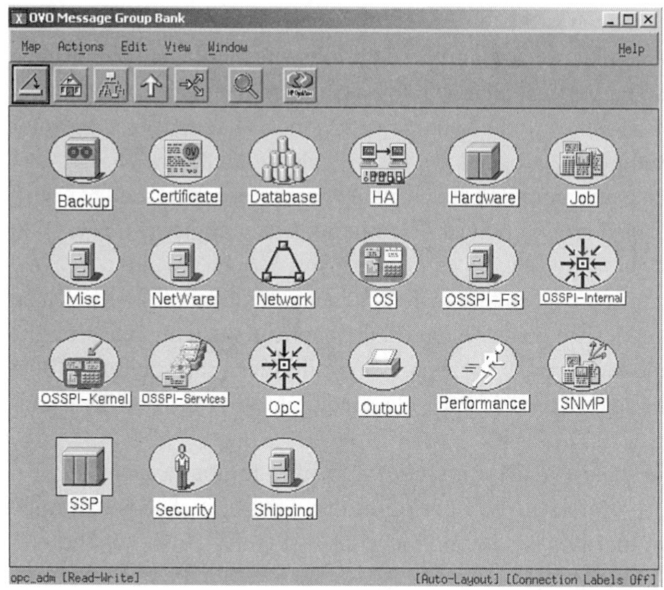

You can change the look of the icon by highlighting it with the left mouse button. Open the pop-up menu with right mouse button. Select Change Symbol Type. This opens the window for the symbol types you may choose from, as shown in Figure 13-15. (Refer to the *Administrator's Reference, Volume I* for more information.)

Figure 13-15 Changed Message Group "Shipping" symbol type.

13.11 USERS AND USER PROFILES

The operator responsibilities and tools are assigned to the operator and to the operator account. Each operator's configuration is located in the User Bank. There are three methods to create a new user and assign responsibilities using the GUI. The first method is to assign a profile. A profile is preconfigured with the node groups, message groups and applications (covered in Section 13.12). The components are typically customized for each operator depending on their responsibilities. The profile is typically named and assigned based upon the operator's role. A profile may contain other profiles.

The same profile is reusable for operators who have similar responsibilities. Pre-configured profiles save time when adding new operators—you just create the new account and apply an existing profile.

The second method is to create the user account and define responsibilities and application tools for each individual account. The third method is to use a combination of both of the other methods. The configuration that is assigned to the operator determines what nodes the operator sees in their OVO console. For example, if an operator is responsible for all the mail servers but not the database servers in the management domain, they will only see messages related to events coming from the mail servers. The next section provides a closer look at configuring a new OVO operator using a profile.

The profile is a method to configure an environment that includes all the attributes that an operator needs to perform their tasks. The profile includes the applications that appear on the desktop, the message group, and node groups. If there are responsibilities necessary in addition to those in a profile, they should be selected for the individual requirement of the specific operator account.

The introduction of *Smart Plug-Ins* (SPIs) includes appropriate operator profiles for managing the environment to which the SPI configuration is assigned. An example of how to assign a profile to an operator is shown in steps 1-8. Fig 13-16 shows the OS-SPI profile.

Figure 13-16 OS-SPI and Administrator profiles.

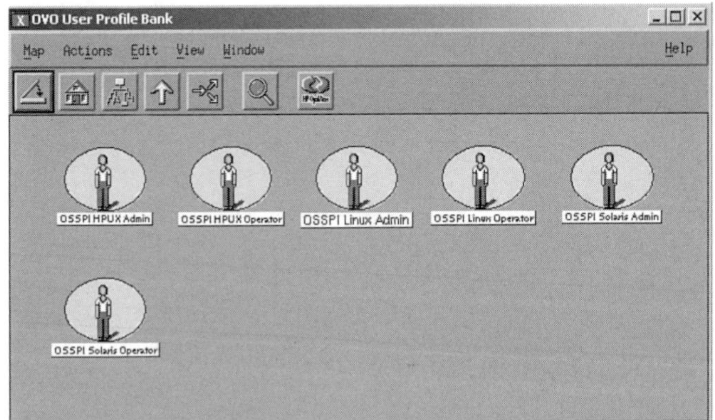

1. Locate the default profiles from the menu by selecting **Window→User Profile Bank**.
2. Open the operators profile bank.
3. From the menu, select **Window→User Bank**.
4. Select the operator icon, right-click, and select modify; this opens the Modify Operator Configuration window.
5. Select the **Profile** button as shown in Figure 13-17.

6. After the operator's profile bank is open, drag and drop the appropriate default SPI profile.

Figure 13-17 Operator Configuration shows the Profile button.

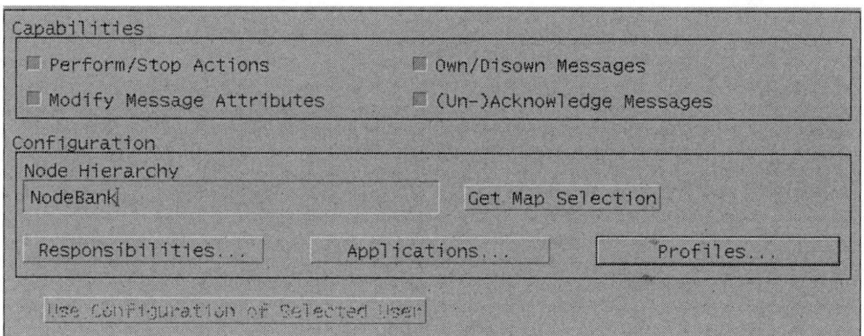

The result of the drag and drop operation is shown in Figure 13-18.

Figure 13-18 SPI Profile assigned to the Operator configuration.

7. After the profile is assigned, close the User Profile Bank and close the Operator Profile.
8. Configure the other features of the Operator's account, which will be covered in Section 13.14, "Configure a New OVO Operator."

13.12 APPLICATIONS

In the operator's GUI, OVO operations console is a primary tool for resolving problems that have been identified and presented in the message browser. After the decision to further investigate a problem is made, the operator should not have to leave the console to do so. Tools are built into the operator's console to help isolate and resolve problems. In the operator's GUI, the tools are provided in the Application Desktop, as shown in Figure 13-19.

Figure 13-19 Application Bank.

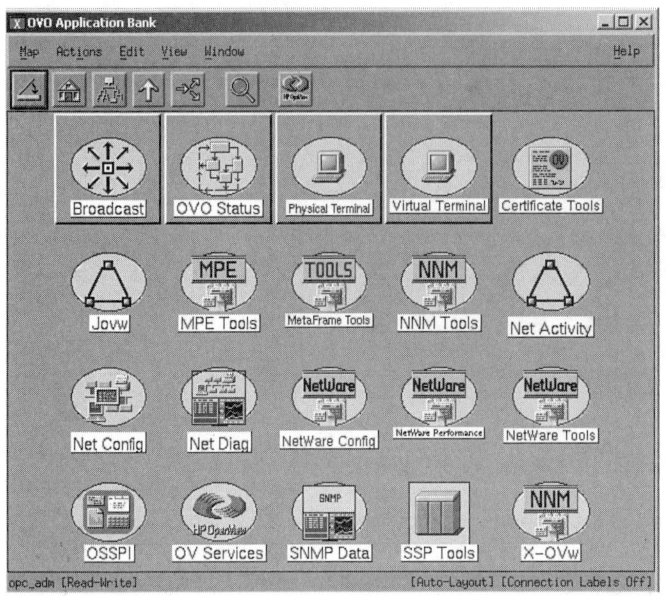

The OVO Administrator has "all" applications available for direct use or for assignment to operators in the Application Bank. This resource area contains symbols that represent categories of tools that are readily available for use. The tools are represented by symbols arranged in a hierarchy starting with a top-level represented by oval shaped symbols, called application groups. If you double-click on the icon, you'll find that the second level contains specific tools for that application group category. The top level of the Application Bank contains square-shaped symbols that are executable. Drag and drop the node onto the application to initialize the program. The Application Bank's oval-shaped symbols represent Application Groups, a collection of applications. Double-click with the mouse on the application group icon to move to the second level of the hierarchy.

The symbols at the second level could represent additional Application Groups within this category if the symbol is oval. There are also square icons, which are ready for use and only require a drag/drop operation, as previously described.

The applications icons are embedded with program instructions that execute programs on the specific node or on the management server. For example, to check the status of a node, drag and drop a managed node symbol from the Node Bank onto the square symbol in the Application Bank called ITO Status. This task executes the command **opcragt –status** on the OVO server and returns the results to the operator console in a separate window.

Customized application techniques are covered in more detail in the User Guide.

Figure 13-20 Application Group.

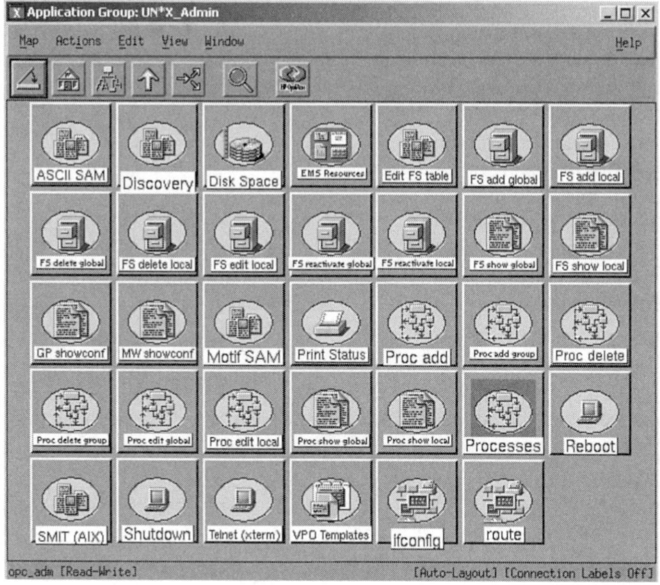

13.13 THE OPERATOR CONSOLE

The primary tasks performed by the operator include following troubleshooting procedures to resolve the problems reported in the message browser. The operators accomplish the problem-solving tasks with OVO tools found inside the operator's console. The problem-solving tasks are outlined here for reference. There are two operator user interfaces, Motif and Java. The two desktops provide the same basic functionality; this is covered in more detail later in this section. However, some of the key differences between the two should help you make decisions on which is right for your operations environment. Table 13-6 is a comparison of some key differences between the Motif and Java user interfaces.

Table 13-6 Comparison of Motif and Java User Interfaces

User Interface Features	Java	Motif
Login Screen	Yes	Yes
UNIX account required	No, just a valid OpenView user account	Yes, operator must log onto UNIX management server, then start up the OpenView X-Windows GUI.
Specify server during login	Yes	No, only connects to the local server where the operator has a valid UNIX account.
X-Server required on the desktop	Only if you plan to execute X applications from the client.	Required to login to the management server. Allows operator to redirect the X Display back to the client.

Table 13-6 Comparison of Motif and Java User Interfaces (Continued)

User Interface Features	Java	Motif
GUI processes use server	No, the GUI processing is only running on the client. A process on the server suppoorts the user connection via a socket.	Yes, X-Windows processes are running on the server for each operator.
Service Views	Yes, service views for the operator environment configured using OpenView Service Navigator are visible in the client console.	No.
Change GUI look and feel	Yes, Motif, Metal, Windows, **Edit→Preferences**	Yes, via X application defaults con figuration file.
Save GUI layout Store the X-Window layout. Select the Menu Item –View.	Yes	Yes
Message Browser change the layout **View→Layout**.	Yes, columns can be moved, hidden, or resized	Yes, only add or remove columns from the display,
Sort messages in Active Message Browser **View→Some**.	Yes, click on the column label	No, requires a new browser,
View Custom Message Attributes	Yes	No
Administrator GUI	No	Yes

The operator's Motif desktop at login, as shown in Figure 13-21, contains five primary windows, Root, Managed Nodes, Message Groups, Application Desktop and Message Browser.

Figure 13-21 OpenView Operator Motif console.

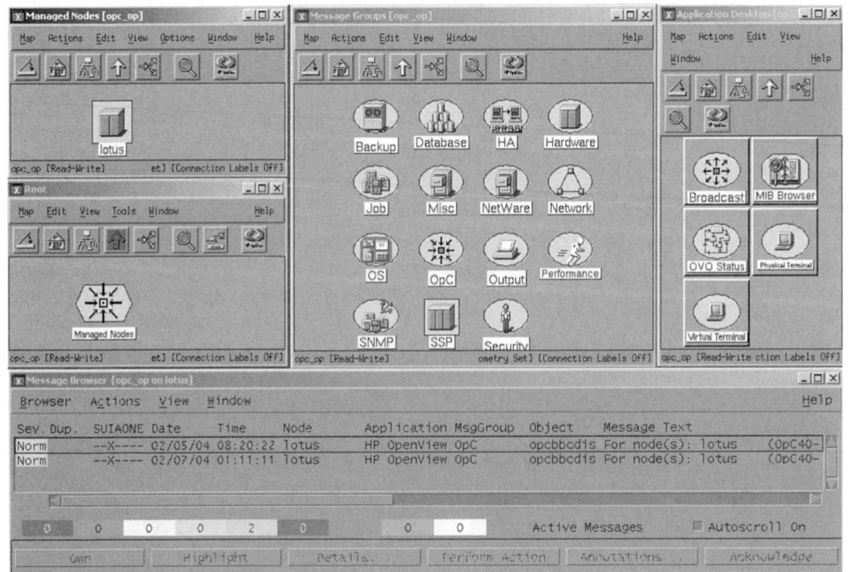

The Java Console contains a list (on the left pane) of the operators managed nodes, message groups, applications, and services (if configured). (Refer to the *OpenView Operator Java Users Guide* for more information). Figure 13-22 is an example of the Operator Java User Interface.

Figure 13-22 OpenView operator Java user interface.

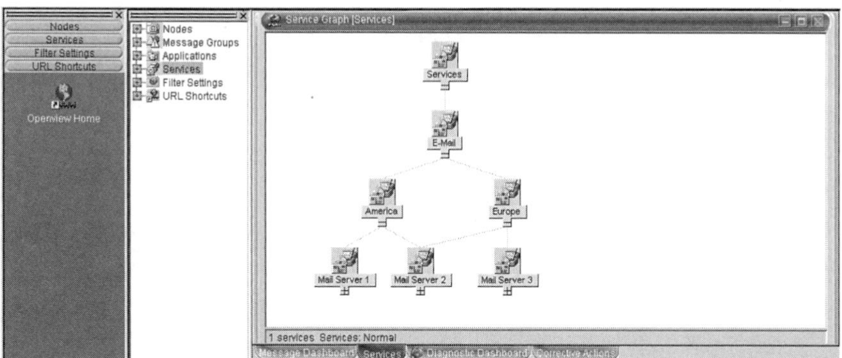

13.14 CONFIGURE A NEW OVO OPERATOR

The administrator is responsible for defining the customized environment for each operator. The operator configuration is controlled through the Motif graphical user interface by logging on as the OVO Administrator. At this time, there are no administrator functions (such as customization, configuration distribution, and so on) available through the Java console. You can also log on as opc_adm in the JAVA GUI, but you will have operational capabilities only. The administrator can define operator responsibilities based on specific skills or roles via a profile. The profile contains all the tools, applications, node groups, and message groups required by the operator. When the operator account is configured with a name, password, preferences, node hierarchy, the profile is added. Use this method to quickly configure many operators based on the roles they have within the enterprise. Every operator will not see all messages; only those that originate from the nodes which are members of the assigned Node Groups and have a Message Group assigned to the user. By limiting the scope of the messages the operator sees, we maintain focus on the important events that cause messages in the browser. This enables the operations, development, support, and other experts with the knowledge of the applications, servers, and network and services experience to own the problem until it is resolved.

The operator relies upon the tools assigned in their profile to get the job done. In some instances, operators require tools that are not included in the profile. After the application is defined in the administrators' application bank window, assign the application to the operator. Assign the operator's application desktop.

For example, if you want to assign the OV Services to one operator and not a profile, open the application bank in the operators' configuration. Open the application bank window and drag and drop the OV Service application group into the operator's application window. The next time the operator logs into the system he will see new menu items and network tools in the root window. She will also see the Internet icon in the root window.

13.14.1 Summary of the Process to Create a New Operator

The following example is meant to give a high-level overview of the major steps required to configure a new operator account.

Step 1. Start opc and login as opc_adm.

Step 2. In the Node Bank, select **Window→User Bank**. This opens the the User Bank.

Step 3 Select **Action→User→Add**. This opens another screen for you to customize the new operator account.

Step 4. Alternately, to modify an existing operator account, select the icon for the account in the User Bank, right-click, and select modify from the pop-up menu.

Step 5. The Add/Modify User window contains the configuration components for a typical OpenView Operator. Define the user account name, password, Preferences, Node Hierarchy, Responsibilities, Applications, and Profile(s).

Step 6. If you have configured a Profile or installed SPIs that contain the components for this operator's role, assign the Profile. The steps to assign a profile were described in Section 13.11, "Profiles and User Banks."

Step 7. If this is the only customization you require at this time, click **OK**.

Step 8. Add the Managed Nodes that will be managed by the operator (covered in Section 13.9.1).

Step 9. Assign the Managed Nodes to appropriate Node Groups (covered in Section 13.9.2).

Note: Steps 8 and 9 are not part of the operator configuration. They are listed here as reminders of additional tasks to complete.

13.14.2 Functional Tests for the Operator Account

When a new operator account is configured (or an existing account modified), perform a few functional tests before you turn the account over to the production operator. Several recommended tests along with suggestions on how to perform them are shown here:

- **Test the login account**—Login as the operator; use the account name/password.
- **Test the message environment**—Use the **opcmsg** command after it is installed.
- **Test the integrated OVO Applications**—From the operator UI, open the application desktop. Select a node and drag and drop the node onto an application.
- **Test the integrated OV Services**—Open the Root window, check to see whether the Internet Icon appears, and drill down (double-click) on the icon to see additional network topology (if applicable, not all operators have this service assigned).
- **Test the integrated tools**—Select items in the Root Menu, for example Tools, SNMP MIB Browser.
- **Test the Message Browser Layout**—Open the message browser; ensure that the messages are arriving from the nodes. Perform this test this after the managed nodes are configured and assigned to the operator.
- **Test the Java Client Console**—Start the Java console and use the operator account to login.

13.15 CONFIGURE THE MANAGEMENT SERVER

There are many configuration tasks for the management server. After the initial installation, customize the server environment. A few of the most popular initial configuration tasks are described in this section.

13.15.1 Initial Message Management

The management server produces messages immediately after installing the agent software, policies, actions, monitors, and commands. The agent software running on the server generates the messages. Many of the messages are duplicates; this happens if the OVO agent detects the same error condition multiple times. If you disable the policies, you will not see the messages from that node in the message browser. Initially, you just want to suppress the duplicate messages. In the next section, we discuss how to control duplicate messages on the management server. Other message suppression concepts are covered in Chapter 14.

13.15.2 Control Duplicate Messages

Some messages in the browser indicate that you have successfully installed the agent or distributed the policies. The other platform- and application-specific messages depend on which policies are installed on the managed node.

In the beginning, just after a new installation, you may find it necessary to reduce the number of duplicate messages that appear in the message browser. You can reduce the amount of redundant information appearing in the message browser by changing the server configuration with the duplicate message suppression feature.

13.15.3 Example Server Duplicate Message Suppression

Select **Actions→Server→Configure**. Select duplicate message suppression from the window shown in Figure 13-23.

This configures the server to display and increment a counter for duplicate messages in the message browser. If there is information that should accompany a message in the form of a note, it is referred to as an annotation. You can either discard the duplicate messages or add them as annotations to the original message.

Figure 13-23 Server duplicate message suppression.

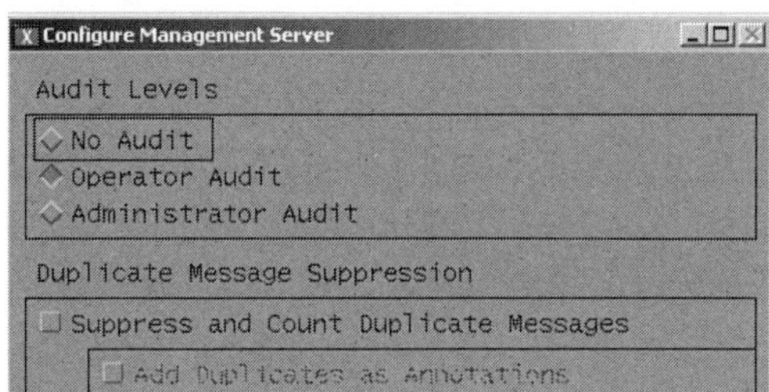

13.15.4 Default OVO X-Window Controls

The Motif *Graphical User Interface* (GUI) has many customizable features. The file /opt/OV/lib/X11/app-defaults/C/Opc controls the X-Window display features for the OpenView Operations GUI. In the next two sections, we look at two of the Motif GUI configuration areas.

13.15.5 Control the Message Group Pop-Up Window

The Message Groups window dominates the screen anytime a new critical message arrives on the server. During the early phases of server configuration, you should control this window right away. The default X-Windows control for this window is called **Opc.alertmsggroupPopup**. The default setting is True. Change the setting to False to prevent this window from popping up to the front of your display for each new critical message. There are three ways to set this control.

First, if you change the setting in the Opc file from True to False, as described previously, you affect the entire server. All users who login via an X-server and launch he OpenView GUI will see the result of the global setting. The configuration will take affect during subsequent operator login session.

The second way to control this window is from the command line during the startup of the OpenView GUI with the **command opc -xrm Opc.alertmsggroupPopup: False**. This controls the window for the individual session.

The third method is creating a file in the users home directory called Xdefaults and place the line in the file **Opc.alertmsggroupPopup: False**.

13.15.6 Colored Lines in the Message Browser

The status color of the lines in the message browser can be displayed across the full width of the line. Edit the file **/opt/Ov/lib/X11/app-defaults/C/OpC**. Remove the comment symbol from the line **Opc.browserColoredLines: True**. Restart your session. You can activate this feature during login for one session with the following command:

opc –xrm Opc.browserColoredLines: True

The other choice is to add this line for an individual account to the users **.Xdefaults** file.

13.16 WORKING FROM THE COMMAND LINE

Many tasks that you will complete using the graphical user interface are also accomplished from the command line. This is important because you might prefer to automate some tasks and perhaps write your own scripts to perform them. For example, you may want to distribute the templates or components for several nodes and with the command **opcragt**, which is easily done. Chapter 14 contains a practical use example for command line distribution.

13.17 PROBLEM SOLVING WITH OPENVIEW OPERATIONS

Documented problem-solving techniques and procedures for the operators are provided with Motif and Java graphical user environments. The tasks usually fall within the following categories:

- Detect a problem
- Investigate the problem
- Solve the problem
- Document the problem solution

In addition to problem-solving tasks, other resources and documentation are available online to help the operator become proficient with OVO as quickly as possible. Download the Java GUI configuration components at http://<management_server>:3443/ITO_OP/. Refer to Figure 13-24.

Figure 13-24 The OpenView Java GUI includes a link to a web-based view for online help and other information.

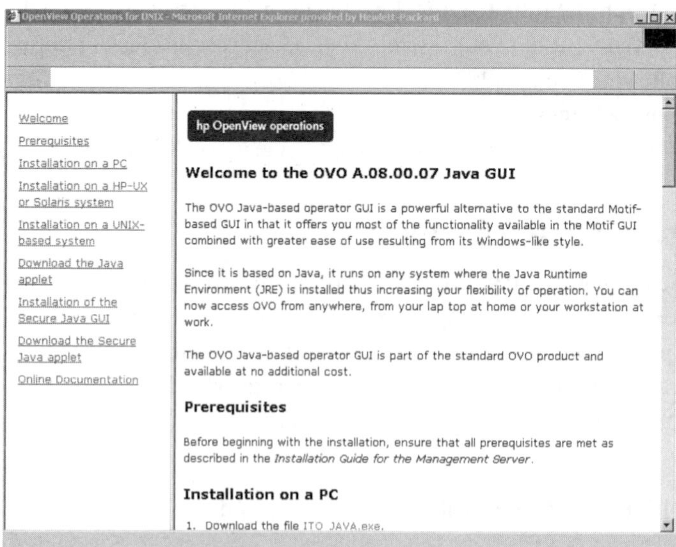

As another example, an operator working from the Java console can select the **Help menu→Contents**. The following web page, shown in Figure 13-25, contains links to information about "What's New," Operator Help, OpenView Navigator Help, and the OV Java GUI Operations Guide.

```
http://<management_server>: 3443/ITO_OP/help/en/ovo/html/index.htm
```

Figure 13-25 OV Operations and Service Navigator Documentation is available online via a user-friendly web-based view.

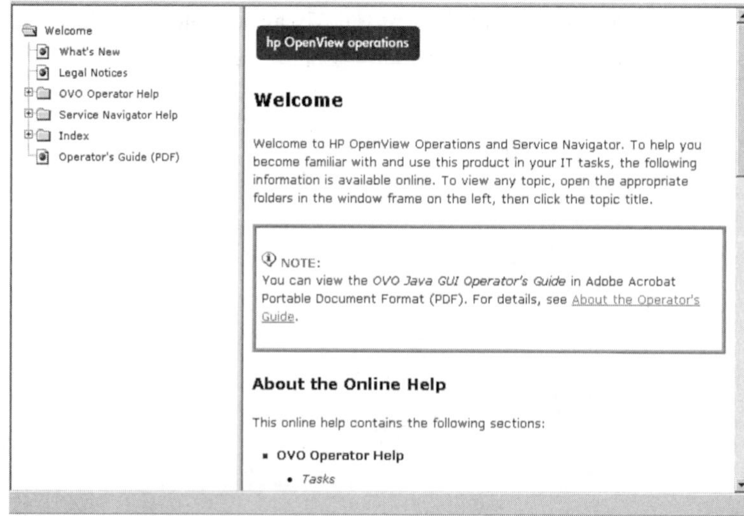

13.18 OVO SERVER AND NODE RESOURCES

One of the most challenging parts of learning about the OpenView platform is remembering what file is located in which directory. The tables in this section are quick references for the binaries, configuration, log, component, and queue files that are located on the server and managed nodes (for HTTPS-based agents and DCE-RPC-based agents). The server stores the platform specific agent configuration files. Reference the *Administrators Reference, Volume 2*, for the agent platform-specific file locations.

13.18.1 Processes and Queue Files

Table 13-6 is a quick reference for most of the OVO processes and associated queue files. During run time the processes use the queues and pipes for inter-process communications and temporary data storage. The information listed in the table is for reference only. Chapter 22 covers additional information about the queue files.

Table 13-6 Management Server Processes and Queue Files

Process Name	Queue/Pipe Files	Description
opcactm Action request Actrespq/p	Actreqq/p	Action manager
	Action response	
opcbbcdist		Configuration adapter (HTTPS based)
opccmm		Subprocess of message receiver, used for bulk transfers
opccsad		Certification Server Adapter
opcctlm	Ctrlq/p Inform control manager of configuration changes	Control Manager
opcdispm	Dispq/p Display Manager to the GUI processes Mpicdmq/p Control display manager Sgmceq/p Display manager change events	Display manager
opcdistm		Distribution manager
opcforwm	Forwmgrq/p	Message forward manager
opcmsgm	Msgkeyq/p Manual acknowledgment Mpicmmq/p Control message manager	Message Manager
opcmsgrb		Message receiver (HTTPS based)
opcmsgrd	Msgmgrq/p Messages and requests	Message receiver

Table 13-6 Management Server Processes and Queue Files (Continued)

Process Name	Queue/Pipe Files	Description
opcsvcm		Service engine
opcttnsm	Ttnsq/p, Ttnsarq/p	Trouble ticket, notification service man-ager
ovoareqsdr	Rqsdbdf Buffer file for request sender Rqsq/p Request sender Input	Request sender
opctramn		Transfer manager
opctss		TCP socket server
opcuiadm		Administrator User Interface
opcuiop		Operator User Interface
opcuiopadm		Administrator Operator User Interface
opcuiwww		Java User Interface manager
ovbbccb		Communication broker (HTTPS based)
ovcd		Control daemon
ovconfd		Configuration and Deploy
ovoareqhdlr		Request handler

13.18.2 Server Directory Structure

The directories on the management server, shown in Figure 13-8, are used for storing the binary (/opt/OV), configuration (/etc/opt/OV), and run time (/var/opt/OV) files. Included for example, are the vendor or customer specific versions of the OVO agent software, actions, commands, and monitors. During distribution, the node-specific flag files are created in the interim distribution directory (/var/opt/OV/share/tmp/OpC/mgmt_sv/distrib) on the server. Prior to transferring the data the configuration is packaged for the appropriate managed node. Details about the OVO agent distribution process are covered in Chapter 14. The Smart Plug-In (add-on components) directories created for the SPI are not included in these tables.

Table 13-7 Management Server Directory Structure

Directory Name	Description
/etc/opt/OV	Parent directory for configuration data.
/etc/opt/OV/share/backgrounds	Background graphics files.
/etc/opt/OV/share/bitmaps/<lang>/OpC	Language-specific bitmaps.
/etc/opt/OV/share/conf/OpC/mgmt_sv/appl	Parent directory for application registration files (ARF's).
/etc/opt/OV/share/conf/OpC/mgmt_sv/reports/<lang>	Language-specific configuration and message reports.
/etc/opt/OV/share/conf/OpC/mgmt_sv/respmgrs	Configuration files for responsible manager configurations.
/etc/opt/OV/share/conf/OpC/mgmt_sv/services/<lang>	Configuration file for Service Navigator.
/etc/opt/OV/share/conf/OpC/mgmt_sv/tmpl_respmgrs	Sample flexible management configuration files.
/etc/opt/OV/share/conf/OpC/mgmt_sv/templates	Templates based on specific character sets.
/etc/opt/OV/share/conf/OpC/mgmt_sv/users	User-specific registration files.

Directory Name	Description
/etc/opt/OV/share/conf/OpC/mgmt_sv/work_respmgrs	Working directory for editing and checking responsible management configuration files
/etc/opt/OV/share/fields/<lang>	OVO-specific fields used within the GUI.
/etc/opt/OV/share/lrf	Local registration files (LRFs).
/etc/opt/OV/share/registration/<lang>	Language-specific application registration files (ARF's).
/etc/opt/OV/share/symbols/<lang>/OPC	Language-specific bitmaps.
/opt/OV	Parent directory for binaries.
/opt/OV/bin/OpC	Binary and GUI files.
/opt/OV/bin/OpC/agtinstall	Agent tools.
/opt/OV/bin/OpC/extern_Intf	External interface files that are used for notification services, trouble ticket integration and physical console connectivity.
/opt/OV/bin/OpC/Install	Installation and distribution utilities.
/opt/OV/bin/OpC/utils	Additional Tools.
/opt/OV/contrib/OpC	Contributed Tools.
/opt/OV/lib	Parent Directory for Shared Libraries.
/opt/OV/lib/nsl	Supported Character Sets.
/opt/OV/lib/X11/app-defaults	Parent directory for X configuration file Opc.
/opt/OV/newconfig	Copies of system startup, application default files, and so on.
/opt/OV/old	Backup copies of the configuration files.
/opt/OV/OpC/config	Directory for configuration uploads.
/opt/OV/OpC/defaults	Directory for configuration uploads.
/opt/OV/OpC/examples/appl	Scripts for application integration.
Refer to man page **opcupload**.	
/opt/OV/OpC/examples/progs	ITO API example programs.
/opt/OV/ReleaseNotes	Final notes not included in the manuals.
/opt/OV/www/htdocs/Ito_op	Java GUI Installation files.
/var/opt/OV	Parent Directory for Run Time Data.
/var/opt/OV/conf/OpC/mgmt_sv	Templates assigned to the management server.
/var/opt/OV/log/OpC/mgmt_sv	Installation and error log files.
/var/opt/OV/share/databases/OpC/mgd_node/customer/<arch>	Parent directory for the customer-specific agent software. Includes commands, programs, scripts and actions
/var/opt/OV/share/databases/OpC/mgd_node/vendor/<arch>	Parent directory for the vendor-specific agent software. Includes commands, programs, scripts and actions
/var/opt/OV/share/help/<lang>/OpC	Language-specific online help files.
/var/opt/OV/share/tmp/OpC/distrib	Staging area for distributions to the managed node.
/var/opt/OV/share/tmp/OpC_appl	Parent directory for temporary files during **opccfgdwn** and **opccfgupld**.
/var/opt/OV/share/tmp/OPC/mgmt_sv	Directory used by processes for temporary data and data exchanges via queues and pipes.

13.18.3 Server Configuration Files

The configuration files in Table 13-8 enable the management server environment to function properly. It is possible to achieve specific process behavior through further customization of the configuration files with the command **ovconfchg**.

Table 13-8 Server Configuration Files

File Name	Description
/etc/opt/OV/conf/OpC/mgmt-sv/svreg	All registered server processes
/etc/opt/OV/share/conf/OpC/mgmt_sv/svreg	Currently registered server processes
/opt/Ov/lib/X11/appp-defaults/C/Opc	X-Window server display control file
escmgr*	Message escalation on the management server
msgforw*	Message forwarding on the management server
outage *	Configuration file for service hours and service outage

* The file is not configured by default. Refer to Chapter 19 for more information.

13.18.4 Managed Node Directory Structure

The following directories on the managed node are used for storing the binary (/opt/OV/bin/OpC), configuration (/var/opt/OV/bin/instrumentation), and run-time (/var/opt/OV) files.

Table 13-9 HP and Solaris Managed Node Directories

Directory Name	Description
/opt/OV/bin/OpC	Programs and commands.
/opt/OV/bin/OpC/install	Programs and commands used during agent or component installation.
/opt/OV/bin/OpC/utils	Programs that are provided in addition to the standard binary command files. The directory contains a README file.
/var/opt/OV/bin/Instrumentation	Automatic and operator actions, commands, monitors.
/var/opt/OV/datafiles/	Coda datafiles.
/var/opt/OV/datafiles/policies	Final versions of the agent configuration files.
/var/opt/OV/log	Log files.
/var/opt/OV/tmp/OpC	Queue files for the agent processes.
/var/opt/OV/tmp/OpC/bin	Temporary location for binary files.
/var/opt/OV/tmp/OpC/distrib	Temporary bulk transfer location for files during distribution.

Note: Refer to the Administrator's Reference Volume 2 for the directory structure of other managed nodes.

13.18.5 Managed Node Configuration Files

The files **nodeinfo** and **opcinfo** (used with prior releases of OVO) are combined into one data file (on HTTPS-based nodes) and the configuration changes to the file are made with either the command **/opt/OV/bin/ovconfget** locally or **/opt/OV/bin/ovconfpar** remotely from the OVO server. Refer to the man pages for details about the commands. The configuration file listed in Table 13-10 are shown for reference only. Please do not modify. This also applies to policies.

Table 13-10 Managed Node Configuration Files

File Name	Description
/var/opt/OV/datafiles/policies /mgrconf.*	Agent message forwarding file
/var/opt/OV/datafiles/policies /primmgr*	_Control switch and automatic action authorization file on the managed node

*This file is configured as part of the manager-to-manager customization. Refer to Chapter 19 for more Information on message forwarding concepts.

13.18.6 Error and Log Files

The error and trace files used with the DCE-RPC and HTTPS agents are shown in Table 13-11. Refer to the HP OpenView Operations Tracing Concepts and User Guide for information on configuring tracing.

Table 13-11 Server Error, Log and Temporary Files

File Name	Description
/var/opt/OV/System.txt	Error file
/var/opt/OV/share/tmp/OpC/mgmt_sv/cfgchg	Configuration change queue file

Refer to the man pages for the command ovconfchg and for more details on how to modify the configuration.

Table 13-12 HP and SUN DCE Node Error, Log, Temporary Files

File Name	Description
/var/opt/OV/tmp/OpC	Agent queue files
/var/opt/OV/log/OpC/opcerror	Agent error log file

Note: Refer to Administrator's Reference Volume 2 for other agent platforms.

13.18.7 System Resource Files

The files listed in Table 13-13 are general system resource files that are modified or created by OpenView during the initial installation of the server or managed node.

Table 13-13 System Resource Files Adapted by OpenView.

File Name	Description
/etc/password	User password file
/etc/group	Group file
/sbin/init.d/opcagt	Agent startup and shutdown script
/etc/rc.config.d/opcagt	Agent startup and shutdown configuration variable file
/sbin/rc3.d/S#opcagt	Startup sequence number linked to the start/stop script
/sbin/rc2.d/K#opcagt	Shutdown sequence number linked to the start/stop script
/etc/services	Internet services, and ito-e-gui for opcuiwww (Java clients) (Server Only).
/etc/inetd.conf	Service configuration for opcuiwww (Server Only).
/var/adm/inetd.sec	Not configured by default install; used to limit access to the service ito-e-gui (Server Only).
/etc/rc.log	Contains system, service and application startup information
/var/adm/syslog/syslog.log	Operating system log file (HP). This file is not used by OVO by default, but may contain information for troubleshooting.
/var/adm/sw/swagent.log	Software installation log

13.19 DOCUMENTATION

The following documentation is available in PDF format (unless otherwise noted) after installation on the management server. The files are located in the directory /opt/OV/www/htdocs/ito_doc/C/manuals.

- Administrator's Reference Volume I
- Administrators Reference Volume II
- Concepts Guide
- Database Entity Diagrams
- Database Schema
- MPE Templates
- Installation Guide for the Management Server
- OpenView Operators Java Guide
- OpenView Navigator User Guide

13.20 TOOLS AND RESOURCES

The management server is installed with a primary web page, `http://<management_server>:3443/ITO/`. This page contains links to many other resources as shown in Figure 13-26.

NOTE: Some of the web links may change without notice.

Figure 13-26 OVO Tools and Resources web page.

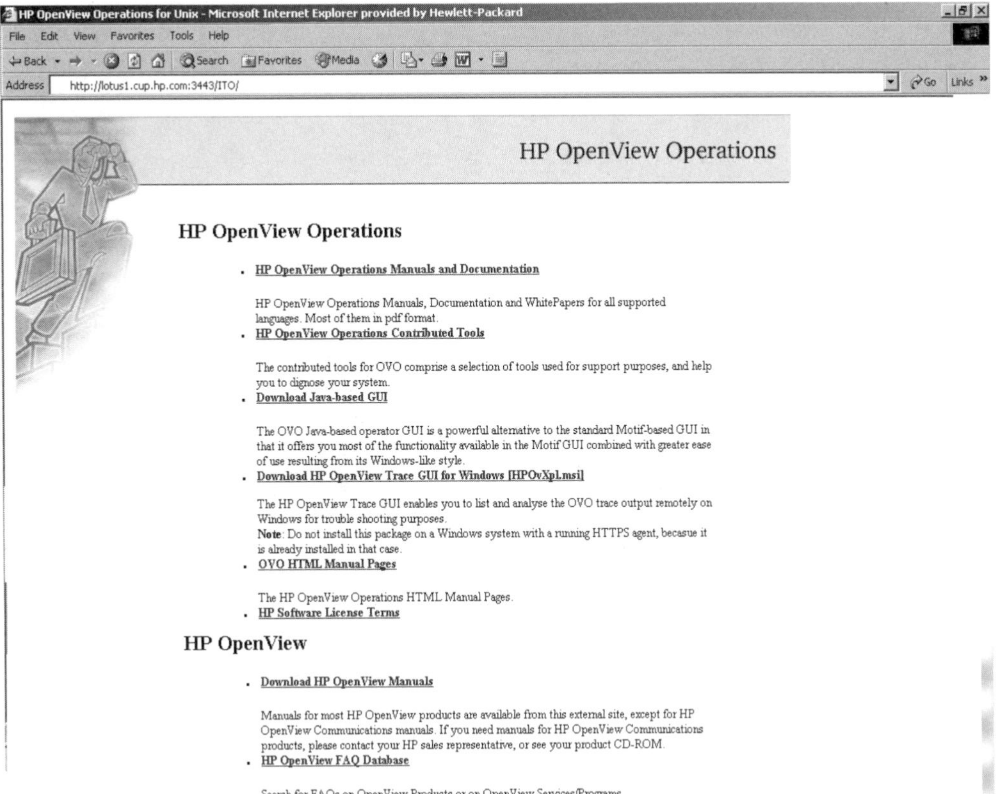

- **Download HP OpenView Software Patches**

  You may download HP OpenView patches from this location. Alternatively, if you have an HP Support Contract for your OpenView products, you may contact the HP Response Center and request patches on DAT tape. Consolidated patches are also available on CD-ROM.
- **Online Support**

  hp OpenView eCare is a fast, efficient way to access interactive technical support tools needed to manage your business and ensure uptime. The information and tools used by hp OpenView phone support experts are now available to you.

Hewlett-Packard

- **Hewlett-Packard**
- **HP OpenView**

Table 13-14 Tools and Resources URL Guide

Document Name	URL
Contributed tools	http://<server>:3443/ITO/contrib.html
Download Java client console	http://<server>:3443/ITO_OP/
Operator Guides for OpenView Operations and Service Navigator	http://<server>:3443/ITO_OP/help/en/ovo/html/Index.htm
OVO HTML man pages	http://<server>:3443/ITO_MAN/
OVO software License terms	http://<server>3443/ITO/LICENSE_ITO.txt
Download OpenView manuals	http://ovweb.external.hp.com/lpe/doc_serv/
OpenView FAQ Database	http://ovweb3.external.hp.com/ovfaq/
Download OpenView patches	http://support.openview.hp.com/support.jsp?FromPROD=ovo
Online E-Care Support*	http://support.openview.hp.com/support.jsp?FromPROD=ovo
Hewlett Packard home page	http://www.hp.com
OpenView home page	http://www.openview.hp.com
*Online E-Care	The E-Care web site provides fast access to OpenView Technical Support Tools.

13.21 SUMMARY OF EXECUTING OVOINSTALL

This section provides a list of the major steps that are accomplished by executing the ovoinstall program.

1. Query the user for information about number of concurrent users, and types of connections. This information is used to access if the available resources are adequate for the installation. If they are not you will get a warning message.
2. Check the system environment for the recommended patches.
3. Install OVO server software (including NNM).
4. Configure the OVO server. (Note: in prior releases of OVO the opcconfig program was used for this step).
5. Install OS SPIs (if selected by the user).
6. Install local OVO agent (if selected by the user).

13.22 SUMMARY

Chapter 13 covered a lot of ground and should be a helpful reference for new and experienced OVO administrators. The chapter included key concepts and best practices for a new enterprise management implementation with OpenView, and touched upon some of the details of the configuration tasks. Finally, the chapter ends with lots of resources and references, which although available from other sources are consolidated here for quick reference. The next chapter continues with more details about the components and how to deploy the OVO configuration.

CHAPTER 14

Agents, Policies and Distribution

One goal of enterprise management is to minimize service-impacting downtime. This goal can be accomplished with the assistance of the OpenView intelligent agent software. The primary function of the agent is to monitor the managed environment and report problems and status information about the health of applications, devices, and services. The agent software components for all supported platforms are initially installed on the management server. After the OVO management domain is defined, the agent software and instrumentation is distributed to the various managed nodes. The agent distribution installs the software onto the node based on architecture and operating system (such as HP, SUN, NT, Linux, IBM, and so on). In general, prior to distribution you should customize the agent, policies, and instrumentation (which includes agent configuration, policy templates, actions, monitors, and commands) to meet the specific needs of the managed environment. The focus of this chapter is to provide an overview of the operation, configuration, and distribution of the agents, policies, and instrumentation.

14.1 THE OVO AGENTS

There are two types of OVO agents, DCE/NCS-based agents and HTTPS-based agents. DCE/NCS-based agents are the traditional agent type and use *remote procedure call* (RPC) services to communicate with the server. HTTPS- based agents, used for highly secure communications, use standard Web security technologies (such as HTTP, SOAP, Proxies, SSL, and so on). Refer to Chapter 20, "Security," for more security information. Both types of agents are referred to in this chapter. The two types of agents are used similarly to manage the nodes. The node communications type is determined when you add the node to the OVO configuration. Select **Actions→Node→Add** to create a new node. The default machine type for the new node is HP PA-RISC (HTTPS), as shown in Figure 14-1. The default communication type is HTTPS, as shown in Figure 14-2.

Figure 14-1 The Add Node window shows the managed node default configuration.

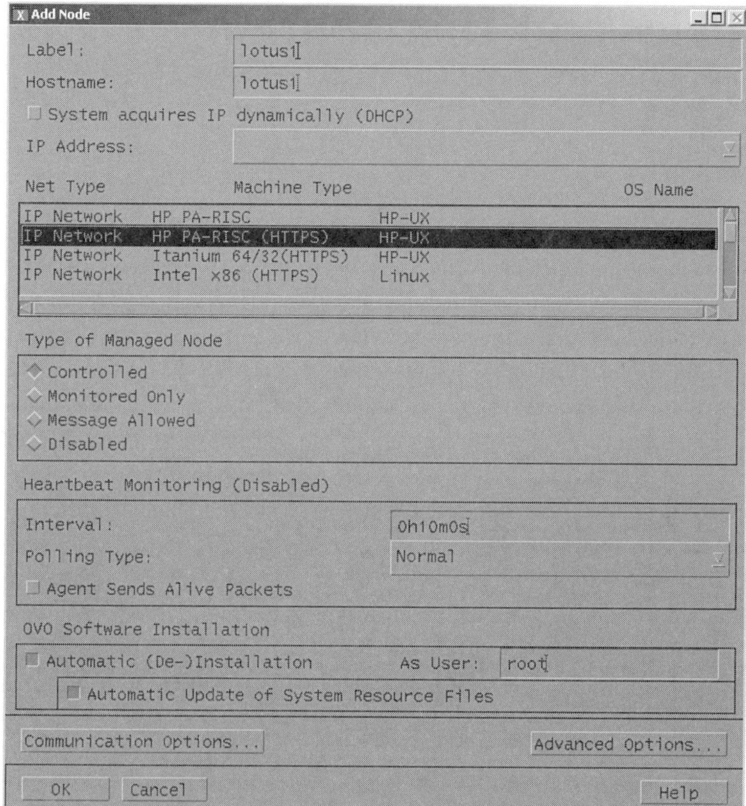

14.1.1 List of Tasks Performed by the Agents

There are many tasks performed by the agent, and the tasks are not limited to the following list:

- Intercept messages from their respective source (logfile, SNMP traps, command line, or API)
- Filter the messages according to the templates and conditions activated on the managed node
- Log messages to a local file that could be used, for example, for debugging
- Buffer messages in the event the agent cannot communicate with the management server
- Execute local automatic actions
- Execute scheduled actions
- Execute operator initiated actions and respond to desktop application requests
- Forward messages to the management server

- Monitor thresholds
- Monitor the health and status of the agent itself
- Pass messages to external programs
- Perform message correlation

14.1.2 The Agent Processes

The agent processes provide the functionality for fault, event, service and performance management. The agent processes are distinguished into two categories, core and sub-agent. The core processes are primarily responsible for controlling agent startup and shutdown, monitoring the status of the other agents, communication functions, distribution, and configuration changes.

The sub-agents extend the functionality of the agent platform to perform tasks, such as reading a logfile, monitoring a threshold, and intercepting a message or an SNMP trap. During operation, the agent processes send or accept information and instructions from other local OVO processes or from the management server. One parent process is responsible for managing the other agents. It starts, stops, and provides status on all of the other agents as required. In order for a subagent to run the policy, templates for the subagent must be installed. Policy templates are referred to as policies on HTTPS-based nodes and are called templates on RPC-based nodes. For example, in order for the message interceptor to run, install the message policy along with the **opcmsg** command. In order for the logfile encapsulator to run, install the logfile components (at least one logfile policy), and so on. Following are descriptions of the HTTPS agent processes:

- **Control Agent (ovcd)**—Parent process, starts/stops/statuses sub-agents, communicates with the local communication broker.
- **Message Agent (opcmsga)—**Sends messages to message receiver on OVO server, sends action responses to the server, interface for programs that access the internal *message stream interface* (MSI), forwards data to other OVO servers, and sends agent alive packet to server. MSI is covered in Section 14.5.3.
- **HTTPS Communication Broker (ovbbccb)—**Listens on port 383 for HTTP connection requests; returns port number of registered programs.
- **Configure/Distribute (ovconfd)—**Distributes policies to the final location on the local file system.
- **Action Agent (opcacta)—**Starts/stops automatic and operator actions; handles command broadcast and other desktop application requests.
- **Logfile Encapsulator (opcle)—**Reads logfile(s), checks the logfile nodes and creates time, and triggers a file to be executed. The file to be executed is used in a case when the actual logfile may be a binary file. The content of the binary file must be converted into ASCII format and stored in a readable file in order for the logfile encapsulator to process the data. The file that is executed is the program that converts the binary file into ASCII format. For example, in order to convert the binary file wtmp, you need to execute the

command **last**. The output from the execution of the command can be redirected to a file (such as /usr/bin/last agent process>/tmp/last.out). This process is referred to as the binary conversion process. Then the file to be read becomes /tmp/last.out.

- **Monitor Agent (opcmona)**—Executes monitor scripts, checks monitor script returned values against threshold, creates message and sends to message agent, handles scheduled actions, and connects to the embedded performance component for performance monitor requests.
- **Message Interceptor (opcmsgi)**—Intercepts messages created with the **opcmsg** command or the *application program interface* (API), evaluates message for match condition, and sends matched message to the message agent.
- **Trap Interceptor (opctrapi)**—Converts SNMP traps to OVO messages, sends messages to the message agent, can register with NNM to obtain incoming traps or listen for traps on port 162.
- **Event Correlation Agent (opceca)**—Correlates events on the node; requires an ECS policy.
- **ECS Annotate Server (opcecaas)**—Starts external programs; requires ECS engine.
- **Security Certificate Client (ovcs)**—Used during installation to allow or deny certificate requests.
- **Performance Agent (coda)**—Embedded performance component; collects performance metrics data.

The RPC-based agent processes, when installed with the default templates, are listed here:

- Control agent (opcctla)
- Message agent (opcmsga)
- BBC Location Broker (llbserver)
- Action agent (opcacta)
- Monitor agent (opcmona)
- Message Interceptor (opcmsgi)
- Trap Interceptor (opctrapi)
- Performance agent (coda)

14.2 THE OVO MANAGEMENT SERVER PROCESSES

In addition to its role as the primary manager for the managed nodes, the server functions as the repository for the agent software and components, including templates (which are converted into policies during distribution) and instrumentation (also known as actions, commands, and monitors). These components allow the OVO administrator to define the systems, devices, and services within the management domain. The components' definition includes specific service levels for monitors, alarms, and corrective actions. The server includes a run-time version of NNM and the OVO Oracle database. The server could also have other OpenView products installed for local use or for distribution to the nodes (such as SPIs, Service Navigator, ECS Designer, and so on).

14.2.1 Tasks Performed by the Server

The tasks performed by the management server include but are not limited to the following:

- Collecting Data from the managed nodes
- Regrouping Messages (see the definition of this later in this chapter)
- Calling appropriate agents for specified tasks, such as perform actions
- Controlling the database interface, ensuring that the database is operational
- Forwarding messages to other OVO servers in larger installations
- Installing agent software onto the managed nodes
- Notifying and updating managed node with configuration changes
- System alive monitoring
- Self monitoring
- Forwarding messages to external processes or notification service interface
- Updating and coordinating user interfaces
- Adding messages to the database
- Correlating duplicate messages
- Routing messages to external processes (such as Event Correlation Manager)
- Installing, tracking, and reporting on OVO licensing

14.2.3 The Management Server Processes

Following are descriptions of the management server processes.

OVO Management Server:

- **Control Manager (opcctlm)**—Started by ovspmd, starts all other OVO server processes except ovoareqsdr and ovoareqhdlr, and spawns database maintenance processes opcdbmsgmv and opchistdwn. Performs license check.
- **Action Manager (opcactm)**—Communicates instructions via the managed node's control agent to the action agents to perform automatic and operator actions, scheduled actions, application startup, and broadcasting. Provides mechanism for external interface instruction text.
- **Message Manager (opcmsgm)**—Receives messages from the managed nodes via the message receiver. Performs message correlation, message regroup, log message to database, add annotations, trigger notifications, and forwards message to trouble ticket and notification manager (opcttnsm).

- **TT & Notify Mgr (opcttnsm)**—Trouble ticket and notification service manager; feeds an external notification interface with the message attributes from OVO. For example, can be configured to send email to responsible operators when a critical message is received.
- **Forward Manager (opcforwm)**—Sends messages to the message receiver on other OVO management servers. Takes input from message manager, action manager (action responses) and the display manager.
- **Service Engine (opcsvcm)**—Service Navigator configuration manager. Maintains service graph and calculates service status, built-in adapters handle client requests.
- **Display Manager (opcdispm)**—Sends message to configured operators, receives input from the message manager, and send GUI action and change requests to action manager or control manager.
- **Distribution. Manager (opcdistm)**—Distributes agent software, communicates with distribution agent on the managed node, controls manager, connects to database, and reads configuration data.
- **Cert. Svr Adapter (opccsad)**—Certificate server adapter.
- **BBC Config Adaptor (opcbbcdist)**—HTTPS Configuration Adapter.
- **Request Sender (ovoareqsdr)**—Sends and receives request for other processes to the control agent.
- **Request Handler (ovoareqhdlr)**—Handles request from registered services.
- **Message Receiver (opcmsgrd)**—DCE-RPC based message and action response receiver daemon, communicates with forward manager on other OVO servers, starts subagent opccmm for socket connection during distribution, and is started by the request sender.
- **Message Receiver (opcmsgrb)**—HTTPS-based message receiver daemon
- **Control Daemon (ovcd)**—Takes input from HTTPS communication broker ovbbccb.
- **BBC Communications Broker (ovbbccb)**—Listens for incoming communication from the managed node on port 383. sent and received.
- **Config and Deploy (ovconfd)**—Configuration and Deploy Component for HTTPS agents; converts templates to policies and pushes configurations to the managed nods.
- **Certification Server (ovcs)**—Security Certificate Server.

Other supporting processes are called for specific tasks as required; they do not appear in the output of the OVO status commands. Some of the supporting processes are listed here:

- **opccmm**—Communication manager, started by message receiver for socket services during distribution to node and data transfer and communication to other servers.
- **opcuiwww**—JAVA GUI process used for client connections to the OVO server. Started by inetd.
- **opctss**—TCP socket server, receives port number from distribution manager.
- **opcuiop**—Operator GUI.
- **opcuiopadm**—Administrator's operator GUI.
- **opcuiadm**—Administrator GUI.

- **opctranm**—Executes file transfer to nodes and remote commands on DCE nodes; used during installation and some SPI discovery.
- **opc**—Called by ovspmd during server startup; triggers startup of the control manager.
- **Event Correlation (opcecm)**—Event correlation manager requires an ECS policy.

14.3 AGENTS ALIVE AND WELL AT ALL TIMES

The server periodically checks the health of the agents. The frequency of the check is configured in the node configuration. The control agent sends status replies to the message receiver on the server. If the network interface is alive (via ping), the server sends an alive-check packet to the control agent. The DCE control agent is the parent process of all the other agents running on the node. When the control agent is not running, the server reports that the control agent is down. If the network interface is down, the server reports that the node is down. The control daemon (ovcd) is the parent process on HTTPS agents.

The agent can send alive checks to the server. This may be more efficient from a network traffic perspective. To configure the "agent sends alive check," modify the node configuration from the Node Add or Node Modify Window. See Figure 14-1.

14.3.1 RPC Service

HTTPS-based node communications is the default (for 8.x managed nodes). You can select the RPC-based node and communication type when you add the node to the OVO configuration. There are prerequisites that must be met prior to installation of the RPC-based agents. Refer to the system vendor's documentation for operating system RPC patch information. Refer to the DCE Agent Concepts and Configuration Guide for platform-specific node communication details.

14.3.2 HTTPS Communication Service

HTTPS-based communications provides information exchanges based on open standard HTTP 1.1 and SOAP. The HTTPS-based process (ovbbccb) runs on the managed node and listens for request on port 383. The HTTPS-based agent communications eliminate the need for DCE/NCS RPC technology and offer more efficient management through firewalls. Refer to the *HP OVO HTTPS Agent Concepts and Configuration Guide* for further details.

14.3.3 Functional Tests for Primary Communications

There are some cases when the node and the server may not communicate. OpenView makes extensive use of the configured name resolution services (DNS, NIS or a host file). Here are questions to ask when you think communication is an issue:

- Are all of the agents running?
- Can the node ping the server?

- Can the server ping the node?
- Can you verify the control agent with opcragt?
- Is the communication service running on the node?
- Are the communication processes running on the server?
- Do the server and the node resolve the same names and addresses for each other?
- Does the node have more than one network interface card? If so,
- Which interface IP address is configured to communicate with the server? And also,
- Which interface IP address for the node is configured on the server?
- Did the node communication type change (i.e. UDP to TCP)?
- Can you verify the path for the network end-to-end connections?
- Can you ping the node's HTTPS process?

If you have tried most of the functional tests and the communication still does not work,it is possible that the queue files have become unusable. As a last resort, it may be necessary to stop the agents, remove the queue files, and restart the agents. Refer to Chapter 22, "Troubleshooting Tips and Techniques," for more information on troubleshooting.

14.4 AGENT INSTALLATION

This section covers four methods used to distribute the agent software and components to the managed node. The first method is called automatic. With this distribution method, you control the activation of the distribution program (inst.sh) from the management server's Motif GUI. The second method is semi-automatic. In this method, some of the tasks are performed from the server and some are performed at the node. This method is primarily used with Microsoft Windows nodes. The third method is manual and is performed from the console of the managed node. The manual method is preferred when the node is outside a firewall. The fourth method uses the server command line. This chapter provides installation examples for an HP-UX and Windows node. Refer to the *DCE Agent Concepts and Configuration Guide*, for platform-specific installation guidelines and requirements.

The agent installation process occurs in several stages. During the first stage, the agent software is installed on the managed node. Methods of installation are described in sections 14.4.1 through section 14.4.6. Agent installation includes transfer of the software from the management server to the node, creating an opc-op (operator) account on the node, and installing startup and shutdown programs for the agent software. The second stage installs the policies and instrumentation components.

14.4.1 Automatic Install

If the distribution is performed from the GUI, the installation script (inst.sh) is executed to handle the tasks and provide status to the administrator at the console. The inst.sh script is also used to de-install the agent software. The inst.sh script performs the following tasks (not necessarily in order):

1. Resolve the node name.
2. Ping the node.
3. Verify root access to the node or prompt the administrator for the root password.
4. Determine the node type.
5. Determine the OVO version if an agent is already installed on the node.
6. Call the distribution manager (opcdistm).
7. Call the configuration and deploy manager (ovconfd for HTTPS nodes).
8. Verify system time between the node and the server. Different time zones are handled automatically. It is important that "normalized" time settings are identical or as close as possible between the agent and server.
9. Choose a file transfer method (ftp,rcp or ssh/scp).
10. Create temporary staging area on the node
11. Modify the resource files so the agent will automatically start upon system boot. The resource files were described in Chapter 13.
12. Create opc user account and group.
13. (Re-) start the agent processes.
14. Perform new installation, update only, or complete redistribution (also called the forced update option) of the policies and instrumentation.
15. Remove previous install log or install error files.
16. Update the installation log file (inst_sum.log).
17. Write errors to the installation error log (inst_err.log).
18. Create and remove the distribution lock file. (Tip: If the distribution is interrupted the lock file should be removed prior to attempting another distribution. The lock file is located on the management server in the directory /var/opt/OV/share/tmp/OpC/mgmt_sv/Inst.lock.)

14.4.2 Semi-automatic Install for Windows Nodes

All steps in the listing shown are performed on the server, except one manual step l. If there is no Domain account, provide some entry at the ITO account password prompt, used to configure the ITO account (opc_op) on the node. This install method assumes that we are doing an installation on a Primary or Backup Domain controller. Within a domain, after the software in installed on the domain controllers, additional nodes contact the domain controller for software distribution. Refer to the node configuration for details on how to configure the node to download software from a domain controller. The first three steps listed here are the same for all nodes prior to agent distribution.

1. Add the node to the node bank.
2. Add the node to a node group.
3. Configure the operator console for the node group.
4. Restart the operator session (if you have created a new node group that modified the operator configuration, this will enable changes to operator configuration to appear in their console).
5. Configure full ftp services on the node. This enables use of the Internet Services Manager in the Admin Tools Application Group.
6. Ensure read/write access to the disk on the managed node for ftp file transfers. Instructions on checking the node for read/write access vary for different Windows operating systems. Consult the system documentation or on-line Windows help.
7. Ensure that there is one NTFS file system on the node.
8. Verify name resolution (node and server).
9. Obtain the managed node administrator password. Test the password (for example, login on the node).
10. Assign the policies to the node from the GUI.
11. Distribute the agent software, policies, and instrumentation (actions commands, and monitors) from the GUI.
12. When prompted by the installation script, supply the Administrator Password.
13. When prompted to provide another password, supply the password that will be used for the OVO Account within the domain.
14. Watch the prompts carefully for the manual step that will instruct you to go to the node and execute the opc_Inst.bat script.
15. When the prompt halts, read the Instruction in the Installation window and go to the node (do not hit the return key on the server command line).
16. At the node in the ftp directory (typically C:\Inetpub\ftproot) the Install process has created a new directory opc_temp. Execute the opc_inst.bat program that has been staged there by the Install process.
17. After the batch script completes, return to the sever and press the return key at the distribution window.
18. The distribution will proceed; press return when the program completes.
19. Test the operation of the node; send a message to the server. You can do this from the command line at the node. For example: /opt/OV/bin/OpC/utils/submit.sh. The submit.sh script sends about five test messages to the message browser.
20. Verify the agent status from the server. You can do this from the command line at the server.
21. For example: opcragt -status <node name>.

14.4.3 Manual Installation

The first five manual installation steps are performed at the command line of the node. The remaining steps are performed on the server:

1. Copy the compressed package for the node type from the server to the node. (via ftp or another method).
2. Uncompress the package in a temporary directory.
3. On Windows nodes, configure a nodeinfo and the opcsetup.inf.
4. Use the software installation method best suited for the node (such as swinstall, opc_inst.bat, pkgadd, rpm, and so on) to install the agent on the node.
5. Activate the agent on the node with the opcactivate command. With the -s option, the script will perform the necessary stops to set up the programs for agent startup and shutdown during system boot.
6. Add the node to the node bank.
7. Add the node to a node group.
8. Assign the node group to the operator and administrator.
9. Restart operator and administrator sessions to ensure that the messages from newly Installed nodes will appear in the message browser(s) for the appropriate operators (including the Administrator).
10. Update the database on the management server with the command opcsv. This command sets the software status flag In the OVO database. This informs the database that the OVO software has been successfully installed on the managed node.
11. Activate heartbeat polling (a server to node periodic check) with the command **opchbp**. This command enables the server to be checked periodically using the configured communication protocol to ping the node and verify the control agent on the node is running.

14.4.3.1 Example: Manually Install HP (DCE/RPC-based) Node

The supported agent software (compressed package_name.Z files) is installed during initial installation of the server. There is a version of the agent software for each transport layer communication protocol. One transport protocol available for communication with the node is *User Datagram Protocol* (UDP), which sends out the transmission but does not guaranteed delivery of the transmission. A more reliable protocol, *Transmission Control Protocol* (TCP), sends the transmission and verifies via acknowledgement signals to and from the node that the transmission was delivered successfully. The choice of UDP or TCP depends on the network environment; although TCP requires more traffic due to the acknowledgement routine on a busy network, it will ensure better stability of the communications between the node and the server. Decide in advance which transport protocol option is best for your environment, TCP or UDP. The compressed installation files contain the agent software, the communications package, and the performance components. If you use the –s option with the opcactivate program, the managed node resource files are configured using the script upd_res.sh. Identify the character code set for the server (check the opcsvinfo file) and the character code set for the node (HP default=ISO885915). The steps to add the node manually are as follows:

1. Add the node to the node bank.
2. Add the node to a node group.
3. Restart the message browser (for messages from the new group).
4. Copy/ftp the compressed agent files from the server into a temporary directory on the node. The files are in the directory /var/opt/OV/share/databases/OpC/mgd_node/vendor/hp/pa-risc/hp-ux11/A.07.10/RPC_DCE_TCP. The file names for an HP-UX node are opc_pkg.Z, com_pkg.Z, perf_pkg.Z and opc_inst.
5. Execute the program opc_inst on the managed node.
6. Execute the program: opcactivate <OVO_server_name> -s <server_name> -cs <HPserver.codeset> -cn <agent.codeset>

Note: The server name shown in the example is the name of the primary management server for this node.

7. Execute the program: opcsw –installed <node_name> on the management server.
8. Execute the program: opchbp –start <node_name> on the management server to start heartbeat polling.
9. Execute the program: opcragt –distrib –template –action –monitor –commands <node> on the management server.
10. Assign the new group to operators as required.
11. Restart the operator sessions.

14.4.3.2 Example Manual Installation Microsoft Windows Node

The procedure to manually install the Microsoft Windows node is outlined here. If the node requires an encrypted Domain Account password for the ITO account, a program (crypt) is provided on the server to create and encrypted password. If the password field is left blank, a generic password is generated by OVO. A sample opcsetup.inf file is shown.

1. Add the node to the node bank.
2. Add the node to a node group or create a new group.
3. Login to the node as the Administrator account.
4. Enable full ftp services on the node.
5. Ensure read/write access to the disk for ftp.
6. Transfer the NT package files from the server. The directory location for the Windows files is /var/opt/OV/share/databases/OpC/mgd_node/vendor/ms/intel/nt/A.07.10/ RPC_DCE_TCP. The files to transfer include: comm_pkg.Z, opc-inst.bat, opc_pkg.Z, opc_pre.bat, opcsetup.inf, perf_pkg.Z, unzip.exe, and unzip.txt.

7. Rename the files with the .Z extension with .zip extensions.
8. Create a nodeinfo file, add the node configuration information, and add the appropriate parameters. An example nodeinfo file is shown here for reference.

```
OPC_MGMTSV_CHARSET iso885915
OPC_NODE_CHARSET ascii
OPC_NODE_TYPE CONTROLLED
OPC_AGENT_LOG_DIR /var/opt/OV/log/OpC
OPC_COMM_TYPE RPC_DCE_TDP
```

9. Edit the opcsetup.inf file and add the drive letter and management server name. An example opcsetup.Inf file is shown here for reference.

```
[Setup Drive]
VOID
[Management Server]
unknown

[Account Password]

[Force User]
Off
[Authentication]
Off


[HP ITO Version]
A.07.22
[Agent Architecture]
ms/intel/nt
```

10. Execute the opc_inst.bat program.
11. Start the agent software: **opcactivate –s <management_server>**.
12. On the server, add the node to the database: **opcsw –installed <node>**.
13. Configure heartbeat polling: **opchbp -start <node_name>**.
14. Distribute policies and instrumentation (via the GUI or the use the **opcragt** command).
16. Add the node group to the operator configuration.
17. Restart the operator session.

14.4.6 Agent Installation using Secure Shell (ssh)

OVO supports the secure shell (ssh) method of installation. The prerequisites for the ssh configuration are assumed. Select the secure shell option, shown in Figure 14-2, from the Node Communications Options window. After the button is selected, additional information about the secure shell installation is available by pressing the F1 key on the keyboard.

Figure 14-2 The Node Communication Options window is used to select the method of communication between the agent and the server.

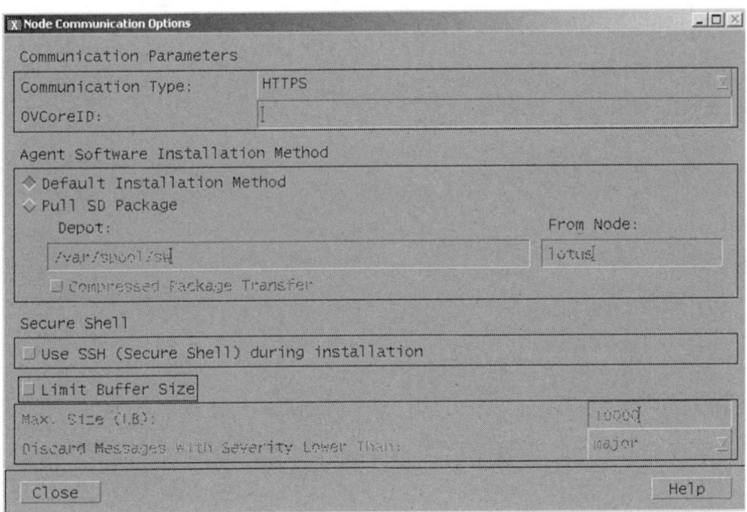

The secure shell installation process is outlined in the online help, as shown in Figure 14-3.

Refer to Chapter 20 for more information about Secure Shell.

Figure 14-3 Secure shell installation process instructs the server to use the secure shell installation method to distribute components over the network to the managed node.

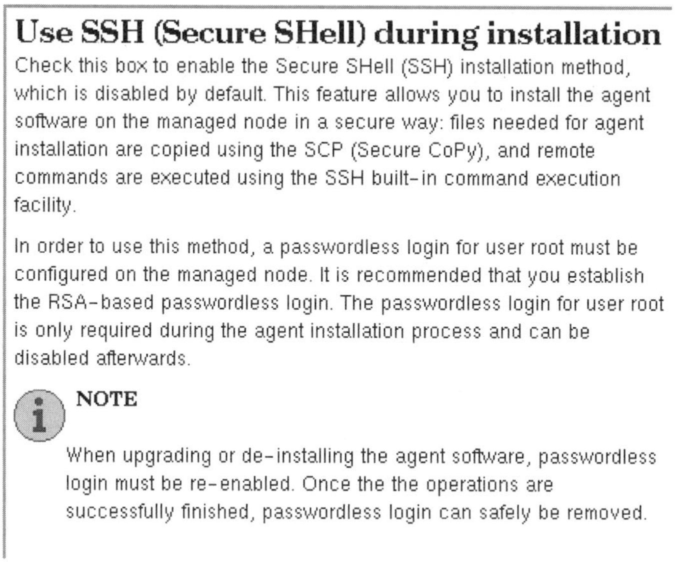

Use SSH (Secure SHell) during installation

Check this box to enable the Secure SHell (SSH) installation method, which is disabled by default. This feature allows you to install the agent software on the managed node in a secure way: files needed for agent installation are copied using the SCP (Secure CoPy), and remote commands are executed using the SSH built-in command execution facility.

In order to use this method, a passwordless login for user root must be configured on the managed node. It is recommended that you establish the RSA-based passwordless login. The passwordless login for user root is only required during the agent installation process and can be disabled afterwards.

NOTE

When upgrading or de-installing the agent software, passwordless login must be re-enabled. Once the the operations are successfully finished, passwordless login can safely be removed.

14.4.5 Command Line Distribution of Agent Components

The commands for agent and component distribution are listed here for reference. Refer to the man page or the online *Administrators Task Guide* for more information.

In some operations environments, it is more feasible to install the agent software, policies, and instrumentation using a program that you create and execute using the name(s) of the nodes that you want to install. Although the details of such a script are outside the scope of this chapter, the commands that are essential for completing the core task are described here for reference. With what has already been discussed in this chapter, some of the commands and concepts are already familiar. Here we assume that the management server is installed and operational.

- Add the node to the OVO database with the command opcnode
  An example of the command syntax is shown here for reference. Check the man page for a detailed description of the command options. This is a very long command line!
  /opt/OV/OpC/utils/opcnode –add_node node_name=lotus_your.domain.com net_type=NETWORK_IP mach_type=MACH_BBC_HP-UX_PARISC group_name=hp_ux node_label=lotus.your.domain.com comm_type=COMM_BBC

- Execute the script /opt/OV/bin/OpC/agtinstall/inst.sh on the server; provide node data at the prompts as requested. A brief transcript of the script is shown here for reference.

```
# /opt/OV/bin/OpC/agtinstall/inst.sh
          ____________________________

          Script /opt/OV/bin/OpC/agtinstall/inst.sh invoked by
root at 11/23/03 00:42:42.
          OVO Software Maintenance on Managed Node(s).
          Enter system(s) for which software maintenance should
be done. More than one system can be specified, if separated by
blank: (empty = stop processing)
=========> lotus.your.domain.com
=========> Preferred IP address of node lotus.your.domain.com
(Return=lotus.your.domain.com)?
Managed Nodes platforms supported by this Management Server:
hp/pa-risc/hp-ux11
hp/pa-risc/HP-UX1100
ip/other/other
linux/x86/linux24
ms/intel/nt
non_ip/other/other
sun/sparc/solaris
sun/sparc/solaris7
=========> Enter platform name for lotus.your.domain.com :hp/pa-
risc/hp-ux11
=========> Automatic update of system resource files
(y|n=default)?y
=========> Automatic (re-)start of OVO services on
(y|n=default)?y
=========> OVO version (V.UU.FF) which should be installed on
system lotus.your.domain.com (Return=latest version)?A.07.14
=========> Pathname of logging directory on system
lotus.your.domain.com(Return=default logging directory)?
=========> Enter distribution method for Agent package (1 = Man-
agement Server based, 2 = Satellite Agent Depot with SD, 3 =
Windows NT installation server 4 = Secure Shell installation
(default=1)?
=========> Login name of superuser for system
lotus.your.domain.com (Return=root)?
```

From this point, the system will continue with the install process. After the installation completes successfully, take the next steps to complete the configuration.

- Check the installation with the program: /opt/OV/bin/OpC/utils/opcnode –list_nodes
  An example of the output from the **opcnode** command is shown here for example.

```
# /opt/OV/bin/OpC/utils/opcnode -list_nodes
List of all Nodes in the OVO database:
=====================================================================
Name            = lotus.your.domain.com
Label           = lotus.your.domain.com
IP-Address      = 10.153.209.61
Network Type    = NETWORK_IP
Machine Type    = MACH_BBC_HP-UX_PARISC
Comm Type       = COMM_BBC
```

- Distribute the policies and instrumentation. An example of the syntax for the command **opcragt** is shown here for reference.

```
   /opt/OV/bin/OpC/opcragt -distrib -templates -actions   \
-monitor -commands lotus.your.domain.com
```

14.5 AGENT CONFIGURATION

The agent configuration is performed through the administrator's GUI or from the command line.

14.5.1 Agent Configuration Files

Information and instructions are provided to the agents via the policies and configuration files. For example, you change the node type from controlled to message allowed via the GUI. After you close the DCE-based node configuration window, the update is immediately sent to the configuration file (nodeinfo) on the managed node and you will see a message about the new configuration in the message browser. HTTPS-based nodes do not use a nodeinfo file. Using the command **opcragt**, you can check or change DCE node configuration parameters. For example, the following configuration variable is set using the **opcragt** command line:

```
# cd /opt/OV/bin/OpC/install
# ./opcragt -set_config_var OPC_MAX_ICMP_PINGS=10 nodename
nodename.domain.yourco.com
Node nodename.domain.yourco.com
Done.
```

The RPC/DCE-based agent configuration files include the following:

- **opcinfo**—Uses variables to customize agent behavior for the specific environment; not affected by the node configuration changes.
- **nodeinfo**—Contains the node configuration information; overwritten if the node configuration is modified.
- **mgrconf**—Configures to what servers the node is allowed to forward messages and determines what servers are allowed to send a request to perform actions on the node. Used within a *manager of managers* (MOM) environment.

Starting with 8.0—HTTPS-based agents, the DCE-RPC files are replaced by a policy configuration file. A policy is a template in XML format. Executing the following commands performs changes to the policy files:

ovconfchg—Manipulates settings files, updates the configuration database, and triggers notification scripts.

ovconfpar—Sets and returns configuration parameters remotely.

ovconfget—Returns specified attributes from the configuration database.

Refer to the *HTTPS Agent Concepts and Configuration Guide* and the man pages for more information on the policy files.

14.5.2 Server Configuration Files

Similar to the configuration and operation on the managed node, the server processes obtain information and instructions for operational behavior during startup via server policies. For example, the server policy for Event Correlation or Server Regrouping could be configured for the server. Refer to Chapter 20 for more information on HTTPS and OVO security components.

The agent and server process behavior can be altered or enhanced using various configuration variables. The server configuration file locations can be determined during the installation by defining two symbolic path definitions, InstallDir and DataDir. The default directories on the UNIX platform are /opt/OV and /var/opt/OV. You can check the runtime directory paths with the command ovpath. Refer to the man page for syntax details.

14.5.3 The Message Stream Interface (MSI)

Some agent components are external programs written using the OpenView *Application Programming Interfaces* (APIs)

The *message stream interface* (MSI) provides a program interface for external programs to obtain OVO messages if the message interface is configured to open the message queues for read/write. The APIs are used to create, read, write, and modify the messages. OVO provides the mechanism to enable MSI input or output via the template, node, and server configuration, and the Advance Options window. The event correlation engine is one example of how OVO uses the MSI.

The MSI is covered in more detail in the *OpenView Developers (Software) Toolkit*. Refer to the OpenView web site `http://openview.hp.com` for links to information for software developers.

14.6 POLICIES

Policies are the heart of the agent configuration. They give the agent intelligence via management rules that enable the agent to intercept events or collect data from information sources. A policy includes a complete set of rules (also called conditions) to handle a single information source such as a logfile. Information for the policies is generally created through the GUI. The policy instructs the agent on how to access the source, and what the "rule" is for managing the source (for example, what events to act on or suppress). The default policy templates are installed on the management server. Many policies are ready to configure out-of-the-box due to the *Smart Plug-In* (SPI) concept used to develop the policies. Refer to Chapter 15, "Smart Plug-Ins," for more information on SPIs. It may be necessary to copy and customize a default policy. For example, you may need multiple policy groups with different monitoring, alarm, and notification thresholds for multiple node groups. After the policy is customized, it is assigned and distributed to the managed node or node group. Prior to distribution to the DCE-based managed node, the policy is also called a template. During distribution the template is converted to a policy. Verify the policies that are deployed with the command **ovpolicy**. This section refers to templates in order to be consistent with the configuration components inside the GUI.

14.6.1 Working with Policy Templates from the GUI

As we have seen in a previous section of this chapter, the template interface in the GUI is called Message Source Templates. After you decide which template type you need, the next steps include:

1. Select that template type from a default group or add a new template group.
2. Create a new template in the template group or copy and rename an existing template into the new group.
3. Add your customizations.
4. Assign the template to the node.
5. Distribute the template.

Look at the template customization concepts. **Select Window→Message Source Templates** to bring up the Template Window, as shown in Figure 14-4. The default templates are listed on the right side. If you double click on the template group name, the left panel displays the detailed list of templates for the group selected from the listing on the right side.

Figure 14-4 The Message Source Templates interface is used to configure the rules/policies for the agent.

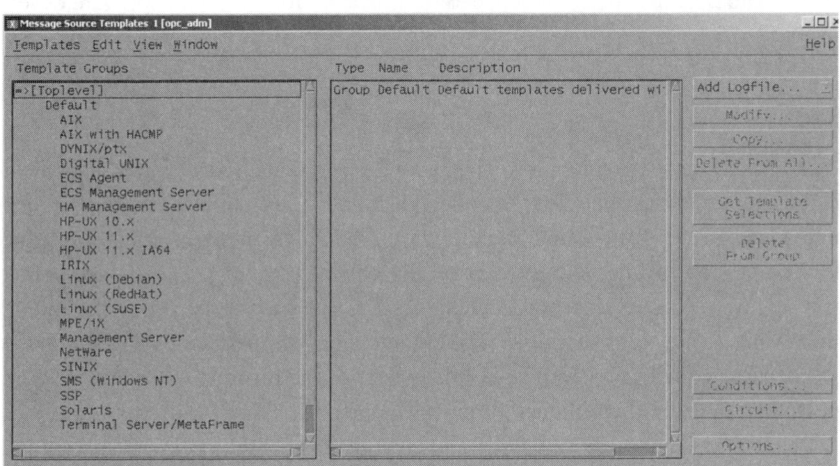

This section provides descriptions of the different template types. Each template type provides a primary template window. After the primary template is configured, add conditions to each template. The conditions determine what "rule" is used to generate a message and if the message is forwarded to the management server or suppressed. When working with the template GUI, you can obtain on-line Help information for each field of a template. Place the cursor in any field of a template to make this the active field and select the F1 key on the keyboard. This opens the HELP interface for the specific field.

14.6.1.1 Logfile Templates

The task of application monitoring extends to periodic evaluation of the entries in an application's logfile (or other event information file). The entries in the logfile are evaluated one line at a time. During parsing, the agent examines a list of conditions for each line of the file. When a match is found between a line in the logfile and a condition, the condition statement triggers further processing as required (for example, to produce a message or execute actions). The parsing of the lines in the logfile continues until a match condition is found and then processing of the logfile stops.

There are two types of log files, ASCII and binary. The list here describes the features of the OVO logfile configuration environment shown in Figure 14-5 and 14-6.

1. OVO reads an ASCII log file without help from other programs.
2. Binary log files require the help of an outside program to extract the content into ASCII format. OVO will read the information from the newly created ASCII file. For an example, examine the Bad logins logfile.

Figure 14-5 Logfile Template window contains the information about a specific template.

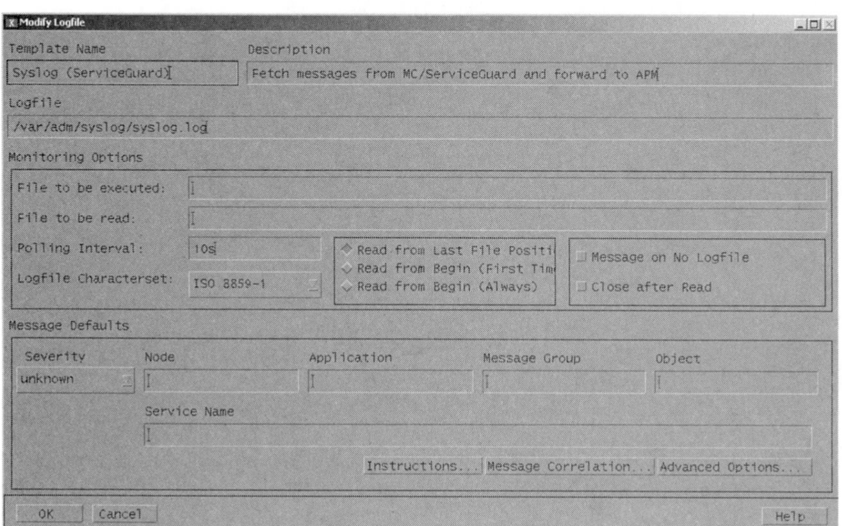

Figure 14-6 Logfile Template Conditions window is used to configure the rules that apply to the agent.

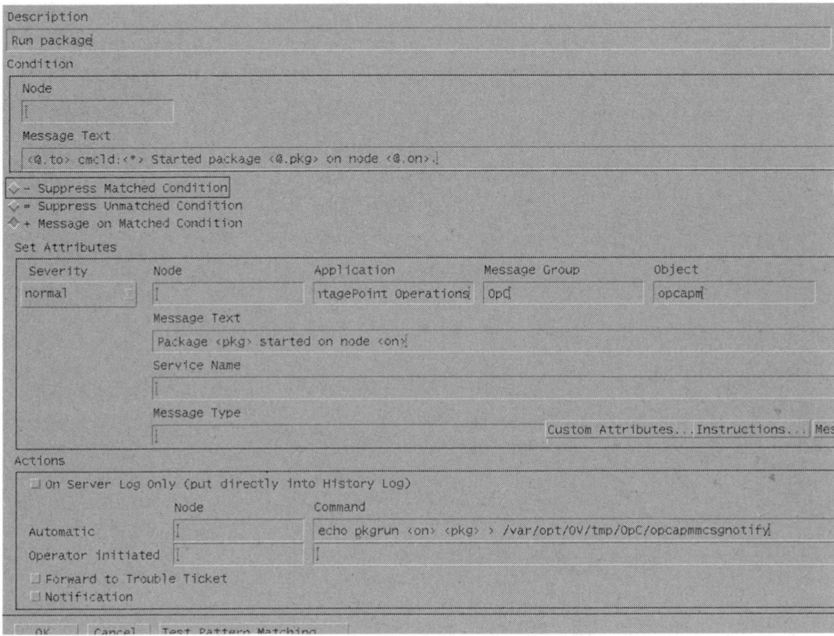

3. In the match conditions section of the template, OVO expects a syntax (similar to grep or sed) to parse each line in the logfile.
4. When a pattern match is found, a message is created using the information found in the attributes section of the template.
5. The conditions determine if the event will be suppressed or if the event will be passed to the server in the form a message.
6. The conditions will cause one of two things to happen when a pattern match is found. Send a message or Suppress the event.

- A shortcut to the pattern match syntax is built into the Template Conditions window. Place your mouse inside the pattern match field and press the right mouse button. This opens a pop-up menu with the pattern match syntax. This also works in the object pattern field for a monitor template condition and the variable bindings of the trap template. This allows you to easily convert a typical input line into the required OVO pattern: For example, to copy an input line from your file and paste it into the match field, highlight the portions of the input pattern you need to replace with a regular expression. Right-click and select the particular regular expression "constructor" which will then replace your highlighted portion of the input line.

- You can test the pattern match syntax against a logfile from the Conditions window by using the test pattern matching button at the bottom of the screen. Provide the name of the logfile. Your pattern will be tested for match and unmatched lines in the logfile. This allows you to immediately correct the pattern syntax to ensure that you filter the correct information. You can test a list of conditions from the Message and Suppress Conditions window.

14.6.1.2 Monitors

A monitor program is used to collect information from a monitored object and send the results of the data collection to the monitor process using the **opcmon** command (or API). The information is evaluated against the values in a monitor template, shown in Figure 14-7, to determine if the monitor value violates the threshold.

Figure 14-7 The Monitor Template window is used to describe the attributes of a monitor.

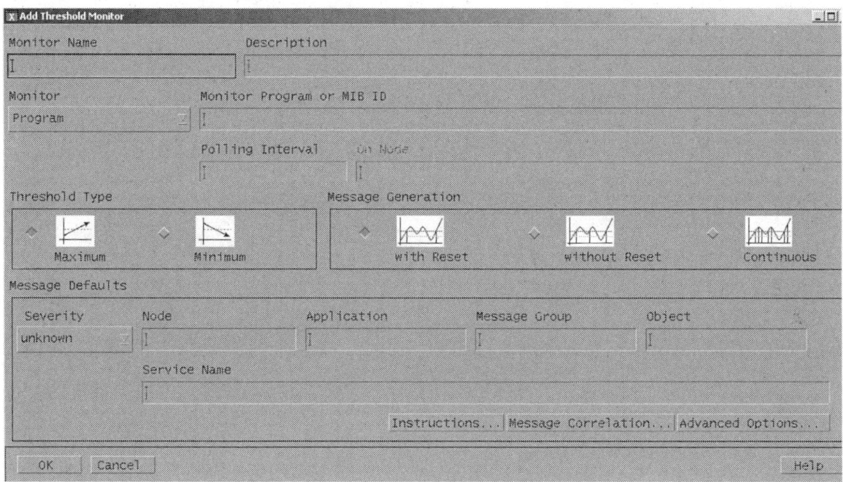

During execution, the monitor template is used by the monitor program to send or suppress messages. The process to accomplish this task is summarized in the following list.

1. The monitor process (opcmona) executes an external program or script to determine the status of system or application run-time parameters. For an example, examine the swap_util monitor template.
2. The external program or script (called a monitor program) submits the value to the agent using the program called opcmon. Refer to the man page for more details about the opcmon program.

3. The agent compares the value against the threshold (high or low) configured in the template.
    - A message is generated based on the threshold criteria.
4. A list of conditions (see Figure 14-24) determines if a message is sent to the server or suppressed.

Figure 14-8 The Monitor Condition window shows an example for cpu utilization.

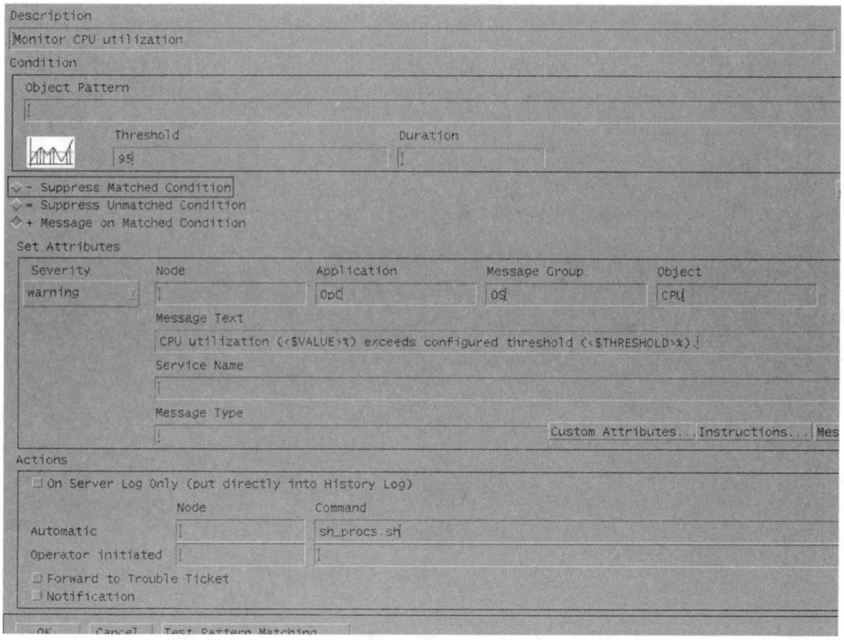

It is possible for OVO to access MIB variables, MS Performance Monitor Logs, and Embedded Performance Component Collections. These sources do not require a script or call to opcmon to their variable values. Select the Program Button on the template window (see Figure 14-4). The other options in the list are MIB Object or External.

The program option without the path assumes that the monitor program is distributed to the managed node along with the policy. The MIB Object requires the MIB ID. External programs provide data to OVO via the program API opcmon. For example, with MS Performance Logs use syntax similar to the following in the Program Monitor field:

NTPerfMon\\FTP Server\\Current Connections_Total

This determines what the number of current FTP connections.

When collecting metric data via the embedded performance component, use syntax similar to the following in the Program Monitor field:

OVPERF\\CODA\\GLOBAL\GBL_CPU_TOTAL_UTIL

The name of the monitor used in the monitor script or monitor program must match the name of the monitor template. Example: opcmon monitor_name=value. The monitor_name and the monitor template name must match.

14.6.1.3 Messages

Message interception is the process of providing parameters to the **opcmsg** command (or API) that will submit the information to the message interceptor for processing and then to the message agent for delivery to the management server. The message command can be executed at the command line or included inside a script or program.

The message and suppression options are summarized in the following list. An example message template window is shown in Figure 14-9.

1. The command (or API) **opcmsg** submits messages to the message template.
2. The message template is configured to check for the attributes of the incoming message.
3. If the message from the **opcmsg** command matches the template conditions, a message is created and sent to the server
4. The message can be suppressed if the conditions list of the template contains the rule for suppressing messages.

Figure 14-9 The Message Template window is used to define a message.

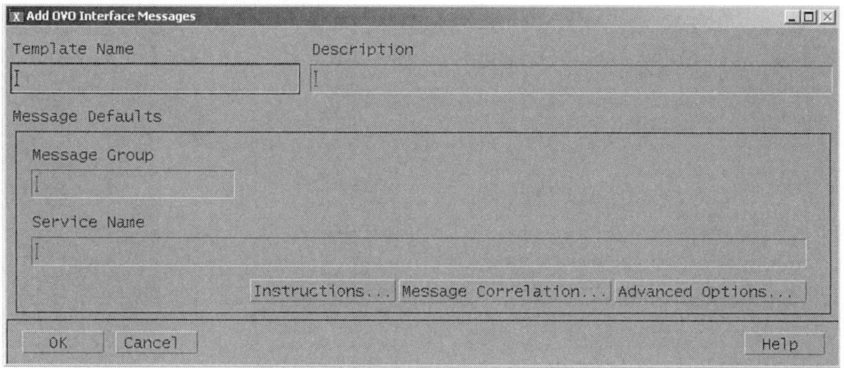

- You can test the pattern match for messages from the command line with the command /opt/OV/bin/OpC/opcmsg. If you want to match specific criteria of a message, include the message attributes on the command line. Example: opcmsg sev=major a=myapp o=process_name msg_g=customer msg_t="Application not running" In this example a=application, o=object, msg_g=message group, msg_t=message text. The required opcmsg d parameters are application, object, and message text; the others are optional.

There are more command line parameters (see the man page). The options in the example have the following meaning: The parameters correspond to the fields in the message browser as follows: sev=Severity, a=Application, o=Object, msg_g=Message Group, msg_t= Message Text. See Figure 14-6 for a pattern match syntax example.

- If you add a parameter to the command line that is not configured in the template, the message will show in the browser as unmatched after the following criteria are met. In cases where the template condition attribute is left blank, this is treated as a match. The empty condition field is treated as "anything goes." Only after all conditions have been examined (in an effort to match) and no match happens, OVO will look at a template "Option" value (such as Forward unmatched messages). If the forward unmatched is enabled, then the unmatched message is sent to the server.

14.6.1.4 Traps

The SNMP trap originates on a device and is an indication of an event that has occurred on the device. If the trap destination at the device is configured to send events to the OVO trap interceptor (opctrapi) running on a managed node or the management server, the trap is processed and converted into a message based on the trap template conditions. An example trap template and trap condition window is shown in Figure 14-10 and 14-11. One advantage of processing the trap on the management server the reduced potential for duplicate events to arrive from multiple agents. The NNM process ovtrapd can pass incoming traps to the opctrapi process, on nodes that run OVO and NNM. Facilitate this type of operation by adding the variable SNMP_SESSION_MODE NO TRAPD to the agent configuration file. Refer to Appendix C for resource information about SNMP.

A summary of the trap template configuration criteria and options is shown in the following list:

1. The criteria used to match a trap are based on the information within the trap. Refer to Chapter 1, "Introduction to NNM, CIV, and SIP," for more information about SNMP.
2. If the criteria for the trap are matched by the configuration of the trap template, a message is generated.
3. The message will contain the attributes configured in the template.
4. The message suppression rule could also apply.
5. The OVO trap template contains over 300 readily available trap conditions that the management server handles.
6. If the OVO node is configured with a trap template, it forwards the traps it receives to the server in the form of a message (if the suppression rule is not applied).

Figure 14-10 A Trap Template instructs the trap process (**opctrapi**).

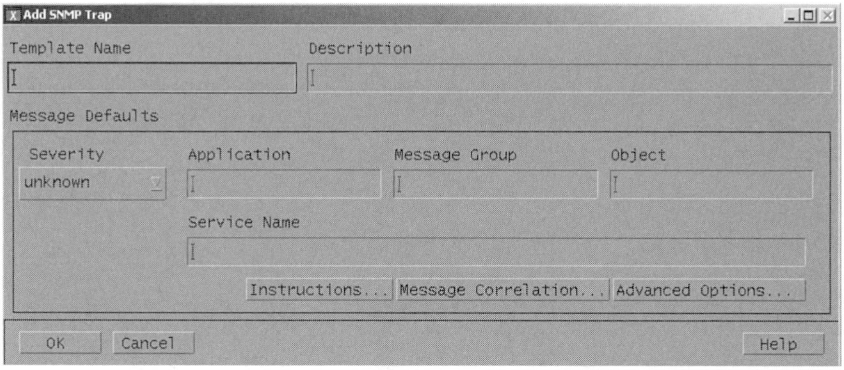

Figure 14-11 Trap Template Condition.

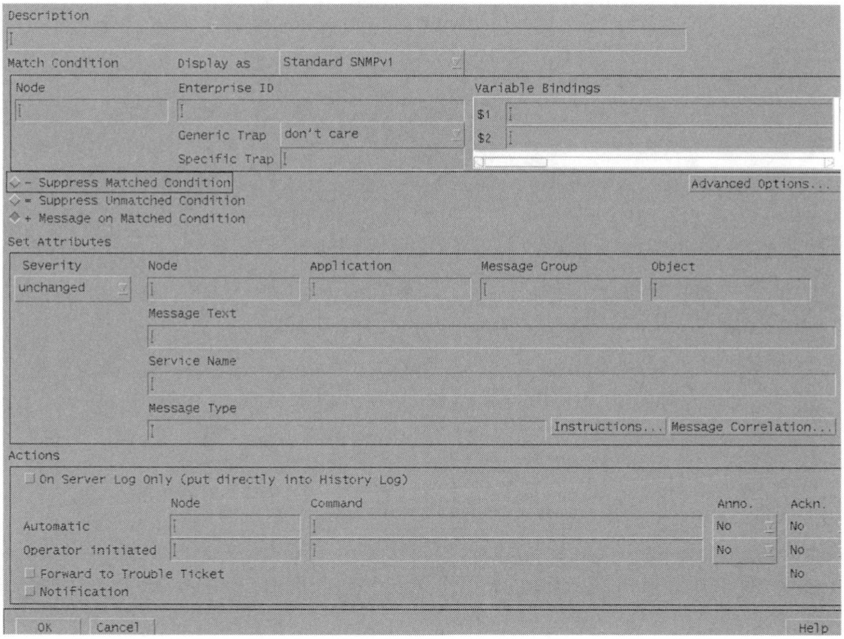

14.6.1.5 Schedule template

During operations, daily, weekly, or monthly routine tasks are generally scheduled via the UNIX cron process. OpenView has an internal environment similar to the cron process. Configure a schedule template, as shown in Figure 14-12, to execute programs and commands at scheduled times. One example of using the schedule plate is recurring download of the database history using the opchistdwn command.

Figure 14-12 Schedule Templates are used to execute programs or commands are pre-determined (scheduled) intervals.

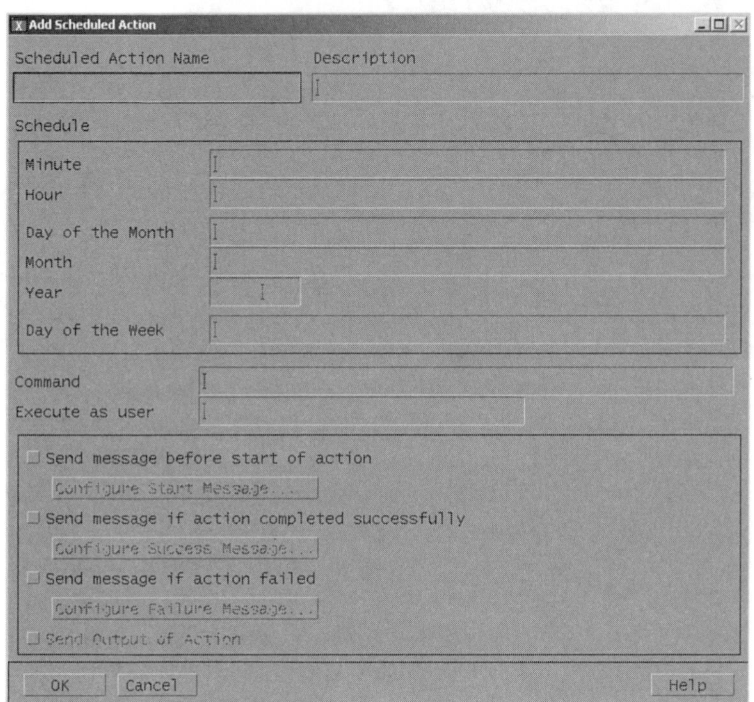

14.6.1.6 Message Forwarding Templates

A message forwarding template (msgforw) instructs the agent to send messages to another server if necessary. This template configuration is covered in more detail in Chapter 19, "Enterprise Management Flexibility with Multiple Servers."

14.6.1.7 Outage Template

The outage template instructs the server buffer to log into the database or ignore messages from the managed nodes based upon service level arrangements or maintenance schedules. This template configuration is covered in more detail in the HP OpenView Operations Concepts Guide.

14.6.1.8 Message Regrouping Template

Messages that arrive on the management server contain a message group attribute. It is possible using the message regroup template to override the message group attribute. If the message is regrouped, it will contain the regrouped message attribute. This feature allows someone who is in on different team to see the regrouped messages. The regroup template is located on the management server. Select **Action→Server→Regroup** to open the regroup template conditions window shown in Figure 14-13.

Figure 14-13 The Regroup Condition changes the original message group attribute on messages that match the regroup condition.

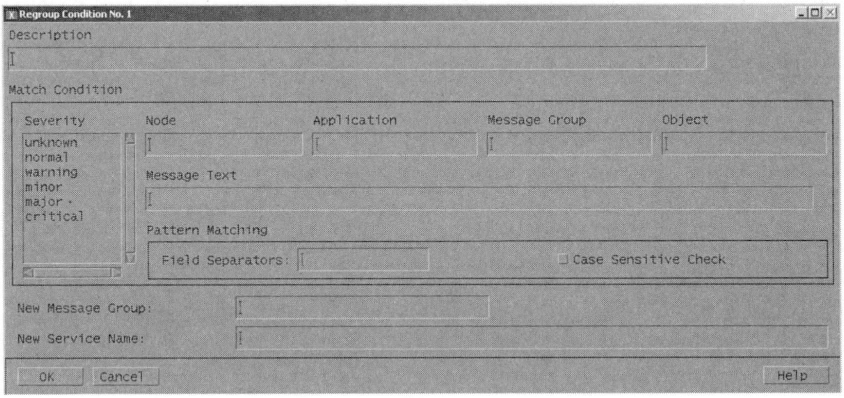

14.6.2 Working with Template Files

Configuration of the templates is done primarily through the GUI. OVO flexible management templates and other specialized templates (such as Service Navigator or Service Hours) are created and modified with a text editor. Refer to Chapter 20 for more information on flexible management templates.

14.6.2.1 Template Format

A brief description of the sections of a typical logfile template is included here for reference. The template has the same information that is required when configuring a template from the GUI. The template name, description, logfile path, and so on are required parameters. The exefile is the file to be executed (as described in Section 14.1.2, "The Agent Processes"). The entries in the logfile are always read from the beginning (ALWAYS FROM BEGIN) and the file is closed after it is read (CLOSE AFTER READ). The default message attributes will set the message SEVERITY, APPLICAITION, MSGGRP, and OBJECT as they are to appear in the message browser. The SERVICE_NAME describes the service that this event will be associated with and is used by the Service Navigator service engine process to update the service views. The file includes a detailed look at the conditions for the template and includes the condition text. The pattern syntax used throughout the template forms the basis upon which the lines in the logfile will be parsed. The default OBJECT attribute is changed to the "<user>" that is the variable defined in the CONDITION TEXT. The message TEXT displays the user name of the failed login, the terminal, host, time, and date of the failed login.

14.6.3 Template Administrator

Planning, organizing, development and implementation of the templates can be a very big job. The configuration, customized scripts, and deployment strategy for the templates requires a dedicated effort. Sometimes the OpenView Administrator is responsible for these tasks in addition to other important duties. However, in many environments an OpenView Template Administrator coordinates template development activities.

Configure the Template Administrator account from the User Bank. Select **Window→User Bank→Action→User→Add**. See Figure 14-14. The Template Administrator manages, and creates the templates that will be deployed into the OVO domain. This OVO account is provided a limited GUI console environment during its OVO session. The GUI interface is the Message Source Template window. See Figure 14-15.

The Template Administrator must inform the OVO Administrator when templates are ready for distribution. The distribution function is performed only from the OPC Administrator GUI or from the command line at the server as root.

Only one OVO Administrator session is allowed at a time, but there can be multiple Template Administrator sessions working in parallel.

Figure 14-14 User configuration interface for the Template Administrator account.

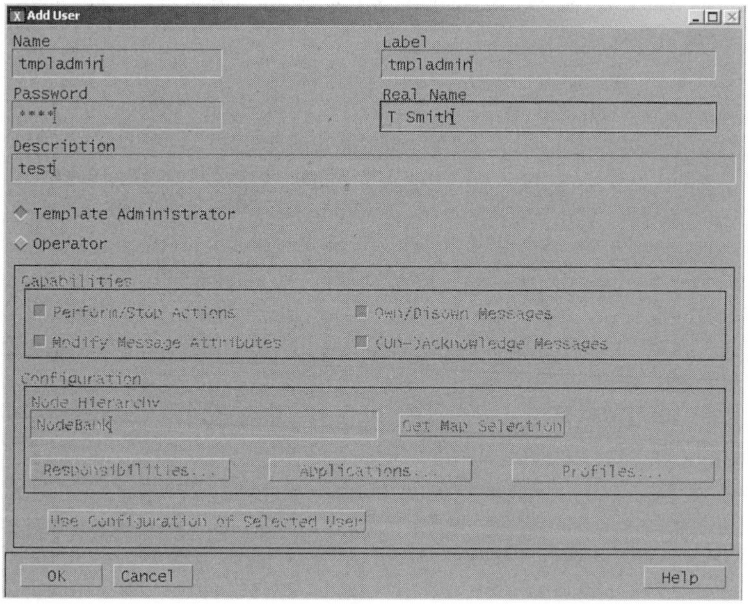

Figure 14-15 Template Administrators work from the GUI for message source templates.

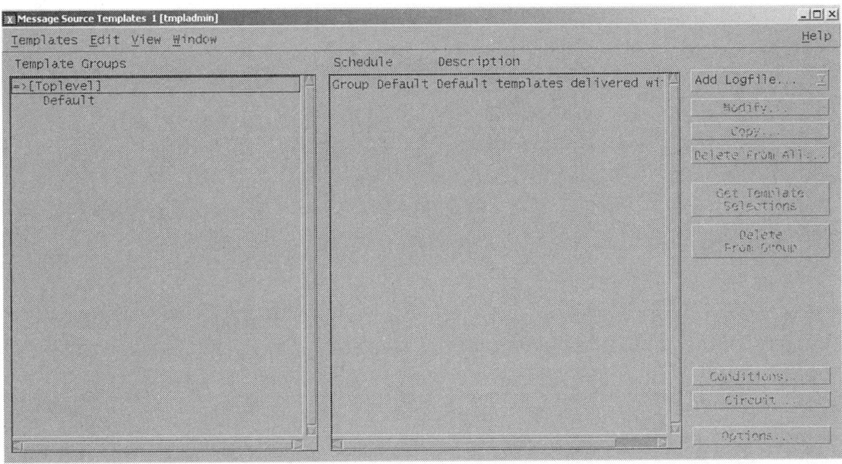

14.6.4 Template Groups

The first step in the process for creating customized template is to create a new template group. This helps organize the templates into logical groups. The default templates are links to one source file. You can see the same template name in multiple template groups. When you change the template in one group it also changes in the other groups. It is the same file. A good practice for template management is to create new template groups, create new templates, or make copies and rename the source templates. With this method during an upgrade, your custom templates are protected. Also, when creating a new template group, provide a name for the template group that will place it alphabetically before the standard template groups. OVO matches the names of the template groups in the order of the template group layout. The template groups are also organized according to the installed SPIs. However, if necessary you can create your own template group as outlined in Section 14.6.4.

14.6.4.1 Process to Create a New Template Group

Follow these steps to create a new template group:

1. Open the Message Source Template window.
2. On the left side of the screen, double-click **Top Level**.
3. Move the mouse to the upper right corner, click and hold down the right-mouse button, and click **Add Logfile**.
4. In the menu list, select **Add Group**.
5. If you open the Logfile Template window, click **Cancel** and try again.
6. Enter a Template Group Name and Description; click **OK** as shown in Figure 14-16.

Figure 14-16 Use the Add Template Group window to create a unique template group.

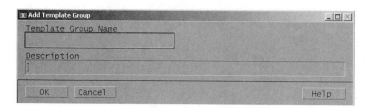

Figure 14-17 shows the new template group Customer_1 in the Message Source Template Window.

Figure 14-17 The name of the custom template group is listed with other templates in the Message Source Templates window (partial view of the window).

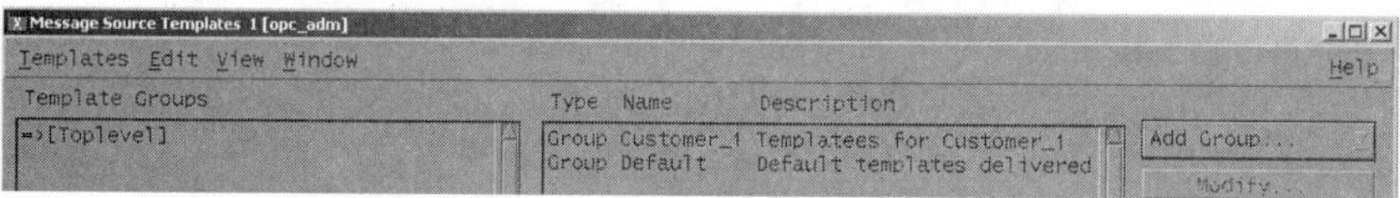

14.6.4.2 Copy and Paste Templates into a Template Group

To use a default template as a baseline for creating your own customized templates, use the following procedure:

1. In the Message Source Template window, the template or template group select (click once to highlight it). This is the template you should copy. Select from the menu **Edit→Copy**.
2. Select the New Message Source Template Group and select from the menu **Edit→Paste**.
3. The template appears in the list. At this point you have created another link to the original template from your new template group. In the next steps, you will create a new name for your copy of the original template and it will no longer be a link to the original.
4. Select the template or template group (click-once to highlight).
5. Select **Copy** from the list of options on the right side of the window.
6. Change the name of the template and select **OK** (or you could begin to work on the template modifications). Just remember to give the template a new name.
7. When the copy is complete, you'll see the new template and the original.
8. Remove the original template from the New Template Group. Select the template and Click-Delete From Group. Be careful: Do not remove the default templates from the Default groups.
9. You now have a new template group that contains a renamed version of the original template.
10. Close the Message Source Template 2 window and select **Templates→Close Window**.

Note: If you need to restore the default configuration, a copy is created during installation and stored in the directory /var/opt/OV/share/tmp/OpC_appl/defaults.

14.6.5 Template Assignment

Check the template to node assignments shown in the Define Configuration window. For example, select the Node Bank and **Actions→Agents→Assign Templates**. After the template assignment is confirmed, click OK. If you need to assign a template, follow the steps in the next list. At this time, the template assignment has made no changes to the agent. The template becomes active on the agent only after distribution of the policy to the managed node.

14.6.5.1 Template to Node Assignment

1. Select the node in the Node Bank.
2. Select **Actions→Agents→Assign Templates**.
3. In the Define Configuration window, select Add.
4. If from the previous copy/paste example the template is still selected in the Message Source Template Window, after the Add Configuration window opens you will see the selected templates or template groups in the list, on the right side. Verify the node for the template on the left side of the Add Configuration window and add a node (or nodes) to the list if necessary. The nodes you add to the list will be assigned the templates on the templates on the right side of the window. Click **OK**. Go to step10.
5. If there are no templates in the list on the Add Configuration window, or if you need to add more templates to the list, click **Open Template Window**.
6. Select the templates or template groups in the Message Source Template window.
7. Leave the Message Source Template window open.
8. Return to the Add Configuration window and click Get the Selected Templates. This will fill in the list of templates.
9. Verify the node list on the right and click OK.
10. In the Define Configuration window, click OK.
11. You are finished with the template to node assignment.
12. There is a difference between assigning single templates to the node versus assigning template groups. When assigning template groups, all member templates will automatically be assigned. As templates are added to existing template groups they are assigned and distributed as members of the group.

14.6.7 Template Files

The template configuration is stored in the database on the management server. During a template distribution to a node, a template file is transferred to the node in binary, encrypted format.

14.6.7.1 Templates on the Management Server

The template files are deployed as required to provide the necessary instrumentation for the agents on the managed node or server. Some specialized template files add additional capability to the agents on the server or node, for example *manager of managers* (MoM). The template files that provide the basis for the flexible management concepts are found in the following directory: /etc/opt/OV/share/conf/OpC/mgmt_sv/templates. Other types of templates that instrument the agent for specialized management, monitoring, corrective actions and alarming could be installed on the server as SPIs. More details of the flexible management templates are covered in Chapter 19.

14.6.7.2 Templates on the Managed Node

The templates are referred to as policies after they are distributed to the managed node. The policy files contain policy data, one file for each policy type. In prior releases, a template file would contain the entire set of templates. The policy files represent each individual template. The policy files are maintained in the directory /var/opt/OV/datafiles/policies. The directory path is identified with the variable $DATADIR where DATADIR=/var/opt/OV. An example of the policy directory contents is shown here for reference.

```
# cd /var/opt/OV/datafiles/policies
# ls -l
total 10
drwxr-xr-x   2 root       root      1024 Nov 22 21:36 le
drwxr-xr-x   2 root       sys       1024 Oct 13 20:08 mgrconf
drwxr-xr-x   2 root       root      1024 Nov 22 21:36 monitor
drwxr-xr-x   2 root       root      1024 Nov 22 21:36 msgi
drwxr-xr-x   2 root       root      1024 Nov 22 21:36 trapi
# cd le
# ls
5324c9f4-fa46-71d7-1fc7-9c99d13d0000_data
5324c9f4-fa46-71d7-1fc7-9c99d13d0000_header.xml
532a13d2-fa46-71d7-1fc7-9c99d13d0000_data
532a13d2-fa46-71d7-1fc7-9c99d13d0000_header.xml
5331f700-fa46-71d7-1fc7-9c99d13d0000_data
5331f700-fa46-71d7-1fc7-9c99d13d0000_header.xml
```

A listing of a policy data file is shown here.

```
# more 5324c9f4-fa46-71d7-1fc7-9c99d13d0000_data
SYNTAX_VERSION 5
LOGFILE "Bad Logs (10.x/11.x HP-UX)"
        DESCRIPTION "History of HP-UX 10.x/11.x bad logins
(/var/adm/btmp logfile)"
```

```
        LOGPATH "/var/adm/btmp"
        EXEFILE "opcfwtmp /tmp/btmp.stat /var/adm/btmp
/tmp/btmp.out"
        READFILE "/tmp/btmp.out"
        INTERVAL "10s"
        CHSET ISO88591
        ALWAYS_FROM_BEGIN
        CLOSE_AFTER_READ
        SEVERITY Warning
        APPLICATION "/usr/bin/login(1) Login"
        MSGGRP "Security"
        MSGCONDITIONS
                DESCRIPTION "Failed remote login"
                CONDITION_ID "53259b2c-fa46-71d7-1fc7-
9c99d13d0000"
                CONDITION
                        TEXT "FAILED <@.user> <@.tty> <@.host>
<*.date> <*.time>"
                SET
                        OBJECT "<user>"
TEXT "Failed login of <user> on <tty> at <time> <date>"
                DESCRIPTION "opcfwtmp failure"
                CONDITION_ID "53277c26-fa46-71d7-1fc7-
9c99d13d0000"
                CONDITION
                        TEXT "opcfwtmp:"
                SET
                        SEVERITY Critical
                        MSGGRP "OpC"
                        OBJECT "opcfwtmp"
                        TEXT "<$MSG_TEXT>"
```

14.6.5 Template Status

Use the **ovpolicy** command to view, activate and deactivate templates on the managed nodes. Use the **opcragt** command (or the Administrator's GUI) to distribute the templates. A template is converted to a policy data file during HTTPS-based distribution. An example of viewing the installed policies is shown here.

```
# ovpolicy -list

List installed policies for host: 'lotus'.
```

```
   TypeName                    Name                              Status
----------------------------------------
'le'                       'Bad Logs (10.x/11.x HP-UX)'      enabled
'le'                       'Cron (10.x/11.x HP-UX)'          enabled
'le'                       'Syslog (ServiceGuard)'           enabled
'mgrconf'                  'OVO authorization'               enabled
'monitor'                  'cpu_util'                        enabled
'monitor'                  'disk_util'                       enabled
'monitor'                  'distrib_mon'                     enabled
'monitor'                  'mondbfile'                       enabled
'monitor'                  'proc_util'                       enabled
'msgi'                     'opcmsg(1|3)'                     enabled
'trapi'                    'SNMP 6.20 Traps'                 enabled
'trapi'                    'SNMP ECS Traps'                  enabled
```

14.6.5.1 ovpolicy and opctemplate

Use the command **ovpolicy** to verify status, install, remove, enable, and disable local policies. The command **opctemplate** is a wrapper command for **ovpolicy**. Refer to the man page for a complete listing of the **ovpolicy** command.

14.6.5.2 Temporarily Disabling and Enabling a Template

It might be necessary to temporarily disable the policies during times of maintenance on applications that are monitored by OVO. This would prevent the agent from sending any information about events or performing actions that are triggered by the policy. When a policy is disabled, there are no messages created for that policy.

Use the command **ovpolicy** (or **opctemplate**) to change or check the status of policies. For example, changing the policy status to disabled prevents the events from a particular policy from arriving in the message browser. Another advantage is that this method does not require completely disabling the entire agent and also avoids the task of unassign and later assign the template. This command requires root user permission.

14.7 ACTIONS, MONITORS, COMMANDS AND EXTERNAL NOTIFICATION SERVICES

The components that are used to supplement the templates are usually created as scripts or programs. The files are referred to collectively as instrumentation. After distribution to the managed node the files are located in the directory /var/opt/OV/bin/instrumentation. A listing of the directory is shown here for reference.

```
# cd /var/opt/OV/bin/instrumentation
# ls
E10000Log.sh          mailq_l.sh          opclpst
ssp_config.sh         ana_disk.sh         mailq_pr.sh
opcnprcs              st_inetd.sh         cpu_mon.sh
mondbfile.sh          opcps               st_mail.sh
disk_mon.sh           mwa_read.sh         perf_alxp.sh
st_syslogd.sh         dist_del.sh         opc_get_ems_resource
proc_mon.sh           swap_mon.sh
dist_mon.sh           opc_sec_v.sh        pv.sh
vp_chk.sh             itogpm.sh           opcdf
sh_procs.sh           last_logs.sh        opcfwtmp
ssp_chk.sh
```

14.7.1 Actions

The templates can be further enhanced to execute programmed automatic or operator-initiated actions on the managed nodes. The configuration interface is found in the actions section of the template. See Figure 14-18 for an example of the Actions and External Services configuration interface on for a template condition.

Figure 14-18 Use the Actions and External Services template interface to configure automaticactions, operator action and activate forwarding to a trouble ticket or notification programs.

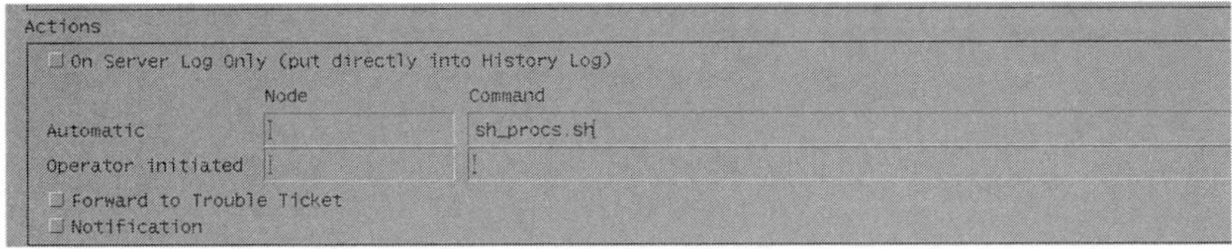

14.7.2 Monitors

A monitor is an external program or script that periodically, based on the template configuration, executes to determine run-time values that are forwarded via the monitor agent to the message agent. The program opcmon is used to send the values to the monitor agent. If the monitor agent evaluates the value and determines it violates the threshold established by the template configuration, a message is created.

14.7.3 Trouble Ticket Interface

The template also provides the configuration interface to instruct the agents to send message attribute information to external programs, such as trouble ticket, paging, and email systems. On the server, enable sending the message to a trouble ticket system. Configure the trouble ticket interface and select Forward to Trouble Ticket (the button is on the Conditions window). Some external application may provide the interface program for the pager program or trouble ticket system. Select **Actions→Utilities→External Notification**. See Figure 14-19.

Figure 14-19 Activate the Trouble Ticket Notification Service using this dialog box.

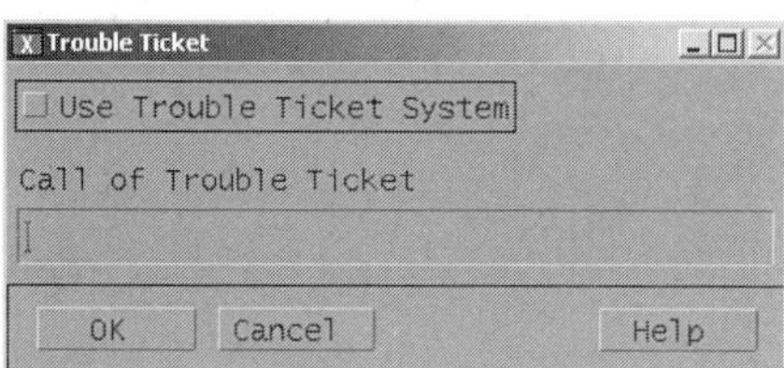

14.7.4 External Services

The external Notification Schedule Configuration interface is found in the actions section of the template. Place a checkmark in the box for a notification service to receive the event notification from OVO via an external program, such as email or pager. Figure 14-18 shows the template interface that selects the Notification Service. The schedule for external notification programs, shown in Figure 14-20, is configured on the management server.

Figure 14-20 The Notification Schedule Configuration interface shows the days of the week and hours of the day to apply the rules for the notification services.

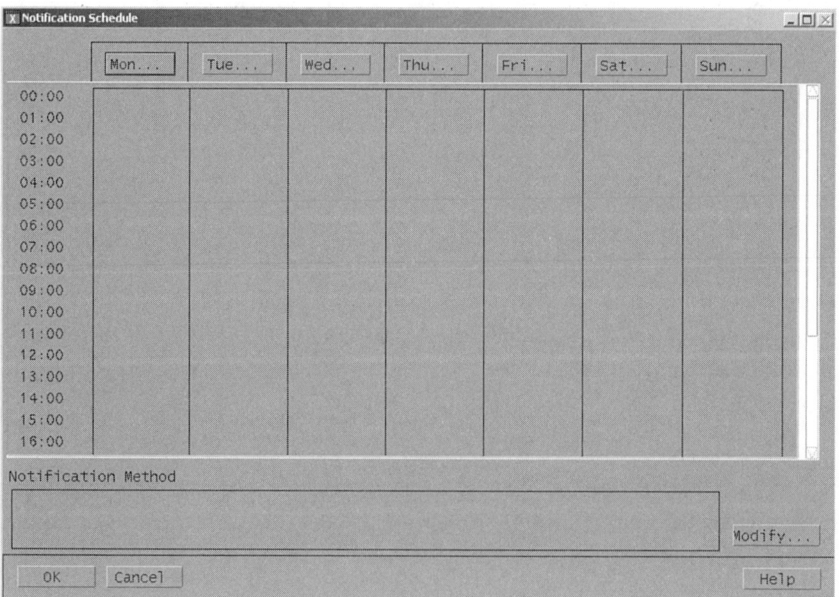

Configure the notification service to send a message using the external notification program at a specific time of the day or day of the week. The configuration process includes the following steps:

1. Select **Actions→Utilities→Notification Service,** if there are notification schedules already configured, the window will show different colors for the vertical bars that represent the start and end of the service schedules.
2. Select Modify, which brings up the configuration dialog box (see Figure 14-21).

Figure 14-21 Notification Method Configuration window determines which program to use for external notifications, such as a pager program.

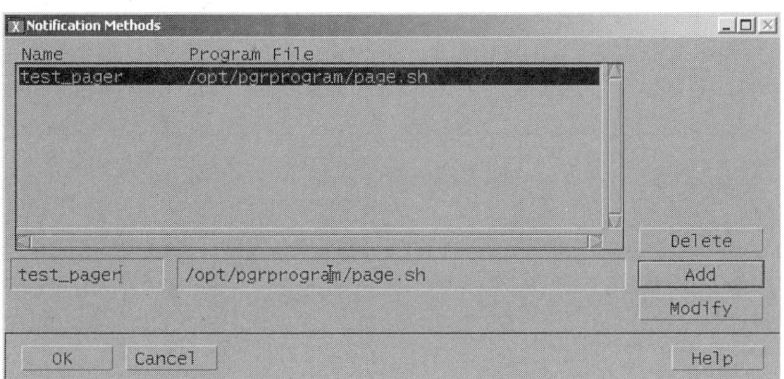

3. Add the name of the program and the full path to the program, as shown in Figure 14-21. Add a second notification method if appropriate. Someone can create the interface program that will take the output of the OVO message and forward the information to the external application (trouble ticket system or pager system). The example shows a pager notification.
4. Create the notification schedule (see Figure 14-20) to send a page or email at the scheduled time. Select the day of the week from the top of the Notification Schedule window.
5. Enter the time to send the page (see Figure 14-22); if there are multiple notification methods, for example page and email, they are indicated with different vertical bars in the notification schedule window.
6. Select **OK**. If there is another type of notification service it will show up in the list. Select the arrow as shown in Figure 14-22 to view the list.
7. For each day, build the desired notification schedules. Figure 14-23 is the result of a notification schedule for each week, a pager schedule for the weekdays during business hours, and a separate email notification schedule for after hours and weekends.

Figure 14-22 The example schedule for the pager system shows the start and end time for pager notifications.

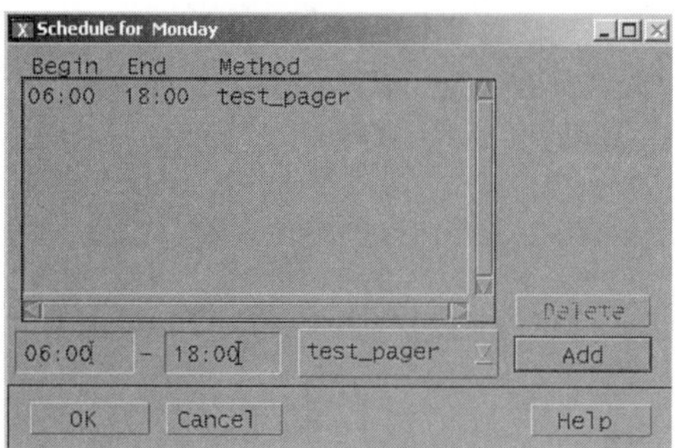

Figure 14-23 A weekly notification schedule could contain multiple notification methods each represented by a different vertical bar.

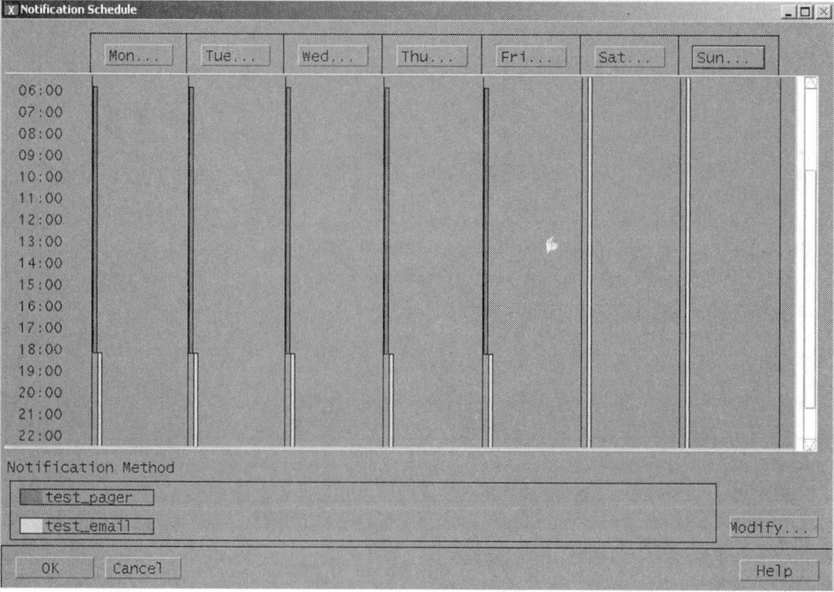

14.8 USING TEMPLATES FOR MESSAGE SUPPRESSION

There are many other concepts related to template configuration that are covered in more detail in the product documentation — this section provides an introduction to the concepts of message management. Normal operation with OVO brings many messages into the message browser. Some of them are extremely important and some may be for information only or not required at all. Occasionally, the same message appears multiple times. As shown in Chapter 13, "Out-of-the-box with OpenView Operations," it is possible to configure the server to display one instance of the message and count the duplicates. However, a better method of avoiding unwanted messages at the source is considering when setting up new policies. You can choose to suppress all messages that match the criteria within the conditions, suppress unmatched messages if they do not match the specific conditions, or send a message if the condition is matched. You create a condition for each possible scenario that could potentially generate a message. Figure 14-24 shows the list of conditions for a system log file.

Figure 14-24 The System Logfile Message and Suppress Conditions window lists the match and suppress conditions in the order they are applied to the messages.

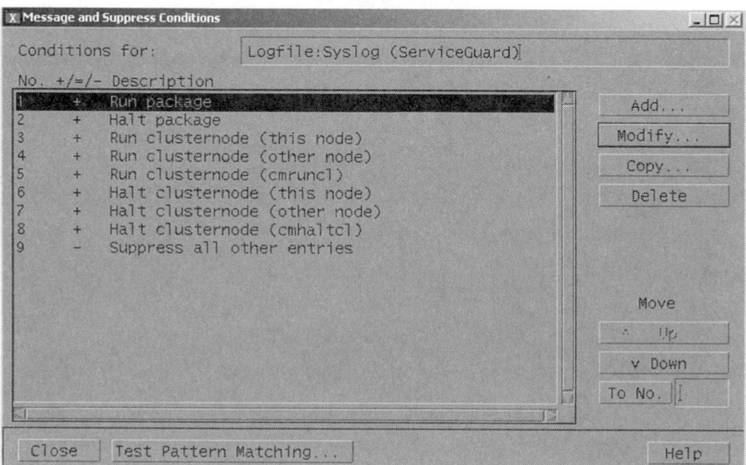

For example, if you are using OVO to monitor the system log file for specific instances, events, or errors, a corresponding condition is created for each different type of event or error that might enter the system log file. The conditions listed in Figure 14-24 indicate eight conditions that, the first matched condition, will send a message to the server (the "+" mean message on matched condition). If there are no match conditions, the last condition in the list (shown with a "-") suppresses messages from all other system log file events. For an example of the suppression condition for the system log file, see Figure 14-25.

Monitor or logfile templates read data sources or files at periodic intervals that you specify in the template policy. The information from the data source is analyzed against the conditions, and either a message is created, the event is suppressed per the message suppression rules, or the message is sent to the server. If there are multiple instances of the same event occurring over a period of time, this could cause the duplicates to eventually accumulate in the message browser. Configure the message suppression policies from within the template conditions window. Select the Message Correlation button located on the template conditions window.

Figure 14-25 The Suppress Condition window defines the text wildcard pattern match <*> for message suppression.

Figure 14-26 The Message Correlation and Duplicate Message Suppression window provides more options to configure rules for message suppress.

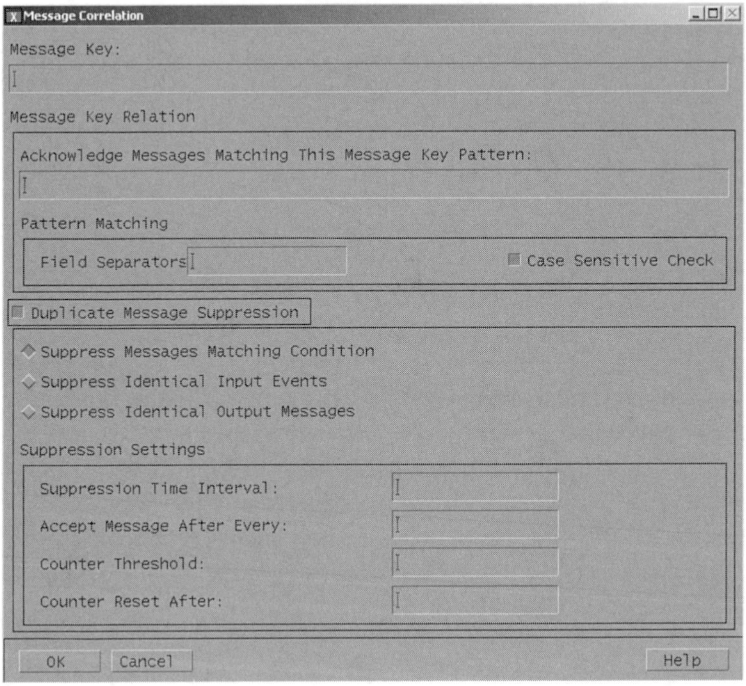

14.9 CONTROL MESSAGES WITH MESSAGE CORRELATION

Message keys correlation is another message management feature, as shown in Figure 14-24. This is configured within the template. The message attributes are analyzed, and if the same message already exists within the browser, it is acknowledged and replace by a successor with similar attributes. The message key can contain fixed text and variables. For example, the disk monitor shown in Figure 14-27 could have a message key automatically generated, as shown in Figure 14-28, for all the conditions for the disk utilization threshold monitor.

Figure 14-27 Configure a threshold monitor, the example template shown, using the program name and a call to the executable program.

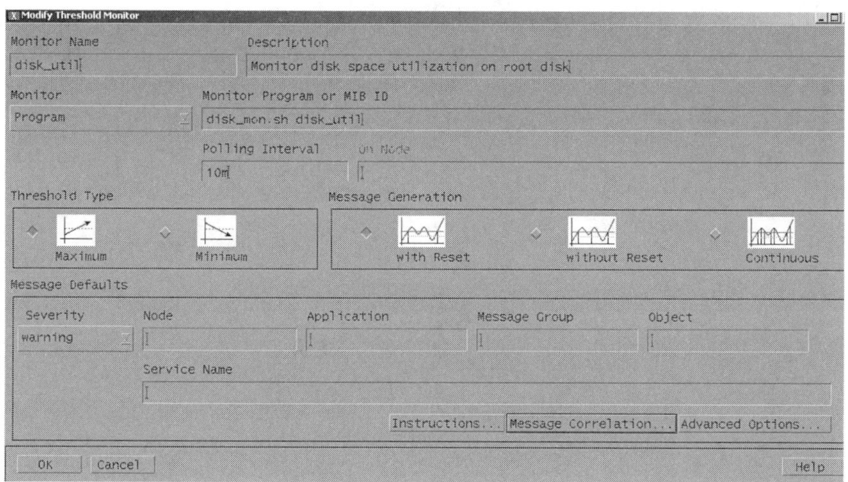

Figure 14-28 The message key for the threshold monitor helps maintain the most current messages in the message browser.

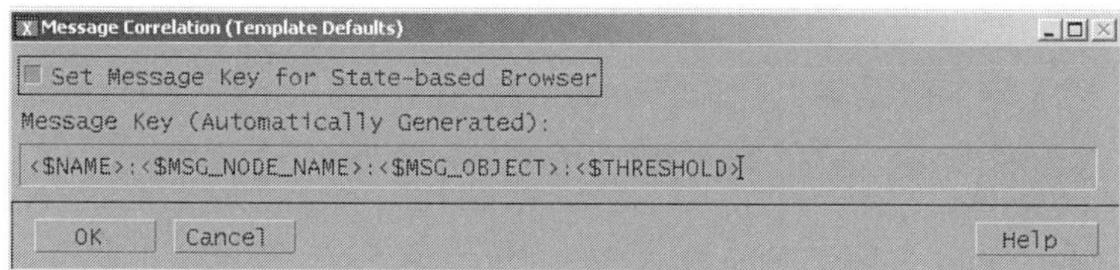

The message key is used to match the message with the same attributes and acknowledge it automatically. This has the advantage of reducing the number of messages in the browser. Another advantage is that the messages in the browser will always show the most current state of the monitored threshold. The message browser is considered state-based when used in conjunction with the message correlation feature.

14.10 DISTRIBUTION

The administrator distributes the policies and instrumentation from the server to managed node. During distribution to the node, the distribution manager is called to establish connection with the node. The ovconfd process on the server pushes the distribution to the node. The ovconfd process on the node ensures that the files are placed into the proper directories and complete the installation process.

The staging area for the distribution is located in the directory /var/opt/OV/share/tmp/OpC/distrib. The server moves the compressed configuration files into this directory. The filename is the hexadecimal format of the node's IP address.

14.10.1 Template Group to Node Group Assignment

Template to node assignment was covered in Section 14.6.5, "Template Assignment." For bulk distribution to many nodes, it is more efficient to assign the node to a node group and perform the distribution to the entire node group. After the templates are assigned to a node group, use the GUI to distribute the templates.

Another feature available is called the hidden node group. Use a "hidden" node group for distribution purposes. The new node group is not assigned to any operators. See Figure 14-29.

Figure 14-29 Create hidden node groups using the Configuration window.

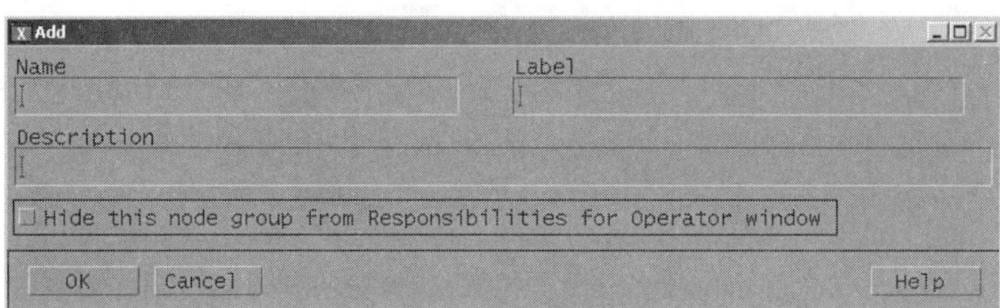

14.10.1.1 Assign the Templates to the Nodes or Node Groups

The steps to assign the template policies to a node group are shown here for reference:

1. From the menu in the Node Bank, select **Actions→Agents→Assign Templates**.
2. Select **Add** to display the Add Configuration window, as shown in Figure 14-30.
3. From the Add Configuration window, select Open Template window as displayed in Figure 14-31.
4. In the Template window, select the template or template group (the selected group in the example is highlighted).

Figure 14-30 The Define Configuration window lists the current template to node and node group assignments.

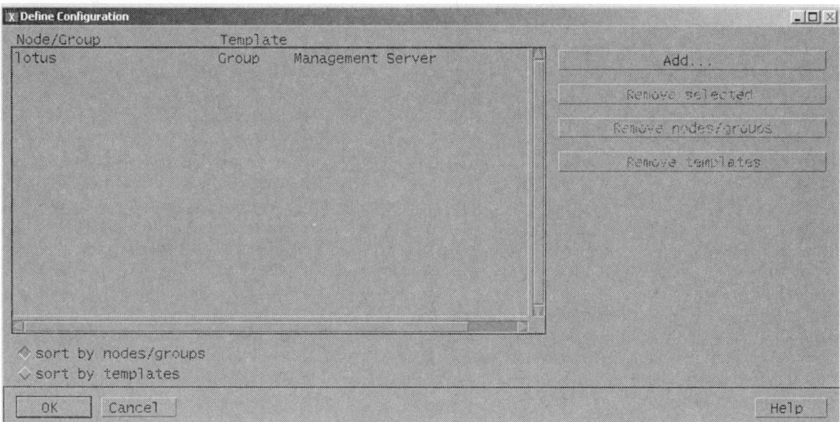

Figure 14-31 The default and custom template groups are listed in the Template window.

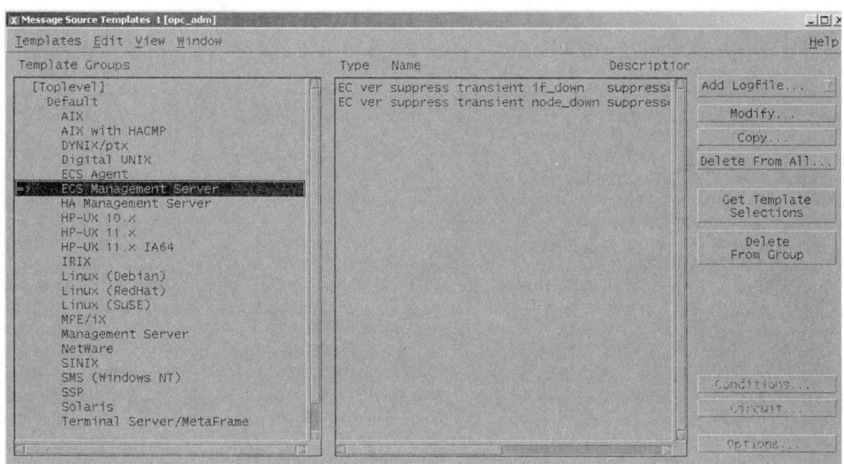

5. In the Add Configuration window, select Get Template Selection. The selected template group appears in the Add Configuration window.
6. Close the Template window.
7. In the Add Configuration window shown in Figure 14-32, click **[OK]**.

Figure 14-32 The Add Configuration window now shows the selected template group and the node group to which it is assigned.

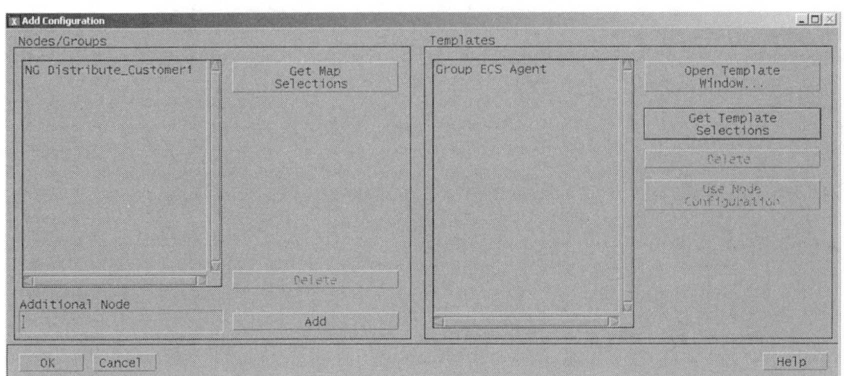

8. Return to the Define Configuration window as shown in Figure 14-33. Click **[OK]**.

Figure 14-33 The Define Configuration window lists the existing and new node group assignments.

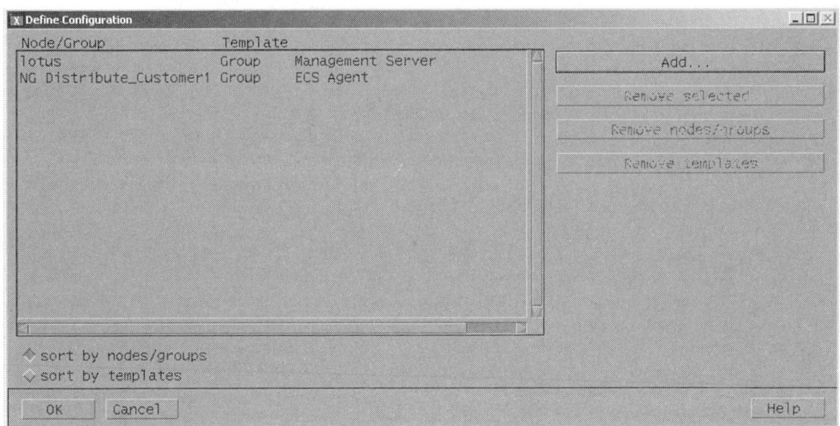

9. From the Node Group menu, highlight the Node Group.

10. From the menu in the Node Bank, select **Actions→Agents→Install/Update Configuration**. Select Templates from the components list, see Figure 14-34. If you have created customized instrumentation, also select Actions, Commands, and Monitors. Click **[OK]**.

Figure 14-34 The distribution of components is controlled from the Install/Update Configuration window.

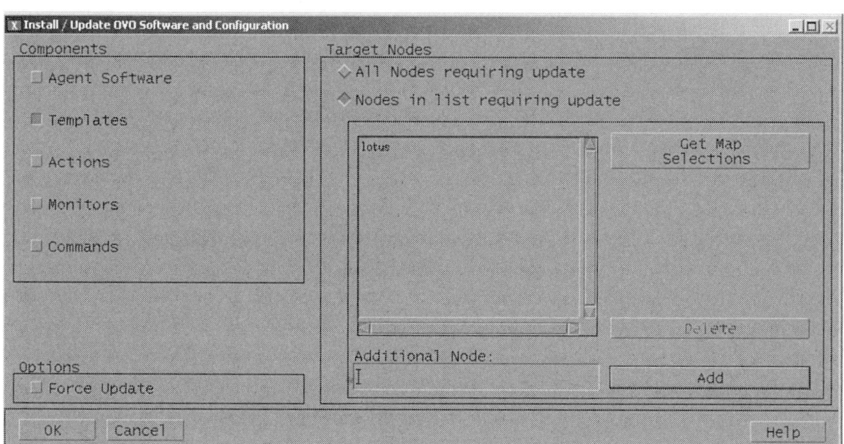

You can distribute templates, actions, monitors, and commands for each distribution, and unless you select the "Force Update" box, you will still only distribute the elements that have changed since the last distribution. This helps avoid distributing templates without their related instrumentation. Selecting the "Force Update" option redistributes all assigned templates and instrumentation for the target node(s). Don't forget to locate customized actions, commands, or monitors in the customer directory path prior to distribution to ensure the latest versions are transferred to the managed node. The customer directory path is /var/opt/OV/share/databases/OpC/mgd_node/customer/<vendor>/<architecture>/<OS>/<actions>|<cmds>|<monitor>.

14.11 SUMMARY

This chapter covered many examples of customizing the OVO environment for production operations. Many of the tasks are performed by the OV system administrator and some tasks are performed by dedicated template administrators. Overall, the chapter demonstrated the flexibility and ease of use for working within the interface or from the command line to define, configure, assign and distribute the built-in components. In the next chapter, we look at some of the add-on components.

CHAPTER 15

Smart Plug-Ins

Smart Plug-Ins (SPIs) are software solutions that integrate out-of-the-box components into the OpenView platform. The components provide instant-on management of application and device availability within the domain. SPIs provide pre-configured templates, message groups, application groups, node groups and instrumentation for different enterprise environments. The advantage is that you spend less time with detailed configuration activities, such as creating templates from scratch. Instead, you can take a pre-defined template and customize it for your need. In this chapter, the Database SPI is used for reference. The features of the SPI include:

- Monitoring and control of enterprise resource planning, database, messaging, and management applications
- Ready to configure out-of-the-box.
- Automatically collect, monitor, process, alarm, and take corrective actions for most events.
- Modular and easily integrates into the OVO platform to extend the management domain.
- Access data from application log files, MIBs, scripts that perform data extraction, and other data sources including database tables.

One of the biggest tasks of the OV system administrator is customizing the tools and components that provide the daily operations view of the environment. The benefits of the SPI include:

- Time savings.
- Improved efficiency through automatically managing important aspects of enterprise applications and services.
- Reduced training costs because multiple SPIs are easily implemented.
- Reduced costs by eliminating redundant integration.

A large variety of SPIs is available, and more are always under development by HP and other vendors. Some of the SPIs require a license to use others are free. Visit http://openview.hp.com/products/spi/index.html for links to the complete SPI product line.

In this chapter, we discuss the general implementation details of an SPI. We also describe the components and resources provided by the SPI.

15.1 INSTALLING AN SPI

This section provides a summary of the general process for installation of the SPI. Complete documentation for each SPI is provided when you purchase or download the SPI. You also have the option of installing some SPIs during the installation of the management platform.

15.1.1 Installation Summary

The summary gives the OVO system administrator a quick look at what it will take to implement your first SPI:

- The OpenView Operations management server must be installed before installing an SPI.
- Install the SPI using the software installation program, swinstall. The source depot will be one of three sources: the OVO bundle, an application CD, or the file downloaded from the web site into a directory of your choice.
- Distribute the SPI software components to the managed (target) node. During the initial distribution SPI actions, monitors, and command components are transferred to the node.
- Configure the SPI components that are used to communicate with the target node. For example: the database configuration file is created and remains on the server. It contains the connect information required for the database instance on the target node.
- Assign and distribute the SPI templates onto the target node. Logfile and Monitor templates are pre-configured with the most common logfile messages strings and monitor metrics. The periodic execution of the collector/analyzer program "dbspicao" checks the oracle alert log or determines the value of a metric. The collector/analyzer program is part of the Oracle SPI. Examples of the types of entries in the alert log or metrics that are pre-configured include ORA-00018 max number of session exceeded and ORA-00206 error writing control file. You can customize the frequency of the check, thresholds, message text, actions, and so on. The complete instructions on customizing the templates and available metrics for each type of database are included with the SPI documentation.

15.2 COMPONENTS OF AN SPI

This section describes the components of an SPI, using the Oracle database SPI as an example. Some of the GUI components that are configured out-of-the box include metric alarms, logfile conditions, applications and tools, performance metrics and reports.

15.2.1 Component in the Message Group Bank

The message groups visually organize the types of messages that are currently in the active message browser. The SPI adds a new message group to identify the types of messages that are produced by the SPI components. The SPI components distributed to the managed node provide the agent with messages that are tailored for the application environment the SPI component is designed to monitor. The SPI for the Oracle database includes message groups, application groups, and node groups components for fault, performance and configuration of the database. These SPI messages are delivered to the message browser with context based on the database instance.

15.2.1.1 Database SPI Message Group-Administrator View

An example of the Database SPI message group is shown in Figure 15-1.

Figure 15-1 Database SPI message groups in the Message Group Bank.

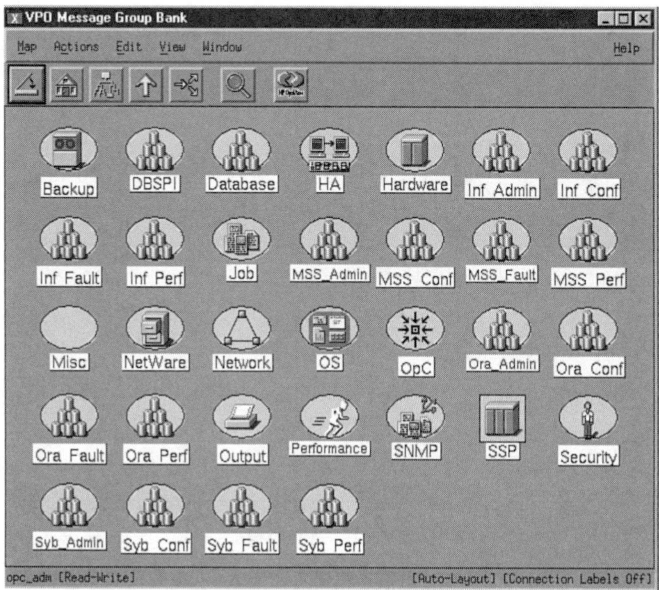

15.2.1.2 Database SPI Message Group-Operator View

The Operator view for Motif and Java includes the appropriate message groups as assigned by the administrator in the responsibility matrix of the user bank or user profile.

15.2.2 Component in the Node Group Bank

The node groups is an important area for defining the operator's responsibilities. SPI node groups are created during installation. The administrator uses one of the node groups for initial discovery of the environment on the managed node. During the discovery process the node is probed to collect data that is used to create some of the management components and files. The SPI node groups, along with other node groups (and the message groups), are used to assign operator responsibilities. The node groups represent the database servers and make is easier to deploy policies, add or remove database nodes.

Note: Not all SPIs have a discovery function.

15.2.2.1 Database SPI Node Groups-Administrator View

Figure 15-2 shows an example of the Database SPI node group(s) that are visible to the OV administrator.

Figure 15-2 Oracle database SPI node groups—OpenView administrators view.

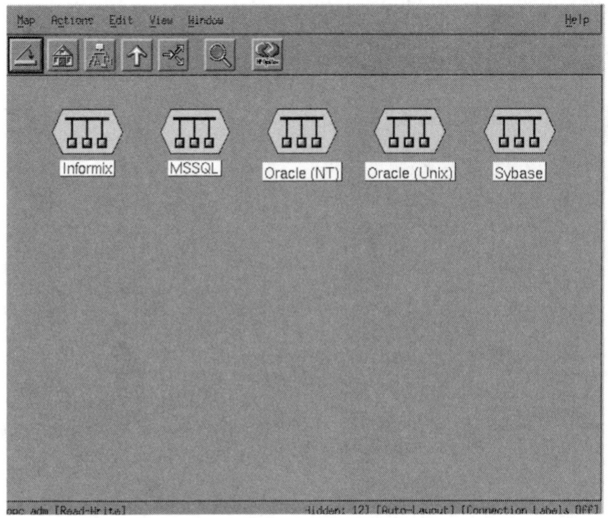

15.2.2.2 Database SPI Node Groups-Operators View

The Operators view for Motif and Java includes the appropriate nodes as assigned by the administrator in the responsibility matrix of the user bank or user profile.

15.2.3 Components in the Application Bank

During installation of the SPI, a new Application Group is created. The Application Group for the SPI contains other application groups for managing the initial configuration of the node, managing the components of the SPI, and de-installing the components when necessary.

15.2.3.1 Database SPI Application Groups

Examples of the Database SPI Application Group Hierarchy within the Application Bank are shown in Figures 15-3, 15-4, 15-5, and 15-6.

Figure 15-3 Application Bank with the Database SPI application group.

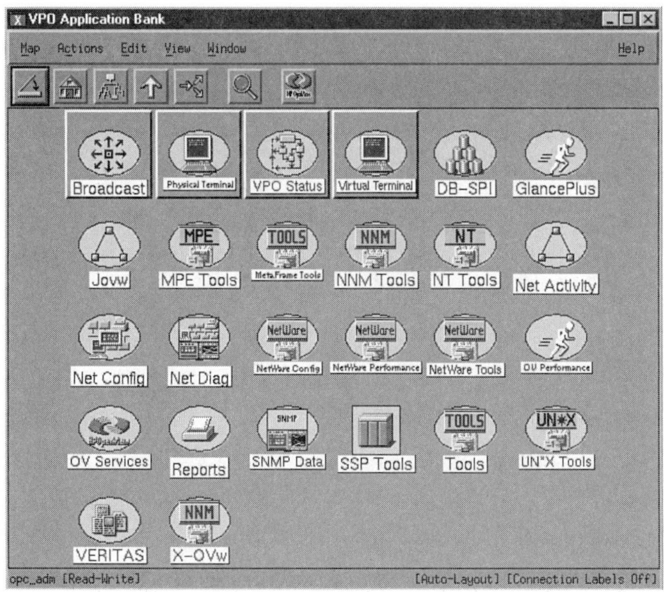

Figure 15-4 View of the Application Group: Database SPI.

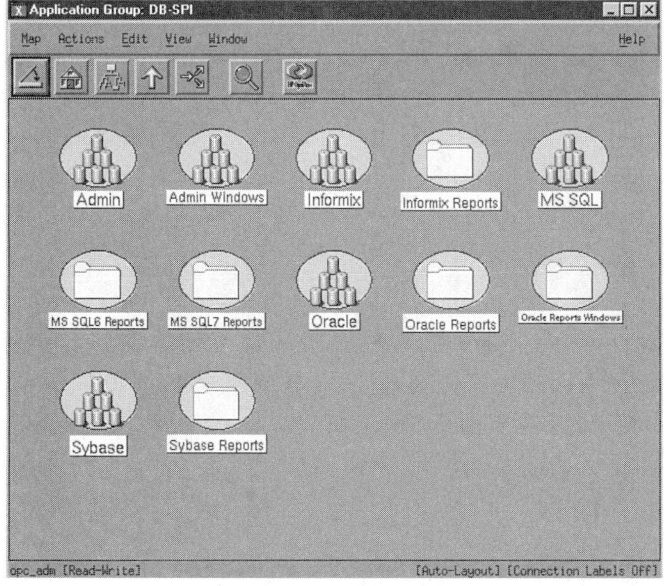

Figure 15-5 Application Group: DBSPI Administrator.

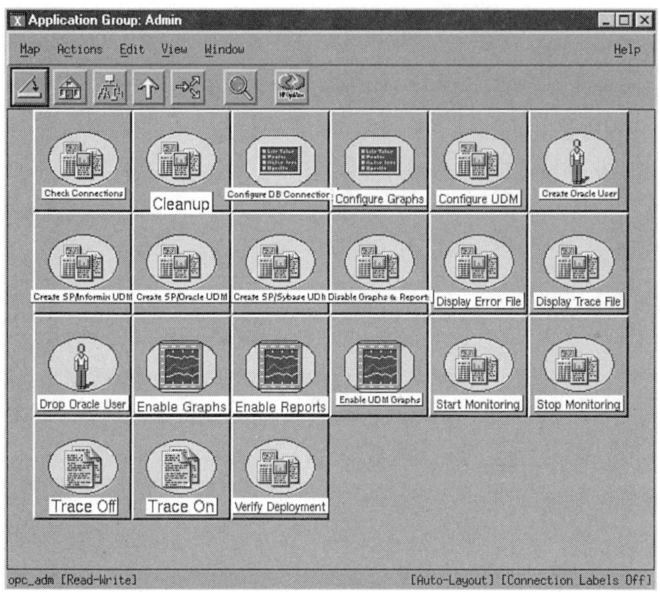

Figure 15-6 Application Group: Oracles

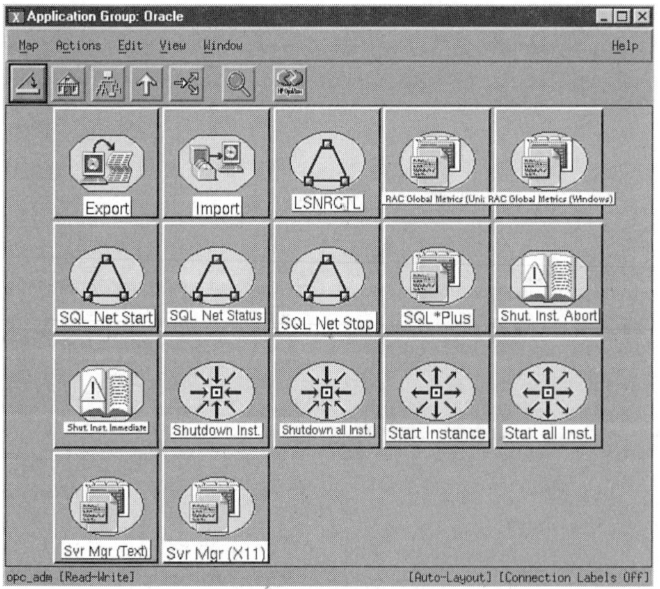

15.2.4 Components in the Message Source Templates

Installing the SPI on the operating system runs the configuration upload command, opccfgupld to add the SPI components to the Message Source Templates environment on the server. The SPI template components are organized into template groups. This helps to simplify the management and distribution tasks. See Figure 15-7.

Figure 15-7 SPI Template group in the Message Source Template window.

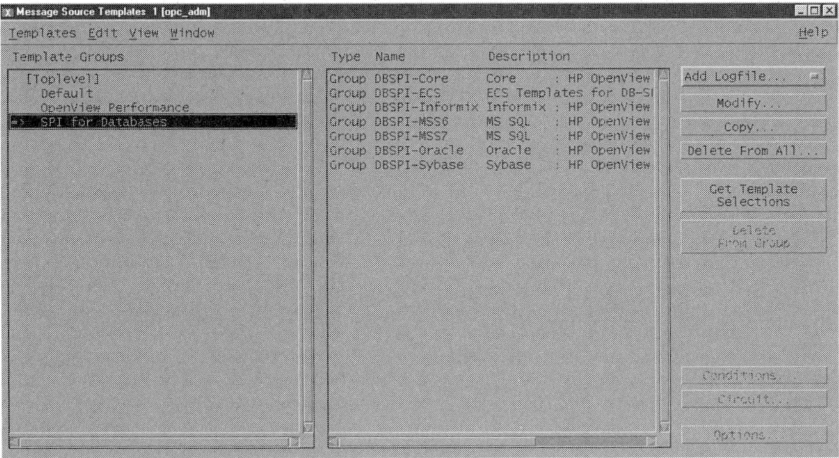

15.2.5 The Message Browser

The message browser is tailored for each operator, and appropriate messages from the SPIs will appear in the active browser or the history browser. Some SPI messages are integrated with actions (automatic or operator) and operator instruction text.

15.2.6 Directories and Files on the Management Server

The SPI files and configuration components are located in the appropriate vendor-specific directories until distribution.

15.2.7 Directories and Files on the Managed Node

After the components for the SPI are installed on the managed node, they are located in the appropriate directories along with other OpenView scripts and programs. The path to the files is vendor-platform specific and is shown in Chapter 14, "Agents, Policies, and Distribution." The SPIs are installed in different directories based on managed node platform.

As an example on the HPUX target node, the locations of the SPI binary components are

- /opt/OV/bin/OpC/action
- /opt/OV/bin/OpC/cmds
- /opt/OV/bin/OpC/monitors

The configuration files are located in the directory /var/opt/OV/<spi>/conf. The trace files are located in the directory /var/opt/OV/<spi>/conf. The log files are located in the directory /var/opt/OV/<spi>/log.

The temporary files used during run-time are located in the directory:/var/opt/OV/<spi>/tmp.

15.3 TYPES OF SPIS

The SPIs provided by Hewlett Packard, Partners and Gallery SPIs are listed in this section for reference. Contact HP for the latest information regarding licensing of the SPI products. The Integrated Solutions Catalog is available at http://www.openview.hp.com/sso/isv/browseapp. This catalog provides a list of vendors that have integrated their products with OpenView.

15.3.1 OpenView SPIs Available from Hewlett Packard

SPIs bundled with the OV Operations Product (like the Operating System SPI) are covered by the OVO license. The SPI provided by HP and partners have separate part numbers, and each SPI requires a separate license. To obtain these products, visit http://openview.hp.com/spis.

1. BEA Tuxedo
2. BEA WebLogic Application Server
3. Broadvision
4. Data Network Devices
5. IBM WebSphere
6. Informix
7. Microsoft .NET
8. Microsoft Active Directory
9. Microsoft Exchange 2000 Server
10. Microsoft SQL Server 2000
11. mySAP.com
12. Oracle
13. PeopleSoft
14. Remedy Action Request System
15. Storage Area Manager
16. Sybase
17. WebMethods
18. Windows +
19. OSSPI for UNIX (Free)

Note: This list is subject to change by HP.

15.3.2 SPIs Available from HP Partners

SPIs provided by HP Partners are ordered with a separate part number and require a license and support from the partner. If you are interested in writing your own SPI for integration with OpenView, you can obtain additional information at `http://openview.hp.com/partners/programs`.. Certified partner SPIs available include the following:

1. Altiris Connection for HP OpenView by Altiris, Inc.
2. e-Sentinel by e-Security, Inc.
3. HERMES SoftLab Siebel eBusiness SPI by Hermes Softlab
4. Notes SPI by nworks
5. UpdateExpert by St. Bernard Software
6. Tripwire for Servers by Tripwire

Note: This list is subject to change by HP.

15.3.3 Free Gallery SPIs

The SPIs available as free downloads from the SPI Gallery web site are not licensed or supported. To obtain these products, visit http://www.openview.hp.com/downloads/spi. The Questions and Answers about the SPI Gallery are available at the following location `http://www.openview.hp.com/products/spi/prod_spi_0003.html`. The following SPIs are available from the SPI Gallery:

1. Ariba
2. ATG Dynamo
3. AXIS SOAP Engine
4. Bluestone Total-e-Business
5. Check Point FireWall-1
6. Cisco PIX Firewall
7. Documentum e-content server
8. HP OpenView storage area manager
9. HP-UX host IDS
10. Inktomi Traffic Server
11. Intershop Enfinity
12. IPlanet Platform
13. ISS RealSecure
14. Microsoft Navision Axapta
15. Nokia WAP Server
16. Portal Infranet
17. Resonate Central Dispatch
18. Sun ONE Application Server
19. Sun ONE Directory Server

20. Sun ONE Identity Server
21. Sun ONE Portal Server
22. Sun ONE Web Services - SOAP engine
23. TIBCO
24. Web Service UDDI Server
25. Integration for Oracle Enterprise Manager
26. Network Node Manager Smart Plug-In for IP Multicast

Note: This list is subject to change by HP.

15.4 SPI DOCUMENTATION AND WHITE PAPERS

Documentation for the SPIs provided by HP is located on the web at `http://ovweb.external.hp.com/lpe/doc-serv/`. A collection of SPI white papers is also available on the web at `http://openview.hp.com/library/index.html`. For reference, the following white papers are available for the Oracle Database:

- Oracle Smart Plug-In
  `http://openview.hp.com/products/spi/spi_oracle/index.html`
- Oracle SPI Metrics Guide: `http://openview.hp.com/products/smart_plug-ins/tech_whitepaper/spi_oracle_metrics_mar02_twp.pdf`
- How to Monitor your Oracle Listeners:
  `http://openview.hp.com/products/smart_plug-ins/tech_whitepaper/spi_oracle_listen_twp.pdf`

15.5 SPI TRAINING

A Database SPI Training Course is available from HP Education, `http://education.hp.com` and delivered via the HP Virtual Classroom. Check the online course catalog and schedule for course numbers U8565S and U8565SR.

15.6 SUMMARY

In this chapter, we have discussed the advantages of using one or more Smart Plug-Ins. You spend less time with detailed configuration activities such as creating templates from scratch. Instead, you can take a pre-defined template and customize it for your needs. In the next chapter, we explore the use of the built-in and add-on performance tools.

## CHAPTER 16

Built-in Performance Tools

Performance management tools are provided with OpenView Operations. These tools are provided out-of-the-box and are ready to use. Tailor the components for your specific environment. In order to utilize some of the tools, you distribute them to the managed node. When deployed, the tools collect metric data and monitor thresholds. When specific thresholds are met, exceeded, or below normal, the tools generate an appropriate message for the operators' view. Other tools are available at the management server. Menus, applications, and commands built into the OpenView administrator and operator consoles provide easy access to many other performance management tools. Programs such as NNM and Oracle include built-in features or add-on components for performance management. In addition, the operating system has many built-in performance tools.

The collection of performance tools that integrate with OpenView Operations allow you to

- Diagnose what is happening in the managed environment right now.
- Characterize what happened this week compared to last week.
- Plan for capacity increases.
- Forecast when you may run out of resources.
- Perform service level management based on transaction response time.
- Optimize application processing.
- Analyze resource utilization.
- Respond to alarm conditions.
- Solve system management problems before they arise.

The purpose for this chapter is to explore the performance management capabilities with OpenView out-of-the-box. We describe the features and look at the differences between the OpenView Embedded Performance Component (OVOA_EPC) and the OpenView Performance Agent (OVPA). Throughout this chapter the OVOA_EPC is referred to as OVOA (OpenView Operations Agent). Other popular performance tools are also discussed. Resources to help you learn more about performance management are provided in Appendix C.

16.1 EMBEDDED PERFORMANCE AGENT (OVOA)

OpenView Operations version 7.0 introduced the embedded performance component. The OVOA is specifically designed to help you get more out-of-the-box performance information. The OVOA is supported on HP-UX, Solaris, Linux, AIX, Tru64, and Windows/NT platforms. While the OVOA collects a fixed set of performance metrics, you can set up threshold monitors through regular templates that only trigger events/messages for a subset of metric threshold violations. The typical installation of the agent software includes

- Control Daemon (ovcd)
- Message Agent (opcmsga)
- Action Agent (opcacta)
- Logfile Encapsulator (opcle)
- Monitor Agent (opcmona)
- Message Interceptor (opcmsgi)
- Trap Interceptor (opctrapi)

The performance data collection and communication agents are

- Embedded Performance Component (coda)—OVOA-EPC
- HTTPS-basedcommunication agent (ovbbccb)

The OVOA facilitates metric data collection and reporting. Along with the performance agent, there is also a dedicated communication program referred to as the HTTPS-based agent. The startup and shutdown of the embedded performance agent and the HTTPS-based agent is the responsibility of the control daemon (ovcd).

16.1.1 OVOA Installation

OVOA installs automatically with the other OVO agents. When performing a manual installation (by copying the agent components) from the server to the node via ssh, ftp, or installing the agent software from a local CD-ROM, the OVOA component (perf_pkg.Z) and the HTTPS-based agent (comm._pkg.Z) are included in the list of selected OVOA components. After the installation, you can check the agent process status with the **ovc** command to confirm that the embedded performance component and the communications component are running.

The performance agent is a registered subagent. This means it can also be stopped and started with the subagent option on the **ovc** command (such as ovc –stop coda). The HTTPS-based agent is not a subagent of the controldaemon, although the control daemon handles startup and shutdown. The output from the agent status command **ovc** is shown here:

```
# ovc -status
ovcd    Control Daemon                 CORE    (1713)   Running
ovbbccb HP OpenView BBC Communications Broker CORE
(1446)   Running
ovconfd HP OpenView Config and Deploy CORE    (1714)   Running
ovcs   HP OpenView Certificate Server SERVER (1715)   Running
opcmsga OVO Message Agent       AGENT,EA      (1733)   Running
```

```
opcacta OVO Action Agent          AGENT,EA                Aborted
opcmsgi OVO Message Interceptor AGENT,EA     (1725)   Running
opcle   OVO Logfile Encapsulator AGENT,EA    (1727)   Running
opcmona      OVO Monitor Agent   AGENT,EA    (1729)   Running
opctrapi OVO SNMP Trap Interceptor AGENT,EA  (1731)   Running
opceca     OVO Event Correlation AGENT,EA             Stopped
opcecaas     ECS Annotate Server AGENT,EA             Stopped
coda         HP OpenView Performance Core    (1734)   Running
```

16.1.2 Performance Data Provided by OVOA

There are over 1000 possible performance metrics available for data collection if you have the right data collection tools. OVOA collects ~120 metrics depending on the vendor platform. ~30 metrics that are common (global) to almost every platform are available via OVOAs data collection environment. Consult the OVOA Metrics Help Text© for details and descriptions of the metrics. Refer to the document `http://ovweb.external.hp.com/ovnsmd/ov_mwa_cm.pdf` for a comparison of OVOA and OVPA metrics. Refer to Appendix C, "Resources," for additional information on performance metrics.

The classes of metrics available are listed here for reference:

- GLOBAL metrics include cpu, disk, network interface, operations, swap, file system, system calls, and table metrics
- CPU (Processor) metrics
- DISK metrics
- NETIF (Network Interface) metrics
- FS (File System) metrics

16.1.3 OVOA versus OVPA

The OVO performance component collects a set of ~30 common system metrics referred to as the "Golden Metrics." A list of the most frequently collected system metrics is provided in Section 16.1.6, "Commands and Files." Use CODA for the data collection of the most common metrics. If it is necessary within your environment to collect additional metrics, consider adding the OpenView Performance Agent.

The embedded performance agent and OpenView Performance Agent can co-exist on the same managed node. With that said, you might wonder why would you need both. On the other hand, how can you decide which one is right for your environment? Let's compare the features of the two performance agents to determine which one best accomplishes the job of monitoring your environment.

Features of the OVOA:

- Included as part of OVO (free!).
- Collects configuration, cpu, swap, disk, memory and network metrics.
- No *Application Response Measurement* (ARM) Support.
- Data is viewable using OpenView Performance Manager (for more information on this product visit `http://openview.hp.com/products/ovperf/index.html`).
- Runs one performance daemon.
- Alarms set via the OVO threshold template.
- No export, extract or customization. Requires OV Reporter for data extraction.
- The OVOA database is not configurable.
- Single metric alarming.

Data is available to some external OV programs such as OV Reporter and OV Performance Manager but cannot be exported for use in "arbitrary" programs. Features of the OVPA:

- Can be purchased as a separate product or in GlancePlus Pak.
- Collects OS, global, application, process-level metrics, network, and user-defined data sources via a data source integration (DSI) and application program interface (API).
- Supports ARM 2.0 extended.
- Data is viewable by PerfView NT and PerfView UX, OVPM UX, and OVPM NT.
- Runs several performance daemons.
- Alarms set in alarmdef file.
- User-defined alarms can be based on any logical combination of metrics.
- Provides extract export, customizable data base, alarming, historical and current data storage.
- Database configuration is provided.
- Data is available to external programs such as OV Reporter and OV Performance Manager and can be exported in various formats so it can be used with almost any other program.
- Multiple metrics can be combined to generate alarms
- Uses DSI metrics from external applications or SPIs can be used to generate alarms

16.1.4 OVOA Configuration

Configuring the managed node for extracting data from the embedded performance component is as easy as configuring a monitor template. In fact, that is the primary method used to extract data from OVOA. The monitor agent periodically collects the metric data, defined within a monitor template. The monitor agent collects the data from the embedded performance subagent through a query interface. The message is then sent to the management server via the message agent if the value of the collected metric violates the defined threshold.

16.1.4.1 Deploy the Embedded Performance Agent Template

Let's walk through an example of configuring and installing an OVOA template on HP-UX:

1. Create a new monitor template (see Figure 16-1) and add the special syntax for the embedded performance agent. The trigger for the data collection is found in the string inside the Monitor Program or MIB field on the template OVPERF\\CODA\\GLOBAL\GBL_CPU\UTIL; each section of the key is described here:
   - OVPERF—keyword for CODA (OVOA)
   - CODA—name of the data source
   - GLOBAL—object class (others include: CPU, NETIF, FS, DISK)
   - GBL_CPU_UTIL—metric
   - Figure 16-1 is an example of the syntax to collect one of the performance metrics. The template data collection syntax for a Window node would look like the following: NTPerfMon\\FTP Server\\Current Connections_Total

Figure 16-1 Create a new OVOA monitor template.

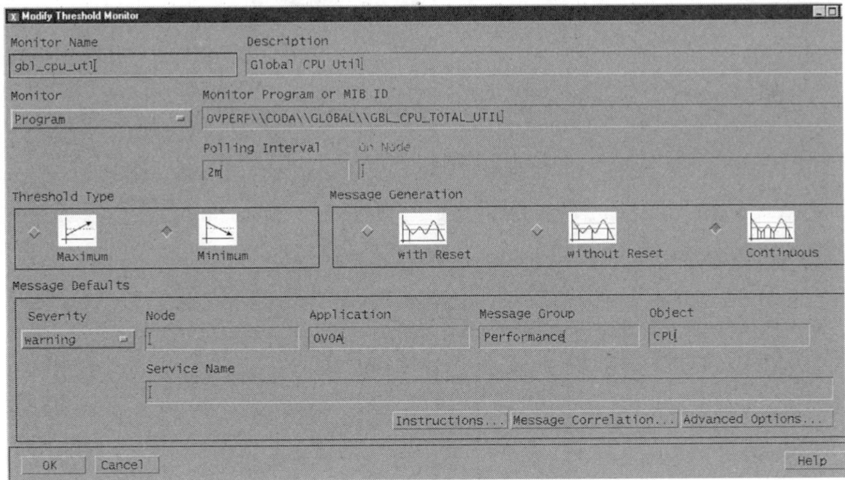

- Create a template condition for the threshold. (See Figure 16.2).

Figure 16-2 A template condition shows the threshold for the GBL_CPU_UTIL metric data collection from the OVOA.

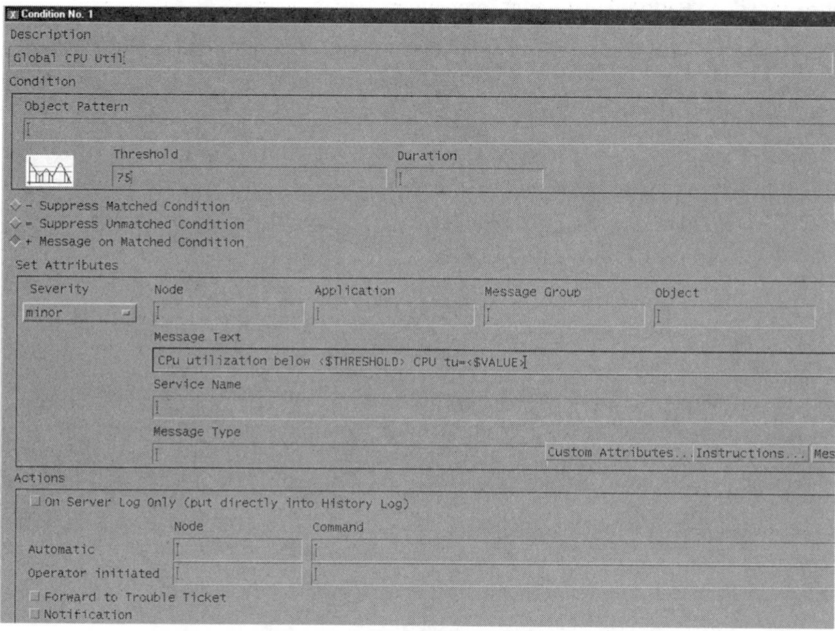

- Assign and distribute the template to the managed node (see Figure 16-3).

Figure 16-3 The OV monitor template distribution process is the same as that for other components.

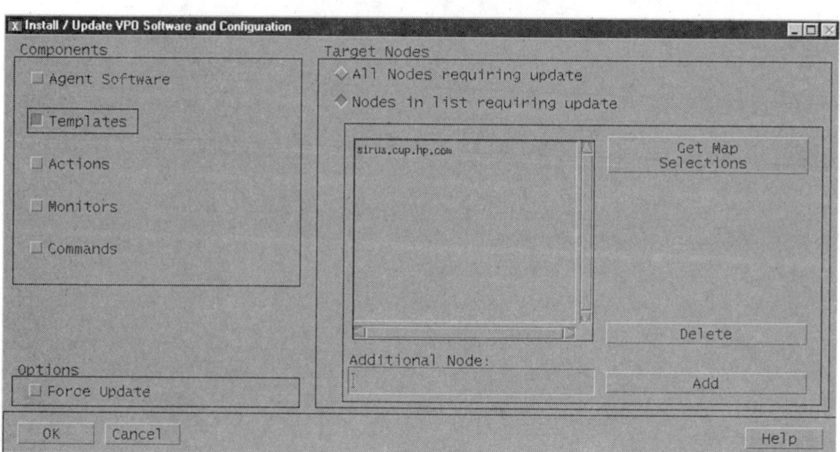

- Check the template distribution on the managed node using the **opctempate** (or **ovpolicy**) command; refer to Figure 16-4.

Figure 16-4 The OVO templates (policies) are shown in the output of the **opctemplate** (**ovpolicy**) command.

```
# opctemplate -l

VPO Enterprise templates (from VPO server on UNIX) :
--------------------------------------------------------------------------------
LOGFILE      "Cron (10.x/11.x HP-UX)"                          enabled
LOGFILE      "Su (10.x/11.x HP-UX)"                            enabled
SNMPTRAP     "SNMP 6.20 Traps"                                 enabled
SNMPTRAP     "SNMP ECS Traps"                                  enabled
OPCMSG       "MsgStormMessages"                                enabled
OPCMSG       "opcmsg(1|3)"                                     enabled
MONITOR      "gbl_cpu_utl"                                     enabled
MONITOR      "disk_util"                                       enabled
MONITOR      "distrib_mon"                                     enabled
MONITOR      "mondbfile"                                       enabled
MONITOR      "proc_util"                                       enabled
MONITOR      "swap_util"                                       enabled
```

- Review the results in the active message browser as shown in Figure 16-5

Figure 16-5 The OVO monitor template distribution status is shown in the message browser.

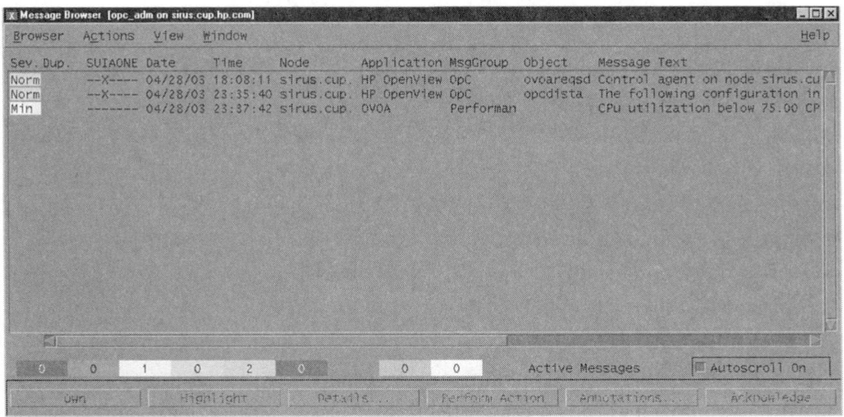

16.1.4.2 The Hook Between opcmona and OVOA

Recall that there is another process, called the HTTPS-based agent, introduced with OVO 7.x. The agent is used as the mechanism for storing the metrics in the database files and provides communication between OVOA and opcmona. As an example, when the monitor agent starts it reads the configuration file for monitors. Using the information from the template, opcmona requests the data specified from OVOA. It communicates to the OVOA via the BBC. The frequency of requests for data (the interval you program in the template) may vary, but the updates to the data files from OVOA are fixed at five-minute intervals. Therefore, the recommendation is to set the monitor template interval at no less than 5 minutes.

16.1.5 Interface with Other Programs

OVOA allows other OpenView programs access to the metrics, such as *OV Performance Manager* (OVPM), SPIs, and *OV Service Reporter* (OVSR). Refer to the OV Performance Agent product documentation (web links are provided in Appendix C) for details on how to integrate these applications with OVOA. Creating and distributing templates that will utilize external programs such as the opcmon (API) is another powerful options which lends itself to more flexibility in that you can parse the output from standard UNIX commands (such as vmstat) to produce a metric value that is returned to the opcmona for evaluation. Refer to Section 16.4 for an example of creating a template for use with the command opcmon.

16.1.6 Commands and Files

OVOA has a command set, files and directories. You can now perform the same task with more than one command. For example, to start and stop the OVOA/CODA process, you could use **opcagt** (OVO 7.x), **ovc** (OVO 8.x) or **codautil** (OVO 7.x and 8.x). Always stop and start the process with the same command.

16.1.6.1 Frequently Used Commands

- **ovc –status**—Display the status of the OV agents.
- **opcsubagt –disable coda**—Disable coda data collection.
- **opcsubagt –enable coda**—Enable coda data collection.
- **codautil –start**—Start coda subagent.
- **codautil –stop**—Stop coda subagent.
- **codautil –obj**—List data sources (new with OVO 7.12 agent patch).
- **codautil –dumpds**—Dump the data source (new with OVO 7.12 agent patch).
- **codautil –status**—Check coda status.
- **codautil –support**—Test the coda data collector.

The output from the **codautil –support** command will print to standard out and display the CODA version, metrics available, and the current collection of metric values. An example of the output from the command **codautil –support** is shown here:

```
=== 04/29/03 00:50:00
Instance: 0
GBL_COLLECTOR: Coda A.07.10.05
GBL_INTERVAL: 300.00
GBL_OSNAME: HP-UX
GBL_OSVERSION: U
GBL_OSRELEASE: B.11.11
GBL_MACHINE: 9000/800
GBL_NUM_CPU: 1
GBL_MEM_PHYS: 786432
GBL_NUM_DISK: 2
```

```
GBL_NUM_NETWORK: 1
GBL_MACHINE_MODEL: 9000/800/A400-44
GBL_STATTIME: 04/29/03 00:55:00
GBL_ACTIVE_CPU: 1
GBL_RUN_QUEUE: 0.19
GBL_CPU_SYS_MODE_UTIL: 0.09
GBL_CPU_USER_MODE_UTIL: 0.37
GBL_CPU_TOTAL_UTIL: 0.46
GBL_DISK_PHYS_IO_RATE: 2.42
GBL_INTERRUPT_RATE: 310.90
GBL_SWAP_SPACE_AVAIL: 2092.09
GBL_SWAP_SPACE_UTIL: 40.50
GBL_MEM_PAGEIN_RATE: 0.03
GBL_MEM_PAGEOUT_RATE: 0.00
GBL_MEM_UTIL: 97.69
GBL_NET_IN_PACKET_RATE: 3.57
GBL_NET_OUT_PACKET_RATE: 1.56
GBL_NET_ERROR_RATE: 0.00
GBL_FS_SPACE_UTIL_PEAK: 77.73
```

16.1.6.2 File Locations

The locations and brief descriptions of the OVOA files for HP-UX, Solaris and LINUX platforms are shown here for reference.

- /var/opt/OV/log/OpC/coda.txt—Coda readme file
- /var/opt/OV/log/coda.log—Logs, OVOA start, stop, open, create, delete, log file rollover, and status messages
- /var/opt/OV/bin/OpC/monitor /ddfcomp_coda, ddflog_coda,ddfcomp_codaAA, ddflog_codaAA—used to create objects inside the coda database
- /var/opt/OV/databases/coda.db—Coda database file and up to five numbered coda database files
- ./tmp/coda_list—Temporary file

16.1.6.3 Data Files

The data for the embedded performance component database log files is extracted every five minutes. It is estimated that 25MB of disk space is required. This estimate is based on the following formula: 1 metric instance = 8 bytes, multiplied by the number of instances and the number of times per day. For example, if you have 3 metrics collected every 5 minutes for one day (288 collection intervals) for 10 disks, multiplied by 8 bytes, the daily collections for the 10 disks would require ~69,120 bytes. Continue this calculation rule for the other objects on the system (such as CPUs, disks, file systems, and so on). So, estimating 25MB (5MB/data file) is really a minimum requirement for the disk capacity to store the data in the embedded performance agent (coda) logs. The log files are created once per week for five weeks. At the end of the fifth week, the sixth log file is created and the first log file is deleted. This is by design and cannot be altered. This process called "rollover" happens every Sunday at 12 a.m.

16.2 THE PERFORMANCE AGENT

The OVPA (formerly called the MeasureWare Agent) captures performance, resource, and transaction data from managed servers or workstations. The program environment uses minimal system resources to collect, log, summarize, timestamp, detect alarm conditions and send notifications to the appropriate applications, such as OVO or NNM. It allows other programs such as OV Performance Manager, OV Reporter and Glance to utilize (extract) the data collected. OVPA utilizes data source integration (DSI) technology to receive alarm on and log data from external data sources such as applications, databases, networks, and other operating systems.

16.2.1 OVPA Installation

OVPA is distributed with OVO and requires a separate license. It is installed from the management server if you select from the menu **Actions→Agent→Install Subagent**, then select MWA as the subagent to be installed. The agent can also be installed from a distribution CD or software depot using swinstall. After installation, the files and programs are located in the directory /opt/perf. Figures 16-6 and 16.7 show the template source for OVPA. Assign and distribute the templates to the managed node where you need to monitor up to as many as 300 metrics and take advantage of the other features offered by OVPA. The OVPA is supported on HP-UX, Solaris, Windows, Tru64, LINUX, and AIX platforms.

Figure 16-6 OVPA Message Source Template Group is shown in the Message Source Template window.

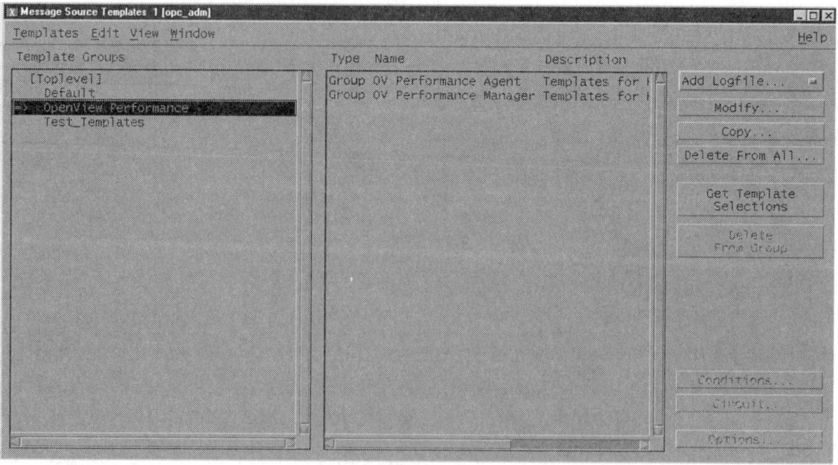

Figure 16-7 OVPA Message Source Template Group contains the default templates listed in the Message Source Template window.

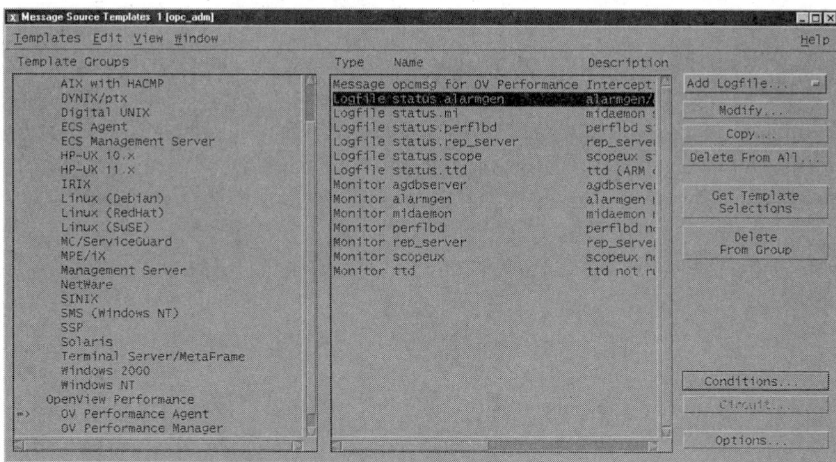

16.2.2 OVPA (3.x) Process Environment

- **RPCD**—HP-UX remote procedure call daemon, provides the endpoint map service for a system. The rpcd program listens on udp and tcp port 111. The endpoint map service is a system-wide database where local RPC servers register binding information associated with their interface identifiers. The endpoint map is maintained by the endpoint map service of the RPC daemon. The endpoint map services are responsible for handling RPC lookups from requesting clients of compatible locally mapped servers. This technology is being phased out of the OpenView platform and replaced by new technology, HTTPS communications programs. Refer to Chapter 14, "Agents, Policies, and Distribution," for more information about the HTTPS-based agent.
- **DCED** (Distributed Computing Environment Daemon)—Solaris (remote procedure process on SUN platforms).
- **rpcss**—Windows (remote procedure process on Microsoft platforms).
- **ovbbccb**—HTTPS-based data communications process.
- **Perflbd**—Reads the perlbd.rc file to obtain data source names and locations. perflbd starts a rep_server process for each configured data source in the perflbd.rc file. perflbd gives the client products (such as OV Performance Manager) some data communication information about the agent. Communication with perflbd is through a TCP socket.
- **Rep_server**—Repository server process that provides access to the data stored in the logfiles. Communication with the rep_server is through RPCs.

- **Agdbserver**—Process that provides access to the alarm generator system database. The database contains information concerning all systems that will be receiving alarms from the agent. Communication with the agdbserver is through RPCs.
- **Alarmgen**—Process that analyzes the data and generates and sends alarm notifications to the alarm daemon in OVPM or the message interceptor in OVO or ovtrapd in NNM.
- **Scopeux**—Collects performance data from the operating system where OVPA is installed. After collecting the data, scopeux summarizes the data and logs it in raw log files based on the specification for data collection defined in the collection parameter (parm) file.
- **Midaemon**—Collects and counts trace data coming from the kernel and translates it for use by OVPA and other performance programs, such as Glance, via a shared memory segment. OVPA's scopeux daemon program attaches to the shared memory interface.
- **DSI**—Data Source Integration logging daemon.
- **Utility**—Manages scopeux log files and analyzes or checks the log files via the repository servers and alarmdef file.
- **Extract**—mwa program for obtaining specific summary or detail data from the repositories.

Note: OVPA 4.x replaces the DCE-RPC based processes and functionality with that of HTTPs-based communications processes. Refer to Section 16.2.8, "OVPA 4.x," for more information about OVPA 4.x.

Figure 16-8 The OVPA 3.x major components are RPC-based processes.

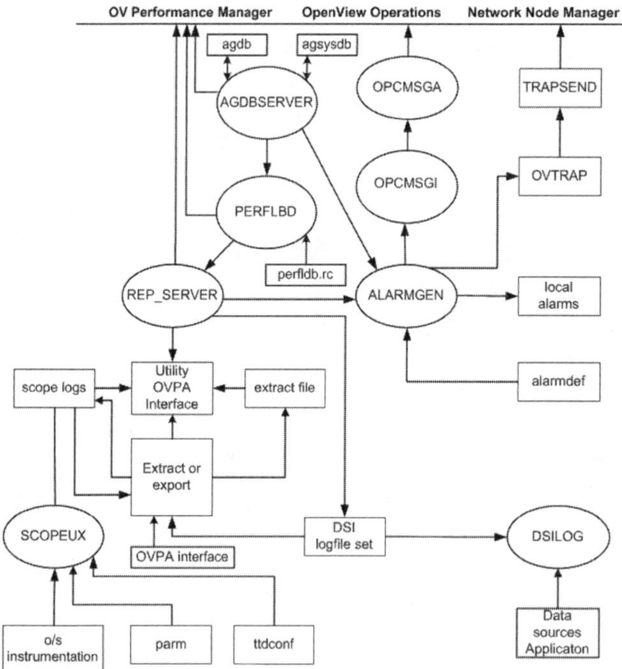

16.2.3 OVPA Startup

The perflbd.rc file is read by the perflbd program during OVPA startup and allows the selected data to be made available for alarm processing and analysis. The default perflbd.rc file contains one entry for a data source named SCOPE that starts a repository server for the scopeux log file set.

The startup sequence for OVPA is as follows:

- Start scopeux (which starts midaemon if it not already running).
- Start transaction tracker (if it is not already running).
- Check for rpcd.
- Start perflbd; this starts the rep_server processes (one at a time) as requested in the perflbd.rc configuration file. Note: This can take some time if the logfiles defined for the data sources are large.
- After the rep_server processes are running, perflbd starts agdbserver.
- Abdbserver starts alarmgen.

After alarmgen is running, connections will be accepted from external programs (such as the HP OpenView Performance Manager).

16.2.4 OVPA Configuration

OVPA has a set of repository severs (called rep_servers) that provide log file data to the alarm generator and other products, such as OV Performance Manager, OVO, NNM and OV Reporter. There is one rep_server for each data source consisting of a scopeux or DSI log file set.

Configure data sources in the /var/opt/perf/perflbd.rc file. A data source is identified with the following syntax within the perflbd.rc file.

```
# cat perflbd.rc
DATASOURCE=SCOPE LOGFILE=/var/opt/perf/datafiles/logglob
```

The DATASOURCE line informs the alarm generator where to find the datafile; the scopeux daemon collects and summarizes performance measurements.

16.2.4.1 Data Source Log File Types

There are several data source LOGFILE types supported. The contents of the data source files are defined here for reference:

- **logglob**—Measurements of global system resource utilization metrics. Global records are logged every 5 minutes.
- **logappl** —Measurements of processes in user-defined application process data.

- **logproc**—Measurements of selected "interesting" processes. Interesting processes are tracked when they first start up, end, or exceed a user-defined threshold for CPU use. Process records are written every 60 seconds and every 5 minutes; the records in logproc are summarized according to the definitions in the parameter file and logged into the logappl file.
- **logdev**—Measurements of individual device performance for disks and volume data, summarized every 5 minutes.
- **logtran**—Measurements of transaction data, summarized every 5 minutes. The transaction-tracking concept is covered in Section 16.3.3 of this chapter.
- **logindx**—Instructions on how to access data in other log files
- **Data Source Integration**—User-defined log file (definition and Configuration covered in Section 16.2.5.2 of this chapter).

16.2.4.2 OVPA Alarm Configuration Example—Contributed by Emil Velez

The example in this section demonstrates the configure information to add to the alarmdef file in order to send performance messages to the OVO message browser if a metric threshold is violated. A brief explanation is provided with each step.

```
# MeasureWare format alarmdef file.  DO NOT REMOVE THIS LINE!
#
# @(#) sample alarm definitions
#
# Sample alarmdef file
#
# edit any lines in this file as desired..

# First come a few sample alarms that illustrate some of the
aspects of
# performance alarming.

# The following alarm, if uncommented, will go off every ten
minutes:
#
#alarm GBL_CPU_TOTAL_UTIL > 0 for 10 minutes
#type = "test"
#start
#  red alert "Test Alarm starting"
#repeat every 10 minutes
#  yellow alert "Test Alarm continuing"
#end
#  reset alert "Test Alarm ending"
#
```

```
# The following application alarm shows the use of the EXEC
statement to
# execute the local action of mailing a message.  Normally, if
the "Other"
# application is using too much cpu, you should determine which
processes
# are causing this activity and then tune your parm file so that
this
# workload is bucketed into one of the application groups appro-
priate for
# your environment.
#alarm OTHER:APP_CPU_TOTAL_UTIL > 10 for 10 minutes
#start {
#  yellow alert "Other application using more than 10 percent of
the cpu"
#  exec "echo 'other application using > 10% cpu' | mail root"
#  }
#end
#  reset alert "Other application cpu warning over"
#

# End of sample alarm section.


# Below are the primary CPU, Disk, Memory, and Network Bottle-
neck alarms.
# For each area, a bottleneck symptom is calculated, and the
resulting
# bottleneck probability is used to define yellow or red alerts.

symptom CPU_Bottleneck type=CPU
rule GBL_CPU_TOTAL_UTIL       > 75   prob 25
rule GBL_CPU_TOTAL_UTIL       > 85   prob 25
rule GBL_CPU_TOTAL_UTIL       > 90   prob 25
rule GBL_PRI_QUEUE            >  3   prob 25

alarm CPU_Bottleneck > 50 for 5 minutes
  type = "CPU"
  start
    if CPU_Bottleneck > 90 then
      red alert "CPU Bottleneck probability= ", CPU_Bottleneck,
"%"
    else
      yellow alert "CPU Bottleneck probability= ", CPU_Bottle-
```

```
neck, "%"
  repeat every 10 minutes
    if CPU_Bottleneck > 90 then
      red alert "CPU Bottleneck probability= ", CPU_Bottleneck,
"%"
    else
      yellow alert "CPU Bottleneck probability= ", CPU_Bottle-
neck, "%"
  end
    reset alert "End of CPU Bottleneck Alert"


symptom Disk_Bottleneck type=DISK
rule GBL_DISK_UTIL_PEAK        > 50   prob GBL_DISK_UTIL_PEAK
rule GBL_DISK_SUBSYSTEM_QUEUE >  3   prob 25

alarm Disk_Bottleneck > 50 for 5 minutes
  type = "Disk"
  start
    if Disk_Bottleneck > 90 then
      red alert "Disk Bottleneck probability= ", Disk_Bottle-
neck, "%"
    else
      yellow alert "Disk Bottleneck probability= ", Disk_Bottle-
neck, "%"
  repeat every 10 minutes
    if Disk_Bottleneck > 90 then
      red alert "Disk Bottleneck probability= ", Disk_Bottle-
neck, "%"
    else
      yellow alert "Disk Bottleneck probability= ", Disk_Bottle-
neck, "%"
  end
    reset alert "End of Disk Bottleneck Alert"


symptom Memory_Bottleneck type=MEMORY
rule GBL_MEM_QUEUE                >    1  prob 20
rule GBL_MEM_PAGE_REQUEST_RATE >   10  prob 20
rule GBL_MEM_PAGE_REQUEST_RATE >   40  prob 20
rule GBL_MEM_PAGEOUT_RATE         >    1  prob 20
rule GBL_MEM_PAGEOUT_RATE         >   10  prob 35
rule GBL_MEM_SWAPOUT_RATE         >    1  prob 35
rule GBL_MEM_SWAPOUT_RATE         >    4  prob 50
```

```
alarm Memory_Bottleneck > 50 for 5 minutes
  type = "Memory"
  start
    if Memory_Bottleneck > 90 then
      red alert "Memory Bottleneck probability= ", Memory_Bot-
tleneck, "%"
    else
      yellow alert "Memory Bottleneck probability= ",
Memory_Bottleneck, "%"
  repeat every 10 minutes
    if Memory_Bottleneck > 90 then
      red alert "Memory Bottleneck probability= ", Memory_Bot-
tleneck, "%"
    else
      yellow alert "Memory Bottleneck probability= ",
Memory_Bottleneck, "%"
  end
    reset alert "End of Memory Bottleneck Alert"


symptom Network_Bottleneck type=NETWORK
rule GBL_NFS_CALL_RATE                > 100  prob 25
rule GBL_NET_COLLISION_1_MIN_RATE     >  60  prob 25  #  1 per
second
rule GBL_NET_COLLISION_1_MIN_RATE     > 600  prob 25  # 10 per
second
rule GBL_NET_COLLISION_1_MIN_RATE     > 3000 prob 25  # 50 per
second
rule GBL_NET_PACKET_RATE              > 150  prob 10
rule GBL_NET_PACKET_RATE              > 300  prob 15
rule GBL_NET_PACKET_RATE              > 500  prob 25
rule GBL_NET_PACKET_RATE              > 1000 prob 25

alarm Network_Bottleneck > 50 for 5 minutes
  type = "Network"
  start
    if Network_Bottleneck > 90 then
      red alert "Network Bottleneck probability= ", Network_Bot-
tleneck, "%"
    else
      yellow alert "Network Bottleneck probability= ",
Network_Bottleneck, "%"
  repeat every 10 minutes
```

```
    if Network_Bottleneck > 90 then
      red alert "Network Bottleneck probability= ", Network_Bot-
tleneck, "%"
    else
      yellow alert "Network Bottleneck probability= ",
Network_Bottleneck, "%"
  end
    reset alert "End of Network Bottleneck Alert"

# The following alarm assumes that on a good network, errors are
rare:
alarm GBL_NET_ERROR_1_MIN_RATE > 10
  type = "Network"
  start
    red alert "Network error rate is greater than ten per
minute"
  end
    reset alert "End of network error rate condition"


# Global swap space utilization alarm:
alarm GBL_SWAP_SPACE_UTIL > 95
  start
    red alert "Global swap space is nearly full"
  end
    reset alert "End of global swap space full condition"

LVOLUME loop
{
if ( lv_space_util > 80 ) then
      {
      if ( lv_dirname == "/var" ) then
        if ( lv_space_util > 80 ) then
           YELLOW ALERT "/var is greater than 80%, currently at:
",lv_space_util
      if ( lv_dirname == "/opt" ) then
        if ( lv_space_util > 92 ) then
          YELLOW ALERT "/opt is greater than 90%, currently at:
",lv_space_util
      if ( lv_dirname == "/usr" ) then
        if ( lv_space_util > 90 ) then
          YELLOW ALERT "/usr is greater than 90%, currently at:
",lv_space_util
      if ( lv_dirname == "/" ) then
```

```
        if ( lv_space_util > 90 ) then
         YELLOW ALERT "/ is greater than 90%, currently at:
",lv_space_util
      if ( lv_dirname == "/home" ) then
        if ( lv_space_util > 70 ) then
           YELLOW ALERT "/home is greater than 70%, currently
at: ",lv_space_util
      if ( lv_dirname == "/opt/maestro" ) then
        if ( lv_space_util > 80 ) then
           YELLOW ALERT "/opt/maestro is greater than 80%, cur-
rently at: ",lv_space_util
      if ( lv_dirname == "/var/opt/perf/datafiles" ) then
        if ( lv_space_util > 95 ) then
           YELLOW ALERT "/var/opt/perf/datafiles is greater than
95%, currently at: ",lv_space_util
      }
}
INCLUDE "/var/opt/perf/nos/nsmdnt2/alarmdef"
```

16.2.4.3 Examples of Measureware Extractions

```
vi report1

REPORT "report 1"
FORMAT ASCII
HEADINGS ON
DATA TYPE GLOBAL
DATE
TIME
GBL_ACTIVE_PROC
GBL_ALIVE_PROC
GBL_COMPLETED_PROC
GBL_CPU_CSWITCH_TIME
GBL_CPU_CSWITCH_UTIL
GBL_DISK_FS_IO
GBL_DISK_FS_IO_RATE
GBL_DISK_FS_READ
GBL_DISK_FS_READ_RATE
GBL_DISK_FS_WRITE
GBL_MEM_PAGEOUT
```

```
GBL_MEM_PAGEOUT_RATE
GBL_MEM_PAGE_REQUEST
GBL_MEM_PAGE_REQUEST_RATE
GBL_MEM_QUEUE
GBL_MEM_SWAP

vi report2
REPORT "report 2"
FORMAT ASCII
HEADINGS ON
DATA TYPE PROCESS
DATE
TIME
YEAR
PROC_CPU_CSWITCH_TIME
PROC_CPU_CSWITCH_UTIL
PROC_CPU_INTERRUPT_TIME
PROC_CPU_INTERRUPT_UTIL
PROC_CPU_NICE_TIME
PROC_CPU_NICE_UTIL
PROC_CPU_NORMAL_TIME
PROC_CPU_NORMAL_UTIL
PROC_CPU_REALTIME_TIME
PROC_CPU_REALTIME_UTIL
PROC_CPU_SYSCALL_TIME
PROC_CPU_SYSCALL_UTIL
PROC_CPU_SYS_MODE_TIME
PROC_DISK_FS_IO
PROC_DISK_FS_IO_RATE
PROC_DISK_FS_READ
PROC_PROC_NAME
PROC_RUN_TIME
PROC_SEM_WAIT_PCT
PROC_TTY
PROC_USER_NAME

# extract -xp -fd -Gg  -b today-1 -e today  -r report1 -f
rxlog.txt
# extract -xp -fd -p  -b today-1 -e today  -r report2 -f
rxlog_proc.txt


REPORT "report 3"
FORMAT ASCII
```

```
HEADINGS ON
DATA TYPE GLOBAL
DATE
DATE_SECONDS
DAY
TIME
YEAR
GBL_ACTIVE_PROC
GBL_ALIVE_PROC
GBL_COMPLETED_PROC
GBL_CPU_HISTOGRAM
GBL_CPU_IDLE_TIME
GBL_CPU_IDLE_UTIL
GBL_CPU_INTERRUPT_TIME
GBL_CPU_INTERRUPT_UTIL
GBL_CPU_SYS_MODE_TIME
GBL_CPU_SYS_MODE_UTIL
GBL_CPU_TOTAL_TIME
GBL_CPU_TOTAL_UTIL
GBL_CPU_USER_MODE_TIME
GBL_CPU_USER_MODE_UTIL
GBL_DISK_CACHE_READ
GBL_DISK_CACHE_READ_RATE
GBL_DISK_HISTOGRAM
GBL_DISK_LOGL_READ
GBL_DISK_LOGL_READ_RATE
GBL_DISK_PHYS_BYTE
GBL_DISK_PHYS_BYTE_RATE
GBL_DISK_PHYS_IO
GBL_DISK_PHYS_IO_RATE
GBL_DISK_PHYS_READ
GBL_DISK_PHYS_READ_BYTE_RATE
GBL_DISK_PHYS_READ_RATE
GBL_DISK_PHYS_WRITE
GBL_DISK_PHYS_WRITE_BYTE_RATE
GBL_DISK_PHYS_WRITE_RATE
GBL_DISK_TIME_PEAK
GBL_DISK_UTIL_PEAK
GBL_FS_SPACE_UTIL_PEAK
GBL_MEM_CACHE_HIT_PCT
GBL_MEM_FREE_UTIL
GBL_MEM_PAGEOUT_RATE
GBL_MEM_PAGE_REQUEST
GBL_MEM_PAGE_REQUEST_RATE
```

```
GBL_MEM_SYS_AND_CACHE_UTIL
GBL_MEM_USER_UTIL
GBL_MEM_UTIL
GBL_NET_IN_PACKET
GBL_NET_IN_PACKET_RATE
GBL_NET_OUT_PACKET
GBL_NET_OUT_PACKET_RATE
GBL_NET_PACKET_RATE
GBL_NUM_NETWORK
GBL_PROC_RUN_TIME
GBL_PROC_SAMPLE
GBL_RUN_QUEUE
GBL_STARTED_PROC
GBL_SWAP_SPACE_UTIL
GBL_SYSCALL_RATE
GBL_WEB_CACHE_HIT_PCT
GBL_WEB_CGI_REQUEST_RATE
GBL_WEB_CONNECTION_RATE
GBL_WEB_FILES_RECEIVED_RATE
GBL_WEB_FILES_SENT_RATE
GBL_WEB_FTP_READ_BYTE_RATE
GBL_WEB_FTP_WRITE_BYTE_RATE
GBL_WEB_GET_REQUEST_RATE
GBL_WEB_GOPHER_READ_BYTE_RATE
GBL_WEB_GOPHER_WRITE_BYTE_RATE
GBL_WEB_HEAD_REQUEST_RATE
GBL_WEB_HTTP_READ_BYTE_RATE
GBL_WEB_HTTP_WRITE_BYTE_RATE
GBL_WEB_ISAPI_REQUEST_RATE
GBL_WEB_LOGON_FAILURES
GBL_WEB_NOT_FOUND_ERRORS
GBL_WEB_OTHER_REQUEST_RATE
GBL_WEB_POST_REQUEST_RATE

REPORT "report 4"
FORMAT ASCII
HEADINGS ON
DATA TYPE PROCESS
DATE
TIME
YEAR
PROC_PROC_NAME
PROC_APP_ID
PROC_CPU_SYS_MODE_TIME
```

```
PROC_CPU_SYS_MODE_UTIL
PROC_CPU_TOTAL_TIME
PROC_CPU_TOTAL_TIME_CUM
PROC_CPU_TOTAL_UTIL
PROC_CPU_TOTAL_UTIL_CUM
PROC_CPU_USER_MODE_TIME
PROC_CPU_USER_MODE_UTIL
PROC_INTEREST
PROC_INTERVAL_ALIVE
PROC_MEM_RES
PROC_MEM_VIRT
PROC_MINOR_FAULT
PROC_PRI
PROC_PROC_IDPROC_RUN_TIME

# extract -xp -fd -Gg  -b today-1 -e today  -r report3.txt -f
rxlog.txt
# extract -xp -fd -p  -b today-1 -e today  -r report4.txt -f
rxlog_proc.txt

Examples of running ovpm from command line

"c:\Program Files\HP Openview\HPOV_IOPS\cgi-bin\analyzer.exe"
   -GRAPHTEMPLATE: CODA "CPU Summary" -SYSTEMNAME: r204c30 -
GRAPHTYPE: TSV

"c:\Program Files\HP Openview\HPOV_IOPS\cgi-bin\analyzer.exe"
        -GRAPHTEMPLATE: CODA "CPU Summary" -SYSTEMNAME: r204c30
```

16.2.4.3 Check the OVPA message interface to OVO

If the OVPA is installed on a managed node where OVO agents are installed, OVPA automatically sends alarms to OVO. If there is no OVO agent on the system, disable the OVO messages setup. OVPA can also send SNMP traps to NNM (agsysdb –add hostname). This is configured in the alarmgen target system database. Check the configuration with the following command: **/opt/perf/bin/agsysdb –l (on HP-UX), /usr/lpp/perf/bin/agsysdb –l** (on AIX) and **c:\rpmtools\bin\agsysdb –l** (on Windows).

The output from the command will look similar to the following:

```
# /opt/perf/bin/agsysdb -l

MeasureWare alarming status:

 SystemDB Version :

 ITO messages : on        Last Error : none
 Exec Actions : on
```

There is more detailed information on the use of this command in the man pages or in the OVPA User's Guide.

16.2.5 Data Source Integration (DSI)

Use the DSI component to implement user defined data sources. For example, you may want to extract the vmstat data every 20 seconds for the User, System, and Idle statistics. The OVPA installation includes the components to check, analyze, and extract the DSI data. SPI's utilize the DSI as a method of collecting application data.

The example in Section 16.2.5.1 demonstrates the steps required to configure a new data source that will send a message to the OVO message browser if a metric threshold is violated. A brief explanation is provided with each step.

16.2.5.1 Data Source Integration Example

The process to implement a DSI log includes the following steps:

Create the Class Specification file

```
# vi /tmp/vmstat.spec
CLASS VMSTATS = 10001;

METRICS

  USER_CPU = 101
  LABEL "USER_CPU";

  SYSTEM_CPU = 102
  LABEL "SYSTEM_CPU";

  IDLE_CPU = 103
  LABEL "%IDLE_CPU";
```

Compile the Class Specification file, and create the logfile set (three new files in the current directory).

```
# sdlcomp /tmp/vmstat.spec /tmp/vmstat.log
sdlcomp
Check class specification syntax.
CLASS VMSTATS = 10001;
METRICS
  USER_CPU = 101
  LABEL "USER_CPU";
  SYSTEM_CPU = 102
  LABEL "SYSTEM_CPU";
  IDLE_CPU = 103
  LABEL "IDLE_CPU";
NOTE: Time stamp inserted as first metric by default.
Syntax check successful.
Update SDL vmstat_log.
Shared memory id used by vmstat_log : 9
Class VMSTATS successfully added to logfile set.
# ls vmstat.log*
vmstat.log          vmstat.log.VMSTATS
vmstat.log.desc
```

Create a format file.

```
# vi /tmp/vmstat.fmt
$numeric $numeric $numeric $numeric $numeric
$numeric $numeric $numeric $numeric $numeric
$numeric $numeric $numeric $numeric $numeric
USER_CPU SYSTEM_CPU IDLE_CPU
```

Note: $number value discounts the first 15 fields from the vmstat output.

Table 16-1 shows the **vmstat** output field descriptions.

Table 16-1 vmstat Command Field Descriptions

Primary Field	Secondary Fields
procs: Information about numbers of processes in various states.	R—In run queue b—Blocked for resources (I/O, paging, and so on) w—Runnable or short sleeper (< 20 secs) but swapped
memory: Information about the usage of virtual and real memory. Virtual pages are considered active if they belong to processes that are running or have run in the last 20 seconds.	avm—Active virtual pages free—Size of the free list

Table 16-1 vmstat Command Field Descriptions

Primary Field	Secondary Fields
page: Information about page faults and paging activity. These are averaged each five seconds, and given in units per second.	re—Page reclaims (without -S) at—Address translation faults (without -S) si—Processes swapped in (with -S) so—Processes swapped out (with -S) pi—Pages paged in po—Pages paged out fr—Pages freed per second de—Anticipated short-term memory shortfall sr—Pages scanned by clock algorithm, per second
faults: Trap/interrupt rate averages per second over last 5 seconds.	in—Device interrupts per second (nonclock) sy—System calls per second cs—CPU context switch rate (switches/sec)
cpu: Breakdown of percentage usage of CPU time for the active processors	us—User time for normal and low priority processes sy—System time id—CPU idle

The vmstat command Column Descriptions (Alternate format)

The column headings and the meaning of each column are:

1. procs: Information about numbers of processes in various states.

```
r       In run queue
b       Blocked for resources (I/O, paging, etc.)
w       Runnable or short sleeper (< 20 secs) but
        swapped
```

```
memory: Information about the usage of virtual and real
memory.  Virtual pages are considered active if they
belong to processes that are running or have run in
the last 20 seconds.

      avm     Active virtual pages
      free    Size of the free list
page: Information about page faults and paging active
ity. These are averaged each five seconds, and given in
units per second.

      re      Page reclaims (without -S)
```

```
        at      Address translation faults (without -S)
        si      Processes swapped in (with -S)
        so      Processes swapped out (with -S)
        pi      Pages paged in
        po      Pages paged out
        fr      Pages freed per second
        de      Anticipated short term memory shortfall
        sr      Pages scanned by clock algorithm, per
                                             second
faults: Trap/interrupt rate averages per second over last 5
seconds.
        in      Device interrupts per second (nonclock)
        sy      System calls per second
        cs      CPU context switch rate (switches/sec)
cpu          Breakdown of percentage usage of CPU time for the
active processors

        us      User time for normal and low priority
        processes
        sy      System time
        id      CPU idl
# vmstat
         procs               memory                        page
faults        cpu
    r     b     w      avm     free    re    at     pi    po     fr
de     sr     in      sy     cs   us sy id
    1     0     0   230390   20390     8     4      0     0      0
0      2    407   1111    158    1  0 99
```

2. Test the dsilog process:

```
# vmstat 20|dsilog /tmp/vmstat.log VMSTATS -f /tmp/vmstat.fmt
-vo
I: 1003415064          0          0          0       10594
1913          0
         0          0          0          0          0
0        110
    211          37      4.0000       2.0000      95.0000
I: 1003415064          0          0          0        8415
1579          0
         0          0          0          0          0
0        108
    144          32      2.0000       1.0000      96.0000
I: 1003415084          0          0          0       10212
```

```
1593          0
         0          0          0          0          0
0        107
    157          37      0.0000      1.0000     99.0000
interval marker
L: 1003414800     2.0000     1.3330    96.6660
Notes:
I: shows incoming data
L: actual data to be logged
```

3. Start the dsilog logging process:

```
# vmstat 20|dsilog /tmp/vmstat.log VMSTATS -f /tmp/vmstat.fmt &
```

4. View the collected DSI data:

```
extract -xp -l /var/opt/perf/vmstat_log -C VMSTATS detail -H -fd
-b first
```

Make the DSI a permanent data source:

```
DATASOURCE=SCOPE LOGFILE=/var/opt/perf/datafiles/logglob
DATASOURCE=DSI_VMSTAT LOGFILE=/tmp/vmstat_log
```

5. Define alarms on DSI data in the /var/opt/perf/alarmdef file:

```
Vi /var/opt/perf/alarmdef (partial listing)
#######DSILOG
alarm DSI_VMSTAT:VMSTATS:USER_CPU>30 for 10 minutes
 start
  critical alert "User CPU exceeded threshold"
 repeat every 15 minutes
  critical alert "User CPU exceeda threshold after 15 minutes"
 end
  reset alert "The User CPU Alert is over"
```

6. Customize graphs in OV Performance Manager:

Refer to the OpenView Performance Manager Documentation for specific implementation and customization details.

16.2.5.2 Definition of Commands and Terms

- **DSI**—Provides the ability to collect, log, correlate, and summarize data from a variety of sources. Common DSI terms and definitions are provided here for reference.
- **sdlcomp**—Tool that creates the DSI log file set (vmstat.log, VMSTAT_log) by reading a specification file.
- **Class Specification File (ASCII)**—Describes the data that is collected using DSI.
- **Class Specification File CLASS** – Defines a group of metrics (USER_CPU, SYSTEM_CPU, and IDLE_CPU) and how they are collected (for example: CLASS name VMSTATS followed by class ID is used internally by DSI; the METRICS values are assigned a unique name and number. Each metric description is terminated with a semi-colon.).
- **Class Specification File LABEL**—Identifies the set of metrics defined by the class.
- **Format File**—Determine what data fields will appear in the final data record and excludes unnecessary information (column headings and data fields). The example format file vmstat.fmt is located in the /tmp directory along with the specification file.
- **Data Feed Process (dsilog)**—Runs continuously in background mode, sending application output to the DSI log file (/tmp/vmstat.log). The vmstat application example shows vmstat (with the list of command line parameters) sending data through a UNIX pipe to the **dsilog** command. The **dsilog** command line parameters include the name of the logfile set, the CLASS name, and data sent to a specific the dsilog file. Syntax checking the specification file with **–vo dsilog** command line option sends the data only to standard output not the actual DSI log file.
- **Preview the data (extract)**—Views the data written to the DSI log file via the **extract** command and writes to an ACSII output file with the name (xfrdCLASS.asc).

16.2.6 OVPA Interface with Other Programs

The Database Smart-Plug In (DB SPI) is one example of a SPI that incorporates data collection capabilities and integrates with OVPM (for graphing and analysis) using the DSI features of OVPA. Installing the DB SPI inserts new entries in the parm file to define the instances of the database as a new application class.

16.2.7 OVPA Commands and Files

- **/opt/per/bin/mwa status**—Checks the OVPA status.
- **/opt/perf/bin/mwa stop**—Stops OVPA.
- **/opt/perf/bin/midaem –T**—Stops midaemon (Also stops active Glance sessions. Glance is described later in this chapter.).

- **/opt/perf/bin/mwa start**—Starts OVPA processes, including midaemon and scopeux.
- **/opt/perf/bin/perfstat –v**—Checks the version and status of the OVPA environment.
- **/opt/perf/bin/ttd –k**—Stop the transaction tracker daemon (refer to the previous section for process description).
- **Parm**—Contains parameters that are used to define applications and processes.
- **Alarmdef** —Defines the conditions that generate alarms.
- **/var/opt/perf/perflbd.rc**—Contains the startup and shutdown commands for the repository servers for each data source that has been configured.
- **/var/opt/perf/status.scope**—Status and error log for scopeux.

The following status files contain diagnostic information from the process environment. The default file size is 1MB, and if the file grows past the limit it is renamed status.filename.old. Use these files to troubleshoot problems that may arise with the processes that generate the files:

- /var/opt/perf/status.alarmgen
- /var/opt/perf/status.perflbd
- /var/opt/perf/status.rep_server
- /var/opt/perf/status.ttd
- /var/opt/perf/status.mi

16.2.8 OVPA 4.x

OVPA 4.x is the same functionally as OVPA 3.x. Origianlly developed for the LINUX platform, OVPA 4.x replaces the DCE-RPC-based components and utilizes OVOA (coda) and the HTTPs-based daemon (ovbbccb) for data collection and communications. The OVOA replaces the functionality of the perflbd and rep-server daemons. The perflbd.rc file is replaced by a datasources file and the alarmgen process is replaced by the perfalarm daemon. Use the **ovpa** command (instead of mwa) to check the OVPA status. The major components of OVPA 4.x are shown in Figure 16-9.

The following status files contain diagnostic information from the process environment. The default file size is 1MB, and if the file grows past the limit it is renamed status.filename.old. Use these files to troubleshoot problems that may arise with the processes that generate the files:

/var/opt/perf/status.scope
/var/opt/perf/status.perfalarm
/var/opt/perf/status.mi
/var/opt/perf/status.ttd
/var/opt/OV/log/coda.log

Figure 16-9 The OVPA 4.x core component for data gathering is coda (OVOA).

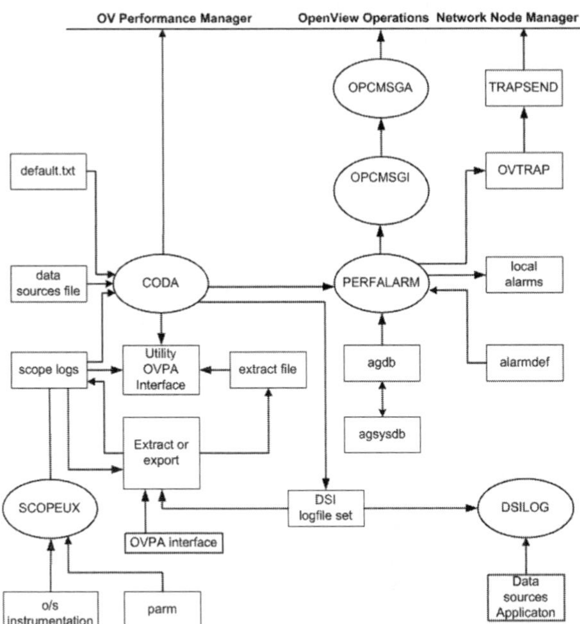

Metric data available from OVPA 4.x is available at: http://ovweb.external.hp.com/ovnsmdps/pdf/metlinux.htm. Installation, release notes, user guides and other documentation is available at the Openview documentation web site: `http://ovweb.external.hp.com/lpe/doc_serv/`.

Note: OVPA 4.x may be changed, upgraded or released by HP for other platforms in the future. Check the OpenView web site for the most up to date product information.

16.2.9 Examples Directory

Example configuration files are located in the directory /opt/perf/examples. The directory includes sample configuration and alarm definition and README files.

16.2.10 Available Metrics

There are over 1000 metrics available for collection on any given system. You can see all the metrics available system-wide with a tool like Glance. OVPA collects a subset of about ~500 metrics on the HP-UX platforms. The OVPA metrics are defined in the text document /opt/perf/paperdocs/mwa/C/methp.txt.

16.3 OTHER PERFORMANCE TOOLS

We have seen two of the most popular tools that collect performance data within the OpenView domain. This section describes some of the other tools that are available to monitor, collect, and analyze collected performance information. Some of the tools are built into the operating system free of charge. Others like Glance and the OV Performance Manager require a license to use.

16.3.1 OV GlancePlus Pack

GlancePlus is a real-time diagnostic tool that displays current performance data directly to a user terminal or workstation. It is designed to help identify and troubleshoot system performance problems as they occur. Figure 16-8 shows the contents of the Glance Application Group, which makes it easy to start, stop, configure and check the status of Glance. The data is displayed for only one node at a time.

Figure 16-10 Glance Application group.

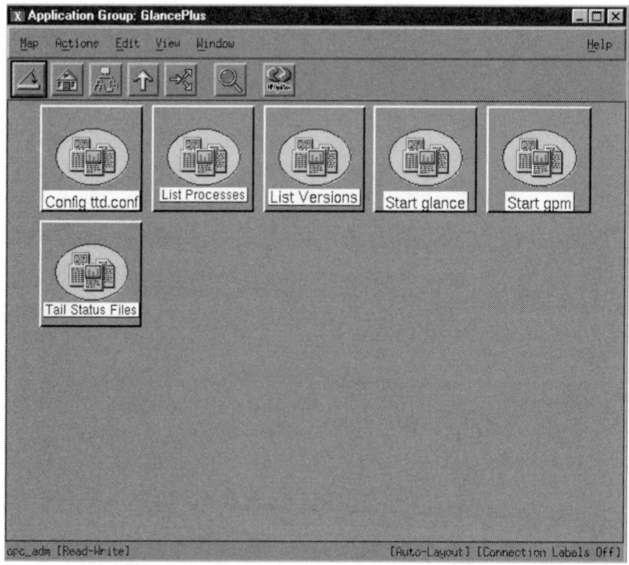

Glance includes two user interfaces: one is character/text-based and the other is a Motif-based graphical interface. Both interfaces allow the user to customize the views of the metric data. Glance is bundled as a separate product or in a combination bundle with OVPA called the GlancePlus Pack. Glance is supported on the following operating systems: HP-UX, LINUX, Solaris, AIX, and Sinix.

Refer to the support documentation available at: `http://support.openview.hp.com` for the most current platform support information.

16.3.2 OpenView Performance Manager (OVPM) 4.x

OVPM 4.x replaces the product called PerfView and provides integrated performance management for multi-vendor distributed networks. OVPM runs on UNIX and Windows platforms, clients connect to OVPM via a web-based interface. It gives you a single interface and a common method for centrally monitoring, analyzing, and graphically forecasting resource measurement data supplied by OVPA.

OVPM also displays information from OV Service Reporter, OV Internet Services and OV Operations. There are three OVPM components as described here:

- **Analyzer**—included with the base product, performs analysis of historical performance data for trend analysis.
- **Monitor**—(add-on) receives, displays and filters alarms
- **Planner** —(add-on) provides the means to forecast future performance in order to facilitate performance management.

16.3.3 Glance versus OV Performance Manager

Although Glance and OVPM both provide metric data in user friendly graphical format, the two programs have unique differences. The features of the two programs are compared in Table 16-2.

Table 16-2 Comparison of Glance and Performance Manager

FEATURES	GLANCE	PERFORMANCE MANAGER
Primary benefit “What is happening right now?” Also, supports historical logging and analysis with extra setup using DSI. Supports Transaction Tracking withextra setup using ARM.	Real-time performance diagnostics; “What has happened over a period of time?”	Data Collection and Trend Analysis
Platforms supported	UNIX Only	Windows NT, Windows 2000, Motif (Analyzer)
User interface	Text Motif	Java Web forms
Startup mechanism	Standalone: glance gpm	Standalone (pm command) Action within OVO Action within OVO Application within OVO
Add-on components Planner	None	Monitor
Base product description	Kernel	Analyzer—Trend-analysis tool with drill-down feature
Process to collect data		Connects to OVO or OVP agents on managed nodes, OV Reporter, SPIs, and OV Internet Services

Table 16-2 Comparison of Glance and Performance Manager (Continued)

FEATURES	GLANCE	PERFORMANCE MANAGER
Drill-down details - View more detail, including process level metrics		Time, Numbers, Global, Application, Process, Disk Device, Logical Vol ume, Network Interface, System Configuration
Connection to multiple data sources	No, view metrics from one system at a time	Yes, view metrics from multiple data sources per across multiple systems
Filters - View a subset of the metrics shown in the graphical table views.		Yes
Graph Types	Line/stacked line Pie	

If you need a more real-time view of the metric data, Glance would provide the best solution. If you plan to analyze the data you are collecting over a period of time to make investment, upgrade, migration, or configuration decisions, Performance Manager provides the best solution.

16.3.3.1 Terms and Definitions Used with Glance

Application Response Measurement (ARM)—Run-time library APIs linked within an application program. During run-time the application transactions are collected and logged and available for graphing.

Transaction Tracking (TT)—Collect, analyze and graph transaction response times, transaction counts, and service level violations that occur within an application during run-time. Requires a LOGTRAN entry in the OVPA parameter file, registration daemon (ttd), configuration file (ttd.conf), and customized application with ARM APIs.

16.3.4 OVPA Applications Integration with OVO

The OVO application bank has an application group called performance. Figure 16-11 shows the performance agent application group that contains (OVPA) applications that provide out-of-the-box integration with OVO. Some of OVPA application group components are listed here for reference:

- Check alarmdef
- Check parm
- Config alarmdef
- Config parm
- Config perflbd.rc
- Config ttd.conf
- List processes
- List versions
- Restart perf agent

- Start perf agent
- Start extract
- Stop perf agent

Figure 16-11 OVPA application group represents the out-of-the box performance tools for use with the performance agent.

16.3.5 Network Node Manager

NNM has built-in performance tools that allow you to check the health of the managed devices in the domain. The tools are built into the menu of the root window of the OVO Administrators console. The information available from within NNM provides the following:

Collect the Performance Data—using snmpCollect

Configure Performance Monitoring Threholds—using snmpCol.conf

Performance Data in text format—using snmpColDump

Performance Data in graphical format—using xnmgraph

Remote Monitoring—using the MIB (RMON)

Capacity Planning—using the current topological information

Store and Report the Performance Data-using the Data Warehouse and Reporting tools

16.3.6 Databases

Many of the performance measures for the database environment within the OV domain can be captured with the OpenView Database SPIs. Refer to the specific database documentation for performance tools that are available.

16.3.7 Operating System Built-in Performance Tools

Commands built into the UNIX operating system can provide valuable information to help collect and analyze performance data for specific system resources. The programs outlined here do not represent every possible tool for all supported OpenView server and agent operating systems. Consult the specific system documentation (man pages on HP) for a detailed listing of the commands and command line options.

16.3.7.1 top

Displays and updates information about the top processes on the system. Summarizes the general state of the system (load average), quantifies amount of memory in use and free, and reports on individual processes active on the system. **top** updates its displays at intervals. On multi-processing systems, top reports on the state of each CPU.

16.3.7.2 sar

Reports on cumulative system activity, including CPU utilization, buffer activity, transfer of data to and from devices, terminal activity, number of specific system calls used, amount of swapping and switching activity, queue lengths, and other kernel tables.

16.3.7.3 vmstat

Quantifies the use of virtual memory by processes on the system; also reports on traps and CPU activity. **vmstat** produces CPU and virtual memory metrics on an interval specified at the command line.

16.3.7.4 iostat

Reports I/O statistics for active disks, terminals, and processor(s)

16.3.7.5 nice

The **nice** command executes a command at a non-default CPU scheduling priority. A nice value influences a program's process scheduling priority. When the nice value is higher than the default schedule priority (19 on HP-UX), the schedule priority for the program is lowered. The nice value is used to compute the priority value; it does not set the priority value.

16.3.7.6 ps

Report the current process status. Use this command to determine if all of the OpenView, user, or other application processes are running. Here is an example of the **ps** command specifically looking for the running Oracle processes: **ps –ef|grep ora**

16.3.7.7 size

Prints the total size of the object file, including the text, data, and unintialized data.

16.3.7.8 swapinfo –t

The **swapinfo** command is used to review the current configuration for device and filesystem swap. Sometimes when you run the OV system check report (more on this in Chapter 17) it will print a warning that there is insufficient swap space configured. System swap space is configured when the operating system is installed. This determines how much virtual memory is available when it becomes necessary for the process vhand to select pages in memory that can be temporarily paged out to the swap space on disk. The swap area also functions as a dump device when necessary.

16.3.7.9 SAM

SAM is the system administration tool provided with the HP-UX operating system. This tool is invaluable when you need quick access to the operating system tools to perform administration tasks. For example, setting up new volume groups, lan cards, users, and tuning the kernel. Activities performed by SAM are logged in the /var/adm/sam/sam.log

16.3.7.10 cron

Cron executes commands and programs at timed intervals. It is helpful for collecting data and performing other important tasks routine tasks regularly.

16.3.7.11 crontab –l

List cron's scheduled jobs.

16.3.7.12 uptime/ruptime

Reports the local or remote system's load average.

16.3.7.13 time and timex

The **time** command reports on the time it takes to execute a command. The **timex** command also reports the time it takes for a command to complete along with additional details if invoked with the –s or –p options.

16.3.7.14 ipcs

Ipcs provides a print to standard out on semaphores message queues and shared memory. You may recall that some of the kernel parameters for OpenView are for semaphores.

16.3.7.15 bdf and df

The **bdf** and **df** commands show information on the current mounted file systems, total capacity, amount used, amount available, percent used, and percent available. These commands also display inode percent used, and the number of used and free inodes.

16.4 OPERATING SYSTEM TOOLS INTEGRATION EXAMPLE

In the previous section, we saw how many operating system data collection tools are available to provide information about the performance of the managment environment. Several of the tools are already integrated within OVO via the Application Bank. Others could add functionality within OVO. The following example demonstrates use of the OVO monitor template to collect file system metrics using the external command **opcmon** to feed the metric data into. The metric value is compared with the threshold and if the threshold is violated a message is created and delivered to the message browser using the **opcmsg** command. Refer to the man pages for the complete command syntax.

The opcmon (API) could be incorporated into scripts or integrated within a scheduled actions template. In the example opcmon is executed from the command line. A brief explanation is provided with each step in the following external monitor program example.

1. Create a monitor template. Refer to section 16.1.4.1 for the overall process to create, customize, assign, and distribute a monitor template.
2. Leave the Monitor Program or MIB field blank and change the monitor type from Program to External. Add the monitor name. See Figure 16-12.

Figure 16-12 The monitor template contains the monitor name and the monitor type is set to External.

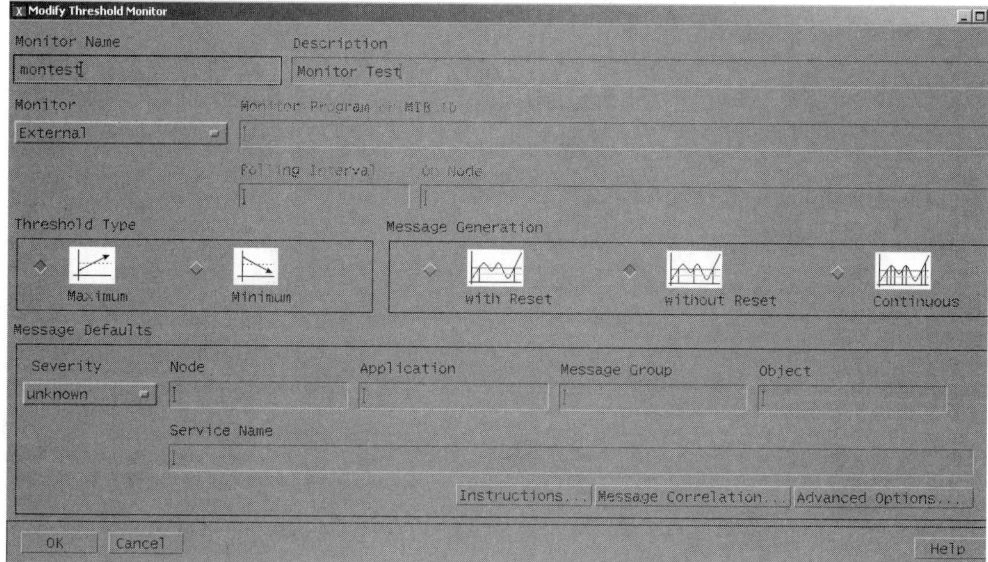

Add a new threshold condition as shown in Figure 16-13.

Figure 16-13 The monitor template condition shows the match conditions (Object Pattern and Threshold) and message attributes (Severity, Message Group and Message Text).

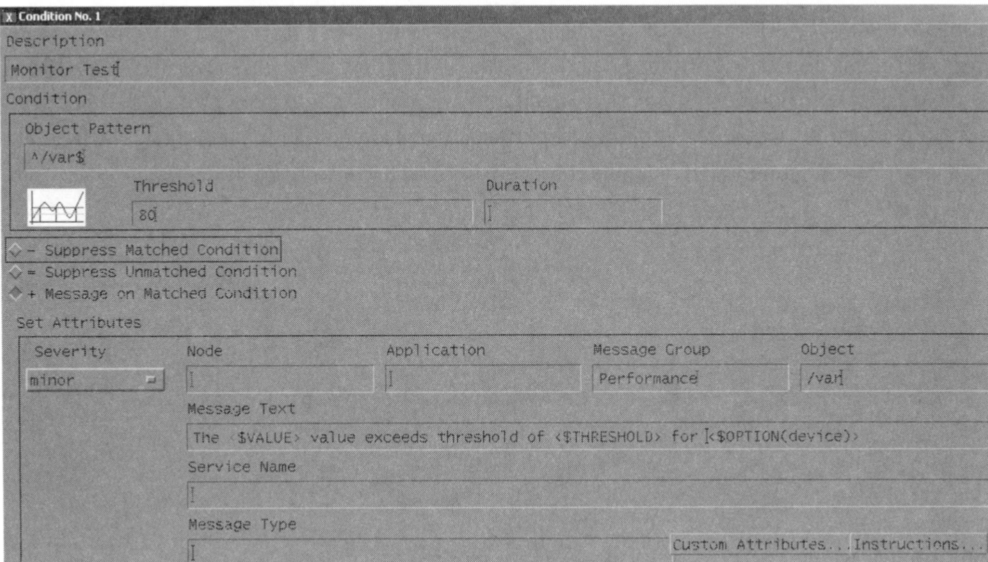

3. Assign and distribute the template to the managed node.
4. Use the **opcmon** command to trigger a performance event that exceeds the template threshold.
5. /opt/OV/bin/OpC/opcmon montest=90 –object /var –option device=/dev/vg00/lvol6
   - View the results in the message browser.

Figure 16-14 The Message Details window shows the results of the matched monitor condition and the custom message text.

Message Details
Node: lotus
Application:
Message Group: Performance
Object: /var
Source: Monitor:montest:Monitor Test
Annotations: 0
Attributes:
Message ID: -bd7e-71d8-11ab-0ff410b70000
Forwarding Manager:
Severity: Minor
Service Name:
Message Key:
Message Type:
Time First Created on Managed Node: 06/13/04 14:10:56
Time First Received on Mgmt. Server: 06/13/04 14:10:56
Number of Duplicates: 0
Time Last Received on Mgmt. Server: 06/13/04 14:10:56
Owned by: at
Message Text
The 90.00 value exceeds threshold of 80.00 for /dev/vg00/lvol6

16.5 DOCUMENTS AND REFERENCES

Refer to Appendix C for documentation and references.

16.6 SUMMARY

The OVO built-in performance tools provide a great start for monitoring the run-time environment. The tools are easily customized and deployed to a variety of managed nodes. One key task of the OVO system administrator is to try to simplify as many routing tasks as possible and let the system perform the work. The tools for performance management help meet this objective. The next chapter covers more system administration tasks, tools and techniques.

CHAPTER 17

Server Administration

There are many OpenView support models operating today that have grown out of the paradigms within the mainframe and distributed computer support environment. In other words, there are primary operators (Tier 1 or Level 1) who monitor and respond to events within the system. When the Tier 1 Operator needs support, she would likely page someone who can take an even closer look at the problem and determine the course of action to resolve the issue. Specialists who are responsible for the applications running on the operating system are working to ensure that the application is healthy and that documented procedures are available for those who are responsible for the daily operations tasks. Vendors are available in this support chain to provide additional break-fix support for any hardware or off-the-shelf software support. If the application is highly customized, likely there are developers on call as well. Take a step back and think about the issues involved with so many people with such a diversity of skills and interests to ensure that the primary service objectives are met or exceeded in the eyes of the customer. The role of system administrator is a key role in coordinating the efforts of many other staff, providing updates to management, and performing important system management and maintenance tasks.

This chapter is an outline of several general OpenView Administration tasks. More specific tasks are outlined in the Administrators Task Guide available via the On-Line Help Interface. Select **Help→On Tasks** for details about how to perform the tasks. You will need to regularly refer to other reference materials as previously listed in Chapter 13, "Out-of-the-box with OpenView Operations." What is important is that you add these items to your administration toolkit and use them as needed.

Throughout this chapter, HP-UX is used for reference. Although specific path names, patch names, and some commands are different between the HP and SUN management platforms, the functionality of the OVO server is the same on both. There are resources listed in Appendix C, "Resources," that are also useful for more information.

This information is subject to change and should be adapted for the specific OV environment within which you work. We strive to provide accurate and usable information, but we accept no responsibility for any mishaps that might occur from the use of information within this section. It is highly recommended that you follow the first rule of system administration: backup often and test the backup often.

17.1 SYSTEM ADMINISTRATION RESPONSIBILITIES

There are many general responsibilities for a system administrator. If you have had the opportunity to administer other types of systems, many of the tasks will seem very familiar, like backup or system shutdown for maintenance. Within many OpenView domains, you'll find more than one administrator. Depending on the size of the enterprise, you might find large teams of administrators and support staff who are located regionally. Many of the accepted responsibilities (from various sources) of a system administrator were outlined in the introduction to Part II of this book, "OpenView Operations." Others include

- Maintain the operating integrity of the system.
- Supervise the periodic maintenance of the system and, when necessary, request field service from system vendors.
- Maintain a log of system problems and communicate them to operators and outside vendors.
- Install and test upgrade and improvements to the hardware and software; notify outside vendors of weaknesses or defects in their software or equipment.
- Coordinate the archiving of data from disk to tape or other media.
- Document the files and software on the system; ensure that outdated or unused files are deleted or archived.
- Monitor and troubleshoot production operations; assist operators in analyzing and using system resources.
- Train operators in the proper use of equipment and specific software procedures.
- Consult with other support staff or software developers on specialized software installed for specific projects.
- Provide new documentation where necessary, and condense, expand, or reinterpret existing written materials from vendors.
- Analyze system utilization and accounting data of work performed on the system.
- Specify and create, where possible, programs that enhance production.
- Maintain awareness of technical development and make recommendations to management on the need for implementing new technology.

17.2 SYSTEM STARTUP AND SHUTDOWN

During system startup and shutdown, programs are executed that cause the OpenView environment to start and stop gracefully. Programs called during startup are sequenced in order to ensure that any program dependencies have been met before executing application startup scripts. Each vendor platform is slightly different. The examples in this section are from the HP-UX 11.11 system startup environment.

The startup and shutdown model uses four components:

1. Execution scripts
2. Configuration variable files
3. Link files
4. Sequencer script

17.2.1 Execution Scripts

Execution scripts read variables from configuration variable files. The OpenView platform relies on the execution of network startup programs (they are not covered here). The startup scripts are located in the directory /sbin/init.d. The execution scripts for OpenView on the management server are as follows:

- SNMP startup scripts (SnmpHpunix,SnmpMaster,SnmpMib2,SnmpTrpDst)
- DCE startup scripts (DCE programs required for OV RPC communications)
- NNM and OVO startup scripts (ov500)
- Oracle startup script (ovoracle)
- OV Agent startup scripts (opcagt)

17.2.2 Configuration Variable Files

Configuration variable files are located in the directory /etc/rc.config.d. These files control the calls to the startup scripts that determine if the programs will start up. One (1) means start up the program and zero (0) means do not start up the program. Some files also contain other variables that are important to the program during startup. For example, the nfs.server file contains the number of nfs server processes (NUM_NFSDs) to startup. For OpenView, the configuration variable files are as follows:

- **SNMP startup variables**—SNMP_HPUNIX_START=1; export SNMP_HPUNIX-START; SNMP_MASTER_START=1; export SNMP_MASTER_START; SNMP_MIB2_START=1; export SNMP_MIB2_START; SNMP_TRAPDEST_START=1; export SNMP_TRAPDEST_START
- **DCE/RPC startup variable**—START_RPCD=1
- **NNM and OVO startup variable**—START_OV500=1
- **Oracle startup variables**—ORACLE=1, OVORALISTENER=1
- **OV Agent startup variables**—OPCAGT_DIR=/opt/OV/bin/OpC; START_LANG=C.iso88591; OPCAGT=1

17.2.3 Link Files

The link files are files that contain the startup or shutdown sequence number in the name of the file. Each file that the link file points to is called in order based on the sequence number assigned to the link. This order ensures that the applications and services start up in such a way that if an application requires the network service, the network service starts before the call for the application to start. There are two sequence link files for each startup script located in the /sbin/init.d directory. One sequence link file determines the startup order and starts with the letter "S" followed by the sequence number. The other sequence link file determines the shutdown order and starts with the letter "K" followed by the sequence number for shutdown. The sequence numbers for the OpenView program startup and shutdown are located in three locations: /sbin/rc1.d, /sbin/rc2.d, and /sbin/rc3.d, and are listed here for reference:

- /sbin/rc1.d/K060ov900→/sbin/init.d/ovoracle
- /sbin/rc1.d/K410Rpcd→/sbin/init.d/rpcd
- /sbin/rc1.d/K435SnmpHpunix→/sbin/init.d/snmpHpunix
- /sbin/rc1.d/K435SnmpMib2→/sbin/init.d/SnmpMib2
- /sbin/rc1.d/K435SnmpTrpDst→/sbin/init.d/SnmpTrpDst
- /sbin/rc1.d/K440SnmpMaster→/sbin/init.d/SnmpMaster
- /sbin/rc2.d/K010OVCtrl --> /sbin/init.d/OVCtrl
- /sbin/rc2.d/K059opcagt→/sbin/init.d/opcagt
- /sbin/rc2.d/K060ov500→/sbin/initd.d/ov500
- /sbin/rc2.d/S560SnmpMaster→/sbin/init.d/SnmpMaster
- /sbin/rc2.d/S565SnmpHpunix→/sbin/init.d/SnmpHpunix
- /sbin/rc2.d/S565SnmpMib2→/sbin/init.d/snmpMib2
- /sbin/rc2.d/S565SnmpTrpDst→/sbin/init.d/SnmpTrpDst
- /sbin/rc2.d/S590Rpcd→/Sbin/init.d/Rpcd
- /sbin/rc3.d/S920 --> /sbin/init.d/OVCtrl
- /sbin/rc3.d/S390ov300→/sbin/initd.d/ovoracle
- /sbin/rc3.d/S940ov500→/sbin/init.d/ov500
- /sbin/rc3.d/S941opcagt →/sbin/init.d/opcagt

Note: The command **opcagt** applies to DCE agents only.

17.2.4 The Sequencer Script

The sequencer script /sbin/rc is responsible for calling the startup scripts for the programs during system boot and ensuring that they start with the system variables and in the correct order. During installation of the OpenView application programs, the startup and shutdown environment is configured on the management server and during agent installation on the managed node in case you enabled the automatic update of system resource files. If any programs fail to startup or shutdown properly, check the sequencer script log file /etc/rc.log for more information.

During system boot, there is a series of transitions that are referred to as run levels. On an HP-UX system there are four run level transitions possible starting from a halted state (run level

0) to run level six. The link files for each run level are located under the directory /sbin/rcX.d, where "X" represents the number for the run level. Each run level directory contains the links to the programs that will be executed during startup or shutdown. The sequence numbers provide the order of precedence for the scripts in each run level directory. At each change of state during startup, the system enters a new run level and the files in the /sbin/init.d directory are executed based on the sequence number for the link found in the directory /sbin/rcX.d.

17.3 FILE SYSTEMS AND DISKS

The requirements for the file system resources for OpenView are outlined in the Installation Guide for the Management Server. The requirements for file system resources change as the system used to store information as the OpenView domain grows. The default configuration for disks can be examined using the *Logical Volume Manager* (LVM) provided with HP-UX as an example for disk storage allocation. Other volume manager products (such as Veritas Volume Manager, also supported on HP-UX) use similar concepts. Disk storage devices are generally assigned to a volume group; the volume group is used to allocate capacity to partitions (called logical volumes). The result of the allocation of logical volumes becomes a file system available for use to store the data for the operating system and applications. Over time, the file system requirements for OpenView may change. In some cases, the allocation of physical disks within volume groups may change if some of the original allocation of capacity is unused. Other reasons to evaluate the allocation of disk and file system resources include changes to the database when additional extents are required and performance issues.

17.3.1 Check the Disks Available on the System

LVM and file system commands to help check the disks and allocation of disk capacity within the system are listed here for reference purposes. Refer to the system documentation for a complete description of the commands.

- **ioscan –funC disk**—Check which disks are physically attached to the system
- **vgdisplay –v**—Display volume groups and logical volumes
- **lvdisplay –v /dev/vg00/lvol1**—Display information about a specific logical volume
- **bdf**—Check which logical volumes are mounted to the file systems
- **more /etc/fstab**—Check that the file systems are mounted during system startup
- **fsck**—Check the file system integrity (requires specific options)

17.3.2 Check the Available Capacity of the File Systems

The file system information is helpful to keep track of potential file systems that will require added capacity or file systems that are not using all the allocated capacity. Refer to the HP-UX System Administration Guide for details. You can also receive regular updates about the file systems if you implement file system monitor templates. You can implement file system monitor templates by creating them or by installing the OS-SPI. The file system listing here is generated from executing the **bdf** command.

```
Filesystem              kbytes     used      avail %used Mounted on
/dev/vg00/lvol3         262144   104752     147585   42% /
/dev/vg00/lvol1         299157    46169     223072   17% /stand
/dev/vg00/lvol6        2097152  1375663     678526   67% /var
/dev/vg00/lvol5        2097152  1078611     954919   53% /usr
/dev/vg01/lvol2        4096000  2845065    1172754   71% /u01
/dev/vg01/lvol1         524288   215234     290673   43% /tmp
/dev/vg00/lvol7        2048000  1569073     449503   78% /opt
/dev/vg00/lvol4         262144     1181     244657    0% /home
/dev/vg01/lvol8        2048000     1607    1918501    0% /backup
```

17. 4 OVO SERVER BACKUP

Backup is a task that you will perform frequently. Restore should be a task you perform less frequently. The backup recommendations here and those from other environments might look similar. In the event of a disaster, the OVO server recovery includes the following three areas for full operations:

1. The operating system and user environment.
2. The application programs.
3. The network configuration.

The recovery concept seems very straightforward at first, look closer at what could be involved. If there is a file system failure, are you prepared for the time it will take to restore the system? Depending on the type of backup that you have performed, it could take you days or hours to recover. Operating system or application failures are often resolved with a patch fix. If the application fails after an upgrade, you could also make the decision to return to a prior release of the program until you work out the bugs in the test environment. What test environment? What does a test environment have to do with a backup? We will talk more about this in the next section of this chapter. The time to recovery also depends on the type of backup strategy you have adopted.

17.4.1 Develop a Backup Procedure

The procedure for backup and recovery should include a regular full-system backup. A full-system backup usually transfers the data to an offline storage media such as tape, CD or removable disk for off site storage. An outline of a backup procedure might include

- In /etc/motd (the message of the day file), display the times the system will be down for maintenance, including scheduled backup times.
- A few minutes before bringing the system down or starting the online backup, broadcast a message to all users that the system will be coming down for maintenance in a few minutes. Use the **/etc/wall** command or the **opcwall** command and give users time to finish what they are doing before they are logged off during system or process shutdown.
- Offline "cold" backups should always be done in single-user mode to prevent users from accessing and using system files during the backup procedure. When bringing the system down, use the **shutdown** command with a grace period option.
- After the system is in single-user mode, execute a **sync** command and check the files' system integrity with the **fsck** command. Take corrective actions for any file system errors.
- Before starting the backup, mount the specified file systems.
- During the backup procedure, log the fsck activity, disk usage data, and commands executed during the backup to a log file and maintain a hardcopy.
- A tape scan file from the tape utility can be generated in /tmp and printed for audit purposes.
- An adequate supply of tapes to a tape pool should be made. Rotate the tapes on a regular basis and do not use tapes beyond their normal life and wear expectancy.
- After the backup is complete, return the system to multi-user mode.
- Consider storing the tapes at an offsite location, a precaution that protects backup in case of catastrophic events like fires, hurricanes, tornadoes, and floods.
- Test the recovery procedure to ensure that the tapes will restore the system information.

Tools from multiple vendors support these backup methods. After you backup the OpenView data using the tools discussed in the next sections, it is still necessary to perform a standard backup of the operating system environment. The backup information provided in this section consists of general guidelines and is not OV-specific. It is recommended to check commercial off-the-shelf backup solutions, such as HP's DataProtector.

Many system administrators use cron or some other type of program to schedule regular system backups. The OpenView schedule template shown in Figure 17-1 is another method for executing a program on a regular schedule (except offline backups). The interface for the template is located within the Message Source Templates Window (**Window→Message Source Templates→Add Schedule**).

Figure 17-1 Schedule template executes programs or commands at the configured intervals.

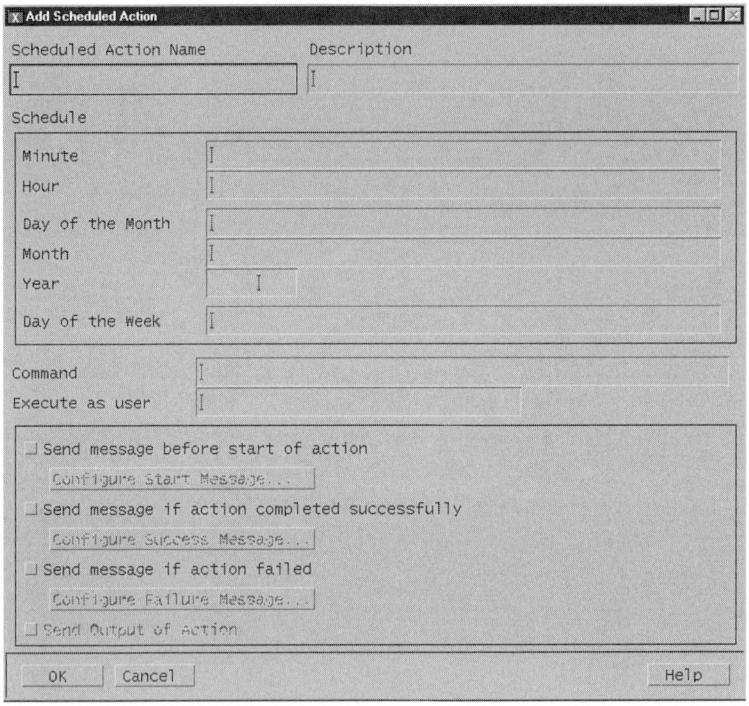

Add Scheduled Action

Scheduled Action Name

Description

Schedule

Minute

Hour

Day of the Month

Month

Year

Day of the Week

Command

Execute as user

Send message before start of action

Configure Start Message...

Send message if action completed successfully

Configure Success Message...

Send message if action failed

Configure Failure Message...

Send Output of Action

OK Cancel Help

17.4.2. OVO Tools to Perform the Backup

Let us look at some of the tools to perform an OpenView backup.

17.4.2.1 Offline Backup

The backup tools opc_backup and opc_restore can be executed from the command line. opc_backup can also be scheduled as part of the routine tasks for daily maintenance. The command line options are for a full backup of the configuration data stored on disk and runtime data stored in the Oracle database. Because some of the data is memory resident during operations, opc_backup requires the shutdown of both the server (including OVO, Oracle and NNM) and GUI processes. If the required downtime is not feasible within your OV operation, consider using the online backup method described in the next section of this chapter.

17.4.2.2 opc_backup Documentation

A brief summary of the **opc_backup** and **opc_recover** commands is provided here for reference purposes. Refer to the on line manual page (man opc_backup) for further details.

SYNOPSIS

opc_backup [-c] [-d <dir>...] [-h] [-n] [-v] [<backup device>]

opc_recover

DESCRIPTION: The command opc_backup saves the HP OpenView Operations (OVO) environment. By default, opc_backup is used interactively but it can also be used non-interactively. The user can choose between two backup methods:

1. A full OVO backup. This saves the OVO and OpenView Installation, consisting of the whole OpenView directory tree and all data contained in the Oracle database openview. Note that parts which are not located in the /opt/OV or /var/opt/OV or /etc/opt/OV sub trees are not backed up. This means that the Oracle binaries are not backed up.
2. An OVO configuration backup only. This saves the entire ITO configuration, consisting of various ITO and OpenView configuration directories and all the data contained in the Oracle database openview. Note that a backup of the OpenView database includes both the currently active and the history messages. If you do not want to back up these messages to save space, acknowledge the active messages and download the history messages using the appropriate ITO administrator GUI functionality or the opchistdwn (1M) command before starting the backup.

Before running opc_backup, make sure that no ITO user interface or any other ITO processes are accessing the database.

The backup is written with the fbackup (1M) command. Symbolic links are NOT resolved, but saved as symbolic links.

The command opc_backup performs the following steps:

* If called in interactive mode, the user is asked for the backup method (full backup or configuration backup).
* Checks for running ITO GUI processes.
* If a full backup is applied and the management server acts as a managed node, the ITO agent processes are stopped. If the management server is in a clustered environment, you must make sure that no ITO agent process is running on any cluster client.
* Stops the OpenView platform services, the ITO server processes and any other OpenView integrated products, by using the ovstop (1m) command. Make sure that no processes access the database either directly or over SQL*Net or Net8, from any other system.
* Starts the SQL*Net or Net8 listener and the Oracle database, if they are not running.
* Extracts all Oracle files needed for a complete backup of the database. This includes the data files, redo log files and control files.
* Performs a shutdown of the Oracle instance.

* If called in interactive mode, the user is asked for additional directories, which should also be backed up. The user can also choose to back up other directories in addition to the ITO configuration and database directories (for example, the directory with the downloaded history messages). Note that symbolic links are not resolved, but are saved as symbolic links.
* Calculates and prints the approximate amount of free space needed for the backup on the backup device.
* If called in interactive mode, the user is asked for the destination to which the backup will be written. You can specify the device file of a tape drive or a file on disk. A device file is assumed, if the backup destination starts with /dev/.
* Writes the backup to the given destination, using the fbackup (1M) command.
* Restarts the Oracle instance.
* Restarts the OpenView platform services, the ITO server processes and any integrated products, by using ovstart (1m).
* If a full backup is applied and the management server system is a managed node, the ITO agent processes are restarted.

With opc_recover, you can restore any ITO configuration, which has been previously backed up using opc_backup. The recovery restores the saved ITO and OpenView directories and the openview database.

The opc_recover script performs the following steps:

* Asks the user whether the backup was applied with the full backup method or with the configuration backup method of opc_backup. (If a full backup was applied, the agent processes must be stopped and various directories must be cleared.)
* If a full backup is applied and the management server acts as a managed node, all ITO agent processes are stopped.

If the management server is in a clustered environment, you must make sure that no agent process is running on any cluster client.

* Stops the OpenView platform services, the ITO server processes and any other OpenView integrated products, by using the ovstop (1m) command.

Make sure that no processes access the database either directly or over SQL*Net or Net8, from any other system.

* Shuts down the Oracle instance and stops the SQL*Net or Net8 listener.
* Asks the user for the source from which the backup must be restored. It is possible to restore a backup from a tape or from a disk file.

If the backup is restored from tape, the user is asked for the device file of the tape drive.

If the backup is restored from disk, the user is asked for the path name of the file from which the backup must be restored.
* Asks the user if the backup should be run in verbose mode. If verbose mode is specified, the restore command, fbackup (1M), is called with the verbose option and displays all restored files.
* Clears the saved OpenView and ITO directories. This is to prevent inconsistencies between the information in the database and the information in the OpenView directories.
If you restore from a full ITO backup, the whole /opt/OV, /var/opt/OV and /etc/opt/OV directory trees are cleared.
If you restore from an ITO configuration backup, the following directories are cleared:

- /var/opt/OV/share/databases
- /etc/opt/OV/share/registration
- /etc/opt/OV/share/conf
- /var/opt/OV/share/tmp/OpC/mgmt_sv
- /var/opt/OV/share/tmp/OpC/distrib

* Restores the backed up directories:
* Restarts the Oracle database processes and the SQL*Net or Net8 listener.
* Restarts the OpenView platform services, the ITO server processes and any integrated products, by using ovstart (1m).
* If a full backup is applied and the management server acts as a managed node, the ITO agent processes are restarted.

FILES
/var/opt/OV/log/OpC/opcbkup.log
The transcript of the opc_backup script will also be written to this logfile. Each time opc_backup is called, it will be overwritten.

/tmp/opcrec.log
The transcript of the opc_recover script will also be written to this logfile. Each time opc_recover is called, it will be overwritten.

SEE ALSO
ORACLE Server - ADMINISTRATION, HP OpenView IT/Operations: Administrator's Reference, fbackup (1M), frecover (1M), opc_backup (5), opcdbreorg (1m), ovstart (1m), ovstop (1m), opc (5)

17.4.2.3 Online Backup with ovbackup.ovpl

The ovbackup.ovpl and ovrestore.ovpl programs make it possible to perform a backup while the OVO GUI and server processes are running. This method is sometimes called the "Hot Backup." This is accomplished by placing the OV processes in a temporarily (only takes a few seconds) paused state and copying the (memory resident, operational and analytical) data to disk. The backup includes the databases of both NNM and OVO configuration data, but not the OV software. Internally, the OVO backup scripts are called by the ovbackup.ovpl program. The OV backup scripts take advantage of Oracle online backup techniques (described in more detail in Chapter 18, "Oracle for OpenView").

17.5 CONFIGURATION DOWNLOAD

The configuration of the OVO environment is stored in tables in the Oracle database. The information is available for external programs such as reporting tools or performance tools. The information is also available for sharing with other OVO servers or for creating a backup server in the event, the primary server is unavailable.

17.5.1 Why Download the Configuration?

Download the configuration to create a backup server. This requires many pre-requisites that will be covered in Chapter 19, "Enterprise Management Flexibility with Multiple Management Servers." You can also download the configuration to save the data in the event that the database is recreated. The default database configuration is installed in the initial stage of configuring the management server. After the enterprise-specific components are configured, this information should be preserved for later use in case it becomes necessary to re-load the customized configuration. Another reason to download the configuration is in case you need to distribute or share parts of the configuration with another OVO server. For example, you might have created several templates that could be reused in another OVO domain.

17.5.2 What Can You Download?

You can download all or any part of the configuration that is stored in the OVO database. The configuration download user interface shown in Figure 17-2 shows what components can be selected. Use the OVO Administrator's GUI or the command **opccfgdwn** to download the components from the command line after you have created a "download spec file" from within the GUI. As an example, Figure 17-3 shows the selection of two templates.

The procedure to create the download specification file is performed within the GUI. Select the following menu items to launch the user interface: **Actions→Server→Download Configuration**.

Figure 17-2 Download Configuration Data window is used to select the specific components you want to download.

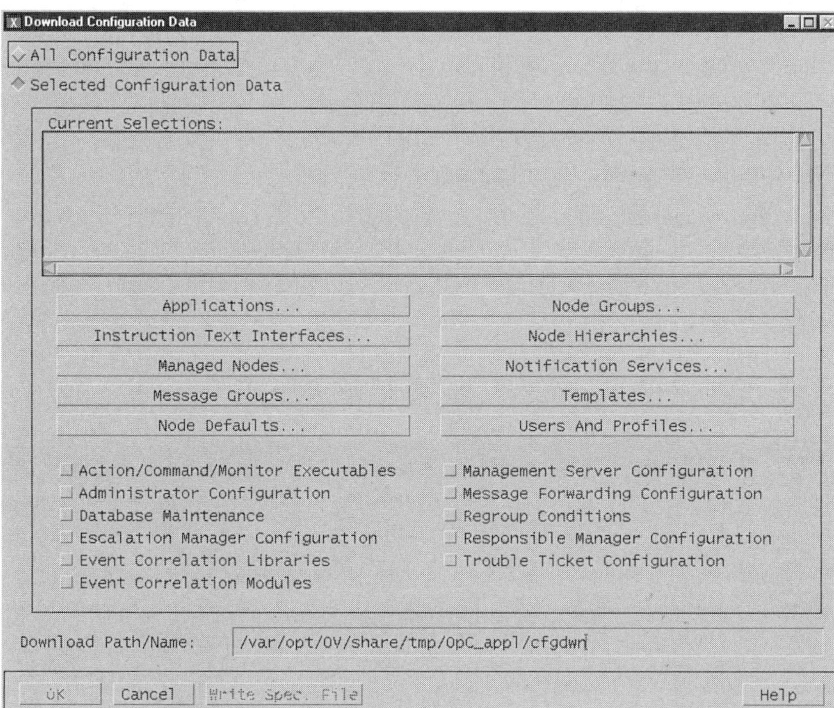

Figure 17-3 Configuration Download—the Components window shows the selection of two templates.

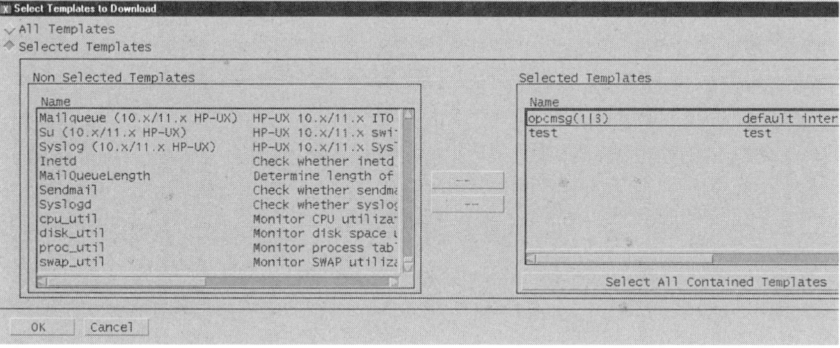

The configuration download window as shown in Figure 17-3 shows an option at the bottom of the window to write the configuration specification file. If this is selected, only the specification file is written to disk. The spec file contains the necessary format that represents the selected components of the configuration. Clicking OK will download the configuration right away. Alternately, after creating the specification file, you can use the **opccfgdwn** command at the command line.

17.5.3 Where Will the Downloaded Configuration End Up?

You specify where you want the download configuration files. The default location is /var/opt/OV/share/tmp/OpC_appl/cfgdwn. The default path is shown in Figure 17-4. The configuration download creates a download specification file (download.dsf) and a database index file in the download directory path.

Figure 17-4 Download selected components into the specified directory path.

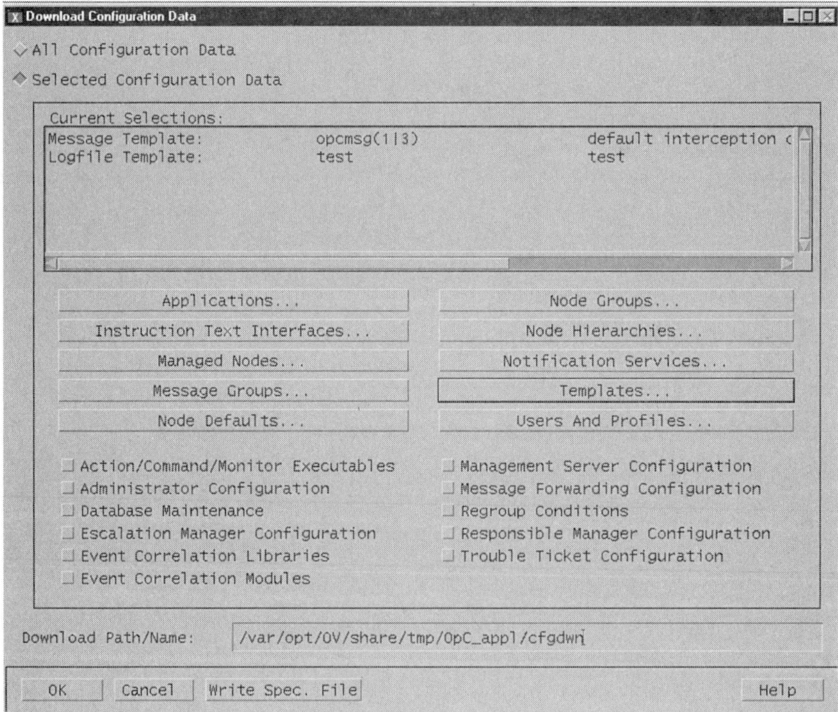

During the configuration download from the GUI, a terminal window is open to provide status, as shown in Figure 17-5.

Figure 17-5 Configuration Download Status window shows the progress of the download process.

```
ITO Download Configuration
+ verifying target filetree
+ parsing download specification file "/var/opt/OV/share/tmp/OpC_appl/cfgdwn/download.dsf"
+ starting download
+  of selected configuration data
 + reading logfile templates from DB
 + downloading template "test"
 + reading interface templates from DB
 + downloading template "opcmsg(1|3)"
+ opccfgdwn finished
Warning:
   Since not 'All Configuration Data' was selected for the download, the
   upload may result in unexpected database contents.
   Try 'man 1m opccfgdwn' for details.

press return:
```

The following listing shows the results of the configuration download into the cfgdwn directory. A subdirectory and the download specification file are created.

```
# ls -l
total 2
drwx——    3 root        sys                  96 Aug  7 22:27 C
-rw-r—r—   1 root        opcgrp               61 Aug  7 22:27 down-
load.dsf
```

This listing shows the contents of a download.dsf specification file:

```
# more download.dsf
INTERFACE_TEMPLATE "opcmsg(1|3)" ;
LOGFILE_TEMPLATE "test" ;
download.dsf: END
```

Looking inside the "C" directory, we find the database index file cfgdwn.idx. You also see the TEMPLATES directory that contains the components of the download. The "C" directory listing is shown here:

```
# ls -lR
total 2
drwx—— 4 root sys       96 Aug  7 22:27 TEMPLATES
-rw——- 1 root sys      440 Aug  7 22:27 cfgdwn.idx

./TEMPLATES:
total 0
drwx—— 2 root sys       96 Aug  7 22:27 INTERFACE
drwx—— 2 root sys       96 Aug  7 22:27 LOGFILE

./TEMPLATES/INTERFACE:
total 4
```

```
-rw——- 1 root   sys     1971 Aug  7 22:27 interface.dat

./TEMPLATES/LOGFILE:
total 2
-rw——- 1 root   sys      739 Aug  7 22:27 logfile.dat
```

17.5.4 How Can You Distribute the Downloaded Configuration?

Prior to jumping right into our discussion on how to distribute a downloaded configuration, let us step back and consider why this process is necessary. One of the reasons you would download the configuration is to ensure that you have a current snapshot of the OpenView server environment. The configuration takes time and resources to set up and you can protect this investment if you take periodic snapshots of the environment as it evolves. The configuration download is one component of the management server environment. Other aspects of the environment were discussed earlier in this chapter. Another reason for performing a configuration download is to keep multiple management server configurations in sync. If you distribute the management and monitoring tasks performed by OVO across multiple servers, any one server could take over for another server in the event of failure. This is possible provided that you are regularly synchronizing the configuration across the servers. In the rest of this section, we discuss the details of the configuration download process.

Use the command **opcmgrdist** on the primary server to distribute the downloaded configuration to the secondary server(s). This assumes that you have set up the second management server(s) to receive the configuration. The steps for this include the following:

- Add the primary server to the node bank and a node group on the secondary server as message allowed.
- Add the secondary server to the node bank and node group on the primary server as message allowed.
- Download the configuration use the GUI or the **opccfgdwn** command.
- Transfer the configuration directory tree (from the primary server) to the configuration directory tree on the secondary server using ftp or rcp or by using the command **opcmgrdist**.
- The configuration could be transferred using the command **opcmgrdist** and specifying the name of the secondary server.
- If you transfer the configuration to the secondary server using the command **opcmgrdist**, a message to confirm the distribution will arrive in the browser on the secondary server.
- The secondary server will get a notification message but the configuration is not automatically uploaded.
- Now follow the steps to upload the configuration as discussed in the next section.

17.6 CONFIGURATION UPLOAD

Configuration upload of the OVO environment is performed using from the command line with **opccfgupld**. There is no GUI interface to perform this task. The command line options will determine if you overwrite the existing configuration (-replace), append to the existing components (-add), or add only new conditions to a template (-subentity).

17.6.1 What Are the Prerequisites for Configuration Upload?

The procedure to upload configuration components is as follows:

1. Stop the OVO management server processes and exit the Administrator GUI if you are uploading any configuration data other than just templates or template groups.
2. Upload the configuration with the command **opccfgupld** from the location of the configuration.
3. After successfully uploading the configuration, restart the OVO server processes if necessary.
4. Restart the Administrator GUI.
5. If necessary, assign and distribute the new components to the managed nodes or assign to the operator.

17.6.2 What If You Only Want to Upload Part of the Configuration?

The following list shows examples of using the **opccfgupld** command. The examples assume that the file tree containing the configuration has already been created by using the **opccfgdwn** command from the Administrator GUI or from the command line. The configuration file tree is assumed to reside in the directory /var/opt/OV/share/tmp/OpC_appl/newConf.

1. Uploading in Add Mode (Default). The file tree in this example contains configuration information for two templates. If one of the templates already exists, it is not overwritten. /opt/OV/bin/OpC/opccfgupld /var/opt/OV/share/tmp/OpC_appl/newConf.
2. Uploading in Replace Mode. Even if the template exists, it is overwritten. /opt/OV/bin/OpC/opccfgupld –replace /var/opt/OV/share/tmp/Opc_appl/newConf.
3. Uploading and adding at the sub-entity level. Assume that a template already has three conditions and you need to add two more conditions sent from an external source. In this case, you should append the new conditions to the end of the existing template. /opt/OV/bin/OpC/opccfgupld –add –subentity /var/opt/OV/share/tmp/OpC_appl/ newConf.

17.6.3 How Can You Create a Backup Server?

Creating a backup server assumes that you have replicated the hardware and software components of the OpenView management platform. This configuration concept is used to provide a backup server for the managed nodes to send their message in the event of failure of the primary OV server. This configuration is covered in more detail in Chapter 19.

17.7 HISTORY DOWNLOAD

The information stored inside the history messages tables in the database will grow without bounds. In other words, it will grow until the database tablespace can no longer be extended because no space is left on the filesystem for automatic extent allocation. In order to avoid this situation or to simply perform housecleaning on the tables, the history download utility is available. Use the command **opchistdwn** to download the configuration periodically. The command **opchistupl** restores the records from a prior **opchistdwn**.

17.7.1 What Is the Process to Download the History Information?

Working from inside the Administrator GUI, select **Actions→Utilities→Database Maintenance**. Figure 17-6 shows the fields that you can fill in to instruct the system and to download the data from the history tables (the section marked History Log). The information can be downloaded on a regular schedule if you provide the time, day, and directory information. You also specify how much data to download. You enter your choice of records; for example, older than 1 day, 1 week, or 30 days. Here we mean extract, because the records are removed from the database tables.

Figure 17-6 The Database Maintenance window us used to perform database maintenance.

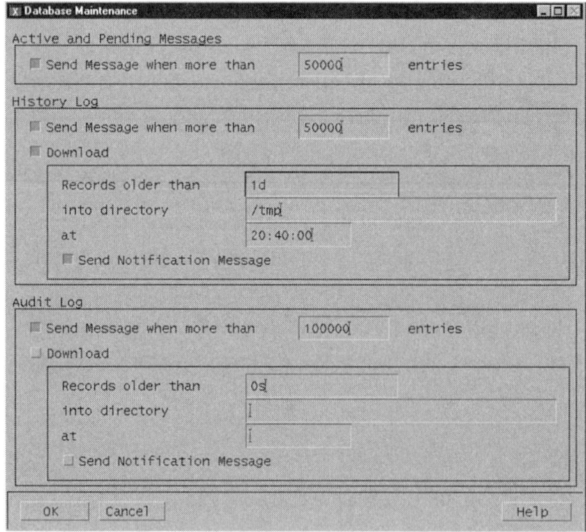

17.8 AUDITING

Periodic system audits may be necessary as part of an enterprise-wide security policy. There are features built into most operating systems to enable a system administrator to perform this task. OpenView has a feature for auditing activities performed while operating within the OV application environment. The audit data can also be downloaded with the command opcauddwn or uploaded with the command opcaudupl. We will discuss this in more detail in Chapter 20, "Security."

17.9 REPORTING

Generate reports from the Administrator or Operators user interface by selecting Reports from the Utility menu. The data for the reports is gathered from the Oracle database by using SQL statements. The reports are formatted and presented in an easy to read format inside a display window. There is no way to control the format or the information within the report because these details are included in the SQL script that collects the data. The report interface allows you to save the report to a file or print to a printer. The reports generated for an Operator are different from those available for an administrator.

You can modify the report layout or add your own reports by modifying or adding your own SQL scripts to the directory /etc/opt/OV/share/conf/OpC/mgmt_sv/reports/C. For modifications, it is recommended that you should copy an existing report to a new file. After doing so, or when adding completely new report scripts, make sure to add them to the oper.rpts and/or admin.rpts configuration files so they will be accessible from the user interface by the respective user categories.

17.9.1 Operator Reports

Look at the reports available for an operator and how the operator generates the report. Figure 17.7 shows the list of reports available for an operator. The operator activates the report interface from the message browser menu. Select **Actions→Utilities→Reports**.

The Operator selects one report from the list. Selecting Apply generates the report in a separate window, as shown in Figure 17-8.

It is possible to use the default reports as a baseline to create your own reports. Use standard structured query language (SQL) or edit the report file to build reports that are unique to your environment. The default operator report file (oper.rpts) is located in the directory /etc/opt/OV/share/conf/OpC/mgmt_sv/reports/C.

Figure 17-7 Operator Reports provide operator's with quick reports about the OVO run-time environment.

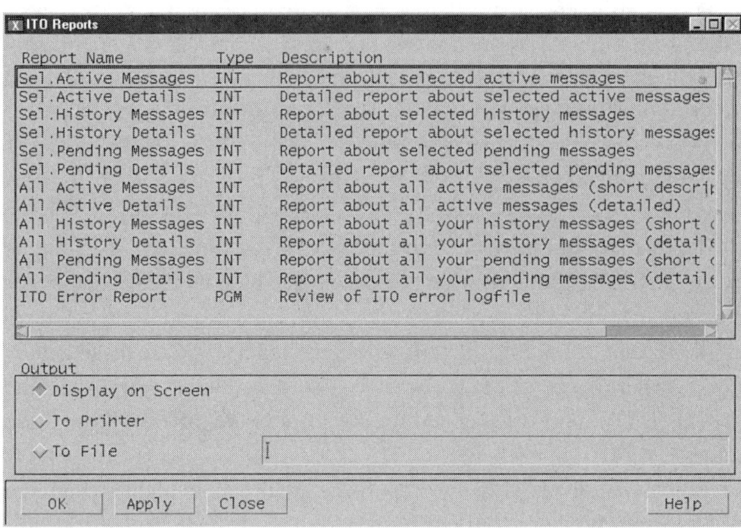

Figure 17-8 Operator report about a selected active message is a report about the messages shown in the Message Browser.

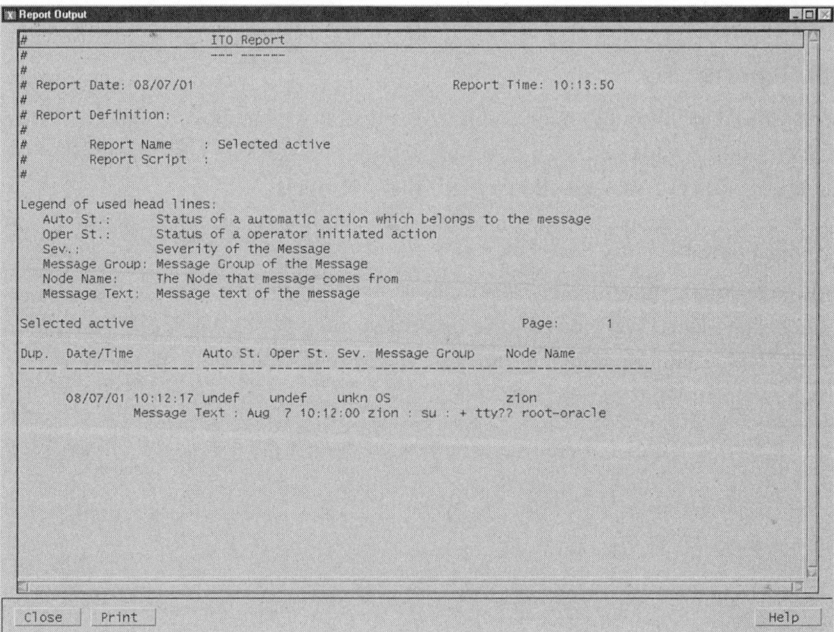

17.9.2 Administrator Reports

The reports available for an Administrator include reports about operators' activities, configuration of templates, and messages, as shown in Figure 17-9. The Administrator generates a report from the Node Bank Menu by selecting **Actions→Utilities→Reports**.

Figure 17-9 Administrator reports contain information about the run-time environment for the OVO system administrator.

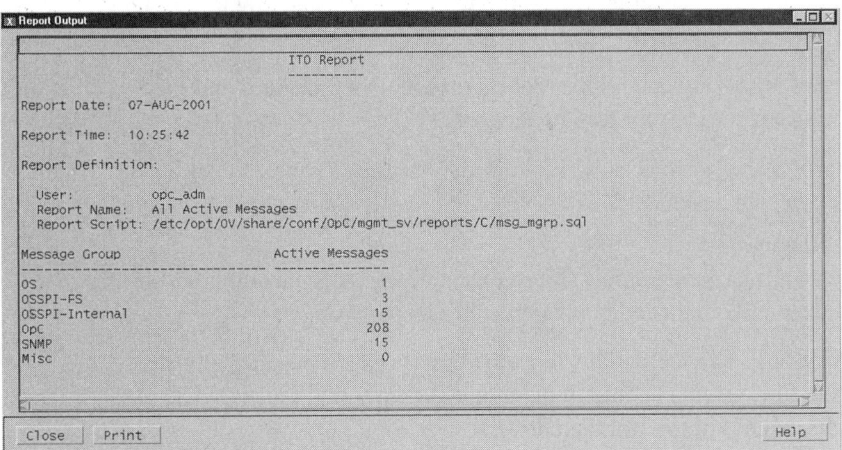

It is possible to use the default reports as a baseline to create your own administrator reports. Use SQL or edit the report file to build reports that are unique to your environment. The default report file (admin.rpts) for the operator is located in the directory /etc/opt/OV/share/conf/OpC/mgmt_sv/reports/C.

17.9.3 External Report Programs

External applications, such as OpenView Reporter, can create reports from data stored in the OV Oracle database. The OV ReportER product requires a separate license and installs on a Windows platform. During the configuration of OV Reporter, you decide which management server database to use for the reports. Integrated OpenView applications such as Smart Plug-Ins or OV Storage Area Manager provide custom reporting facilities to provide information for their specific environments. Refer to the product documentation for details on the integration with OV Reporter. Further enhanced and customized reports are available with the addition of Seagate Crystal Reports®. (OV Report contains and uses Crystal Reports.) The advantages of using the external report tools include customization, portability, and publishing the reports via the web. Additional information about OpenView Reporter is found at `http://docs.hp.com/HP-UXHP-UX/onlinedocs/netsys/OV_ReporterConcepts.pdf`.

17.9.4 Sample Reports from OV Storage Area Manager

Several report categories and a description of three reports from each category are shown here. There are more reports available in each category. Consult the OVSAM documentation for report integration details. Also, refer to the documentation that comes with the OV Storage Area Manager SPI.

- **Inventory Reports**
  Inventory of Hosts—This report lists the managed hosts and their attributes discovered in the storage network..

  Inventory of NAS Devices—This reports lists the NAS devices and their attributes discovered in the storage network..

  Inventory of Storage Devices—This reports lists the storage devices and their attributes discovered.
- **Capacity Reports**
  Capacity of Hosts—This report summarizes the capacity information for the file systems on the managed hosts in the storage network.

  Capacity of NAS Devices—This report summarizes the capacity information for the file systems visible to the managed hosts that are on NAS devices discovered in the storage network.

  Capacity of Storage Devices—This report summarizes the capacity information on storage devices discovered in the storage network.
- **Customer-Based Reports**
  Capacity of NAS Devices—By customer, this report summarizes the capacity information for the file systems visible to the managed hosts that are on NAS devices discovered in the storage network.

  Capacity of Storage Devices—By customer, this report summarizes the capacity information on storage devices discovered in the storage network.

  Capacity of Volumes—By customer, this report summarizes the capacity information for the file systems contained on managed hosts and NAS devices discovered in the storage network.

17.10 UTILITIES AND CONTRIBUTED TOOLS

There are many tools and utilities provided with the OpenView platform that will help the OV administrator perform analysis and troubleshooting tasks.

17.10.1 Utility Programs

The utility programs are located in the directory /opt/OV/bin/OpC/utils. The programs in the utils directory are listed in Table 17-1 with a brief description of each for reference. Usage examples of some of the utilities immediately follow the table.

Table 17-1 OVO Utilities

<table>
<tr><th>Program Name</th><th>Usage Options</th><th>Description</th></tr>
<tr><td>ecsmgr</td><td></td><td>ECS correlation engine manager. ecsmgr can be used to alter the correlation engine's configuration.</td></tr>
<tr><td>inst_usr.sh</td><td></td><td>Check and install ITO user
on UNIX systems.</td></tr>
<tr><td>opc_time_diff</td><td>[file1] [file2] threshold or
–t [file1] [file2]</td><td>Prints filename exceeding threshold time difference (in min). Option -t prints the time difference in minutes; File2 should be the newer one.</td></tr>
<tr><td>opcecsact</td><td><ACK|CORRIND|SHOW
CORR> <message_id>
[,message_id]</td><td>Handles the action for ECS SNMP traps. The first parameter defines the action:
CORRIND: Attaches an annotation to indicate that the event has correlated child events.
SHOWCORR: Retrives the correlation tree of child events for a given parent event.
The second parameter must be a message ID or a list of message IDs.</td></tr>
<tr><td>opcerr
error</td><td>opcerr -h | <errcode>

[<errcode>...]</td><td>Gets details and instructions for an ITO

message.</td></tr>
<tr><td>opcgetcorrevts</td><td>opcgetcorrevts <msgid></td><td>See also the man page opcgetcorrevts(1M).
vdumpevents(1M)</td></tr>
<tr><td>opcnls</td><td></td><td>Check for a valid agent codeset.</td></tr>
<tr><td>opcnode</td><td>-add_node | -del_node
| -chg_commtype | -list_nodes
| -add_group | -del_group
| -list_ass_nodes | -list_groups |
-assign_templ|-deassign_templ
| -list_ass_templs | -list_templs |
-assign_node | -deassign_node
Attributes:
node_name=<node_name>
node_label=<node_label>
group_name=<nodegrp_name>
group_label=<group_label>
net_type=<network_type>
mach_type=<machine_type>
comm_type=<comm_type>
node_list='<list>'
templ_type=<templ_type></td><td>Maintains nodes, node groups and template assignments.
See also the man page opcnode (1M).</td></tr>
</table>

opcpat	[-h] [-i] [-q] [-fp <patternfile>] [-fv <valuefile>] [-o <outfile>]	Test program for ITO pattern matching. See also the man page opcpat(1).
opcseldist		Controls the distribution of selected files in the actions|cmds|monitors directories on the management server to selected managed nodes. An example of using the selective distribution command for only allowing distribution of the required Smart Plug-in binaries that is actually required on each node.
opcsvcdcode		
opcsvnls	opcsvnls [-c] [-l] [-t] [-o <codeset>] -c : get codeset for locale -l : get language for locale -o <cset>: get locale for codeset -v <cset>:check if <codeset> is a valid ITO codeset -k <cset1> <cset2>:check compatiblity -d : dump internal tables	Determines language of ITO manage ment server.
opctempl	opctempl { -get <templ_name> <templ_type> <file> } |{ -add <file> } | { -modify ~<file> }	Maintains templates in files. See also the man page opctempl (1M). Restrictions: This command can only be issued by the root user. To enable other users to execute this command, the system administrator must change the file's attributes and copy it to a location which is included in the variable.
ovtrap2opc	ovtrap2opc <trapd_conf_file> <template_name> <application>	Converts trapd.conf file and uploads it into database. See also the man page ovtrap2opc (1M). See also opccfgupld(1M) and trapd.conf (4)
submit.sh	submit.sh	Generates test message for OVO.

See also HP OpenView IT/Operations: ITO Administrator's Guide to Online Information and man opc(5).

17.10.1.1 Utility Programs Usage Examples

- opcerr OpC10-001—Gets details and instructions for an ITO error message.
- opcnode -add_node node_name=fancy.ben.kape.com \ net_type=NETWORK_IP mach_type=MACH_HP11_PA_RISC \ group_name=hp_ux—Adds the HP-UX 11.0 node fancy.ben.kape.com with network type IP and assigns it to the node group hp_ux.
- opcnode -assign_template -templ_name="HP-UX 10.x/11.x"\ templ_type=TEMPLATE_GROUP node_name=fancy.ben.kape.com \ net_type=NETWORK_IP—Assigns a template group to a node.

- opcnode -chg_commtype node_list="fancy.ben.kape.com server.ben.kape.com" \ comm_type=COMM_DCE_TCP—Changes the node communication type.
- opcnode -list_ass_nodes group_name=hp_ux—Lists all nodes, which are assigned to the node group hp_ux.
- ovtrap2opc /etc/opt/OV/share/conf/C/trapd.conf "SNMP Traps" snmptraps.

17.10.2 Contributed Tools

The contributed (unsupported) tools are located in the directory /opt/OV/contrib/OpC. The programs in the contrib directory are listed in Table 17-2 with a brief description of each for reference. Usage examples of some of the tools are found in other chapters. For example, **opc_odc**, which creates a report about the database configuration is found in Chapter 18. Another tool **itochecker** is covered in more detail in Chapter 22, "Troubleshooting Tools and Techniques."

Table 17-2 Server (S) and Agent (A) Contributed Tools

Program Name	Usage	Description
opcchgaddr	S	Changes the node address in the OVO database See also man page opcchgaddr (1M).
opc_reset_ports	S	Resets the port range in the database to the default value.
opcsvctemplchk	S	Identifies comma-separated service names within templates or conditions. Comma-separated service names within templates and conditions are not supported with VPO A.06.00 or OVO A.07.00.
win_logpath_set	S	Sets the logpath of Windows managed nodes to /usr/OV/log/OpC; with VPO A.6.00 and OVO A.07.00 the node name in the logpath is no longer supported.
opccfgtest	S	Checks if the APIs are working correctly. For use by HP support only.
itochecker	S	Checks many aspects of your system and writes reports that can be sent to the support center. See also man page itochecker (1M).
itosend	S	Mails the itochecker results to HP listguis.
checkuiwww	S	Checks for open GUI connections. Checks both Motif and Java GUI connections.
lsof	S	Prints a list of all open files. This is an OpenSource utility needed by listguis. You need a dedicated version for each OS version. See also `ftp://vic.cc.purdue.edu/pub/tools/unix/lsof`.
opcdbck	S	Checks the database tables for consistency. See also the README file in the contrib. Directory.
opc.checkfile	S	Opcdbck configuraton file.
opc_odc	S	Collects information about the database configuration. The data collected is written to an output file /tmp/opc_odc.log.

Table 17-2 Server (S) and Agent (A) Contributed Tools

Program Name	Usage	Description
opcsrvtst	S	Shows nodes of this server along with info from opc.hosts.
lb_admin	S	NCS support tool. (Solaris Server only.)
stacktrace	S	Analyzes core files.
opcdfchk	A	Checks the agent buffer file. For use by HP support only.
opcsystst	A	Checks network configuration.
opcrpccp	A	Manages the name server use for RPC applications.
opcqchk	A	Dumps the contents of a message queue.
lb_admin	A	NCS support tool. (Solaris, Pyramid, Olivetti, OSF, SCO, Dynix, NCR, Irix, SINIX.)
stacktrace_agt	A	Analyzes core files to find out the function stack trace. It's only available on HP-UX agents for now. The tool is the same, as on the server, it only has to be installed with a different name to avoid problems while de-installing the agent.

View the contents of the contrib. directory via the web: `http://<mgmt_svr>:3443/ITO/index.html`
Also, refer to the README file located in the directory /opt/OV/contrib./OpC.
The location of the contributed tools by vendor platform:
HP-UX:/opt/OV/contrib./OpC
NT:/usr/OV/contrib./OpC
AIX:/usr/lpp/contrib./OpC
OSF:/usr/opt/OV/contrib./OpC

17.11 SUMMARY

There are many system administration tasks covered within this chapter. The information helps new OVO system administrators define the scope of work for operating and maintaining a new OpenView enterprise management environment. Experienced administrators should find resources and techniques that add to existing system management toolkits. The next chapter covers the OVO database environment.

CHAPTER 18

Oracle for OpenView

The Oracle database is the central repository for the OpenView Operations. The database is part of the overall OpenView systems management environment. After the operating system is installed and configured for OpenView, you can begin the installation of *Oracle for OpenView* (OfO) or the Enterprise Edition of Oracle. Installation of OfO was covered in Chapter 13, "Out-of-the-box with OpenView Operations." The product installation follows a standard procedure for installation of an Oracle database. An order for HP OpenView Operations for UNIX does not include the product OfO. OfO must be ordered separately. The installation procedure for OfO is documented in the *OpenView Operations Installation Guide* (refer to Appendix C, "Resources," for more information on the documentation). Post-installation of the database, install the OpenView application software components (which include NNM), then execute the database configuration script (opcconfig) for the OpenView environment. During the run-time operations process, applications, scripts, and users interact with the database. The user interface provides the primary connectivity required for database interaction. Database transactions performed through the GUI occur transparent to the operator. External applications and scripts also cause transactions to occur within the database. For example, a report request from within the OpenView GUI (**Actions →Utilities→Reports**) calls for the execution of an SQL script (provided with OpenView) to query the database; collect, format, and present the data in a display window; and save the report to disk or send the report to a printer. This is one example of how the user is allowed to interact with the database transparently. Other interactions with the database may require direct access via the command line.

In some enterprise environments, the OpenView System Administrator is responsible for the role of Database Administrator. The responsibilities of a Database Administrator are similar to the role of a system administrator. The similar tasks include: database backup; add, modify, and delete user accounts; customize scripts to enable users interact with the database transparently; monitor database performance; and install, upgrade, and apply patches as required. In companies that use databases throughout the enterprise, Database Administrators take the responsibility for managing OfO. This ensures a consistent approach to database management across the enterprise.

The OpenView Administrator should learn as much as possible about Oracle for OpenView. This chapter is just a beginning. The sections presented provide an overview of the database environment. Details about the OpenView Operations database help you become familiar with the concepts and terms necessary to successfully interact with the system, peers, and DBA colleagues.

18.1 DATABASE TERMINOLOGY

- **Archive log mode**—Keep copies of all transactions from the redo logs.
- **Cold backup**—Shuts down the database prior to performing a backup.
- **Control file**—Used to test the database integrity during startup.
- **Database**—Program that manipulates one or more data files.
- **Data dictionary**—Tables and views that are a read-only database reference.
- **Data warehouse**—Repository of data about related objects.
- **Hot backup**—Database is running while performing a backup.
- **Instance**—A set of server processes that has its own *Shared Global Area* (SGA), an area of shared memory.
- **Index**—Mini copy of table entries used for rapid access to the data.
- **Non-arvhive log mode**—No save of redo log before it is overwritten.
- **Redo logs**—Keep track of database changes.
- **System Identifier (SID)**—Identifies each database interface.
- **Table**—A database object that holds the data.
- **Tablespace**—A collection of one or more datafiles.
- **Transaction**—Sequence of SQL statements that manipulate the database.
- **View** —A custom presentation of the database table information.
- **Import and export**—Used to perform logical backup and recovery of database objects. Allows extraction of database objects into flat files that can be stored or moved to another database.

18.2 DATABASE STRUCTURES

The general database has three types of environments (referred to as structures or components), including physical, logical, and memory resident. These structures combine to provide the run-time database environment sometimes referred to generically as the database instance.

18.2.1 Logical Components

- **Schema**—A collection of database objects owned by a database user. The schema objects include database structures like tales, views, and indexes.
- **Table**—Contains rows and columns and holds the data.
- **Views**—A customized query of the database that presents data from one or more tables or other views.
- **Index**—Speed up the data retrieval from tables. Similar to the index of a book.

- **Clusters**—Groups of tables that are physically stored together, share common columns, and are used together.
- **Data block**—Corresponds to the bytes of physical space on the disk. This is the finest granularity of data storage.
- **Extents**—An allocation of contiguous data blocks.
- **Segments**—A set of extents allocated for specific use within the logical structure of the database. Segment types include data, index, temporary, and rollback.
- **Tablespace**—A group of related structures that are allocated as a (tablespace) storage unit. The tablespace contains one or more datafiles. The size of the datafile determines the size of the tablespace. The combined storage capacity of the tablespaces determines the total storage capacity of the database.
- **Other**—There are other logical database structures, such partitions, sequences, roles, privileges, snapshots, triggers, packages, functions and links, that are not covered in this section because they are part of the standard database environment.

18.2.2 Physical Components

- **Datafiles**—Data storage containers assigned to the tablespace. Data in the datafile are read as needed during normal database operation and stored in memory buffers.
- **Redo log files**—Record all changes made to the data. Used for database recovery. Redo log files are overwritten regularly.
- **Control files**—Contain information about the physical structure and status of the database (such as database name, names and locations of the datafiles and redo log files). Control files are critical to the operation of the database.
- **Archive log files**—Store the database transactions (copied from the redo log files) in the event that database recovery becomes necessary.
- **Parameter file**—Used during database startup to allocate and designate storage buffers and file locations and to assign run time database environment variables.
- **Trace files**—Designated files that capture database process information.

18.2.3 Memory Components

- **Shared Global Area (SGA)**—Shared by all database server processes and client processes and includes the following memory structures: shared pool (dictionary cache and shared SQL cache), database buffer, redo log buffer, and java pool.
- **Program Global Area (PGA)** — Used by single Oracle server process to contain the sort area, session information, cursor state, and stack space.
- **Shared Pool**—Stores data dictionary and shared SQL areas.

- **Data dictionary cache**—Contains table and column definitions and user privilege information.
- **Library cache** —Stores information about the most recently used SQL statements (statement text, parse code and execution plan).
- **Database buffer cache**—Stores the most recently used blocks of database data.
- **Rollback segment (called Undo segment in Oracle 9.i**)—Like tables and indexes, rollback segments exist in data files and parts of them are brought into the database buffer cache when required. Before making any change, the server process saves the old value into a rollback segment. This information is used to undo changes if a transaction is rolled back, ensure that other transactions to not see uncommitted changes, and recover the database to a consistent state in case of failures.
- **Redo log buffer**—Stores log changes made to the database. The redo entries are written to the redo log file, which is used if recovery becomes necessary. Records changes made through the instance: the block that changed, the location of the change, and the new value. Circular buffer: it is reused after it is filled up, but only after all the old redo entries are recorded in the redo log files.

18.2.4 User Processes

The user process is started when the users requests an OpenView session. The user process exits when the user session terminates. User processes facilitate user transactions with the database and sends calls to the dedicated server process. For example, **opcuiwww** is a JAVA client (user) process.

18.2.5 Dedicated Server Processes

Dedicated server processes run on the management server and provide services for the OpenView user process. The dedicated server uses an exclusive PGA. For example, oraopenview is a dedicated server process.

18.2.6 Background Processes

The processes shown here make up the database server processes. They must run continuously, otherwise OVO cannot connect to the database. Start or stop the processes with the script /sbin/init.d/ovoracle start (or stop).

- **Database writer (dbwr)**—Writes to datafile, database buffer cache, redo log buffer, and undo segments.
- **Log writer (lgwr)**—Flushes the redo log buffers when and update or commit are executed.
- **Checkpoint (chkp)**—Synchronizes the three major database files and removes uncommitted data from the data file.
- **System monitor (smon)**—Used to clean/free up server resources, such as locks, after a database crash.
- **Process monitor (pmon)**—Cleans up client resource files (for example, after a user process terminates).

- **Archiver (arch)**—Copies the online redo log files to the archival log file.
- **Dispatcher**—(optional) Presents only when shared server configuration is used. Responsible for routing requests from connected user process to shared server processes and returning responses back the user processes.
- **Recoverer (reco)**—(optional) Resolves distributed transactions that are pending to a network or system failure in a distributed database.
- **Listener**—Responsible for receiving incoming client connection requests and directing them to the appropriate service.

18.3 ENVIRONMENT VARIABLES

During database installation and session startup, the environment variables tell the database where to find important information and define system parameters required for database operations. The environment variables follow the version of the database and are subject to change.

18.3.1 User Environment

The variables are defined by the user before database installation in the root users and oracle users profiles located in the user's home directory. The list below shows the common variables set for the OpenView database:

ORACLE_TERM—Preferred terminal type

ORACLE_BASE—Path for Oracle data

ORACLE_HOME—Location of Oracle software

ORACLE_SID—Instance name

NLS_LANG—Character set

SHLIB_PATH—Path to shared libraries

PATH—Path includes Oracle binaries

An example listing from the root users profile is shown here:

```
export ORACLE_BASE=/opt/oracle
export ORACLE_HOME=$ORACLE_BASE/product/9.2.0
export ORACLE_SID=openview
export ORACLE_TERM=ansi
export SHLIB_PATH=$ORACLE_HOME/lib32
export NLS_LANG=american_america.WE8ISO8859P15
export PATH=$PATH:$ORACLE_HOME/bin
```

18.4 DATABASE FILES AND DIRECTORY LOCATIONS

Oracle recommends following a standard called *Optimal Flexible Architecture* (OFA) for installation, configuration, location, naming and layout of the database objects, files and directories.

OFA is designed to:

- Organize large amounts of complicated software and data on disk to avoid device bottlenecks and poor performance
- Facilitate routine administrative tasks, such as software and data backup, which are often vulnerable to data corruption
- Facilitate switching between multiple Oracle databases
- Adequately manage and administer database growth
- Help eliminate fragmentation of free space in the data dictionary, isolate other fragmentation, and minimize resource contention

Refer to Appendix C, "Resources," for more information on OFA.

The installation of the database files follows the environment variables configured before installation of the database. During installation, a check to confirm the location of the files is performed. The following directories are under the directory path $ORACLE_HOME/product/<db_version>:

Bin—Binary for all products

Dbs—Database files, init<SID>.ora, and sql.bsq script

Lib—Oracle product libraries

Orainst—Installation files and programs

Rdbms—Server files, scripts, and libraries required for the database

Plsql—PL/SQL, procedural option

Sqlplus—SQL*Plus

Network—Oracle Net8 (in version 8.X)/SQL*Net (in version 7.x)

Svrmgrl—Server Manager

Admin—Administrative scripts

Demo—Demonstration scripts and data files

Doc—README files

Install—Product installation scripts

Lib—Product libraries

Log—Log files

18.5 DATABASE STARTUP AND SHUTDOWN

The database startup and shutdown scripts are located in the standard system location for startup at system boot time. If it becomes necessary to stop or restart the database after system boot utilize execute the scripts or commands at the command line.

18.5.1 Automatic Database Startup and Shutdown

At system boot time, the database startup is controlled by two configuration variables (ORACLE and LISTENER) located in the file /etc/rc.config.d/ovoracle. If the variable is equal to 1 (one), the database will startup. If the variable is equal to 0 (zero), the database will not startup. The script that executes the database startup commands is /sbin/init.d/ovoracle (/etc/init.d/ovoracle on Solaris). The database startup occurs in sequence based on the sequence numbers assigned to the ovoracle link files in the directories /sbin/rc3.d for startup sequence and /sbin/rc1.d for the shutdown/sequence. Also, the file /etc/oratab can start or prevent database startup.

Depending on user response to the automatic database startup question during the OVO server installation, the value of the Oracle database and listener process startup variables will be set to 0 or 1. If the database does not start automatically, you must make sure that it is started using some other mechanism before starting the OVO server.

18.5.2 Manual Database Startup and Shutdown

Manual database stop or restart sometimes becomes necessary. One reason for this would be to configure the database for archive log mode or after making changes to the parameter (initialization) file. The commands to stop the database are executed by the privileged user oracle. The following example demonstrates the commands to login to the database and perform a manual shutdown:

```
# su - oracle
$ sqlplus
SQL*Plus: Release 9.2.0.2.0 - Production on Sat Jan 10 12:34:53
2004

Copyright © 1982, 2002, Oracle Corporation.  All rights
reserved.
Enter user-name: system
Enter password:
Connected to:
Oracle9i Enterprise Edition Release 9.2.0.2.0 - 64bit Production
JServer Release 9.2.0.2.0 - Production
SQL> connect sys/<password> as sysdba
Connected.
SQL> shutdown
Database closed.
```

```
Database dismounted.
ORACLE instance shut down.
SQL> startup
ORACLE instance started.

Total System Global Area  267479512 bytes
Fixed Size                   735704 bytes
Variable Size             184549376 bytes
Database Buffers           81920000 bytes
Redo Buffers                 274432 bytes
Database mounted.
Database opened.
```

18.5.2.1 Database Shutdown Command Line Options

- **Shutdown (no options)**—The execution of the **shutdown** command stops the database, provided that there are no processes connected to the database and or outstanding transactions. If executed with processes connected the command will hang indefinitely.
- **Shutdown normal**—Same as shutdown; wait for all users to disconnect. During shutdown, no new user connections are accepted. The database and redo log buffers are flushed to disk. Physical files are synchronized. The normal shutdown does not require instance recovery when the database restarts.
- **Shutdown transactional**—Same as shutdown normal, except all users are disconnected after their current transactions complete.
- **Shutdown immediate**—Current sessions are terminated and all users are logged off, current transactions are rolled back. No new user login sessions are accepted. The database and redo log buffers are flushed to disk. The physical files are synchronized. No instance recovery is required when the database restarts.
- **Shutdown abort**—Terminate current sessions and log off all users. Accept no new request for login. Buffer cache is not flushed to disk. Physical files are not synchronized. Active transactions are not rolled back. Instance recovery is required when the database restarts. This may become necessary if the database is deadlocked and the shutdown immediate does not work. If this becomes necessary, you need to perform the following steps to bring the database back to a consistent state: shutdown abort, startup, and shutdown.

18.6 DATABASE QUERIES

Oracle uses a *structured query language* (SQL) to enable you to search the database objects and gather the information you need. The format of the database statements follows a specific syntax that includes the command, object, and source table from which to extract the data. In order to extract the data using SQL, you could execute a pre-existing script, write a script that contains the SQL statements you need, or execute the SQL statement at the database command line.

18.6.1 Basics of Writing SQL Statements

The following is true of SQL statements:

- Begin at the SQL prompt
- Can be entered on one or more lines
- Line wraps are indicated with a number at the beginning of the continued line
- Are not case sensitive, unless indicated
- Clauses are usually placed on separate lines for readability and editing
- Tabs and indents can be used to make the code more readable
- Keywords cannot be split across lines or abbreviated
- Keywords typically are entered in uppercase
- All other words, such as table names and columns, are lowercase
- One statement can be entered at a time for processing
- End with semicolon
- Choose the rows in a table
- Choose the columns in a table
- Select data from multiple tables

18.6.2 Examples of Database Queries using SQL

Login to the database. Use the **sqlplus** command to execute several SQL statements:

```
# sqlplus
SQL*Plus: Release 9.2.0.2.0 - Production on Sat Jan 10 12:57:48
2004

Copyright © 1982, 2002, Oracle Corporation.  All rights
reserved.
Enter user-name: opc_op/opc_op@ov_net
Connected to:
Oracle9i Enterprise Edition Release 9.2.0.2.0 - 64bit Production
JServer Release 9.2.0.2.0 - Production
SQL> select count(*) from opc_act_messages;
COUNT(*)
139
SQL>
```

18.7 DATABASE REPORT

The computer output shown here is a listing from a report you can produce with the database utility program /opt/OV/bin/OpC/utils/opc_odc. This report gives you everything you need to know about the database immediately after installation or after periodic changes. The information collected by the program includes collecting data about the Oracle installation; detecting some Oracle problems and printing corresponding errors or warnings; listing the information about the database tablespaces, tables, and configuration; and listing database run-time parameters that determine utilization of the operating system resources. The output from executing the utility program is stored in the /tmp directory by default. The complete output is provided here for reference purposes. The database internal structure is subject to change by HP. Refer to the OVO Release Notes and OpenView database schema and entity relationship documentation for the most current information about the OVO database.

```
# ./opc_odc
Oracle data collector tool opc_odc.
Called on Sat Jan 10 19:24:51 PST 2004.

OS:  11.11
SYS: 9000/785/J5600
UNAME: lotus
HOSTNAME: lotus
PHYS. MEMORY: 1024 MB
SWAP: 2048 MB
Please enter the value for the ORACLE_SID [openview]:
Please enter the value for ORACLE_BASE [/opt/oracle]:
Please enter ORACLE_HOME [/opt/oracle/product/9.2.0]:
Checking connection to DB openview...
Can connect to database openview.
Dumping Oracle tables ..
Checking Oracle Errors in the Dump files ..
Checking sqlnet ..

opc_odc finished. See the logfile /tmp/opc_odc.log for a
detailed protocol
```

The output from the opc_odc tool is shown here. Some of the output is summarized.

```
Oracle data collector tool opc_odc.
Called on Sat Jan 10 12:15:59 PST 2004.

OS:  11.11
SYS: 9000/785/J5600
UNAME: lotus
HOSTNAME: lotus
PHYS. MEMORY: 1024 MB
```

```
SWAP: 2048 MB
Checking existence of OV database
OV database configuration file /etc/opt/OV/share/conf/ovdbconf:
DB_VENDOR Oracle
DB_NAME openview
DB_RELEASE 9.2.0
DB_TIME_STAMP "Thu, Oct 9, 2003 03:34:42 AM"
DB_USER ovdb
ORACLE_SID openview
ORACLE_HOME /opt/oracle/product/9.2.0
ORACLE_BASE /opt/oracle
DBA_USER oracle
DATA_DIR /ora_db
CREATE_DIR /opt/oracle/admin/openview/create
INDEX_DIR /ora_db
ADMIN_DIR /opt/oracle
OS_AUTHENT_PREFIX
CHARACTER_SET WE8ISO8859P15
BASE_DATA_TS_SIZE 25
BASE_INDEX_TS_SIZE 5
DATA_TS_SIZE 25
INDEX_TS_SIZE
TEMP_TS_SIZE 2
DATA_TS_EXTENT_SIZE 2
DATA_TS_MAX_SIZE 500
INDEX_TS_EXTENT_SIZE
ECHO_CMD echo
PROMPT TRUE
DBA_PROGRAM sqlplus
OV_USER ovdb
DBA_LOGFILE /var/opt/OV/share/log/sqlplus_log
ORACLE_BASE_REV 9
ORACLE_SECOND_REV 2
NLS_LANG american_america.WE8ISO8859P15
ITO_DATADIR /ora_db
ITO_INDEXDIR /ora_db

OpC configuration file /opt/OV/bin/OpC/install/opcsvinfo:

# File:          opcsvinfo
# Description:   Installation Information of ITO Management
Server
# Package:       HP OpenView IT/Operations
#
# © Copyright 2003 Hewlett-Packard Development Company, L.P.
OPC_INSTALLED_VERSION A.08.00.06
```

```
OPC_MGMT_SERVER lotus
OPC_MGMTSV_CHARSET iso885915
OPC_INSTALLATION_TIME 10/09/03 03:27:01
OPC_SG FALSE

DATABASE ov_net
Oracle DBA user:
oracle:APWUxRlsuHnvc:101:101:,,,:/home/oracle:/usr/bin/sh

#
# File: initopenview.ora
#

control_files              = (/ora_db/control01.ctl,
/ora_db/control02.ctl,
/ora_db/control03.ctl)

background_dump_dest       = /opt/oracle/admin/openview/bdump
core_dump_dest             = /opt/oracle/admin/openview/cdump
user_dump_dest             = /opt/oracle/admin/openview/udump

# log_archive_start          = true
# log_archive_dest           = /opt/oracle/admin/openview/arch/
# log_archive_format         = "T%TS%S.ARC" # if you want automatic
archiving

db_block_size              = 8192
db_name                    = openview
rollback_segments          = (r01,r02,r03,r04)
os_authent_prefix          = ""

# tuning parameters
db_files = 50
db_file_multiblock_read_count = 16                          #
MEDIUM
db_block_buffers = 10000                                      #
MEDIUM
shared_pool_size = 128000000                                  #
LARGE
log_checkpoint_interval = 99999
processes = 50                                                   #
SMALL
dml_locks = 100                                                  #
SMALL
log_buffer = 65536
max_dump_file_size = 10240 #limit trace file size to 5 Meg ea
```

```
open_cursors = 1024
compatible=9.0.0.0.0
sort_area_size=262144
#
# End of file initopenview.ora
#
#

# This file is used by ORACLE utilities.  It is created by
root.sh
# and updated by the Database Configuration Assistant when cre-
ating
# a database.

# A colon, ':', is used as the field terminator.  A new line
terminates
# the entry.  Lines beginning with a pound sign, '#', are com-
ments.
#
# Entries are of the form:
#   $ORACLE_SID:$ORACLE_HOME:<N|Y>:
#
# The first and second fields are the system identifier and home
# directory of the database respectively.  The third filed indi-
cates
# to the dbstart utility that the database should , "Y", or
should not,
# "N", be brought up at system boot time.
#
# Multiple entries with the same $ORACLE_SID are not allowed.
#
#
# *:/opt/oracle/product/9.2.0:N
*:/opt/oracle/product/9.2.0:N
openview:/opt/oracle/product/9.2.0:N
Checking connection to database openview as Oracle DBA.
Checking connection to DB openview...
Can connect to database openview.
Checking connection to database as ITO user opc_op.
OpC user:
opc_op:*:777:77:OpC default operator:/home/opc_op:/usr/bin/ksh
Can connect to database as user opc_op.
Checking the ITO tables.
All ITO tables exist.
```

```
Dumping Oracle tables ..
Total System Global Area  267479512 bytes
Fixed Size                   735704 bytes
Variable Size             184549376 bytes
Database Buffers           81920000 bytes
Redo Buffers                 274432 bytes

NAME                                  TYPE        VALUE
____________    ______- ___________-
O7_DICTIONARY_ACCESSIBILITY          boolean     FALSE
active_instance_count                integer
aq_tm_processes                      integer     0
archive_lag_target                   integer     0
audit_file_dest                      string      ?/rdbms/audit
audit_sys_operations                 boolean     FALSE
audit_trail                          string      NONE
background_core_dump                 string      partial
background_dump_dest                 string
/opt/oracle/admin/openview/bdump
backup_tape_io_slaves                boolean     FALSE
bitmap_merge_area_size               integer     1048576
blank_trimming                       boolean     FALSE
buffer_pool_keep                     string
buffer_pool_recycle                  string
circuits                             integer     0
cluster_database                     boolean     FALSE
cluster_database_instances           integer     1
cluster_interconnects                string
commit_point_strength                integer     1
compatible                           string      9.0.0.0.0
control_file_record_keep_time        integer     7
control_files                        string      /ora_db/con-
trol01.ctl,
/ora_db/control02.ctl,
/ora_db/control03.ctl
core_dump_dest                       string
/opt/oracle/admin/openview/cdump
cpu_count                            integer     2
create_bitmap_area_size              integer     8388608
cursor_sharing                       string      EXACT
cursor_space_for_time                boolean     FALSE
db_16k_cache_size                    big integer 0
db_2k_cache_size                     big integer 0
```

```
NAME                               TYPE        VALUE
---------------------- -------
db_32k_cache_size                  big integer 0
db_4k_cache_size                   big integer 0
db_8k_cache_size                   big integer 0
db_block_buffers                   integer     10000
db_block_checking                  boolean     FALSE
db_block_checksum                  boolean     TRUE
db_block_size                      integer     8192
db_cache_advice                    string      ON
db_cache_size                      big integer 0
db_create_file_dest                string
db_create_online_log_dest_1        string
db_create_online_log_dest_2        string
db_create_online_log_dest_3        string
db_create_online_log_dest_4        string
db_create_online_log_dest_5        string
db_domain                          string
db_file_multiblock_read_count      integer     16
db_file_name_convert               string
db_files                           integer     50
db_keep_cache_size                 big integer 0
db_name                            string      openview
db_recycle_cache_size              big integer 0
db_writer_processes                integer     1
dblink_encrypt_login               boolean     FALSE
dbwr_io_slaves                     integer     0
dg_broker_config_file1             string      ?/dbs/dr1@.dat
dg_broker_config_file2             string      ?/dbs/dr2@.dat
dg_broker_start                    boolean     FALSE
disk_asynch_io                     boolean     TRUE
dispatchers                        string
distributed_lock_timeout           integer     60
dml_locks                          integer     100
drs_start                          boolean     FALSE
enqueue_resources                  integer     205
event                              string
fal_client                         string
fal_server                         string
fast_start_io_target               integer     0
fast_start_mttr_target             integer     0
fast_start_parallel_rollback       string      LOW
file_mapping                       boolean     FALSE
filesystemio_options               string      asynch
```

```
fixed_date                          string
gc_files_to_locks                   string

NAME                                TYPE        VALUE
------------------------------------ -------
global_context_pool_size            string
global_names                        boolean     FALSE
hash_area_size                      integer     524288
hash_join_enabled                   boolean     TRUE
hi_shared_memory_address            integer     0
HP-UX_sched_noage                   integer     0
hs_autoregister                     boolean     TRUE
ifile                               file
instance_groups                     string
instance_name                       string      openview
instance_number                     integer     0
java_max_sessionspace_size          integer     0
java_pool_size                      big integer 33554432
java_soft_sessionspace_limit        integer     0
job_queue_processes                 integer     0
large_pool_size                     big integer 0
license_max_sessions                integer     0
license_max_users                   integer     0
license_sessions_warning            integer     0
local_listener                      string
lock_name_space                     string
lock_sga                            boolean     FALSE
log_archive_dest                    string
log_archive_dest_1                  string
log_archive_dest_10                 string
log_archive_dest_2                  string
log_archive_dest_3                  string
log_archive_dest_4                  string
log_archive_dest_5                  string
log_archive_dest_6                  string
log_archive_dest_7                  string
log_archive_dest_8                  string
log_archive_dest_9                  string
log_archive_dest_state_1            string      enable
log_archive_dest_state_10           string      enable
log_archive_dest_state_2            string      enable
log_archive_dest_state_3            string      enable
log_archive_dest_state_4            string      enable
log_archive_dest_state_5            string      enable
```

```
log_archive_dest_state_6            string      enable
log_archive_dest_state_7            string      enable
log_archive_dest_state_8            string      enable
log_archive_dest_state_9            string      enable
log_archive_duplex_dest             string

NAME                                TYPE        VALUE
-------------------- -------
log_archive_format                  string      %t_%s.dbf
log_archive_max_processes           integer     2
log_archive_min_succeed_dest        integer     1
log_archive_start                   boolean     FALSE
log_archive_trace                   integer     0
log_buffer                          integer     65536
log_checkpoint_interval             integer     99999
log_checkpoint_timeout              integer     1800
log_checkpoints_to_alert            boolean     FALSE
log_file_name_convert               string
log_parallelism                     integer     1
logmnr_max_persistent_sessions      integer     1
max_commit_propagation_delay        integer     700
max_dispatchers                     integer     5
max_dump_file_size                  string      10240
max_enabled_roles                   integer     30
max_rollback_segments               integer     30
max_shared_servers                  integer     20
mts_circuits                        integer     0
mts_dispatchers                     string
mts_listener_address                string
mts_max_dispatchers                 integer     5
mts_max_servers                     integer     20
mts_multiple_listeners              boolean     FALSE
mts_servers                         integer     0
mts_service                         string      openview
mts_sessions                        integer     0
nls_calendar                        string
nls_comp                            string
nls_currency                        string
nls_date_format                     string
nls_date_language                   string
nls_dual_currency                   string
nls_iso_currency                    string
nls_language                        string      AMERICAN
nls_length_semantics                string      BYTE
```

```
nls_nchar_conv_excp                  string     FALSE
nls_numeric_characters               string
nls_sort                             string
nls_territory                        string     AMERICA
nls_time_format                      string
nls_time_tz_format                   string
nls_timestamp_format                 string
nls_timestamp_tz_format              string

NAME                                 TYPE       VALUE
------------------------------------ -------
object_cache_max_size_percent        integer    10
object_cache_optimal_size            integer    102400
olap_page_pool_size                  integer    33554432
open_cursors                         integer    1024
open_links                           integer    4
open_links_per_instance              integer    4
optimizer_dynamic_sampling           integer    1
optimizer_features_enable            string     9.2.0
optimizer_index_caching              integer    0
optimizer_index_cost_adj             integer    100
optimizer_max_permutations           integer    2000
optimizer_mode                       string     CHOOSE
oracle_trace_collection_name         string
oracle_trace_collection_path         string
?/otrace/admin/cdf
oracle_trace_collection_size         integer    5242880
oracle_trace_enable                  boolean    FALSE
oracle_trace_facility_name           string     oracled
oracle_trace_facility_path           string
?/otrace/admin/fdf
os_authent_prefix                    string
os_roles                             boolean    FALSE
parallel_adaptive_multi_user         boolean    FALSE
parallel_automatic_tuning            boolean    FALSE
parallel_execution_message_size      integer    2152
parallel_instance_group              string
parallel_max_servers                 integer    5
parallel_min_percent                 integer    0
parallel_min_servers                 integer    0
parallel_server                      boolean    FALSE
parallel_server_instances            integer    1
parallel_threads_per_cpu             integer    2
partition_view_enabled               boolean    FALSE
```

```
pga_aggregate_target                    big integer 0
plsql_compiler_flags                    string      INTERPRETED
plsql_native_c_compiler                 string
plsql_native_library_dir                string
plsql_native_library_subdir_count       integer     0
plsql_native_linker                     string
plsql_native_make_file_name             string
plsql_native_make_utility               string
plsql_v2_compatibility                  boolean     FALSE
pre_page_sga                            boolean     FALSE
processes                               integer     50
query_rewrite_enabled                   string      false
query_rewrite_integrity                 string      enforced

NAME                                    TYPE        VALUE
------------------------------------ -------
rdbms_server_dn                         string
read_only_open_delayed                  boolean     FALSE
recovery_parallelism                    integer     0
remote_archive_enable                   string      true
remote_dependencies_mode                string      TIMESTAMP
remote_listener                         string
remote_login_passwordfile               string      NONE
remote_os_authent                       boolean     FALSE
remote_os_roles                         boolean     FALSE
replication_dependency_tracking         boolean     TRUE
resource_limit                          boolean     FALSE
resource_manager_plan                   string
rollback_segments                       string      r01, r02, r03,
r04
row_locking                             string      always
serial_reuse                            string      DISABLE
serializable                            boolean     FALSE
service_names                           string      openview
session_cached_cursors                  integer     0
session_max_open_files                  integer     10
sessions                                integer     60
sga_max_size                            big integer 267479512
shadow_core_dump                        string      partial
shared_memory_address                   integer     0
shared_pool_reserved_size               big integer 6710886
shared_pool_size                        big integer 134217728
shared_server_sessions                  integer     0
shared_servers                          integer     0
```

```
sort_area_retained_size              integer     0
sort_area_size                       integer     262144
spfile                               string
sql92_security                       boolean     FALSE
sql_trace                            boolean     FALSE
sql_version                          string      NATIVE
standby_archive_dest                 string      ?/dbs/arch
standby_file_management              string      MANUAL
star_transformation_enabled          string      FALSE
statistics_level                     string      TYPICAL
tape_asynch_io                       boolean     TRUE
thread                               integer     0
timed_os_statistics                  integer     0
timed_statistics                     boolean     TRUE
trace_enabled                        boolean     TRUE
tracefile_identifier                 string
transaction_auditing                 boolean     TRUE

NAME                                 TYPE        VALUE
——————————————————— ——————-
transactions                         integer     66
transactions_per_rollback_segment    integer     5
undo_management                      string      MANUAL
undo_retention                       integer     900
undo_suppress_errors                 boolean     FALSE
undo_tablespace                      string
use_indirect_data_buffers            boolean     FALSE
user_dump_dest                       string
/opt/oracle/admin/openview/udump
utl_file_dir                         string
workarea_size_policy                 string      MANUAL

TABLESPACE_ BLOCK  INITIAL   NEXT    MIN  MAX PCT
NAME:    SIZE   EXTENT    EXT     EXT  EXT INC

SYSTEM          8192   16384   16384  505  50  0
TEMP         8192  106496    5242880   1  505  0
RBS1         8192 5242880    5242880   2  505  0
TOOLS        8192  106496     1048576  1  505  0
OPC_TEMP     8192 1048576     1048576  1    0  1048576
OPC_1        8192   65536              1
OPC_2        8192   65536              1 2147483645
65536
OPC_3        8192   65536              1 2147483645
6553
```

```
OPC_4         8192   65536              1 2147483645
65536 6
OPC_5         8192   65536              1 2147483645
65536
OPC_6         8192   65536              1 2147483645
65536
OPC_7         8192   65536              1 2147483645
65536
OPC_8         8192   65536              1
OPC_9         8192   65536              1 2147483645
65536
OPC_10        8192   65536              1 2147483645
65536
OPC_INDEX1    8192   65536              1 2147483645
65536
OPC_INDEX2    8192   65536              1 2147483645
65536
OPC_INDEX3    8192   65536              1 2147483645
65536

Note: The following database parameters are not shown in the
summary output shown.
STATUS, CONTENTS, LOGGING, FOR EXTENT,_MAN
ALLOCATION, PLU, SEGMENT
18 rows selected.

FILE                      FILE  TABLESPACE  BYTES_BLOCKS STATUS
NAME                      ID    NAME
/ora_db/system_1.dbf       1 SYSTEM     125829120  15360 AVAILABLE
/ora_db/temp_1.dbf         2 TEMP         2097152    256 AVAILABLE
/ora_db/RBS1_1.dbf         3 RBS1        47185920   5760 AVAILABLE
/ora_db/OPC_1_1.dbf        5 OPC_1        4194304    512 AVAILABLE
/ora_db/OPC_2_1.dbf        6 OPC_2        5242880    640 AVAILABLE
/ora_db/OPC_3_1.dbf        7 OPC_3        1048576    128 AVAILABLE
/ora_db/OPC_4_1.dbf        8 OPC_4       27262976   3328 AVAILABLE
/ora_db/OPC_5_1.dbf        9 OPC_5        1048576    128 AVAILABLE
/ora_db/OPC_6_1.dbf       10 OPC_6        4194304    512 AVAILABLE
/ora_db/OPC_7_1.dbf       11 OPC_7        4194304    512 AVAILABLE
/ora_db/OPC_8_1.dbf       12 OPC_8        4194304    512 AVAILABLE
/ora_db/OPC_9_1.dbf       13 OPC_9        6291456    768 AVAILABLE
/ora_db/OPC_10_1.dbf      14 OPC_10       6291456    768 AVAILABLE
/ora_db/OPC_INDEX1_1.dbf 15 OPC_INDEX1 13631488 1664 AVAIL.
/ora_db/OPC_INDEX2_1.dbf 16 OPC_INDEX2 10485760 1280 AVAIL.
/ora_db/OPC_INDEX3_1.dbf 17 OPC_INDEX3 10485760 1280 AVAIL.
```

```
Note: The following database parameters are not shown in the
summary listing.
RELATIVE_FNO, AUT, MAXBYTES, MAXBLOCKS, INCREMENT_BY,
USER_BYTES,  USER_BLOCKS

GROUP#       STATUS  TYPE   MEMBER

1            STALE   ONLINE /ora_db/redo01.log

2            STALE   ONLINE /ora_db/redo02.log

3                    ONLINE /ora_db/redo03.log

TABLESPACE_NAME                     FREE_BLOCKS  FREE_BYTE
_______________ ______- _____

OPC_1                                       472    3866624
OPC_10                                      744    6094848
OPC_2                                       600    4915200
OPC_3                                        48     393216
OPC_4                                      1344   11010048
OPC_5                                       120     983040
OPC_6                                       472    3866624
OPC_7                                       496    4063232
OPC_8                                       488    3997696
OPC_9                                       744    6094848
OPC_INDEX1                                 1512   12386304
OPC_INDEX2                                 1208    9895936
OPC_INDEX3                                 1256   10289152
RBS1                                        639    5234688
SYSTEM                                       98     802816
TEMP                                        255    2088960
TOOLS                                       127    1040384

17 rows selected.

TABLESPACE_NAME, FILE_ID, BLOCK_ID, BYTES, BLOCKS, RELATIVE_FNO

Note: The following parameters are not shown in the next sec-
tion: INITIAL_EXTENT   NEXT_EXTENT
```

```
TABLE_NAME                TABLESPACE_NAME
-------
OPC_ACT_MESSAGES          OPC_1
OPC_ACT_CUST_ATTRIB       OPC_1
OPC_SERVICE               OPC_10
OPC_SERVICE_LOG           OPC_10
OPC_MSG_TEXT              OPC_2
OPC_ORIG_MSG_TEXT         OPC_2
OPC_ANNOTATION            OPC_2
OPC_ANNO_TEXT             OPC_2
OPC_NODE_NAMES            OPC_3
OPC_NODE_ALT_NAME         OPC_3
OPC_NODE_ALT_ADDR         OPC_3
OPC_NODE_ALT_V6_ADDR      OPC_3
OPC_USER_DATA             OPC_4
OPC_CAPABILITIES          OPC_4
OPC_OP_PROFILES           OPC_4

TABLE_NAME       TABLESPACE_NAME
OPC_NODES                   OPC_4
OPC_CLUSTER_MAP             OPC_4
OPC_NET_MACHINE             OPC_4
OPC_CHSETS                  OPC_4
OPC_COMM_TYPE               OPC_4
OPC_NET_SEC_TYPES OPC_4
OPC_PLTFRM_FAMILY           OPC_4
OPC_AGENT_STATUS            OPC_4
OPC_NODE_GROUPS             OPC_4
OPC_NODES_IN_GROUP          OPC_4
OPC_MESSAGE_GROUPS          OPC_4
OPC_APPLICATION             OPC_4
OPC_INTEGR_APPL             OPC_4
OPC_APPL_LOGIN              OPC_4
OPC_OV_APPL                 OPC_4
OPC_APPL_GROUPS             OPC_4
OPC_APPL_NODE_LIST          OPC_4
OPC_APPL_IN_GROUP           OPC_4
OPC_APPLGRP_IN_GRP          OPC_4
OPC_OP_REALM                OPC_4
OPC_OP_DESK                 OPC_4
OPC_OP_GROUP_DESK           OPC_4
OPC_AUDIT                   OPC_4
```

```
OPC_AUDIT_PARAM          OPC_4
OPC_DB_MAINTENANCE       OPC_4
OPC_NOTIF_SERVICES       OPC_4
OPC_NOTIF_SCHEDULE       OPC_4
OPC_TROUBLE_TICKET       OPC_4
OPC_NODE_CONFIG          OPC_4
OPC_NODE_DEFAULTS        OPC_4
OPC_TEMP_OBJECT_LIST     OPC_4
OPC_TEMP_APPL_LIST       OPC_4
OPC_TEMP_MSGGRP_LIST     OPC_4
OPC_TEMP_NODE_LIST       OPC_4
OPC_TEMP_TEMPL           OPC_4
OPC_INSTR_INTERF         OPC_4
OPC_INSTRUCTIONS         OPC_4
OPC_SYMBOLS              OPC_4
OPC_ESCAL_ASSIGN_M       OPC_4
OPC_APPRESP_ID_LST       OPC_4
OPC_COND_OPER_LIST       OPC_4
OPC_FORWARD_MSGS         OPC_4



TABLE_NAME                      TABLESPACE_NAME
OPC_TGRP_ON_NGRP                OPC_4
OPC_TGRP_ON_NODE                OPC_4
OPC_TEMPL_ON_NGRP               OPC_4
OPC_TMPL_ON_NODE                OPC_4
OPC_TGRP_IN_TGRP                OPC_4
OPC_TEMPL_IN_TGRP               OPC_4
OPC_TEMP_SERVICE_LIST           OPC_4
OPC_APPL_PLATFORMS              OPC_4
OPC_OP_BROWSER_SET_CMA          OPC_4
OPC_CMA_NAMES                   OPC_4
OPC_COND_CUST_ATTRIB            OPC_4
OPC_SERVICE_MSGS                OPC_4
OPC_OP_SERVICES                 OPC_4
OPC_CHANGE_STATUS               OPC_4
OPC_MSG_KEY_REL                 OPC_4
OPC_NODEHIER_LAYOUT             OPC_4
OPC_NODEHIERS                   OPC_4
OPC_COND_STAT_VAR               OPC_4
OPC_OP_BROWSER_SET_OBJ          OPC_4
```

```
OPC_OP_BROWSER_SET              OPC_4
OPC_MONITOR_COND                OPC_4
OPC_TEMPL_GROUPS                OPC_4
OPC_EC_SOURCE                   OPC_4
OPC_COND_TYPE_LIST              OPC_4
OPC_MPI_REG_CONDS               OPC_4
OPC_OPEN_MPIS                   OPC_4
OPC_MGMTSV_CONFIG               OPC_4
OPC_NODE_PATTERN                OPC_4
OPC_OP_OV_GEOMETRY              OPC_4
OPC_OP_DEFAULTS                 OPC_4
OPC_OP_RUNTIME                  OPC_4
OPC_SOURCE_TEMPL                OPC_4
OPC_TEMPL_STATUS                OPC_4
OPC_TEMPL_OPTIONS               OPC_4
OPC_LOGFILE_SOURCE              OPC_4
OPC_CONSOLE_SOURCE              OPC_4
OPC_INTERF_SOURCE               OPC_4
OPC_MONITOR_SOURCE              OPC_4
OPC_SCHED_SOURCE                OPC_4
OPC_TRAP_SOURCE                 OPC_4
OPC_MSG_COND                    OPC_4
OPC_RGR_COND                    OPC_4



TABLE_NAME                      TABLESPACE_NAME
OPC_TRAP_COND                   OPC_4
OPC_COND                        OPC_4
OPC_COND_SEV_LIST               OPC_4
OPC_COND_APPL_LIST              OPC_4
OPC_COND_MGRP_LIST              OPC_4
OPC_COND_OBJ_LIST               OPC_4
OPC_COND_NODE_LIST              OPC_4
OPC_COND_TEXT                   OPC_4
OPC_SNMP_VARIABLES              OPC_4
OPC_HIST_MESSAGES               OPC_6
OPC_HIST_CUST_ATTRIB            OPC_6
OPC_HIST_MSG_TEXT               OPC_7
OPC_HIST_ORIG_TEXT              OPC_8
OPC_HIST_ANNOTATION             OPC_9
OPC_HIST_ANNO_TEXT              OPC_9
```

```
OPC_TMP_VISIBLE_PROFILE
OPC_TMP_VISIBLE_NODE
OPC_TMP_VISIBLE_NODE2
OPC_TMP_VISIBLE_PATTERN
OPC_TMP_VISIBLE_MSGGRP
OPC_TMP_VALID_MSGGRP
OPC_TMP_MISC_MSGGRP
OPC_TMP_VISIBLE_SERVICE
OPC_TMP_MSG_ID
OPC_TMP_MSG_ID_SERVICE
OPC_TMP_FILTER_APPL
OPC_TMP_FILTER_OBJ
OPC_TMP_FILTER_CMA
OPC_TMP_FILTER_NODE
OPC_TMP_FILTER_PATTERN
OPC_TMP_FILTER_PATTERN_NODE
OPC_TMP_FILTER_MSGGRP
OPC_TMP_FILTER_SERVICE
132 rows selected.

Disconnected from Oracle9i Enterprise Edition Release 9.2.0.2.0
- 64bit Production
JServer Release 9.2.0.2.0 - Production
SQL> exit
List of Tables with their Record Counts as of 10-JAN-04 12:20:18
Total Records in OPC_ACT_CUST_ATTRIB            ::          0
Total Records in OPC_ACT_MESSAGES               ::        139
Total Records in OPC_AGENT_STATUS               ::          0
Total Records in OPC_ANNOTATION                 ::         60
Total Records in OPC_ANNO_TEXT                  ::         60
Total Records in OPC_APPLGRP_IN_GRP             ::         20
Total Records in OPC_APPLICATION                ::        201
Total Records in OPC_APPL_GROUPS                ::         20
Total Records in OPC_APPL_IN_GROUP              ::        201
Total Records in OPC_APPL_LOGIN                 ::         13
Total Records in OPC_APPL_NODE_LIST             ::         21
Total Records in OPC_APPL_PLATFORMS             ::          0
Total Records in OPC_APPRESP_ID_LST             ::          4
Total Records in OPC_AUDIT                      ::        206
Total Records in OPC_AUDIT_PARAM                ::        181
Total Records in OPC_CAPABILITIES               ::          4
Total Records in OPC_CHANGE_STATUS              ::         27
Total Records in OPC_CHSETS                     ::         37
```

```
Total Records in OPC_CLUSTER_MAP            ::       0
Total Records in OPC_CMA_NAMES              ::       0
Total Records in OPC_COMM_TYPE              ::      12
Total Records in OPC_COND                   ::    1038
Total Records in OPC_COND_APPL_LIST         ::     606
Total Records in OPC_COND_CUST_ATTRIB       ::       0
Total Records in OPC_COND_MGRP_LIST         ::      17
Total Records in OPC_COND_NODE_LIST         ::     234
Total Records in OPC_COND_OBJ_LIST          ::       7
Total Records in OPC_COND_OPER_LIST         ::       4
Total Records in OPC_COND_SEV_LIST          ::    1038
Total Records in OPC_COND_STAT_VAR          ::       0
Total Records in OPC_COND_TEXT              ::    2789
Total Records in OPC_COND_TYPE_LIST         ::       4
Total Records in OPC_CONSOLE_SOURCE         ::       1
Total Records in OPC_DB_MAINTENANCE         ::       1
Total Records in OPC_EC_SOURCE              ::       3
Total Records in OPC_ESCAL_ASSIGN_M         ::       0
Total Records in OPC_FORWARD_MSGS           ::       0
Total Records in OPC_HIST_ANNOTATION        ::       0
Total Records in OPC_HIST_ANNO_TEXT         ::       0
Total Records in OPC_HIST_CUST_ATTRIB       ::       0
Total Records in OPC_HIST_MESSAGES          ::       0
Total Records in OPC_HIST_MSG_TEXT          ::       0
Total Records in OPC_HIST_ORIG_TEXT         ::       0
Total Records in OPC_INSTRUCTIONS           ::    2881
Total Records in OPC_INSTR_INTERF           ::       0
Total Records in OPC_INTEGR_APPL            ::     142
Total Records in OPC_INTERF_SOURCE          ::       2
Total Records in OPC_LOGFILE_SOURCE         ::      47
Total Records in OPC_MESSAGE_GROUPS         ::      16
Total Records in OPC_MGMTSV_CONFIG          ::       1
Total Records in OPC_MONITOR_COND           ::      55
Total Records in OPC_MONITOR_SOURCE         ::      45
Total Records in OPC_MPI_REG_CONDS          ::       4
Total Records in OPC_MSG_COND               ::    1773
Total Records in OPC_MSG_KEY_REL            ::      23
Total Records in OPC_MSG_TEXT               ::     216
Total Records in OPC_NET_MACHINE            ::       8
Total Records in OPC_NET_SEC_TYPES          ::      14
Total Records in OPC_NODEHIERS              ::       1
Total Records in OPC_NODEHIER_LAYOUT        ::       3
Total Records in OPC_NODES                  ::       2
Total Records in OPC_NODES_IN_GROUP         ::       2
```

```
Total Records in OPC_NODE_ALT_ADDR              ::       0
Total Records in OPC_NODE_ALT_NAME              ::       0
Total Records in OPC_NODE_ALT_V6_ADDR           ::       0
Total Records in OPC_NODE_CONFIG                ::      18
Total Records in OPC_NODE_DEFAULTS              ::       8
Total Records in OPC_NODE_GROUPS                ::       2
Total Records in OPC_NODE_NAMES                 ::       3
Total Records in OPC_NODE_PATTERN               ::       0
Total Records in OPC_NOTIF_SCHEDULE             ::       0
Total Records in OPC_NOTIF_SERVICES             ::       0
Total Records in OPC_OPEN_MPIS                  ::       4
Total Records in OPC_OP_BROWSER_SET             ::       1
Total Records in OPC_OP_BROWSER_SET_CMA         ::       0
Total Records in OPC_OP_BROWSER_SET_OBJ         ::       2
Total Records in OPC_OP_DEFAULTS                ::       4
Total Records in OPC_OP_DESK                    ::      21
Total Records in OPC_OP_GROUP_DESK              ::      26
Total Records in OPC_OP_OV_GEOMETRY             ::      12
Total Records in OPC_OP_PROFILES                ::       0
Total Records in OPC_OP_REALM                   ::      79
Total Records in OPC_OP_RUNTIME                 ::       0
Total Records in OPC_OP_SERVICES                ::       0
Total Records in OPC_ORIG_MSG_TEXT              ::     156
Total Records in OPC_OV_APPL                    ::      54
Total Records in OPC_PLTFRM_FAMILY              ::       2
Total Records in OPC_RGR_COND                   ::       0
Total Records in OPC_SCHED_SOURCE               ::       0
Total Records in OPC_SERVICE                    ::       0
Total Records in OPC_SERVICE_LOG                ::       0
Total Records in OPC_SERVICE_MSGS               ::       0
Total Records in OPC_SNMP_VARIABLES             ::       2
Total Records in OPC_SOURCE_TEMPL               ::     103
Total Records in OPC_SYMBOLS                    ::      63
Total Records in OPC_TEMPL_GROUPS               ::      33
Total Records in OPC_TEMPL_IN_TGRP              ::     182
Total Records in OPC_TEMPL_ON_NGRP              ::       0
Total Records in OPC_TEMPL_OPTIONS              ::     100
Total Records in OPC_TEMPL_STATUS               ::       0
Total Records in OPC_TEMP_APPL_LIST             ::       0
Total Records in OPC_TEMP_MSGGRP_LIST           ::       0
Total Records in OPC_TEMP_NODE_LIST             ::       0
Total Records in OPC_TEMP_OBJECT_LIST           ::       0
Total Records in OPC_TEMP_SERVICE_LIST          ::       0
Total Records in OPC_TEMP_TEMPL                 ::       0
```

```
Total Records in OPC_TGRP_IN_TGRP                    ::        32
Total Records in OPC_TGRP_ON_NGRP                    ::         0
Total Records in OPC_TGRP_ON_NODE                    ::         3
Total Records in OPC_TMPL_ON_NODE                    ::         0
Total Records in OPC_TMP_FILTER_APPL                 ::         0
Total Records in OPC_TMP_FILTER_CMA                  ::         0
Total Records in OPC_TMP_FILTER_MSGGRP               ::         0
Total Records in OPC_TMP_FILTER_NODE                 ::         0
Total Records in OPC_TMP_FILTER_OBJ                  ::         0
Total Records in OPC_TMP_FILTER_PATTERN              ::         0
Total Records in OPC_TMP_FILTER_PATTERN_NODE         ::         0
Total Records in OPC_TMP_FILTER_SERVICE              ::         0
Total Records in OPC_TMP_MISC_MSGGRP                 ::         0
Total Records in OPC_TMP_MSG_ID                      ::         0
Total Records in OPC_TMP_MSG_ID_SERVICE              ::         0
Total Records in OPC_TMP_VALID_MSGGRP                ::         0
Total Records in OPC_TMP_VISIBLE_MSGGRP              ::         0
Total Records in OPC_TMP_VISIBLE_NODE                ::         0
Total Records in OPC_TMP_VISIBLE_NODE2               ::         0
Total Records in OPC_TMP_VISIBLE_PATTERN             ::         0
Total Records in OPC_TMP_VISIBLE_PROFILE             ::         0
Total Records in OPC_TMP_VISIBLE_SERVICE             ::         0
Total Records in OPC_TRAP_COND                       ::       833
Total Records in OPC_TRAP_SOURCE                     ::         5
Total Records in OPC_TROUBLE_TICKET                  ::         1
Total Records in OPC_USER_DATA                       ::         4
Note: Index Detail, Referential Constraints, and Block Details
are not shown in the summary output.

*++++++++++++++++++++++++++++++++++++++++++++++++++++++++++++++++
•     Files in the Oracle Dump Destination
+++++++++++++++++++++++++++++++++++++++++++++++++++++++++++++++++
Note the complete file listing is not shown in the summary out-
put.
/bin/ls -l /opt/oracle/admin/openview/bdump
total 266
Checking Oracle Errors in the Dump files ..
/opt/oracle/admin/openview/bdump/alert_openview.log:ORA-00130:
invalid listener address
'(ADDRESS=(PROTOCOL=TCP)(HOST=)(PORT=1521))'
/opt/oracle/admin/openview/bdump/alert_openview.log:ORA-00130:
invalid listener address
'(ADDRESS=(PROTOCOL=TCP)(HOST=)(PORT=1521))'
```

```
/opt/oracle/admin/openview/bdump/alert_openview.log:ORA-00130:
invalid listener address
'(ADDRESS=(PROTOCOL=TCP)(HOST=)(PORT=1521))'

*+++++++++++++++++++++++++++++++++++++++++++++++++++++++++++++
•     Dump last 200 Messages of alert_openview.log
++++++++++++++++++++++++++++++++++++++++++++++++++++++++++++++

tail -200 /opt/oracle/admin/openview/bdump/alert_openview.log
  background_dump_dest      = /opt/oracle/admin/openview/bdump
  user_dump_dest            = /opt/oracle/admin/openview/udump
  max_dump_file_size        = 10240
  core_dump_dest            = /opt/oracle/admin/openview/cdump
  sort_area_size            = 262144
  db_name                   = openview
  open_cursors              = 1024
  os_authent_prefix         =
PMON started with pid=2
DBW0 started with pid=3
LGWR started with pid=4
CKPT started with pid=5
SMON started with pid=6
RECO started with pid=7
Mon Jan 12 00:03:49 2004
ALTER DATABASE   MOUNT
Mon Jan 12 00:03:53 2004
Successful mount of redo thread 1, with mount id 2485429285.
Mon Jan 12 00:03:53 2004
Database mounted in Exclusive Mode.
Completed: ALTER DATABASE   MOUNT
Mon Jan 12 00:03:54 2004
ALTER DATABASE OPEN
Mon Jan 12 00:03:54 2004
Thread 1 opened at log sequence 101
Current log# 2 seq# 101 mem# 0: /ora_db/redo02.log
Successful open of redo thread 1.
Mon Jan 12 00:03:54 2004
MTTR advisory is disabled because FAST_START_MTTR_TARGET is not
set
Mon Jan 12 00:03:54 2004
SMON: enabling cache recovery
SMON: enabling tx recovery
```

```
Mon Jan 12 00:03:55 2004
Database Characterset is WE8ISO8859P15
replication_dependency_tracking turned off (no async multimaster
replication found)
Completed: ALTER DATABASE OPEN
Sat Jan 10 18:46:46 2004
Shutting down instance: further logons disabled
Shutting down instance (normal)
License high water mark = 2
Sat Jan 10 18:46:46 2004
ALTER DATABASE CLOSE NORMAL
Sat Jan 10 18:46:46 2004
SMON: disabling tx recovery
SMON: disabling cache recovery
Sat Jan 10 18:46:46 2004
Shutting down archive processes
Archiving is disabled
Archive process shutdown avoided: 0 active
Thread 1 closed at log sequence 101
Successful close of redo thread 1.
Sat Jan 10 18:46:47 2004
Completed: ALTER DATABASE CLOSE NORMAL
Sat Jan 10 18:46:47 2004
ALTER DATABASE DISMOUNT
Completed: ALTER DATABASE DISMOUNT
ARCH: Archiving is disabled
Shutting down archive processes
Archiving is disabled
Archive process shutdown avoided: 0 active
ARCH: Archiving is disabled
Shutting down archive processes
Archiving is disabled
Archive process shutdown avoided: 0 active
Sat Jan 10 18:55:55 2004
Starting ORACLE instance (normal)
LICENSE_MAX_SESSION = 0
LICENSE_SESSIONS_WARNING = 0
SCN scheme 1
Using log_archive_dest parameter default value
LICENSE_MAX_USERS = 0
SYS auditing is disabled
Starting up ORACLE RDBMS Version: 9.2.0.2.0.
System parameters with non-default values:
  processes                = 50
```

```
  shared_pool_size          = 134217728
  control_files             = /ora_db/control01.ctl, /ora_db/con-
trol02.ctl, /ora_db/control03.ctl
  db_block_buffers          = 10000
  db_block_size             = 8192
  compatible                = 9.0.0.0.0
  log_buffer                = 65536
log_checkpoint_interval   = 99999
db_files                  = 50
db_file_multiblock_read_count= 16
  dml_locks                 = 100
  rollback_segments         = r01, r02, r03, r04
  background_dump_dest      = /opt/oracle/admin/openview/bdump
  user_dump_dest            = /opt/oracle/admin/openview/udump
  max_dump_file_size        = 10240
  core_dump_dest            = /opt/oracle/admin/openview/cdump
  sort_area_size            = 262144
  db_name                   = openview
  open_cursors              = 1024
  os_authent_prefix         =
PMON started with pid=2
DBW0 started with pid=3
LGWR started with pid=4
CKPT started with pid=5
SMON started with pid=6
RECO started with pid=7
Sat Jan 10 18:55:57 2004
ALTER DATABASE   MOUNT
Sat Jan 10 18:56:01 2004
Successful mount of redo thread 1, with mount id 2485556221.
Sat Jan 10 18:56:01 2004
Database mounted in Exclusive Mode.
Completed: ALTER DATABASE   MOUNT
Sat Jan 10 18:56:01 2004
ALTER DATABASE OPEN
Sat Jan 10 18:56:02 2004
Thread 1 opened at log sequence 101
Current log# 2 seq# 101 mem# 0: /ora_db/redo02.log
Successful open of redo thread 1.
Sat Jan 10 18:56:02 2004
MTTR advisory is disabled because FAST_START_MTTR_TARGET is not
set
Sat Jan 10 18:56:02 2004
SMON: enabling cache recovery
```

```
SMON: enabling tx recovery
Sat Jan 10 18:56:02 2004
Database Characterset is WE8ISO8859P15
replication_dependency_tracking turned off (no async multimaster
replication found)
Completed: ALTER DATABASE OPEN
Starting ORACLE instance (normal)
Sat Jan 10 20:13:44 2004
Starting ORACLE instance (normal)
LICENSE_MAX_SESSION = 0
LICENSE_SESSIONS_WARNING = 0
SCN scheme 1
Using log_archive_dest parameter default value
LICENSE_MAX_USERS = 0
SYS auditing is disabled
Starting up ORACLE RDBMS Version: 9.2.0.2.0.
System parameters with non-default values:
  processes                = 50
  shared_pool_size         = 134217728
  control_files            = /ora_db/control01.ctl, /ora_db/con-
trol02.ctl, /ora_db/control03.ctl
  db_block_buffers         = 10000
  db_block_size            = 8192
  compatible               = 9.0.0.0.0
  log_buffer               = 65536
log_checkpoint_interval  = 99999
db_files                 = 50
db_file_multiblock_read_count= 16
  dml_locks                = 100
  rollback_segments        = r01, r02, r03, r04
  background_dump_dest     = /opt/oracle/admin/openview/bdump
  user_dump_dest           = /opt/oracle/admin/openview/udump
  max_dump_file_size       = 10240
  core_dump_dest           = /opt/oracle/admin/openview/cdump
  sort_area_size           = 262144
  db_name                  = openview
  open_cursors             = 1024
  os_authent_prefix        =
PMON started with pid=2
DBW0 started with pid=3
LGWR started with pid=4
CKPT started with pid=5
SMON started with pid=6
RECO started with pid=7
```

```
Sat Jan 10 20:13:46 2004
ALTER DATABASE   MOUNT
Sat Jan 10 20:13:51 2004
Successful mount of redo thread 1, with mount id 2485562682.
Sat Jan 10 20:13:51 2004
Database mounted in Exclusive Mode.
Completed: ALTER DATABASE   MOUNT
Sat Jan 10 20:13:51 2004
ALTER DATABASE OPEN
Sat Jan 10 20:13:51 2004
Beginning crash recovery of 1 threads
Sat Jan 10 20:13:51 2004
Started first pass scan
Sat Jan 10 20:13:52 2004
Completed first pass scan
89 redo blocks read, 12 data blocks need recovery
Sat Jan 10 20:13:52 2004
Started recovery at
Thread 1: logseq 101, block 961, scn 0.0
Recovery of Online Redo Log: Thread 1 Group 2 Seq 101 Reading
mem 0
Mem# 0 errs 0: /ora_db/redo02.log
Sat Jan 10 20:13:53 2004
Ended recovery at
Thread 1: logseq 101, block 1050, scn 0.1000291
12 data blocks read, 12 data blocks written, 89 redo blocks read
Crash recovery completed successfully
Sat Jan 10 20:13:54 2004
Thread 1 advanced to log sequence 102
Thread 1 opened at log sequence 102
Current log# 3 seq# 102 mem# 0: /ora_db/redo03.log
Successful open of redo thread 1.
Sat Jan 10 20:13:54 2004
MTTR advisory is disabled because FAST_START_MTTR_TARGET is not
set
Sat Jan 10 20:13:54 2004
SMON: enabling cache recovery
SMON: enabling tx recovery
Sat Jan 10 20:13:55 2004
Database Characterset is WE8ISO8859P15
replication_dependency_tracking turned off (no async multimaster
replication found)
Completed: ALTER DATABASE OPEN
```

```
Starting ORACLE instance (normal)


Checking sqlnet ..

*+++++++++++++++++++++++++++++++++++++++++++++++++++++++++++++++
•     Check net files in /etc
++++++++++++++++++++++++++++++++++++++++++++++++++++++++++++++++

/bin/ls -l /etc/*.ora
/etc/*.ora not found

*+++++++++++++++++++++++++++++++++++++++++++++++++++++++++++++++
•     Check net files in /etc
++++++++++++++++++++++++++++++++++++++++++++++++++++++++++++++++
more /etc/*.ora
/etc/*.ora: No such file or directory

*+++++++++++++++++++++++++++++++++++++++++++++++++++++++++++++++
•     Check net files in
/opt/oracle/product/9.2.0/network/admin/*.ora
++++++++++++++++++++++++++++++++++++++++++++++++++++++++++++++++

/bin/ls -l /opt/oracle/product/9.2.0/network/admin/listener.ora
/opt/oracle/product/9.2.0/network/admin/snmp_ro.ora /opt/ora-
cle/product/9.2.0/network/admin/snmp_rw.ora /opt/oracle/prod-
uct/9.2.0/network/admin/sqlnet.ora
/opt/oracle/product/9.2.0/network/admin/tnsnames.ora /opt/ora-
cle/product/9.2.0/network/admin/tnsnav.ora
•     rw-r—r—   1 root       sys            715 Oct  9 03:49
/opt/oracle/product/9.2.0/network/admin/listener.ora
•     rw-rw-r—   1 oracle     dba             86 Oct  7 10:57
/opt/oracle/product/9.2.0/network/admin/snmp_ro.ora
•     rw-rw-r—   1 oracle     dba              0 Oct  7 10:57
/opt/oracle/product/9.2.0/network/admin/snmp_rw.ora
•     rw-r—r—   1 root       sys            352 Oct  9 03:49
/opt/oracle/product/9.2.0/network/admin/sqlnet.ora
•     rw-r—r—   1 root       sys            492 Oct  9 03:49
/opt/oracle/product/9.2.0/network/admin/tnsnames.ora
•     rw-r—r—   1 root       sys            275 Oct  9 03:49
/opt/oracle/product/9.2.0/network/admin/tnsnav.ora
```

```
*++++++++++++++++++++++++++++++++++++++++++++++++++++++++++++++++
•     Check net files in /opt/oracle/product/9.2.0..
+++++++++++++++++++++++++++++++++++++++++++++++++++++++++++++++++

more /opt/oracle/product/9.2.0/network/admin/listener.ora
/opt/oracle/product/9.2.0/network/admin/snmp_ro.ora /opt/
oracle/product/9.2.0/network/admin/snmp_rw.ora /opt/oracle/
product/9.2.0/network/admin/sqlnet.ora /opt/oracle/
product/9.2.0/network/admin/tnsnames.ora /opt/oracle/
product/9.2.0/network/admin/tnsnav.ora

# FILENAME: listener.ora
# DATE....: Jan 7 1999
# NETWORK.: openview
# NODE....: Server
# SERVICE.: LISTENER
# COMMENT.: For use with HP OpenView IT/Operations
LISTENER =
(ADDRESS_LIST =
(ADDRESS=
(PROTOCOL=IPC)
(KEY= openview)
        )
(ADDRESS =
(PROTOCOL = TCP)
(HOST = lotus)
(PORT = 1521)
        )
  )
STARTUP_WAIT_TIME_LISTENER = 0
CONNECT_TIMEOUT_LISTENER = 10
LOG_DIRECTORY_LISTENER = /opt/oracle/product/9.2.0/network/log
LOG_FILE_LISTENER = listener
SID_LIST_LISTENER =
(SID_LIST =
(SID_DESC =
(SID_NAME=openview)
(ORACLE_HOME=/opt/oracle/product/9.2.0)
    )
  )
```

```
TRACE_LEVEL_LISTENER = OFF
snmp.visibleservices = ()
ifile = /opt/oracle/product/9.2.0/network/admin/snmp_rw.ora
# FILENAME: sqlnet.ora
# DATE....: Jan 7 1999
# NETWORK.: openview
# NODE....: Client + Server
# SERVICE.: C_OPENVIEW_COMMUNITY
# COMMENT.: For use with HP OpenView IT/Operations
TRACE_LEVEL_CLIENT = OFF
TRACE_DIRECTORY_CLIENT = /opt/oracle/product/9.2.0/network/log
LOG_DIRECTORY_CLIENT = /opt/oracle/product/9.2.0/network/log
# FILENAME: tnsnames.ora
# DATE....: Jan 7 1999
# NETWORK.: openview
# NODE....: Client
# SERVICE.: C_OPENVIEW_COMMUNITY
# COMMENT.: For use with HP OpenView IT/Operations
ov_net =
(DESCRIPTION=
(ADDRESS_LIST=
(ADDRESS =  (PROTOCOL = IPC)(KEY =openview))
(ADDRESS =
(COMMUNITY=OPENVIEW_COMMUNITY)
(PROTOCOL=TCP)
(HOST=lotus)
(PORT=1521)
        )
    )
(CONNECT_DATA=
(SID=openview)
    )
  )
# FILENAME: tnsnav.ora
# DATE....: Jan 7 1999
# NETWORK.: openview
# NODE....: Client
# SERVICE.: C_OPENVIEW_COMMUNITY
# COMMENT.: For use with HP OpenView IT/Operations
LOCAL_COMMUNITIES =
(COMMUNITY_LIST =
(COMMUNITY = OPENVIEW_COMMUNITY)
  )
```

```
*+++++++++++++++++++++++++++++++++++++++++++++++++++++++++++++++
•      Check TNS_ADMIN..
++++++++++++++++++++++++++++++++++++++++++++++++++++++++++++++++

echo

Checking Listener status

++++++++++++++++++++++++++++++++++++++++++++++++++++++++++++++++


LSNRCTL for HP-UX: Version 9.2.0.2.0 - Production on 10-JAN-2004
12:20:41
Copyright © 1991, 2002, Oracle Corporation.  All rights
reserved.
Connecting to (ADDRESS=(PROTOCOL=IPC)(KEY=openview))
STATUS of the LISTENER
Alias                     LISTENER
Version                   TNSLSNR for HP-UX: Version 9.2.0.2.0 -
Production
Start Date                10-JAN-2004 12:13:32
Uptime                    0 days 0 hr. 7 min. 9 sec
Trace Level               off
Security                  OFF
SNMP                      OFF
Listener Parameter File
/opt/oracle/product/9.2.0/network/admin/listener.ora
Listener Log File
/opt/oracle/product/9.2.0/network/log/listener.log
Listening Endpoints Summary...
  (DESCRIPTION=(ADDRESS=(PROTOCOL=ipc)(KEY=openview)))
  (DESCRIPTION=(ADDRESS=(PROTOCOL=tcp)(HOST=lotus)(PORT=1521)))
Services Summary...
Service "openview" has 2 instance(s).
  Instance "openview", status UNKNOWN, has 1 handler(s) for this
service...
  Instance "openview", status READY, has 1 handler(s) for this
service...
The command completed successfully


Checking tnsping ov_net

++++++++++++++++++++++++++++++++++++++++++++++++++++++++++++++++
```

```
TNS Ping Utility for HP-UX: Version 9.2.0.2.0 - Production on
10-JAN-2004 12:20:41

Copyright © 1997 Oracle Corporation.  All rights reserved.

Used parameter files:
/opt/oracle/product/9.2.0/network/admin/sqlnet.ora


Used TNSNAMES adapter to resolve the alias
Attempting to contact (DESCRIPTION= (ADDRESS_LIST= (ADDRESS =
(PROTOCOL = IPC)(KEY =openview)) (ADDRESS = (COMMUNITY=OPEN-
VIEW_COMMUNITY) (PROTOCOL=TCP) (HOST=lotus) (PORT=1521))) (CON-
NECT_DATA= (SID=openview)))
OK (100 msec)


Checking trcroute  ov_net

++++++++++++++++++++++++++++++++++++++++++++++++++++++++++++++++


Trace Route Utility for HP-UX: Version 9.2.0.2.0 - Production on
10-JAN-2004 12:20:42

Copyright © 1999 Oracle Corporation.  All rights reserved.

Route of TrcRoute:
---------

Node: Client            Time and address of entry into node:
10-JAN-2004 12:20:42 ADDRESS= PROTOCOL=IPC  KEY=openview
Node: Server            Time and address of entry into node:
10-JAN-2004 12:20:42

*+++++++++++++++++++++++++++++++++++++++++++++++++++++++++++++++
•     Check uptime
++++++++++++++++++++++++++++++++++++++++++++++++++++++++++++++++

uptime
8:20pm  up 9 mins,  1 user,  load average: 0.38, 0.29, 0.15
```

```
*++++++++++++++++++++++++++++++++++++++++++++++++++++++++++++++++++++
•     Print Shell Environment
+++++++++++++++++++++++++++++++++++++++++++++++++++++++++++++++++++++

env
_=/usr/bin/env
OV_ADM_DIR=/opt/oracle
MANPATH=/usr/share/man/%L:/usr/share/man:/usr/contrib/man/%L:/us
r/contrib/man:/usr/local/man/%L:/usr/local/man:/opt/upgrade/shar
e/man/%L:/opt/upgrade/share/man:/opt/pd/share/man/%L:/opt/pd/sha
re/man:/opt/pd/share/man/%L:/opt/pd/share/man:/opt/pd/share/man/
%L:/opt/pd/share/man:/opt/resmon/share/man:/opt/hparray/share/ma
n/%L:/opt/hparray/share/man:/opt/scr/share/man:/usr/dt/share/man
://opt/perl/man:/opt/ignite/share/man/%L:/opt/ignite/share/man:/
opt/OV/man:/opt/graphics/common/man:/opt/OV/man:/opt/OV/man
SHLIB_PATH=/opt/oracle/product/9.2.0/lib32:/opt/oracle/prod-
uct/9.2.0/lib
DBA_TOOL=/opt/oracle/product/9.2.0/bin/sqlplus
OV_DATA_DIR=/ora_db
PATH=/usr/sbin:/usr/bin:/usr/ccs/bin:/usr/contrib/bin:/opt/hpar-
ray/bin:/opt/nettladm/bin:/opt/upgrade/bin:/opt/fcms/bin:/usr/bi
n/X11:/usr/contrib/bin/X11:/opt/pd/bin:/opt/resmon/bin:/opt/scr/
bin:/opt/atok/bin:/opt/egb/bin://opt/perl/bin:/usr/sbin/diag/con
trib:/opt/vje/bin:/opt/ignite/bin:/opt/graphics/common/bin:/opt/
OV/bin:/opt/OV/bin/OpC:/opt/OV/bin/OpC/utils:/opt/OV/bin/OpC/ins
tall:/opt/OV/contrib/OpC:/sbin:/home/root:/opt/oracle/prod-
uct/9.2.0/bin
NLS_LANG=american_america.WE8ISO8859P15
COLUMNS=80
ORACLE_BASE=/opt/oracle
OV_INDEX_DIR=/ora_db
OV_DBA_USER=oracle
WINDOWID=4194330
EDITOR=vi
LOGNAME=root
DBA_ERR_GREP=MGR-
MAIL=/var/mail/root
DBA_TOOL_NAME=sqlplus
ORACLE_SID=openview
ERASE=^H
OV_OS_PREFIX=
ITO_INDEXDIR=/ora_db
SQLNET_CONF_DIR=/opt/oracle/product/9.2.0/network/admin
DBUSER=oracle
OV_CHARSET=WE8ISO8859P15
DISPLAY=10.10.210.60:0.0
```

```
ORA_USER=oracle
SHELL=/sbin/sh
ORACLE_TERM=ansi
ITO_DATADIR=/ora_db
HOME=/
TERM=hpterm
ORACLE_HOME=/opt/oracle/product/9.2.0
DB_CONNECT=ov_net
PWD=/opt/OV/contrib/OpC
TZ=PST8PDT
LINES=24


*+++++++++++++++++++++++++++++++++++++++++++++++++++++++++++++++
•     Report amount of free disc space
++++++++++++++++++++++++++++++++++++++++++++++++++++++++++++++++

bdf
Filesystem           kbytes    used   avail %used Mounted on
/dev/vg00/lvol3      204800   79691  117293   40% /
/dev/vg00/lvol1      299157   68632  200609   25% /stand
/dev/vg00/lvol8     2609152  682383 1806416   27% /var
/dev/vg00/lvol7     1658880 1560690   92077   94% /usr
/dev/vg00/lvol4      122880  118063    4519   96% /tmp
/dev/vg01/lvol1     3072000 2957535  107361   96% /ovo_8
/dev/vg01/lvol4     1228800  300612  870240   26% /ora_db
/dev/vg00/lvol6      503808  487846   15024   97% /opt
/dev/vg01/lvol3     3584000 2327889 1177652   66% /opt/oracle
/dev/vg01/lvol2     1228800  984015  229526   81% /opt/OV
/dev/vg00/lvol5       20480    1417   17873    7% /home
/dev/dsk/c0t0d0      142958  142958       0  100% /SD_CDROM


*+++++++++++++++++++++++++++++++++++++++++++++++++++++++++++++++
•     Disk Utilization at /ora_db
++++++++++++++++++++++++++++++++++++++++++++++++++++++++++++++++

du -s /ora_db
598284     /ora_db
```

```
*+++++++++++++++++++++++++++++++++++++++++++++++++++++++++++
•     Collect performance information / Part 1
++++++++++++++++++++++++++++++++++++++++++++++++++++++++++++

iostat -t
              tty              cpu
            tin tout    us  ni  sy  id
               0   30    6  10   8  77

  device    bps      sps     msps

  c3t6d0      0      0.0      1.0
  c3t5d0      0      0.0      1.0
  c3t4d0      0      0.0      1.0
  c0t0d0      0      0.0      1.0



*+++++++++++++++++++++++++++++++++++++++++++++++++++++++++++
•     Collect performance information / Part 2
++++++++++++++++++++++++++++++++++++++++++++++++++++++++++++

vmstat -s
0 swap ins
0 swap outs
0 pages swapped in
0 pages swapped out
810394 total address trans. faults taken
603584 page ins
0 page outs
51536 pages paged in
0 pages paged out
789060 reclaims from free list
595960 total page reclaims
76 intransit blocking page faults
597878 zero fill pages created
331594 zero fill page faults
1339274 executable fill pages created
51752 executable fill page faults
0 swap text pages found in free list
95110 inode text pages found in free list
0 revolutions of the clock hand
```

```
100726 pages scanned for page out
0 pages freed by the clock daemon
325099 cpu context switches
380801 device interrupts
905970 traps
6374669 system calls
22490 Page Select Size Successes for Page size 4K
87558 Page Select Size Successes for Page size 16K
274 Page Select Size Successes for Page size 64K
15 Page Select Size Successes for Page size 256K
283 Page Select Size Successes for Page size 1M
8 Page Select Size Successes for Page size 4M
5 Page Select Size Successes for Page size 64M
22490 Page Select Size Failures for Page size 16K
2150 Page Select Size Failures for Page size 64K
2424 Page Select Size Failures for Page size 256K
2439 Page Select Size Failures for Page size 1M
2722 Page Select Size Failures for Page size 4M
2730 Page Select Size Failures for Page size 16M
2730 Page Select Size Failures for Page size 64M
326268 Page Allocate Successes for Page size 4K
79889 Page Allocate Successes for Page size 16K
286 Page Allocate Successes for Page size 64K
15 Page Allocate Successes for Page size 256K
308 Page Allocate Successes for Page size 1M
8 Page Allocate Successes for Page size 4M
5 Page Allocate Successes for Page size 64M
566 Page Demotions for Page size 16K



*++++++++++++++++++++++++++++++++++++++++++++++++++++++++++++++
•     Collect performance information / Part 3
+++++++++++++++++++++++++++++++++++++++++++++++++++++++++++++++

vmstat
        procs              memory                        page
faults       cpu
    r     b      w       avm     free     re     at     pi    po     fr
de     sr      in       sy     cs  us sy id
1      0      0   173523    76537  932   177     95     0      0     0
187     509  11870    605   16   8 77
```

```
*+++++++++++++++++++++++++++++++++++++++++++++++++++++++++++++++++
•     Check for Oracle processes
+++++++++++++++++++++++++++++++++++++++++++++++++++++++++++++++++

ps -ef | grep ora
  oracle  1638     1  0 20:13:46 ?        0:00 ora_lgwr_openview
  oracle  1634     1  0 20:13:45 ?        0:00 ora_pmon_openview
  oracle  1636     1  0 20:13:46 ?        0:00 ora_dbw0_openview
  oracle  1569     1  0 20:13:31 ?        0:00 /opt/oracle/prod-
uct/9.2.0/bin/tnslsnr LISTENER -inherit
  oracle  1640     1  0 20:13:46 ?        0:00 ora_ckpt_openview
  oracle  1642     1  0 20:13:46 ?        0:00 ora_smon_openview
  oracle  1644     1  0 20:13:46 ?        0:00 ora_reco_openview
    root  4594  2807  1 20:20:44 ttyp1    0:00 grep ora



*+++++++++++++++++++++++++++++++++++++++++++++++++++++++++++++++++
•     Report Global Process status (Note: Summarized Output)
+++++++++++++++++++++++++++++++++++++++++++++++++++++++++++++++++

ps -efl
  F S      UID   PID  PPID  C PRI NI             ADDR    SZ
WCHAN    STIME TTY       TIME COMD
1001 S   oracle  1569     1  0 154 20        42111340   766
9772c0 20:13:31 ?         0:00
/opt/oracle/product/9.2.0/bin/tnslsnr LISTENER -inherit
1001 S   oracle  1640     1  0 156 20        41e5fd80 16976
b027a4 20:13:46 ?         0:00 ora_ckpt_openview
1001 S   oracle  1642     1  0 156 20        41f79e40 17008
b027ac 20:13:46 ?         0:00 ora_smon_openview
1001 S   oracle  1644     1  0 156 20        41e5fec0 16992
b027b4 20:13:46 ?         0:00 ora_reco_openview
    1 S     root  1752     1  0 154 20        422d1600   176
977280 20:14:04 ?         0:00 ovspmd -U
  1 S     root  1805     1  0 158 20        427e8180   101
42210040 20:14:58 ?         0:00 /sbin/sh /usr/dt/bin/dtrc
  1 R     root  1777     1  0 152 20        422854c0 3386
- 20:14:19 ?          0:00 /opt/OV/bin/ovdbrun -c
/var/opt/OV/share/databases/analysis/def
  1 S     root  1753  1752  0 154 20        422d1740    98
9772c0 20:14:05 ?         0:00 ovsessionmgr
  1 S     root  1825     1  0 154 20        41c84d40    70
977280 20:15:00 ?         0:00 /usr/sbin/stm/uut/bin/tools/moni-
```

```
tor/disk_em
  1 S      root  1767  1752  0 154 20         42089d40   93
977280 20:14:14 ?          0:00 ovtrapd
2401 R      bin  1757  1752  0 152 20         42285880 4548
- 20:14:06 ?          0:07 ovrequestd -s
2001 S      bin  1761  1760  0 168 20         4234ca40  183
4235d168 20:14:07 ?          0:00 /opt/OV/httpd/bin/httpd
  1 R      root  1790  1772  0 152 20         425a4e40  323
- 20:14:43 ?          0:00 /opt/OV/lbin/eaagt/opcle
2001 S      bin  1762  1760  0 154 20         4234cb80  183
42370168 20:14:07 ?          0:00 /opt/OV/httpd/bin/httpd
2001 S      bin  1763  1760  0 168 20         4234ccc0  183
423aa168 20:14:07 ?          0:00 /opt/OV/httpd/bin/httpd
2001 S      bin  1764  1760  0 168 20         4234ce00  183
423b8168 20:14:07 ?          0:00 /opt/OV/httpd/bin/httpd
2001 S      bin  1765  1760  0 168 20         423c1080  183
423c0168 20:14:07 ?          0:00 /opt/OV/httpd/bin/httpd
2001 S      bin  1768  1752  0 154 20         4242b180  283
9772c0 20:14:14 ?          0:00 ovactiond
  1 R      root  1769  1752  0 152 20         4242b400 1020
- 20:14:15 ?          0:00 ovalarmsrv
  1 S      root  1770  1752  0 154 20         4242b680  140
9772c0 20:14:15 ?          0:00 genannosrvr -a orch_async
  1 S      root  1771  1752  0 154 20         422d1240  124
977280 20:14:15 ?          0:00 ovdbcheck -ovspmd
401 R      root  1772     1  0 152 20         4242b900 1481
- 20:14:15 ?          0:03 /opt/OV/bin/ovcd
401 R      root  1782  1772  0 152 20         425a4440 1395
- 20:14:30 ?          0:00 /opt/OV/lbin/conf/ovconfd
401 R      root  1778  1772  0 152 20         424fe200  405
- 20:14:20 ?          0:00 /opt/OV/bin/ovcs
401 R      root  1776     1  0 152 20         4242be00 1558
- 20:14:17 ?          0:01 /opt/OV/bin/ovbbccb
  1 R      root  1788  1772  0 152 20         425a4bc0  281
- 20:14:39 ?          0:00 /opt/OV/lbin/eaagt/opcmsgi
401 R      root  1797  1772  0 152 20         425a4a80  657
- 20:14:54 ?          0:00 /opt/OV/lbin/perf/coda
  1 R      root  1792  1772  0 152 20         424fec00  502
- 20:14:47 ?          0:01 /opt/OV/lbin/eaagt/opcmona
  1 R      root  1794  1772  0 152 20         425a4d00 1027
- 20:14:50 ?          0:01 /opt/OV/lbin/eaagt/opctrapi
401 R      root  1796  1772  0 152 20         42745480  648
- 20:14:53 ?          0:01 /opt/OV/lbin/eaagt/opcmsga
    1 S      root  2807  2638 12 158 24         42ad5340  155
42b5b040 20:15:59 ttyp1      0:00 /sbin/sh ./opc_odc
```

```
*+++++++++++++++++++++++++++++++++++++++++++++++++++++++++++++++
•     Collect Information about Shared Memory and Semaphore
Usage
+++++++++++++++++++++++++++++++++++++++++++++++++++++++++++++++

ipcs
IPC status from /dev/kmem as of Sat Jan 10 12:20:44 2004
T       ID     KEY          MODE          OWNER      GROUP
Message Queues:
q        0 0x3c1c0555 -Rrw—w—w-        root       root
q        1 0x3e1c0555 —rw-r—r—         root       root
Shared Memory:
m        0 0x411c05cc—rw-rw-rw-        root       root
m        1 0x4e0c0002 —rw-rw-rw-       root       root
m        2 0x412009c5 —rw-rw-rw-       root       root
m        3 0x301c3e75 —rw-rw-rw-       root       root
m        4 0x501c7b09 —r—r—r—          root       other
m        5 0x00000000 —rw———-          root       root
m     9478 0x00000000 —rw-r——-         oracle     dba
m        7 0x00000000 —rw-r——-         oracle     dba
m        8 0x96e866c0 —rw-r——-         oracle     dba
m     2825 0x00000000 D-rw———-         root       root
m       10 0x01205edf—rw-rw-rw-        root       root
m       11 0x01206297 —rw-rw-rw-       root       root
m       12 0x012062b0 —rw-rw-rw-       root       root
m       13 0x012062a0 —rw-rw-rw-       root       root
m      270 0x012062a8 —rw-rw-rw-       root       root
m      271 0x01206300 —rw-rw-rw-       root       root
m      272 0x012063e0 —rw-rw-rw-       root       root
m       17 0x01206352 —rw-rw-rw-       root       root
m       18 0x012063d3 —rw-rw-rw-       root       root
m       19 0x012063d9 —rw-rw-rw-       root       root
m       20 0x012063d8 —rw-rw-rw-       root       root
m      277 0x431c8850 —rw-rw-rw-       daemon     daemon
Semaphores:
s        0 0x411c05cc—ra-ra-ra-        root       root
s        1 0x4e0c0002 —ra-ra-ra-       root       root
s        2 0x412009c5 —ra-ra-ra-       root       root
s        3 0x00446f6e—ra-r—r—          root       root
s        4 0x00446f6d—ra-r—r—          root       root
s        5 0x01090522 —ra-r—r—         root       root
s        6 0x311c3e75 —ra-ra-ra-       root       root
s        7 0x4004c1d3 —ra-ra-ra-       root       root
s        8 0x4004c1d4 —ra-ra-ra-       root       root
```

```
s        9 0x501c7b09 —ra-ra-ra-      root      other
s       10 0x4004c1d8 —ra-ra-ra-      root       root
s       11 0x4004c1d9 —ra-ra-ra-      root       root
s       12 0x612007c0 —ra-ra-ra-      root       root
s       13 0x732007c0 —ra-ra-ra-      root       root
s       14 0x702007c0 —ra-ra-ra-      root       root
s       15 0x692007c0 —ra-ra-ra-      root       root
s       16 0x752007c0 —ra-ra-ra-      root       root
s       17 0x632007c0 —ra-ra-ra-      root       root
s       18 0x642007c0 —ra-ra-ra-      root       root
s       19 0x662007c0 —ra-ra-ra-      root       root
s       20 0x6c2007c0 —ra-ra-ra-      root       root
s       21 0x6d2007c0 —ra-ra-ra-      root       root
s       22 0x6f2007c0 —ra-ra-ra-      root       root
s       23 0x410c01f1 —ra-ra-ra-      root       root
s      444 0xa467d1a8 —ra-r—-         oracle     dba
s       25 0x522007c0 —ra-ra-ra-      root       root
s       26 0x013d8483 —ra-r—r—        root       root
s       27 0x01205ee6 —ra-ra-ra-      root       root
s       28 0x01205ecd—ra-ra-ra-       root       root
s       29 0x012062ba—ra-ra-ra-       root       root
s       30 0x01206322 —ra-ra-ra-      root       root
s      171 0x0120635e—ra-ra-ra-       root       root
s      172 0x012063b7 —ra-ra-ra-      root       root
s      173 0x012063e8 —ra-ra-ra-      root       root
s       34 0x012063c4 —ra-ra-ra-      root       root
s       35 0x012063d6 —ra-ra-ra-      root       root
s       36 0x012063da—ra-ra-ra-       root       root
s       37 0x012063de—ra-ra-ra-       root       root
s      178 0x4c1c8850 —ra-r—r—        daemon     daemon

opc_odc finished. See the logfile /tmp/opc_odc.log for a
detailed protocol.
```

18.8 DATABASE TOOLS AND RESOURCES

Out-of-the-box database tools and resources are found in the following directories; the programs were listed with descriptions in Chapter 17, "Server Administration." This listing shows the programs that are useful for database operations.

Contributed tools:

- /opt/OV/contrib./OpC/itochecker
- /opt/OV/contrib/OpC/opcdbck
- /opt/OV/contrib/OpC/opc_odc

Database-tuning document:

- /opt/OV/ReleaseNotes/opc_db.tuning

Local web site with links to OpenView resources:

- `http://<management_server_name>:3443/ITO/`

18.9 SUMMARY

The OVO database is powerful, and although it is not necessary to become a database expert to work with OVO, it is recommended that you become familiar with basic database concepts and terminology. This helps when planning and resolving with a DBA or support resources and any issues or configuration changes you think are necessary in order to optimize the operation of the database.

CHAPTER 19

Enterprise Management Flexibility with Multiple Management Servers

The flexible management concept helps distribute the application, system, and network management tasks to OpenView servers enterprise-wide. The location of the servers depends on the business requirements. The model for distributed management supports locating the systems at different sites within the same city, different states, or different countries. Implementing the OpenView distributed management server architecture requires detailed planning.

Enterprise management policies are used as a basis for the development of *service level agreements* (SLAs). The SLAs guide the OpenView distributed management design and implementation. When the detailed design plan is developed, the enterprise management needs become a roadmap for how the OVO agents are utilized to help meet the requirements of the SLAs. The company policies, in conjunction with the OpenView design plan, help define the operation's support plans. The support plan may centralized some operations and distribute others at the regional level.

The use of embedded notification and alert technology may include sending pager messages, forwarding messages to a trouble ticket system, or high-availability failover. When multiple management servers send and receive information over the network, a reliable high-speed transport is essential. Other considerations include time zone synchronizations if the machines are located in multiple time zones and send messages from one time zone to another.

This chapter is an overview of the flexible management features built into OVO.

19.1 DISTRIBUTED OPENVIEW SERVER CONCEPTS

OVO management servers are authorized to perform the following tasks on the managed nodes:

- Receive messages
- Assume responsibility for the node
- Update the agent software
- Update the license information
- Perform actions
- Distribute customized configurations

Expand these basic application, systems, and network management concepts when multiple OpenView management servers work together to provide an enterprise-wide solution. The multiple management server concepts are often called *manager of manager* (MoM). Questions that help guide the basic MoM configuration details should include:

- Which messages are sent to other servers?
- Which management servers will participate in the configuration?
- How will the servers be authorized to perform actions on remote nodes?
- How will the servers maintain consistent configurations?

Other questions (not covered in this chapter) that are very important include:

- How many servers are required?
- Will distributed NNM servers provide additional infrastructure support?
- How will you implement the systems management policies that guide the configuration?
- What types of monitors already exist?
- How will the existing monitors integrate with OVO?

In general, the flexible management configuration implements two key concepts. The first enables a node to send messages to different management servers. The second involves multiple management servers that communicate and send messages to each other.

19.1.1 Backup Server

If the original management server is unavailable, a backup management server is prepared to take over. This is sometimes called the backup server or failover solution. This solution is implemented without the use of *high availability* (HA) cluster technology, but requires additional hardware and software.

19.1.2 Competence Center and Escalation

In the competence or expertise center concept, some messages are filtered at the original management server and then sent to a second management server for further analysis and troubleshooting by software or hardware specialists. The system is programmed to send the filtered messages to the second management server automatically. As an option, a selected message escalation to the competence center is triggered by an operator in the message browser.

19.1.3 Follow-the-sun

Enterprise operations that are twenty-four hours and seven days (24x7) require distributed systems management operations across different time zones. This follow-the-sun model enables the support functions to shift time zones. Automatic action responses, notifications, and event monitors continue to operate seamlessly and, if necessary, messages are forwarded to systems located in different regions.

19.2 TERMINOLOGY

When there are multiple management servers, it is helpful to use new terms and concepts to understand the configuration.

19.2.1 OpenView Domain

This term refers to the managed devices that send messages and events to an OpenView management server. The management server has responsibility for the devices within the domain. The responsibilities of the management server were described in Chapter 14, "Agents, Policies, and Distribution."

19.2.2 Message Forwarding

Events are transformed into messages on the managed node using an SNMP trap interceptor, program monitor, message interceptor, console monitor, or message interceptor. After converting the intercepted event into an OVO message, the message is sent to a management server. This process is called message forwarding.

19.2.2 Responsible Manager

The responsible manager is the server to which the managed node is authorized to send messages. The responsible manager configuration is defined inside a configuration file that could reside on a managed node or a management server.

19.2.3 Primary Manager

A primary manager is the management server is authorized to configure the agent, deploy policies and execute actions. The information about which manager currently is primary resides on the managed node.

19.2.4 Original Manager

The original management server distributes the initial OpenView configuration to the managed node. The initial configuration includes the agent software, templates, and configuration components such as programs, files, or scripts.

19.2.5 Secondary and Action Allowed Managers

The secondary manager is authorized to become a primary management server in the event of a failure or takeover. The authorized manager configuration resides in a file on the managed node. It is important to define all relevant managers as secondary, including the primary manager. If this is not done it will not be possible for the primary manager to resume responsibility for the node.

An action-allowed manager is authorized to execute actions on the managed node. Typically all secondary managers are also declared as action-allowed.

19.2.6 Failover/Takeover/Failback/Takeback

A failover is triggered when a secondary manager becomes the primary manager. The process is generally performed manually but can be automated. The command that triggers the failover (sometimes called takeover) is issued from a secondary manager. The **opcragt** command (with appropriate options) is sent across the network to the managed nodes and instructs them to begin forwarding the necessary (OPC_PRIMARY_MGR) messages to the new primary server. If the calling server is an authorized secondary manager, the node responds by sending messages to the new primary server. The secondary server is now the primary manager. In order for the original primary server to resume responsibility for the managed nodes, it must also issue the same command to instruct the nodes to report to a new primary manager. This process is sometimes called failback or takeback.

In some environments, the failover and takeback process is automated in the event that the primary node is not responding. If other management servers periodically check the primary server (via ping) and it is not responding, the secondary manager automatically triggers a failover.

19.2.7 Escalation

Some or all messages can be selected from the message browser and forwarded (escalated) to another server. One key difference in the escalation process is that it is initiated manually by the operator. The other message-forwarding concepts, once configured, happen automatically. The server to which the message is sent is called an escalation manager. The operator initiates an escalation through the GUI. The escalate button will display in the pop-up menu or message details for a selected message. If the message matches an escalation rule, the operator can initiate the escalation by selecting the escalate button for the selected message. The escalation configuration resides on the management server. After a message is escalated, it is flagged as 'escalated to' or 'from.' Message escalation is determined by configuration rules.

19.2.8 Switch Control Responsibility

Messages forwarded from one manager to another can allow the target manager to have full control of the message. This means that the standard message actions are available, such as acknowledge, own, escalate (if configured), operator initiated actions, and add annotations. When the message is acknowledged on the second server, it is automatically acknowledged on the original server. Alternatively, a message can be forwarded as read-only from one management server to another. Messages that arrive at the target management server without switch control have the attribute flag set to read-only and cannot be forwarded or escalated. Non-switch control messages allow local acknowledgement and annotations. The non-switch control messages are called notification messages. Several configurable parameters define the behavior of switch control messages. The switch control parameters are in the ovconfchg on the server, and have to be set up in dedicated forwarding configuration files, as explained in Section 19-5. Sample configuration files, templates and configuration parameters are presented in other sections of this chapter.

19.2.9 Sync Configurations

When multiple management servers have responsibilities and authority to become primary managers, the configurations of the servers must be kept synchronized. If, for example, a message from a node, arrives on a secondary manager for which it has no configuration, the message is discarded. It is recommended that the configuration be regularly synchronized. The process to synchronize the configuration requires a configuration download from one manager and a configuration upload on the other managers.

19.3 DIRECTORIES

The files and directories necessary to configure the flexible management concepts (discussed in Section 19.3.1 and 19.5.1) are available for immediate use after installation.

19.3.1 Directories on the Management Server

The directories and files installed on the management server include many sample configuration files that are ready to customize for the specific flexible management or *manager of manager* (MoM) concept. It is a good practice to preserve the default copies of the files and create working copies for the customized configuration. The directories on the management server are in the path /etc/opt/OV/share/conf/OpC/mgmt_sv.

19.3.1.1 respmgrs

This directory is initially empty until you finalize the configuration and copy the production files into this directory. Some of the files in this directory are distributed to the managed node. We will cover the details of what files are distributed to the node in Section 19.5.4. Other files in this directory remain on the local server and are read by the server processes.

19.3.1.2 tmpl_respmgrs

This directory contains sample templates for the various flexible management configurations. The names of the files (such as follow-the-sun) provide a guide to the type of file. Some files have generic names (such as example.M2), and it is necessary to read the content of the file to determine how it may apply to a particular configuration.

19.3.1.3 work_repmgrs

This directory serves as a work area. Prior to changing a sample template, copy it into the work_respmgrs directory. Customize the sample template and save it with a new name. Some sample templates must retain their original name (such as escmgr and msgforw). The new name for the template will dictate how the template is used after it is read by the server or agent processes. Details about the template naming conventions are covered in Sections 19.5.2, "Management Server Templates" and 19.5.4, "Template Distribution." After the template is checked, copy the file into the respmgrs (production) directory.

19.4 COMMANDS AND UTILITIES

This section provides descriptions and examples of the frequently used commands:

- **opcragt**—Remotely administer agent process; includes template distribution and trigger for MoM failover/takeover.
- **opcmomchk**—Check flexible management configuration files.
- **opccfgdwn**—Download configuration data from the OVO database to flat files.
- **opccfgupld**—Upload configuration from flat files into the OVO database.
- **opcmgrdist**—Distribute the OVO configuration between management servers.
- **opcsv**—Administer manager services running on the management server.
- **opc_ip_addr**—Converts IP address to hexidecimal format.

19.5 TEMPLATES

Most of the template configurations within OVO use the graphical user interface. The MoM templates do not have a GUI. The templates are in ascii format. Use an ASCII text editor to configure the template. MoM sample templates are pre-configured with the most popular multiple server scenarios. After the template is customized, check the template syntax with the utility opcmomchk.

19.5.1 Template Types

The template type defines the rules for message filtering and forwarding provided to the message agents and the message managers. The overall template types are

- **Time**—Describes the criteria for what time the specific rules and conditions apply for message match or suppression.
- **Message forwarding**—Describes the roles and responsibilities of the management servers and how agent and server processes handle messages based on match and suppress criteria.
- **Escalation**—Describes criteria for sending a message to another server via an operator initiated escalation of a selected message.
- **Service**—Describes the service hierarchy for use with Service Navigator. (Refer to the HP OpenView Service Navigator Concepts and Configuration Guide for additional information about Service Navigator.)

19.5.2 Management Server Templates

Templates on the management server provide instructions for message forwarding, service outage, service management, and escalations. The corresponding template names are

- msgforw
- escmgr
- outage
- service (use with Service Navigator; not covered in this chapter)

The template files listed will reside in the ./respmgrs directory and must have the names as shown.

The allnodes template is created on the manager and distributed to the managed node. If you require special rules within the node template for some nodes and not others, copy and rename the allnodes file with a unique file name. This is covered in more detail in Section 19.5.4.1.

19.5.2.1 Template Activation

Perform MoM template activation on the server with either a server process restart or session restart. See the template descriptions for the proper method to activate the template. Perform template distribution to activate MoM template on the managed node, which triggers the agent to read the MoM configuration file.

19.5.3 Managed Node Templates

MoM templates for certain scenarios (such as backup-server and follow-the-sun) reside on the managed node and define message-forwarding rules and secondary server authorization. The message agent reads the template during agent startup. The mgrconf file is the MoM template on the managed node after it has been distributed from the OVO server. Do not modify this file manually.

19.5.4 Template Distribution

The MoM template distribution process is the same process used for other templates. Through the GUI, select **Actions→Agents→Install/Update Templates**. Use the **opcragt** command (with the appropriate options) for command line template distribution.

Prior to distribution, locate the customized template in the production directory (respmgrs). During distribution, the distribution manager will check for new or updated templates in the respmgrs directory.

19.5.4.1 Template File Names that Change after Distribution

The MoM template for the managed node is either called allnodes or a name that represents the IP address converted to hex number format. If the name is allnodes, this template is distributed to all the selected managed nodes during distribution. If the name of the template is a converted IP address for one of the nodes, it means that the configuration is different from the allnodes file. The IP address template file is only distributed to the node with the IP address that is the same as the hex number of the template file.

19.5.4.2 Convert IP Address to Hex Number

A utility program, **opc_ip_addr**, is available in the directory /opt/OV/bin/OpC/install to help with the math conversion of the IP address.

```
#/opt/OV/bin/OpC/install/opc_ip_addr lotus
lotus=192.168.16.2=c0a81002
```

19.5.4.2 Rename the allnodes File for a Specific Node

Here is an example of the process to change the name of the file for distribution to a specific node:

```
# ls -l /etc/opt/OV/share/conf/OpC/mgmt_sv/respmgrs

total 6
-r—r—r—    1 root       sys          2098 Aug 14 15:23 allnodes
drwx——     2 root       sys            96 Dec  2  2000 lastdistr
```

```
# cp allnodes c0a81002

# ls -l
total 12
-r—r—r—   1 root       sys              2098 Aug 14 15:23 allnodes
-r—r—r—   1 root       sys              2098 Aug 14 15:25 c0a81002
drwx——    2 root       sys                96 Dec  2  2000 lastdistr
```

After adding the custom changes to the new file c0a81002, distribute to the managed node (lotus in the prior example) either with the GUI or with the command **opcragt**.

19.5.5 Template Syntax

The templates are written with a syntax that describes how the agent will handle the messages that are filtered (for match or suppress conditions) by the template. The logic of the template is organized from the top with a section to define time criteria. The message must match the time criteria (if it is specified) in addition to the other template conditions. The time criteria is set to #none if it does not apply.

Each section of the template begins with a section label in all capital letters. The section label is plural and the subsections' labels are singular. Multiple sub-sections can follow a section label. Descriptions and comments help make the templates easier to understand. Comments follow the symbol (#). Two good rules-of-thumb are to use comments liberally throughout the template and use offset lines for readability. The symbol "e" used in the syntax descriptions represents an empty string. An "OR" condition is represented by the symbol "|". Days of the week are spelled out. The time is represented by a twenty-four-hour format. Dates are specified by the month (two-digits), the day, (two-digits), the year (four digits).

19.5.5.1 Time Template

A sample time template "followthesun" and the syntax chart are shown here for reference. The template is followed by brief descriptions of the syntax. A time template defines generic time ranges (e.g DAYTIME = 8:00-18:00). These definitions have to be referenced in message rules later in the template file in order to become active. You may want to specify that Database messages during DAYTIME are sent to another manager. The time template configuration is illustrated here:

```
TIMETEMPLATES
# time template 1
      TIMETEMPLATE "shift1"
        DESCRIPTION "Time Template 1 "
        # Time template for shift1
        # this includes the time from 17:00 to 24:00  and from
0:00 to 6:00
        # on the weekday Monday to Friday
```

```
            TIMETMPLCONDS
                TIMETMPLCOND
                   TIME FROM 0:00 TO 6:00
                   WEEKDAY FROM Monday TO Friday
                TIMETMPLCOND
                   TIME FROM 17:00 TO 24:00
                   WEEKDAY FROM Monday TO Friday
       TIMETEMPLATE "shift2"
         DESCRIPTION "Time Template 2 "
         # Time template for shift2
         # this includes the time from 6:00 to 17:00
         # on the weekday Monday to Friday
            TIMETMPLCONDS
                TIMETMPLCOND
                   TIME FROM 6:00 TO 17:00
                   WEEKDAY FROM Monday TO Friday
         # time template 3
       TIMETEMPLATE "shift3"
         DESCRIPTION "Time Template 3 "
         # Time template for shift3
         # this includes the time from 0:00 to 24:00 (the whole
day)
         # on the weekday Saturday and Sunday
            TIMETMPLCONDS
                TIMETMPLCOND
                   TIME FROM 0:00 TO 24:00
                   WEEKDAY FROM Saturday TO Sunday
```

19.5.5.2 Keywords for the Time Templates

TIMETEMPLATES—Define one or more time templates in the section labeled TIME-TEMPLATES.

TIMETEMPLATE—Define the individual templates with the key TIMETEMPLATE and include elements for message match or suppress time. Give each time template a unique name and DESCRIPTION surrounded by double quotes.

TIMETMPLCONDS—Multiple time template conditions can follow the section label.

TIMETMPLCOND—Define the match or suppress time criteria. Valid time criteria are based on Universal Standard Time (UST). (Reference Appendix C for more information on UST.)

TIMECONDTYPE—The start of the time filter criteria begins with the key TIME FROM and ends with the key TO. The time is further defined by the specification of additional parameters within the time condition type WEEKDAY ON the DAY (of the week or multiple days) or the exact DATE.

19.5.5.3 Time Template Syntax

The full keyword syntax list is shown here.

```
timetmpls      ::=
<timetmpls> TIMETEMPLATE <string>
DESCRIPTION   <string>
                       <conditions> | e
conditions ::=
TIMETMPLCONDS <timetmplconds> | e
timetmplconds ::=
<timetmplconds> TIMETMPLCOND <timetmplcond> | e
timetmplcond ::=
[TIMECONDTYPE <timecondtype>]
[TIME FROM  <time> TO <time>]
[WEEKDAY <weekday>]
[DATE  <exact_date>] | e
timecondtype ::=
Match| Suppress
time ::=
<hh>:<mm>
weekday ::=
ON <day> | FROM <day> TO <day>
exact_date ::=
ON <date> | FROM <date> TO <date>
day ::=
Monday|Tuesday|Wednesday|Thursday|Friday|Saturday|Sunday
date ::=
<mm>/<dd>/<yyyy> | <mm>/<dd>/*
```

19.5.5.4 Message Template

The sample template "followthesun" is shown here. The responsible manager configuration template sections with brief syntax descriptions immediately follow the template.The following illustration is the second part of the template file that was described in Section 19.5.5.1.

```
#
# Responsible Manager Configurations for follow-the-sun func-
tionality
```

```
#
RESPMGRCONFIGS
   RESPMGRCONFIG
   DESCRIPTION "responsible managers M1 "
      SECONDARYMANAGERS
         SECONDARYMANAGER
            NODE IP 0.0.0.0 "M1"
            DESCRIPTION "secondary manager M1"
         SECONDARYMANAGER
            NODE IP 0.0.0.0 "M2"
            DESCRIPTION "secondary manager M2"
         SECONDARYMANAGER
            NODE IP 0.0.0.0 "M3"
            DESCRIPTION "secondary manager M3"
      ACTIONALLOWMANAGERS
         ACTIONALLOWMANAGER
            NODE IP 0.0.0.0 "M1"
            DESCRIPTION "action allowed manager M1"
         ACTIONALLOWMANAGER
            NODE IP 0.0.0.0 "M2"
            DESCRIPTION "action allowed manager M2"
         ACTIONALLOWMANAGER
            NODE IP 0.0.0.0 "M3"
            DESCRIPTION "action allowed manager M3"
      MSGTARGETRULES
         MSGTARGETRULE
         DESCRIPTION "target rule description "
            MSGTARGETRULECONDS
            # for all messages
            MSGTARGETMANAGERS
               MSGTARGETMANAGER
     # target manager from 17:00 to 24:00 and 00:00 to 6:00
               # from Monday to Friday
                  TIMETEMPLATE "shift1"
                  OPCMGR IP 0.0.0.0 "M1"
               # target manager from 6:00 to 17:00
               # from Monday to Friday
               MSGTARGETMANAGER
                  TIMETEMPLATE "shift2"
                  OPCMGR IP 0.0.0.0 "M2"
               # target manager on the whole weekend
               MSGTARGETMANAGER
                  TIMETEMPLATE "shift3"
                  OPCMGR IP 0.0.0.0 "M3"
```

19.5.5.4 Keywords for Responsible Manager Configuration

RESPMGRCONFIGS—Begins the description of the configuration for the responsible managers (primary, secondary, and action-allowed or escalation).

RESPMGRCONFIG—Begins the responsible manager configuration.

DESCRIPTION—A string containing a short manager description.

SECONDARYMANAGERS—A secondary ITO manager for an agent has permission to take over responsibility and to become the primary ITO manager for an agent.

SECONDARYMANAGER—Begins the configuration for a specific secondary manager.

NODE—The NODE IP of the SECONDARYMANAGER.

DESCRIPTION—A string that contains the description of the SECONDARY MANAGER.

ACTIONALLOWMANAGERS—An ITO manager that is allowed to execute actions (via the ITO Action Agent) on the managed node and to which the action response (such as command broadcast) is sent. Only the primary ITO manager has the possibility to configure "action allowed" managers for an agent.

NODE—The NODE IP of the SECONDARYMANAGER.

DESCRIPTION—A string containing a short description of the SECONDARY MANAGER.

MSGTARGETRULE and MSGTARGETRULES—Rules to configure the MSGTARGETMANAGER.

DESCRIPTION—A string containing the description of the MSGTARGETRULE.

MSGTARGETMANAGER and MSGTARGET MANAGERS—Define a manager to which the agents send messages and action responses belonging to the OVO messages (result of automatic actions). Only the primary OVO manager has the possibility to configure "message target" managers for an agent. An OVO message is sent to exactly one OVO manager. This is also used to escalate messages from one manager to another manager.

TIMETEMPLATENAME—The name of the corresponding timetemplate.

OPCMGR—The NODE IP of the ITO Manager.

MSGCONTROLLINGMGR—Attribute for a "message target" manager in order to be able to switch control of a message themselves

NOTIFYMGR—Attribute for a "message target" manager in order to notify themselves. This is set by default if no attribute is defined for the "message target" manager.

ACKNONLOCALMGR—Attribute for a message rule to force a direct acknowledgement of a notification message on a "source" management server.

MSGTARGETRULECONDS, MSGTARGETRULECOND—These conditions tell the agent to which manager the specific messages have to be sent based on message attributes and/or time. The message agent evaluates the message target conditions by reading the file mgrconf (for example, on HP- UX 11.x: /var/opt/OV/conf/OpC/mgrconf). If the mgrconf file does not exist, the messages are sent according to the info stored in the /var/opt/OV/conf/OpC/primmgr file. If the primmgr file does not exist, messages are sent according to the info stored in the opcinfo (or equivalent schema) file.

DESCRIPTION—A string containing the description of the Messagetargetrule Condition. The message target conditions are also used to specify the escalation rules. In this case, the ITO manager evaluates the file /etc/opt/OV/share/conf/OpC/mgmt_sv/respmgrs/escmgrs and escalates the message to the appropriate target managers.

SEVERITY—Six types of the severity are available: Unknown, Normal, Warning, Minor, Major or Critical

NODE—A node can be given in different ways, for example: NODE IP 0.0.0.0 hpbbn; If the node is defined in the format IP <ipaddress> or IP <ipaddress> <string> you should normally use the ipaddress "0.0.0.0". The real ipaddress will then be resolved by the name services. It also useful to set the <string> containing the name of the system to $OPC_PRIMARY_MGR and the <ipaddress> to "0.0.0.0".

APPLICATION—A string containing the application name, such as "Omniback."

MSGGRP—A string containing the name of the message group, such as "Backup."

OBJECT—A string containing the name of the object, such as "/dev/cartridge."

MSGTYPE—A string containing the description of the message type.

MSGCONDTYPE—Two condition types are possible:

Match—True when this msgtype matched.

Suppress—True when this msgtype is not matched.

19.5.5.5 Forwarding All Messages with Time Criteria

The template syntax for forwarding all messages with no message filtering rules is shown as follows in the sample template. The segment of the template shows that the MSGTARGETRULECONDS is left with only a placeholder to indicate that all messages are forwarded and that other rules may apply, but there are no message filters based on message attributes. (In other words, the example demonstrates, that all messages go to manager M1 during "shift1." At other times subsequent rules apply.) MSGTARGETMANAGERS identifies the servers to which the messages are forwarded. The message target manager criteria will apply to the messages that occur during the time window called "shift1" in the TIMETEMPLATE. The MSGTARGETMANAGER includes the unique node identifier OPCMGR to which the messages are forwarded. The use of the IP

0.0.0.0 means that the local name resolution process should be used. The local name resolution could be the hosts file, NIS or DNS. The unique name of the server is on the line labeled OPCMGR IP 0.0.0.0 “M1”. Replace the M1 with the actual server name. The OPCMGR message target could also be represented with the variable "$OPC_PRIMARY_MGR".

```
MSGTARGETRULES
         MSGTARGETRULE
         DESCRIPTION "target rule description "
            MSGTARGETRULECONDS
            # for all messages
            MSGTARGETMANAGERS
               MSGTARGETMANAGER
     # target manager from 17:00 to 24:00 and 00:00 to 6:00
               # from Monday to Friday
                  TIMETEMPLATE "shift1"
                  OPCMGR IP 0.0.0.0 "M1"
```

If the time for sending messages is twenty-four hours, seven days per week, use the special variable $OPC_ALWAYS.

19.5.5.6 Forwarding Some Messages without Time Criteria

The following example template example.M2 defines a MSGTARGETRULECOND condition for messages that have a MSGGRP (message group) attribute “databases.” If the message group condition matches, the message is sent to the MSGTARGETMANAGER every time it occurs. The 24x7 clock is defined with the TIMETEMPLATE label by using the variable $OPC_ALWAYS.

```
MSGTARGETRULES
        MSGTARGETRULE
            DESCRIPTION "database messages"
            MSGTARGETRULECONDS
                MSGTARGETRULECOND
                    DESCRIPTION "Condition 1"
                    MSGGRP "databases"
            MSGTARGETMANAGERS
                MSGTARGETMANAGER
                    # every time
                    TIMETEMPLATE "$OPC_ALWAYS"
                    OPCMGR IP 0.0.0.0 "M1"
```

19.5.5.7 Forwarding Messages to the Primary Manager

The template example.M2 time template "shift1" defines the hours during which all other messages MSGTARGETRULE and MSGTARGETCONDS are both empty. When no message target rule or message target condition is defined, all the unmatched events are sent to the MSGTARGETMANAGER. The name of the target manager is represented with the variable $OPC_PRIMARY_MGR, which means to send the messages to the current primary manager.

```
MSGTARGETRULE
    DESCRIPTION "other messages"
    MSGTARGETRULECONDS
    MSGTARGETMANAGERS
        MSGTARGETMANAGER
            TIMETEMPLATE "shift1"
            OPCMGR IP 0.0.0.0 "$OPC_PRIMARY_MGR"
            # the actual manager name is stored
            # in an extra config file on the agent
```

19.5.5.8 Message-forwarding Syntax

The full keyword syntax is shown below.

```
Respmgrconfigs ::=
<respmgrconfigs> RESPMGRCONFIG DESCRIPTION <string> <respmgr-
conds> | e

respmgrconds ::=
SECONDARYMANAGERS <secondmgrs> ACTIONALLOWMANAGERS <actallowm-
grs> [MSGTARGETRULES <msgtargetrules>]

secondmgrs ::=
<secondmgrs> SECONDARYMANAGER NODE <node> [DESCRIPTION <string>]
| e

actallowmgrs ::=
<actallowmgrs> ACTIONALLOWMANGER NODE <node>[DESCRIPTION
<string>] | e

msgtargetrules ::=
<msgtargetrules> MSGTARGETRULE DESCRIPTION <string> <msgtar-
getrule> | e

msgtargetrule ::= MSGTARGETRULECONDS <mtrconditions>
MSGTARGETMANAGERS <msgtargetmgrs> |
MSGTARGETRULECONDS <mtrconditions>
```

```
MSGTARGETMANAGERS <msgtargetmgrs> ACKNONLOCALMGR

mtrconditions ::=
<mtrconditions> MSGTARGETRULECOND DESCRIPTION <string> <mtrcond>
| e

mtrcond ::=
<mtrcond> SEVERITY <severity> |
<mtrcond> NODE <nodelist> |
<mtrcond> APPLICATION <string> |
<mtrcond> MSGGRP <string> |
<mtrcond> OBJECT <string> |
<mtrcond> MSGCONDTYPE <msgcondtype> | e

msgtargetmgrs  ::=
<msgtargetmgrs> MSGTARGETMANAGER TIMETEMPLATE <string> OPCMGR
<node> |
<msgtargetmgrs> MSGTARGETMANAGER TIMETEMPLATE <string> OPCMGR
<node> MSGCONTROLLINGMGR |
<msgtargetmgrs> MSGTARGETMANAGER TIMETEMPLATE <string> OPCMGR
<node> NOTIFYMGR | e

severity ::=
Unknown | Normal | Warning | Minor | Major |Critical

nodelist ::=
<node> | <nodelist> <node>

msgcondtype ::=
Match | Suppress

node ::=
IP <ipaddress> | IP <ipaddress> <string> |OTHER <string>

String ::=
"any alphanumeric string"

ipaddress ::=
<digits>.<digits>.<digits>.<digits>
```

19.5.6 Sample MoM Templates

The sample templates provided out-of-the-box are described here for reference. Refer to the *OpenView Operations Concepts Guide* for more information.

- **escmgr template**—Example template for the escalation feature. It is the template of management server M1. Example scenario: There are two management servers, M1 and M2. Management server M2 is allowed to escalate each message, at any time, to management server M1.
- **hierarchy template**—Example template for escalation of messages to the Central Server MC. It is the template of management server MX (where X stands for 1,2,3…).
- **backup-server template**—Example template for configuring a backup server. This template applies to management server M1. Example scenario: There are two responsible management servers, M1 and M2, where management server M2 is a possible backup server for management server M1.
- **followthesun template**—Example template for the follow-the-sun feature. It is the template of management server (installation server) M2 for managed node A. Example scenario: There are three different responsible management servers, M1, M2, and M3. The responsibilities for node A are defined as follows: management server M1 is responsible for node A on weekdays from Monday to Friday from 17:00 to 24:00 and 0:00 to 6:00; management server M2 is responsible for node A on weekdays from Monday to Friday from 6:00 to 17:00; management server M3 is responsible for node A on weekends, Saturday and Sunday, from 0:00 to 24:00.
- **service template**—Example template for service-oriented message distribution (competence centers). It is the template of management server M1 for all managed nodes. Example scenario: There are three management servers, *Database Service Center* (DBSVC), *Application Service Center* (APSVC), and a *Local Manager* (M1). Independent of the time, each managed node of the Local Manager M1 sends its events as follows: events of "DATABASE" to Database Service Center DBSVC, and events of the applications "FINANCE" and "CAD" to APSVC. Other events (without "DATABASE," "FINANCE," and "CAD") are sent to the Local Manager M1.
- **example.m2 template—**Example template for a combination of follow-the-sun and service center features. It is the template of management server (primary manager) M2 for managed nodes C and D. Example scenario: There are three different responsible management servers, M1, M2, and M3 and two managed nodes, C and D. The primary manager for these nodes is management server M2. In the period from 6:00 to 18:00, Node C and Node D send their events (without DB events) to the primary manager. In the period from 18:00 to 6:00, Node C and Node D send their events (without DB events) to management server M3. The DB events of both nodes are always sent to the competence center M1.

- **example.m3 template**—Example template for the follow-the-sun feature. It is the template of the management server (primary manager) M3 for managed nodes E and F. Example scenario: There are two responsible management servers, M2 and M3, and two managed nodes, E and F. The primary manager for these nodes is management server M3. In the time period from 6:00 to 18:00, Nodes E and F send their events to the responsible manager M2. In the period from 18:00 to 6:00 Node E and Node F send their events to the management server M3.
- **hierarchy.agt template**—Example template for the hierarchical management feature. It is the template for all nodes of management server M1. Example scenario: There are two management servers, M1 and MC. Management server M1 is configured as the primary manager for all nodes. Management server MC is configured as an action-allowed manager for all nodes. This allows the Management server MC to perform actions on the distributed managed node.
- **hierarchy.sv template**—Example template for the hierarchical management feature. It is the template of the local managed node M1. Example scenario: There are two management servers, M1 and MC. This template makes sure that all regional management server (M1) messages are sent to the central management server MC.
- **hier.specmgr template**—Example template for hierarchical management configuration. It is the template of the central/regional management server. Example scenario: There are regional management servers (for example, M1) and one central management server MC. All SNMP messages are sent to the $OPC_PRIMARY_MGR .and all other messages are sent to the central management server MC.
- **hier.time.spec template**—Example template for hierarchical management configuration. Example scenario: This template is similar to the hier.specmgr template but it is time-based. There are two shifts: daytime (8:00 - 18:00) and nighttime (not between 6:00 - 18:00). During the daytime, all SNMP messages are sent to the $OPC_PRIMARY_MGR. All other messages are sent to the central management server MC. During the nighttime all messages are sent to the central management server MC.
- **hier.time.all template**—Example template for the hierarchical management feature. This template describes a message scenario for use on the local management server M1. Example scenario: There are regional management servers (for example M1) and one central management server MC. There are two shifts: daytime (8:00 - 18:00) and nighttime (not between 6:00 - 18:00). During the daytime all messages are sent to the $OPC_PRIMARY_MGR .and during the nighttime all messages are sent to the central management server MC.
- **msgforw template**—Example template for the message-forwarding feature. Template msgforw of local management server. Example scenario: There are five management servers dbexpert, dbnotify, applinfo, master, and the local management server. All DATABASE messages are sent to the management servers dbexpert, dbnotify, and the local management server. The control of the message is passed to dbexpert. On the local management server, the DATABASE messages are acknowledged directly. All messages

concerning CAD applications are sent to the management servers applinfo for information (no control). All critical messages coming from nodes x1 or x2 are sent to management server master for information (no control).

19.6 MESSAGE FORWARDING

There are two types of message-forwarding configurations. They can be used separately or in combination. One type of message forwarding instructs the managed node to send messages to a different management server. The MoM template called allnodes or hex_address is transferred to the managed node and renamed mgrconf during a normal template distribution. The manager-to-manager message forwarding is a configuration that instructs the management servers to forward messages to other managers. The file msgforw resides on the servers that participate in the message-forwarding scenarios.

19.6.1 Message-Forwarding Cookbook

After the message-forwarding scenario is determined, select the appropriate sample templates, rename, and distribute to the node or rename msgforw for server-to-server message forwarding.

19.6.2.1 Management server configuration tasks

This section lists the general tasks to configure message forwarding between the multiple management servers and the managed nodes.

1. Add the forward managers to the primary manager's node bank as a message allowed node.
2. Add the primary manager to the forward manager's node bank as a message allowed node.
3. Add the forward managers to a node group on the primary manager.
4. Add the primary manager to a node group on the forward manager.
5. Copy the message-forwarding sample template from the tmpl_respmgrs directory to the work_respmgrs directory.
6. Edit the template; add the names of the responsible target (forward) forward managers.
7. Add the appropriate attributes for message control, notification or acknowledgement. (Refer to Section 19.3.3 for a definition of the attributes)
8. If necessary, edit the server configuration file **ovconfchg** to modify the default message-forwarding behavior.
9. Use the opcmomchk utility to syntax check the template.
10. Move the message-forwarding template to the respmgrs directory.
11. Create the managed node message-forwarding template by renaming the file (allnodes or hex_address).

12. If this file is for server to server message forwarding, rename the file msgforw.
13. Distribute the configuration to the other management servers. This step is performed to ensure that the servers have the appropriate attributes in the database to receive messages from nodes in other domains.
14. Restart the management server processes to activate the message-forwarding template on the server.
15. Test the configuration. Create test messages (using opcmsg) that match the conditions of the message-forwarding templates.

19.6.2.3 Message Forwarding Attributes

The message attributes described in this section are used within the MSGTARGETRULECONDS of the template and define processing instructions for the message after it arrives on the MSG-TARGETMANAGER server.

Message forwarding attributes include the following:

- **MSGCONTROLLINGMGR**—Within the message-forwarding template, assign this attribute to each manager that should get a switch-control copy of the message from the managed node.
- **NOTIFYMGR**—Assign this attribute to managers that receive notify messages from the managed node.
- **ACKNONLOCALMGR**—This attribute, when assigned to the messages sent to the primary server, causes the message to automatically acknowledge and transfer directly to the history browser.

19.7 BUILDING A BACKUP SERVER

The relationship between the management server (the primary server) and the managed node is extended to other servers that will have responsibility for the node in the event of a primary server failure. The backup server should be installed following the standard OpenView Management server procedure.

19.7.1 OpenView Failover Concepts

If a failover or takeover becomes necessary it means that the primary server where the node normally sends its messages is no longer available to receive information from its managed nodes. A surrogate server must assume responsibility for the nodes. When the primary server is available, it must resume responsibility for the managed nodes. Therefore, both servers including the primary and all secondary servers must maintain consistent configurations to minimize the time it takes to failover and failback.

1. Configure the management responsibilities (authorization) file called allnodes. Next, install and configure the backup server. Distribution of the all nodes file is final step prior to testing the setup.
2. Download the configuration data. In the GUI, select **Action→Server→Download Configuration**.
3. Install the backup server.
4. Distribute the downloaded configuration data to the backup server with the command **opcmgrdist**.
5. Stop all services on the backup server with **ovstop opc**.
6. Upload the configuration data to the backup server with the command **opccfgupld**.
7. Start the services on the backup server with **ovstart opc**.
8. Distribute the allnodes file and test the backup server. Switch to the backup server using the command on the backup server, **opcragt –primmgr <node_name>**.

19.8 ESCALATIONS

The operator performs message escalation from the message browser. After a message is escalated, the message details contain information about the escalation, as shown in Figure 19.1. The configuration steps for message escalation are outlined in the next section.

19.8.1 Process Steps to Create the Escalation Template

1. Add the escalation manager to the source manager's node bank as a message allowed node.
2. Add the source manager to the escalation manager's node bank as a message allowed node.
3. Add the escalation manager to a node group on the primary manager.
4. Add the primary manager to a node group on the escalation manager.
5. Copy the escmgr template from the tmpl_respmgrs directory to the work_respmgrs directory on the source manager.
6. Edit the template; replace the name of their server "M1" with the name of the escalation manager.
7. Use the opcmomchk utility to check the syntax of the escalation template.
8. Move the escmgr template to the respmgrs directory.
9. Restart the OVO session.
10. Test the message escalation. Select a message in the browser, open the details or the pop-up menu, and select escalate. In the message details there is a new button, "Escalate." The message should appear on the escalation manager.

19.8.2 Sample Escalation Template

The sample template escmgr in this example enables messages escalation a manager to a manager called tahiti. The managed node would also have a MoM configuration file that authorizes tahiti to perform actions and/or become a secondary manager.

```
# Sample Escalation Template.
# This template allows Servers to escalate messages to
# the another system.
#TIMETEMPLATES
# None
# Responsible Manager Configurations
#
RESPMGRCONFIGS
    RESPMGRCONFIG
DESCRIPTION "Responsible mgrs"
        SECONDARYMANAGERS
        ACTIONALLOWMANAGERS
    MSGTARGETRULES
        MSGTARGETRULE
      DESCRIPTION "Management Server tahiti"
            MSGTARGETRULECONDS
            MSGTARGETMANAGERS
            MSGTARGETMANAGER
            TIMETEMPLATE "$OPC_ALWAYS"

                OPCMGR IP 0.0.0.0 "tahiti"
```

19.9 CONFIGURATION VARIABLES

Use the following variables when necessary to modify the default message-forwarding behavior. Add the variables to the ovconfchg on the management servers as required.

```
OPC_ACCEPT_CTRL_SWTCH_ACKN TRUE
#Accepts acknowledgment for control-switched messages from other
management servers.

OPC_ACCEPT_CTRL_SWTCH_MSGS TRUE
#Accepts control-switched messages from other management
servers.
```

```
OPC_ACCEPT_NOTIF_MSSGS TRUE
#Accepts notification messages from other management servers.

OPC_FORW_CTRL_SWTCH_TO_TT TRUE
#Forwards control-switch messages to a trouble ticket or a noti-
fication service.

OPC_FORW_NOTIF_TO_TT FALSE
#Forwards notification messages to a trouble ticket or a notifi-
cation service.

OPC_ONE_LINE_MSG_FORWARD FALSE
#Controls forwarding in larger manager hierarchies.

OPC_SEND_ACKN_TO_CTRL_SWTCH TRUE
#Sends acknowledgements to control-switched messages.

OPC_SEND_ANNO_TO_CTRL_SWTCH TRUE
#Sends annotations to control-switched messages.

OPC_SEND_ANNO_TO_NOTIF TRUE
#Sends annotation to notification messages.

OPC_SEND_ANT_TO_CTRL_SWTCH TRUE
#Sends action-related data to control-switched messages.

OPC_SEND_ANT_TO_NOTIF TRUE
Sends action-related data to notification messages.
```

19.10 SUMMARY

In larger environments, multiple management servers become essential. The advantages include minimized use of network bandwidth for message transmission between the agents and servers, configuration of nodes within a specific region to report to a regional server, message forwarding and configuration control between multiple servers. This chapter provided configuration details and many examples of how to accomplish multiple management server scenarios. There are some concepts that were not covered, such as the outage scenario which describes the criteria for scheduled maintenance, unscheduled downtime, and service hours based on service level agreements (SLAs). Refer to the HP OpenView Operations Concepts Guide for more information. In the next chapter we take a high level look at many security concepts that are related to OpenView.

PART 3

OpenView Best Practices

In this section, we share some information on best practices for OpenView. This is a very general and broad topic, but in Part 3, three chapters provide information that will help you plan and document (Chapter 21), secure (Chapter 20) and take effective corrective action actions (Chapters 21 and 22) when necessary in the OpenView systems environment.

CHAPTER 20

Security

OpenView Operations (OVO) offers server, user, and process security checks during communications between the management server and the managed nodes. Authentication checks include server and node names, user passwords, process transaction requests, and data exchanges over the network media. For example, the managed node verifies that a requesting management server is authorized to request information from the node prior to sending messages or allowing data distribution.

Opportunities exist to make all levels of the OpenView communications model more secure if necessary. With OVO 8.0, the nodes that are located outside the firewall are now easily managed using the new built-in Internet secure agent. OVO also supports secure shell (as an add-on) for message forwarding, application transactions, and data exchanges over the network.

The primary communications model (up to version 7.10) was RPC based. The RPC clients and servers exist on the OVO nodes and servers. These programs run as dedicated processes during normal operations and play an important role in the data exchange methodology. Non-RPC-based agent communication options such as secure hypertext transfer protocol (HTTPS)-based agents are also available for communications between the server and managed nodes.

This chapter outlines the three primary OpenView communications models, including RPC, non-RPC, and HTTP at a high level along with relevant reference information on the standard network protocols used to implement the technology. Examples are used throughout the chapter as we cover the security aspects of the process, password, network, data, and user environments. Popular security enhancements are also discussed. Refer to Appendix C, "Resources," for information on security-related resources.

20.1 DCE-RPC PROCESSES AND COMMUNICATIONS

In the RPC-based communications model, several OVO servers communicate directly with OVO processes on the managed node. They are referred to as the open agents. These processes are running at all times and are responsible for tasks ranging from checking the health of the managed node to forking helper programs during configuration distribution. The processes start (**opcsv –start**) and stop (**opcsv –stop**) along with the other management server processes.

20.1.1 Open Agents' Advantages

Introduced to allow easier development of new agent software for multiple managed node platforms, the open agents make it easier to add agents (sub-agents) or policies (such as smart plug-ins) to an existing management server without many programming code changes. One key benefit is that new agents can take immediate advantage of the server binaries and any new instrumentation is distributed using the general installation script (inst.sh).

20.1.1.1 RPC-based Open Agent Functional Areas

The open agent concept enables implementation of OpenView system management technology across multiple platforms. Through the development and use of shared open agent resources, a variety of agents are integrated into the management server environment, such as NT, Solaris, LINUX, AIX, and others. The agents and components for these platforms are initially installed on the management server and distributed to the managed node using the same distribution mechanism from the server. The distribution mechanism from the command line or GUI requires access to database tables. The initiating processes ensure the correct communications and query the database to build the configuration file for the node.

20.1.1.2 Agent Software Distribution

RPC-based OpenView processes rely on the remote procedure call daemon (rpcd) during distribution and update operations. The process name varies depending on the platform; check the managed node installation instructions for the naming convention of the local remote procedure call process.

20.1.1.3 Open Agent Process Descriptions

Open agent processes are shown in Figure 20-1 from the output of the **opcsv** command.

Each open agent performs a unique task in facilitating agent and server communications. The processes are described in the following list:

- **ovoareqsdr**—The request sender informs the control agent to start, stop, or update their local OVO agents. The request sender is also responsible for OVO self-monitoring of the management server processes and heath checks via heartbeat polling of the managed nodes.
- **opcbbcdist**—The distribution manager distributes the node-specific configurations, scripts, and programs for automatic and operator actions to the managed node in response to requests from the distribution agent on the node. The distribution manager forks other processes as required such as the opctss sub-process and the inter-management server communications process called opccmm.
- **opcmsgrd**—The message receiver collects all messages from the managed nodes.

Figure 20-1 OpenView Open Agent Server Processes are used for consistent information exchanges between the various heterogeneous agents and the management server.

```
OVO Management Server status:
-----------------------------
Control Manager       opcctlm      (1772) is running
Action Manager        opcactm      (1779) is running
Message Manager       opcmsgm      (1780) is running
TT & Notify Mgr       opcttnsm     (1781) is running
Forward Manager       opcforwm     (1782) is running
Service Engine        opcsvcm      (1787) is running
Cert. Srv Adapter     opccsad          isn't running
BBC config adapter    opcbbcdist   (1786) is running
Display Manager       opcdispm     (1783) is running
Distrib. Manager      opcdistm     (1784) is running


Open Agent Management status:
-----------------------------
Request Sender        ovoareqsdr   (1490) is running
Request Handler       ovoareqhdlr  (1769) is running
Message Receiver (BBC) opcmsgrb      (1770) is running
Message Receiver      opcmsgrd     (1771) is running

Ctrl-Core and Server Extensions status:
---------------------------------------
Control Daemon (ovcd) not running
#
```

20.2 GENERAL TCP/IP AND RPC COMMUNICATIONS

Warning, this section is full of technical jargon. This section explains concepts that are common to the UNIX operating system. Although, as an OVO administrator it is not necessary to become a UNIX guru, it is helpful to have an understanding of the UNIX operating system. In this section, we will take a high-level look at how the operating system facilitates process-to-process communications. UNIX maintains file descriptor values inside tables. Tables created for each user contain information on all open files. I/O is handled via file descriptors. File descriptors provide access to files (via information stored in the files' node). A pipe file appears as filetype "p" (lowercase letter "p"), and these files are used with function calls for inter-process communication. For example, check the pipe files in the temporary directory used during runtime by the OVO processes on management server with the command **ls –l /var/opt/OV/share/tmp/OpC/mgmt_sv**. UNIX pipes allow processes to communicate. Pipes allow the output of one process to serve as input to another. There are many different forms of inter-process communications that are created using system calls.

Sockets are communication mechanisms used between running processes in UNIX TCP/IP environments. Sockets define the communication mechanism and an *application program interface* (API) for building client/server applications. The socket is defined by an IP address and a port number. For example, to view a socket connection, use the command **netstat –an**. There are several different types of sockets possible depending on the port numbers. Refer to the file /etc/services to see a listing of the well-known TCP port numbers configured on your system. Some popular connections are established using a Stream socket=TCP or Datagram socket=UDP (port 23 is typically used for telnet sessions and port 80 is primarily used for web services). A socket is much like a file identifier for open, close, read, and write system calls. The information required to establish the connection with the remote system is defined in the TCP header.

Remote Procedure Calls (RPCs) make your request for remote service seem like a local system call. An RPC request is sent to the remote system and from the user perspective it seems to execute a local system call (or command), and you wait to get the results back at your system. You can view the key information about the RPC environment with the commands **rpcinfo –t** or **rpcinfo –u**.

It's important that OpenView takes advantage of the standards-based communication mechanism, which can be made more secure by using built-in features (such as inetd.sec or shadow passwords) or by installation of additional operating system components in the form of security patches or applications. At a minimum, you should always maintain the OVO environment with the most current security-related patches. The discussion on how to secure the standard operating system environment is well covered in many other sources. Refer to Appendix C for additional resources.

20.3 NON-RPC AGENTS

Vulnerabilities in the RPC services have prompted a move toward OpenView communications agents that no longer rely upon the RPCs. The security issues related to the RPC services are documented at the *Computer Emergency Response Team* (CERT) Incident Note IN-99-04 at `http://www.cert.org/incident_notes/IN-99-04.html`. For now, OVO will continue to support the use of RPC-based communication (with the recommended security patches for RPC installed) and non-RPC-based communications. However, as of OVO 8.0, the HTTPS-based agent has been introduced. Read additional information on the non-RPC-based communication model in the DCE RPC Communication without Endpoint Mapper White Paper, available at `http://ovweb.external.hp.com/lpe/doc_serv/`.

20.4 HTTP PROXY AGENT

It is now possible to manage important business resources that reside outside the firewall such as web servers, transaction servers, and others with the OpenView HTTPS-based agent. This proxy agent, also called the OpenView communication broker (ovbbccb) agent, is based upon well-known Web security technology such as *Secure Socket Layer* (SSL) , *Simple Object Access Protocol* (SOAP), Proxies, and HTTP. Communication in the HTTPS-based environment provides single-port (383 by default) out-of-the-box Internet security. The security model is based on SSL/PKI encryption and server and client certificates for authentication.

Implement the HTTP-based agents from the management server automatic distribution via the GUI or transfer the package software to the managed node. Configure the certificates for secure agent/server network communication using SSL after the agent software is installed. The certificate configuration is built in to the GUI. Refer to the *OpenView Operations HTTPS Agent Concepts and Configuration Guide* for implementation details.

20.5 USERS AND PASSWORDS

During installation of the managed node, the operations account opc_op is created. The installation process of the OpenView agent creates the account on the managed node. The name of the account for example on a UNIX node is opc_op. You can view this account after the agent is installed using the command line, as shown in Figure 20-2.

Figure 20-2 OpenView Operations User account security includes authentication during login and when performing operations during run-time.

```
-> grep opc_op /etc/passwd
opc_op:*:777:77:OpC default operator:/home/opc_op:/usr/bin/ksh
```

The account is made secure during installation and prevents direct login. Operations that require a local account on the managed node utilize the opc_op account. Such operations include operator actions, broadcast commands, and applications launches from the operator's list of applications on the application desktop in the MOTIF console or in the navigation pane in the JAVA console.

20.5.1 Administrators

The OVO Administrator's privileges are that of a root user on any system managed by OVO. These privileges are required to perform the systems management tasks. See Chapter 13, "Out-of-the-box with OpenView Operations," for details of the OVO Administration tasks. As an example, during agent distribution from the management server the root password is required on the managed node. For easy access, there is sometimes a .rhosts file enabled on the server and the node to make the distribution process more user friendly (no password authentication check with .rhosts).

When the .rhosts is not allowed for security reasons, the OpenView administrator will be prompted for the managed node root password during the agent installation. In large environments where there are regional and central server administrators, coordination is essential to develop the most effective method of configuration distribution. When root passwords are not allowed over the network, the OpenView agent can be installed manually. In addition, OVO added the option to user SSH for installing agents over the network. This requires a separate ssh installation on the managed nodes and the server. Later in Section 20.8.7, "Secure Socket Layer (SSL)," you will find more information about implementing SSL.

20.5.2 Operators

Operators perform some tasks utilizing the privileges of the root user on the managed node. Operator-initiated actions, for example, could be programs or commands that require root privilege to execute. Automatic actions are not executed by the operator but by OVO itself. The operator is restricted to perform the tasks as root while performing these tasks. OVO also makes available the broadcast command application. This feature allows an operator to initiate the call to a command that will execute on one or multiple nodes simultaneously. Some operations management tasks require administrator privileges and these are performed as authority permits within the operator's environment. Security features built into the operator's console can restrict operators from performing certain tasks. The operators' configurations determine what messages, applications, and features of OVO are enabled during their sessions.

20.6 FILES AND DATA

Integrity of the files and data is very important to the success of an OpenView system management environment. It is recommended that frequent backups be performed of the OVO runtime and configuration data. The Oracle database provides data protection via passwords and restrictions on data access. Periodic audits of the file system reduce the risk of data security vulnerabilities. One way to check for files and directories with open permissions is with the **find** command, as shown in the following examples:

Use the find command to check for files with all permissions open to the world:

 # find / -type –f -perm 777 –print

Use the find command to check for directories with all permissions open to the world:

#find / -type –d –perm 777 –print

20.7 AUDITS

In most secure environments, requirements for computer audits are determined by the company security policies. Some companies may not require computer audits. The audit levels built into OVO include the following:

- No Audit
- Operator Audit (default setting)
- Administrator Audit

Changes to the audit levels take effect at the next operator or administrator session. Audit areas are in nine categories for the administrator, from user login and logoff to executing an action such as database maintenance through the graphical user interface. The complete list of Administrator Full Audit Areas is shown here for reference:

- **User**—Login, logoff, change password
- **Actions, Applications, Broadcasts**—Start, add, modify, delete
- **Message Source Templates**—Add, modify, delete templates, actions, conditions
- **Managed Nodes**—Configuration, distribution, changes, template assignments
- **Node Groups**—Add, modify, delete, node assignments
- **User Configuration**—Add, modify, delete
- **Database Maintenance**
- **Trouble Ticket and Notification Service**

Enable, disable or modify the audit configuration through the Administrator's GUI (**Actions→Server→Configure**), as shown in Figure 20-3.

Figure 20-3 Use the OpenView Audit Configuration window to enable or disable Administrator and Operator level audits functions.

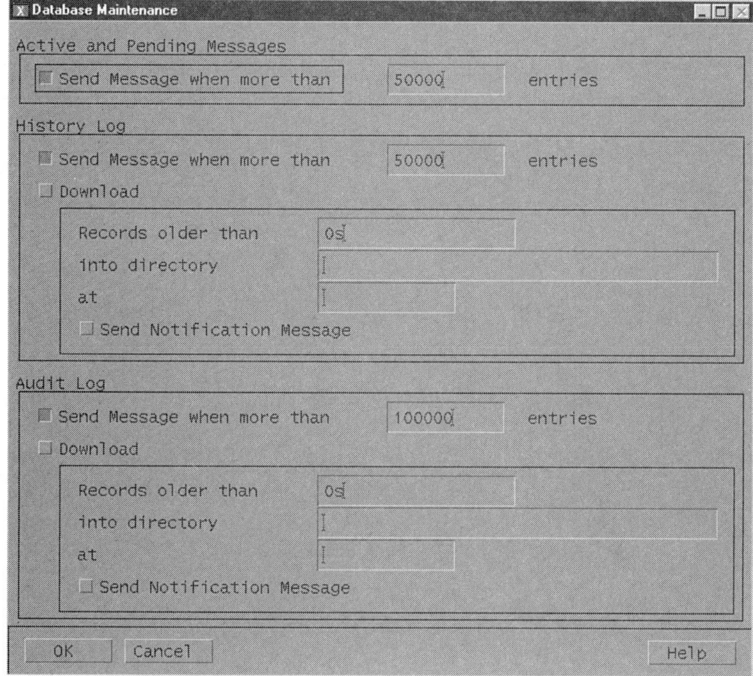

Warning: Making the audit level configuration available to the administrator may pose a security risk in itself. The OVO Administrator could easily disable auditing temporarily to abuse OVOs capabilities in the managed environment without leaving any trace in the audit trail. If you require permanent full auditing without giving the administrator the option to change the audit level, run the command **/opt/OV/bin/OpC/opc_audit_secure**, which will lock the audit level and not allow the administrator to change it back.

See Appendix C for a complete reference to the definition of a computer audit provided by the authors of the book *Security in Distributed Computing*, Glen Bruce and Bob Dempsey. They state, "Computer auditing involves the independent review of computer controls, and the delivery of a formal report detailing its findings against acceptable standards."

The OVO Report interface contains a list of audit reports that are easily produced for record-keeping purposes. It is also recommended that the audit information be downloaded regularly from the database. This function is also available through the GUI (**Actions→Utilities→Reports**) as shown in Figure 20-4.

Figure 20-4 OpenView Audit Reports are created from the data stored in the database.

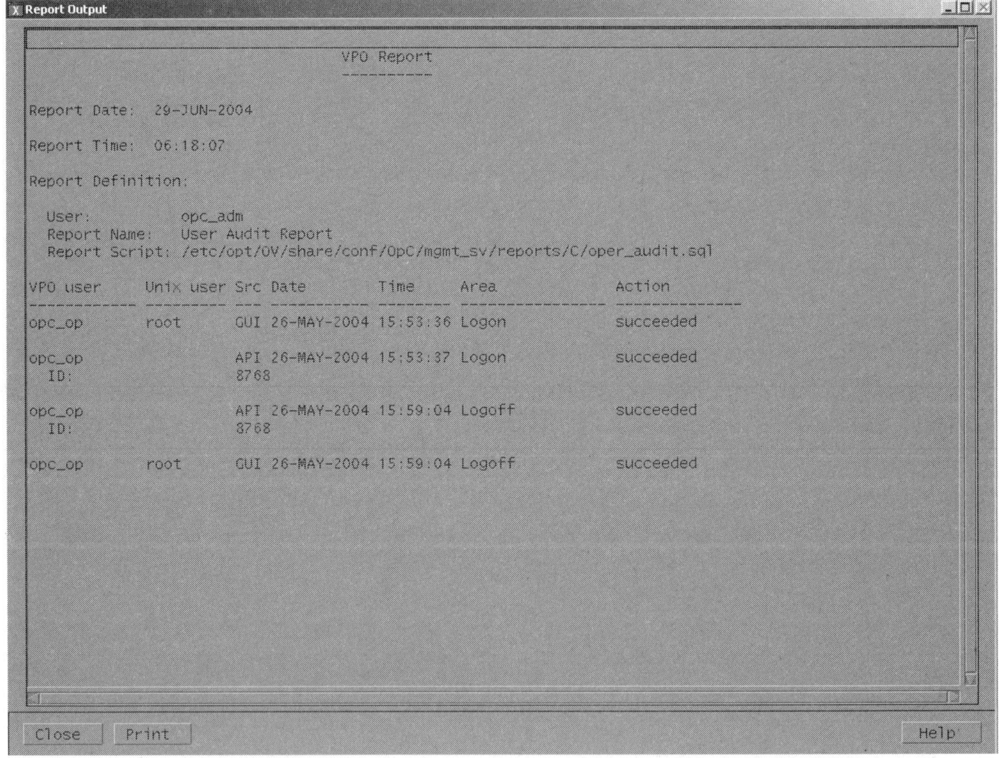

Download the Audit data from the database through the Database Maintenance Window (**Actions→Utilities→Database Maintenance**) as shown in Figure 20-5.

Figure 20-5 This view shows how to download audit data from the database.

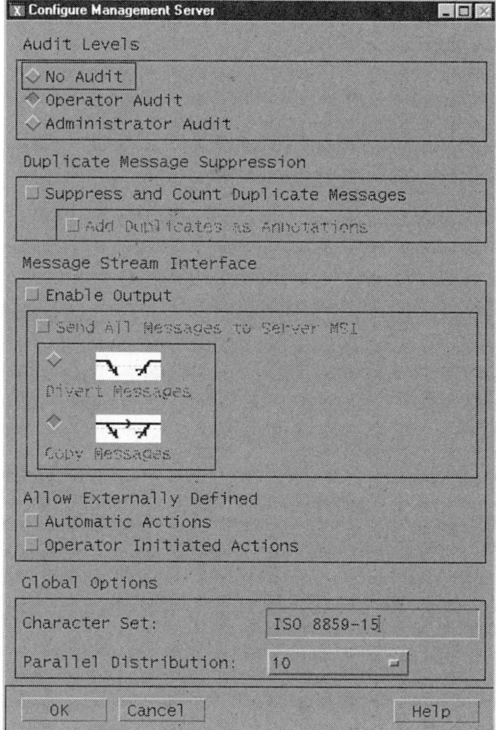

20.8 ENHANCED SECURITY

OpenView supports industry standard system security features. These features introduce multiple layers of security enhancements. Some of these are at the socket layer and go up through the application layer. In this section, we discuss some of the most popular security components available for TCP/IP environments. When the enhanced security options are installed on the management server, you have the option to choose the security method to configure on a node-by-node basis.

20.8.1 Data Encryption Standard (DES)—Private Key

DES is a single-symmetric key used for encryption and decryption. The key is a single large random-number (from 64 up to 128 bits), used by the client and server to encrypt and decrypt messages. Here is an example of how the algorithm works: Node A sends a message that is encrypted with the *fully qualified domain name* (FQDN) of the node. A message arrives at the server after transmission over the network is decrypted using the client's FQDN. When authenticated, the message moves to the next upstream process. The message is decrypted and authentication of the server is performed on the managed node by a decryption routine.

20.8.2 RSA—Public Key

Developed by Ronald Rivest, Adi Shamir, and Leonard Aldeman, RSA differs from DES because the encryption algorithm uses two keys. RSA is based on a standard called *Public-Key Cryptography* (PKC). Originally based on the ANSI draft standard X9.42 an algorithm developed by Diffie-Hellman, one key is private and the other key is public. The size of the key generated by the algorithm is up to 512 bits. The PKC servers keep users' public keys. The server validates the users' ownership of their public keys. Here is an example of how the algorithm works: Node A sends a message to server encrypted with the server's public key. At the server, the server's private key is used to decrypt the message. When the server sends a message to the client, it is encrypted with the client's public key and decrypted by the client using a private key known only to the client.

20.8.3 Kerberos

Kerberos was developed as part of the Massachusetts Institute of Technology project Athena (and specified in RFC 1510). Kerberos is an add-on service that provides authentication and can be used with many network protocols including RPC. Kerberos uses *Data Encryption Standard* (DES) encryption to protect data as it travels across the network. DES uses tickets (also called keys) that are encrypted with a secret password and the ticket can only be decrypted at the other end with the same secret password. The secret password is stored on the Kerberos server.

The Kerberos server provides a centralized authentication service. This key distribution function is to mutually authenticate clients to servers. There are three services involved in completion of the user or process authentication: *Key Distribution Center* (KDC), *Authentication Service* (AS), and *Ticket Granting Service* (TGS). The six steps in the authentication process are outlined here for reference:

1. Request for TGT
2. Get TGT plus session key
3. Request ticket for specific service
4. Get service-ticket plus session key
5. Request service
6. Provide server authentication

This authentication method initiates the client-server data exchange. Subsequent exchanges do not utilize all six steps and can be summarized as follows:

- Steps 1 and 2 are performed per user login
- Steps 3 and 4 are performed once per service request
- Steps 5 and 6 are performed once per service session

20.8.4 Distributed Compute Environment (DCE)

Distributed Computer Environment (DCE), developed by the *Open Software Foundation* (OSF) provides configuration management, distributed file sharing, remote procedure calls, and user authentication. DCE enhances the Kerberos authentication model by using a combination of packet encryption, time-based authentication credentials, and a security server (called a "trusted third-party"). The DCE security server maintains an access control list similar to a database of users, servers, and security policies (this collection of data is referred to as the registry service). Authenticated RPC requires that each DCE principal (user, application program, computer, DCE cell, or DCE service) use a key known only to the client and the security server. The key is generated from a users secret password and is maintained by the registry service. Clients and servers use authenticated RPC based on the key (also called a ticket). The steps involved with obtaining the ticket are outlined here for reference:

1. The RPC client reads its password from the key file on the node.
2. The RPC client logs in and gets a login context (name/password) from the security server.
3. When authenticated, the RPC client sends the RPC request.
4. The RPC server checks the ticket with the password in the key file on the server.

The RPC client on the managed node is the message agent (opcmsga) process. The RPC server on the managed node is the control agent (opcctla) process. On the management server, the message receiver is the RPC server.

The base DCE client components include the shared libraries and daemons (rpcd/dced). Out-of-the-box, the DCE client components include the features for authenticated RPC. The configuration steps must be performed on every node within that will use DCE/RPC security.

The security services are configured on the managed nodes, which become members of a DCE cell. The cell includes a security server located on a managed node or the management server. A utility program called dce_config provides a menu-driven interface to help configure the local node into the cell. When configured for DCE/RPC, the management server will not communicate with nodes that are not members of the DCE cell.

20.8.5 GSS APIs

The *Generic Security Service* (GSS)-*Application Program Interface* (API) is provided with OVAS as a customizable security solution that enables you to develop and implement your own security requirements. GSS is defined by RFC-2743 and is incorporated as OVO's security protocol. When installed, the GSS functionality is enabled for the managed node communications via **Actions→Node→Modify→Communications**. Select Network Security Protocol GSS. This option adds a new line item to the nodeinfo file OPC_NSP_TYPE GSS_API_V2.

OVO ANS only provides the interfaces for a GSS-compliant encryption product to be "plugged-in." OVO ANS does not provide this encryption by itself.

20.8.6 HTTP and S-HTTP

SSL encryption for HTTP ensures the integrity of transactions and the confidentiality of information exchanged via HTTP. The early development of the S-HTTP is a joint effort between *Enterprise Integration Technologies* (EIT) and the *National Center for Supercomputing Applications* (NCSA) at the University of Illinois and RSA Data Security. Several S-HTTP web servers are based on RSA's public-key cryptography and EIT's Secure HTTP software. S-HTTP provides application-level transaction security and supports digital signatures at the application level. OpenView uses the Public-Key Encryption model provided by Entrust.

Additional information about HTTP and S-HTTP can be found at `http://www.dmc.ie/maim2002/mairead/practice/projects/MP4/indes.html` and `http://www.eit.com/projects/s-http`. Also refer to the HP OpenView Operations HTTPS Agent Concepts and Configuration Guide.

20.8.7 Secure Socket Layer (SSL)

SSL is an application-independent protocol. Sockets live at layer-5 of the OSI model. Sockets are either connection-oriented or connectionless. Connection-oriented sockets allow data flow (back and forth as needed) between the client and server. As socket, when established, represents the IP address and a known port number and is represented as follows:

10.2.12.14:23 represents the IP address and the well known telnet port

Sockets are used locally for *inter-process communications* (IPC) and for Internet connections, as shown in the previous example. In using a TCP Socket, the connection setup uses a file descriptor for subsequent read and write operations. Check the established connections with the command **netstat –in** from the command line. Basic operation of SSL transmissions include the following steps:

1. Client sends server a "hello" message
2. Server sends over its certificate (includes server's public key)
3. Client creates session-key and sends it encrypted to the server
4. Server encrypts future communications with client's session key.
5. Additional information about the SSL protocol is available at `http://home.netscape.com/security/techbriefs`

SSL helps secure the JAVA client console. This prevents eavesdropping of the passwords and message information that traverses the network between the client console and the management server. The client components are a component of the OVAS add-on package. After the OVAS secure JAVA client is installed on the server, distribution to the clients follows the standard procedure via `http://<management_server_name>:8880/ITO_OP`. The two files installed from the management server are ito_op.jar and ito_ssl.jar. The authentication certificates are generated on the server with the opcca utility provided with OVAS. The certificate is installed on the client in addition to the two (dot) jar files. The handshake protocol is initiated using SSL when you startup the JAVA client console. When the session initiates, the JAVA client GUI displays a closed padlock icon.

20.8.8 PAM Authentication

The *HP Configuration Guide for Kerberos Products on HP-UX* states the following about PAM authentication: "HP-UX provides Kerberos authentication as part of the Pluggable Authentication Module (PAM) architecture that is specified in RFC 86 of the Open Group. PAM allows multiple authentication technologies to coexist on HP-UX. A configuration file determines which authentication module to use, in a manner transparent to the applications that use the PAM library."

OVO user accounts exist in two places on the management server, the database and the password file. The account names and passwords for each configured OVO user are authenticated by the PAM modules that are installed on the management server operating system. PAM authentication is configured in the /etc/pam.conf files. The configuration requires valid entries for each user in the OVO database (new users are added via the GUI) and the /etc/passwd file (with entries for all users accounts that access OVO).

20.8.9 SOAP (XML)

The World Wide Web Consortium (`www.w3c.org`) defines SOAP Version 1.2 as a lightweight protocol intended for exchanging structured information in a decentralized, distributed environment. It uses XML technologies to define an extensible messaging framework providing a message construct that can be exchanged over a variety of underlying protocols. The framework has been designed to be independent of any particular programming model and other implementation specific semantics.

SOAP (XML) technology replaces the DCE-RPCs for use with the HTTPS-based agent.

20.9 GENERAL SECURITY MEASURES

Proactive steps in security protection include, but are not limited to, the following:

- Check the system for new accounts added to the password file
- Check for change in the system files
- Check for changes to file and directory permissions
- Check for any new SUID or SGID programs
- Check for changes to .rhosts files or, better yet, eliminate them
- Check for changes to the hosts.eqiv file
- Review contents of user owned (.) dot files
- Check start-up scripts and programs called
- Check for hidden files and directories

20.10 SUDO

Sudo is a public domain software program. It provides a layer of control on the use of root user privileges available during a session. The root account is the only account on the system with unrestricted privileges. If a security policy is adopted and requires a mechanism that restricts the root user privileges, Sudo is a program adopted by many UNIX system administrators. Advantages of Sudo include:

- Selected root user privileges can be distributed as required to operators
- The root password is not required to execute commands with Sudo
- Commands executed via Sudo are logged
- Root user privileges can be revoked without changes to the root password
- Privileged users and their privileges are maintained in a secure list

20.10.1 Download the Public Domain Sudo Program

Obtain the software from the HP Public Software Domain at `http://software.hp.com`. The depot name is sudo-x.x.xxx-sd-xx.xx.depot.

Download the software to the public domain software directory on the server. The example uses the directory /opt. After downloading the depot, install it using the command **swinstall –s /opt/xxxxxxxx.depot –x allow_incompatible=true sudo**

20.11 SECURE SHELL (SSH) FOR HP-UX

Secure Shell (SSH) is a client/server application that enables secure communications for login file transfers and remote command execution between distributed computer systems. SSH uses public-key encryption for authentication. The basic authentication model for public-key encryption was described in Sections 20.8.1 and 20.8.2 of this chapter. The overall five-step ssh authentication process is outlined here for reference:

1. Client requests a connection to a remote server.
2. The server running the secure shell daemon (sshd) checks the requestors ID.
3. The server sends the client a key.
4. The client provides the key to the local secure shell daemon (sshd).
5. The local sshd sends the key back to the remote server sshd to finish the authentication process.
6. The secure session is now initiated between the client and the server.

20.11.1 General Installation and Configuration

Resources that provide details on the installation of secure shell programs are provided in Appendix C. The OVO Administrator will require remote access privileges on the client and the server or work with the UNIX system administrator of the managed node to configure the ssh client components.

Obtain a version of ssh authorized for use within the United States
Unpack and install the software
Edit the secure shell daemon startup configuration files
Generate the security keys
Distribute the public key to the remote systems
Add the path to the ssh client program to your PATH
Test your connection

20.11.2 OVO Agent Installation Using SSH

OpenView supports use of SSH for installation of the agent software on the managed nodes. Update existing nodes to enable the secure shell installation method with the SSH update utility itosshupdate. After the decision is made to use the secure shell for agent distribution, modify the managed node configuration to support the new secure shell policy. Edit the node configuration by selecting **Actions→Node→Modify→Communications** and selecting Use SSH (Secure Shell) during installation. Refer to Appendix C for additional information.

20.12 THE FIREWALL

A firewall, as defined in *Cisco© Press's Dictionary of Internetworking Terms and Acronyms*, is a "router or access server, or several routers or access servers, designated as a buffer between any connected public networks and a private network. A firewall router uses access lists and other methods to ensure the security of the private network." The HTTPS-based agent makes it possible to configure and support nodes outside the firewall. A firewall configuration might be necessary to communicate with the managed nodes in one of the following three locations:

- **The demilitarized zone (DMZ)**—Usual location for web servers, ftp servers, and b2b transaction servers.
- **Internet**—Untrusted areas of the internetwork; outside the DMZ.
- **Intranet**—Trusted area for devices within the private network(s).

Information on configuring OpenView for DCE (NCS)/RPC-based communications can be found in the document, "Firewall Configuration White Paper," available at `http://ovweb.external.hp.com/lpe/doc_serv/`.

The *HTTPS Agent Concepts and Configuration Guide* contains detail on configuring the HTTPS-based agent for use with firewalls.

20.12.1 Proxy Filter

Communication sessions between the management server and the managed node that travel through the Internet may require a proxy filter. A "proxy" filter is a firewall that authenticates user (or application) sessions that originate inside the firewall and allows the communication to proceed to the destination, outside the firewall. The proxy firewall generally configures port

8080 to receive, authenticate, and forward inbound or outbound network traffic. Communications to/from the management server might originate from the following processes: certificate server (ovcs), config/deploy component (ovconfgd), remote control (opcragt), request sender (ovoareqsdr), message receiver (opcmsgrb), and configuration adaptor (opcbbcdist). The communications from an OVO managed node originating from the message agent first contact the "proxy" firewall (on the default port 8088) where authentication takes place and the traffic is forwarded to the destination inside the firewall. The HTTPS-based agent can take advantage of the proxy concept for secure communications. The proxy environment requires additional application software such as Apache©, which is not provided by the OVO installation. Read more about firewall and proxy filters at `http://www.itsecurity.com/dictionary/dictionary.htm`.

20.13 SUMMARY

The importance of security goes without saying, except you have to say it often. Constant reminders and validation are two keys to maintain the secure environment of the OpenView domain. The primary domain server has root access to each managed node. When the domain is spread across regions and sometimes continents, the security aspects are even more important and complex. The transmission of the OpenView data and communications between the managed node and the server over short (LAN) or long distance (WAN) networks should raise some issues for the security teams. The data transmitted includes passwords in either compressed or encrypted form depending on how the systems are configured. The flexibility of OpenView to support a number of different security enhancements is an important feature. The OV administrator is responsible for implementing the OV components using the native security built into the product and using the enhanced security add-on modules as required.

CHAPTER 21

Plan, Document, Take Corrective Actions, Administer Changes

It is imperative that the *OpenView Operations* (OVO) architecture and processes be well planned and documented. It is also crucial that you have management buy-in for this project because you will likely need co-operation between teams, such as application development, network configuration, and client access. For example, OVO requires that an OVO agent be installed on each monitored system. Typically, the OVO administrator and the client administrator are different engineers and may report to different managers. You will need to get approval from the system administrator to install the OVO agent on the client.

During the planning phase, you should keep accurate documentation such as network architecture, supported platforms, and monitored applications. You should also document which templates are assigned and distributed to which nodes. The OVO documentation should evolve with the project.

The purpose of corrective actions is to return the application (or whatever caused the OVO message to appear in the browser) back to its normal state. Corrective actions can be configured as automatic or manual from the user interface. Corrective actions may include restarting processes, sending email, or linking to a trouble ticketing system such as *OpenView Service Desk* (OVSD).

Changes in the OVO environment may include adding templates and template conditions, rewriting scripts that are executed by templates, adding nodes to the node bank, or simply adding OVO operators. As your monitored enterprise evolves with new systems and applications, so should your OVO node bank, application bank, operator bank, and message source templates. Administering changes includes acting on OVO messages, updating the OVO environment, and updating documentation. Networks, systems, and applications are continuously evolving. Applications and database server versions change. New hardware and new users are deployed. As such, the administration of application monitoring needs to constantly change. New OVO agents need to be distributed, new templates need to be created, and new operators need to be configured.

21.1 PLANNING THE OVO ENVIRONMENT

During the planning phase, determine what types of systems and applications will be monitored. Devise a list of supported operating systems and applications. Determine which applications may be monitored using existing solutions or *Smart Plug-Ins* (SPIs). Refer to Chapter 15, "Smart Plug-Ins," for a detailed discussion of Smart Plug-Ins. Determine which applications require custom template and application development.

You may want to begin your planning with a network diagram. NNM discovery can assist in documenting the network layout.[1] Custom discovery and mapping of your network can be accomplished via NNM's auto-discovery feature and the use of a seed file (refer to Chapter 5, "Network Discovery"). You may find that your network actually looks different than expected. In this case, it may be prudent to revisit some of the initial planning. For example, if systems are not discovered by NNM, it could be due to a firewall blocking the ICMP requests. In this case, you may want to deploy a NNM collection station on the other side of the firewall for NNM to communicate to clients. Depending on the location of the OVO server, you may be required to open firewall ports for communication between the OVO server and its clients.

The location of OVO servers should be placed strategically throughout your enterprise. Typically, OVO servers are located in a Network Operating Center where the operations staff has access and control of the servers. You should consider whether they should to be placed behind firewalls for security purposes. If firewalls are required, opening firewall ports between the OVO server and clients will need to be included in the plan.

After the required systems have been accurately discovered by NNM, the OVO administrator needs to configure the managed enterprise. This entails defining Node Groups, Message Groups, Template Groups, Operators, and distributing agents and the required templates to the managed nodes. See Chapter 12, "Introduction to OVO," for a detailed description of these topics.

OVO corrective actions can be automated and/or manual. Consider that you are monitoring the **sendmail** process on a UNIX system. An OVO agent determines that the process is no longer running. OVO allows you to define a corrective action that will attempt to restart the process without manual intervention. It also allows you to define an operator-initiated action that will restart the process with customizable command options. Customization of OVO application monitoring needs to be well planned.

The OVO administrator is responsible for the overall configuration of OVO. This includes creating and adding nodes, node groups, templates, applications, message groups and operators. The three types of OVO users are defined as follows:

- **Administrator**—Responsible for the overall configuration.
- **Template Administrator**—Responsible for template creation and modification.
- **Operator**—Responsible for the day-to-day operation of the environment, using the Message Browser as the central monitoring component.

1 The underlying NNM processes are automatically installed and integrated when you install OVO.

The OVO administrator can begin the configuration plan by determining which nodes to monitor, which message groups to create, which applications are required, and the responsibilities of each operator. Figure 21-1 depicts the administrator's configuration responsibilities and the outcome of the operator's view of OVO.

Figure 21-1 The OVO administrator is responsible for creating and adding nodes, node groups, message groups, applications, and operators.

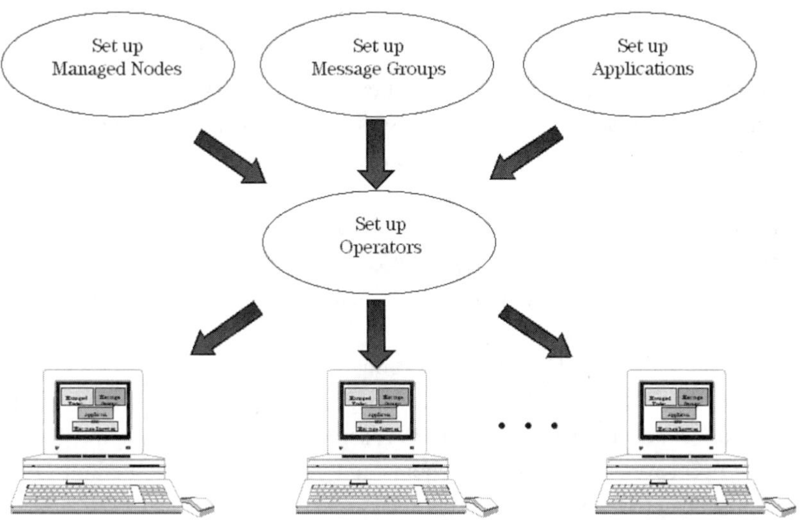

The following is a list of questions that may help in the OVO planning phase:

1. How many OVO servers are required?
2. Which OS will the server run on?
3. Where will the server be located?
4. Do firewalls exist between the OVO server and client?
5. Which systems/apps need to be monitored?
6. Which systems/ apps are mission critical?
7. What service levels are required? (Platinum, Gold, Silver, Bronze)
8. Which templates need to be assigned?
9. Who will deal with the problems?
10. Will OVO be linked to a external notification system?
11. Which SPIs are available to monitor applications?
12. How many operators are required?
13. What node groups should be configured?
14. What message groups should be configured?
15. How many template administrators are required?
16. Which applications require template and/or application development?

After these questions have been addressed, the administrator can begin configuring the OVO environment. Template administrators can assist in creating and modifying templates and integrating SPIs. The administrator is the only user capable of assigning and distributing templates.

Note: The opcnode command can be used for routine maintenance such as adding and removing nodes, and assigning, deassigning, and distributing templates.

21.1.1 Architecture

To create a network diagram, obtain a list of router IP addresses for the networks you intend on managing. Implement a seed file to include these IP addresses. Allow NNM to discover your network. If necessary, tweak the seed file and re-discover the network. Repeat until desired systems have been discovered by NNM.

Determine the number of OVO servers required to manage your enterprise. If you are managing fewer than 1000 systems, most likely a single OVO server will suffice. However, this depends on variables such as the number of templates distributed to the servers, the polling frequency, and the horsepower of the OVO server.

Determine OVO server locations. This should be done in conjunction with the network design team to ensure communication with all necessary managed nodes. List client locations and ensure that you have network connectivity between the OVO server and the client systems. If firewalls exist between the OVO sever and any of the clients and you are using the default OVO ports, the firewall ports will need to be opened.

21.1.2 The Systems

Determine the platform to be used as the OVO server. Current server platforms include HP-UX and Solaris.[2] The OVO Windows product is a different implementation and can also be used as the management server. See Chapter 25, "OVOW Implementation Tasks," for details. This chapter is focused on the OVO product for UNIX.

Determine the platform's type to be supported as managed nodes. Currently supported agent platforms include:[3]

- HP-UX
- Solaris
- AIX
- Linux
- Tru64

2 At the time this manuscript was written, OVO Windows was the product available for a Windows management system. OVO-W is similar to OVO-UNIX but did not originate from the same application software. The OVO product is in the process of being ported to Windows.

3 Refer to the Installation Guide for the Management Server for a complete list of supported operating system versions.

- Window NT
- Windows 2000
- Windows XP
- Novell Netware
- ptx
- SINIX

After the management server and the managed nodes have been determined, you are ready to determine which applications need to be monitored.

21.1.3 The Applications

OVO monitors applications. You should be able to list all applications that will be supported by the OVO environment. In addition to listing the applications, you need to know what components of the application need to be monitored. For example, you might want to monitor log files, resource utilization, or process status.

Distinguish between mission critical and non-mission critical applications. After determining the mission critical applications, you can begin researching whether a solution already exists for your particular application. Determine whether a SPI exists that can monitor your application sufficiently.

Consider monitoring the following list of mission critical applications:

- SAP R3
- OVSD Application Server
- WebSphere
- MicroSoft Exchange Server
- Citrix
- Radia

From the previous list, SPIs exist for the three applications: SAP R3, WebSphere, and Microsoft Exchange Server. The work for these applications is not complete yet. Each SPI needs to be configured and appropriate components (templates, monitors, and commands) need to be assigned and distributed to the appropriate systems. A good rule of thumb is to begin with at least one template administrator for each application and/or SPI used in OVO. As template administrators gain experience, they will be able to more effectively handle more template and SPI responsibilities. You shouldn't expect one administrator to do all of the work for the monitoring of these applications.[4]

4 During an on-site experience for a large OVO implementation, the OVO customer employed 20 full time template administrators, one for each monitored application. This is not an uncommon practice.

Consider the first mission-critical application in the list, SAP R3. The SAP R3 Smart Plug-In guide consists of 322 pages. The following topics are included in the document:

1. Installing and Configuring the SMART Plug-In for SAP R/3
   - Phase 1: Installation Tasks
   - Phase 2: VPO Administration Tasks
   - Phase 3: SAP-Specific Tasks
2. Customizing Smart Plug-In Monitors
3. Installing and Customizing the Performance Monitor
4. Other Methods for Configuring and Customizing
5. Using the Smart Plug-In for SAP R/3
6. Service Views

As you have probably guessed, implementing the SAP R3 SPI, as with most SPIs, is not a trivial task. In order to implement the SPI, you will need to coordinate between the OVO administrator, the template administrator, and SAP R3 experienced engineers. Typically the OVO administrator has no prior SAP R3 experience and the SAP R3 engineer has no prior OVO experience. This makes for an interesting implementation.

An actual implementation of the SAP R3 SPI involved 2 OVO administrators and 2 SAP R3 experts working together over a month-long period. After two weeks of work, we were able to successfully get an SAP R3 message in the OVO message browser as well as display SAP R3 service views in the *OpenView Service Navigator* (OVSN).[5]

Now consider monitoring an application for which no available SPI exists, such as Radia. Radia is an inventory and software distribution application available for multiple platforms. In an actual implementation, the *Radia Configuration Servers* (RCS) are located in various geographical locations throughout the world. The primary RCS is on a Windows XP system and several secondary RCSs are on HP-UX 11 systems. Listed here are the components to be monitored on the UNIX systems:

HP-UX processes—**znfytmgr**, **ztoptask**, **zlogmgr**, **zbldpmgr**, **ztrymgr**, **ztcpmgr**, **zclkmgr**, **zutilmgr**, **zrexxmgr**

HP-UX logfiles—**nvd101_manager.log**, **radish.log**

Because there is no Radia SPI template, development is required to monitor the above processes and logfiles. A single template with multiple message conditions can be used to monitor the processes. A log file encapsulator template will be required to monitor each of the logfiles. Implementation details should be handled by the template administrator. The administrator assigns and distributes the templates.

5 OVSN is an XML-based product that provides a service view in order to perform root cause analysis.

21.2 OVO DOCUMENTATION

OVO administrators should consider documentation that includes network layout, nodes, node groups, templates, applications, operator configuration, and SPIs. Both OVO and NNM can be used to gather documentation. Much of the documentation gathering can be automated using OVO commands. Additional documentation may include screen captures of the user interface.

OVO operators can also provide documentation via the Message Browser. If an operator determines a solution to a recurring problem, he or she can add an annotation to the message. This annotation might describe a fix that can be automated in OVO. The administrator can then modify the associated message source template to execute an automatic action that would resolve the recurring problem alleviating user intervention.

21.2.1 Documenting the Network Layout

The network layout can play a critical role in determining outages. For example, assume that a distributed application consists of components located in different geographical regions. OVO may be reporting a problem that appears to be an application that is down, when in reality a network outage has prevented the application from communicating with a database server located in a different geographical region. Another similar scenario is a client that is trying to access an application located in a different geographical region. Both examples appear to be an application outage, but may also be caused by a network outage.

The ovw GUI can be used to capture the network layout. Document important submaps that contain mission critical devices such as database and application servers. You may also want to document the network submaps that include the client systems that require access to the applications. Use a screen-capturing tool such as Paint Shop Pro® for capturing screen shots of network maps for documentation.

21.2.2 Documenting Nodes, Node Groups, and Templates

The OVO command **opcnode**[6] can be executed from the command line to list Node Groups, Message Groups, Template Groups, and so on, for accurate documentation. Refer to the manpage on **opcnode**. This utility helps immensely when documenting OVO customizations. Listed here are some examples of the **opcnode** command.

The following command lists all nodes in the OVO node bank. This command also displays the symbol label, IP address, network type, machine type, and communication type:

```
opcnode -list_nodes
```

6 The opcnode command requires root access.

Sample output:

```
  List of all Nodes in the ITO database:
=================================================================
Name           = xback1.hp.com
Label          = xback1
IP-Address     = 20.32.122.15
Network Type = MACH_S400, NETWORK_IP, CONSOLE_TEMPLATE, COMM_NCS
Machine Type = MACH_OTHER, NETWORK_NO_NODE, UNKNOWN_TEMPLATE,
COMM_UNSPEC_COMM
Comm Type      = MACH_S400, NETWORK_IP, CONSOLE_TEMPLATE, COMM_NCS
=============================================================
Name           = xnaodws.atl.hp.com
Label          = xnaodws1
IP-Address     = 20.32.12.15
Network Type = MACH_S400, NETWORK_IP, CONSOLE_TEMPLATE, COMM_NCS
Machine Type = MACH_WINNT
Comm Type      = MACH_S700, OPCMSG_TEMPLATE, COMM_DCE_TCP
=============================================================
Name           = xshell.hp.com
Label          = xshell
IP-Address     = 12.32.122.15
Network Type = MACH_S400, NETWORK_IP, CONSOLE_TEMPLATE, COMM_NCS
Machine Type = MACH_HP11_PA_RISC
Comm Type      = MACH_S800, COMM_DCE_UDP
=============================================================
Operation successfully completed.
```

The next **opcnode** command lists all node groups defined in OVO:

opcnode -list_groups

Sample output:

```
List of all Node Groups in the ITO database:

=================================================================
Name           = Agent_Check_NT
Label          = Agent_Check_NT
Description    = Custom Agent check for Windows NT Systems
=================================================================
Name           = Agent_Check_UX
Label          = Agent_Check_UX
Description    = Custom Agent check for HP-UX Systems
=================================================================
```

```
Name           = hp-ux
Label          = hp-ux
Description    = HP-UX Systems
==========================================================
Name           = VirtualVault
Label          = VirtualVault
Description    = node group for VirtualVault systems
==========================================================
Name           = net_devices
Label          = net_devices
Description    = Network Devices
Operation successfully completed.
```

This **opcnode** command allows you to display all nodes in the node group listeded from the previous command.[7] The following lists all nodes assigned to the **hp-ux** node group:

```
opcnode -list_ass_nodes group_name=hp-ux
```

Sample output of the above command:

```
List of Nodes assigned to 'HP-ux':

==========================================================

Name           = xback1.hp.com
Label          = xback1
==========================================================
Name           = xaodws.hp.com
Label          = xaodws
==========================================================
Name           = x3107nt.hp.com
Label          = x3107nt1
==========================================================
Name           = xsdrpt1.hp.com
Label          = xsdrpt1
==========================================================
Name           = xaodfs1.hp.com
Label          = xaodfs1
==========================================================
Name           = xaod001.hp.com
Label          = xaod001
==========================================================
```

7 OVO allows you to group nodes together by including common nodes in a node group. Templates can be assigned to a group of nodes as well as individual nodes.

```
Name          = xodsext.hp.com
Label         = xodsext
============================================================

Operation successfully completed.
```

The following opcnode command displays the templates assigned to the node named jasmine. If the template administrator is descriptive with template naming, this list is self-documenting. Otherwise, you may want to include additional information about the template and template conditions with your documentation.

opcnode -list_ass_templs node_name=jasmine net_type=NETWORK_IP

Sample output:

```
List of Templates and Template Groups assigned to 'jasmine':
============================================================
|MSG| mwa_4.3_UX
|SCH| housekeep_1.1_SCHED_UX11
|GRP| Agent Up Check
|GRP| HP WAN Monitoring
|GRP| Health Check
|GRP| MB:HP-UX 11
|GRP| MC/SG physical Management Server
|GRP| OPC: Core Infrastructure
|GRP| OS:HP-UX 11.x
|GRP| System Monitoring
============================================================
Operation successfully completed.
```

The output of **opcnode** can be saved to a file.[8] When you are comfortable using the **opcnode** command, you can develop scripts to automate the documentation of your OVO environment. SPIs typically consist of a group of templates, applications, commands, and actions. The commands may be scripts or binary executables. Your documentation should include nodes, node groups, and templates.

21.2.3 Documenting Applications and Operator Configuration

Each operator is assigned a group of applications designed to assist him or her in returning the managed node back to a normal state. It is important that the OVO administrator assign the applications to an operator based on the operator's responsibilities. For example, an HP-UX operator

8 The **opcnode** command is not limited to displaying information. It can be used to modify the OVO environment. **opcnode** allows you to assign and de-assign templates as well as add and remove nodes to and from node groups.

should have access HP-UX applications that would allow problem resolution for HP-UX systems. An Oracle® operator should have access to the appropriate database applications.

Operators must be configured with a set of responsibilities in order to see messages in the browser. An operator is configured by assigning node groups and/or message groups to the operator. Configuration of the operators should be documented to verify that an operator is actually receiving messages. A screen capture of the operator configuration from the administrator GUI is good way to document operator configuration.

Operator configuration also includes applications and application groups assigned to an operator. A screen capture of an operator's application desktop such as the one shown in Figure 21-2 is a good way to document assigned applications.

Figure 21-2 Documenting the operator's application desktop ensures that each operator has access to the necessary tools.

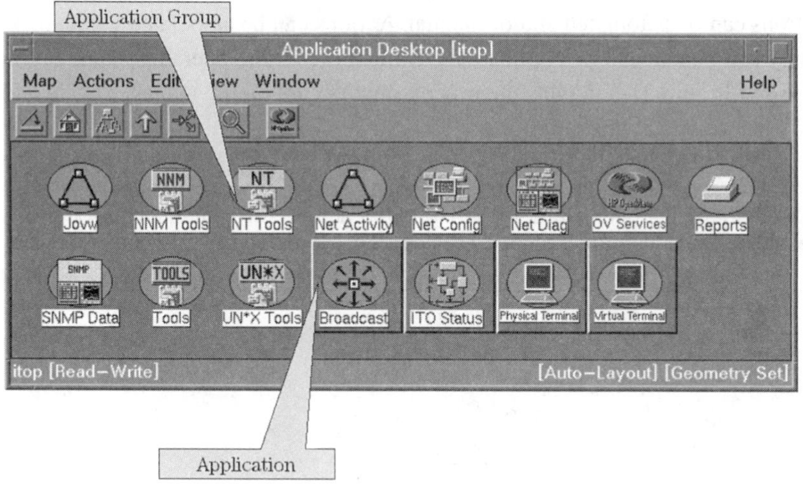

21.2.4 Documenting SPIs

SPIs typically consist of a group of templates, applications, commands, and actions. The commands may be scripts or binary executables. SPIs can be documented similarly to templates and applications. In addition to documenting the templates and applications, you should provide a directory listing of scripts and executables defined by the SPIs implemented in OVO.

21.2.5 Operator Documentation

While operators do not have access to modify the message source templates, they have the ability to add annotations (notes) to a message in the message browser. For example, an operator determines how to resolve an issue by logging into the system and executing a command. If this is a recurring problem, the operator can include details of the solution by adding an annotation to the message.

When the OVO administrator reviews the annotation provided by the operator, he or she might do one of several things. If the solution is simple and requires the execution of a command and executing this command always resolves the problem, this command can be added as an automatic (or operator-initiated) action to the message source template.

Another way the administrator may handle a problem is to create an application that would perform the task that resolves the problem. In this case, the operator is forced to execute the application—the action is not automatic.

In addition, the administrator could add procedures to the Instructions field of the message source template condition. In this example, the documentation has come full circle from the administrator to the operator back to the administrator. The documentation cycle should continue throughout the lifecycle of OVO.

21.3 CORRECTIVE ACTIONS

OVO corrective actions can be automated and/or manual. Actions can be associated with a message template or they can be standalone applications available from the operator's application desktop. The diagram in Figure 21-3 depicts the process that occurs on the managed node and management server when using automatic actions.

Figure 21-3 An automatic action is configured in the message source template. A message is intercepted by the OVO agent, conditions are applied, and the action is executed locally on the managed node. Results of the action are passed to the management server and appear in the message browser.

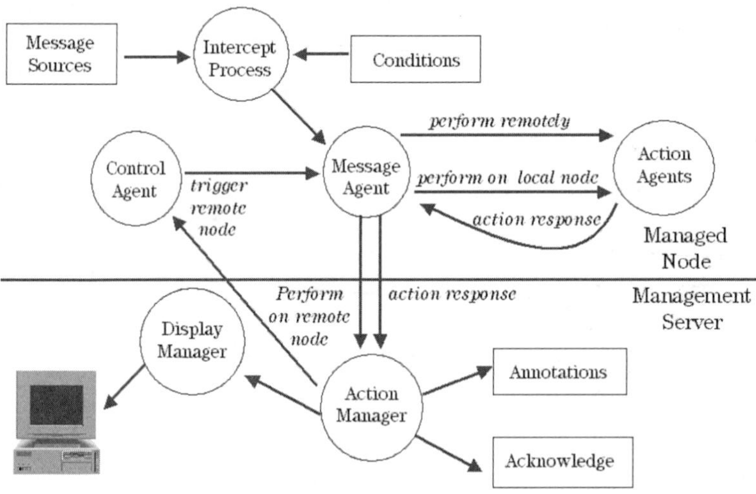

Assume that OVO is configured to monitor the UNIX **sendmail** process on a managed node. An OVO agent indicates that the **sendmail** process is no longer running on the node by a message in the browser. The OVO administrator has the ability to define a corrective action that will attempt to restart the process without manual intervention. Automatic actions are configured in the message source template.

Consider the following scenario: the operator receives a message that the UNIX **sendmail** process is not running on node abc123. The message may look something like this:

```
Sev SUIAONE  Date       Time       Node     Application   MsgGroup    Object
Message Text
Crit         01/01/04   15:03:04   abc123   sendmail      email       process
Sendmail is not running
```

The operator uses the Virtual Terminal application from the application desktop to login the system from which the message originated and executes the command

```
/sbin/init.d/sendmail start
```

Executing this command restarts the **sendmail** process (solving the problem). The operator should notify the appropriate template administrator how the problem was resolved. The template administrator may opt to add this command to the message condition that captured the terminated **sendmail** process. After modifying the template condition, the template needs to be re-distributed to all managed nodes to which it is assigned.

Recall the meaning of the flags in the message indicator column labeled **SUIAONE**; in particular, the columns **I**, **A**, **O** and **N**. These flags are indicators that the operator can use to determine if there are **actions**, **instructions** (automatic or operator initiated), and/or **notes** associated with a message.

An X in the I column indicates that instructions are available to the operator in the Message Details window. An operator cannot add instructions to a message. Only administrators and template administrators can add instructions. The operator should pay attention to this column because instructions indicate that procedures may exist to assist the operator in resolving the problem.

An S in the A column indicates that an automatic action is configured in the template that captured the message and that it ran successfully. An F indicates that the configured automatic action failed. Details for why an action failed can be found in the annotations if the template is configured to save the output. An R in the A column indicates that the action is currently running. The operator can check the status and has the option to re-run the automatic action.

An X in the O column indicates that an operator-initiated action exists for this message. This action requires operator intervention. An S indicates the operator-initiated action ran successfully, an F indicates that it failed, and an R indicates that it is currently running.

An X in the N column indicates that there are annotations (notes) associated with the message. An operator can add as many annotations as necessary to a message. The annotations are useful when the operator needs to refer to a previous message that has been resolved.

The administrator can define automatic actions and operator-initiated actions that will attempt to return a managed node back to its normal state. Operator-initiated actions are convenient for more complicated scenarios that require decision-making by an operator. Sometimes it is necessary for an operator to perform status checks before initiating an action. If the operator needs to perform a series of actions for a specific problem, the administrator may opt to use a combination of instructions, operator-initiated actions, and applications. Applications available in the operator's application can also be used in problem resolution.

21.4 Changing the OVO Environment

As your managed enterprise grows and changes, so must the OVO monitoring. Changes include the managed nodes, the node groups, templates, applications, message groups, and operator workspaces. The administrator is responsible for making most of the modifications. However, as the managed environment grows, administering changes to OVO may become overwhelming for a single individual. For that reason, the OVO administrator can create template administrators that have the ability to create and modify templates.

21.4.1 Administrator Changes

The administrator adds nodes to the node bank, creates node groups, adds nodes to node groups, creates applications, integrates SPIs, and adds and configures operators and template administrators. The administrator should solicit feedback from the operators and template administrators in order to better manage the enterprise.

21.4.2 Template Administrator Changes

The purpose of the template administrator role is to create and maintain message source's templates, commands, and actions in support of monitoring applications. A large managed environment might include many template administrators. Template administrators are typically specialized in different areas, such as operating systems, database applications, or specific SPIs. This allows the configuration of OVO to be distributed among many engineers. As more applications are added to the managed enterprise, more template administrators may be necessary.

21.4.3 Operator Changes

The operator has limited ability to make modifications in OVO. While the ability is limited, the changes and feedback to the OVO administrator made by an operator are essential to a successful OVO implementation. The focal point of the day-to-day activities in OVO is the message browser. The operator receives a message, interprets the message, and takes some action based on the information provided in the message.

The operator has the ability to make modifications to the message in a number of ways. Consider the earlier **sendmail** scenario where the operator discovers the fix for a recurring problem. The operator receives a message indicating that the **sendmail** process is no longer running. The operator logs into the system and issues a command to restart the process.

If executing a command restarts the **sendmail** process (resolving the problem), the operator should notify the appropriate template administrator how the problem was resolved. The template administrator may opt to add this command to the message condition that captured the terminated **sendmail** process. After modifying the template condition, the template needs to be re-distributed to all managed nodes to which it is assigned. All three OVO users are involved in this change:

- The operator resolves the recurring problem and notifies the template administrator
- The template administrator updates the message source template with an automatic action
- The administrator re-distributes the message source template to assigned managed nodes

21.5 SUMMARY

The OpenView Operations architecture and processes should be well planned and documented. Accurate documentation including network architecture, supported platforms, monitored applications, nodes, node groups, and template assignment should be kept in order to make the OVO implementation successful. OVO documentation should evolve with the project.

Corrective actions can be included in message source templates in order to return the application to its normal state. Corrective actions can be achieved automatic or manual. Corrective actions may include restarting processes, sending email, or linking to an external notification system.

Changes in the OVO environment include adding templates and template conditions, rewriting scripts that are executed by templates, adding nodes to the node bank, and adding operators. Administering changes include acting on OVO messages, updating the OVO environment, and updating documentation. Changes are made by the OVO administrator and template administrator.

CHAPTER 22

Troubleshooting Tools and Techniques

Troubleshooting techniques are developed through experience, trial and error, collaboration, and determination. When an event occurs that will cause system or application downtime, the number one priority is get it working again as quickly as possible. If the event is something that you are familiar with, you will approach the issue with confidence due to your experience. When the event is new and one that you have not personally resolved, you are likely to tread with a more cautious mindset. The confidence comes with experience; the techniques used are generally a combination of proven solutions. If the solution is documented from the application or system vendor, it has been tested and will most likely bring the system or application online with the least downtime. Collaboration with colleagues is important when the issue falls outside the realm of familiar territory. It never hurts to ask a question or two of those who might have seen a similar situation and have more current experience. Finally, determination is the final essential quality for someone facing the troubleshooting task even when the situation they face may be unfamiliar.

The task of troubleshooting a problem has three key components: a clear problem definition followed by appropriate data collection and analysis. The purpose of this chapter is to provide general guidelines, introduce some techniques for troubleshooting, and provide information on how to obtain additional resources to resolve common OVO issues. This chapter does not substitute for the *Administrators Reference Guide for OpenView Operations*.

22.1 DATA GATHERING TECHNIQUES AND TOOLS

Questions you might ask to begin the troubleshooting process include:

- Are there planned maintenance activities happening at this time?
- What is the complete error message?
- What versions of the OpenView software products are in use?
- What versions of the operating system are running on the server and agent?
- What server or agent hardware platform is involved?
- Where did the error occur? On the server or the node?
- When did the error initially occur?
- Can the problem be repeated?
- Have there been any recent changes to the system (such as new software)?
- What is the status of the OpenView processes?

- Did any error messages appear in the log files?
- Are there any errors in the itochecker report?
- Do the processes start and stop properly?
- Do you have the current patches installed for the agent, server, and operating system?
- Do you have a current system backup?
- Did the failed process produce a core file?
- Are unplanned maintenance activities happening now?

The troubleshooting recommendations and resource information presented in this chapter are adopted from known best practices. Due to the dynamic nature of the environment, it is important to check for the most current OpenView problem resolution resources available online at `http://support.openview.hp.com`. Determine whether the issue you face today may have already been resolved with a patch or documented resolution process. This chapter presents general guidelines to isolate the issues into the correct categories and collect the necessary information to begin the troubleshooting process.

22.1.1 Check for Errors

Error messages from OpenView are reported to the user via a variety of sources. The error message sources are the log files, the graphical user interface, and the shell. In the graphical user interface, the error messages may appear in a pop-up window as the result of an illegal operation or in the message browser within the message text. There are a few log files that contain important information about the normal operation of the system and when necessary error messages when an operation within the OV environment did not complete successfully. For example, after installing an operating system or OV patch you should check the installation log files for any errors.

22.1.1.1 Review the Log Files

The log files that may contain important system operation and error messages are described here for reference purposes. Refer to the Administrator Guide for the platform-specific location of the log files:

- **opcerrror**—Server and agent run time error log (on DCE agent)
- **system.txt**—Server and agent run time error log file (on HTTPS-based agent)
- **install.log**—Management server installation log file
- **inst_err.log**—Management server install error log file
- **inst_sum.log**—Summary of managed node installation
- **opccfgupld.log**—Configuration upload log file
- **alert_<SID>.log**—Oracle database alert log file
- **operating system and subsystem error log files**—(check the files that are appropriate in your operating environment)

22.1.1.2 OVO Errors

If an OVO error message has been produced, check the meaning and possible resolutions using the **opcerr** command. The message will start with the string OpC" and contain a body and tail as shown in the following example.

```
# tail /var/opt/OV/log/OpC/opcerror|grep ERROR

07/16/04 10:31:36 ERROR opctrapi  (Trap Interceptor)(1907)
[opcevti.cpp:1460]:
Receiving SNMP PDU failed: Lost connection with pmd/ovEvent process
(application disconnected). Trying to reinitialize. (OpC30-204)

# /opt/OV/bin/OpC/utils/opcerr 30 204
MESSAGE OpC30-204:
Receiving SNMP PDU failed: .... Trying to reinitialize.
INSTRUCTION:
The VPO event interceptor could not get a SNMP PDU although it was
informed that there is one available. The SNMP API message <snmp-msg>
gives
more information.
The event interceptor tries to reconnect to pmd.
```

The OVO error messages are organized into categories based upon the number in the body (such as OpC20-xxxx). The OVO error categories with examples are shown in Table 22-1.

Table 22-1 OVO Error Message Categories

Error Category	Error Number	Sample Description
Internal Messages	OpC10-0001	Insufficient memory
Public Routines	OpC20-0001	Invalid queue descriptor
Agent Processes	OpC30-0001	Invalid request to assemble
Manager Processes	OpC40-0001	Can't open pipe [x1]
Database Access	OpC50-0001	Database inconsistency detected
Internal Database Messages	OpC51-0022	Retry
Messages used by the commands (API)	OpC53-0150	Usage: opchistupl <file>
Configuration upload/download	OpC54-0002	Unknown option
Database Install/upgrade	OpC55-0016	Already exists
User Interface	OpC60-0005	User name must be entered
NT Installation	OpC130-0010	Setup program started (preinit)
Security	OpC140-0116	Secret key for <x1> not found

Refer to the online Help for the complete Error Messages Reference Guide.

22.1.1.3 Oracle Errors

Some Oracle database error messages have two parts ORA-xxxx. When you need to gather more information about the error, use the utility program $ORACLE_HOME/bin/oerr. This program will produce useful information about the error and troubleshooting tips. The error message categories are shown in Table 22-2.

Table 22-2 Oracle Error Message Categories

Message Numbers	Categories
00000-00099	Oracle Server
00200-00249	Control files
00250-00299	Archiving and recovery
00300-00379	Redo log files
00440-00485	Background processes
00700-00709	Dictionary cache
00900-00999	Parsing of SQL statements
01100-01250	The database and its support files
01400-01489	SQL execution errors
01500-01699	DBA set of SQL commands
02376-02399	Resources
04030-04039	Memory and the shared pool
04040-04069	Stored procedures
12100-12299	SQL*Net
12500-12699	SQL*Net
12700-12799	Use of the multilingual options

If there is a message in the message browser from the Oracle database, the message text will include the error message number. With this information, you can check the message with the **oerr** command as shown in the next example. Sometimes the error messages are very complex and could signal major trouble. If you are not sure what corrective action is required, report the error to your Database Administrator or support vendor.

```
# $ORACLE_HOME/bin/oerr ORA 01547

01547, 00000, "warning: RECOVER succeeded but OPEN RESETLOGS
would get error below"

// *Cause: Media recovery with one of the incomplete re//covery
options ended without error.  However, if the //ALTER DATABASE
OPEN RESETLOGS command were attempted now, //it would fail with
the specified error. The most likely //cause of this error is
forgetting to restore one or more //datafiles from a suffi-
ciently old backup before executing //the incomplete recovery.
```

```
// *Action: Rerun the incomplete media recovery using dif//fer-
ent datafile backups, a different control file, or different
stop criteria.
```

Some Oracle error messages are very generic, not fatal and provide codes that can only be interpreted by contacting a DBA.

22.1.2 Check, Stop, or Start the OpenView Processes

The process check is one of the best places to start checking the run-time environment. Ensure that the correct processes are running, determine why they are not, or restart the processes. If the OVO processes will not stop, check the process table with the **ps** command. If necessary remove them with the **kill** command.

22.1.2.1 Check Server and Agent Process Status

The processes running during normal operations of the server are as follows:

- Control Manager (opcctlm)
- Action Manager (opcactm)
- Message Manager (opcmsgm)
- TT & Notify Manager (opcttnsm)
- Forward Manager (opcforwm)
- Service Engine (opcsvcm)
- Certification Server Adaptor (opccsad)
- BBC configuration adaptor (opcbbcdist)
- Display Manager (opcdispm)
- Distribution Manager (opcdistm)
- Request Sender (ovoareqsdr)
- Request Handler (ovoareqhdlr)
- Message Receiver (BBC opcmsgrb)
- Message Receiver (opcmsgrd)
- Control Daemon (ovcd)
- BBC Communications Broker (ovbbccb)
- Configuration and Deploy Component (ovconfd)
- Certificate Server (ovcs)

From the command line of the management server, use the following commands to verify that the correct processes are running:

- **opcsv**: Check the management server processes
- **opcsv –status**: check the management server processes
- **ovstatus –c**: Check the OpenView platform (NNM)
- **opcsv –stop**: Stop the server processes
- **opcsv –start**: Start the server processes

The results of the opcsv command are shown here:

```
#opcsv
OVO Management Server status:
-----------------------------
Control Manager      opcctlm      (3847) is running
Action Manager       opcactm      (3856) is running
Message Manager      opcmsgm      (3857) is running
TT & Notify Mgr      opcttnsm     (3858) is running
Forward Manager      opcforwm     (3859) is running
Service Engine       opcsvcm      (3864) is running
Cert. Srv Adapter    opccsad      (3862) is running
BBC config adapter   opcbbcdist   (3863) is running
Display Manager      opcdispm     (3860) is running
Distrib. Manager     opcdistm     (3861) is running
Open Agent Management status:
-----------------------------
Request Sender         ovoareqsdr   (3843) is running
Request Handler        ovoareqhdlr  (3846) is running
Message Receiver (BBC) opcmsgrb     (3848) is running
Message Receiver       opcmsgrd     (3849) is running

Ctrl-Core and Server Extensions status:
---------------------------------------
Control Daemon               ovcd       (1460) is running
BBC Communications Broker    ovbbccb    (1467) is running
Config and Deploy            ovconfd    (1457) is running
Certificate Server           ovcs       (1469) is running
```

From the command line of the server, verify that the correct processes are running on the managed node; if necessary, restart the processes:

- **opcragt-status-all**: Check the status of all configured agents
- **opcragt-status <node_name>**: Check the status of a specific node
- **opcragt-stop<node_name>**: Stop the agent processes

Many of the processes running during normal operation of the agent (depending on the deployed policy) are as follows:

- Control Daemon (ovcd)
- HTTPS Communication Broker (ovbbccb)
- Configuration and Deploy Component (ovconfd)
- Certificate Server (ovcs)
- Message Agent (opcmsga)
- Action Agent (opcacta)
- Message Interceptor (opcmsgi)
- Logfile Encapsulator (opcle)
- Monitor Agent (opcmona)
- SNMP Trap Interceptor (opctrapi)
- Event Correlation Agent (opceca)
- ECS Annotate Server Agent (opcecaas)
- Embedded Performance Component (coda)

The output from the **ovc** command is shown here:

```
# ovc
ovcd     Control Daemon                               CORE   (4314)    Running
ovbbccb HP OpenView BBC Communications Broker CORE   (1467)    Running
ovconfd      HP OpenView Config and Deploy     CORE   (4315)    Running
ovcs         HP OpenView Certificate Server   SERVER (4320)    Running
opcmsga      OVO Message Agent            AGENT,EA       (4321)    Running
opcacta      OVO Action Agent             AGENT,EA       (4322)    Running
opcmsgi      OVO Message Interceptor      AGENT,EA       (4323)    Running
opcle        OVO Logfile Encapsulator     AGENT,EA       (4325)    Running
opcmona      OVO Monitor Agent            AGENT,EA       (4327)    Running
opctrapi     OVO SNMP Trap Interceptor    AGENT,EA       (4329)    Running
opceca       OVO Event Correlation        AGENT,EA                 Stopped
opcecaas     ECS Annotate Server          AGENT,EA                 Stopped
coda         HP OpenView Performance Core                (4331)    Running
```

From the command line of the HTTPS-based managed node, verify that the correct processes are running; if necessary, restart the processes.

- **ovc**: Check the status of the agent
- **ovc –status**: Check the agent status
- **ovc –start**: Start all agent processes
- **ovc –stop**: Stop all agent processes except the control agent
- **ovc –kill**: Stop all agent process, including the control agent

Note: the ovc command is available on HTTPs-based nodes only. Check the agent status of DCE-based nodes with the opcagt command.

22.1.3 Utilize the Online Help

During troubleshooting, it is helpful to have all the necessary information and resources at your fingertips. The online resources provided within the OpenView platform make access to important information easy. Inside each graphical window there is a HELP button on the menu. As shown in Figure 22-1, you can obtain help about the typical administrator tasks, icons, and errors. There is also a search engine, a glossary of terms, and instructions on how to use the built-in help.

Figure 22-1 OpenView Operation online help.

```
 # tail /var/opt/OV/log/OpC/opcerror|grep ERROR
 07/16/04 10:31:36 ERROR opctrapi  (Trap Interceptor)(1907)
[opcevti.cpp:1460]:
 Receiving SNMP PDU failed: Lost connection with pmd/ovEvent
process
 (application disconnected). Trying to reinitialize.
(OpC30-204)

 # /opt/OV/bin/OpC/utils/opcerr 30 204
 MESSAGE OpC30-204:
 Receiving SNMP PDU failed: .... Trying to reinitialize.
 INSTRUCTION:
 The VPO event interceptor could not get a SNMP PDU although
it was
 informed that there is one available. The SNMP API message
<snmp-msg> gives
 more information.
 The event interceptor tries to reconnect to pmd.
```

22.1.4 The itochecker Report

OVO provides utilities out-of-the box to assist with troubleshooting. One utility, the itochecker, provides an overall check of your OVO environment. You can use the itochecker report to help isolate a problem. With the itochecker, you can generate a report that will provide important information about the state of the configuration on the management server environment. Read the man page for usage details. In this section, an example is provided of how to create a full report and a display of the results. The report provides a good overall look at the OVO environment. The primary areas of interest are any categories that show errors.

22.1.4.1 Run the itochecker Report

1. Run the report:
   # /opt/OV/contrib/OpC/itochecker –a
2. Extract an HTML report file from the compressed tar file:
   # zcat /tmp/ITO_rpt/ITO_rpt.tar.Z | tar xvf - report.html
3. View the report in the browser with the command
   /opt/netscape/netscape report.html

This listing is the main menu of the report; the hyperlinks guide you to additional details about the specific areas in each category. Use this report to get a quick indication of any signs of trouble within the OVO environment.

```
ITOCHECKER REPORT
Thu Feb 5 08:22:43 PST 2004
Management Server: nuema
System Environment Check
Name Resolution   OK
System Info OK
Number Of Processes / System Load    OK
DCE Status and Patchlevel    OK
System file permissions    OK
OS Patches    OK
OVO EnvironmentCheck
OVO Version/Package & ECS Designer    N/A
Server Processes    OK
Kernel Parameters    WARNING
OVO Patches    OK
Installed OVO filesets    OK
OVO Binaries: Version and Patches    OK
OVO Libraries: Version and Patches    OK
Disk space in DB and OVO Directories    OK
Pending Data in Distribution Directory    WARNING
OpCdecoded Config Files    OK
Cluster Information    N/A
core File Information    OK
opcinfo and opcerror Files    OK
Elements in Server Queues    OK
Elements in Agent Queues    OK
File permissions and ownershipOK
Database Check
Database Info    OK
Database Queries    OK
```

```
OVO Database Check
Agent Entries in DB <-> Agent Entries in Filesystem    OK
Diskspace in Oracle Directory    OK
Nodes Check
Nodes Check    OK
Nodes Check Statistics    OK
Java GUI / Service Navigator
Java Version / Path    OK
Content of dir /opt/OV/www/htdocs/ito_op    OK
Content of dir /etc/opt/OV/share/conf/OpC/mgmt_sv/opcsvcm    OK
Check number of configured services and loggings    OK
Output of /opt/OV/contrib/OpC/stacktrace -svc    OK
```

Created by itochecker version A.08.00

22.2 FUNCTIONAL CHECKS

The functional checks are helpful when you need to determine overall operability of the OVO environment. When the functional checks do not result in the desired outcome, the next step is to plan time for the necessary troubleshooting, configuration changes, or perhaps a patch fix. In order to isolate the problem, ensure that you have collected as much system information as possible. Also, perform the initial data gathering and basic troubleshooting prior to placing a support call, if necessary. Table 22-3 provides a listing of OVO functional checks.

Table 22-3 OpenView Operations Functional Test—Checklist

Check the following areas	Procedure	Notes
1. Are all of the management server processes running?	opcsv	Restart the processes. Investigate why the process was not running.
2. What is the version of the management server software?	opcsv -version	Verify the current patch level for the management server. Upgrade if necessary.
3. Are all of the managed node processes running?	ovc	Check the error log file for possible reasons the process is down. Restart the processes.
4. What is the patch version of the managed node software?	opcagt -version	Try to maintain the current patch release.
5. Check the installed version of . managed node software and the sub-agent components from the management server	opcragt –agent_ version <node>	This is also a quick way to check the communications between the server and the node. If this fails to verify, the node is managed by this server. It may be necessary to restart the processes on the node.
6. Check for OVO errors on the DCE managed node.	tail /var/opt/OV/log/ opcerror	If there are error messages in the file, check for resolutions via the eCare problem resolution web site. It may be necessary to log a support call via ltrc.hp.com.

Check the following areas	Procedure	Notes
7. Check the OVO errors on the HTTPS managed node.	tail /var/opt/OV/log/ System.txt	
8. Check the remote procedure call service (RPC), verify that the DCE/(NCS) or RPC-based agents are registered.	rpccp show mapping opcmsgrd opcdistm opcdispm RPC processes on the node: rpcd (HP) opcctla dced (RPC) llbserver (NCS)	RPC processes on the server:
9. Check the status of the Oracle processes.	ps –ef|grep ora	If the oracle processes are not run ning, the OVO processes will not start.
10. Verify the Oracle listener.	lsnrctl status	If the listener lsnrctl start is not running, restart it. The database must be open in order for the listener to start properly. You may need the help from a DBA to restart the database.
11. Check the OpenView platform background processes and services (NNM).	ovstatus -c	If the OpenView background processes are not running, OVO processes will not start.
12. Verify hostname resolution from the server.	nslookup <node>	The OpenView platform utilizes nslookup <local_server_name> name resolution lookup services, this information must be correct within the DNS, NIS or local host file. Note: The command nsquery is becoming more useful for hostname or IP lookups. It provides more detailed information.
13. Verify hostname resolution from the managed node.	nslookup <server> nslookup <local_ node_name>	
14. Check network connectivity from the server.	ping <node>	ping tests may indicate certain net work delays that can be viewed with OpenView as a node down. Intermittent ping failures should be investigated and resolved.
15. Check network connectivity from the managed node	ping <server>	If the node is unable to ping the server; messages are buffered until the server is available.
16. Check the name resolution service configuration file.	more /etc/nsswitch.conf	Verify the search order. If using multi-homed hosts, see #17.

Table 22-3 OpenView Operations Functional Test—Checklist (Continued)

Check the following areas	Procedure	Notes
17. Is the node multi-homed?	Add an entry with the second IP_ADDRESS HOSTNAME into a file that you create s on the server called /etc/opt/OV/share/conf/ OpC/mgmt_sv/opc.host	The file has the same format as the /etc/hosts file. After the file is cre ated restart the server processes. Any changes to the file require process restart.
18. Operator and Administrator login.	ps -eflgrep ui ps -eflgrep opcuiwww	Each operator (including the admin-istrator) should have a unique login account for security purposes.
19. Login to OVO using the operator account to ensure that the environment displays the correct information based upon the operators responsibilities.		
20. Check the Oracle environmental variables	cat /etc/opt/OV/share/ conf/ovdbconf	
21. Check the Oracle environmental variable within the user Oracle shell environment.	su – oracle	envlgrep ORA
Note: Compare this output to the listing found in Chapter 23. It may be necessary to consult with a DBA to verify the health of the OVO oracle database. The oracle user account requires the correct environment for installation and configuration of the database and during runtime operations.		
22. Check for all the environmental variables within the user oracle shell environment	su – oracle env > /tmp/ora_env.out more /tmp/ora_env.out	System environment variables are also important, such as the PATH, MANPATH, LANG, and so on.
23. Check connectivity to the Oracle database	1. su – oracle 2. sqlplus opc_op/ 3. Exit	Oracle 8.x and 9.x
Note: It may be necessary to check with a DBA to gain access to the database using the privileged user accounts.		
24. Check remote connections to the database.	1. su – oracle 2.sqlplus opc_op/ opc_op@ov_net	
25. Check the error logs.		Refer to Section 22.1.1.
26. Clean up pending template distributions.	ll /var/opt/OV/share/ tmp/OpC/distrib rm /var/opt/OV/share/ tmp/OpC/distrib/*	If the distribution failed, a message will periodically appear in the message browser; remove the files from the distribution directory.
27. Check the integrity of the queue files	/opt/OV/contrib/OpC/ opcqchk <queue_file>	If this program presents a menu and basic opera-tions can be performed the queue file is OK.

Check the following areas	Procedure	Notes
28. Test message data flow in general	opcmsg a=a o=o msg_t=test	If the message appears in the browser message flow is OK.
29. Messages should appear in the browser of the assigned operator if not check the following:	1. Check the operator's responsibilities 2. Use local logging for the policy to check whether a. the agent actually recieves the input event. b. the event is suppressed or not c. rule out duplicate message suppression and message/event correlatoiin. d. check history browser, message could have been configured to go directly to history tables in the database. 3. Review policy inventory on the managed node using the command ovpolicy or opctemplate. 4. Use the opcpat command to verify pattern syntax is correct. See the man pages for use of the opcpat command.	
30. Test action execution.	Use command broadcast and run a command (i.e. hostname)	If successful actions work in general
31 Verify agent status	opcragt <node_name)	This displays agent status and tests basic connectivity
32. Test basic HTTPS connectivity	bbcutil -ping <node>	Execute the command on the managed node
33. Test HTTPS agent security certificates	ovcert -list	
34. Test connectivity of DCE agent	rpccp show mapping	
35. Utilize the trace facility	If necessary to further investigation configure XPL tracing	Refer to the Tracing Concepts and Users Guide for more information about XPL tracing and logging.

22.2.1 When the Processes Will Not Start

If you perform the functional check and the processes will not start, it could be due to corrupt queue or pipe files. Corrupt queue files occur on rare occasions if the OS or physical disk buffers have not been flushed to disk successfully. These files can be removed from the server or node while the OVO processes are not running. If it becomes necessary to remove the queue files, be aware they contain data that will be lost. However, if you have tried everything else and you are still experiencing problems with agent or server processes, move the queue files. Check the integrity of the OVO processes by moving the queue files temporarily, then restart the agent. If the agent starts, return the original queue file; this will minimize data loss. If necessary remove the queue files and restart the processes. The queue files will be recreated.

22.2.1.1 Procedure to Remove the Queue Files on the Server

1. Exit all OVO GUIs.
2. Stop the management server processes: **ovstop ovoacomm**.
3. Erase the OVO temporary files: **rm /var/opt/OV/share/tmp/OpC/mgmt_sv/***.
4. Restart the management server processes: **ovstart opc**.
5. Restart the GUI: **opc**.

22.2.1.2 Procedure to Remove the Queue Files on the Node

1. Stop all the managed node processes: **opcagt –kill**.
2. Erase the OVO temporary files: **rm /var/opt/OV/tmp/OpC/***.
3. Verify that all of the process have stopped: **ps –eaf|grep opc**.
4. Restart the managed node processes: **opcagt -start**.

22.3 PROBLEM SOLVING

The tools built into the OVO user environment help you solve and manage incidents as they arrive in the message browser. The messages indicate that the agent on the managed node recognized an event and the message about the event is forwarded to the server. The event-processing mechanism depends upon a variety of resources that must all function properly. When diagnosing problems within the OpenView environment using a structured approach to problem solving (described earlier in Section 22.1 of this chapter), it is important to isolate the problem and use proven methods to determine the root cause of the problem. The OpenView processing environment is organized into the following functional categories:

- Installation /De-installation
- Client/Server Communications
- Error handling
- Networking
- Database(s)
- Event and Message processing
- Background Processes and Services (NNM)
- Policies
- Client/Server Configuration
- Applications (out-of-the-box and add-on)
- Graphical User Interface (MOTIF or JAVA)
- Agents and Sub-Agents
- Smart Plug-Ins
- Backup/Recovery
- Security (built-in and add-on)
- High Availability (Service Guard, Veritas, Solaris, AIX, Tru-64)
- Various Vendor-specific operating system environments (HP, Sun, IBM, Microsoft, LINUX, Sequent)

When you decide where to begin the troubleshooting process (such as the management server or managed node), you can locate the specific problem-solving resources. The most current information on diagnosing and resolving OVO problems is available at the OpenView support web site: `http://support.openview.hp.com`. The documentation, troubleshooting tools, software patches, and access to a worldwide OpenView user and support community are just a click away!

22.4 SELF-HEALING SERVICES (SHS)

When you experience a particular problem with the OpenView platform, wouldn't it be nice if the server took some initiative to diagnose and help you resolve the problem more quickly? Some timesaving tasks could include initial data collection, problem categorization, search for relevant eCare documents, notify the appropriate support staff that an incident has happened, and contact HP and report the problem. Taking this dream to another level, after the system contacts HP, they would immediately analyze the reported problem and send you an analysis report with relevant recommendations on how to resolve the problem. Wow, that sounds like a great idea, but when will it be available for OpenView? This dream is already a reality. A sample analysis report is shown here for reference.

```
Report Available - HP OpenView Self-Healing Services
This message has been automatically generated. Please do not
reply to this message.
```

```
Your recently submitted HP OpenView Self-Healing Services inci-
dent has been analyzed, a report has been generated and it is
available on the HP OpenView Support web site. Please view your
HP OpenView Analysis Report at the following web address (HP
Passport sign-in required):
 -
https://support.openview.hp.com/software/analysis/report?inci-
dent=00306E2C804F-1089649416-625345064-1073641417572

Incident Summary:

 Date/Time:          Jan 9, 2004 9:43:37 AM GMT
 Machine Name:       tester
 Application:        self-healing services
 ID:                 00306E2C804F-1089649416-625345064-
1073641417572
 Short Description: Test

After you sign-in with an HP Passport account, you may need to
provide the HP OpenView Support system handle which was used to
submit the incident. You can find this system handle in the HP
OpenView Self-Healing Services client profile located on the
system from which this incident was submitted.

This report will provide you with customized information and
assistance to help you solve your software difficulties and keep
your systems running smoothly. In the event that you require
personal assistance, you will also be able to initiate a support
case for this incident from the analysis report.

Thank you!

HP OpenView Self-Healing Services Team
```

SHS installs on the management server in two phases. The *Instant Support Enterprise Edition* (ISEE) client must be installed first. This client software is responsible for communication with database and analysis servers located within HP regional sites. These HP servers run the SHS application software within a secure environment. The software is responsible for receipt of the incoming request from the client (ISEE). Refer to the ISEE web site, `http://www.hp.com/hps/hardware/hw_instant.html`, for more information about how ISEE is utilized for the datacenter, desktop or distributed environment. Download the current ISEE client at `http://www.software.hp.com/`. The ISEE client sends encrypted incident information to the HP analysis and problem diagnosis servers. This is done seamlessly without operator intervention. The client and server perform authentication checks prior to incident data transfer using encrypted private and public keys. The SHS client provides the user interface and incident management infrastructure, which performs the tasks of monitoring the OV management server for errors, analyzing the error message, and sending local information messages to the administrator. If the incident requires further analysis (per the configuration) it is sent to the HP servers using the HTTP port. The SHS environment supports a secure proxy for Internet communications.

These capabilities are available for the OpenView server platform free of charge. You can find out more about SHS and download the client software from: `http://support.openview.hp.com/self_healing.jsp`. Read the SHS documentation for installation instructions.

22.5 SUMMARY

Troubleshooting, problem analysis and root cause determination requires patience, determination, and experience. As a new OpenView administrator it is important to fully characterize problems in order to begin troubleshooting on the correct path. Although you may start out on one path and end up on another in order to resolve a complex problem, over time the most important skill will become patience. You will need this quality in order to describe the problem to others who may be able to help you determine the root cause of the problem faster such that you implement correct solutions and minimize system downtime.

PART 4

OpenView Operations for Windows

OpenView Operations for Windows (OVOW) extends services management flexibility within the IT organization. The Microsoft Windows-centric operations and performance management solution manages a heterogeneous enterprise environment. The startup-planning scenario is similar for the Windows and UNIX management platforms. The decision to utilize one or both types of OVO management servers will drive the details of the implementation tasks which are based upon the organizations enterprise-wide service, application, system and network management requirements. This section introduces the overall concepts and features of the OVOW management platform.

CHAPTER 23

Introducing OVO for Windows

When you decide to invest in an OpenView enterprise management solution, *OpenView Operations for Windows* (OVOW) will likely become part of the discussion. This includes unique features, installation, training, and operational interface details. The operational objectives of OVOW are the same as those for *OVO for UNIX* (OVOU). Both products provide a real-time view of which events are impacting the ability of the enterprise to deliver services to end customers and minimize service impacts when infrastructure components are offline due to planned or unplanned downtime. This chapter contains information to introduce the HP OVOW product.

23.1 ARCHITECTURE

Let's start by taking a high-level view of OVOW and comparing it to OVOU. The agent technology is functionally the same between the two products. They differ here when the OVOW agent takes advantage of the unique features of the Windows architecture. Some differences are easier to adjust to than others; for example, OVOW policies are similar conceptually to templates that are referred to in OVOU. Table 23-1 shows common platform-specific differences.

Table 23-1 OVOU and OVOW Platform Features

OVOU Platform*	OVOW Platform*
Oracle Database XWindows capability UNIX remsh access for applications Integrated out-of-the box with NNM Service management requires separate configuration of the product using XML-based template files and additional commands	MSDE, MS/SQL Close integration with other OVO Windows products Version control of policies Extensive reports and graphs for performance data Hyperbolic service tree in the console
Operator's console JAVA user interface or Applet (could also be XWindows/Motif with OVO 8 and below)	Visual Basic tools for managing windows systems VB Script and JScript tools Operator and Administrator GUI Integrates with MMC (MMC is discussed later in this chapter.) Discovery of Windows nodes WMI Event Policy Management Service management integrated out-of-the box

*The list is not inclusive

OVOW is a three-tier architecture consisting of the management server, console and the managed nodes. Out-of-the-box, the product includes the following components: a database, automatic discovery, message policies, performance, reporting and graphing tools. The Windows-specific polices that are provided with OVOW are listed here for reference; consult the OVO Windows documentation for the most current list of policies.

The OVOW agents and policies are designed to process and act upon data from the following event sources:

- Windows Event Logfiles (NT/Win2K)
- Perflib (NT/Win2K)
- WMI Store (NT/Win2K)
- System Logfiles
- External Messages (opcmsg command and API)
- SNMP Events
- Custom metrics made available by external programs or scripts

23.1.1 Management Server

The OVO administrator performs system management functions such as deploying agents and policies for all managed nodes via the server. Service management data and policy configurations are stored on the server along with the messages and event notifications.

The server platform uses *Microsoft Management Console* (MMC), *Windows Management Instrumentation* (WMI), and the *Distributed Component Object Model* (DCOM) as core technologies. The OVOW application is a snap-in to the MMC and requires the MMC in order to run. Service management data, and policy configuration information is stored on the server.

23.1.1.1 Microsoft Management Console

The MMC handles the user interface for OVOW. It is the Windows 2000 common application GUI for administering the operating system. OVOW requires MMC to operate.

23.1.1.2 Web-Based Enterprise Management and WMI

WMI is the Microsoft implementation of *Web-Based Enterprise Management* (WEBM) to develop a standard technology for accessing management information in an enterprise environment. WEBM is an industry standard initiative by the *Distributed Management Task Force* (DMTF). For additional information, visit `http://www.dmtf.org/standards/wbem/`.

23.1.1.3 Component Object Model and DCOM

The *Component Object Model* (COM) provides functions that enable diverse applications to interoperate. DCOM is a protocol that provides support for objects running on the server to communicate with remote systems over the network.

23.1.2 OVOW Management Console

The console provides a *graphical user interface* (GUI) to perform routine management tasks, such as

- Service and node discovery (refer to Chapter 25, "OVOW Implementation Tasks," for additional information about discovery)
- Configuring, editing and deploying policies
- Accessing, editing, and maintaining data, such as messages, graphs, and service views.

23.1.3 Managed Nodes

The agent runs on the managed node and sends exceptions (messages) to the management server based on the deployed policies. The node responds to requests from the server to execute or disable a policy. Performance data collected on the node is made available for viewing in the message browser as monitored thresholds or other graphical performance management or reporting tools. In the event that communications with the server are interrupted, the agent continues to operate, storing messages locally and performing automatic actions. When the server communication is re-established, the stored messages are forwarded to the server.

23.2 INSTALLATION

Before installing the management platform, develop a plan. See Chapter 13, "Out-of-the-box with HP OpenView Operations," for implementation planning. Read the *HP OpenView Operations/Performance for Windows Installation Guide*. It is also recommended that you test the installation on a non-production server if possible to become familiar with OVOW prior to implementation into production. The products installed on the management server are delivered on a CD media kit.

23.2.3 Product Summary

The initial installation of the OVOW management platform includes the following products:

- ***OpenView Operations for Windows* (OVOW)**—Management client/server and console for heterogeneous service, application, systems management.
- **OpenView Reporter**
- **OpenView *Network Node Manager* (NNM)**—Network management.
- **OpenView NNM Adaptor**—Automatic discovery of NNM nodes.
- **OpenView Problem Diagnosis**—Performs network path analysis, and presents end-to-end path information.
- **OpenView Problem Diagnosis Add-On Module (NDAOM)**—Provides detailed information on network performance; requires Performance Diagnosis.

- **OpenView Performance Agent**—Collects performance information.
- **OpenView Performance Manager**—Displays performance information.
- ***Microsoft SQL Server 2000 Desktop Edition*** **(MSDE)**—Database, can be upgraded to SQL Server 2000 Enterprise or Standard Edition.
- **PERL**—Provides support for policies and tools.
- **JAVA Runtime Environment**—Runs JAVA GUI programs.
- **JAVA Application Launcher**—Supports the graphing components.

Smart Plug-Ins:

- Windows Operating System
- UNIX Operating System
- Web Servers
- Microsoft Active Directory Server
- Microsoft Exchange Server
- Microsoft SQL Server
- Informix
- Oracle
- Sybase
- Microsoft Enterprise Servers
- mySAP.com
- BEA WebLogic Application Server
- IBM WebSphere

Note: During the guided installation process, select the products and components that are appropriate for your enterprise solution.

23.2.4 Installation Summary

Prior to the installation, verify that you have met all prerequisites for hardware and software. They are documented in the *HP OpenView Operations Performance for Windows Installation Guide*. The installation summary provides a high-level look at the installation tasks as shown in the following list:

- **Starting the installer**—If you need to review a transcript of the installation, the installer writes to the OVInstaller_install.log. The file is overwritten each time the installer is run.
- **System requirements checks**—Checks things such as Administrator privileges, prior versions of the product, operating system, memory, disk and version of the installer. Errors are showstoppers.

- **Start install wizard**—The product selection list contains the required (OVOW) and optional (SPIs, HP OpenView Reporter) applications. Select the server and console on the same platform or console only install option. Database account password, license acceptance and OVOW server account setup questions.
- **Check product prerequisites**
- **Install the software packages** - The files for the server, console, agents and optional (selected) packages are transferred from the CD's to disk.
- **Install complete**—Registry updates, launch the OVOW tutorial.

23.2.5 Product Directory Structure

Program files are transferred from the CD onto the file system into the following directories by default:

OVInstallDir = <drive>:\Program Files\ HP OpenView

OVDataDir = <drive>:\Program Files\ HP OpenView\Data

OVAgentInstallDir = <OVInstallDir>\packages = agent software

OVAgentDataDir = <OVAgentInstallDir>

OVDataDir\HP OVInstall = server/console install/upgrade log files

OVDataDir\HP OVInstall = <package>_install.log files

<drive>:\SystemRootDir = installer log file

<drive>:\SysTemp = OVOW agent install log file

23.2.6 Product Documentation

The product documentation is available from the OpenView support web site, `http://ovweb.external.hp.com/lpe/doc_serv/`. After installation, the product guides are also found on the management server in the directory <OVInstalldir>\NLS\1033\Manuals\. The OVOW documentation is listed here for reference.

- HP OpenView Operations/Performance for Windows Installation Guide
- HP OpenView Operations/Performance for Windows Upgrade Guide—upgrade instructions from prior versions of OVOW to the current version.
- HPOV Auto Pass Users Guide—Information on obtaining permanent license passwords.
- OVO Readme—OVOW Release information

Other documents are available for each addition software application, SPI, or product component installed on the management server.

23.2.7 Product Demonstration

The HP OpenView Integrated service Assurance for Windows is a live demonstration program that explains the OVOW components. The demonstration is viewable via the web at `http://www.openview.hp.com/demos/index.html.`

23.2.8 Training

After the installation is complete, a self-guided tutorial displays to help you become more familiar with the primary system administration tasks.

Visit `http://education.hp.com` to view course outlines and schedule OpenView training classes.

23.3 EXPLORING THE FEATURES OF THE CONSOLE

The windows management console provides a "single pane of glass" for managing the enterprise. Built into the console are all of the tools required to focus on services, sort messages, modify, view and deploy policies, utilize tools and much more. Here are some of the features of the management console:

- **Console navigation tree (left side of the console)**—Managed nodes, services and tools listed hierarchically.
- **Details pane (right side of the console)**– Provides graphic views of the service map and a list view of the active message browser (or filtered message browser).
- **Toolbar**
- **Servers folder**—Hierarchy of service and its supporting software tools.
- **Nodes folder**—Hierarchy of the managed nodes.
- **Service map**—Graphical view of services and nodes, capability to drill down to view root cause a problem on the impacted service and impacts on other services. The services displayed in the map are discovered automatically using the deployed policies and instrumentation.
- **Active message browser**—Messages from managed nodes and services, allows message filtering based on attributes such as severity, application, message text, and so on.

The console, as shown in Figure 23-1, can be installed on a separate computer for more management flexibility.

Figure 23-1 OpenView Operations for Windows console.

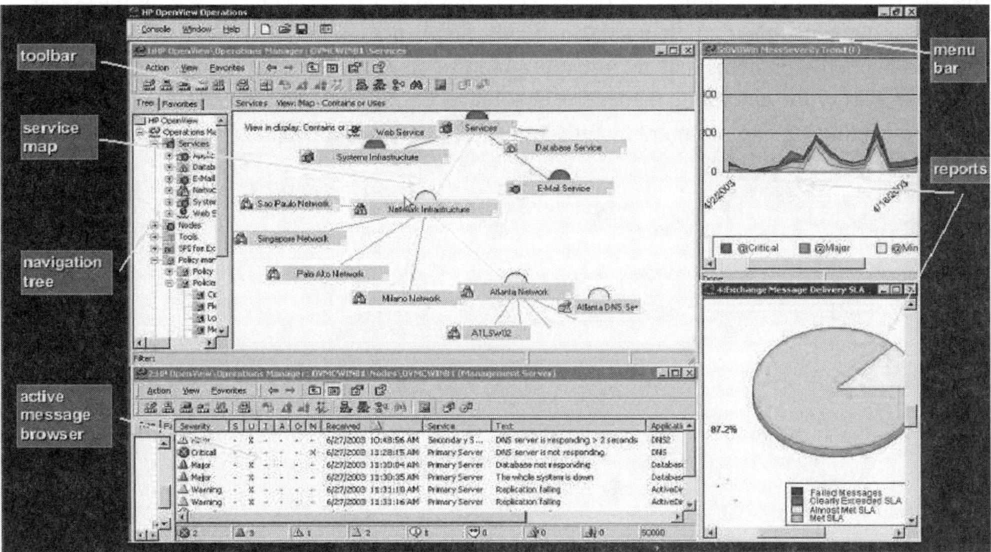

23.4 MESSAGE PROCESSING

Similar to OVOU, OVOW uses intelligent agents to monitor events and collect information for further processing. Event sources include log files, SNMP events, performance metrics and messages generated externally using the message API. The events are processed, presented, and acted upon either automatically or with operator assistance. In order to process the event, the agent is directed through configuration policies what events to monitor and process.

23.4.1 Policies, Actions and Tools

A policy contains rules that determine what objects to monitor. The object is the source of an event that would trigger further action by the agent. For example, the policy might direct the agent to suppress an event or generate a message as a result of the object exceeding a specific threshold. Messages that are processed and filtered based on attributes such as node, application, object, severity, and descriptive text are forwarded to the server and appear in the active message browser. Actions are planned responses to the specific event. An action can be performed automatically at the managed node or with operator assistance after the message arrives on the server. Built-in tools such as executable commands give the user more flexibility to respond to problems.

Finding the root cause of an event is important in analyzing and making a problem determination. The service console allows an operator to drill down on a service to view the root cause of the problem and or take further action to resolve the problem.

23.5 SUMMARY

The OVOW product introduced in this chapter has many similarities to the more familiar OVOU product. It may be necessary in some environments to utilize one or both of these platforms to provide the most efficient solution to your end customers. The advantages of introducing OVOW in environments that are already Windows-centric will make the decision to include OVOW as part of the enterprise management solution easier.

We continue to explore more features of OVOW in the next chapter.

CHAPTER 24

OVO Windows and OVO UNIX Interoperability

The two products *OVO Windows* (OVOW) and *OVO UNIX* (OVOU), as mentioned previously, are designed for enterprise-wide management. If the skills of your company's staff are primarily strong with the Windows operating system, it may be more effective to introduce a Windows-centric management platform. This advantage of OVOW makes it an attractive compliment to OVOU. If you decide to take advantage of the two types of management platforms to gain the flexibility and span of administration to multiple teams it is necessary to look closer at how the two server platforms work cooperatively. This chapter contains information on the areas in which the two products OVOW/OVOU may interoperate. One formal definition of interoperability is offered here for reference: 1. The ability of systems, units, or forces to provide services to and accept services from other systems, units or forces and to use the services so exchanged to enable them to operate effectively together. [JP1] 2. The condition achieved among communications-electronics systems or items of communications-electronics equipment when information or services can be exchanged directly and satisfactorily between them and/or their users. The degree of interoperability should be defined when referring to specific cases. [JP1] (188). So, with that in mind, let's take a look at the built-in communication, resource, and service exchanges that are possible between OVOW and OVOU.

24.1 OVOW and OVOU Communications

The servers are both TCP/IP-based which means that basic communications via commands such as ping allow administrators from either server to verify that network connectivity is in tact. It may be necessary to test connectivity and report the information back to the users at the console in a more structured way. Why not take advantage of the built-in communication and monitoring tools?

24.1.1 Server-to-Server Alive Checks

The servers could also periodically probe for services and resource availability via SNMP. Both servers support the integrated OpenView application *Network Node Manager* (NNM) and therefore have the inherent capability to utilize the SNMP applications provided by NNM. NNM is installed with the management server on OVOU. NNM is a plug-in to the MMC on OVOW.

When installed, NNM's management functionality is available to periodically check for remote nodes, as discussed in earlier chapters. In this section, the focus is on the SNMP monitoring capability of OVO.

An OVO monitor could provide status information into the message browser about the state of the other management server(s). If an MIB monitor periodically probes a device, an OpenView agent is not required. But it is necessary to have the SNMP components configured, which would normally happen as part of the initial operating system installation. The following references provide information on how SNMP is implemented on the OpenView server platforms:

- **HPUX SNMP Information**—`http://managementsoftware.hp.com/products/snmp/prod_snmp_0003.html.`
- **Solaris SNMP Information**—`http://www.sun.com/servers/entry/docs/817-2559-11.pdf.`
- **Windows SNMP Information**—`http://www.microsoft.com/resources/documentation/WindowsServ/2003/enterprise/proddocs/en-us/Default.asp?url=/resources/documentation/WindowsServ/2003/enterprise/proddocs/en-us/sag_snmpservice.asp.`

In addition to installing the SNMP components, after creating a monitor policy, a device icon (represents the MIB monitored OV server), should appear as a message allowed node within the node configuration of the server.

24.2 Message Forwarding

Message forwarding is very common within the OVO environment. See Figure 24-1. When there are many managed nodes perhaps in different buildings, regions, or countries, a message flow plan becomes extremely important. Things to consider include:

- What messages will the node forward to the server?
- What messages will the OVOW forward to OVOU?
- What messages will OVOU servers forward?

These considerations are important because the message flow causes a higher load on the network. Take a careful look at the traffic on the network before, during, and after the implementation of OpenView. These network metrics and other requirements (such as message suppression) will guide the decisions about what messages will flow into the server's OV database.

The message forwarding configuration concept was described in Chapter 19, "Enterprise Management Flexibility with Multiple Servers." Refer to the OpenView Concepts Guide for more information.

Figure 24-1 Message and policy interoperability between OVOW and OVOU.

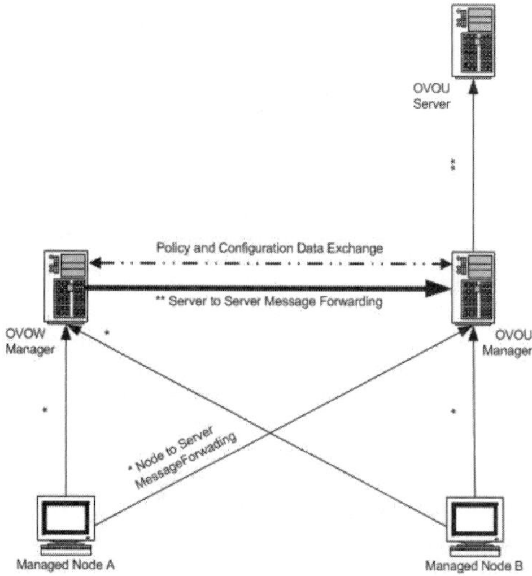

24.2.1 Message Forwarding Rules

In general, message forwarding is a flexible configuration, allowing messages to pass from one system to another. However, as you might expect, there are a few restrictions. The message forwarding rules are described with scenarios in this section for reference. Refer to Figure 24-1.

- Windows managed nodes A and B send messages to their respective primary managers, as shown in the diagram by the vertical lines from the nodes to the servers.
- Upon switch-control (using the tool SwitchMgmtServer), managed node A sends messages to OVOU, the new primary manager (per instructions in a MultipleActionManager policy) as shown by the diagonal line from node A to OVOU.
- Upon switch-control (using the tool SwitchMgmtServer), managed node B sends messages to OVOW, the new primary manager (per instructions in a MultipleActionManagers policy)
- Messages from OVOW managed nodes can be forwarded to the OVOU server (this is done by defining a message forwarding rule within a policy).
- Messages from an OVOW server that are forwarded to an OVOU server can be forwarded from there to another OVOU server. This is shown in the illustration by the one-way arrow from the OVOW manager to the OVOU manager. Then the vertical arrow leads to a third system, which is another OVOU manager.

24.3 Policy, Template, and Service Data Exchange

When the environment supports multiple management servers, it is practical for OVO Administrators to develop policies and templates that are shared among the servers. In other words, if you build the policy for one server it is transferred to other servers as required. The OV commands to facilitate the policy and template data exchange are executed from the command line and or the GUI.

24.3.1 OVOW to OVOU

For example, to distribute a policy from the OVOW server to the OVOU server, use the following guidelines:

- Use the utility program **ovpmutil** to download the policy from the OVOW server.
- Use the utility program **ovpmutil** to extract the policy data into a file.
- Transfer the policy file to the OVOU server.
- Use the utility program **iconv** to convert the codeset from OVOW to OVOU.
- Use the utility program **opctempl** to upload (import) the OVOW policy.
- Use the command **ovpmutil** to extract the service tree into an XML file.

24.3.2 OVOU to OVOW

Template exchange from OVOU to OVOW should follow the guidelines listed here:

- Use the command **opccfgdwn** to download the template from OVOU (this can also be done via the GUI by selecting **Actions→Server→Configuration Download**).
- Transfer the template file from OVOU to the OVOW server.
- Use the utility program **importpolicies** to import the OVOU template.

24.3.3 Interoperability Commands

Several programs help facilitate the interoperability between OVOW and OVOU. The definitions of some of the OVOW commands are shown here for reference; these commands are also found in the online help. The OVOU commands are also listed without full syntax (refer to Appendix A).

ovpmutil—ovpmutil is a tool that allows you to perform some configuration tasks from the command line. The tool can be used to

- Deploy policies.
- Download or upload policy, tool, or service information from the management server.
- Convert downloaded information between structured storage format and ASCII format.
- Register policies or policy groups.

Command syntax:

```
OvPMUtil [<flag-list>] <parameter-list>
```

Flag list:

```
[ -[?] [HELP] ] = Usage information
```

Parameter list:

```
DEP [(/p | /pg) /<policyname>] [(/n | /ng)<nodename>] [/c
(TRUE|FALSE)] [/e (TRUE|FALSE)][/t <type>][/v <version>]
PCV [/x]|[/c [/v <version>][/n <name>][/i]] <filenamelist>
REG <policyfilename> /g <policygrouppath>
CFG <conftype> [UPL <configfilename>]|[DNL [/p <subtree>]
[/t <targetdir>][/a]]
```

DEP (deploy) options:

```
DEP [(/p | /pg) /<policyname>] [(/n | /ng)<nodename>] [/c
(TRUE|FALSE)][/e (TRUE|FALSE)][/t <type>][/v <version>]
<policyname>
```

This required parameter indicates the name of the policy or policy group to be deployed. It must contain the path to the policy as shown in the console tree, starting under Policy groups. Use /p to indicate a policy, or /pg to indicate a policy group. The path must begin with a backslash ("\"), and policy groups within the path are separated with a backslash ("\"). If the name of a policy group contains spaces, the entire path must be enclosed in quotation marks.

`<nodename>`

This required parameter indicates the name of the node or node group on which the policy will be deployed. It must contain the path to the node as shown in the console tree, starting under Nodes. Use /n to indicate a node, or /ng to indicate a node group. The path must begin with a backslash ("\"), and node groups within the path are separated with a backslash ("\"). If the name of a node group contains spaces, the entire path must be enclosed in quotation marks.

`/c`

(check version) If this optional parameter is set to FALSE, no version check is made, and the policy is deployed even if a newer version of that policy is already deployed on the node. If the parameter is TRUE (or absent), the policy will only be deployed if no newer version of the policy is deployed on the node.

`/e`

(enable) If this optional parameter is set to FALSE, the policies are disabled on the node after deployment. If this parameter is TRUE (or absent), the policy or policy group is enabled after deployment.

`/t <type>`

If this optional parameter is set, the policy will only be deployed if it is a policy of the given policy type. Only the original English names may be used, and must be enclosed in quotation marks, for example "Logfile Entry" or "Windows Management Interface". This parameter is not valid when a policy group is deployed.

```
/v <version>
```

If this optional parameter is set, the policy will only be deployed if it matches the given version. This parameter is not valid when a policy group is deployed.

PCV (Policy Conversion) Options:

Converts a policy structured storage file into two ASCII files (*.header and *.data), or converts the ASCII files into a policy structured storage file.

```
PCV [(/x <filenamelist> | /c <filenamelist>)]] [/v
<version>] [/n <name>][/i]] <filenamelist>
/x <filenamelist>
```

Extracts the structured policy store from <filenamelist>, which is a list of policy files (downloaded using ovpmutil CFG DNL) to be converted. The downloaded policy (which is a structured storage file) will be extracted into the header stream (*.header) containing the policy management information (for example, name, version, LogicalID, InstanceID and Checksum) and the data stream (*.data) containing the policy definition. Multiple structured storage files can be extracted by listing them separated with a space.

```
/c <filenamelist>
```

Combines the *.header and *.data files into a structured policy store. The filename list has the same format as for /x .

```
/v <version>
```

This optional parameter changes the version information of the policy to <version> during combination (the InstanceID and Checksum are also be updated). This option is not valid when the /x option is used.

```
/n <name>
```

This optional parameter changes the name given to the policy (new LogicalID, InstanceID is created and Checksum is updated).

```
i
```

If this optional parameter is specified, just the InstanceID (and Checksum) information of the policy is updated. If not specified and the Checksum does not match the data stream, an error is generated.

```
<filenamelist>
```

See previous description of /x.

CFG (Configuration Upload/Download) options:

```
CFG (POL|SVC|TLS)[UPL <configfilename>]|[DNL [/p <subtree>]
[/t <targetdir>][/a]]
CFG (POL|SVC|TLS)
```

Uploads or downloads the policy, service, or tool configuration.

POL = policy configuration

SVC = service configuration

TLS = tools configuration

```
UPL <configfilename>
```

Uploads a structured storage file created with the DNL option.

```
DNL
```

Downloads the policy, service, or tools configuration from PMAD and puts it into Structured Storage Files

```
/p <subtree>
```

This parameter is only valid for configuration download. For policies, it must contain a PATH from which policies are downloaded recursively. It must contain the path to the policy as shown in the console tree, starting under Policy groups. The path must begin with a backslash ("\"), and policy groups within the path are separated with a backslash ("\"). If the name of a policy group contains spaces, the entire path must be enclosed in quotation marks.

For services/tools configuration this parameter is the RELPATH of the item at which the recursive enumeration will begin. It defaults to the respective root item.

```
/t <targetdir>
```

This optional parameter indicates where the downloaded structured storage files should be written. If not specified, the configuration information is stored in the root directory (".") of the current drive.

```
/a
```

If this optional parameter is specified, all registered policies with all registered versions are downloaded into the file system.

REG (register) options:

```
REG <policyfilename> /g <policygrouppath>
```

The REG option is only useful when you want to upload a policy that does not have a structured storage file, or that should be uploaded to a location that is different from the policy's original location.

```
<policyfilename>
```

Name of a policyfile (structured store containing policy name and version information in the header as well as the stream in the data part) to be registered in the system.

`<policygrouppath>`

This is an optional parameter. It must contain PATH. If specified, the registered policy is also assigned to the group specified in <policygrouppath>.

Examples of using ovpmutil:

Download a policy and convert to ASCII format:

1. Download the policy **disk_monitor** from the policy group **Server Policies** to the test directory on the C Drive:

```
ovpmutil CFG POL DNL /p "\Server Policies\disk_monitor" /t
c:/test
```

2. Convert a downloaded structured storage file to an ASCII header and data file:

```
ovpmutil PCV /x C:\test\disk_monitor_CC832F49-A8BC-
11D3-A45F-080009DC628C /t c:/test
```

3. Deploy all **Logfile Entry** policies in the policy group Server Policies to the node **parsnip**, even if a newer version is already deployed on the node:

```
ovpmutil DEP /pg "Server Policies" /n "\email
servers\parsnip" /c FALSE /t Logfile Entry
```

Import Policies—The tool Import Policies imports OpenView Operations for UNIX templates into OpenView Operations for Windows. The templates must be from OpenView Operations for UNIX version 5.33 or higher.

Usage:

```
ImportPolicies/f <policy file>
                [/g <policy group>]
                [/r | /d]
                [/c ASCII|/c UTF8|/c ISO81|/c ISO82|/c ISO85|
                 /c ROMAN8|
                 /c SJIS|/c EUCJP|/c GB2312|/c BIG5|/c EUCTW|
                 /c EUCKR]
```

All imported policies are stored in subdirectories of the policy directory Policy Management\Policy Groups\Imports From File.

Policy File (/f)—The policy file contains one or more templates that will be imported as policies into OpenView Operations for Windows. This file is created by the config download command (opccfgdwn) on an OpenView Operations for UNIX server. For every template contained in the file, a new policy will be added to OpenView Operations for Windows.

Note: Refer to the *HP OpenView Operations for UNIX Administrator's Reference Volume I* for information about downloading template files.

This table shows the OpenView Operations for UNIX message source types and shows the policy type to which they are converted:

Message Source Type	Policy Type
Logfiles	Logfile Entry or Windows Event Log
SNMP Trap	SNMP Interceptor
Message Interface	Open Message Interface
Threshold Monitor	Measurement Threshold
Scheduled Action	Scheduled Task

Other OVOU message source types cannot be imported into OVOW.

Policy Group (/g)—If this optional parameter is given, the policies of the file are stored in the policy group "...\Imports From File\<policy group>". If the given group doesn't exist, it will be created.

If the /g option is omitted, a new policy group named with the current date and time will be created and used.

Replace (/r) Flag—Use this option if you want to replace any existing policies within <policy group> that have the same name as any template that you are importing.

CAUTION: The old policy is replaced and cannot be recovered. If neither the /r nor /d flag is used, policies that have the same name as an existing policy contained in <policy group> will not be imported.

Duplicate (/d) Flag—Use this option if you want to import policies that have the same name as existing polices in the same <policy group> without overwriting them. The policies will have different GUIDs.

If neither the /r nor /d flags is used, policies to be imported that have the same name as a policy contained in <policy group> will not be imported.

Codeset (/c)—This parameter must be set if the policy file contains non-ASCII characters (for example, a download file from an English OVOU server is encoded in iso8859-1, a download file from a Japanese OVOU server is encoded in Shift-JIS). In this case, the policies will be converted to the multibyte Unicode encoding UTF8 before adding to OVOW. (This is necessary because within OVOW all polices are stored in a Unicode encoding.)

If omitted, it is assumed that the given file (<policy file>) only contains ASCII data.

Convert OVOU Operations templates to OVOW policies:

1. Download the OpenView Operations for UNIX Operations 5.33 or higher templates from the OpenView Operations server using the OpenView Operations command **opccfgdwn** (see OpenView Operations for UNIX Operations documentation) to a config download package.
2. Copy the download package to the OpenView Operations for Windows management server.
3. If any template names contain any special characters, open the config download package and remove them. Special characters are not allowed in policy file names.
4. Upload OpenView Operations for UNIX Operations 5.33 or higher templates to the OpenView Operations for Windows management server, where they become OpenView Operations for Windows policies. Use the command **ImportPolicies**, as described previously.
5. Customize the OpenView Operations for Windows policies as required.
6. In OpenView Operations for Windows, deploy the newly customized OpenView Operations for Windows policies on the appropriate managed nodes.

OVO UNIX Interoperability Commands:

opctempl

opccfgdwn

opccfgupld

24.4 Comparing Features of OVOU and OVOW

In discussing the interoperability between the two types of OV servers, it is interesting to note what features they have in common and key areas where they differ. Table 24-1 compares the features of OVOU and OVOW. The list is for reference purposes and is not all-inclusive.

Table 24-1 OVOU and OVOW Comparison

Description	OVOW	OVOU
Application Bank	Tools tree	Yes
Auditing	N/A	Yes
Automatic Service Discover via SPI	Yes	N/A
Custom Message Attributes	N/A	Yes
Database	MSDE, can upgrade to SQL Server	Oracle
ECS correlation	N/A	Yes
Encryption	N/A	Yes
Heartbeat polling	Registry	GUI and command line
History download	Registry	GUI and command line

Description	OVOW	OVOU
Management server in a cluster configuration	N/A	HP MC/Service Guard Veritas Sun
Message group bank	N/A, assign message groups via user role	Yes
Message synchronization	Only with another OVOW server	Only with another OVOU server
MPE/iX console support	N/A	Yes, via MPE/iX, template
MSI correlation	N/A	Yes
Multiple administrators	Yes	N/A
Managed nodes	Nodes	Yes
NNM Integration	Installs NNM Adapter; NNM must be installed separately	NNM installation out-of-the-box
Notification Interface	Via WMI	Built-in
OpenView Reporter Lite	Integrates out-of-the box	N/A
Operator initiated actions	Operator Initiated Commands	Yes
ovtrap2opc	N/A	Yes
PERL script support	Yes	Yes
PKI	N/A	Yes
primmgr file and opcragt -primmgr	N/A	Yes
SPI for Active Directory	Yes	N/A
Store (log) embedded performance agent metrics for graphing	Yes	N/A
Template	Policy	Yes, non-HTTPS
Template versioning	Yes	N/A
Trouble Ticket interface	Via WMI	Built-in
User bank and user profile bank	User Roles	Yes
UNIX agent deployment	Manual	Automatic
User authentication		PAM
User rights in OpenView controlled via operating system	Yes	N/A
VB Script support	Yes	N/A
Web-based event browser	Yes	N/A
WMI monitoring policies	Yes	N/A

There are many differences between the two products. Some of the templates' differences are shown in Table 24-2 for reference.

Table 24-2 OVOW and OVOU Template Comparison

Template Type	OVOW	OVOU
ASCII configuration files for SPIs	Config File	N/A
Flexible Management	Yes	msgforw template
Logfile	Logfile Entry and Windows Event Log	Logfile encapsulator template
Threshold	Measurement Threshold	Monitor template
Add variables to the nodeinfo file	Node Info	N/A

Table 24-2 OVOW and OVOU Template Comparison (Continued)

Template Type	OVOW	OVOU
Messages	Open Message Interface	Yes
Schedule	Scheduled Task	Scheduled action
Service Auto-Discovery	Included with SPIs	N/A
SNMP	SNMP Trap Interceptor	Trap template
Intercept WMI and WBEM messages and signals	Windows Management Interface	N/A

24.5 Summary

Utilizing a combination of Windows and UNIX platforms within the enterprise management environment may be necessary for overall management flexibility. The interoperability between the two platforms helps facilitate ease of use and ease of data exchanges when necessary.

CHAPTER 25

OVOW Implementation Tasks

This chapter outlines the overall steps in implementing OVOW. Out-of-the-box features such as service discovery are discussed. The implementation tasks include ensuring that the network prerequisites are configured on the management server (such as DNS or a local host file). Node information is collected initially via SNMP, so the SNMP community name for the nodes must be known on the server. Refer to the OVOW online help for additional information.

25.1 AUTO-DISCOVERY AND AUTO-DEPLOYMENT

Learning which nodes and services are on the local network is referred to as *discovery*. There are two types of discovery implemented with OVOW. Fast out-of-the-box implementation with OVOW includes service and node discovery.

25.1.1 Service Discovery

The OVO Windows OS *Smart Plug-In* (SPI) provides the catalyst that initiates service discovery on supported Windows managed notes. Deploy the service auto-discovery policy to the node. This is done automatically when SPIs are installed. Manually configure service discovery and select **Policy Management→Policies grouped by type→Service Auto Discovery** from the console tree. After a service is discovered, policies are distributed to the managed node and the service map updates with the display of the services that are running on the node. Resources discovered include but are not limited to hardware, operating system, and applications. An example of the service discovery map is shown in Figure 25-1.

Figure 25-1 An example of an OVOW service discovery map.

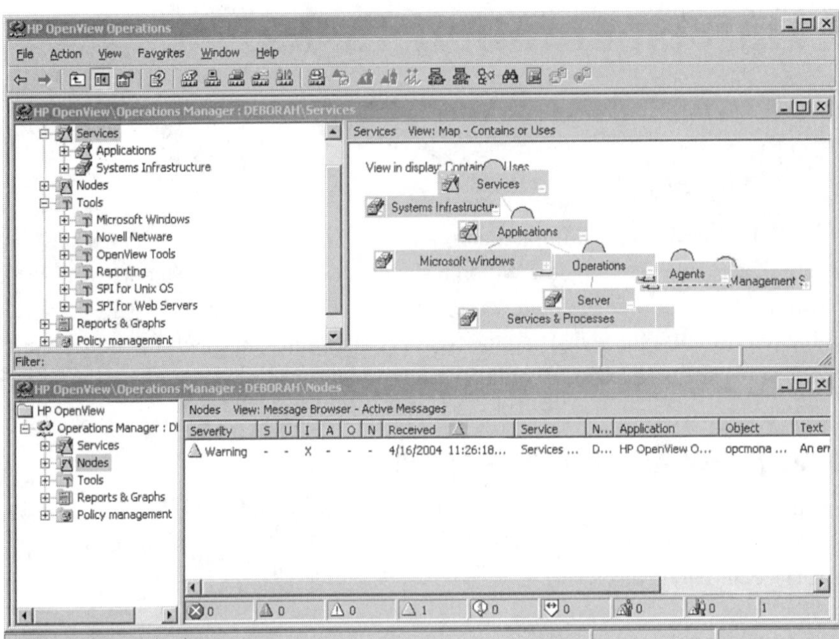

25.1.2 Node Discovery

Discovered nodes are listed in the nodes tree of the management console. Policies are automatically deployed to the Windows managed nodes. DNS, or the management server's local host file, is used to discover the UNIX nodes.

25.2 ADD NODES

If a node is not added automatically, add it manually. **Select Configure→Nodes** from the Nodes folder in the console tree to add nodes manually. See Figure 25-2 for an example node configuration.

Figure 25-2 OVOW example node configuration.

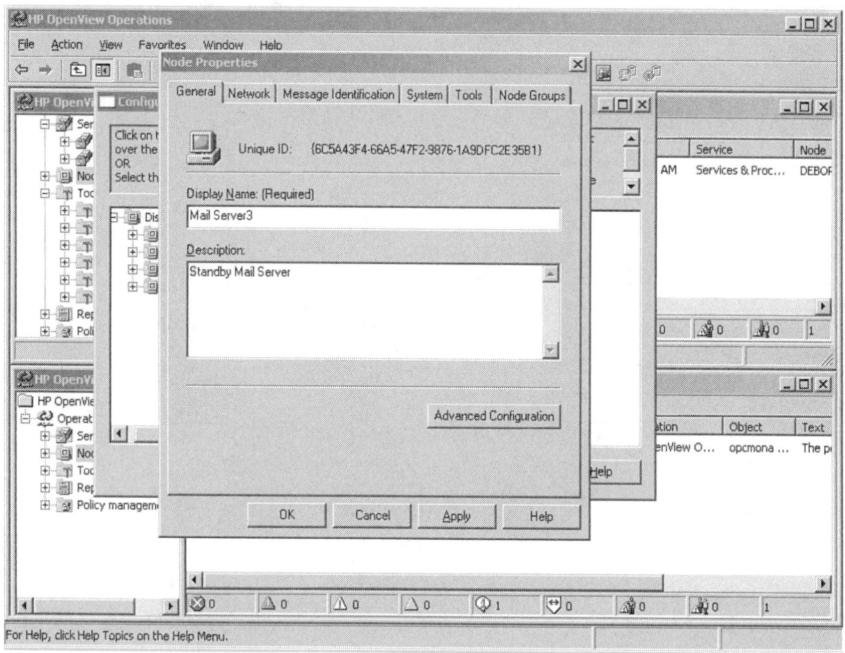

25.3 CREATE AND DEPLOY POLICIES

Policies are organized into different policy types. Each policy type gives instruction to the agent about what events, services and devices to monitor on the managed node. Policies are organized into policy groups. To create a policy group, select the **Policy management→Policy groups→ New Policy Group** from the console tree. The source of the event is defined as a new policy within the policy group. Use the built-in policy editor to build new policies. The policy editor for a measurement threshold will ask for information such as short name, description, source type, program name, and polling interval. See Figure 25-3 for an example of using the policy editor.

Figure 25-3 OVOW example of the policy editor.

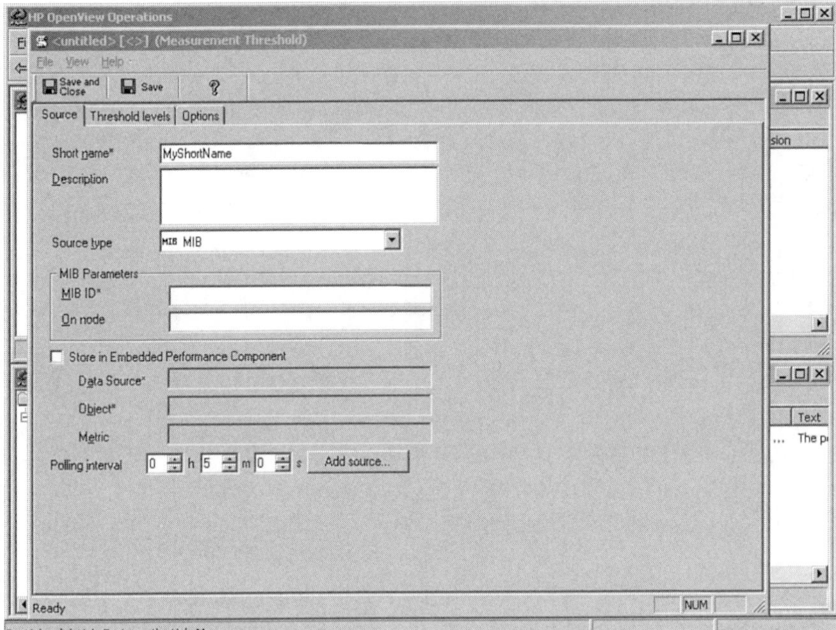

25.4 TOOLS, AUTOMATIC COMMANDS, AND SERVICES

Complete the configuration through addition of tools, commands, and services. These components add important capabilities to the systems management toolkit. Services could include commands that are executed as a result of specific service events.

25.4.1 Tools

Tools are applications used by the operator to perform tasks and resolve problems within the service management environment. Tools are executed on nodes upon which the tool is configured. The system administrator can assign tools to users and thus restrict who can execute specific applications within the environment. To configure tools, select the Tools folder in the console tree (see Figure 25-4).

Figure 25-4 OVOW example tools configuration.

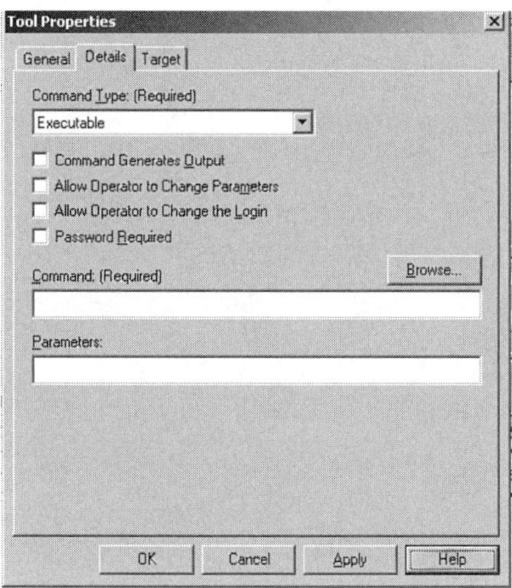

25.4.2 Automatic Commands

Automatic commands are similar to automatic actions. To configure automatic commands, select a Policy Group, use the policy editor to change a policy rule, and add the automatic command (see Figure 25-5).

25.4.3 Services

Initial service discovery may be a good start in showing what events are taking place on the node. It may be necessary to add additional service components. Use the Service Editor to define services and service dependencies that appear in the service map. To create a new service from the console tree, select **Configure Services→Applications→Add component**. To associate a message with a service, select the policy and define the message attributes for the start, continue, and end messages within the service configuration (see Figure 25-6).

Figure 25-5 OVOW example of automatic commands configuration.

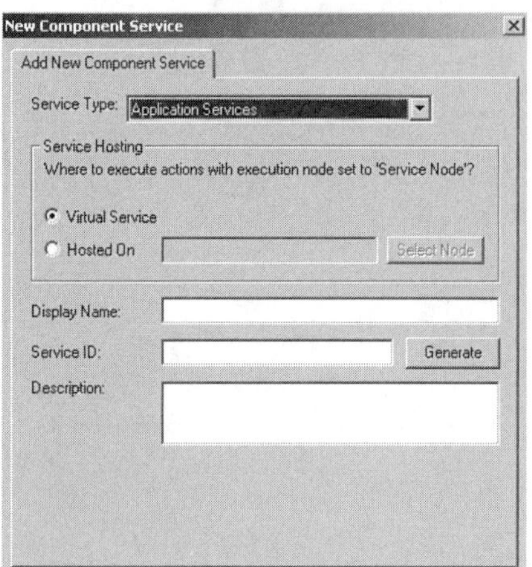

Figure 25-6 OVOW example service.

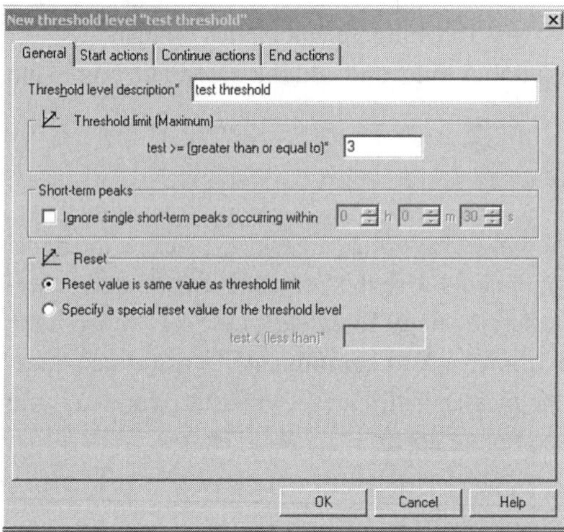

25.5 SUMMARY

This chapter provides a high-level introduction to the OVOW platform to OVOU administrators or managers. Refer to the documentation available for download from `http://ovweb.external.hp.com/lpe/doc_serv/`.

APPENDIX A

OpenView Commands Quick Reference Guide

A.1 NETWORK NODE MANAGER COMMANDS

findroute—Determine IP routing using SNMP requests

ipmap—Display map of network discovered by netmon

loadhosts—Load IP topology database from /etc/hosts

netmon—Discover and monitor nodes on the network

nmdemandpoll—Poll a node for information

opcctrlovw—Remote server for NNM

ovactiond—Execute shell command upon receipt of an event

ovaddobj—Object registration utility

ovalarmadm—Command used in NNM event subsystem

ovalarmsrv—Background process for NNM event subsystem

ovbackup.ovpl—HP OpenView NNM backup utility

ovchange_locale_mapping—Specify the codeset in use by the HP

ovcoldelsql—Delete SNMP trend data from the NNM data warehouse

ovcolmigo—Migrate pre-NNM 6.0 SNMP trend data in the Oracle database

ovcolqsql—Query data collector data residing in a relational

ovcolsum—Summarize/aggregate SNMP trend data in the NNM data

ovcoltosql—Export NNM data collector data to the NNM data warehouse

ovconfadmin.ovpl—Administer the files in the $OV_CONF directory

ovdbcheck—Validate NNM relational database dependencies

ovdbdebug—Provide troubleshooting information for the NNM data

ovdbsetup—Configure NNM relational database, non-embedded only

ovdelobj—HP OpenView object deregistration utility

ovdumpevents—Dump the contents of the NNM event database

ovdwconfig.ovpl—Configure NNM data warehouse

ovdwevent—Export/trim NNM events to/from the NNM data warehouse

ovdweventflt—Create filters for event exporting for the NNM data

ovdwloader—Reload data into the NNM data warehouse

ovdwquery—Query the NNM data warehouse using SQL

ovdwtopo—Perform topology maintenance for NNM data warehouse

ovdwtrend—Perform NNM data warehouse maintenance for SNMP trend

ovdwunloader—Unload data into the NNM data warehouse for migrating

ovevent—Generate an event and send it to the NNM event subsystem

ovexec—Prompt for login information, then execute command

ovexprguru—Facilitate the invocation of **xnmgraph**

ovfiltercheck—Parse filter definition files and, optionally, statements

ovfiltertest—Test filter definitions against the object database

ovhelp—NNM help subsystem

ovhtpasswd—Create and update the passwords for web launcher authentication

ovmapcount—Check ovw map reference counts

ovmapdump—Print the contents of the NNM map database

ovmapsnap—Create a snapshot of an NNM map

ovnnmPassword—Request, install, and view license passwords

ovnnmversion—Print out NNM version installed

ovobjprint—Display the contents of the object database

ovpause—Pause HP OpenView platforms service processes

ovrepld—Gather remote topology information to be merged in with local topology

ovrequestd—Run programs based on a schedule

ovrestore.ovpl—HP OpenView NNM restore utility

ovresume—Resume NNM service processes

ovsessionmgr—Background process to support HP OpenView web launcher

ovspmd—NNM process management process

ovstart—Start NNM managed processes

ovstatus—Report status of NNM managed processes

ovstop—Stop NNM managed processes

ovtopmd—NNM Topology Manager Process for IP discovery and layout

ovtopodump—Print out the contents of the IP topology database

ovtopofix—Correct inconsistencies between ovtopmd and ovwdb

ovtrap2opc—Convert trapd.conf file and upload it into database

ovtrapd—Receive and buffer SNMP traps within the NNM event subsystem

ovuispmd—HP OpenView NNM user interface

ovversion—Print out version of OpenView products installed

ovw—HP OpenView NNM GUI

ovwchgrp—Command equivalent to using -g option with ovwperms

ovwchmod—Command equivalent to using -m option with ovwperms

ovwchown—Command equivalent to using -u option with ovwperms

ovwdb—Background process that maintains the object database

ovweb—Start a web browser with a specified URL

ovwperms—NNM map permission listing and changing

ovwrs—Spawn/respawn the graphical user interface

ovwsetupclient—Configure a distributed ovw client system

pmd—HP OpenView Postmaster process

rbdf—Check remote disk space using SNMP requests

regverify – Check registration files

remotepoweron—Send special MagicPacket™ to remotely wake up a machine

request_list—Cause **ovrequestd** to list requests it is working on

rnetstat—List network information of a remote SNMP node

rping—Send remote packet echo using ICMP Echo requests

snmpColDump—ASCII dump/modify data collected by snmpCollect

snmpCollect—Collect, compare, and store SNMP MIB values

snmpbulk—Query node for information using an SNMPv2 GetBulk request

snmpnotify—Issue an SNMP notification (Trap or Inform request)

snmpset—Issue an SNMP set request

snmptrap—Issue an SNMP Version 1 Trap

snmpwalk—Query a node repeatedly using SNMP

xnmappmon—Terminal output encapsulation tool

xnmcollect—Maintain data collector configuration/MIB expressions

xnmevents— Browse alarms (GUI); (command line) load/delete event definitions

xnmgraph—Line-graphing tool

xnmloadmib—Load and unload SNMP MIBs

xnmpolling—Network polling configuration

xnmsnmpconf—SNMP configuration utility

xnmtopoconf—Configure access to remote collection stations

xnmtrap—Configure the NNM event system

A.2 CUSTOMER VIEWS AND SERVICE INFORMATION PORTAL COMMANDS

ovcustomer

create_organization—Creates an organization based on the customer ype and customer name specified

add_associations_to_org—Adds the NNM selection name or IP addresses to the specified association

create_location—Defines one of the four site types: general, NOC, POP, or peering_point

set_location—Adds devices to locations

set_field—Sets the object attributes **isServer**, **isCPE**, and **isKeyDevice**

remove_associations_to_org—Removes NNM selection name from specified association

delete_organization—Deletes the organization from CV

unset_location—Removes the specified location from the organization

delete_location—Deletes the specified location from CV

unset_field—Removes the specified object attribute

print _organization—Lists the organization information

print_associated_organization—Lists the organization type, organization name and external key for the specified selection name or IP address

print_associated_interface—Lists information about interfaces associated with objects

print_associated_node—Lists information about nodes associated with objects

ovcustomer help print—List all print commands

ovcustomer help print_a—List print_assocation commands

ovcustomer help print_l—List print_location commands

ovcustomer help print_o—List print_organization commands

A.3 OPENVIEW OPERATIONS COMMANDS

call_sqlplus.sh—Run an SQL*Plus report using the ITO database

install—Install commands

ito_op—HP OpenView Operations Java UI

opc—graphical user interface for HP OpenView Operations

opc_audit_secure—Lock the audit level in the OVO database

opc_backup—Back up the HP OpenView Operations configuration

opc_recover—Recover the HP OpenView Operations configuration

opcack—Externally acknowledge active messages of selected operator

opcackmsg—Externally acknowledge active message

opcackmsgs—Externally acknowledge active messages with specific message attributes

opcadddbf—Add a new datafile to an Oracle tablespace

opcagt—Administer agent services for HP OpenView Operations

opcagtdbcfg—Parse AgentPlatform and perform DB updates

opcagtreg—Register subagent

opcannoadd—Add an annotation to a message

opcauddwn—Download Operations audit entries to a file

opcaudupl—Upload audit information into HP OpenView Operations

opccfgdwn—Download configuration data from the ITO database to flat files

opccfgout—Configure variables for scheduled outage; update the OVO outage

opccfgupld—Upload configuration from flat files into the ITO

opcdbidx—HP OpenView Operations database troubleshooting tool

opcdbinit—Fill HP OpenView Operations database with default configuration

opcdbinst—Create or destroy HP OpenView Operations database

opcdbpwd—HP OpenView Operations database password tool

opcdbreorg—Re-organize HP OpenView Operations database

opcdbsetup—Create the ITO DB tables and load the initial configuration

opcdbupgr—Upgrade the HP OpenView Operations database

opcdcode—View HP OpenView Operations encrypted template files

opcgetcorrevts—Print correlated child events

opcgetmsgdet—Obtain some message details

opcgetmsgids—Get current message IDs to an original message ID

opchbp—Switch HP OpenView Operations heartbeat polling

opchistdwn—Download Operations history messages to a file

opchistupl—Upload history messages into HP OpenView Operations

opcnode—Maintain nodes, node groups and template assignments in OVO

opcmack—Acknowledge a message of HP OpenView Operations

opcmapnode—Find NNM server for a specified node

opcmgrdist—Distribute HP OpenView Operations configuration

opcmomchk—Check "Flexible Management" configuration files

opcmon—Forward monitored object value to HP OpenView Operations

opcmsg—Submit a message for HP OpenView Operations

opcpat—Test program for HP OpenView Operations pattern matching

opcragt—Remotely administer agent processes on HP OpenView Operations

opcseapplmerge—Merge applications and application groups

opcsebinarymerge—Merge executables

opcsecfgcheck—Test consistency of data references for ITO-SE

opcseldist—Check the syntax of configuration files for selective distribution

opcsekey—Set login information for HP OpenView Operations

opcservice—Configure services in HP OpenView Operations

opcsesubproductadd—Adding all the ITO-SE config data

opcsesubproductdel—Delete a whole subproduct from ITO-SE

opcsetempladd—Add template(s) or template group(s) to ITO-SE

opcsetempldel —Delete a template(s) or template

opcsetemplmerge—Merge, add, or delete a template

opcskm—Secret Key Management Tool

opcsqlnetconf—HP OpenView Operations SQL*Net configuration tool

opcsv—Administer manager services of HP OpenView Operations

opcsvcconv— Convert service files for HP OpenView Operations

opcsvcdwn—Download Operations service status logs to a file

opcsvcterm—Terminal access to the HP OpenView Navigator

opcsvcupl—Upload service status logs into HP OpenView Operations

opcsvskm—Secret Key Management Tool

opcsw—Set software status in HP OpenView Operations database

opctempl—Maintain templates in files in HP OpenView Operations

opctemplate —Enable or disable OVO templates

opctmpldwn—OVO template download and encryption tool

opcwall—Inform HP OpenView Operations users

APPENDIX B

Hostname Resolution

A lot of money is spent on network and systems management systems in order to be *proactive* when managing systems and networks. And in order to be truly proactive, the problem must be detected and resolved without the customer knowing there was a problem. To do this, the products work correctly. For network and systems management products to work correctly, hostname naming services such as the /etc/hosts file, NIS, and DNS must be properly configured. Configuring these services incorrectly will result in hostnames being out-of-sync in various databases, missed OpenView Operations messages, multiple objects in the NNM topology, and forwarded traps with different hostnames. There are times that products won't even install because the product cannot determine the hostname of the system. Most of these problems can keep you in *reactive* mode.

B.1 THE DEFINITION OF HOSTNAME

There should not to be a unique or independent hostname for every interface within the system. Literally, there is only *one* hostname for a system and any other name for a system is known as an alias. Using grandiose host-naming schemes as the alias instead of using it as the official hostname provides the same functionality as when used as an *official hostname*. Ensure that the forward lookups return all the IP addresses for that system (a feature only available using the DNS) and the reverse address lookups for the IP addresses for that system return the same official hostname as a *Fully Qualified Domain Name* (FQDN). In addition, ensure that the official hostname and its aliases are entered into name services using only lower case. Following these simple steps will provide you with few "name and address" resolution problems.

Many administrators improperly configure hostname naming services (/etc/hosts, NIS, and the DNS) for multi-homed hosts by configuring a separate official hostname for each interface, and then configure the opc_hosts file so that OpenView Operations will resolve the IP address to the proper hostname. This gets them out of the predicament in which they just put themselves by incorrectly configuring hostname naming services! The same scenario applies to authentication and configuration files such as .rhosts, hosts.equiv, inetd.sec, fstab, vfstab, and so on.

Configuring the sometimes numerous configuration and authentication files can be quite time consuming, especially when using /etc/hosts or NIS as the primary source of hostname and IP address resolution. When using either of these services as a source of resolution, only one IP will be resolved for a given hostname. This increases labor costs and the costs of owning the products because each alias must be added to authorization files if the service is to be allowed from each interface of an authorized host.

B.2 SETTING A SYSTEMS HOSTNAME

The hostname is set by the operating system. In HP-UX, the hostname is set at boot time by the startup script /sbin/init.d/hostname using the HOSTNAME variable set in the file /etc/rc.config.d/netconf. The IP addresses for all Ethernet interfaces are defined in /etc/rc.config.d/netconf. Each Ethernet interface name and its associated subnet mask, IP address, Broadcast address, and Interface state is assigned the same unique index number for that Interface Name/IP address combination. All Ethernet interfaces defined in /etc/rc.config.d/netconf are set at boot time by the startup script /sbin/init.d/net. The interfaces themselves are configured by the "ifconfig-ing," the interface with its associated IP address in /etc/rc.config.d/netconf, and not by resolving an alias to its IP.

In Solaris, the hostname is configured in the file /etc/nodename and is set at boot time by the /etc/rcS.d/S30rootusr.sh script. It is not set by using the **hostname** command, but by using the **uname** command with the –S option which sets both the *uname* and the *hostname* to the same name simultaneously. The IP addresses are configured for each interface by placing the hostname alias for an interface within the appropriate configuration file in /etc/hostname.<interface_type>0-9. The IP addresses are set at boot time by the /etc/rcS.d/S30rootusr.sh by retrieving the hostname alias from each file, resolving that hostname to the IP address, retrieving the IP netmask from /etc/netmasks file, and configuring the associated IP and netmask to the appropriate interface. Many times, the hostname alias in each /etc/hostname.<interface_type>0-9 is incorrectly inserted into hostname naming services (/etc/hosts, NIS hosts map, and the DNS) as an official hostname for resolution, such as the second column of the hosts file or file used to create the NIS hosts map. The S30rootusr.sh file will function properly with the hostname alias in the third or fourth column of the /etc/hosts file.

This hostname returned by the **hostname** command is commonly known as the *short* hostname, meaning that it is unqualified, or has no DNS domain attached to it. It should not be set to an FQDN. The UNIX operating system and subsequent programs retrieve the hostname of the current host with the *gethostname()* system call. Many products will then try to fully qualify the hostname to find what is commonly known as the official hostname from a naming service such as /etc/hosts, NIS, or DNS. The official hostname is the second column of the /etc/hosts file or file used to create the NIS hosts map. It should always be the FQDN. The DNS always returns a FQDN.

B.2.1 Incorrect /etc/hosts, NIS, and DNS Configuration

"My hostnames in one product don't match those within Network Node Manager." "The hostnames in all my NMS products come up differently in each products database." "I can only remsh or rcp from specific hosts." or "When Network Node Manager does a configuration check, hostnames for the map icons get changed, so I turn the configuration check off."

Do these comments sound familiar? It is because each product uses a different algorithm for retrieving the hostname for a multi-homed system, and the naming service it used for obtaining the hostname from the IP did not resolve to the same fully qualified (with domain) hostname, or FQDN, as another product.

To prevent this from occurring, the entries within /etc/hosts, NIS, and the DNS for a particular host and IP address must match each other. Each IP must resolve to an FQDN. Each IP on a multi-homed host must resolve to the same FQDN. The DNS always returns an FQDN and the /etc/hosts and NIS should as well. Everything else is an alias (/etc/hosts, NIS) or an additional address record (DNS). The *pointer records* (PTR), or address-to-name records, within DNS must all "point" to the same official hostname for a multi-homed host. The PTR records should not point to an alias.

The network and systems management products, even ARPA services, benefit from a correct configuration of each naming service. It prevents one from turning off processes, such as NNM's configuration check, that are designed to help give a snapshot of how a particular host is configured within the network. It makes administration of UNIX and authentication simpler and easier.

B.3 ARE /ETC/HOSTS, NIS, AND DNS CONFIGURED PROPERLY?

Are multi-homed hosts (hosts that have more than one IP interface) resolving to different *official hostnames*? If they are, most likely you have seen the aforementioned problems. Configuring multi-homed hosts within any naming service with separate *official hostnames* causes nothing but problems, especially when used with an NMS. If the official hostname in /etc/hosts does not match that of the NIS hosts map and the DNS, it causes problems. When separate official hostnames are configured within any naming service it adds additional administration to every file that is used to authenticate a host for a particular service. For NFS, r-commands, or OpenView products, every official hostname will need to be entered into the particular authentication file or any file used for authentication or configuration (/etc/exports, .rhosts, inetd.sec, netgroups, and so on) to ensure that authentication functions properly when an IP packet comes from a different interface. The administration time required to configure a host for each service adds up, and makes administration more cumbersome.

B.3.1 Proper Configuration of Naming Services

Whether or not OpenView products are used, standard UNIX services will also benefit from properly configuring these name services. The correct configuration of name services first requires the forward lookup, hostname to IP, and return all the IP addresses for the given hostname. The latter can only be done using the DNS. It cannot be done with an /etc/hosts file or the NIS hosts map. The /etc/hosts file and NIS hosts map are searched sequentially and stop at the first resolution. The inability to return all the addresses for a host can prevent authentication between client and server in some products. This is because the hostname sent within the IP datagram does not resolve to the source address from the IP packet. It could also fail because the source address does not resolve to a resolvable IP address in the product's authorization file.

The second requirement is that all reverse address lookups, IP address to hostname, for the IP addresses on a particular system point to the same official hostname or FQDN. This prevents multiple node names to appear for the same system in various databases, traps, and so on. It also makes certain that authentication between client and server functions correctly no matter what interface the packet is sent from.

Configuring name services as described reduces the amount of administration of service authentication files and provides a more reliable resolution for all system processes, services, and OpenView products.

B.3.2 NNM, SNMP, and Hostname Resolution

Some companies purchase NNM to manage their enterprise and refuse to run an SNMP agent on their systems because they believe SNMP is a security issue. That debate will not be discussed here. If there is no running SNMP agent on the managed system, NNM has nothing to interrogate to determine the number of interfaces, IP addresses, and netmasks associated with that system. NNM only knows the IP addresses in its *object* database. In order to correlate these IP addresses to a particular system, NNM must do a reverse address lookup on the IP address to retrieve the hostname. Hostnames that match are placed in the same node container object in the *topology* database; hostnames that don't match are deemed as separate hosts and added to the *topology* database as such. Therefore, separate hosts are exactly what will be seen in the NNM maps. With no SNMP agent to interrogate, NNM has no way to determine the

- Network protocol
- System model
- Number of interfaces
- Protocol of each interface
- Subnet mask
- IP address(es) of each interface
- Loopback address(es)
- And more

If no SNMP agent is running, NNM cannot determine if IP addresses are software loop-back, non-migratable IP addresses, or migratable IP addresses. All the addresses are deemed non-migratable IP addresses. There will also be no SNMP traps sent from the node.

When NNM has an SNMP agent to interrogate, it retrieves the interface information from the ifInterface branch of the MIB-II tree and uses this information to create the

- Network protocol
- System model
- Number of interfaces
- Protocol of each interface
- Subnet mask
- IP address(es) of each interface
- Loopback address(es)
- And so on

NNM associates all the IP addresses retrieved from the ifTable table of the SNMP agent of a specific node and properly associates each interface with the appropriate container object. NNM then determines a hostname by using the following rules:

1. If a non-migratable[1] software loopback IP address (other than 127.0.0.1) exists and resolves to an IP hostname, and both are true, that hostname will be used.
2. If not, NNM uses the lowest numbered[2] non-migratable IP address that resolves to an IP hostname.
3. If no IP addresses resolve to an IP hostname, the lowest numbered, non-migratable IP address is formatted as a string and used as a hostname.

When no SNMP agent is running on a system and the reverse-address resolution of the discovered IP addresses resolve to different hostnames, then NNM will have an inaccurate topology database. This inaccuracy will also be reflected in the IP map. In addition, other network management software that determines the hostname from reverse address resolution may not have determined the same hostname as NNM. It gets very confusing for operators.

Sometimes SNMP agents can also give NNM an inaccurate topology database, even with properly configured hostname resolution. If a multi-homed host shows up as separate nodes in the NNM map, use the following test to determine if there may be a problem with the agent:

1. Check to see if all SNMP agents of the same type exhibit the same problem.
2. Select a node that shows up in the map as separate hosts.
3. Change both the read and write community strings on the node so that NNM can no longer query the SNMP Agent.
4. Ensure that all IPs for the node resolve to the same FQDN.
5. Run **xnmsnmpconf –clearCache** on the management server.
6. Run **nnmdemandpoll** against the node from the management server
   The two node container objects will become one container object. NNM now is relying solely on reverse address lookups to determine what IP addresses belong to a node container object. There may be a problem with the SNMP agent on the system. See if there is an updated agent and ensure that you have the latest NNM patches installed.

1 A non-migratable IP address is an address that is permanently assigned to the interface. A migratable IP address is an IP address that is not permanently assigned to an interface on a system from M/C ServiceGuard. The migratable IP address is only available when the M/C ServiceGuard package is running and located on the node on which the package is currently running.

2 The "lowest numbered" IP address is determined by using a byte-by-bye comparison of the IP addresses.

B.3.2.1 Properly Configured /etc/hosts

The Official Hostname

The second column in any host file is the official hostname to which that IP address belongs. There is only one official hostname for a given system.. Always use the FQDN in the second column within the /etc/hosts file and NIS hosts master map. Hosts outside its DNS domain will resolve it as an FQDN, and it is a best practice to always make it an FQDN.

Any host outside the DNS domain of another host will use the FQDN to communicate with one another. If a process from a client resolves its official hostname to a short hostname through /etc/hosts and sends that name to a server in another domain, there is the possibility the client will not be authenticated. The server authentication process may take the source address from packet of the client and resolve the address to an FQDN through the DNS. Then take that resolved hostname and compare it to the short hostname that came in the client IP packet and deny authentication because they do not match.

The official hostname within the second column of /etc/hosts is used to determine the domain in Sendmail. The resolver will determine the domain using the official hosts name if the domain is not set in /etc/resolv.conf. Sendmail uses this entry to determine the domain name if the $j macro is not defined in sendmail.cf. Properly setting the official hostname in /etc/hosts can save configuration of files elsewhere on every system.

The /etc/nsswitch.conf File

The configuration of the name-service switch file, /etc/nsswitch.conf, determines what service or "database" source will be used for retrieving data within a particular database. It determines the order of use and when to switch from one service to another. The operating system uses this file to retrieve information on a number of items, such as password, groups, hosts, and so on. Here we will be dealing with the different databases from which to retrieve host information; a host's IP address and a host's official hostname.

The file has a simple syntax and the HP-UX manual page covers this completely. The following syntax will be used for demonstration purposes: <database> : <source> [<criteria>] <source>

The <database> entry can be one of many, such as passwd, group, hosts, and so on. The <source> that can be configured for data retrieval includes files, nis, nisplus, dns, or ldap, and the <criteria> by which the name service will "switch" or not switch from one <source> to another is based on the status of the particular <source>. The <criteria> can be based on the status of SUCCESS, UNAVAIL, NOTFOUND, and TRYAGAIN. Only the configuration of the hosts <database> using files, nis, and dns as a <source> with the <criteria> [NOTFOUND = continue] will be discussed here. It appears to be the best solution overall.

Using the <criteria> [NOTFOUND = continue] instructs the name-service switch to continue to the next <service> if the requested database entry was not found in the database. The following syntax instructs the name service switch to look in the local files (/etc/hosts) first, and if the requested host is not found to "continue" looking in the DNS:

hosts: files [NOTFOUND=continue] dns

Is this the best configuration for the /etc/nsswitch.conf file? It is, if the majority of hosts that are to be resolved are listed in the /etc/hosts file and the system must perform a number of resolutions, such as NNM. The DNS is the preferred name service to use for OpenView products, but it must be properly configured. Proper DNS configuration is found in section B.XX

The primary <source> should be the most accurate and reliable service.; Most clients can be configured as in Figure B-2 and without impacting performance. Placing DNS or NIS to be queried first may require any configuration file used in startup scripts to be configured with the IP address versus a hostname or alias. There is no network configured at boot, and when configuring the interface there is no way for the system to query the DNS or NIS to resolve the hostname to an IP address to configure the interface with the appropriate address. Until the *domainname* is set and the *ypbind* process is started, there is no way to query an NIS server for hostname resolution.

The /etc/hosts File

A properly configured hosts file should look like the hosts file in Figure B-1. The first column is the IP address, the second the FQDN (or official hostname), the third column and beyond can be any alias. This example uses the short hostname in the third column and then an alias using the short hostname and the associated network interface. Using all lower case will prevent other hostname resolution problems.

Ensure that the first entry line of the local host file is the IP of the network to which the default route is set, which is generally the fastest link. Using the /etc/hosts file as configured in Figure B-1, and communicating with ovwsrv from this system (itself), the 192.168.1.3 address will always be used. To connect to the IP address on lan0's interface, use either ovwsrv or ovwsrv-lan0. To connect to the IP address on lan1's interface use ovwsrv-lan1. Using the alias will always resolve to the IP address to which you want to connect. Configuring NIS and DNS using this methodology (which will be discussed later) will prove to be effective. Any aliasing scheme can be used in columns 3 and beyond in the /etc/hosts file and the NIS master map.

Figure B-1 A properly configured /etc/hosts file will have an FQDN in the second column with the hostname and aliases following.

```
127.0.0.1  loopback  localhost

192.168.1.3 ovwsrv.nsr.hp.com  ovwsrv  ovwsrv-lan0

172.32.16.3  ovwsrv.nsr.hp.com  ovwsrv  ovwsrv-lan1
```

Figure B-2 Figure B-2 shows an /etc/nsswitch.conf configuration file that will try to resolve a hostname first within /etc/hosts and then, if not found, use the DNS.

```
passwd:  compat
group:   compat
hosts:   files [ NOTFOUND = continue ] dns
...
```

Figure B-3 The output from netstat –rn shows the routing table. This table shows the route a packet will take based on its destination address.

Routing Tables

Dest/Netmask	Gateway	Flags	Use	Interface	Pmtu
127.0.0.1	127.0.0.1	UH	10258	lo0	4136
192.168.1.3	192.168.1.3	UH	20795	lan0	1500
172.32.16.3	172.32.16.3	UH	1643	lan1	1500
192.168.1.0	192.168.1.3	U	0	lan0	1500
172.32.16.3	172.32.16.0	U	0	lan1	1500
127.0.0.0	127.0.0.1	U	0	lo0	4136
default	192.168.1.3	UG	0	lan0	1500

How Hostname Resolution Determines Route Determination

Based on the configuration of the /etc/nsswitch.conf file in Figure B-2, the local host will resolve the hostname (ovwsrv) from the *gethosbytname* system call from the /etc/hosts file asovwsrv.nsr.hp.com with an IP of 192.168.1.3. Communication with ovwsrv will take place internally based on the routing table in Figure B-3. Packets bound for 192.168.1.3 are routed to 193.168.1.3, which is a host route. The Gateway column is known as the *immediate gateway* for reaching the destination in the Destination/Netmask column. Some systems may show this route or gateway as 127.0.0.1. If the network cable were removed, the system would still be able to communicate with itself. The same situation applies to using the alias ovwsrv-lan0. The system will resolve ovwsrv-lan0 as ovwsrv.nsr.hp.com with an IP of 192.168.1.3 and internally communicate through lan0 based on the routing table in Figure B-3.

The same functionality exists when communicating with 172.31.16.3 (ovwsrv-lan1), but the only way to resolve a hostname to 172.31.16.3 using the /etc/hosts file in Figure B-1 is to use the alias ovwsrv-lan1. This system will resolve ovwsrv-lan1 to an official hostname of ovwsrv.nsr.hp.com with an IP of 172.31.16.3, and packets bound for ovwsrv-lan1 (172.31.16.3) will communicate internally via the lan1 interface. This communication is based on the routing table in Figure B-3, which shows the route to 172.31.16.3 as an internal route to 172.31.16.3.

Any packet not bound for a local host route in the routing table will be checked against the next immediate gateway. In this instance, the destination address will be checked against the netmask of local networks 192.168.1.0/255.255.255.0 and 172.132.16.0/255.255.255.0. When a hostname is resolved to an IP address that falls within either of these two networks, but not IP addresses 192.168.1.3 or 172.31.16.3, the packet is sent to the gateway for that specific network, such as 192.168.1.3 (lan0) for IP addresses in 192.168.1.0 and 172.31.16.3 (lan1) for IP addresses 172.31.16.0. The source address for these packets will be either 192.168.1.3 or 172.31.16.3. The source address will be 192.168.1.3 for all packets destined for 192.168.1.0/255.255.255.0 and will be 172.31.16.3 for packets bound for 172.31.16.0/255.255.255.

If the destination address does not fall within any of the aforementioned routes, then it is sent to the default route, 192.168.1.1 with a source address of 192.168.1.3. This gives an example on how name resolution determines the route a packet will take to its destination.

B.3.3 Properly Configured NIS

B.3.3.1 The Domain Name

One of the first things that must be done when configuring an NIS domain is to determine the NIS domain name. Few system administrators know that within Solaris there are some system scripts and configuration files (sendmail.main, sendmail.subsidiary, X, and so on) that actually use the NIS domain name to determine the DNS domain. They also use it do create the FQDN of the system. Scripts will truncate the defined NIS domain name (returned from the *domainname()* command) to the first period (dot) if it (the domain name) does not begin with a period to determine the DNS domain name. The script then attaches that domain name to the hostname from *hostname()* command to create an FQDN for the local host. If the NIS domain name is set to a name that is not a sub-domain of the DNS domain, hostname resolution fails for that FQDN for the local host's name. If the NIS domain name begins with a period, it assumes that the NIS domainname is the actual DNS domain and attaches it to the hostname to create a FQDN for the host.

The NIS domain within the Solaris OS, including SunOS, and HP-UX is to be configured as a sub-domain of the DNS domain, but it is not defined within DNS for host resolution within the DNS. The NIS domain itself is *only the domain to which the NIS clients bind to retrieve NIS services*, but is associated with the DNS domain by creating the NIS domain name as a sub-domain of the host's respective DNS domain. This makes NIS configuration flexible, but many administrators configure it incorrectly, adding time to perform hostname resolution for some things and even impairing system performance in some instances.

Setting up an NIS domain within the DNS domain nsr.hp.com for a group of administrative assistants could be done with an NIS domain of admin.nsr.hp.com. Within the host file and DNS hosts would reside in the nsr.hp.com DNS domain, such as ovwsrv.nsr.hp.com. All systems would be configured to bind to the NIS domain admin.nsr.hp.com.The scripts and configuration files that build the FQDN for lookup will truncate the "admin," the NIS sub domain, from the domain name retrieved from *domainname()* command and leave the DNS .nsr.hp.com. In essence, hostname + (domain name – NIS sub domain) = Fully Qualified Domain Name.

When using the Solaris operating system, the NIS domain can be configured to the DNS domain by setting the domain name to begin with a period (dot); for example, .nsr.hp.com. It can be set whether or not NIS is actually used by the system. This prevents those Solaris scripts that truncate to the first period from doing so and accurately builds the FQDN of the system for lookup, though it should be able to lookup the short hostname properly through the other naming services. Without modification of the startup scripts in /sbin/init.d, HP-UX will not set the domain name unless the system is also configured as an NIS client or NIS server.

The CDE Calendar Manager Service Daemon

HP-UX does not have any startup scripts or configuration files that truncate anything from the domain name retrieved from the *domainname(1M)* command to use in conjunction with the *hostname(1M)* command in the creation of an FQDN. The domain name will only be set if the NIS server or client is configured. But on both HP-UX and Solaris, the CDE calendar manager service daemon (/usr/dt/bin/rpc.cmsd) does create an FQDN as described previously. It will truncate the NIS domain name if configured as part of the DNS domain name and combine it with the hostname from the *gethostname()* system call to create a FQDN. It will then place it in *every entry* created by the user in the users callog file in /var/spool/calendar. Both the HP-UX and Solaris CDE rpc.cmsd will create a properly configured FQDN under the following circumstances:

- Removal of the NIS sub-domain of the domain name returned by *domainname(1M)* added to the hostname from *hostname(1M)* results in a resolvable FQDN.
- Removal of the leading dot of the domain name returned by *domainname(1M)* and added to the hostname from *hostname(1M)* results in a resolvable FQDN.
- The domain name returned by *domainname(1M)* added to the hostname from *hostname(1M)* results in a resolvable FQDN.

If the NIS domain name is not set as a sub-domain of the DNS domain, or set equal to the DNS domain (beginning with a period) in which a host resides, the CDE calendar manager service daemon creates an FQDN of a host that does not exist and places the invalid FQDN in the user's call log file in the /var/spool/calendar directory. As the user adds calendar entries, the callog file grows larger and more entries will contain the invalid FQDN. The calendar manager service daemon will try to resolve the invalid FQDN for every entry in the user's callog file to contact the host. Eventually the calendar program will appear to be hung when running the calendar program. In actuality, the hostname resolution has to time out for every entry through every naming service listed in /etc/nsswitch.conf trying to resolve the invalid FQDN. It's not noticeable at first, but as a user's calendar gains entries it becomes slower and slower and eventually the user calls to complain that the calendar program "hangs." This problem is due to the incorrect configuration of the NIS domainname.

On a system that has no NIS domain name configured, the CDE calendar manager service daemon uses the short hostname returned from the *gethostname()* system call in the users callog file in the /var/spool/calendar directory. The calendar manager service daemon will resolve the short hostname and work correctly.

Sendmail and NIS

When the sendmail daemon is started, it tries to fully qualify the host's hostname in order to use a FQDN in the message header for the return address (without site hiding configured) for mail that passes through it. Sendmail attempts to determine the FQDN, or canonical name, through the naming services configured in /etc/nsswitch.conf and assign it to the $j macro, assign the domain name to the $m macro (version 8), and the short hostname to the $w macro. If it cannot resolve a FQDN for the hostname, it uses the short hostname. If it can only resolve a short hostname, the sendmail daemon will continually generate syslog messages stating it cannot fully qualify the hostname.

Sendmail is most peculiar when it is trying to fully qualify the hostname within /etc/hosts or NIS. If Sendmail cannot find an FQDN for the short hostname in the second column of the line /etc/hosts file or NIS hosts map, it checks for an FQDN in the third column and then the fourth, and so on, until it finds one on that line. It doesn't matter if the FQDN is correct or not, it will use the first one it finds for $j and $m. If it doesn't find one, it uses the short hostname.

In SunOS, Sendmail's $m is set to the NIS domain by retrieving the domain name that was set at boot time. If the domain name begins with a period or a plus sign, the first character is truncated and the remainder is set to $m. If the domain name does not begin with a plus sign or a period, the whole domain is assigned to $m. In older Sun versions of sendmail.cf files, such as sendmail.main and sendmail.subsidiary, the rule sets would truncate the first sub-domain of the domain name if it did not begin with a period and assign the rest of the domain to $m.

B.3.3.1.1 The NIS Hosts Map

The NIS hosts map needs to be configured just as the /etc/hosts file. It provides hostname resolution just as an /etc/hosts file does, only it is a map that used in by all clients bound to the NIS domain. Just as in the /etc/hosts file, the order of multi-homed hosts within the host's file used as the NIS master file for the NIS master map is extremely important when using the short hostname to connect to a system. The resolution is sequential just as it is with the /etc/hosts file. The first entry for each host should be the primary interface to which all other systems will connect when using the host's actual hostname. The first line with the hostname to be resolved will be used to determine the IP address (first column) for connection to that system. System authentication remains as described earlier in the /etc/hosts section. Use an alias versus the hostname to connect to any specific interface on a host.

All systems using NIS will resolve hostnames and IP addresses to the same to the same host or IP. Though multiple IP addresses are configured to a single hostname in the NIS map, only one IP will be given. Just like using the /etc/hosts file, only the first one will be given.There is no *sortlist* feature within NIS as there is with DNS to allow for sorting of IP addresses for multihomed hosts in a given order.

Putting It All Together using NIS

Figure B-4 is the NIS hosts map from the NIS server. On the OpenView server ovwsrv.nsr.hp.com, the /etc/nsswitch.conf file is configured as it looks in Figure B-5, and the hosts file as Figure B-1. The OpenView NNM server will discover the node xyzzy. The node xyzzy has the same /etc/nsswitch.conf configuration as Figure B-5, and its host's file like Figure B-6. NNM has retrieved a list of IPs from the default routers' arp cache and pings 192.168.1.9, queries the SNMP agent, and retrieves the interfaces from xyzzy's iftable and builds the node container object with two Ethernet LAN interfaces with the IP addresses 192.168.1.9 and 172.31.16.9. With 172.31.16.9 being the lowest numbered, non-migratable IP address, NNM attempts to reversely resolve this IP to find a hostname for the newly discovered node as described here.

1. A reverse lookup is used to find a host with an IP of 172.31.16.9; the nsswitch.conf file states to first use the /etc/hosts file for resolution for the hosts name service.
2. The /etc/hosts file is searched for an IP address of 172.31.16.9.
3. No IP is found with the IP address of 172.31.16.9, return to /etc/nsswitch.conf.
4. The /etc/nsswitch.conf file states that for hosts name service, continue the search in NIS if the name is not found in the /etc/hosts file. The NIS host map is queried for resolution.
5. Resolution for the IP address of 172.31.16.9 is found in the NIS map. The official hostname is an FQDN of xyzzy.nsr.hp.com.

The host is entered into the NNM database with a FQDN, xyzzy.nsr.hp.com. The domain name is truncated from the FQDN and the short hostname, xyzzy, is used as the label of the node object on the map.

Figure B-4 Figure B-4 contains a portion of the NIS hosts map from the NIS server.

```
127.0.0.1 loopback localhost

192.168.1.3 ovwsrv.nsr.hp.com ovwsrv ovwsrv-lan0
172.32.16.3 ovwsrv.nsr.hp.com ovwsrv ovwsrv-lan1
192.168.1.6 nfssrv.nsr.hp.com nfssrv nfssrv-lan0
172.32.16.6 nfssrv.nsr.hp.com nfssrv nfssrv-lan1
192.168.1.9 xyzzy.nsr.hp.com xyzzy xyzzy-lan0
172.32.16.9 xyzzy.nsr.hp.com xyzzy xyzzy-lan1
172.18.4.18 hp712.nsr.hp.com hp712 hp712-lan0
172.19.8.123 hpe35.nsr.hp.com hpe35 hpe35-lan0
```

Figure B-5 On node ovwsrv.nsr.hp.com, the /etc/nsswitch.conf configuration file will try to resolve a hostname first within /etc/hosts and then, if not found, use the NIS.

```
passwd:   compat
group:    compat
hosts:    files [ NOTFOUND = continue ] nis
...
```

Figure B-6 Figure B-6 shows the /etc/hosts file for host xyzzy.nsr.hp.com.

```
127.0.0.1   loopback   localhost

192.168.1.9 xyzzy.nsr.hp.com  xyzzy  xyzzy-lan0
172.32.16.9  xyzzy.nsr.hp.com  xyzzy  xyzzy-lan1
```

Any application or process on the management server ovwsrv, that communicates with the host xyzzy.nsr.hp.com will follow the same flow to find the IP of the hostname xyzzy. The process will not resolve the hostname xyzzy.nsr.hp.com by the FQDN or short hostname in its local hosts file. The resolution will continue to search for the hostname in the NIS host map. There it will retrieve the IP address of 192.168.1.9 for either the short hostname xyzzy, or its FQDN, because it is the first in the list. Based on the routing table in back in Figure B-3, the packet will be sent to the immediate gateway 193.168.1.3 and sent out lan0 where 192.168.1.9 will be listening and pick it up and continue communication. While communicating with each other, the source address of packets from the NNM server, ovwsrv.nsr.hp.com, will be 192.168.1.3 and the source address of packets from the host, xyzzy.nsr.hp.com, will be 192.168.1.9.

Tip: Configuring the NIS master /etc/hosts file as shown in Figure B-4 facilitates the use of h2n or HP's hosts_to_named script. That is, IP address in the first column, FQDN of the host in the second column, and aliases for the IP in the third and following columns. With either script, a hosts file is parsed to create domain name service db files. This /etc/hosts format, used in conjunction with hosts_to_named or h2n, create perfect DNS db files. Using this scheme in an NIS master hosts map allows for the use of one hosts file to create both the NIS hosts map and DNS db files. It will also give you the same resolution results in NIS and DNS. The only difference being NIS will only resolve one IP for a multi-homed host as where DNS will resolve all the IP addresses for the host.

B.3.3.1.2 Network File System (NFS) and NIS

Mounting remote files using NFS can be done in two ways: static mounts, which are configured in a mount list, /etc/fstab (HP-UX) or /etc/vfstab (Solaris), or automounts, which are configured through an NIS map. Whichever way is used, the NFS mount should mount the servers closest interface to the client. There are several ways to ensure that this occurs. Both poor hostname resolution and incorrect NFS configuration will give poor NFS performance and even failure to work as it should.

Figure B-7 shows a network that contains a router, two NFS clients (xyzzy and ovwsrv), and an NFS server (nfssrv). Each has two interfaces, lan0 on the 192.168.1.0 network and lan1 on the 172.31.16.0 network. The lan0 interfaces are the primary interfaces and the lan1 interfaces are for the NFS traffic. To mount the /home directory from nfssrv on each client xyzzy and ovwsrv, an entry must be made in each of the clients mount list:

```
nfssrv:/home      /home   nfs   defaults   0 0 #   HP-UX fstab entry
nfssrv:/home -    /home   nfs   -          yes     intr,bg   # Solaris vfstab entry
```

If either of the previous entries is used in the respective operating systems mount list, the behavior will not be as expected. NFS traffic takes place over the 192.168.1.0 network and not the 172.31.16.0 network as designed. Both clients will resolve nfssrv through the NIS host map (as configured in Figure B-4) to 192.168.1.6 because it is the first entry in the NIS host map that contains the alias nfssrv. All the other entries for nfssrv are ignored. All NFS communication will be through lan0 and not through lan1 based on the server and clients routing table. In order to get the expected results, a different alias for nfssrv must be used within the mount list:

```
nfssrv-lan1:/home     /home   defaults 0 0     # HP-UX fstab entry
nfssrv-lan1:/home -   /home   nfs       - yes   intr,bg   # Solaris vfstab entry
```

These entries resolve nfssrv-lan1 to 172.31.16.6 through the NIS host map because it is the only entry with the alias nfssrv-lan1 and, based on the routing table of the clients and server, NFS communication between client and server will be over the 172.31.16.0 network through lan1 of both systems. The official hostname remains a FQDN for all IP addresses and functionality of OpenView NNM and Operations remain undisturbed.

The Netmasks File

The /etc/netmasks file is used to determine the subnet mask of a network on Solaris. The contents of the netmask file are the IP network and its respective subnet mask for each network on a single line.

```
172.31.0.0      255.255.255.0
192.168.1.0     255.255.255.0
```

The /etc/netmasks file does support both standard and variable length subnetting of the network column. Using a single NIS netmasks map for HP-UX NIS clients is not supported. HP-UX NFS does not read the NIS netmasks map, it only reads the /etc/netmasks file. The automounter (AutoFS) in both Solaris and HP-UX uses the networks and netmasks within the /etc/netmasks file to determine the clients local subnet. This ensures the automounter mounts an NFS server on a local subnet versus traversing a router for a specific mount point.

Figure B-7 The network diagram in Figure B-7 is used with the supplied text in demonstrating the importance of good hostname resolution and NFS configuration.

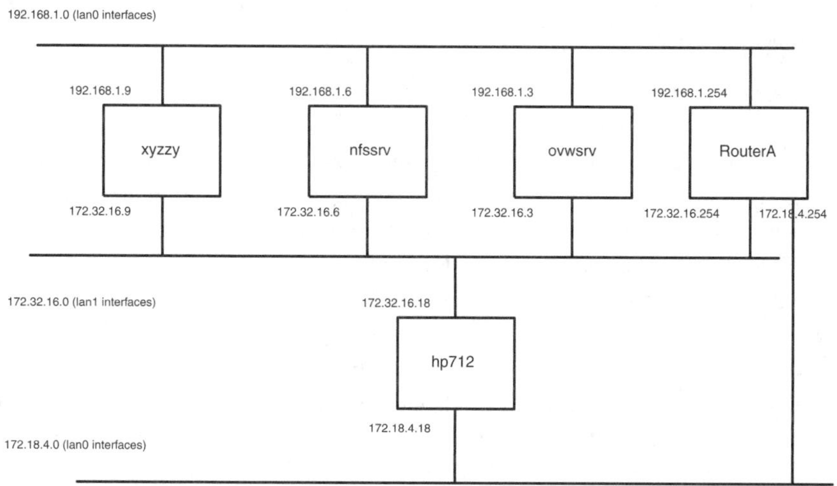

Automounted Directories

The automounter is used to automatically mount NFS filesystems as needed and unmount them when no longer in use. Using Figure B-7 as the network and NFS server and client layout, the mount for /home in the NIS automount map is configured so that NFS traffic is now over 192.168.1.0 network:

```
/home        nfssrv-lan0:/home
```

All clients in the NIS domain would mount their home directory to nfssrv-lan0 (192.168.1.6). The hosts ovwsrv and xyzzy have no problem with this configuration. All NFS traffic runs over the 192.168.1.0 network. The node hp712 begins to see "238 NFS server not responding" errors in the syslog. These errors are seen because the default route on hp712 is set to 172.32.16.254. The node hp712 mounts /home on nfssrv-lan0 via routera (172.32.16.254). The source address of the NFS IP packets from hp712 is 172.32.16.18 and the destination address is 192.168.1.6. When the host nfssrv receives the packet, its sees the source address is 172.32.16.18. According to the routing table in nfssrv, the route to the 172.32.16.0 network is via its immediate gateway, 172.32.16.6. The host nfssrv redirects the packet to hp712 via 172.32.15.6. The packet is received by hp712 and acted upon. But hp712 is still waiting for a response from 192.168.1.6 and it appears the NFS server is not responding.

Because the NFS server has multiple interfaces, list all the unique aliases of interfaces in the automount map (replicated file systems). The hostname alone for a system cannot be used when using NIS as the name service. When NIS is used as the name service it will only return the one IP address (192.168.1.6). Configure the automount map using replicated file systems as shown in this example:

/home nfssrv-lan0,nfssrv-lan1:/home

In order to use an automount map with replicated file systems, the proper netmasks for the IP networks must be entered in the /etc/netmasks file. This ensures that a client, such as hp712 in Figure B-7, will mount an NFS file system from a local interface (172.32.16.18) to 172.32.16.6 and not send packets through routera and having nfssrv redirect them through a local interface. The OpenView products continue to work properly.

B.3.3.1.3 The r-commands and NIS

The r-commands are made up of clients and servers and act against the "remote" client specified with the command. The clients are remsh (HP remote shell), rsh (Solaris remote shell), rlogin (remote login), rexec (remote execute), and rcp (remote copy). The servers are remshd (remote shell daemon), rexecd (remote execute daemon), and rlogind (remote login daemon).

There are two files that can be configured to allow authorization of execution of the r-commands on a remote host: /etc/hosts.equiv and a .rhosts file within a user's home directory. The /etc/hosts.equiv file can globally authorize a host or specific users from a host for use of rcp, remsh, or rlogin. The users .rhosts file authorizes the local user and any a remote user from a specific host. Each file can be used to deny access as well authorize access.

Using either of these authentication files in conjunction with NIS to allow remote access from a specific host requires at least the entry of the hostname alias of the interface from which the request will come. If access to host is authorized from either interface of the node hp712, then both aliases hp712-lan0 and hp712-lan1 must be in the /etc/hosts.equiv file or the users .rhosts file, otherwise only requests from the alias listed will be authorized access.

When the request comes from the client (HP-UX), it appears the server daemon resolves the hosts (aliases) listed in each file (/etc/hosts.equiv or a users .rhosts) to an IP address and matches it to the source address of the IP packet. In Figure B-7, if only the hostname is used, such as hp712, then only r-commands from 172.18.4.18 will be authorized to use r-commands on a host because hp712 resolves to IP 172.18.4.18 on every node. Resolving hp712-lan0 will give the IP of 172.18.4.18 and hp712-lan1 resolves to the IP of 172.31.16.8. The use of both aliases are required in the .rhosts file for authorization of either interface when using NIS as the naming service. Even when NIS is configured to use DNS as the resolver for hosts, NIS will only return one IP address for a given host.

Solaris appears to provide authorization by resolving the IP of the source address to the official hostname and matching the resolved hostname to that of one in the authorization file (/etc/hosts.equiv or .rhosts). Thus, if IP to hostname resolution resolves to unique official hostnames, then each hostname must be in the authorization file. Resolving the IPs to a single hostname requires only one host to be in the authorization file.

B.3.3.1.4 OpenView Operations and NIS

OpenView hostname and IP resolution works no differently that any what has been previously explained, but it relies heavily on the official hostname, especially in an enterprise environment where the OpenView products are configured in Manager of Manager and Distributed Internet Discovery and Monitoring configurations. The information given here is to help the administrator better understand how to setup NIS in order that the entire system will benefit when resolving hostnames and IP addresses and how some products use the NIS domain to create an FQDN. Configuring the NIS domain name incorrectly can add administration overhead and hostname resolution failures. In mission critical applications where correct hostname resolution is imperative and communications between systems must take place within milliseconds, there is no time for invalid data or lookup failures because of incorrect configuration of the system. Improper configuration degrades system and application performance by wasting CPU and memory resources.

B.3.3.1.5 OpenView Operations and Agent Communication

Using Figure B-4 as the hosts file or NIS map, an administrator adds the node to the node bank OpenView Operations using only the IP address 172.31.16.9. OVO resolves the IP address to the hostname.

If an administrator uses the hostname when adding a node to the node bank, OVO resolves the hostname to all possible IP addresses. Using NIS as the naming service supplies only the first hostname found; using the DNS provides a popup-menu of all the IP addresses resolved for the hostname.

The administrator should know what IP address is used as the primary interface, here the administrator chooses to use address 172.31.16.9. All communication takes place between the manager and client over what IP network? The answer is 192.168.1.0, because using NIS as the naming service provides only resolves the first host name found to an IP address. In the example given here, it is the 192.168.1.9 address that is resolved for the nodes' hostname on the management server.

An agent on any managed node will "bind to" the first active network interface's IP address. An administrator doesn't have much control over this; often it is the order of the network interfaces, which is determined by the motherboard or backplane of the system. It can be overridden by setting the IP in the opcinfo file.

If an agent sends an opcmsg to the management server, it includes in what is called the rpc "payload" both its IP address and its hostname as it is resolved on the client. The management server will use this IP and hostname information to authenticate the agent sending the information. The management server will query the configured naming services to attempt to match them to a node entry in the node bank. If the management server is successful, the message is accepted. If no match can be established, such in the case that the agent sent a short hostname and the naming service on the manager returns a FQDN or the IP is un-resolvable, then the message is dropped. It is assumed that the agent is an impostor and is trying to gain unauthorized access to the server.

The opc.hosts file can be used to establish an authorization match, but it is not meant to replace incorrectly configured naming services. Naming services should be properly configured.

Because NIS returns only one IP for a given hostname and it is the IP that matches the first instance of the hostname in the NIS hosts map, the second IP address for the managed node is never resolved using the short hostname. The message is discarded and not placed in the operator browser. A properly configured DNS server will return all IP addresses for a multi-homed host and this scenario will be avoided.

Using short hostnames within the official hostname column of the NIS map can cause havoc when the configuration of the nsswitch.conf file is set to use NIS and then the DNS and the NIS server is becomes unavailable. Both NNM and OVO would have set all the hostnames within both their respective databases to the short hostname. The DNS only returns FQDNs, and during a configuration check of the nodes, NNM changes all the hostnames within its database from a short hostname to an FQDN. As long as the NIS server is not responding, all events in the NNM Alarm browser will resolve the hostname to the FQDN. Events captured by the OpenView agent's trap interceptor will also be a FQDN, which may or may not match a node in the node bank for a message entry in the message browser. When the NIS server returns to operation, NNM's configuration check of the nodes will return the hostnames in its database to the short hostname. There is an OpenView-specific trap for the occurrence of a hostname change. If it is enabled, the number of traps can be enormous.

B.3.3.2 OpenView Products and the DNS

OpenView products must have definitive hostname and IP address resolution, especially when configured in a Distributed Internet Discovery and Monitoring or Manager of Manager environment. Every system must resolve each host to the same IP address(es) and each IP address resolve to the proper and same FQDN. The DNS is the *only* naming service that is used by all the platforms and by all the operating systems on which the OpenView products run or OpenView products and agents manage. The DNS is the best naming service to use for resolving hostnames and IP addresses, whether or not any OpenView product are used in an enterprise. The DNS can provide all the IP addresses for a single hostname in addition to distinct host aliases across disparate domains. NIS can only lookup information of any kind within a single NIS domain. NIS does not traverse NIS domains; there is no NIS hierarchy. Configuring the DNS in order that everything works properly is a simple task once it is thoroughly understood.

B.3.3.3 Properly Configuring the DNS

B.3.3.3.1 The /etc/resolv.conf File

The specifics of DNS resolution for the local host are configured within the /etc/resolv.conf file. Its configuration specifies what DNS domain(s) to search, and which nameservers to utilize for the search for hostname and IP address resolution. Later versions of the resolver code, such as used in HP-UX 11.11, allow for the additional behavioral options such as a sortlist that will give priority to specified IP address ranges on multi-homed hosts.

A typical /etc/resolv.conf file:

```
domain      nsr.hp.com
sortlist 192.168.1.0/255.255.255.0
nameserver 0.0.0.0
nameserver 192.168.1.3
nameserver 10.4.3.2
```

The *domain* entry is the local domain name. If this line is omitted, the domain is determined by the hostname returned by *gethostname()*, truncated after the first dot. If the official hostname in the second column in the /etc/hosts file is not an FQDN, the resolver assumes the root domain.

The *nameserver* entry contains the IP address of the nameserver to use for querying. A maximum of three nameservers can be listed in the file. All others are ignored. The entry "nameserver 0.0.0.0" tells the resolver that this host is a nameserver and to query itself for resolution. Any other IP address assigned to the system will also work on this line. Seeing the 0.0.0.0 entry should immediately trigger in the mind that this system is a nameserver over having to "resolve" in the mind the IP to the hostname. If the /etc/resolv.conf file has only a single domain or search line, this too tells the resolver to use the local system as a DNS server.

The *search* option sets a list of domains (up to six) for hostname lookup. The first domain within the *search* list must be the local domain to enable the use of short hostnames within authentication files, such as .rhosts and inetd.sec. If a host is not found within the first domain in the search list, the resolver will continue the search through every domain in the search list until it finds a match. If no match is found in any of the domains within the search list, the search either stops, or continues with the next naming service as defined by the configuration of /etc/nsswitch.conf.

The *sortlist* option (HP-UX 11.11, Solaris 8/9) tells the resolver in what order to sort the IP addresses of a multi-homed host, thus allowing connectivity to nodes through specific IP addresses over other IP addresses configured on a system. A total of 10 pairs of IP address/subnet mask (subnet mask is optional) entries, separated by white space, can be specified.

It is highly recommended that all management and collection stations be caching only name servers. NNM and OVO are forward and reverse address lookup intensive. As well they should be; it is how they begin communication for what they manage.

B.3.3.3.2 Forward Lookups

Forward lookups are "name-to-address" mappings within a DNS *DOMAIN* db file. When a host is resolved by OVO, it needs to know every IP address associated with that host. To ensure that specific IP addresses are returned others, the *sortlist* option can be configured in the clients /etc/resolv.conf file (if the resolver supports it). The sortlist can also be applied within the named.conf file of the DNS server itself to indicate preferred networks in answer to queries. To use the sortlist in conjunction with the DNS server itself, the DNS server must reside on the same network as the client making the request.

The DNS allows for the inclusion of unique names for the same IP address within its forward lookup dbs. This capability allows for the retrieval of all the IP addresses associated with a particular hostname and a single IP address for a different hostname. In the example in Figure B-8, we have just that. The resolution of ovwsrv using the DNS as configured in Figure B-8 will resolve two addresses for the host ovwsrv.nsr.hp.com, 192.168.1.3 and 172.31.16.3. The resolution of the alias ovwsrv-lan0 will resolve only the 192.168.1.3 address and the resolution of ovwsrv-lan1 will resolve only the 172.31.16.3 address. This behavior is what most administrators wish to see.

If a CNAME record is used in place of an additional A record for ovwsrv-lan0 (or any alias), the DNS will resolve both addresses for ovwsrv. This is not the behavior most administrators wish to see in resolving an alias for a host. A CNAME for a uni-homed host will give the same resolution "look and feel" as /etc/hosts and the NIS hosts map.

Using the DNS for hostname resolution is preferred over NIS because the DNS allows for both forward and reverse address lookups within any DNS domain. NIS, on the other hand, only allows for hostname resolution within the local NIS domain.

Figure B-8 Figure B-8 shows a correctly configured DNS address file.

```
ovwsrv          IN    A    192.168.1.3
ovwsrv-lan0     IN    A    192.168.1.3
ovwsrv          IN    A    172.32.16.3
ovwsrv-lan1     IN    A    172.32.16.3

xyzzy           IN    A    192.168.1.9
xyzzy-lan0      IN    A    192.168.1.9
xyzzy           N     A    172.32.16.9
xyzzy-lan1      IN    A    172.32.16.9

hp712           IN    A    172.18.4.18
hp712-lan0      IN    A    172.18.4.18
hp712           IN    A    172.32.16.18
hp712-lan1      IN    A    172.18.4.18

hpe35           IN    A    172.19.8.123
hpe35-lan0      IN    A    172.19.8.123

nfssrv          IN    A    192.168.1.6
nfssrv-lan0     IN    A    192.168.1.6
nfssrv          IN    A    172.32.16.6
nfssrf-lan1     IN    A    172.32.16.6
```

B.3.3.3.3 Reverse Lookups

Reverse-address lookups are "address-to-name" mappings within a DNS *ADDRESS* db file and allow only one unique name per IP address. All IP addresses for a multi-homed host must resolve to the same FQDN in order for all the products and services to function properly.

Figure B-9 shows a simulated db.192.168.1 or db.172.31.16 DNS file (without the SOA record) since the example networks are using the same host in each network. A resolution of 192.168.1.3 or 172.31.16.3 will return ovwsrv.nsr.hp.com. Any process resolving either IP will receive the same FQDN.

Figure B-9 Figure B-9 is an in-addr file that could be used for networks 192.168.1 or 172.31.16.

```
3    IN    PTR    ovwsrv.nsr.hp.com.
9    IN    PTR    xyzzy.nsr.hp.com.
6    IN    PTR    nfssrv.nsr.hp.com.
```

B.3.3.3.4 Testing Resolution: nsquery versus nslookup

On HP-UX, either the nslookup or nsquery command will traverse the /etc/nsswitch.conf file and provide the source (/etc/hosts, NIS, or DNS) from which the resolution came. The nslookup command is not accurate when it comes to forward address lookup of mult-homed hosts within the DNS. The nslookup command "round robins" the IP addresses of multi-homed hosts whether or not the *sortlist* option is configured in the /etc/resolv.conf file. The exception is when one of the resolved IP addresses is on the same network as both the host requesting resolution and the DNS server itself (HP-UX only, Solaris round robins). HP-UX 11.x provides the **nsquery** command in /usr/contrib/bin and provides more accurate resolution. The **nsquery** command does traverse the /etc/nsswitch.conf file for the services to query for resolution and will sort the returned IP addresses according to the *sortlist* option configured in /etc/resolv.conf.

The **nslookup** command provided with Solaris does not traverse the /etc/nsswitch.conf file, it only queries the DNS. If a hostname is not resolved using nslookup on Solaris, either the resolver is not configured, the configured DNS servers are not operational, the host does not exist in the DNS as queried, or it doesn't exist in the DNS. It does not mean that the host does not exist within /etc/hosts or NIS. A "ping –s <hostname>" will resolve the <hostname> using /etc/nsswitch.conf file and the ICMP echo will show the IP address to which it resolved. The nsquery command is not provided with the Solaris operating system. The ping command doesn't state where the resolution came from, but it does state the IP address it is pinging for the host given on the command line.

Dig can also be used, but currently must be downloaded for either platform.

B.3.3.4 Sendmail and the DNS

A mail server using sendmail relies on the accuracy of the DNS to deliver electronic mail as much as an OpenView management server does to manage the nodes and networks within the enterprise. Sendmail uses hostname naming services, such as the DNS, to retrieve the IP address of the destination host and to determine the host from which the mail came, or the host(s) through which mail has been relayed. Only through the DNS can sendmail determine if there is a mail exchange record (MX) for the destination host. An MX record tells sendmail to send the mail to a specific host or hosts when delivering e-mail. This host can be the same host or a host specifically configured to receive mail, such as a mail host or mail server.

If name resolution is configured to use the DNS and sendmail cannot resolve an FQDN through NIS or the /etc/hosts file, sendmail will try to resolve the $j and $w macros through the DNS. If the host is a mail server or mail host, it needs to utilize the DNS to deliver and receive mail.

B.3.3.5 NFS and the DNS

Mounting NFS file systems using hostname resolution from the DNS is no different from using the described /etc/hosts and NIS hosts map. Configuring alias names with an additional IP address within the forward address DNS db resolves the alias to a single IP address. Using the hostname alias in a static mount within /etc/fstab or within an automount map will resolve the alias to the appropriate IP address for mounting through the desired network interface at the NFS server.

The benefit of using the DNS in conjunction with the replicated filesystems option is that the automounter configuration only requires the actual hostname. DNS will return all the IP addresses for the multi-homed host.

/home nfssrv:/home

This also requires the /etc/networks file to be configured with the correct network class and network netmask on the client. The previous line in the automount map is configured to use the actual hostname of the NFS server, nfssrv. The /etc/nsswitch.conf file is configured to use the host file first then the DNS server for resolution of hostnames on the client hp712. The /etc/netmasks file on hp712 contains the following for this scenario:

```
172.31.0.0   255.255.255.0
172.18.0.0   255.255.255.0
```

Refer to Figure B-7 for the network topology.

When the automouter on hp712 needs to mount a specific directory, such as /home from the NFS server nfssrv, the automounter will resolve the hostname nfssrv and receive two IP addresses for the hostname. The automounter will then, through an algorithm using /etc/netmasks file, determine that the IP address 172.31.16.6 is local to that of nfssrv and that the interface responds (is up). The client hp712 requests the mount from the nfssrv at 172.31.16.6 through 172.31.16.0 at lan1 based on its own routing table, which shows a local network route. All NFS communication for this mount point takes place between the NFS server and client over the 172.31.16.0 network. The source and destination packets between the two systems will be either 172.31.16.6 or 172.31.16.18, and each system's routing table states that the 172.31.16.0 is a local route out of a local interface.

Configuring hosts xyzzy and ovwsrv where both interfaces for the hosts are on the same networks as the NFS server and using the same automount map configuration for /home as hp712 results in the mount occurring over either interface.

B.3.3.6 The r-commands and the DNS

The r-commands function the same way with DNS as they do when using an /etc/hosts file or the NIS hosts map. The value added by using the DNS again is the ability to retrieve multiple IP addresses for a single hostname. When using NIS for hostname resolution, all host aliases must be in the /etc/hosts.equiv file or a users .rhosts file to allow remote access to a node from any interface from a specific system. The more interfaces, the more entries that are required. Using DNS as the hostname naming service requires using only one entry for the host within /etc/hosts.equiv or a .rhosts file because all the addresses can be returned for the host.

Having additional address records for the host alias, such as hp712-lan0, still allows for "r-command-ing" to, telnet-ing to, or ping-ing to a specific interface. The resolution of the hostname alias through the DNS (just like with NIS) returns the specific IP address. Resolution of the hostname alias through the DNS also allows for the denial of r-commands from specific interfaces, whether the host alias is configured in the authorization file itself or you are adding them to a specific netgroup designed explicitly for use within the authorization file for denial of access using those interfaces. The reverse address lookup is always the same official hostname.

B.3.3.7 Traceroute

Many will believe that the **traceroute** command is now "broken" because configuring each IP for a multi-homed host to reversely resolve to the same hostname will no longer resolve to the hostname alias configured as host-interface. This is true, it no longer will resolve to the hostname alias, but to the actual hostname of the multi-homed host. But the command still works as designed.

The standard **traceroute** command only resolves the IP of the interface in which the packet exits a host and does not resolve the IP of the interface in which a packet enters a host. When the **traceroute** command begins giving an asterisk (*), it is always either the "goesinta or "goesouta" interface on the next hop after the last good hop. The command does not provide what the next hop will be and therefore a login to the last good hop is required to determine the route in which the packet is to take. That telnet will most likely be to the loopback interface, which would also be aliased in the preferred host-naming service.

HP has a traceroute-like command named **findroute** that is supplied with NNM. The program traces the route via SNMP and gives the hostname and both the entering and exiting interface the packet traversed through each multi-homed host to the destination. It also allows for the tracing of packets between two disparate systems other than the host from which it is run. If the SNMP agent on each host in the route is not accessible to **findroute**, the trace fails at the first host to which the SNMP agent is not accessible.

Using **findroute** to find the route from ovwsrv to hp712 on the sample network in Figure B-7 would occur like this: If ovwsrv is configured to use the DNS and its resolver has a sortlist option included with 172.18.0.0, it is the preferred network with a netmask of 255.255.255.0. Running **findroute** on ovwsrv to find the route from ovwsrv to hp712 will result in the resolution of the 172.18.4.18 IP address for hp712.nsr.hp.com. Based on the routing table in ovwsrv, the packet will leave ovwsrv out lan0 to the default router routera.nsr.hp.com (192.168.1.254) and out routera.nsr.hp.com 172.18.4.254 interface to hp712.nsr.hp.com (172.18.8.18). The output of **findroute** on the command line would look like this:

```
findroute hp712.nsr.hp.com
```

Source	Source Address	Next Hop	Next Hop Address
ovwsrv.nsr.hp	192.168.1.3	routera.nsr.hp	192.168.1.254
routera.nsr.hp	172.18.4.254	hp712.nsr.hp.	172.18.4.18

Note that both interfaces of routera are included in the "found route." If the 172.18.4.254 interface of router 1 is not up, the 192.16.1.254 interface is still displayed as the next hop. Using standard traceroute will only provide the "goesouta" interface, and if the interface is not functional, traceroute will not resolve the IP to the name of the router and a splat, or an asterisk will be displayed.

Executing find route from the NNM GUI provides the output in a window and highlights the route on the NNM map, including the interfaces it traversed. Opening a multi-homed container object shows the highlighted interfaces. If the container object is opened as a separate submap, the interface can be selected and the interface in the multi-homed host and the connector line on the IP Map will be highlighted.

B.3.4 Windows NT and Hostname Resolution

Hostname resolution within Microsoft Windows products resolves the names of TCP/IP resources if the resource does not connect using NetBIOS. Hostname naming services can be can a local host file or the DNS. The location of the local host file itself is Windows product dependent. For Windows NT or Windows 2000, it is found in the %Systemroot\System32\Drivers\etc directory. The IP address and hostname entries within the host file are configured just as described in previous paragraphs for the UNIX host file.

The resolution of a host within both Windows NT and Windows 2000 uses the following order:

Local host file
DNS
NetBIOS

The order of using the DNS or NetBIOS can be changed by modifying the following registry entry (Windows NT):

```
HKEY_LOCAL_MACHINE\SYSTEM\CurrentControlSet\Services\Tcip\Para-
meters\DnsNbtLookupOrder
Value Type: REG_SZ - Character string
Valid Range: 0 (DNS first) or 1 (NetBIOS first)
Default: 0 (DNS)
```

The 0 value specifies that DNS name resolution takes priority over NBT name resolution. A value of 1 will place NBT name resolution over DNS name resolution. Windows 2000 resolves through DNS by default. The can be changed by the same registry entry listed previously.

B.4 SUMMARY

NNM, OVO, and other network and systems management products, as well as the UNIX system in general, benefit greatly from proper configuration of hostname naming services. There are many other services and server configurations that rely on hostname resolution that are not mentioned here, such as XDMCP, MC/ServiceGuard, and hp webadmin. There is too much at stake to not have hostname resolution resolve properly. Without proper resolution the NMS cannot function properly or provides accurate events, alarms, and correlation. These will be missed because of hostname authentication issues. If a company wants a world class network, systems, and service management system, that company must have a first class hostname naming service.

APPENDIX C

Resources

The resources listed in this section provide Internet links to additional information, tools and articles relevant for specific OpenView system administration or general system administration topics.

C.1 BOOKS

`http://docs.hp.com`—Hewlett Packard Documentation

`http://www.phptr.com`—Prentice Hall Technical Books

`http://www.bookpool.com`—Discount Technical Books

`http://www.hp.com/hpbooks`—Hewlett Packard Books

`http://www.tatteredcover.com`—Bookstore with locator for out of print books

C.2 CERTIFICATION

`http://h10017.www1.hp.com/certification/index.html`—HP Certified Professional Program

`http://www.CertMag.com`—*Certification Magazine*

C.3 DATABASES

`http://www.ibm.com`–IBM (DB2)

`http://www.informix.com`–INFORMIX

`http://www.microsoft.com`—MICROSOFT (SQL Server)

`http://www.oracle.com`—Oracle Home Page

`http://otn.oracle.com/index.html`—Oracle Technology Network

`http://www.sybase.com`—SYBASE

C.4 HP INFORMATION AND RESOURCES

`http://www.hp.com`

`http://itrc.hp.com`—HP Information Resources/HP Forums

`http://h21007.www2.hp.com/`—Developer and Partner Solution Programs

C.5 JAVA

`http://www.javasoft.com`

`http://java.sun.com`

C.6 LDAP

`http://www.interex.org/pubcontent/enterprise/jan02/framelin.html`—LDAP Article

C.7 MANAGED NODES

http://www.hp.com—DEC, HP-UX, MPE

`http://www.ibm.com`—IBM

`http://www.linux.org`—LINUX

`http://www.microsoft.com`—NT/W2000/XP

`http://www.novell.com`—Novell

`http://www.sgi.com`—SGI

`http://www.siemens.com/index.jsp`—SIEMENS

`http://www.sun.com`—SUN

`http://h30097.www3.hp.com/products.html`—Tru64 UNIX Products

`http://jazz.external.hpcom/src/vt3k`—MPE vt3k software (for use with OVO)

C.8 MIBS

`http://www.isi.edu/cgi-bin/iana/enterprise.pl`—Enterprise Number lookup

`http://www.mibdepot.com`

`www.sins.com.au/netmon/mibload.html`

`ftp://veneria.isi.edu`

C.9 NETWORKING AND SERVICE MANAGEMENT

`http://openview.hp.com/solutions/nsm/index.html`—Network Service Management

`www.itil.co.uk`—Information Techology Infrastructure Library

`www.itsmf.com`—Service Management Forum

`www.cisco.com`—Network Products and Technical Resources

`http://searchnetworking.techtarget.com`—Network Technology Trends

`http://www.ntp.org`—Network Time Protocol

C.10 OPENVIEW SELF HEALING SERVICES

`http://support.openview.hp.com/self_healing.jsp`—Self-healing client monitors the application log files for Network Node Manager and OpenView Operations looking for errors within the application.

C.11 OPENVIEW DOCUMENTATION, SUPPORT, AND PRODUCT RESOURCES

`http://openview.hp.com`—OpenView Home Page

`http://support.openview.hp.com`—OpenView Support and Resources

`http://www.webware.hp.com`—OpenView Software Licenses

C. 12 PERFORMANCE

`http://openview.hp.com/products/performance/twp/ovperf_twp_metrics_sep03.pdf`–OV Performance Agent and Embedded Performance Component Metrics Chart

`http://ovweb.external.hp.com/ovnsmdps/pdf/perfagent_metrics.html`—OV Performance Agents Help Text

`http://openview.hp.com/400/products/performance/twp/ovperf_twp_arm_oct03.pdf`—ARM Instrumentation in HP OpenView Performance Products

`http://forums1.itrc.hp.com/service/forums/categoryhome.do?categoryId=166`–Forum discussions concerning OpenView Glance, MeasureWare, Performance Insight, and OpenView VantagePoint Performance

`http://www.openview.hp.com/products/ovperf/index.html`—Performance Manager, Monitor, Agent Overview

`http://ovweb.external.hp.com/ovnsmdps/pdf/ovpm4.0_releasenotes.pdf`—OpenView Performance Manager Release Notes

C. 13 RFCS

http://www.internic.net—Source for published RFCs

C.14 SECURITY

http://www.cert.org—Computer Emergency Response Team, computer security alerts

http://www.ciac.llnl.gov—Computer Security services

http://wwww.microsoft/security—Microsoft security patches

http://www.nist.gov—National Institute of Standards and Technology (NIST)

http://www.nist.gov/itl—NIST Information Technology Lab—computer security standards

C.15 SOFTWARE

http://openview.hp.com/products/operations_for_hpux/twp/ovoux_twp_eaf_jul02.pdf—*Enhanced Administration* (EAF) for HP OpenView Operations

http://www.hp.com/large/events/2003/openview_web—OpenView Product Demonstrations

http://www.openview.hp.com/demos/index.html—OpenView Product Demonstrations

http://www.openview.hp.com/downloads/downloads.html—OpenView Product Downloads

http://www.software.hp.com—HP Software Depot

http://www.w3.org—World Wide Web Consortium

C.16 SNMP

ftp://ovweb.external.hp.com/pub/NNM62/SnmpAgent

http://www.snmp.com—SNMP Research

http://www.cisco.com/univercd/cc/td/doc/product/software/ios120/120newft/120t3/snmp3.htm—Cisco SNMP v3 documentation

http://www.snmplink.org—SNMP and MIB information

C.17 SYSTEM ADMINISTRATION

http://www.sage.org—The System Administrators Guild

http://searchnetworking.techtarget.com/—Network Administration Resourses

http://www.samag.com—UNIX and LINUX System Administration

http://www.ugu.com—UNIX GURU Universe

http://bhami.com/rosetta.html—System Administration Universal Translator

C.18 TRAINING

http://education.hp.com

http://www.globalknowledge.com

C.19 TROUBLESHOOTING

http://www.troubleshooters.com/troubleshooters.htm

C.20 USER GROUPS

http://www.interex.org—HP-UX user group

http://www.ovforum.org—OpenView user group

http://www.usenix.org—Association for Advanced Computing Systems

C.21 UNIX

http://www.ugu.org—UNIX resources, UNIX command/tip of the day

http://bhami.com/rosetta.html—Multi-vendor platform support commands and resources

C.22 WHITE PAPERS

http://ovweb.external.hp.com/lpe/doc_serv_

INDEX

E

O

Q-R

U-V

W

X-Z